# SALES LAW

## DOMESTIC AND INTERNATIONAL

### REVISED EDITION

By

**CLAYTON P. GILLETTE**
Professor of Law
New York University School of Law

**STEVEN D. WALT**
Professor of Law
University of Virginia School of Law

## CONCEPTS AND INSIGHTS SERIES

New York, New York
FOUNDATION PRESS
2002

Cover Design: Keith Stout
Cover Art: Drawing of a 15th Century Stained Glass window in Chartres Cathedral, north-western France, circa 1400.
Getty Images Archive.

395 Hudson Street
New York, NY 10014
Phone Toll Free 1–877–888–1330
Fax (212) 367–6799
fdpress.com

ISBN 1–58778–447–5

 TEXT IS PRINTED ON 10% POST CONSUMER RECYCLED PAPER

*To the memory of my parents*

C.P.G.

*To my mother and the memory of my father*

S.D.W.

*

# PREFACE

This book describes and analyzes the law of sales under Article 2 of the Uniform Commercial Code ("UCC") and under the United Nations Convention on Contracts for the International Sale of Goods (the "CISG" or "Convention"). There already exist several excellent works on these bodies of law. One might reasonably inquire what is different about this effort.

We believe that our approach adds to the existing work in two ways. First, we do not attempt to describe all the provisions under these bodies of law. Our assumption is that many of the provisions of the relevant law are self-explanatory and that restating them or citing to cases that apply them does little to provide additional understanding. We therefore concentrate on those provisions that have been most problematic and try to provide an analytical framework that students can apply even to provisions that we do not discuss explicitly. Thus, we intend to offer a theoretical treatment of Sales Law rather than merely a descriptive one.

We are admittedly normative in this approach. We ask what legal rules should be adopted and how existing rules should be interpreted and applied. Commercial law does not comprise an abstract, arbitrary set of principles. Rather, the drafter and applier of relevant rules acts against some framework of what commercial law is intended to achieve. The UCC speaks of interpretive principles in very broad strokes, such as the admonition in § 1-102 to liberally construe its provisions to promote purposes and policies such as "to simplify, clarify and modernize the law governing commercial transactions." Our assumption is that a more frank confrontation with the law of commercial law is necessary. We could simplify and clarify commercial law with rules such as "buyer always wins," or "all disputes will be resolved by coin flips." Obviously, no one would think that such rules were preferable to a law predicated on some normative basis. But what should that normative basis be? In this book, we analyze and critique commercial law by reference to those principles that have been the subject of current debates about the proper direction of commercial law. These include such principles as allocating risks to parties in the best position to avoid them, respecting the autonomy of commercial parties, and minimizing social waste by allowing parties who value goods most highly the possibility of obtaining them. We believe that it is only through familiarity with these modes of analysis that the student of commercial law can make appropriate choices among competing commercial rules and appropriate interpretations of existing rules.

The second feature of our approach that is worth emphasizing is our simultaneous treatment of international and domestic commercial law. The dramatic increase in international commerce makes this effort necessary. Improvements in transportation, communication, and payment devices have made international sales more common, and the open world economy has made such transactions economically feasible. The attorney who is unfamiliar with legal principles that apply to international transactions will be ill-prepared to face the inevitable surge in commerce. We therefore attempt to compare domestic commercial law principles with those generated under the CISG and to analyze the most obvious areas of difference.

We have written this volume at a time when proposed revisions of the UCC are in a state of flux. We discuss some of the proposed changes, since they reflect recent thinking on commercial law, even if they are never enacted. If we are correct that the student of commercial law should look to underlying principles rather than simply become familiar with doctrinal provisions, then the analyses that we offer should be readily applicable to commercial rules, regardless of their form. Nevertheless, we try to indicate those areas in which the proposed revisions would make significant changes from current law.

Finally, we admit to some frustration in trying to inform the reader about the context of cases decided under the CISG. Few of the cases have been translated into English, though this situation is improving. Some of the translations contain awkward phrasing that make us wonder whether the translation accurately reflects the court's reasoning. We have relied primarily on the compilation of cases decided under the CISG in the original language, with abstracts in English, in Michael Joachim Bonell, UNILEX International Case Law & Bibliography on the UN Convention on Contracts for the International Sale of Goods (1995), and on the datbase maintained by Pace University School of Law and available at http://www.cisg.law.pace.edu/.

We are grateful to Kevin Kordana and George Triantis for comments on the manuscript and to John Dolan for comments on Chapter 11. Brian Jennings and Nathan Pietila provided excellent research assistance. Finally, we are grateful to Deans Robert Scott, John Jeffries, and John Sexton for the time and support necessary to complete this project.

# TABLE OF CONTENTS

CHAPTER 1
INTRODUCTION TO SALES LAW

## I. Introduction to Article 2 of the UCC

Sales law involves legal doctrines that regulate the relationship between the parties involved in an exchange of goods for a price. As a general matter, sales law only addresses transfers of tangible personal property, not real estate or intangibles such as intellectual property rights. Sales law, therefore, is a subset of contract law. Unlike general contract law doctrine, which has evolved primarily through the common law process of judicial decision, sales law is found in statutory law. For domestic transactions, the primary statute is Article 2 of the Uniform Commercial Code ("UCC"), which has been enacted as part of the statutory law of every state other than Louisiana, as well as the District of Columbia and the Virgin Islands. As we will see, state law has been augmented by certain provisions of federal law, particularly in the area of consumer sales. For international transactions in goods, the United Nations Convention on Contracts for the International Sale of Goods (the "CISG" or "Convention") has quickly become a major source of law, at least for those countries that have agreed to be bound by its provisions. As of this writing, 59 nations are Contracting States (as signatories to the CISG are called) under the CISG. These include major commercial nations, such as the United States, Germany, France, Canada, and China. But some major commercial countries, notably Great Britain and Japan, have not yet become Contracting States.

The UCC was originally promulgated under the auspices of the American Law Institute ("ALI") and the National Conference of Commissioners on Uniform State Laws ("NCCUSL") in the 1940s in order to bring a greater level of certainty and predictability to an increasingly national commercial system. The UCC was intended to deal not only with sales, but with a range of transactions involving commercial parties, from the use of negotiable instruments to secured transactions. The entire project was headed by Professor Karl Llewellyn of the Columbia Law School. Much of the UCC, and Article 2 in particular, reveals Llewellyn's commitment to legal realism and to his desire to allow commercial parties to dictate the proper scope and doctrine of the law that was to govern their practices. Llewellyn assumed that these parties were in a better position than judges or legislators to determine socially desirable commercial arrangements. Thus, in many ways the UCC seeks primarily to give state sanction to private rules developed by merchants. This is clear both from § 1-102(3) [Rev. 1-302(a)[1]], which permits parties to contract out of the rule supplied by the UCC, and from the inclusion of several provisions that contain vague, almost vacuous, admonitions of proper commercial conduct. Llewellyn believed that the courts that would inevitably be required to interpret these provisions should do so by reference to the practices of the trade under investigation, rather than by the imposition of some external standard of appropriate commercial conduct. Thus, one finds multiple sections requiring courts to make judgments by reference to "reasonableness" or "commercial reasonableness"[2] and to incorporate "trade practices" and "course of dealing"[3] into their constructions of contracts between commercial parties.

Notwithstanding their general reliance on commercial parties within a trade to establish legal standards of conduct, the drafters of the UCC were willing to provide some guidance to both commercial parties (and their legal advisors) and courts as to the meaning of the UCC's provisions. Each provision is followed by an "Official Comment" which elucidates the intended application of the provision's terms. While these Comments generally have not been enacted by legislatures and generally do not have the force of law,[4] courts (and students) typically take great solace from these statements in interpreting UCC provisions. Indeed, early versions of the UCC authorized courts to consult the Comments when interpreting specific provisions. In addition, states frequently have little in the way of legislative history that would provide an alternative interpretative aid. It is essential to recall, however, that the drafters did not consistently revise the Comments as they were revising the corresponding provisions. Thus, while the student of the UCC may take

---

[1] All references to "Rev." Article 1 are to Revised Article 1. Unprefixed references are to pre-Revision Article 1.

[2] See, e.g., §§ 2-206(2), 2-207(1), 2-715(1).

[3] See, e.g., § 2-316(3)(c).

[4] The Iowa legislature has adopted the following nonuniform provision:
To the extent that they are consistent with the Iowa statutory text, the 1972 Official Comments to the Uniform Commercial Code are evidence of legislative intent as to the meaning of this chapter as amended. However, prior drafts of the Official Text and Comments may not be used to ascertain legislative intent.
Iowa Code § 554.11109 (1997).

significant comfort in the analysis found in the Comments, it is always necessary to distinguish those interpretive guides from the provisions that alone constitute the law.

Regardless of what courts ought to do, commentators have found that, as a practical matter, courts use the Comments in at least one of three ways. First, courts employ the Comments to assist in exposition of the UCC as well as to describe and explain the meaning of each provision. Second, they have used the Comments to fill gaps in areas not specifically addressed by the text of a provision, but arguably subsumed within it. For instance, § 2-504 imposes duties on the seller when the sales contract allows or requires a carrier to transport the goods to the buyer. The section applies only when "the contract does not require [the seller] to deliver them at a particular destination." This implies that a seller's duties under a sales contract requiring him to deliver at a particular destination may be different.   Section 2-504, however, is silent about when a contract requires the seller to deliver goods to a particular destination.   The silence can be a problem when the sales contract calling for carriage fails to expressly address the matter. Official Comment 5 to § 2-503 fills the gap, stating that "...under this Article the 'shipment' contract is regarded as the normal one and the 'destination' contract as the variant type." A "shipment" contract does not require the seller to deliver goods to a particular destination. Thus, given Comment 5, § 2-504 applies to sales contracts that simply call for transport by a carrier. A contract merely requiring the seller to "arrange for delivery" is an example.

Finally, courts may use the Comments to confirm a view of the provision that they advocate on some independent grounds. For instance, a court may find it makes good policy sense to apply § 2-504 to sales contracts that call simply for the seller to "arrange for delivery." These contracts, the court may find, do not "require [the seller] to deliver" the goods "at a particular destination." Buyers typically may have different preferences for the details of carriage concerning delivery at the destination, as well as better information and risk-bearing abilities in the matter than their sellers. They typically may know more than their sellers about the condition of the goods when delivered to them by the carrier. If so, buyers may be in a superior position to negotiate desirable terms with the carrier concerning the specifics of delivery at the destination, according to the court. The court could conclude that in the circumstances carriage costs are lower for most buyers when sellers enter into "shipment" contracts. Having reached that conclusion on these grounds, the court may further justify it by finding the outcome consistent with the Official Comment: "shipment" contracts are the "normal" carriage contract, "destination" contracts "deviant."

The drafters of the UCC also recognized that the practices they wanted to regulate or leave to self-regulation of the particular trade could change over time. In order to make clear that courts were to allow legal doctrine to keep apace with those changes, the drafters explicitly indicated that courts were to construe UCC provisions liberally to promote its underlying purposes and policies. Those policies explicitly include the modernization of commercial law and recognition of "the continued expansion of commercial practices through custom, usage and agreement of the parties."[5]

Notwithstanding these efforts to allow commercial practices to evolve without changes in statutory commercial law, many commentators and practitioners have found that a law drafted in the 1940s is inadequate for the 1990s. Technological innovations, such as computerization, made prior means of doing business obsolete, and have resulted in changes in statutory law affecting the UCC. Important among these changes are the Electronic Signatures in Global and National Commerce Act ("Esign"), the Uniform Electronic Transactions Act (UETA), and the Uniform Computer Information Transactions Act (UCITA). In addition, the appearance and persistence of difficult issues have led to conflicting judicial interpretations that threaten the uniformity of commercial law. As a result, most of the UCC has recently been subjected to revision efforts. The latest approved revision is Article 1, the UCC's general provisions. Changes to Article 1 of the UCC and non-UCC law such as UCITA are discussed or noted where relevant.

In May 2001, a drafting committee promulgated a draft proposing some organizational and substantive revisions of Article 2. Much of the draft leaves existing Article 2's provisions unchanged. Nevertheless, the draft has proven to be very controversial. The key point of contention has been the scope of Article 2. The membership of the ALI approved the draft proposals, which did not alter the existing scope provision, at its 2001 annual meeting. At the subsequent NCCUSL meeting, however, the drafting committee was asked to approve a new scope section that attempted to define the reach and limits of Article 2 with respect to "smart goods" and other computer-related goods such as software. The NCCUSL membership then defeated a motion to adopt the revision project containing the new scope provision. This leaves the revision of

---

[5] § 1-102(2)(b); Rev. § 1-103(a)(2).

Article 2 is disarray. As of this writing, the ALI and NCCUSL are attempting to resolve their differences about the scope of Article 2. It remains unclear whether any revision will be forthcoming. Because of the substantive proposals reflect the most recent thinking on sales law, we discuss them in this text and compare them to current law. We refer to these proposals as the Proposed Revision (or to a "Proposed" section). All references are to the May 2001draft of the Drafting Committee.

## II. The United Nations Convention on Contracts for the International Sale of Goods

As the international sale of goods has increased, so have the pressures to bring to international trade the same level of legal uniformity and certainty that the UCC has made possible for domestic transactions. Efforts to create greater uniformity in international sales date back to the 1930s, when the International Institute for the Unification of Private Law (UNIDROIT) began work on treaties that would govern international commercial transactions. UNIDROIT ceased its efforts during and immediately after World War II, but ultimately submitted a draft to a diplomatic conference in The Hague in 1964. The conference adopted two conventions, one on the international sale of goods and the other on the formation of contracts for the international sale of goods. These conventions were criticized as insufficiently international in scope and too tied to the legal traditions of continental Western Europe. As a result, the conventions were not widely adopted.

Subsequently, the United Nations Commission on International Trade Law (UNCITRAL), organized in 1966, convened an additional conference to determine whether the Hague treaties could be modified to generate wider acceptance. The result was a series of meetings in Vienna, attended by 62 nations, that led to the adoption in 1980 of the United Nations Convention on Contracts for the International Sale of Goods. Under Article 99 of the CISG, it became effective a year after deposit of the tenth instrument of adherence. As a result, the CISG went into effect among 11 nations in 1988.

Many of the principles underlying the CISG should be familiar to a student of the UCC. Primary among these is the principle of freedom of contract, or "party autonomy." Under Article 6, parties to a contract may exclude the application of the CISG or derogate from or vary the effect of any of its provisions. The exclusion of the CISG may mean that parties have selected the law of a particular jurisdiction to govern their transaction, or that the parties have negotiated between themselves a contract term that reflects their particular transaction, even though that term is inconsistent with the CISG provision covering the same issue. In either case, the parties' selection will trump the CISG. We discuss in Chapter 2 the extent to whether implied versus express exclusions of the CISG is permissible.

Article 7(1) of the CISG also explicitly admonishes courts to recognize and adhere to the international character of the Convention and to promote uniformity. Some courts have responded to the appeal for "internationality" by balancing the dictates of different legal doctrines, including those of Contracting States not involved in the transaction at issue. For instance, in a Swiss case,[6] the court concluded that, under Article 39 of the CISG, a Swiss buyer who wished to reject goods had to notify an Italian seller within a reasonable time after discovery of any nonconformity. The court then had to determine the appropriate time limit for giving the requisite notice. The court considered that the German legal system imposed a relatively short, eight-day, period for giving notice, while Anglo-American and Dutch systems allowed buyers several months to give notice. The court concluded that a one-month period for giving notice constituted a compromise that would advance the international nature of the CISG.

It remains to be seen how successful the admonition of uniformity will be. As we will see, provisions of the CISG are written with sufficient vagueness as to require substantial interpretation. Respect for uniformity requires that courts construing these provisions pay substantial attention to precedents of courts in other jurisdictions that have adopted the CISG. This could cause courts to be relatively proactive in their interpretations of the CISG in order to articulate precedents that will then become authoritative, if not binding, for subsequent courts. More realistically, however, it is difficult to imagine a court deferring to the decisions of foreign legal systems to interpret a convention of which that court's country is a signatory. A United States court, we suspect, is unlikely to adopt an interpretation of a CISG provision favored by a Lithuanian court or a Ugandan court simply because that decision was promulgated first. This is true not only because each court system is likely to be somewhat nationalistic in its desire to shape law under the CISG. Difficulties of identification and translation also make it hard for the judicial system of one Contracting State to have easy access to authoritative versions of the decisions of every other Contracting State.

---

[6] Obergericht Kanton Luzern, 11 95 123/357, 8/1/97 (Switzerland), 1 UNILEX D.1997-2 (M.J. Bonell, ed).

The problems of access to decisions, although still significant, are less serious than they once were. In 1988, UNCITRAL established the CLOUT ("case law on UNCITRAL texts") reporting system for collecting and publishing abstracts of court decisions and arbitral awards relating to the texts produced by UNCITRAL (<http://www.un.or.en-index.htm>). Almost all are reports of final decisions. CLOUT's abstracts are submitted by national correspondents who monitor, collect and summarize decisions and awards in one of the United Nation's official languages. To date over 250 cases involving CISG have been reported. The full text of some of them appear in the UNILEX reports. In light of divergent interpretations of CISG's provisions, UNCITRAL is considering establishing an editorial board in the CLOUT system. The board would summarize and comment on trends in the application of CISG. Its apparent function would be to reduce divergence in interpretation based on ignorance of patterns of CISG's interpretation in national courts and arbitral tribunals. Some degree of uniformity, however, also may be achieved by careful judicial use of the legislative history of the drafting process. A rich documentary history of the Vienna Conference has been compiled,[7] and contains earlier drafts of the CISG and commentaries by parties during their deliberations. The 1978 draft contains a Secretariat Commentary, much of which remains relevant. It is important, however, to recall that this draft, and hence the Secretariat Commentary, precedes the 1980 version of the CISG that was ultimately adopted.

## III. Principles of Sales Contracts—Herein of Default Rules.

Our emphasis on freedom of contract principles in the UCC and the CISG reveals a particular understanding of the function of commercial law. After all, if parties are permitted to deviate from legislatively created legal doctrine, then why have that doctrine in the first place? Why wouldn't parties simply draft their agreements according to their preferences without any background rules of law?

The answer to this question, we believe, lies primarily in the concept of transactions costs. Contracting is an expensive process, as parties must decide which terms they prefer, negotiate those terms with their trading partners, and reduce their agreement to writing. These costs are reduced significantly if the law provides a background set of rules that the parties can accept through contractual silence. In this event, parties

---

[7] See Documentary History of the Uniform Law for International Sales (J.O. Honnold ed., 1989).

need not negotiate or draft terms, since their failure to address particular issues will cause courts to fill in the contractual gaps with the state-supplied "off-the-rack" provision. There may be situations in which particular parties desire terms other than those supplied by the state, even though they will have to incur costs they would have been able to avoid had they accepted the default rule. For instance, legal doctrine may place the risk of loss on sellers during transit, but a particular buyer may prefer to accept the risk of loss at an earlier time. (Perhaps the buyer enjoys an advantage in obtaining insurance or wants to make sure that the goods are packaged in a particular way.) To the extent that we allow parties to deviate from the state-supplied doctrine, legal rules are *default rules*. They apply unless the parties have decided otherwise. They are to be contrasted, therefore, with *mandatory rules*, from which parties cannot deviate even if they desire to do so. For the most part, the transaction-cost-reducing function of legal default rules operates properly only if the state-supplied rule reflects what a majority of commercial parties would prefer. Otherwise, the purpose of the rule will be defeated as most commercial parties bargain away from the default, thereby incurring the very costs that the rule was intended to avoid. As long as the default rule reflects the preferences of the majority of relevant actors, however, total transactions costs will be minimized.

Nevertheless, the very existence of the default rule may have some effect on the risk allocations in the ultimate transaction. Assume, for instance, that the default rule places the risk of loss on seller in a situation where the buyer believes it faces an additional expected loss of $2 as a result of the legal risk allocation. The buyer may believe, for example, that there is a 2 percent greater risk that a good will suffer $100 worth of damage if the seller bears the risk of loss than if the buyer bears it. Under these circumstances, the buyer might negotiate to bear the risk of loss, perhaps for a decrease in the sales price. If, however, the buyer anticipates that the costs of negotiating with the seller will exceed $2, then the buyer is better off accepting the default rule than contracting out of it, even though, transactions costs aside, the buyer would have preferred the alternative allocation of risk of loss.

Even in commercial law, however, legal rules are not necessarily intended to minimize transactions costs. Sometimes legal rules impose an obligation on parties because, left to their own devices, they would reach a solution that was contrary to the interests of nonparties. Price-fixing arrangements, for instance, might be perfectly acceptable to the parties to the contract, but impose costs on others who do not have an opportunity to bargain for a different rule. We can think of actions that impose costs on nonparties as the "externalization" of those costs. Costs of the transaction that are realized by the parties to the transaction, conversely, are "internalized." Rules that protect nonparties tend to be mandatory, rather than default rules, since parties would frequently bargain away from them if given the opportunity to do so.

In addition, some legal rules pursue paternalism. Legal rules could protect parties from bargains they would otherwise make against their own interest. The classic case is the rule against contracts for slavery. One defense for such rules is that we fear that individuals who face short-term needs will underestimate the long-term costs of such a contract and enter into it, only to regret their decision at a later time. In short, as opposed to the case of externalities, in which we fear that contracting parties will be inattentive to the interests of others, we allow courts to invalidate parties' volitional contracts where we fear that individuals will be insufficiently attentive to their own interests or where we believe that parties are incapable of attending to their own interests. Where we wish paternalistically to protect people from their own bad judgment, a mandatory rule again may be appropriate. One example of such a rule is the "unconscionability" doctrine of § 2-302, which allows a court to refuse to enforce the bargain made by the parties because it is too one-sided.

Nevertheless, there are other occasions on which we feel strongly about what bargain the parties should reach, but not so strongly as to prohibit them from bargaining for a different rule. In this case, we might state a rule as a default rule to indicate a social preference, or to call special attention to the option presented by the default rule and ensure that parties who bargain away from that rule incur significant costs that might lead them to think seriously about the appropriateness of their actions. Examples of this function of default rules are more difficult to find in Article 2, perhaps because those provisions envision relatively sophisticated buyers and sellers. But other parts of the UCC which deal with a mix of sophisticated and less sophisticated parties contain rules that have this characteristic. For instance, under Article 9 of the UCC, certain creditors are required to notify their debtors of pending sale of the collateral after foreclosure. This obligation may not be waived or varied as a general matter, but a debtor may sign a statement after default that renounces or modifies the right to notification of sale.[8] The default rule of notification provides a social preference for that rule and induces parties to adhere to it. It also signals the debtor who is asked to sign a

---

[8] § 9-624(a).

post-default waiver that the request involves an extraordinary act and thus encourages contemplation about whether a waiver is appropriate. At the same time, the default nature of the rule suggests that there may be sufficient cases in which a waiver would be appropriate that we do not want to prohibit waivers by making notification mandatory.

A final use for default rules involves what has become known as "information forcing." Rules with this characteristic purport to solve problems that arise when one party has more information relating to a transaction than another party. Under these circumstances, we say that the parties have "asymmetric information." Assume, for instance, that a widget buyer expects to suffer $1000 in damages if the good being sold does not operate properly, even though most buyers in the same position would only suffer $10 in damages. (Maybe our buyer has an unusually profitable downstream contract that can be filled only if the widget operates properly.) If the seller is unaware of the buyer's unique situation and knows only what happens when more typical buyers purchase widgets, the seller will only take precautions sufficient to avoid the standard $10 in damages rather than this buyer's idiosyncratic $1000 damages. Nevertheless, the seller might be in a superior position to avoid the $1000 loss by ensuring proper operation of the widget. If that is the case, we would want the seller to take the precaution to avoid the wasteful loss from materializing. But seller will do so (and charge buyer a price accordingly) only if it is aware of buyer's greater than average potential loss.

A default rule that requires an ignorant seller only to compensate the average expected damage, but that makes a knowledgeable seller responsible for all damages induces, or "forces," the buyer to convey the relevant information to the seller. In this way, buyers will take advantage of their superior information about the transaction by conveying the information to sellers, and sellers will take advantage of their superior ability to avoid losses by taking precautions in an amount equal to the higher expected loss. Since each party performs that act that it is best positioned to perform, the parties are presumably doing what each would agree to do, since that assignment of responsibilities will minimize the costs of the transaction. If a seller were responsible for its buyer's idiosyncratic and unknown damages, for instance, the cost of contracting would increase. The seller would likely incur higher bargaining costs to negotiate a liability cap, or invest more than the expected value of transactional breakdown to ensure that goods performed properly, or charge more for goods, in order to insure against the occasional idiosyncratically high damage award when goods did not perform properly. These consequences suggest that most commercial parties would prefer a default rule that induced the party with superior information to disclose it. Thus, information-forcing default rules are likely to be majoritarian rules as well. We discuss this principle further in Chapter 3.

## IV. Commercial Contracts as Discrete and Relational Contracts — Herein of Reputation

### A. Reputation and Relational Contracts

If default rules truly reflect the preferences of a majority of transacting parties, then written contracts should be relatively incomplete. That is, they will not provide for every future contingency that might materialize during the contract term. Parties will spend little time dickering over terms because the gaps created by their silence are filled by the default terms to which they presumably would have agreed had they negotiated explicitly. Commercial sales contracts, however, may be incomplete for other reasons. The difficulty or cost of foreseeing all contingencies may prevent complete contracting. Parties who anticipate that their interaction will span a significant time period will have difficulty anticipating all the risks that might materialize during their relationship. They will therefore be reluctant to attempt an explicit allocation of all risks. They might fear that they will allocate a risk to a party who is less able to avoid it when the contingency threatens to materialize. Alternatively, parties will not want to invest significant time negotiating the allocation of risks that seem remote. The low probability of an event makes the expected value of some risks not worth the cost of deciding how to allocate them. For instance, it is unlikely that the parties to a 20-year contract for the supply of lumber produced in Oregon will spend much time allocating the risk of Oregon seceding from the Union and placing an embargo on lumber shipments to the remaining states.

Another reason for incomplete contracting is the cost of a court verifying contingencies provided for in a contract. Judicial enforcement of the contract requires a court to observe that a contracted-for contingency has occurred, and the court may have difficulty acquiring reliable information necessary to do so. In such circumstances, parties may decide not to provide for such contingencies.[9]

---

[9] Much of the legal literature on incomplete contracts relies on intuitive hunches about the presence of these factors. For criticism of the unformalized basis of incomplete contracting, see Kirsten Foss & Nicolai J. Foss, *Theoretical Isolation in Contract Theory: Suppressing Margins and Entrepreneurship*, 7

An important type of incomplete contract are "relational" contracts. Relational contracts are characterized by long-term arrangements, heightened uncertainty at the negotiation stage about future consequences of present acts, and the investment of resources unique to the transaction and thus not easily usable in other transactions. These characteristics induce the parties to accommodate each other's needs during the period of performance, even though no explicit contractual allocation requires such an accommodation. The fact that each party has invested in the transaction makes it more difficult to exit from the relationship even when things go better than expected for one party and worse than expected for the other. Instead, the relational character of the contract induces each party to accommodate the interests of the other. For instance, a shipper of coal who constructs a railroad track to serve a particular customer is likely to act in a manner that preserves the relationship with the customer because the track is otherwise useless and creating a new track with a replacement customer would be costly. If the customer has purchased railroad coal cars that cannot easily be moved to other tracks, the parties have created a relationship in which each has incentives to care for the interests of the other rather than to take advantage of the other party's weakness.

The long-term nature of the transactions reinforces the tendency towards accommodation, since each party may be wary that at some future point it will need the assistance of the other party. Thus, each party has an incentive to realize the maximum joint gains of their transaction, that is, to maximize their combined benefits, even though doing so on a particular occasion requires one of the parties to sacrifice an opportunity to obtain personal gains at the expense of another. We contrast this result with activity in which one party takes advantage of the other's vulnerability, even though the gains to the selfish party are outweighed by the losses to the other party. (In the text selfish parties are described as acting "strategically" or "opportunistically.") In a relational situation, the joint interests of the parties would be served by forgoing the selfish action. For instance, one party might maximize joint interests by agreeing to price concessions where the contract term required sales to occur at a fixed price, but the market price of the goods had declined dramatically from the parties' expectations when they first entered into the contract.

The lesson to be learned is that even where a contract fails to allocate

---

J. Econ. Meth. 313 (2000); Jean Tirole, *Incomplete Contracting: Where Do We Stand?*, 67 Econometrica 741 (1999).

certain risks, parties in a relational contract may still be able to protect themselves. Commercial parties in such relationships have incentives to work matters out as the contract is implemented, to forgive small deviations from contract requirements, or to accede to demands of the other party rather than instigate litigation or cancel the contract. To suggest that parties to relational contracts have incentives to cooperate, however, is not to suggest that the law should require them to cooperate. There may be valid reasons for courts to allow behavior that might be considered opportunistic. We discuss this issue when we explore the scope of permissible excuse in Chapter 6.

Relational contracts therefore are to be distinguished from "discrete" transactions, characterized by the "one-shot" deal in which parties face each other, transact, and do not meet again. The salient distinction between these types of contracts is the extent to which the parties will confront each other in a subsequent interaction, that is, the likelihood that they will be "repeat players." Their repeated interactions cause the parties to care about their reputations at least as much as their legal rights. While legal rights are clearly important, commercial parties may often ignore their rights and rely on reputation rather than fear of lawsuits to reduce opportunistic or strategic behavior by trading partners. Lawsuits are expensive to initiate and, even if successful, are unlikely to be fully compensatory. Damages in commercial contract suits will rarely cover litigation costs or the lost value of the award between the time of breach and the time of recovery. Informal norms, such as refusing to cooperate with or transact with a party who has a reputation for acting selfishly, may be much more effective than legal rules in dissuading commercial parties from acting in an opportunistic manner.

## B. Reputation without Repetition

Reputation will also matter where parties do not interact frequently, but where they are both members of the same trade or industry and members of the trade or industry can easily disseminate reliable information about each other. Under these conditions, if I enter into a discrete transaction with one member of the network, any strategic behavior in which I engage can quickly become known to others, and they may be less willing to deal with me in the future. Reputation within a network of related actors may be particularly important in international law. Parties to international sales may be unfamiliar with their trading partners, and be suspicious about mutual performance because geographic distance and differences in legal regimes can render contract enforcement difficult. Thus, parties to international contracts may rely on the reputation of potential trading partners before entering into even a discrete transaction.

As the above discussion implies, reputation affects legal rules in at least two ways. First, reputation reduces the need for legal constraints on strategic behavior because legal sanctions may be secondary to informal sanctions. Threats by members of an industry to shun parties who violate the norms of the trade will be a more effective sanction than the possibility of damages for a breach at some point in the future. Law becomes necessary, however, when reputation is ineffective. Assume, for instance, that a seller is on the verge of bankruptcy, but may be able to avoid business failure by chiseling on a particular contract. Reputational constraints may not prevent the seller from acting improperly, since failure to do so means that there will be no business to enjoy a good reputation. The threat of legal liability, however, may forestall the misconduct if damages can be collected against the seller individually and not just from the defunct business.

Second, the force of reputation justifies a limited judicial role in the construction of commercial contracts. Reputation gives commercial parties incentives to act reasonably and in accordance with industry or trade standards, in order to avoid retaliation. It is largely for this reason that Llewellyn's appeal to commercial practices to complete the interstices of the law makes sense. If commercial actors have significant extra-legal incentives to act in a manner that is consistent with joint welfare, and if the pursuit of joint welfare has limited negative effects on nonparties, then there is less need to impose some externally generated standard on those parties. Thus, it makes sense for a court that is interpreting vague statutory admonitions to act "reasonably" or in "good faith," to consider the conduct of persons in the trade rather than to decide independently what parties should have done in the situation. It is largely for this reason that we frequently see judges invoke the principle that courts do not rewrite contracts for parties or intervene to relieve parties from allegedly improvident bargains.[10]

---

[10] See, e.g., Marriott Corp. v. Dasta Construction Co., 26 F.3d 1057 (11th Cir. 1994); Envirotech Corp. v. Halco Eng'g, Inc., 364 S.E.2d 215, 220 (Va. 1988) ("[W]here, as here, experienced parties agree to allocate unknown or undeterminable risks, they should be held to their bargain; courts, or juries, should not be permitted to rewrite the agreement").

# CHAPTER 2
# GOVERNING LAW

## I. Scope of Sales Law Under Article 2

### A. Definition of "Goods"

The UCC covers a substantial variety of commercial transactions ranging from sales, leases, transactions intended for security, and bulk sales, to transactions in investment securities. Each of the Articles of the UCC governs a particular type of transaction and provides rules unique to that transaction. It is necessary, therefore, to determine how a transaction should be classified for purposes of the UCC. Examination of the scope section of Article 2 offers a deceptively simple explanation of what transactions fall within its purview.

Although Article 2 is titled "Sales," § 2-102 states that Article 2 covers what might be considered a much broader range of dealings: "transactions in goods." Revised 2-102 leaves the provision unchanged. At first glance, "transactions in goods" would appear to subsume virtually all segments of commercial contracting. We begin with an analysis of that phrase to introduce students to the "jigsaw puzzle" nature of the UCC and the unique definitions that the UCC employs. The jigsaw puzzle is evident once one realizes that analysis of one provision of Article 2 typically requires simultaneous analysis of related provisions. Often the relationship among provisions is simply definitional. A term used in one provision will be defined in another. It is essential to pay attention to the definitions of terms within the UCC, since they frequently vary from ordinary language definitions of the same terms. Through an examination of these definitions, we will see how Article 2 actually embraces a narrower range of commercial dealings than the plain English definition of the phrase "transactions in goods" implies.

A hypothetical is helpful here. Assume that Buyer and Seller enter into a contract for the purchase of a desk that Buyer has picked out of Seller's catalogue. The desk must be manufactured by Seller and delivery time is estimated at six weeks. The day after the contract is signed, Seller repudiates on the grounds that a decision has been made to discontinue that desk model. Section 2-102 informs us that the rights of the parties are governed by Article 2 of the UCC if the contract was a "transaction in goods." But was it?

Certainly there was some form of "transaction" involved. The UCC contains no special definition of that term, so we resort to plain English meanings within which our contract between Buyer and Seller would easily fall. But the definition of "goods" is more complicated. Section 2-105(1) defines goods as "things (including specially manufactured goods) which are movable at the time of identification to the contract for sale." Thus, from the outset, it is clear that Article 2 does not govern transactions in real estate or fixtures that have become part of real estate by virtue of their immovability. There are some specific exclusions from the definition of goods, such as money in which the price is to be paid, investment securities, and things in action. But any other "movable" items fall within the definition of goods. The desk at issue, however, has not yet been manufactured, so there is no "thing" to be movable. One might initially imagine, therefore, that the transaction does not involve a good. But recall that the definition requires that movability be determined not as of the time that the contract is made, but as of the time of "identification to the contract for sale." Indeed, Article 2 recognizes that goods subject to its provisions will not always exist at the time the contract is made, since it explicitly refers to "future goods," those goods that are not existing or identified, as a subset of "goods." Future goods, therefore, remain subject to Article 2 if they are movable at the time they are identified to the contract for sale.

Note also that the definition of "goods" in terms of a contract for sale substantially restricts the scope of Article 2. Although the grant of a security interest in a book collection would certainly be a transaction in movables, that transaction is not governed by Article 2 because it does not involve a "contract for sale." Nor would a lease of movable equipment be included within Article 2, because a lease (at least a "true" lease, rather than one that simply takes the form of a leasehold interest while providing the parties with rights that are usually associated with a purchase) is not a sale. It is through the definition of "goods," therefore, that we come to understand how Article 2 is limited to sales law.

Does the desk qualify as something "movable at the time of identification to the contract for sale"? Note that no "sale" of the desk has yet occurred. Section 2-106(1) defines "sale" as the passing of title from seller to buyer for a price. Title may pass at such time as the parties agree. In most cases, however, (and let us assume in our hypothetical) the parties will be silent with respect to the passage of title. In those cases, the default rule will apply. The default provided by § 2-401(2) provides that title passes when the seller has completed performance with respect to the delivery of the goods. In our hypothetical, of course, that has not happened, so no sale has occurred.

Recall, however, that application of Article 2 does not require a "sale;" instead it requires a "contract for sale." That term can include both a present sale of goods and a contract to sell goods at a future time.[1] By entering into an agreement to sell the desk when it is manufactured, that is, to have the title pass once Seller had performed its obligation of manufacture, Buyer and Seller agreed to enter into a contract to sell the desk at that future time. They have thereby entered into a "contract for sale."

The definition of "goods" next requires that the goods be movable not when the contract for sale is entered into, but when the goods at issue are "identified" to the contract for sale. Is that condition satisfied in our hypothetical? The time of identification is governed by § 2-501. Under that provision, goods are identified to the contract for sale at the time the contract is made if it is for the sale of goods that are already existing and identified. This definition seems inherently circular: it curiously provides that present goods can be "identified" to the contract when they are "identified." But the thought behind the language seems relatively clear: If I purchase a desk off the floor of a furniture store, the goods are identified when I make the contract with respect to that particular desk.

In our hypothetical, however, we are not concerned with existing goods, but with future goods. In that case, and subject to exceptions for special goods such as unborn animals or growing crops, identification occurs when the goods have been manufactured and are shipped, marked, or otherwise designated by the seller as the subject matter of the contract. Identification, then, typically cannot occur until the goods are in the form they must take before they are tendered to the buyer. If tender involves shipment of items that the seller is required to assemble, then the goods are not identified until assembly, even if the seller has all the separate parts.[2] Thus, once Seller completes manufacture of the desk and designates it as the one that has been made in satisfaction of Buyer's contract, that designation constitutes an identification to the contract. If the desk will be "movable" at that time, the contract with respect to it is a transaction in goods and is subject to Article 2.[3]

---

[1] § 2-106(1).

[2] See Kit Car World v. Skolnick, 616 So. 2d 1051 (Fla. App. 1993).

[3] Goods that are fungible, like sand, gas, or oil, pose additional identification questions. See, e.g., Piney Woods Country Life School v. Shell Oil Co., 726 F.2d 225 (5th Cir. 1984).

One last problem remains, however. The contract with respect to this desk has been repudiated. Manufacture of the desk will never be completed. Thus, no identification will ever occur and it will never become movable. This might be thought to take the transaction out of the definition of goods. Nevertheless, § 2-610 explicitly covers repudiation, so the drafters obviously intended Article 2 to apply even where contracts were not fully performed. The better interpretation, then, would be that the transaction involves goods, notwithstanding that this conclusion requires us to construe § 2-105(1) to include things that *are movable* at the time of identification to the contract for sale or that *would have been* movable at such time had they come into existence. As a result, the desk would be a "good." A repudiated contract for construction of a house, however, would not fall within the scope of Article 2, since it would not involve a movable "thing" and thus would not be a transaction in a "good." Just to complicate matters more, however, you should recognize that contracts concerning "mobile homes" have typically been included within Article 2, even if alleged defects giving rise to the dispute arose after the home was "blocked up" on a lot.[4]

As the above discussion indicates, definitions in the UCC are not always precise. They may not even be helpful. Section 2-103(1)(d), for instance, defines a "seller" to be "a person who sells or contracts to sell goods."[5] Thus, the definition provides the great insight that one who sells is a "seller." Definitions may also be too vague to be useful without additional interpretation. Section 1-204(3) provides that an action is taken "seasonably" when "it is taken at or within the time agreed or if no time is agreed at or within a reasonable time."[6] Since a "reasonable time" is as open-ended as "seasonable," § 1-204(3)'s definition does not increase clarity. Some other interpretive tool is necessary to provide meaning to the definition. That tool is typically an understanding and application of the policy underlying the UCC or a particular provision. In the chapters that follow, therefore, we will offer explanations for various provisions in order provide the student with analytical tools for

---

[4] See, e.g., Jorgensen v. Pressnall, 545 P.2d 1382 (Or. 1976).

[5] § 2-103(1)(d). Since § 2-106(1) defines a "sale" to be "the passing of title from the seller to the buyer for a price," § 2-103(1)(d) defines a "seller" to be one who passes title to the buyer for a price. Section 2-106(1) clarifies what selling involves; § 2-103(1)(d) does not.

[6] § 1-204(3).

interpretation.

### B. Merchants

A good example of the use of policy to resolve definitional ambiguity concerns the definition of a "merchant" under Article 2. Many provisions of the UCC impose a different standard of conduct on merchants than on non-merchants, so the distinction can be important. Section 2-104(1) defines a "merchant" roughly as a person (a) who deals in goods of the kind, or (b) who represents himself as having knowledge or skill peculiar to the practices or goods involved in a transaction, or (c) whose employment of an intermediary with particular skills makes it reasonable to attribute such knowledge or skill to the employer.

Interpretation of this provision has arisen largely in litigation over application of § 2-201(2) to farmers. Section 2-201(2) provides a merchant exception to the UCC Statute of Frauds requirement. Under § 2-201(2), a contract is enforceable against a merchant, even if it has not signed a legally sufficient memorandum, if the merchant fails to object to the contents of a written confirmation of the contract from another merchant within ten days of receiving it and enforceable against the sender. *Nelson v. Union Equity Co-operative Exchange*[7] presents a typical fact pattern. The farmer entered into an oral contract with a grain silo, promising to deliver wheat at a fixed price at a future time. Subsequently the grain silo sent the farmer written confirmation of the transaction, and he failed to respond. The market price of wheat later increased and the farmer refused to perform. When the silo sued for damages, the farmer raised the lack of a legally sufficient memorandum signed by him as a defense. The silo was indisputably a merchant and the confirmation was enforceable against it. Hence the silo could enforce the contract only if the farmer was also a merchant for purposes of § 2-201(2). The court concluded that the farmer was a merchant, as he made his livelihood by raising and selling crops, and was a "professional" with respect to those practices. A vigorous dissent contended that the farmer only made a "casual sale" of wheat once a year and could not be designated a merchant.

The terms of § 2-104(1) alone do not decide the farmer's status. Nothing in those terms informs us how many times, and under what circumstances, a farmer must sell wheat to "deal in goods of the kind."

---

[7] 548 S.W.2d 352 (Tex. 1977); cf. John F. Dolan, *The Merchant Class of Article 2: Farmers, Doctors, and Others*, 1977 Wash. U.L.Q. 1.

Nor does the definition tell us to which "practices" § 2-104(1) refers: growing wheat, selling wheat, entering into a forward contract for wheat, or responding to a written confirmation of a contract. It is not even clear how we should define the seller's "occupation" to which § 2-104(1) refers: a wheat farmer or an occasional seller of wheat? (Of course, the dissent may have been a bit disingenuous in referring to the farmer as a "casual" seller. One who makes only one sale a year, but who receives all of his annual income from that one sale and who makes a similar sale every year in order to obtain income is a very different kind of seller than a consumer who once a year sells household goods at a yard sale.) Thus, the plain statutory language of § 2-104(1), even when supplemented by dictionary definitions, is inconclusive.

A better way to determine the merchant status of farmers is to identify the underlying purpose of the Statute of Frauds and determine whether holding farmers to the standard of merchants satisfies that purpose. As we discuss at length in Chapter 5, § 2-201(2)'s purpose is to allow parties to enforce a contract without a signed writing from the recipient where the parties nevertheless likely intended a contract for sale. Section 2-201(2) is easily justified by the comparative size of contracting costs associated with obtaining a signed writing and responding to a confirmation. Even the court in *Nelson* recognized that it is cheaper for the recipient to respond to a confirmation than for the sender to obtain a signed writing from the recipient. The recipient reads its mail and, at least where parties are highly likely to understand the business nature of the confirmation, can be expected to understand and object to the contents of a confirmation that contains disputed terms. The sender would have to incur higher costs in obtaining a signed writing from the recipient. Since most confirmations in business contexts can be expected to conform to the transaction agreed to by the parties (in which case the recipient need take no action to verify the contract), contracting costs are reduced by placing the cost of responding to a confirmation on the recipient.

Is a farmer a member of the class of recipients whose failure to respond to a confirmation is reliable evidence that a contract exists? Clearly, yes, since the class includes most people in business. A farmer therefore is a merchant under § 2-201(2). Comment 1 to § 2-104 agrees: "For purposes of these sections [i.e., §§ 2-201(2), 2-205, 2-207 and 2-209] almost every person in business would, therefore, be deemed to be a 'merchant'...." The weight of case law reaches the same result.[8]

There is an obvious corollary to definition by reference to statutory purpose: someone can be a merchant under § 2-201(2) but not under other sections of Article 2. For instance, a farmer might not be a merchant under § 2-314, which creates an implied warranty of merchantability of goods. A § 2-314 warranty, by its terms, only arises when the seller is a merchant with respect to the type of goods sold. As we discuss in Chapter 8, warranty is a risk-allocating device based on the contracting parties' comparative abilities to reduce or eliminate the relevant risk of nonconformity in the goods. An implied warranty of merchantability allocates the risk to the seller only when the seller can take precautions with respect to the nonconformity at less cost than can the buyer. The class of sellers who have a comparative advantage at risk-reducing is smaller than the class of recipients whose failure to respond to a written confirmation is reliable evidence of a contract. So a farmer might be a nonmerchant for purposes of a § 2-314 warranty but a merchant for purposes of § 2-201(2). Comment 1 to § 2-104 agrees: "Obviously this qualification [§ 2-314(1)'s condition that "the seller is a merchant with respect to goods of that kind"] restricts the implied warranty to a much smaller group than everyone who is engaged in business and requires a professional status as to particular kinds of goods." The section-by-section status of a party is a simple consequence of the UCC's reliance on statutory purpose in defining terms.

### C. Mixed Sales and Services

Transactions frequently involve a combination of sales and services, such as when a photographer contracts to take pictures at a wedding, or when a carpenter constructs cabinets and installs them in a kitchen. Courts have used various tests to determine the applicability of Article 2 in these circumstances. Typically, courts have asked whether "the predominant factor . . . , the thrust, the purpose [of the transaction] . . . is a transaction of sale with labor incidentally involved."[9] Even where the buyer appears to have been primarily concerned with the provision of

---

[8] See, e.g., Regents of the University of Minnesota v. Chief Industries, Inc., 106 F.3d 1409 (8th Cir. 1997).

[9] See, e.g., Bonebrake v. Cox, 499 F.2d 951, 960 (8th Cir. 1974) (installation of bowling lanes and equipment constitutes a sale of goods); Ward v. Puregro Co., 913 P.2d 582 (Idaho 1996) (fertilizer application contract fell outside Article 2).

labor, a complaint about the quality of a particular good supplied by the laborer may give rise to application of Article 2. For instance, in *Anthony Pools v. Sheehan*,[10] the plaintiffs contended that the defendant had breached a warranty with respect to a diving board that was part of a new swimming pool. The court noted that if it were to apply the "predominant purpose" test, no quality warranty would apply, since the predominant purpose of the contract was for construction of a swimming pool. Nevertheless, the court concluded that the diving board was a separate accessory sold by the defendant and had not been structurally integrated into the swimming pool. Standing alone, the court found, the diving board was a good, subject to the implied warranties of Article 2.

An alternative means for analyzing "mixed sales" cases is to ask whether the basis of the buyer's complaint is the seller's labor or a defect in the goods. For instance, no Article 2 warranty may attach if an electrician improperly installs wires, causing a fire. The same electrician, however, may make and breach a warranty by properly installing wires that are themselves defective, notwithstanding that they were properly installed. This "gravamen of the action" test. It will not easily resolve all cases, however. For instance, it is not clear whether a buyer who asserts that a custom-made entertainment unit fails to support the weight of an average television set is complaining about the "service" of selecting and installing the offending shelf or the "good" of the shelf itself. Of course, the predominant purpose test sometimes can be just as difficult to apply. Predominance usually is measured by factors such as the relative proportions of the contract price reflecting the cost of goods and services. These proportions can be difficult to determine, and their comparison a matter of degree.

The tests not only reach different results in some "mixed sales" cases. They also have different consequences for the law applied in them. A predominant purpose test selects a single set of legal rules to govern all aspects of a "mixed sales" transaction. If the goods aspect of the transaction predominates, Article 2 applies to the entire transaction, including its services aspects. If the services aspect predominates, non-UCC law controls the entire transaction, including the goods aspect. The "gravamen" test does not select a single set of legal rules to govern the entire transaction. This is because it selects law issue by issue. If the complaint is based on the services aspect of the transaction, non-UCC law control that aspect. Article 2 still governs complaints based on the

---

[10] 455 A.2d 434 (Md. 1983).

goods. Thus, where a transaction presents multiple issues going to provision of goods and services, different law would apply to different issues.

Although the majority of courts adopt the predominant purpose test, the case against its use is strong. Article 2 contains a set of default rules that arguably are efficient for majority of sales of goods. That set includes specific rules concerning delivery, transfer of title, acceptance and inspection, implied warranties, and recoverable damages. Most parties prefer them given the tangible nature of goods, as well as generalizations about their production, buyers' uses, and predictable injuries resulting from nonconformities. Parties might have different preferences if the subject matter is different and these generalizations do not hold. For example, an implied warranty of merchantability places the risk of a result on the seller: the goods must be suitable for the buyer's ordinary purposes. If the provision of a service is uncertain in its outcome, or the preference of its recipients unpredictable, most parties might prefer to allocate the risk of result to the recipient. In that case, an implied warranty is inefficient as a default rule for services contracts. As another example, consider a contract not involving a sale. Contracts involving licenses of intellectual property, for instance, do not transfer title. Even when a license transfers title, the default rule transfers title on the execution of the license.[11] Under § 2-401(2)'s basic rule, however, title passes at the point of delivery of the goods. Therefore, Article 2's default rule for passage of title is inappropriate for the non-sale aspects of transactions requiring delivery.

*Advent Systems Ltd. v. Unisys Corp.*,[12] illustrates the difficulty created by the predominant purpose's "one law" approach. The contract in *Advent Systems* called for Advent to provide computer software under a non-exclusive license that was to be packaged with hardware into a "document management system." Advent's obligations also included supplying and training technical personnel to help in its construction and installation. As such the transaction involved the sale of goods (hardware), a license of intellectual property (software) and the provision of services (supplying and training personnel). The court, motivated by the UCC's underlying purpose of modernizing and unifying the law of

---

[11] See, e.g., Lorin Brennan, *Why Article 2 Cannot Apply to Software*, 38 Duquesne L. Rev. 459, 517 (1999) (describing default rule under Copyright Act).

[12] 925 F.2d 670 (3d Cir. 1991).

commercial transactions,[13]　found that computer programs constitute goods once they are "implanted in the medium" that makes them distributable to and usable by computer operators.[14] Applying the predominant purpose test, the court determined that the contract's main objective was to transfer "products" rather than to provide services.[15] It concluded that under § 2-102 Article 2 applied to the entire transaction.

We think that the conclusion is wrong. Section 2-102 provides that Article 2 applies to transactions in goods, "[u]nless the context otherwise requires." The *Advent Systems* court in effect uses the predominant purpose test to find that the context "requires" Article 2's application to all aspects of the transaction. However, this is a poor test to rely upon, for two reasons. First, in the case of software, the predominant purpose test asks the wrong question: is the goods or services aspect of the transaction its predominant purpose? The question is irrelevant where the inquiry concerns the provision of intellectual property, not goods or services. Second, Article 2's default rules arguably are inappropriate for the sales and services aspects of the transaction in *Advent Systems*. Software is intellectual property, and it is typically licensed, not sold. Further, warranties of merchantability usually do not extend to services, such as supplying and training personnel. The efficient default rules for these aspects of the transaction therefore may not be Article 2's default rules. For both reasons, the transaction does not "require" application of Article 2 to its intellectual property and services aspects even when the context "requires" Article 2's application to the computer hardware. The predominant purpose test is incapable of reaching this result because it applies a single set of default rules to the entire transaction. The result could be reached under gravamen of the action test.

UCITA handles the scope issue presented by "mixed transactions"

---

[13] See § 1-102(2)(a), (c); Rev. § 1-103(a)(1), (3).

[14] See 925 F.2d at 676. The court's determination can be questioned on narrowly statutory grounds. Section 2-105(1)'s definition of goods requires that they be "movable at the time of identification to the contract." If the software referred to in the parties' agreement existed at the time and later was to be installed in the document management system, it could not be considered "movable" at the time it was identified to the contract. See § 2-501(1).

[15] Accord NMP Corp. v. Parametric Tech. Corp., 958 F. Supp. 1536 (N.D. Okla. 1997).

differently from the *Advent Systems* court. Under § 103(a), UCITA applies to computer information transactions. Section 102(11) in turn defines "computer information transaction "to include agreements to transfer or license of computer information. UCITA's general scope rule, contained in § 103(b)(1), adopts the "gravamen" test: different subject matters are governed by different law.[16] Under it, if a transaction includes both goods and computer information, UCITA "applies to the part of the transaction involving the computer information..." In this case Article 2 applies to the goods, assuming that the transaction involved their sale. There are two basic exceptions to UCITA's general scope rule. One concerns transactions involving copies of computer information or associated documentation. Because § 102(10) defines "computer information" to include both, UCITA applies to the copies and documentation as well as to the computer information. UCITA displaces other law. The second exception works to displace UCITA when a copy of a computer program is embedded in sold or leased goods. It applies to the sale or lease of "smart goods." Under § 103(b)(1), if a copy of a computer program is contained in sold or leased goods, UCITA applies to the copy and the computer program only if the goods are a computer or "computer peripheral," or the material purpose of the transaction of the type is ordinarily is to give access to or use of the computer program.[17] If the goods are not computers or computer peripherals or not provided to give access or use, UCITA does not apply to the computer program or the copy of it. For example, the a chip controlling an anti-skid brake system in a car typically would fall within the second exception. Article 2 would apply to both the sale of the car and the computer program controlling the system.

UCITA's general scope rule selects applicable law by subject matter. Under *Advent Systems'* facts UCITA applies to the computer software and the copies containing them, and Article 2 to the computer hardware. The agreement to provide a "document management system" apparently called for the software to be delivered in disk form or some other tangible medium.[18] Because the required media are copies containing computer information, § 103(b)(1)'s first exception controls, and UCITA applies

---

[16] See UCITA § 103 Official Comment 4(b)(1).

[17] See UCITA § 103(b)(1)(A), (B).

[18] See 925 F.2d at 676.

to both the copies and the computer information contained in them. The computer hardware called for in the "document management system," as a good, would continue to be governed by Article 2.[19]   Had the sales agreement called for the seller to deliver the hardware with the software installed, UCITA still would apply to the software and Article 2 to the hardware.   This is because the hardware is a computer, and § 103(b)(1)(A) applies UCITA to a computer program if the goods are computers in which it is contained when sold.  Thus, in either case, § 103(b)(1)'s second exception to its general rule is inapplicable and UCITA is not be displaced by other law.  Article 2 and its default rules therefore apply to the computer hardware; UCITA and its default rules apply to the software and copies of software.  To date, UCITA has been adopted by several states.  Where UCITA is not controlling law, a court must decide under § 2-102 whether Article 2 extends to all aspects of "mixed transactions."

## D.  Leases and Other Transactional Forms

The formal designation or structure that the parties give to their transaction does not necessarily determine its inclusion within or exclusion from Article 2.  For instance, § 2-102 removes from the Article any transaction *intended* to operate as a security transaction, notwithstanding that it takes the formal structure of a sale.  Assume, for instance, that Seller agrees to sell a stamp collection to Buyer on January 1 for $100, while simultaneously agreeing to repurchase the same collection from Buyer on July 1 for $105.  Notwithstanding that the parties have structured their transaction as a contract for sale (indeed, as two sales), we might pierce the parties' formal arrangement and identify the transaction as a secured loan with a 6-month maturity at an annual

---

[19] On *Advent System*'s facts, under UCITA law other than UCITA or Article 2 probably governs the services aspect of transaction.  Section 103(b)(3) applies UCITA's general rule to transactions involving subject matters other than those governed by the UCC: UCITA governs only aspects of the transaction involving computer information.  Non-UCITA law governs its other aspects.  The subsection contains an exception making UCITA applicable to the entire transaction "if the computer information or informational rights, or access to them, is the primary subject matter."  The exception is a variant of the predominant purpose test. See § 103 Official Comment 4(b)(2).  Because the agreement in *Advent Systems* was for the delivery of a "document management system," the supply and training of personnel probably was not its "primary" subject.  Thus, § 103(b)(3)'s exception is inapplicable and neither the UCC nor UCITA governs the services aspect of the agreement.

interest rate of 10 percent. Once we reach that conclusion, the transaction, regardless of form, is "intended for security" and falls outside the scope of Article 2.

Most of the cases that address whether a particular transactional form constitutes a "sale" for Article 2 purposes involve the distinction between a sale and a lease. For the most part, little now turns on the issue, since most states have adopted Article 2A, which applies many Article 2 sales concepts to leases. Nevertheless, there are some differences between the two Articles, so that it remains necessary to understand when each one applies. For instance, the rights of a lessor to recover a leased good from a third-party transferee are greater than the rights of a seller to recover the same good after the buyer's default,[20] and the distinction between a lease and sale may be crucial where the lessor/seller ends up in bankruptcy.[21]

Mere designation of a transaction as a "lease" does not mean that courts will respect that label. Courts have determined that a transaction denominated by the parties as a lease may still constitute a sale where the indicia of a sale exist. Those indicia primarily concern the passage of title to the designated "lessee." Even the definition of "lease" within Article 2A lends itself to this analysis, since the scope section of that Article provides that it applies to any transaction "that creates a lease,"[22] and a "lease" consists of "a transfer of the right to possession and use of goods for a term," but excludes a sale as defined in § 1-206.[23]

The criteria that courts have applied to discern the existence of a lease or sale are essentially those that the UCC employs to distinguish a "security interest" from a lease. Section 1-201(37) defines a security interest by reference to an "economic reality" test as applied to "the facts of each case." A transaction structured as a lease will be interpreted as a sale subject to a security interest if (1) the lessee has an obligation to continue paying consideration for the term of the lease, (2) the lessee cannot terminate the obligation until the end of the leasehold, and (3) the purported reversionary interest of the lessor is essentially meaningless.

---

[20] Compare §§ 2-507, 2-702 with § 2A-525(2).

[21] See Richard L. Barnes, *Distinguishing Sales and Leases: A Primer on the Scope and Purpose of UCC Article 2A*, 25 U. Mem. L. Rev. 873 (1995).

[22] § 2A-102.

[23] § 2A-103(1)(j).

The purely nominal nature of the reversionary interest may be evidenced by a showing that (1) the original term of the lease is equal to or greater than the remaining economic life of the goods, (2) the lessee is obligated to renew the lease for the remaining economic life of the goods or to become the owner of the goods, (3) the lessee has an option to renew the lease for the remaining economic life of the goods for no more than nominal additional consideration other than compliance with the lease, or (4) the lessee has an option to become the owner of the goods for no more than nominal additional consideration at the end of the lease. In any of these cases, the inference may be drawn that the lessee was always intended to retain the good until the end of its useful economic life, which essentially permits the "lessee" to obtain all the benefits that accrue with the passage of title. Revised § 1-203, which replaces § 1-201(37), leaves its substance essentially unchanged.

In applying § 1-201(37)'s factors, courts have primarily paid attention to the rights and duties of the parties at the end of the purported leasehold. Some courts appear to focus solely on whether there is an option to purchase the goods for nominal consideration at the end of the "lease." But the existence of "nominal" consideration is not always clear. An agreement that allowed a lessee to purchase the property "at a mutually agreeable purchase price" at the end of the lease period was deemed not nominal on the assumption that an arm's length bargain would reflect the current market price of the good.[24] But an agreement that a lessee was to pay a flat sum followed by a monthly payment for 60 months and that transferred title to the lessee at the end of the leasehold was not a lease as a matter of law.[25] Similarly, a $100 purchase price at the end of the lease for goods that had been leased for a total of $2 million was considered nominal.[26]

At bottom, the judgment about whether the transaction involves a lease or a sale requires a common sense intuition about who is the owner of the goods. Inquiries into such issues as residual value, options to purchase, termination rights and the like are essentially surrogates for more direct investigations about ownership. To apply this proposition, assume that Susan and Bill have entered into a written agreement

---

[24] Aerospace Corp. v. Comdisco, Inc., 1997 WL 259205 at 2.

[25] In re Southern Star Foods, Inc., 202 B.R. 784, 788 (E.D. Okla. 1996).

[26] In re American General Aircraft Corp., 190 B.R. 275, 278 (N.D. Miss. 1995).

concerning a machine that has a useful life of ten years. Machines of the type that is the subject of the agreement typically sell for $120,000 and have no salvage value at the end of their useful life. (We ignore interest rates in the following discussion for the sake of simplicity.) If the terms of the agreement require Susan to sell the machine to Bill for $120,000, payment to be made in 120 monthly installments of $1000 and recite that "Susan retains title to the machine until Bill makes all payments due under this agreement," we would find that the parties had entered into a conditional sale. The effect of Susan's retention of title is to secure payment of what looks like the full purchase price of the good over the useful life of the good. Regardless of whether we denominate this transaction a 10-year lease with a purchase option of $0, or a conditional sale, ownership of the machine vests in Bill and Susan has a security interest to secure payment of the purchase price.

Now assume that the terms of the agreement state that "Susan agrees to lease the machine to Bill for ten years at $1000 per month. At the end of the lease term, Bill is required to return the machine to Susan." We would still find that there is a secured sale. No residual interest remains at the end of the lease term, so there is nothing of value to return to the lessor. Because Bill bears the risk of fluctuation of the asset's value during the entire useful life of the asset, we would find that Bill is the owner of the machine.[27]

Next assume that the terms of the agreement recite that "Susan agrees to lease the machine to Bill for one year at $10,000 per month. Bill has the option to purchase the machine at the end of the year for $10." Again, this looks like a secured sale. Bill has paid the full price of the good during a period shorter than its useful life, and thus, as a practical matter, is unlikely to return a machine that has a substantial value for which he has paid. He will undoubtedly exercise his option to purchase because the option price, $10, is so much less than the remaining value

---

[27]A common variant in automobile leases is an open-ended lease with a terminal rent adjustment clauses (TRAC). These leases provide for a sale of vehicle by the lessor at the end of the lease term. A TRAC adjusts rent based on the depreciation of the vehicle during the term and the sale price received by the lessor. Because the sale places the upside and downside risks on the lessee, the lessee "owns" the automobile. The sale price partly determines the cost of the use to the lessee while she owns the vehicle. Case law is divided as to the whether a lease containing a TRAC is a true lease or secured sale; compare *In re Tulsa Port Warehouse Co.*, 690 F.2d 809 (10th Cir. 1982) (secured sale) with *Sharer v. Creative Leasing, Inc.*, 612 So.2d 1191 (Ala. 1993) (true lease).

of the machine ($108,000 using straight-line depreciation). What a deal! Furthermore, exercising the option allows him to recover the benefit of the payments he has already made. He is the owner of the machine.

Assume that the terms of the agreement state that "Susan agrees to lease the machine to Bill for $1000 per month for one year. Bill has the option to buy the machine at the end of the term for $110,000." This arrangement makes the determination of ownership difficult, because the parties have effectively split the risks that we normally attribute to ownership. Bill gets the upside risk of any increase in the market value of the good during the year, while Susan takes the downside risk. The issue is not whether the machine has value at the end of the initial term, but who gets that value. Here, the option price of $110,000 is about equivalent to the expected fair market value of the good at the end of the term, $108,000. We cannot say that the option price is nominal relative to the fair market value of the good. Thus, this looks like a true lease.

Suppose that the terms of the agreement provide that "Susan agrees to lease the machine to Bill for $10,000 per month for one year, with the option to renew the lease at $10 per month for each of the following nine years. Bill agrees to return the machine to Susan at the end of the lease term." Again, we would find that the option price is so small compared to the fair market value of the machine at the time the option is exercised that renewal of the lease for the remainder of the machine's useful life is a near certainty. This makes the consideration "nominal" for purposes of § 1-201(37) and the transaction is properly classified as a sale.

Finally, assume in the previous example that the agreement gives Bill a right to terminate the lease at any time during the year. None of § 1-201(37)'s factors make this a secured sale because the factors apply only to leases that do not contain a right to terminate. Nonetheless, the transaction is a secured sale. Given that the option is small compared to machine's fair market value, Bill is unlikely to exercise his right to terminate the lease. Because the lease therefore is likely to remain in effect until the time at which Bill has a right to renew, and the option price for renewal is "nominal," Bill again is likely to renew the lease for the remainder of the machine's useful life. Functionally, Bill "owns" the machine, even though he has the right to terminate the lease.

## II. The Scope of the CISG

### A. Choice of Law as a General Problem in Sales Law

Like Article 2 of the UCC, the CISG does not apply to all commercial transactions. The provisions of the CISG describe the kinds of transactions that fall within and outside of its reach. But the scope provision of the CISG does double duty. It also constitutes a choice of law provision that determines the circumstances under which the substantive provisions of the CISG apply.

To see the importance of the choice of law function of the CISG, consider first how the UCC handles choice of law issues. Section 1-105 of the UCC contains a general choice of law provision that applies to all Articles of the UCC. Under this provision, the UCC as adopted in a particular state will apply to any transaction that bears an "appropriate relation" to the state. In addition, the UCC explicitly permits the parties to agree that their rights and duties under a transaction will be governed by the law of any state to which the transaction bears a reasonable relation. Thus, parties who wish to have their transaction governed by the UCC have substantial discretion to opt into its provisions explicitly, and courts sitting in jurisdictions that have adopted the UCC may reach quite freely for the forum state's version of that body of law, subject only to constitutional limits on due process. Note, for instance, that the UCC permits application of forum law if there exists "an appropriate" relation to the forum state. Although some courts have recently interpreted "appropriate relation" as the "most significant relation,"[28] this test actually allows application of forum law even if some other jurisdiction has *more* significant contacts with, and hence an arguably "more appropriate" relation with the transaction.[29] Assume, for instance, that a Kansas seller entered into a contract with a Nebraska buyer in which all negotiations took place in Nebraska, performance was to occur in Nebraska, and the defect of which the buyer complained materialized in Nebraska. If the seller were to bring an action for the price of the goods in Kansas, the Kansas court would presumably be able to apply that state's law, since one of its citizens was a party to the contract, notwithstanding that the most significant contacts between the parties arose in Nebraska.

In domestic transactions, the widespread adoption of the UCC renders choice of law somewhat superfluous, although state variations in Article 2 and case law may create occasional instances in which choice of law matters significantly. But the ability of parties whose transaction

---

[28] See, e.g., Hadar v. Concordia Yacht Builders, Inc., 886 F. Supp. 1082, 1093 (S.D.N.Y. 1995).

[29] See, e.g., Atlanta Corp. v. Ohio Valley Provision Co., 414 A.2d 123 (Pa. 1980).

has some relationship with a jurisdiction that has adopted the UCC to have that body of law govern their agreement remains important in international transactions. Here, courts may feel both a certain fealty to domestic law and be somewhat concerned about the need to learn a foreign body of law if they do not apply domestic law. This is not to say that application of domestic law is unwarranted; it is only to say that United States courts are likely to seize the broad grant of jurisdiction in the UCC choice of law provision.

In *Callahan Equipment v. Markarian*,[30] for instance, some of the payments of the contract price were telexed from Iran to New Jersey, while other payments were made by the buyer in the United States. Suit was brought by the seller in New Jersey. The court determined that New Jersey law applied, in large part because the payment was to have occurred in that state, and the buyer's failure to pay was the basis of the lawsuit. This reasoning seem a bit contrived. It implies that had the buyer sued the seller in New Jersey for nonperformance, Iranian law would be have applied, since that would have been the jurisdiction in which the expected performance did not occur. A more defensible rationale for the result is that § 1-105(1) permits the forum state to apply its law if the transaction bears an "appropriate" relation to the forum, and the transaction in *Callahan Equipment* did so. The court hinted at this rationale when it declared that New Jersey's contacts were "sufficient" to justify application of New Jersey law.

Courts, however, are not necessarily chauvinistic in their application of domestic law. In *Madaus v. November Hill Farm, Inc.*,[31] a Virginia buyer contracted to purchase a horse from a German seller. The buyer attempted to rescind the contract after taking delivery, on the grounds that the horse was lame. The seller then brought an action in Virginia to recover the purchase price for the horse. Although defendant contended that Virginia bore "an appropriate relation" to the transaction, so that the UCC could apply, the court concluded that German law should govern the transaction. The court rejected a broad reading of § 1-105 and instead interpreted that provision as incorporating previously established state choice-of-law rules of the forum state. Since pre-UCC state law provided that the law of the place of performance governed questions concerning the performance of a contract, and the horse was delivered by the seller

---

[30] 34 U.C.C. Rep. Serv. 1503 (D.N.J. 1982).

[31] 630 F. Supp. 1246 (W.D. Va. 1986).

in Germany, the court concluded that Virginia looked to German law as controlling the rights of the parties. Similarly, the court found that German law governed the buyer's claims concerning the validity of the contract. Again, the court did not determine that Virginia had no "appropriate relation" to the contract. Rather it concluded that pre-UCC law, which it subsumed within § 1-105, looked to the law of the place where the contract was made to decide questions of validity.

These cases demonstrate that, at least in the face of contractual silence, the choice of law issue in international transactions has been highly uncertain. Revised Article 1 alters the UCC's choice of law rules without reducing this uncertainty. Revised § 1-301(c) generally provides that when the parties' agreement is silent as to applicable law, the forum's conflicts of law principles select applicable law. It thereby eliminates the pro-forum bias of § 1-105(1)'s "appropriate relation" test. Revised 1-301(c) instead requires neutrality: the same principles the forum uses to determine law governing non-UCC transactions apply to UCC transactions. However, unpredictability in applying conflict of laws principles remains. Although they need not have a pro-forum bias, predominant conflicts principles are vague and produce divergent results between, and sometimes within, jurisdictions. They are no clearer in application than the "appropriate relation" test.

Revised 1-301(b)(2) gives parties in an international transaction unlimited freedom to choose law, subject to restrictions in the case of consumer transactions. An "international transaction" under § 1-301(a)(2) is a transaction bearing a "reasonable relation" to a country other than the United States. International transactions exclude domestic transactions, and Revised § 1-301(b)(1) enforces a choice of state law if the state law chosen bears a "relation" to the transaction. Uncertainty in determining the "reasonableness" of a relation under § 1-105(1) is retained in Revised § 1-301(a)(2). The only difference is that the uncertainty now goes to distinguishing international from domestic transactions. Doubts about whether a transaction bears a reasonable relation to a state are replaced by doubts about whether the transaction is international or domestic. By its own terms, § 1-301(a)(2) determines international status based on facts about the transaction. More easily verifiable facts as to the identity or location of the parties by themselves apparently are irrelevant. Because the international nature of a transaction requires a "reasonable relation" to foreign elements, the uncertainty in determining "reasonableness" of a relation remains under § 1-301(a)(2).

The uncertainty in applicable law is present not just when the UCC governs but also under other law. For example, in the absence of choice, the basis presumption of the European Community Convention on the Law Applicable to Contractual Obligations selects the law of the place of performance "characteristic" of the contract.[32] Under the same circumstances, the Inter-American Convention on the Law Applicable to International Contracts selects the law of the place having the "closest ties" to the contract.[33] Even when results are predictable, the rules do not provide the basis for the prediction. In a sense, the choice of law issue under the UCC's "appropriate relation" test is comparatively unimportant because the uniformity of domestic sales law makes the consequences of choice of law less dramatic. Thus, one potential potential benefit of the CISG is to bring to international sales contracts the same degree of uniformity in substantive law that the UCC has brought to domestic contracts.

In order to perform that function, the CISG must provide fairly comprehensive guidelines about the conditions under which its substantive provisions apply. According to Article 1(1), the CISG applies where either of two criteria is satisfied. First, the CISG applies to contracts for the sale of goods between parties whose places of business are in different countries, each of which is a party to the CISG (a "Contracting State"). Second, the CISG applies to contracts for the sale of goods between parties whose places of business are in different countries, if the rules of private international law (that is, choice of law rules) would apply the law of a Contracting State to the transaction. Note that these jurisdictional criteria depend initially on the places of business of the parties being in different countries, so that a contract between two domestic parties will never be subject to the CISG, even if the contract involves negotiations, production, or performance with a second country. Note also that the second basis for application may be limited. As discussed below, a Contracting State may declare that it will not be bound by that jurisdictional predicate.

Some examples reveal the intricacies of these seemingly simple jurisdictional doctrines. Assume that a French corporation based in France and a New York-based corporation agree that the latter will ship goods to a plant of the former operating in Japan, where France and the

---

[32]Article 4(1), 33 Int'l Legal Mat. 733 (1994).

[33]Article 9, id.

United States are Contracting States, but Japan is not. A dispute arises about whether the goods were of merchantable quality and the French corporation sues the United States corporation for breach of warranty in New York. The court should apply the CISG to the dispute. Since both parties have places of business in different Contracting States, the CISG governs under Article 1(1)(a). This would be the result whether New York applied New York law or French law to the case. If the court applied the law of the forum, New York law, the CISG would apply because it constitutes federal law adopted by the Congress that, by virtue of the Supremacy Clause of the Constitution, trumps conflicting state law such as the UCC. Thus, § 1-105 would have no relevance in this situation. A New York court would not be entitled to apply New York on the grounds that the transaction had "an appropriate relation" to New York, since that provision has been superseded by federal law where the transaction falls within the scope of the CISG.

If the New York court applied French law, again Article 1(1)(a) would govern since France has also adopted the CISG. Alternatively, if the French corporation brought its action against the New York seller in France, a French court would look to CISG. No conflict between New York law and French law would arise, because each jurisdiction would be applying the same provisions of the CISG.

Assume that French nationals start a company in New Jersey and enter into the same contract with a New York corporation for the shipment of goods to Japan. If the same dispute were to arise, Article 1(1)(a) would not dictate application of the CISG, since all that matters for those purposes is the location of the place of business of the parties, not their nationality or the place where the contract is to be performed. Here the parties both have their place of business in the United States. Note that the flip side of this argument means that the CISG could apply even though all parties are to perform in a single country. Assume that a French corporation involved in construction sends its agent to New York to negotiate for the purchase and shipment of goods from the New York seller to the French buyer's construction project in Virginia. This contract would be governed by the CISG even though the goods never cross an international boundary since the parties have their places of business in different Contracting States.

Assume that in the preceding example, the French corporation sends its agent to negotiate the shipment of raw materials from New York to a processing plant wholly owned by the French corporation, but located in Virginia. Thus, the French corporation is not simply involved in a construction project in the United States. Now the CISG would apply only if the Virginia plant is not a "place of business" under Article 1; if that plant is a "place of business," then both parties would have a "place of business" in the same Contracting State (the United States) and domestic law would apply. Under Article 10, if a party has more than one place of business, the relevant place of business is the one with the "closest relationship to the contract and its performance." Here, the French corporation sent an agent from France to New York to negotiate the contract, but the goods are being shipped to Virginia. Thus, the court would have to decide which of these jurisdictions bore the "closest relationship" to the transaction. Perhaps if the dispute arose out of the negotiation, e.g., a claim that the contract was improperly formed, the relevant place of business would be considered France, from where the negotiator came. In that case, the CISG would apply. But if the dispute arose out of the quality of the goods, then Virginia, where the goods were to be used, might be considered the jurisdiction with the "closest relationship" to the transaction. In that case, both parties would be deemed to have their "place of business" in the United States and the CISG would not apply under Article 1(1)(a).

But recall that Article 1(1)(a) is not the exclusive means by which the CISG can apply. Assume that a Japanese-based corporation and a United States corporation, based in New York, negotiate a contract in New York that the latter will ship goods to a construction project in Virginia managed by the Japanese corporation. The United States is a Contracting State, but Japan is not. When a dispute arises about the quality of the goods, the Japanese corporation sues the United States corporation in New York. Now Article 1(1)(a) would not apply; although the parties have places of business in different states, they are not different Contracting States, since Japan is not a Contracting State at all. Nevertheless, the negotiation of the contract and performance of the contract all occur in the United States, and the forum is a court in the United States. These contacts with the United States may well be sufficient for the court to determine that the rules of private international law dictate that United States law governs the transaction. Because the United States is a Contracting State, and those rules dictate that its law applies, Article 1(1)(b) suggests that the CISG applies to the transaction.

There is, however, an anomaly in this result. When the United States decides to subordinate its domestic law to international law, it is presumably doing so in the name of achieving some degree of uniformity in international sales law. This subordination of domestic interests appears to be reasonable, as long as it is reciprocal, that is, as long as other countries are similarly willing to apply uniform international law to a relevant dispute. But non-Contracting States, such as Japan in the example, have indicated that they are not willing to accept uniform law in preference to their own. For instance, if the same dispute between these parties were brought in a Japanese court, rather than a United States court, and the court were to apply Japanese law there would be no claim that the CISG applied, since Japan is not a Contracting State.[34] The result is that, while Japanese law could apply to a transaction between Japanese and American businesses, substantive United States law (without the CISG) would not have any chance of being applied to the transaction. Thus, there is less reason for the United States to subordinate its domestic law to international law when dealing with a party located in a nation that would not subordinate its domestic law if the same dispute were heard in one of its courts.

For this reason, Article 95 permits a Contracting State to create a reservation to the effect that it will not be bound by Article 1(1)(b). The United States has exercised this right under Article 95.[35] Thus, a United States court hearing a dispute between parties to an international sales contract, where the parties were not residents of different Contracting States, would not apply the CISG notwithstanding Article 1(1)(b). Instead, the court would presumably apply either the law of the other jurisdiction or the UCC pursuant to § 1-105.

In jurisdictions that have not adopted an Article 95 reservation, Article 1(1)(b) will require analysis of whether private international law rules look to the law of the state that has adopted the CISG. For instance, the case of *OLG Koblenz*[36] arose between a German party and an Italian

---

[34] Of course, the Japanese court could apply rules of private international law and find that, under those principles, United States law, rather than Japanese law, applies to the transaction.

[35] See Message from the President Containing a Legal Analysis of the UN Convention on Contracts for the International Sale of Goods, S. Treaty Doc. No. 98-9, Sept. 21, 1983, pp. 21-22, reprinted in 22 Int'l Legal Mat. 1368, 1380 (1984). The State Department also indicated that Article 1(1)(b) was uncertain insofar as it relied on the vagaries of private international law. The reservation of Article 95 leaves the equally uncertain inquiry of whose law should apply to the transaction in the absence of the CISG. To date China, the Czech Republic, Singapore, and Slovakia also have Article 95 reservations.

[36] 2 U 1795/89, February 23, 1990 (Germany), 1 UNILEX D. 1990-2 (M.J. Bonell, ed.). Translated at 14 J.L. & Com. 226 (1995).

party at a time after the CISG had gone into effect in Italy, but before it went into effect in Germany. The German court looked to domestic law on choice of law, and concluded that German law selected the law of the country that had the closest connection with the contract as the governing law for the contract. The court then determined that the relevant country was the one in which the seller was to perform the contract or in which the seller had his domicile or place of business at the time of the conclusion of the contract. Since that country was Italy, Italian law was to apply; and since the CISG was part of Italian law, Article 1(1)(b) applied and made the contract subject to the substantive provisions of the CISG.

The ability to confuse choice of law issues is well illustrated by the case of *OLG Düsseldorf*.[37] A German buyer purchased from an Indiana seller a machine to be installed in a Russian furniture combine. After the German buyer was required to make repairs due to defects in the machine, it sued the Indiana seller in Germany to recover the costs of repair from the seller and to obtain indemnification arising out of the defects, including personal injuries that a Russian operator had suffered. At the time that the contract had been entered into, the United States was a Contracting State, but Germany was not. The court concluded that Article 1(1)(b) governed the contract. That conclusion would have been correct if Article 1(1)(b) applied to the contract, since the contract was between parties with places of business in two different states and rules of private international law may well have applied the law of the Indiana seller. But given the United States' Article 95 reservation, Article 1(1)(b) simply does not apply to transactions between parties with a place of business in the United States and parties with a place of business in a non-Contracting State. Thus, the decision of the court was clearly wrong.

In accordance with the CISG principle of party autonomy, these jurisdictional rules may be modified by the parties. Article 6 provides that the parties may opt out of the CISG or modify virtually any of its provisions. Two issues remain: (1) how do parties opt out, and (2) can parties opt in as well as out? Article 6 is silent on both issues, and relevant diplomatic history is inconclusive. The Uniform Law on International Sales (ULIS), the CISG's predecessor, explicitly allowed

---

[37] 17 U 73/93, July 2, 1993 (Germany), 1 UNILEX, D. 1993-21 (M.J. Bonell, ed.).

both express and implicit opting out.[38] The CISG's diplomatic history reveals that different countries had different responses to the issue of opting out. Some countries wanted any opting out to be express, while other countries favored allowing opting out by implication. For instance, trade usage derogating from CISG is an instance of an implicit opt out. Article 6 reflects a compromise between these positions that offers no clear answer on the issue. Another unresolved issue concerns what constitutes an implicit rejection of CISG's application, even assuming Article 6 permits it. Consider a clause in a contract stating that "This contract shall be governed by the law of the State of New York." Does the language signal the parties' intention not to have CISG applicable to their contract? Two views are possible.[39] One view contends that the reference to New York law only indicates an intention to have New York domestic law fill gaps in the CISG, not to exclude it. After all, by virtue of the Supremacy Clause, the CISG is part of New York law. The opposing view is that the clause indicates an intent to displace the CISG by New York domestic law. Otherwise, the parties would not have gone to the trouble of providing for the CISG when it already applies to their contract. Setting New York domestic law as a gap-filler, without further specificity, is not cost-justified.

In answer to questions posed in Senate hearings prior to the United States' adoption of the CISG, the State Department considered three different ways that contractual parties might handle the issue of CISG's application. First, they could make no reference to choice of law or to the CISG, in which case Article 1 would govern the issue of whether the CISG applies. Second, they could expressly state that the CISG does not apply, in which case the court would instead apply its own choice of law rules. If the state whose law was selected had adopted the CISG, the State Department believed, the forum should apply that state's sales law *without* the CISG, thus respecting the intent of the parties to have different substantive provisions govern the contract. Third, the parties could explicitly provide that the CISG would not be applicable, but also designate applicable law. For instance, the parties might draft a provision

---

[38] See ULIS art. 3, 834 U.N.T.S. 107 (1972).

[39] Compare ICC Court of Arbitration (Paris), August 23, 1994, 1 UNILEX D.1994-20 (M. Bonell ed.) (choice of law of Contracting State an implicit exclusion) with Ceramique Culinaire de France, S.A. v. Musgrave Ltd., Cour de Cassation (France), December 17, 1996, 1 UNILEX D.1996-11 (M. Bonell ed.) (choice not an implicit exclusion).

that states:

> The rights and obligations of the parties under this contract
> shall not be governed by the 1980 United Nations Convention
> on Contracts for the International Sale of Goods. Rather,
> these rights and obligations shall be governed by the Uniform
> Commercial Code as adopted by the State of New York.

In this case, the forum would again apply the selected state law in lieu of
the CISG. The State Department's analysis, while compelling, applies
primarily to its observation about how courts in the United States would
interpret such clauses. It is conceivable that courts in other jurisdictions
would be more or less reluctant to allow parties parties to displace the
CISG. The question as to whether the CISG recognizes implicit opt outs
remains open.

Can parties to a transaction that would not otherwise qualify for
application of the CISG agree to have their contract governed by its
terms? The question is whether parties have the ability to opt in to the
CISG. Assume that neither Brazil nor Japan is a Contracting State, but
that corporations having places of business in those countries enter into
a contract for the delivery of goods in New York and agree that New
York law will govern the contract. Arguably, their choice of law clause
includes the CISG as incorporated into New York law. ULIS, the CISG's
predecessor, explicitly allowed opting in on these facts.[40] The Secretariat
Commentary on the 1978 Draft of Article 1 suggests that this would be
the proper result under the CISG too. It provides that "if two parties from
different States have designated the law of a Contracting State as the law
of the contract, this Convention is applicable even though the parties have
not specifically mentioned the Convention,"[41] and the statement does not
appear to be limited to those situations in which the contracting parties
have their places of business in Contracting States.

Article 1's language does not support the Secretariat's suggestion that

---

[40] See ULIS art. 4, 834 U.N.T.S. 107 (1972).

[41] Commentary on the Draft Convention on Contracts for the International
Sale of Goods, Prepared by the Secretariat, Doc.A/CONF.97/5 (1979), reprinted
in Documentary History of the Uniform Law for International Sales 405 at para.
8 (J.O. Honnold ed., 1989); see also First Committee Deliberations, 3d Meeting,
A/Conf.97/C.1/SR.4 (1980), reprinted in id. at 473 (paras. 60-61) (former
German Democratic Republic proposal to expressly allow opting in rejected as
unnecessary; "principles of autonomy of the will of the parties" already allow it).

the CISG itself allows opting in. Rather, the forum's conflict of laws rules, not the CISG, dete rmine whether the parties' choice of New York law (including the CISG) is to be given effect. In most legal systems that choice would be honored. This is because they respect almost unlimited party autonomy: parties are free to select the law applicable to their contract, with very few restrictions. Section 1-105(1), however, limits party autonomy because it requires a "reasonable relation" between the law chosen and the transaction. The requirement of "reasonableness" restricts the freedom to select law. Since the transaction in the example has New York contacts, the limitation in this case probably would not prevent enforcement of the parties' choice of New York law. A harder case is one in which the parties select the CISG directly, not via the law of a Contracting State. Here conflict of laws rules respecting party autonomy do not automatically select the CISG, because the parties have chosen the CISG, not the law of a particular legal system. The same is true under § 1-105(1), which governs the selection of the law of "a state or nation." In our view, the choice of the CISG should be given effect. The CISG in effect contains almost default terms. Thus, by selecting the CISG, parties are selecting the terms of their contract. If there is nothing objectionable about honoring the terms of a contract, enforcing the selection of the CISG is unobjectionable too.[42]

In cases of doubt, courts may apply the CISG broadly for a variety of reasons. First, it constitutes the most modern statement of international sales law. Second, the very existence of the CISG may reduce uncertainty about the relevant law and reduce the search that a court would otherwise have to make into governing law. Third, application of the CISG will foster uniformity and thus clarify the law of international sales. Perhaps all of these reasons underlie the application of the CISG by an arbitrator in a dispute concerning the buyer's examination of goods

---

[42] Revised Article 1 reaches the same conclusion. Revised § 1-301 does not address cases in which parties select rules other than those of a legal system. However, Official Comment 2 discusses parties' selection of non-legal codes and concludes that "the principles of Section 1-302 allowing parties broad freedom of contract...are adequate for this purpose." Revised § 1-302(a) allows parties to vary by agreement almost all of the UCC's rules. Thus, the Official Comment allows parties to displace rules under Revised § 1-301 that would otherwise apply to their agreement. In effect, the Comment treats choice of law as an ordinary term of a contract.

and notification of nonconformities.[43] The contract was entered into in 1979, prior to the time that the CISG was concluded. Thus, by its own terms, the CISG did not apply to the contract, and neither party's country was a Contracting State. Nevertheless, the arbitrator concluded that the CISG was the best source of the prevailing trade usages that did apply to the contract. The buyer had complied with the requirements of the CISG, which were more flexible than the requirements of the domestic law of the seller, and more consistent with "generally accepted trade usages." In addition, the arbitrator found, the seller had acted in a manner inconsistent with the CISG and thus had forfeited its right to claim the buyer's noncompliance with notice requirements. Notably, the court did not simply reach these conclusions by reference to trade custom, but instead explicitly invoked the specific provisions of the CISG in a contract to which that body of law quite clearly applied, at best, only by analogy.

## B.  Types of Transactions Subject to the CISG

Efforts to decipher the scope of the CISG reveal the very different drafting styles of the UCC and the Convention. As we have seen, the UCC has many of the characteristics of a jigsaw puzzle, so that understanding one provision often requires reference to other provisions. The provisions of the CISG are more self-contained or independent, and terms are used with less precision. The problem of imprecision is exacerbated by the fact that the CISG has been promulgated in six different languages—Arabic, Chinese, English, French, Russian, and Spanish—each of which is considered equally authoritative to the others, notwithstanding their inevitable conflicts.

Article 1(1) states that the CISG applies to "contracts of the sale of goods." The CISG, however, contains no definitional provision equivalent to § 2-105 of the UCC, which defines "goods." Thus, mixed transactions and transactions that are sales (or that are not sales) in form, but not sales (or sales) in substance pose at least the same difficulties under the CISG as under the UCC. Nevertheless, the use of the term "goods," which has an accepted legal meaning, combined with exclusions in subsequent Articles that further illuminate the drafters' intent, suggests that the CISG is intended only to cover contracts that concern movable and tangible property. Sales of buildings, land, and intangible rights are

---

[43] ICC Arbitration Case No. 5713 (France 1989).

excluded.[44]   Similarly, the CISG fails to define "sale."  One court excludes distributorship agreements from the CISG's scope unless they contain definite terms of sale for specified good.[45]  Although Article 3, discussed below, indicates that contracts for the supply of goods to be manufactured may still constitute sales, there is no provision concerning leases or means of distinguishing leases from sales.

These definitional omissions must be filled by reference to the CISG provisions that govern contractual gaps generally. Article 7 provides that questions concerning matters governed by the CISG, but not expressly settled in it, are to be settled in conformity with that document's general principles and in conformity with the law applicable under the rules of private international law. Presumably, this latter provision directs courts to resolve definitional issues under the law of the jurisdiction that governs the contract as selected by conflict of laws principles. At the same time, Article 7(1) dictates that the CISG provisions are to be interpreted with regard to its international character and to the need to promote uniformity in its application. Once courts have filled gaps in the CISG in a particular way such as by articulating factors that distinguish between a sale and a lease, the admonition to ensure uniformity would appear to require subsequent courts to follow those early decisions, even if they lead to results that vary from decisions in the jurisdiction whose law would otherwise apply.

Reference to previous gap-filling decisions makes sense if we are to attain anything like the international uniformity to which the CISG aspires. At the same time, uniformity may mean sacrificing optimal legal principles. The desire for uniformity privileges the first decisions to be reached on matters "governed" by the Convention, but not "expressly

---

[44] Honnold suggests that the inference is even stronger in non-English versions of the CISG.  The French and Spanish versions, for instance, use phrases, *marchandises* and *mercaserías* respectively, that apply only to movable tangible assets.  See John O. Honnold, Uniform Law for International Sales Under the 1980 United Nations Convention 52 (3d ed. 1999). For an inference from the use of *"marchandises"* in the French version to the effect that the coverage is not limited to movable tangible assets, see Commentary on the UN Convention on Contracts for the International Sale of Goods (CISG) 23 (Peter Schlechtriem ed., 2d ed. 1999).

[45] See Helen Kaminski PTY. Ltd. v. Marketing Australian Products, Inc., 1997 Lexis 10630 (S.D.N.Y. 1997); cf. Obergericht Kanton Luzern (Switzerland), January 8, 1997, 1 UNILEX D.1997-2 (M.J. Bonell ed.).

settled" in it. Those decisions, however, are not necessarily reached by the courts most competent to deal with the issue. A court in a country that has little experience with leases or in which the lease/sale distinction has little history will not necessarily understand the subtleties and nuances that have been the basis for multiple decisions in other countries. In addition, courts deciding cases that arise subsequent to early decisions will have the advantage of seeing how the earlier-stated rules work in practice. In an ideal world, they would have the opportunity to alter those rules where adjustment was appropriate. But the admonition to "promote uniformity" may frustrate efforts to adjust or correct earlier interpretations and applications of substantive provisions.

Perhaps our concern is overstated. Regardless of the exhortation towards uniformity, we doubt that courts of one nation will defer substantially to decisions elsewhere. Wholly apart from problems of accessibility and translation—problems that exist today, but that are already being addressed by the CLOUT reporting system—we imagine that only rarely will we see, for instance, United States courts deferring to judgments of Belarus, Ghana, or Iraq to decide issues relevant to the commercial interests of American litigants.

### C. Exclusions

The CISG contains some specific exclusions that clarify the scope issue. Article 2 removes most consumer transactions from the CISG. Consumer transactions involve the purchase of goods for "personal, family or household use." This exclusion recognizes that different countries have very different legal cultures with respect to the application of doctrines such as caveat emptor in consumer transactions. Thus, the CISG does not purport to arbitrate between countries with and without consumer legislation. The exclusion, however, applies only if the seller neither knew nor ought to have known that the goods were bought for such use. This objective test will certainly exclude the sale of souvenirs or film to tourists. But assume that our tourist purchases a good in a market typically frequented by commercial parties, such as a marble table that is usually used in conference rooms but occasionally in residences. That purchaser will have the obligation of informing the seller of the good's intended use if the transaction is to be excluded from the CISG.

Many of Article 2's exclusions suggest that the drafters were only trying to regulate sales of tangible items, rather than less tangible rights or claims. For instance, sales of stocks, negotiable instruments, and money fall outside the CISG.[46] At the same time, other intangibles, such as computer programs or rights of intellectual property, are not excluded, at least explicitly.[47] Some exclusions avoid difficult questions of whether something is or is not a good. For instance, Article 2(f) excludes sales of electricity, and thus eludes the debate that has surrounded the classification of electricity under the UCC. Other exclusions, such as sales by auction or by authority of law relate to the manner of the sale rather than the subject of the sale. The moving force between inclusion and exclusion therefore is more complicated than the simple division into tangible and intangible. As in the case of consumer goods, which are clearly "goods," exclusion in many cases reveals the desire to achieve consensus on a general law of sales among various nations from different legal cultures. Excluded transactions tend to be those that are the subject of substantial domestic regulations, many of which are inconsistent with the regulations of other jurisdictions. For instance, sales of ships, vessels, hovercraft, or aircraft (excluded in Article 2(e)) are often subject to special registration requirements. Any effort to create uniform regulations with respect to such issues might have been thought to have been unavailing from the start. Exclusion therefore appears to have been preferable to efforts to impose regulations on countries that may have resisted sufficiently to reject the entire Convention.

### D. Mixed Sales and Service Contracts

Contracts that concern pure services are not subject to the CISG. As in the UCC, however, there will be cases in which sales and services are intertwined. Article 3 attempts to address the applicability of the CISG in this situation. Article 3(1) includes contracts to manufacture goods within "sales," unless the party who orders the goods supplies a "substantial part" of the materials necessary for the good's production. This provision may expand the scope of "sale" under domestic law. For instance, German law treats contracts for the manufacture of custom-made goods as contracts for manufacture, which are treated separately from contracts for sale. Nevertheless, German courts have properly

---

[46] See Article 2(d).

[47] For a case holding that the sale of standard software constitutes a sale of goods, see Landgericht Munchen (Germany), February 8, 1995, 1 UNILEX D.1995-3.1 (M.J. Bonell ed.). For a broader discussion of the issue, see Arthur Fakes, *The Application of the United Nations Convention on Contracts for the International Sale of Goods to Computer, Software, and Database Transactions*, 3 Software L.J. 559, 582-84 (1990).

applied the CISG to manufacturing contracts between businesses of different Contracting States. But under Article 3(2), contracts fall outside the CISG if the preponderant part of the obligations of the party who furnishes the goods consists of supplying labor or other services. Thus, if the buyer provides raw materials or components to the seller and the seller only assembles and delivers the goods, the contract falls outside the CISG. The CISG did not apply, for instance, to a contract that required a buyer of brooms to provide the seller with many of the materials necessary to manufacture of the finished product.[48] But a contract for the dismantling, transportation, and re-assembly of a hangar was a contract for sale under the CISG because the supply of services was not the preponderant part of the contractual obligations, as measured by the contract price.[49]

The "substantial part" exclusion under Article 3(1) reveals both an interpretive difficulty and the problem inherent in having multiple authoritative versions of the same document. Assume that buyer orders computers from seller and supplies to seller a processor manufactured by a third party. Has the buyer supplied a "substantial part" of the materials necessary for the good's production? The cases we discussed above interpret substantiality in a quantitative manner. On this interpretation, if the processor, for instance, accounted for only one-third of the value of the computer, we might say that the CISG still applied. Even if we interpret "substantial" quantitatively, it does not necessarily imply a "majority" of the value of the finished good. After all, Article 3(2) refers to "the preponderant part" of the contract, a term that does imply "majority." Thus, one may argue that the use of some other phrase in Article 3(1) was intended to avoid any intimation that the CISG required the supply of a majority of materials.

But "substantiality" may also be qualitative, in which case supplying the processor may take the transaction outside of the CISG. Indeed, the qualitative interpretation is supported by the French version of Article 3, which applies the exclusion of Article 3(1) where the buyer supplies "une parte essentielle," or an "essential" part of the materials necessary for manufacture of the goods. Thus, in our hypothetical, the buyer would be

---

[48] See Fa. N. GmbH v. Fa.N. GesmbH & Co., Oberster Gerichtshof (Austria), October 27, 1994, 1 UNILEX D. 1994-27 (M.J. Bonell, ed.).

[49] Marques Roque Joachim v. La Sarl Holding Manin Riviere, RG 93/4879, Cour d'Appel de Grenoble, Chambre Commerciale, April 4, 1995 (France), 1 UNILEX D. 1995-14(M.J. Bonell, ed.).

more likely to fall outside the CISG by virtue of supplying the processor if the French conception of Article 3 applied. It is tempting to say that the qualitative conception is appropriate under French law and the quantitative under United States law. But any such conclusion flies directly in the face of the admonition of Article 7 that courts are to give due regard to the international character of the CISG and to promote uniformity in its application.

The qualitative aspect of substantiality is evident in a French decision, *Societe A.M.D. Electronique v. Rosenberger SIAM S.p.A.*[50] In that case, an Italian producer of electronic components ordered adapters from a French seller. The contract required the adapters to be produced according to the buyer's specifications and design and prohibited the seller from making any use of the adapters other than selling them to buyer. The court held that these restrictions placed the transaction within the Article 3(1) exclusion. The decision seems questionable at best, insofar as the buyer provided no raw materials or goods to seller. Rather, the contractual restrictions only limited what seller could do with its own goods. Those restrictions do not appear to affect the role of the seller as a manufacturer of goods, and thus the facts seem to fit the scenario of a sale that the CISG was intended to cover.

The best way to avoid these uncertainties is to treat them as an invitation to write a more specific contract. As we noted in our earlier discussion, Article 6 of the CISG permits the parties to exclude the application of the Convention from their transaction or to vary from its effect. Thus, where the parties are unsure of the CISG's application or meaning, a specific term embodying the parties' intent would be most appropriate.

### E. Leases

As in the case of the UCC, restricting the application of the CISG to "contracts of sale" requires distinguishing between sales and other forms of transactions, such as leases, and determining whether to defer to the formal structure designated by the parties.[51] Unlike the UCC, the CISG provides no guidance for distinguishing a lease or deferring to the parties' intent. This gap is likely to be filled by courts in particular cases making

---

[50] Cour d'Appel de Chambery, May 25, 1993 (France), 1 UNILEX D.1993-17 (M.J. Bonell, ed.).

[51] An Austrian court declined to apply the CISG to a lease in 1 Ob 525/93 (Austria), 1 UNILEX D. 1993-20.1 (M.J. Bonell, ed.).

reference to their own domestic law on the issue. For instance, we would expect a court sitting in Virginia and confronted with an issue of whether a transaction constitutes a sale or lease for purposes of the CISG to make that determination by applying the criteria of UCC § 1-201(37). As we noted above, however, reliance on domestic law to fill gaps in CISG will inevitably undermine the norm of Article 7(1). That provision admonishes courts to have regard to the international character of the CISG and to the need to promote uniformity in its application. Thus, our hypothetical court arguably should defer to (or at least consider) determinations made in the courts of other Contracting States relating to the sale/lease distinction before invoking domestic law on the issue.

### F. The Principle of Issue-Displacement

The CISG excludes from coverage not only certain types of contracts, but also particular issues affecting contracts that are covered. Article 4 provides that the CISG controls only the formation of the contract and the rights and obligations of the contracting parties. Article 4(a) excludes from the CISG matters affecting the "validity" of the contract, and Article 4(b) excludes questions of property rights in the goods sold. The language of Article 4 suggests that other issues may also be governed by domestic law.

Article 4 therefore implicates a principle of issue-displacement: When the CISG defines an issue and resolves it, domestic law addressing the issue is displaced; when the CISG either does not address the issue or leaves its resolution to domestic law, domestic law continues to govern. Given the CISG's limited scope, there must be some way to determine when it addresses an issue concerning the sales contract and when it does not. Often it is easy to tell when the CISG speaks to an issue. For example, assume that a party to a contract governed by the CISG contends that it is not bound because the parties' agreement was never put in writing and relevant domestic law refuses to enforce contracts not memorialized by a writing. Article 11 provides explicitly that the sales contract need not be concluded or evidenced by a writing. Thus, CISG resolves the issue and, according to the principle of issue-displacement, contrary domestic law is inapplicable. This is true even if domestic law labels a writing requirement a matter of "validity."

Another easy example concerns damages. Article 5 declares that the CISG does not govern the seller's liability to any person for death or personal injury caused by the goods. Suppose nonconforming goods sold to the buyer injure a bystander. Suppose too that the bystander recovers damages from the buyer in tort and the buyer in turn seeks to recover this amount from the seller. The CISG governs the question. True, given Article 5, the CISG does not control the seller's liability, if any, to the injured person. But that is not the question here. Here the buyer seeks to recover for a loss it has sustained resulting from the nonconformity in the goods it sold (liability to the injured person). Article 74 defines consequential damages and includes among them loss resulting from a party's breach. Since the buyer's liability to the bystander is a loss resulting from the seller's breach, it is a type of consequential damage sustained by the buyer. Thus, the CISG defines the issue raised by the buyer and resolves it. Domestic law concerning the buyer's rights against its seller is therefore displaced.

Sometimes, however, it can be difficult to tell whether the CISG addresses an issue. Consider, for instance, matters of validity. As we indicate above, Article 4 excludes validity from the scope of the CISG. But the question always is whether an issue presented is one of validity under *the CISG*. Domestic law concepts of validity are not controlling. At the same time, because the CISG does not define validity, there is no way of saying with certainty which particular matters the CISG considers matters of validity. This becomes a problem, for instance, with respect to the extent to which domestic law controls issues of alleged unconscionability, which we discuss in Chapter 5.

Another difficult example concerns the potential simultaneous application of domestic law and the CISG. This occurs when the same set of facts triggers both the CISG and domestic law. A common illustration is the application of tort law in the same circumstances that the CISG applies. For instance, under some domestic tort law, a breach of warranty also can give rise to tort liability based on fraud or negligent misrepresentation. In general, contract and tort liability can differ in their respective statutes of limitation, notice requirements, measures of damage, and privity requirements (if any). Does domestic tort law continue to govern when the CISG applies? The principle of issue-displacement gives an answer. In our view, not original to us,[52] if facts trigger the CISG's application, domestic law triggered by the same facts is displaced. If additional facts are involved which trigger domestic law alone, domestic law continues to apply. So, for instance, if tort liability based on fraud arises from the same set of facts as a breach of warranty arising under the CISG, the domestic law of fraud no longer applies. If fraud involves a fact not involved in a breach of warranty (e.g.,

---

[52] See Honnold, supra note 44, at 67-68.

knowledge by the seller of the nonconformity), the law of fraud continues to govern.

# CHAPTER 3
## FORMATION OF THE CONTRACT

## I. Introduction: The Evaluation of Formation Rules

Rules of contract formation describe the conditions under which a binding contract is concluded. The formation rules of both Article 2 and the CISG supplement and in some cases alter common law rules. Given these differences, we need both to understand and evaluate the rules. Roughly, three different types of criteria are available: moral, coordination, and efficiency. The three criteria sometimes recommend the same formation rule. For instance, a rule of formation coordinates contracting behavior by indicating what steps parties must take before the state will recognize that they have entered into a binding obligation. Thus, the rule reduces uncertainty, and hence decreases the contracting costs of parties. A formation rule, therefore, might be an efficient rule. For that matter, the rule might also be a morally acceptable one. But selection of the same rule does not mean that the criteria of selection are the same.

The moral criterion focuses on particular interests that require protection from the state's authority to impose contractual obligations. These interests can be communitarian interests of solidarity or altruism or individual interests in freedom. An interest might be the freedom not to have legal obligations imposed on one without one's consent. Or it might be distributional in nature: the interest in being exposed to a risk of being contractually bound only if the other contracting parties are exposed to the same risk. Consider the interest in freedom from imposition of unconsented-to legal obligations. The rule that the offer can dictate the medium through which acceptance is communicated respects the offeror's interest. So too does the rule that, absent course of performance or other prior indication by the offeree, silence by the offeree in the face of an offer does not constitute acceptance. A rule that allows a response to constitute acceptance, whatever medium is demanded by the offeror, or that allows the offeror to consider the offeree's silence as acceptance seemingly create unwilled obligations. Such rules are morally impermissible.

Nevertheless, moral criteria for formation rules, although initially plausible, are too indeterminate to be persuasive. They do not in fact place limits on the state's authority to impose obligations on a party. Take again the assumed interest in freedom from unconsented obligations. A rule allowing silence to constitute consent need not impair this interest. After all, the offeree need not be bound against its will. To avoid being bound, it can indicate nonacceptance by rejecting the offer. Silence in the face of an offer conjoined with the possibility of rejection does not mean that the offeree's resulting obligation is imposed on it. It only means that the offeree bears the cost of indicating its nonacceptance. Suppose the additional cost amounts to an imposition of an unwilled obligation. If so, the contrary rule which requires the offeree to indicate its acceptance *also* imposes an unwilled obligation, because offerees are put to the cost of indicating their assent to the offer. The trouble here is a general one. Formation rules may impose different contracting costs on parties. But all formation rules are consistent with the freedom not to have obligations imposed as long as parties can avoid the operation of such rules. Nonmandatory formation rules allow parties to contract by means other than those provided for in the rule. Because moral criteria look only to the interest protected, they cannot prefer one nonmandatory formation rule over another. No moral limits therefore are placed on the state's authority to adopt nonmandatory formation rules.

A second standard for evaluating formation rules is coordination. This criterion assesses formation rules by how well they allow parties to coordinate their indications of whether a contract has been concluded or avoided. Prospective parties to a contract would clearly prefer having a rule that indicates when an agreement is binding. Such a rule allows them to engage in behavior with the confidence that other contracting parties, and courts, will attach legal significance to their behavior. These parties are less concerned with the substance of the formation rules. In familiar game theoretic terms, formation rules describe a pure coordination game, in which the players are more concerned that everyone engage in the same behavior than they are in the nature of the behavior. For instance, prior to the time that automobiles are manufactured with steering wheels on one side of the car or the other, drivers should be relatively indifferent as to whether they are required to drive on the right or the left. They are more concerned that everyone drive on the same side. Consider, in this context, the mailbox rule, which provides that an acceptance of an offer transmitted through an authorized medium is effective upon dispatch. Once adopted, the rule coordinates contracting behavior by creating identical expectations among contracting parties. The offeror expects that a contract can be concluded prior to receiving the acceptance transmitted. The offeree can treat dispatch as creating a contract. Given the mailbox rule, both parties can estimate the consequences of an authorized dispatch of acceptance and rely accordingly. Rules in force provide a basis for convergent expectations of the parties. Of course, for the same reason, the parties would be equally satisfied with the receipt rule if that were the adopted rule.

There are two difficulties with using the coordination criterion as a standard for evaluating formation rules. The first is indeterminacy. Where there is more than one way to coordinate, the criterion does not give us a basis for deciding among them. This might be acceptable if the available ways to coordinate were entirely equal in all respects, so that different parties did not have different preferences among them. But this will rarely be the case. Even with respect to the choice between the mailbox rule and the receipt rule, offerors will have a different preference than offerees, even though both would prefer *either* rule to *no* rule. The second difficulty with the coordination criterion is that it is often inapplicable. The coordination criterion, in most cases, does not select among potential coordination points. Because the occurrence of pure coordination is rare, the ultimate decision among potential coordination points will have to be made on the basis of some other criterion.

The third criterion is efficiency. The efficiency criterion evaluates a rule by the benefits and costs in applying it. Roughly, the criterion recommends the rule whose operation maximizes the difference between aggregate benefits and costs. In this way the efficiency criterion, unlike the coordination criterion, is sensitive to the costs imposed by different formation rules.

An example may help illustrate the efficiency criterion's application. Consider the rule that, absent course of performance or circumstances indicating otherwise, acceptance requires an affirmative response. An alternative possible rule is that, unless circumstances indicate otherwise, silence operates as acceptance. The associated benefits and costs of two rules can be compared in a rough fashion to determine their efficiency.[1] The "affirmative response" requirement diminishes the net value of the contract to the offeree by the amount of the cost of its response, but saves the offeree the costs of rejection and saves the offeror the costs of uncertainty about whether the contract has been accepted. Acceptance by silence, on the other hand, avoids imposing acceptance costs on the offeree but imposes on that party the costs of rejection, because silence

---

[1] The comparison below is based loosely on Avery Katz, *Transaction Costs and the Legal Mechanics of Exchange: When Should Silence in the Face of an Offer Be Construed as Acceptance?*, 9 J. L. Econ. & Org. 77 (1993); Avery Katz, *The Strategic Structure of Offer and Acceptance: Game Theory and Contract Formation*, 89 Mich. L. Rev. 215 (1990).

will constitute acceptance. In addition, acceptance by silence may leave the offeree more uncertain about the existence of a contract. Whether acceptance by affirmative response or acceptance by silence imposes the fewest costs depends on (1) the probability that offers in general will be accepted, and (2) the relative costs of offeree acceptance, offeree rejection, and offeree uncertainty. The higher the probability that an offer will be accepted (so that offerors would rarely have to incur any costs of rejection) and the lower the costs of offeror uncertainty about the status of outstanding offers, the more we would want to have an acceptance by silence rule. Conversely, if offers are less likely than not to be accepted, the costs of silence will increase and we would prefer an affirmative response rule.

As presented, there is much to dispute in the above rough analysis. The analysis assumes that the value of rejected and accepted offers to their respective offerees is the same. It also assumes that the costs of accepting and rejecting offers is the same. Reasonable people can disagree as to whether offers are in general more likely than not to be accepted. Lastly, this assumption could be overly broad: some sorts of offers might be more likely than not to be accepted, others less likely. These controversial assumptions affect the estimate of costs imposed on offerees under each rule considered. They indirectly therefore also bear on the case for preferring one formation rule over another. But none bears on the criteria for preferring one rule over the other. The operative criteria is one of efficiency.

## II. Offer and Acceptance

The formation rules applicable to contracts governed by Article 2 are a mixture of UCC-supplied and common law rules. Common law formation rules are incorporated by § 1-103, which provides that, "unless displaced by particular provisions of this Act [i.e., the UCC]," principles of law and equity "shall supplement its provisions." In general, UCC provisions either replicate, supplement or displace extra-UCC law. Replication occurs when the UCC just reproduces in statute what decisional law otherwise provides. Elimination of the effect of contracts under seal and the regulatory effect of unconscionability on contracts are two examples.[2] Other UCC provisions are consistent with non-UCC law on particular matters. They simply supplement the relevant extra-UCC law. Two examples are the treatment of commercial impracticability and

---

[2] See §§ 2-203 (seals inoperative), 2-302 (unconscionability).

the good faith requirement on performance.[3]  Some provisions of the UCC displace application of inconsistent rules underwritten by non-UCC principles of law and equity. The "mirror image" rule, the pre-existing duty rule for effective modifications, and (arguably) common law consignments are excluded by provisions of Article 2 inconsistent with them.[4]  Section 1-103, therefore, displaces formation rules inconsistent with those provided by Article 2 and supplements Article 2's rules with rules consistent with them.    Section 1-103 is not self-applying. Difficulties therefore can arise as to which common law rules are displaced and which rules supplement Article 2's provisions.

## A.  Article 2's Approach to Formation Rules

In general, there are two approaches that can be taken to rules governing contract formation. One is to analyze contract formation in terms of formal offer and acceptance, and lapse, rejection, and revocation. A contract, on this approach, is a bargain initiated by an offer and concluded by an acceptance. Familiar common law rules concerning the mechanics of assent are of this sort. An offer is an indication of a willingness to enter a contract such that the person to whom it is addressed is justified in believing that assent will conclude the contract. An acceptance is a commitment by the offeree to the terms proposed by the offer, with no variation however minor. An offer is effective only on communication to the offeree prior to acceptance.  An acceptance concludes a contract on dispatch when dispatch occurs in a manner and medium authorized by the offer. Communication of the acceptance to the offeror is required, absent circumstances in which lack of notice is reasonable.  Offers are terminated by revocation, rejection or lapse. Revocation of an offer occurs upon knowledge of the offeree, direct or indirect, of the offeror's intention not to enter into a contract. Rejection occurs when the offeree fails to make an effective acceptance. Lapse occurs when the offer is terminated by either its terms or the expiration of a reasonable time or the death or incapacity of the offeror. A second

---

[3] See §§ 1-203, 2-615.

[4] See §§ 2-207, 2-209, 2-326. Official Comment 1 to § 1-103 requires "express displacement," something more than the text of § 1-103 requires. The additional requirement arguably is inconsistent with § 1-102's mandate to interpret the UCC liberally. On occasion the difference between the text of § 1-103 and the associated comment is decisive. For a case in which the dispute between majority and dissent in effect turns on the issue, see Warder & Lee Elevator v. Britten, 274 N.W.2d 339 (Iowa 1979).

approach is simply to find a contract where there is consent to an agreement. Here there is no need to analyze contract formation in terms of a formal offer and acceptance. It is sufficient that the parties reached agreement or acted in a manner suggestive of agreement.

Article 2 follows civil law and takes the second, "agreement," approach. At the same time it preserves elements of the first, "offer and acceptance," approach. A short series of interconnected UCC provisions shows the presence of the "agreement" approach. Section 2-204 provides general formation requirements, as its heading makes clear ("Formation in General"). (Section 1-109 makes headings to sections of the UCC part of the sections themselves.) Subsection (1) of § 2-204 provides that "a contract for sale of goods may be made in any manner sufficient to show agreement, including conduct of the parties which recognizes the existence of such a contract." "Agreement" in turn is defined by § 1-201(3): "...the bargain of the parties in fact as found in their language or by implication from other circumstances...." Hence § 2-204(1) treats the agreement of the parties as sufficient to create a contract for sale. Notice that "agreement" does not require an acceptance of an offer to conclude a contract. It simply requires a bargain, however the bargain is indicated ("shown"). So Article 2's general approach to contract formation is centered on the "agreement," not on the offer and acceptance. Section 2-204(2) supports this conclusion. It provides that "an agreement sufficient to constitute a contract for sale may be found even though the moment of its making is undetermined." If contract formation required an offer and an acceptance, then in principle the moment at which a contract was concluded would be determined. If an agreement only requires that there be a bargain, the moment at which the bargain was concluded need not be definite.

Article 2, however, retains elements of an "offer and acceptance" approach to contract formation by presupposing the continued operation of some common law mechanics of formation. Section 2-205, for instance, treats particular sorts of offers made by merchants as irrevocable, even absent consideration. The assumption is that an offer continues to operate as an element in the creation of a contract under Article 2. Section 2-207(1), by allowing an acceptance that varies the terms of an offer to conclude a contract, presupposes that an acceptance concludes a contract. Section 2-206 makes the same assumption. Subsection (1)(a) of § 2-206 rejects the common law default rule on the manner and medium of acceptance: "an offer to make a contract shall be construed as inviting acceptance in any manner and by any medium reasonable in the circumstances...."[5]  Section 2-206 therefore alters only the type of acceptance an offer invites. Considered alone, it preserves the requirement that there be an acceptance.

In principle, Article 2's different approaches are not inconsistent. Article 2's "agreement" approach allows, but does not require, contracts to be concluded without an offer and acceptance. Article 2's "offer and acceptance" approach simply states some of the rules for contract formation by offer and acceptance when this avenue is used to form a contract.[6] (Other rules are provided by common law formation rules, supplemented by § 1-103.)  Section 2-206, for example, requires an acceptance to conclude a contract only when an offer invites it.  Section 2-204 allows a contract to be formed by other means absent an offer.  In practice, Article 2's different approaches to contract formation usually yield the same result.  To see this, realize that there are four sorts of possible cases.  Only in one is there a possible conflict in the result yielded by the two approaches to formation. (1) *Performance, agreement cases*.  The parties partly or fully perform.  There also is an acceptance of an offer operating to conclude a contract. (2) *No performance, no agreement cases*.  The parties fail to undertake any of the duties typically called for under the sales contract, such as tendering delivery or making payment.  At the same time there is insufficient evidence that the parties intended to conclude a contract. (3) *Performance, disagreement over terms cases*.  The parties partly or fully perform.  At the same time they dispute what the agreement required by way of performance. (4) *No performance, agreement cases*.  There has been no performance typically required by a contract of sale.  However, sufficient evidence exists that the parties have concluded a contract.

"Agreement" and "offer and acceptance" approaches give different answers only in (4): *no performance, agreement cases. Performance, agreement* cases do not present an issue of contract formation because there is no dispute that a contract has been concluded.  Behavioral evidence indicates agreement, and there is acceptance of an offer.  In *no performance, no agreement* cases there is no behavioral evidence to conclude that the parties reached agreement under § 2-204(1).  Likewise, given the absence of an offer and acceptance, a contract has not been

---

[5] See also § 2-206, Official Comment 1 (second sentence).

[6] Cf. Gasmark, Ltd. v. Kimbell Energy Corp., 868 S.W.2d 925, 928 (Tex. Ct. App. 1994) (parties can agree to enter into binding agreement using common law rules of offer and acceptance).

concluded under § 2-206(1). *Performance, disagreement over terms* cases do not raise an issue as to whether a contract has been concluded. This is because behavioral evidence indicates that a contract has been concluded under § 2-204(2) as well as via an acceptance of an offer. The dispute is over the terms of a concededly concluded contract. Different answers are possible only in *no performance, agreement* cases. Here there is no behavioral evidence indicating agreement because performance is lacking. At the same time there can be communications between the parties that conclude a contract. In these cases there may be no manifestation of assent under § 2-204(1) even though there can be an acceptance of an offer under § 2-206(1). Whether such cases occur depends on whether a court will construe the acceptance as "sufficient to show agreement" under § 2-204(1) in the circumstances.

### B. Irrevocable Offers Under Article 2

As noted, Article 2's "offer and acceptance" approach alters some important common law formation rules. One change concerns the irrevocability of offers. At common law an offer is revocable prior to acceptance without consideration. Section 2-205 treats a limited class of offers ("firm offers") as irrevocable even without consideration. Under § 2-205, a written offer by a merchant is irrevocable when by its terms the offer gives assurances that it will remain open. If the offer states a period during which it will remain open, the offer is irrevocable for that period. If no period is stated, the offer is irrevocable for a "reasonable time." Whether or not the offer states a period during which the offer remains open, it is irrevocable for at most three months. What constitutes an offer is undefined by Article 2 and, accordingly, left to pre-UCC law under § 1-103.

Section 2-205's "firm offer" rule is for the most part clear and its application relatively uncontroversial. The dearth of cases whose results turn on the rule suggests as much. But difficulties in its interpretation are possible. Consider the facts of *Mid-South Packers, Inc. v. Shoney's Inc.,*[7] the best known case exemplifying § 2-205's operation. Mid-South Packers, the seller, negotiated with Shoney's, the buyer, for the sale of pork products over a period of time. During the negotiations, on April 17, 1982, Mid-South gave Shoney's a letter stating the prices of the products and the terms of sale. The letter also stated that Mid-South would inform Shoney's 45 days prior to changing the price of the pork products. It said nothing about the duration during which the products

---

[7] 761 F.2d 1117 (5th Cir. 1985).

described in the letter would be available at the stated prices. Shoney's began ordering from Mid-South. On August 12, 1982, Mid-South informed Shoney's of a price change. Shoney's continued to order pork products. Subsequently, Mid-South sued to recover the difference between the old and new prices for orders placed after August 12. The court found that on August 12 Mid-South had effectively revoked the April 17 offer by replacing it with an offer at higher prices.

The court's reasoning is significant. It assumed that "at most" Mid-South had made a firm offer to Shoney's on April 17. Given that the offer contained no statement of duration, it was irrevocable until July 17 at the latest. Mid-South's notification to Shoney's occurred on August 12, after the period during which Mid-South's offer remained open. It therefore could amount to a revocation of its April 17 offer. So the court's assumption that a firm offer "at most" was made was unimportant. But suppose Mid-South had notified Shoney's of the price rise on May 1. Whether the notification revoked the April 17 would depend on whether the offer was firm under § 2-205. If so, then it would have remained open for a "reasonable time," possibly lasting through May 1. If not, Mid-South's notification on May 1 could revoke the April 17 offer. Hence it would be necessary to determine whether Mid-South had made a firm offer, a determination that was unnecessary on the facts of *Mid-South Packers*. The determination turns on whether, under § 2-205, Mid-South's April 12 letter contained an "assurance that it will be held open...."

The answer is not self-evident. For one thing, Mid-South's letter did not expressly state that its offer would remain open for any period of time. (On the other hand, the § 2-205 requirement of "assurances" does not demand an express statement that the offer is irrevocable.[8]) Even without such a requirement, different answers are possible. The letter apparently contained merely price quotations associated with described pork products. It did not state that the products would be available for purchase by Shoney's during a specified period. The letter therefore could be a conditional offer: "If we (Mid-South) do not revoke the offer, we offer to sell you (Shoney's) described pork products at the following prices...." Construed in this way, there is no "assurance" that the offer will be held open for any period. Alternatively, Mid-South's statement of price could be read to presuppose that the offer would remain open.

---

[8] But cf. Ivey's Plumbing & Electric Co., Inc. v. Petrocheim Maintenance Inc., 463 F. Supp. 543, 551 n.4 (N.D. Miss. 1978).

The statement of price would be an offer to sell at particular prices over an unspecified period. Mid-South's letter, on this reading, could express an unconditional offer: "We (Mid-South) offer to sell you (Shoney's) the described pork products at the following prices during an unspecified period...." This reading treats Mid-South's letter as giving "assurances" that its offer will remain open. Both interpretations of the letter are plausible. Mid-South's promise to notify Shoney's within 45 days of any price change does not favor either interpretation. That could be a promise to sell Shoney's products at stated prices and to notify it of price changes 45 days prior to their becoming effective, *if* the offer of sale has not been revoked. Alternatively, a promise of notification could be taken as a promise to keep an offer open prior to notification being given. The case is a close one. Given § 2-205's requirement that a writing "give assurance...," we think that to be a firm offer, an offer has to indicate by its terms that it is irrevocable. Absent other evidence, we conclude that Mid-South's offer does not satisfy § 2-205 and is not irrevocable. Our reasoning stems from the same rationale that justifies § 2-205 generally.

Section 2-205 is justified by its efficiency-enhancing features. An irrevocable offer requires the offeror to be bound should the offeree accept. If its cost of performance increases during that period, the offeror's profit decreases. (By standing ready to perform should the offer be accepted, the offeror also may lose valuable opportunities.) If its performance cost decreases, the offeror's profit will not increase. This is because competitors will make offers on the same terms, thereby preventing the offeror from receiving an increased profit on the sale. Thus, an irrevocable offer increases the cost of making offers as compared with a rule allowing for unrestricted revocation of offers. Increased cost reduces the number of offers forthcoming as well as the precautions taken by prospective offerors against making statements which could be construed as offers. On the benefit side, an irrevocable offer not only conveys information to the offeree about the value of the offer. It also benefits the offeror by giving time to assess its value and to rely by making particular investments. For both reasons, an irrevocable offer is a valuable asset to the offeree. Whether a rule governing irrevocable offers is justified depends on whether it yields a net benefit in reducing contracting costs.

Section 2-205 arguably does so. Notice first that § 2-205 applies only to written offers made by merchants. A merchant, as defined by § 2-104(1), includes "a person who deals in goods of the kind or otherwise by his occupation holds himself out as having knowledge or skill" relating to the goods sold. Merchants generally will have a lot more information about the goods than their buyers. The merchant will know about the capacity of its goods and their suitability to the buyer's intended uses. (It also has more accurate information than nonmerchant sellers possess.) This is valuable information to the buyer in the sense that its decision or terms of purchase could be affected. Buyers therefore would prefer to have the information. Merchant sellers would prefer to provide the information. The problem is that sometimes it is difficult for a merchant seller credibly to convey information about product attributes to a buyer. Information conveyed can be discounted either as "puffing" or simply because the buyer is not initially in a good position to evaluate it. Section 2-205 provides a means by which information can be conveyed to the buyer and simultaneously indicate that it is valuable information. Sellers who make firm offers are committed to treat the offer as irrevocable for a period. Doing so exposes the seller to adverse changes in market conditions or foregone sales and therefore increases its costs of performance. A willingness to risk such exposure therefore conveys to the buyer the seller's assessment of the value of the product to the buyer. The seller is less likely to be "puffing." Also, since the offer is irrevocable for a period, the buyer will be more willing to invest in assessing the offer, since it knows that the offer will not be revoked during the assessment process. So both merchant sellers and buyers would prefer that firm offers are enforceable.

There is a corresponding cost to the seller in making a firm offer: the seller is exposed to adverse changes in market conditions or foregone sales during the period in which the offer remains open. Whether the exposure is cost-justified depends on the marginal benefit of extending a firm offer. Since marginal benefits cannot be reliably estimated by a third party, the seller would prefer to determine unilaterally the supply of firm offers it will produce. For the same reason, the seller would prefer a clear rule for producing firm offers to one in which irrevocability turns on vague features of the offer. Section 2-205 satisfies both preferences. The § 2-205 requirement of a signed writing allows the seller unilateral control over the making of an irrevocable offer. And § 2-205's requirement that the "written offer gives assurance" that it will remain open allows a seller to trigger § 2-205's application with confidence that an unintended irrevocable offer will not be found ex post.

### C. The CISG's Formation Rules

The CISG adopts an "offer and acceptance" approach to contract formation. Article 23 provides that "a contract is concluded at the moment when an acceptance of an offer becomes effective in accordance with the provisions of this Convention." No other article allows a contract to be concluded other than by an acceptance of an offer. There is therefore no counterpart in the CISG to § 2-204(1). A Contracting State, however, can opt out of the CISG's formation rules by making a reservation or declaration to that effect. Subject to this qualification, some of the CISG's formation rules differ from the UCC's and its supplemental common law formation rules. Take the points in order.

### 1. Opting Out of the CISG's Formation Rules

The CISG's formation rules appear in Part II, in Articles 14-23. Article 92(1) allows a Contracting State to make a reservation excluding application of Part II. Article 94(1) allows a Contracting State to declare that Part II's formation rules will not apply under specified conditions.[9] The effect of both Articles is to exclude the CISG's formation rules from application to a contract of sale otherwise within the CISG's scope. Their operation is easily illustrated. Assume that Seller's place of business is in State A and Buyer's place of business is in State B and that the CISG otherwise applies to their sales contract. Also assume that State A has made a reservation under Article 92(1) and State B has not. The consequence of State A's reservation is stated in Article 92(2): State A is not considered a Contracting State with respect to issues concerning the formation of Seller and Buyer's sales contract. Suppose now the issue arises as to whether a contract has been concluded by Seller and Buyer. Since State A is not considered a Contracting State with respect to the issue, Seller is treated as having its place of business in a non-Contracting State. Article l(l)(a) therefore does not apply to have the CISG govern the issue. So Part II of CISG governs only if Article l(l)(b) leads to the CISG's application. Article l(l)(b) provides that the CISG applies when conflicts principles ("rules of private international law") "lead to the application of the law of a Contracting State." There are two possibilities, assuming conflicts principles select the law of either Seller or Buyer's state. If the law of Seller's state is selected (State A), it is not considered a "Contracting State." State A's Article 92 reservation says so. Hence its domestic law governing formation rules will apply. Alternatively, if conflicts principles select the law of Buyer's state (State B), its domestic law applies. State B is a Contracting State which has not made a reservation excluding Part II of the CISG. Accordingly, under Article l(l)(b), it is a "Contracting State." Therefore, if State B's law is selected, the CISG's formation rules govern the issue.

---

[9] To date Denmark, Finland, Norway and Sweden have made an Article 92 reservation; Finland and Sweden have made an Article 94 declaration.

## 2. The CISG's Formation Rules Illustrated: Six Hypotheticals

The CISG's formation rules are for the most part identical to the rules in Article 2 and non-UCC law. But there are some important differences. One is the treatment of offer-varying acceptances, which we consider below. Other differences concern the point at which a contract is concluded, the effectiveness of a rejection, and the revocability of an offer. They are illustrated by the following six hypotheticals. In each hypothetical Seller is the offeror and Buyer the offeree, and the CISG otherwise applies. Assume throughout that Seller and Buyer have never dealt with each other before and there is no applicable trade usage. The question in each case is whether a contract has been formed.

> (1) Seller dispatches an offer which is received by Buyer on January 1. Buyer responds on that date by dispatching a letter which reads "I accept your offer...." Seller receives Buyer's letter on January 6. It opens the letter on January 8.

A contract has been concluded on January 6, the date of receipt by the offeror. Articles 18, 23, and 24 yield the result. Under Article 23, a contract is concluded "at the moment when an acceptance becomes effective...." An acceptance becomes effective, under Article 18(2), "at the moment the indication of assent reaches the offeror." Under Article 24, an offer "reaches" the offeror when, among other events, it is delivered to the offeror or his place of business. Since Buyer's acceptance reached Seller on January 6, it became effective on that date. A contract therefore was concluded on January 6. The fact that Seller receives actual notice of Buyer's acceptance on January 8 is irrelevant. So too is the fact that the acceptance was dispatched on January 1. Under the common law "mailbox rule" which supplements the UCC's formation rules via § 1-103, a different result would be reached. The contract would be concluded on January 1, the date on which Buyer dispatched its acceptance through a "reasonable" medium.[10]

> (2) Again, Seller dispatches an offer to Buyer which Buyer receives. On January 1 Buyer dispatches a letter to Seller saying "I accept your offer...." Buyer subsequently changes her mind and sends a fax on January 2 saying "I reject your offer...." The fax is received by Seller on January 2. Seller receives Buyer's letter on January 4.

No contract is concluded. The result follows from Articles 17, 18, and

---

[10] Cf. § 2-206(1).

23.  As in Hypothetical (1), under Article 23, a contract is concluded when the acceptance of an offer becomes effective.  Under Article 17, an offer is terminated when a rejection reaches the offeror.  Once the offer is terminated, an acceptance received by the offeror does not become effective under Article 18(2).  Hence, again under Article 23, no contract is concluded.  Since Buyer's rejection reached Seller on January 2, before Seller received Buyer's acceptance, the rejection operated to terminate Seller's offer.  Buyer's subsequently received acceptance therefore does not operate to conclude a contract.  The result under common law would be similar: If the offeror relied on the rejection, it can treat the offer as terminated.  The CISG and common law differ in result only when the offeror does not rely on the rejection.  This is because the CISG adopts a "receipt" rule for both acceptances and rejections.  Common law adopts a "dispatch" rule for acceptances, a "receipt" rule for rejections, and a limited exception to the "dispatch" rule in the case of an overtaking rejection.  The CISG requires no exception.

> (3) The same facts as in Hypothetical (2) except that on January 1 Buyer dispatches a letter saying "I reject your offer..." On January 2 Buyer changes its mind and sends a fax saying "I accept your offer..."

A contract is concluded.  As in Hypothetical (2), Articles 17, 18, and 23 yield the result.  Again, under Article 23, a contract is concluded by an effective acceptance.  Buyer's acceptance in its January 2 fax became effective when it reached Seller, on January 2.  A contract therefore was concluded on that date.  The rejection received by Seller on January 4 does not terminate Seller's offer because a contract was already formed.  The result under common law would be the same.  Since Buyer's acceptance was received by Seller prior to the rejection, there is no conflict between a "dispatch" rule for acceptances and a "receipt" rule for rejections.

> (4) Seller dispatches a letter to Buyer saying "I offer you...." Buyer receives the letter and begins to make changes in its place of business to accommodate the goods it intends to buy from Seller.  Later, Buyer receives a letter from Seller saying "I revoke my offer to you...." Buyer immediately dispatches a letter to Seller saying "I accept your offer...."

No contract has been concluded.  Articles 16 and 18 yield the result.  Under Article 16(1), an offer is revocable at any time prior to the dispatch of an acceptance.  Buyer made changes to its business but did not dispatch its acceptance until after it received Seller's revocation.

Therefore, Seller's offer was revocable and revoked. So Buyer's subsequent dispatch of acceptance is not effective to conclude a contract under Article 18(1). Article 18(3) does not change the result. Under that provision, the offeree, by trade usage, course of performance or the like, can indicate its acceptance without notifying the offeror. Given such facts, preparatory measures to performance therefore could indicate acceptance. Hypothetical (4)'s assumptions exclude such facts.

We think the result in the Hypothetical is not so bad. True, Buyer has relied on Seller's offer and perhaps even intended its preparations to indicate its acceptance. But arguably the cost of giving notice of acceptance should be placed on Buyer. After all, if Buyer's reliance constitutes acceptance or makes an offer irrevocable, a difficult proof problem is presented: establishing reliance. The problem is present whether Seller or Buyer seeks to prove that there was or was not acceptance. Negative effects are produced to the extent that persons other than the contracting parties, that is, other users of the judicial system, have to bear some of associated proof costs. Article 18(3) reduces these effects by requiring a particular act rather than ambiguous "performance" to constitute acceptance. Because trade usage, course of performance and the like similarly reduce ambiguity, Article 18(3) allows acceptance to be given in that manner.

> (5) On January 1 Buyer receives an offer previously dispatched by Seller which says "I offer you..." Buyer dispatches to Seller an acceptance by letter on January 2. Seller sends a letter to Buyer on January 3 saying "I revoke my offer of January 1." Buyer receives the revocation letter on January 4. Seller receives Buyer's letter of acceptance on January 5.

A contract has been concluded on January 5. Articles 15, 16, 18, and 23 yield the result. Under Article 15(2), an offer is withdrawn, even if irrevocable by its terms, if the withdrawal reaches the offeree before or at the same time as it receives the offer. Since Buyer received Seller's offer on January 1 and the revocation on January 4, Seller's offer is not effectively withdrawn. Under Article 16(1), an offer is revocable until the offeree has dispatched an acceptance. Revocation is effective under the Article only on receipt by the offeree. The negative implication of Article 16(1) is that an offer is *irrevocable* after acceptance has been dispatched. Since Buyer dispatched an acceptance on January 2 but received Seller's revocation on January 4, Seller's revocation is ineffective. Therefore, Seller's offer continued to be open as of January 5, the date Seller received Buyer's acceptance. Under Article 18(2), Buyer's acceptance became effective on January 5. So, under Article 23, the acceptance concludes a contract on that date.

Notice a consequence of the CISG's determination as to when an offer becomes irrevocable. Combined with Article 18(2)'s "receipt" rule for an effective acceptance, the offeree can speculate at the offeror's expense. For once an acceptance is dispatched, Article 16(1)'s negative implication is that the offer is irrevocable, as just noted. But an acceptance does not become effective, according to Article 18(2), until it reaches the offeror. The two rules in conjunction allow the offeree to dispatch an acceptance and observe the market. Its dispatch operates to render the offer irrevocable. Between the time of dispatch and its receipt by the offeror, the offeree can treat the offer as an option contract in the strict sense with no option price. If the market declines, the offeree can simply dispatch a rejection calculated to be received by the offeror prior to the receipt of the acceptance. For instance, the original acceptance might be sent by mail, and the subsequent rejection by fax. Article 17 treats a rejection received as terminating the offer. The subsequently arriving acceptance therefore is not an effective acceptance under Article 18(2). Alternatively, if the market increases, the offeror can do nothing. The acceptance is effective upon receipt by the offeror, and a contract is concluded. In either case, the offeree need pay nothing for the option of having the offer remain open. The common law "mailbox" rule, by treating the acceptance as effective upon dispatch, eliminates this possibility.

We are not upset by the possibility allowed by the CISG's formation rules for two reasons. First, the CISG's formation rules are default rules only. Parties can opt out of them, as Article 6 expressly allows. Hence, offerors can opt out of Article 16(1) by stipulating in the offer, for instance, that it is revocable at any time prior to receiving acceptance. The stipulation eliminates the offer as a zero-price option contract available to the offeree. Not knowing whether more offerors would prefer Article 16(1) to its common law counterpart or the converse, Article 16(1) is not unreasonable a priori. Second, and more important, we suspect that the combination of Articles 16(1) and 18(2) produces an arguably defensible default rule. Sellers are likely to be buyers as frequently as buyers are likely to be sellers, and the goods bought and sold subject to the same extent of volatility in price. (General Motors is not as likely to buy cars as it is to sell them, but it is just as likely that it will sell cars as it will to buy products that are subject to the same changes in price over similar periods as its cars.) If so, both buyers and sellers will be exposed to speculation at the other's expense. The combination of Articles 16(1) and 18(2) therefore is likely to be neutral in its distributional or efficiency effects.

> (6) On January 1, Seller dispatches a letter to Buyer which reads: "I offer to sell you ..., but you must let me know by the end of the month whether you accept the offer." Seller tells Buyer on January 5 that it revokes the offer. On January 6, Buyer faxes an acceptance to Seller, which is received the same day.

A contract may or may not be concluded. It will depend on whether Seller's offer is revocable. This in turn depends on the interpretation given to Article 16(2). Here the CISG is unclear, the result of a compromise between civil law and common law delegates to the Vienna Conference. At common law, an offer is revocable at any time prior to acceptance unless an option contract is created. Since no option contract was created in the hypothetical, Seller's offer is revocable, even if stated to be irrevocable. Even if Article 2 of the UCC applied, the result would not change. Seller's offer is not a firm offer under § 2-205 because it does not give assurances that the offer would be held open.

Under the CISG, Seller's offer may or may not be irrevocable. Article 16(2)(a) provides that an offer cannot be revoked if "it indicates, whether by stating a fixed time for acceptance or otherwise, that it is irrevocable." Seller's offer states a fixed time for acceptance. But it also requires that the offer "indicate[] that it is irrevocable." Therefore, the question is whether stating a fixed time within which acceptance is to occur indicates irrevocability. There are two possibilities. One is that the offeror, by stating a fixed period of time, is merely indicating that the offer lapses after that period. There is no indication that the offer cannot be revoked prior to that fixed time. Alternatively, the indication could be that the offer is irrevocable within the fixed period. A demand for acceptance within a fixed period is consistent with both "lapse" and "irrevocability." The CISG does not resolve the ambiguity.

Article 16(2)(a) is a good example of the CISG leaving provisions vague to achieve consensus.[11] The price of consensus, of course, is to risk nonuniform treatment of the revocability of offers under Article 16(2)(a). Civil law countries probably would interpret the fixing of a period for acceptance as indicating irrevocability. Common law

---

[11] See Arthur Rosett, *Critical Reflections on the United Nations Convention on Contracts for the International Sale of Goods*, 45 Ohio St. L. J. 265 (1984).

countries are much less likely to do so.[12]   Article 7 can help achieve uniformity to an extent. Its prescription to interpret the CISG's provisions in order to "promote uniformity in its application" requires courts to coordinate interpretations to some extent.   But there is a first mover problem of sorts here. Given an initial interpretation of Article 16(2)(a), inertia favors following that interpretation, whatever the initial interpretation.  We interpret Article 16(2)(a) to require an "indication" that the offer is irrevocable, and consider fixing a time for acceptance, *without more*, as insufficient to "indicate" irrevocability.  We do not know whether more offerors would prefer to make irrevocable offers rather than revocable ones.  In our judgment the cost to an offeror of making an offer irrevocable is equal to the cost of making it revocable: a simple stipulation in the offer to the effect that it is revocable or irrevocable.   Hence the irrevocability of offers is not better than revocability, or vice versa, as a default rule.  But offerors prefer a clear well-defined rule as to the revocability of their offers to a vague one.  A vague rule creates uncertainty about its application, and imposes on offerors costs of avoiding having their offers treated as irrevocable when they prefer the offers to be revocable.  These offerors therefore must take precautions against having their offers treated as irrevocable when the offer stipulates a fixed time for acceptance or "otherwise."   Pre-contractual precautions do not produce anything of value.   At one extreme, precautions might take the form of not making an offer at all. A rule that requires clear indications of irrevocability relieves offerors of taking such precautions.   It also avoids the risk of judicial misinterpretation of the parties' intent.  Our conclusion therefore is that Article 16(2)(a) is better interpreted to find that an offer is irrevocable only when its terms indicate irrevocability other than merely fixing a time for acceptance.

### III.  Offer-Varying Acceptance: The Battles of the Forms

When a purported acceptance contains terms not included in the offer, at least two questions arise. One is whether a contract exists at all. The second question assumes that a contract is concluded and asks what its terms include.  If the purported acceptance does not conclude a contract but the parties' behavior indicates that they have contracted, there is an additional question concerning the terms of that contract.

---

[12] See Gyula Eorsi, *Revocability of Offer*, Commentary on the International Sales Law: The 1980 Vienna Sales Convention 150 (C.M. Bianca & M.J. Bonell eds., 1987).

Article 2 of the UCC addresses all three questions in § 2-207; the CISG addresses the first question in Article 19, and the second and third questions by a combination of Articles 14, 18 and 19. Article 2 and the CISG give different answers to the three questions.

## A. Under Article 2

### 1. Introduction

Section 2-207 is not a model of statutory draftsmanship. A close reading of the section reveals its shortcomings. To begin with, it is designed principally to address the "Battle of the Forms" that arises where the parties exchange standardized writings such as a purchase order and order acknowledgement. Only some of the terms of the writings will have been individually negotiated. The others will have been prepared in advance for repeated use in a range of transactions. Since the parties exchange their own standardized forms, not all of the terms of the writings exchanged are the same. And if each party includes in its own forms terms most favorable to it, the forms "battle." Four separate problems can be presented by acceptances that vary the terms of offers. First, if a written confirmation follows an oral agreement, do the terms of the confirmation become part of the contract? Second, if the writings exchanged contain nonidentical terms, is a contract created? Third, if the contract is created despite non-identical terms, what are its terms? Fourth, if the writings exchanged do not create a contract, but the parties' conduct recognizes that a contract is in existence, what are its terms?

Subsection (1) addresses two "battles" involving writings. One is present when an oral agreement has *already* been reached. Subsequently, a written confirmation concerning the terms of the agreement is sent by one or more of the parties: "...a written confirmation which is sent...operates as an acceptance even though it states terms additional or different from those offered or agreed upon...." Perhaps the oral agreement contained skeletal terms — say, just item, price and delivery date. The written confirmation contains other ("additional") or conflicting ("different") terms. Subsection (1) provides that in either case the confirmation remains an "acceptance," not a rejection and counteroffer.

This part of subsection (1) is odd in itself. Obviously a confirmation containing terms additional to or different from those contained in the oral agreement cannot serve as a rejection and counteroffer. The oral agreement already exists. The party sending the confirmation cannot unilaterally alter the nature or terms of the agreement. It does not matter what the party says in its confirmation. That is in part why the clause following the comma in the subsection ("unless...") has no application to this situation. Hence § 2-207's drafters could have intended the part of subsection (1) to address the question of contract terms, not contract formation.

The other "battle" subsection (1) addresses concerns the exchange of writings by an offeror and offeree. In this situation § 2-207(1) answers the question as to whether the writings create a contract. The subsection says that an offeree's writing constitutes an "acceptance" if it is "[a] definite and seasonable expression of acceptance [sic]...even though it states terms additional or different from those offered or agreed upon, unless acceptance is expressly made conditional on assent to the additional or different terms." It follows that the writing does not constitute an acceptance but rather a rejection and counteroffer if either of two conditions is satisfied: the writing is not a definite and seasonable expression of acceptance or if the acceptance is made expressly conditional on the offeror's assent to additional or different terms.

The conditions are not transparent in meaning. Clearly, § 2-207(1) displaces the mirror image rule: the rule that a response to an offer is an acceptance only if it is identical to the offer. But § 2-207(1) is unclear as to when an offer-varying response operates as an acceptance sufficient to conclude a contract. If I offer you a Porsche at $40,000 and you respond "I accept, but at $1000, not $40,000," does your response amount to a "definite...expresssion of acceptance"? Or suppose I offer a Porsche at $40,000 and you respond "I accept at your price, but you must paint the car, deliver it to me, guarantee its performance over its life, and maintain insurance for the first 30 days"? Sometimes the terms of a response differ or supplement those of an offer so much as to not operate as an acceptance, whatever the label put on the response (e.g., "acceptance").[13] The trouble comes in determining the point at which the difference is great enough. The standard of assent in § 2-204(2), although sometimes invoked, is unhelpful here. Under § 2-204(1), the parties' conduct can indicate recognition of a contract. But that evidence is unavailable where the performance has not begun or completed, and the parties have

---

[13] See, e.g., General Electric Co. v. G. Siempenkamp GmbH & Co., 29 F.3d 1095, 1099 (6th Cir. 1994).

exchanged only writings.[14]  Similarly, § 2-207(1) is unclear as to when a response is made "expressly conditional" on the offeror's assent to its additional or different terms.  Obviously, responses which mimic the relevant statutory language work: "My acceptance is expressly conditional on...," or "My acceptance is conditional on..." will do.  But what about "My acceptance is subject to...," "My acceptance must be on...," "My acceptance is only on..."?

Subsection (2) determines the fate of the "additional terms...to the contract..." referred to in subsection (1).  Again, § 2-207(1) refers to two sorts of contracts: an agreement followed by a written confirmation and writings exchanged which contain non-identical terms.  They are "the contract" to which § 2-207(2) provides the terms.  Under § 2-207(2), "additional" terms included in a written confirmation are not part of "the contract."  They are merely "proposals for addition to the contract."  The terms of the contract initially include only those contained in the offer-- the writing to which the acceptance is a response or the oral agreement which the written confirmation follows.  If at least one of the parties is not a merchant, that ends of the matter:  The additional terms in the acceptance do not become part of the contract.  Note that here the corollary to the mirror image rule, the "last shot" doctrine, is replaced by its reverse, a "first shot" doctrine of sorts.  The "last shot" doctrine provides that where a response alters the terms of the offer, and performance follows, the terms of the contract are those of the last writing received prior to performance.  Subsection (1) allows an offer-varying response to operate as an acceptance.  And  § 2-207(2) provides that the contract thereby created is on the terms of the first writing or oral agreement.  Subsection (2) therefore provides a sort of "first shot" doctrine.

If the parties are merchants, the matter is more complicated.  As in the case of a nonmerchant, the additional terms in the offeree's responsive writing are "proposals for additions to the contract."  They are not incorporated into the contract if (a) the offer restricts acceptance to the terms of the offer, (b) the additional terms are material alterations of the contract, or (c) if the offeror makes a timely objection to their inclusion

---

[14] The problem is not solved by appealing to UCC gap-filling terms, as is permitted by 2-204(3): "Even though one or more terms are left open a contract for sale does not fail for indefiniteness if the parties have intended to make a contract...."  An independent standard is necessary to determine whether a party's response indicates an intent to contract when its terms are different enough from the terms of the offer.

in the contract. In other words, the additional terms in the acceptance become part of the contract if the offeror's writing fails to limit acceptance to its terms, the terms of the acceptance are non-material alterations of the contract, *and* the offeror fails to make a timely objection to their inclusion in the contract.

### 2. Problems in § 2-207's Interpretation

It is unclear whether "terms" in § 2-207(2) includes only "additional" terms or also what § 2-207(1) describes as "different" terms. The language of § 2-207(2) is limited to "additional" terms. Subsection (1), however, refers to responses that "state terms additional to or different from" the terms of an offer. And Official Comment 3 to § 2-207, which describes the workings of § 2-207(2), expressly applies the subsection to different terms as well. Subsection (2)'s drafting history is obscure but appears to indicate that "different" was dropped from § 2-207(2) by mistake.[15] Most courts have invoked Comment 3 to construe subsection (2) to apply to both "additional" and "different" terms. So construed, the subsection specifies when additional or different terms in a responsive writing will become part of the contract either recognized or formed under subsection (1). We see absolutely no reason for limiting subsection (2) to "additional" terms. Doing so has the further vice of leaving unresolved how "different" terms are to be handled under § 2-207(2).

Both § 2-207 and its Official Comments are silent as to what the statutory terms "additional" and "different" mean. In an intuitive sense, the words are synonyms: different terms are additional, and additional terms are different. However, 2-207(1) distinguishes between the two sorts of terms. The most plausible possibility is that "different" terms are terms in a response which are either contrary to or contradict a term in the offer. "Blue widgets" in the response is contrary to "green widgets" in the offer. "All warranties" in the response contradicts "no warranties" in the offer. "Additional" terms are terms that are consistent with the terms of the offer but not entailed by them. "Blue widget" in the response is an additional term when the offer speaks only of "widgets." The distinction between "additional" and "different" is unimportant if § 2-207(2) is read to apply to both sorts of terms. If § 2-207(2) is limited to

---

[15] Cf. Spring 1951 draft of Article 2, where both § 2-207(1) and (2) are limited to "additional" terms, and November 1951 Final Draft, where § 2-207(1) refers to "additional or different terms" and § 2-207(2) refers to "additional" terms (12 Uniform Commercial Code Drafts 51-51, 425-26 (E. Kelly ed. 1984)).

additional terms, it is crucial.

Section 2-207(2) provides that the offering-varying terms in an acceptance under § 2-207(1) constitute a "proposal." Subsection (2)(b) also provides that the terms do not become part of the contract when they "materially alter it." So a determination is needed as to when a term in the acceptance materially alters a term in the offer. Roughly, there are three possible standards of "materiality." Some courts have applied a *per se* rule: All additional (or different) terms in an acceptance are material alterations. A second standard is comparative in nature. Under the standard, a term is considered materially altering if it is significantly different from what is usual and customary in a particular business. The standard, in other words, compares the term with predominant trade usage. For instance, arbitration clauses are common in contracts within the textile industry. A contract a buyer enters into to purchase textiles is likely to contain such a clause. A seller's acknowledgment form containing an arbitration clause would not constitute a materially altering term.    The third standard also is comparative in nature but is individualized. A term is materially altering, according to it, when including it would significantly reduce the value of the contract to the offeror. This standard, unlike the second one, looks to the particular offeror, not to trade usage and typical offerors. Of course, the standard will often reach the same results as are reached under the second standard because the offerer often expects terms typically included in contracts in the particular trade.

Consider now the second unresolved statutory issue embedded in § 2-207(2): the effect of additional or different terms on the terms of the offer. Suppose the offer does not limit acceptance to its terms. Suppose also that the offeree's responsive writing contains different terms. And suppose the offeror fails to make a timely objection to their inclusion. Does the contract include or exclude the offeree's different term? Courts and commentators have taken four positions on the matter. Three of the four positions reach the same conclusion. One position considers the different terms a material alteration of the terms of the offer. It concludes that, under § 2-207(2)(b), they do not become part of the contract. A second position asserts that different terms in a responsive writing are objectionable to the offeror. Because different terms are objectionable to the offeror, "notification of objection to them has already been given" under § 2-207(2)(c). Hence, as in the first position, different terms do not become part of the contract under § 2-207(2). The third position reaches the same conclusion by reading subsection (2) literally and ignoring associated Comments. The position notes that subsection (2) applies only to additional terms, not to different terms. It infers from the restriction that therefore the offeree's different terms never would become part of the contract. They simply drop out.

The fourth position yields different results from the other three positions. As with the other positions, it treats different terms which either are contrary to or contradictory to terms in the offer. However, the fourth position draws a different consequence from the presence of different terms. Since terms in the offeror and offeree's writings conflict, it concludes that *both* terms drop out. The conflicting terms "knock out" each other. Neither parties' terms become part of the contract under § 2-207(2). A majority of courts endorse this position.[16] We think that the position is wrong. For one thing, it lacks statutory support. Even if subsection (2) is read to apply to both additional and different terms, under § 2-207(2) either the terms of the *offeree's* writing are included in the contract or they drop out. None of the terms of the offeror's writing are contemplated to drop out. The statutory language in this respect is clear: "Between merchants *such terms* become part of the contract unless...." "Such terms" refers to the terms of the offeree's writing. Further, no support for the position can be had from Official Comment 6. Comment 6 discusses conflicting *confirmations*. They are conflicting confirmations of an oral agreement. The Comment has no application where an oral agreement is not already present. Hence it has no application to cases in which a contract is formed under § 2-207(1) on the basis of an exchange of writings. Lastly, as an interpretive matter, the position is strange. For if the drafters had wanted both the offeror and offeree's terms to cancel each other when they conflict, they knew how to say so. They said so in § 2-207(3): "... the particular contract consist[s] of those terms on which the writings of the parties agree...." Terms which "agree" are neither additional nor different terms. If the drafters did not provide for terms to cancel each other in § 2-207(3), there must be a reason. The plausible reason is that where the offeror and offeree's terms conflict, only the offeree's conflicting terms drop out. The fourth position might be "fairer" to the offeree. But it lacks statutory support.

Section 2-207(3) is fairly straightforward. Like subsection (2), it provides the terms of a contract. But the subsection applies only if § 2-207(1) does not apply and where the parties' conduct indicates that they

---

[16] See Northrup Corp. v. Litronic Industries, 29 F.3d 1173, 1178 (7th Cir. 1994); Weyburn-Barel, Inc. v. Zagar, Inc., 1996 Lexis 16988 (W.D. Mich. 1996).

have contracted: "Conduct by both parties which recognizes the existence of a contract is sufficient to establish a contract for sale although the writings of the parties do not otherwise establish a contract." Subsection (1) applies where the writings of the parties *do* establish a contract. This occurs, again in either of two circumstances: when a written confirmation follows an oral agreement or when the offeree's responsive writing contains a definite and seasonable indication of assent without expressly conditional language. If the "writings establish a contract" under § 2-207(1), § 2-207(2) applies, not § 2-207(3). As noted, subsection (2) provides the terms of the contract formed or recognized under subsection (1). Hence subsection (3) applies only if subsection (2) does not apply.

Given § 2-207(1) and (2), § 2-207(3) makes sense. Contracts recognized or created by an exchange of writings are governed by subsection (1). Subsection (2) provides the terms of such contracts. Section 2-207(3) applies only if writings do not recognize or recreate a contract under subsection (1). Subsection (1) in turn does not recognize or create a contract when a responsive writing either is not a "reasonably definite and seasonable" expression of acceptance or it is made expressly conditional on the offeror's assent to additional or different terms. In either case something else is required to recognize or create a contract. The "something else" is conduct. Under subsection (3), conduct, not writings, recognizes the existence of a contract. The subsection provides the terms of the contract formed by the parties' conduct.

The terms of the contract governed by subsection (3) fall into two categories. One category consists of terms on which the offeror and offeree's writings agree. These are terms common to both writings. Terms that the writings do not share in common drop out: they are "knocked out" and form no part of the resulting contract. In this way different or additional terms in both the offer and offeree's writings are eliminated. The terms of the resulting contract are not those of the last communication dispatched prior to performance. The "knock out" doctrine therefore rejects the corollary of the mirror image rule: the "last shot" doctrine. A second consists of gap fillers provided by the UCC where the parties have been silent. Examples include § 2-305 (price), § 2-308 (place of delivery), § 2-309 (time for performance), § 2-310 (time for payment), § 2-312 (implied warranty of title), § 2-314 (implied warranty of merchantability), and § 2-315 (implied warranty of fitness for a particular purpose). Subsection (3) refers to them as "supplementary terms." The parties' contract includes terms common to the parties' writings and the terms supplied "supplemented" by the Code. Two obvious consequences follow. One is that where terms common to the parties' writings exclude a gap filling term provided by the UCC, the UCC-supplied term does not become part of the contract. The second consequence bears on the "knock out" doctrine: where the terms of the parties' writings differ, and one of the differing terms is identical to a UCC-supplied gap filler, the UCC-supplied term "supplements" the terms common to both parties' writings. The UCC-supplied term therefore reintroduces into the contract a term eliminated by operation of the knock out doctrine.

The Proposed Revision of Article 2 considerably simplifies the handling of offer-varying acceptances. As with current § 2-207, the Proposed Revision divides the problem acceptance into a question of contract formation and a question of the terms of the concluded contract. Proposed § 2-206(3) replicates current § 2-207(1), thus denying the mirror image rule. As with current § 2-207(1), however, we are not told when a response constitutes a "definite and seasonable expression of acceptance." Proposed § 2-207 sets the terms of contracts, however they are formed. It also eliminates the difference between "additional" and "different" terms, and makes the materiality of an alteration in term irrelevant. Basically, the section adopts the knock out rule for all contracts: terms common to the parties' records become part of the contract. All other terms in their records are excluded. The parties' contract also includes supplementary terms supplied by the UCC as well as terms to which the parties have agreed. In this way Proposed § 2-207 removes most objections based on complexity and uncertainty in statute.

Whether Proposed § 2-207 supplies efficient terms is more controversial. Proposed § 2-207's knock out rule supplements the parties' agreement with UCC default terms, even when one party's record attempts to exclude them. This imposes terms a party has signaled it would prefer not apply to its contract. Default terms, such as implied warranties or recoverable consequential damages, arguably allocate risk according to the comparative risk-reducing capacities of the majority of contracting parties. As default terms, they apply unless parties prefer other terms instead. By attempting to exclude default terms in a record, a party indicates its preference for other terms. The preference presumptively shows that default terms do not optimally allocate risk affecting the parties' contract. Proposed § 2-207's knock out rule nonetheless imposes these terms. A court may lack information necessary to select optimal terms to govern the parties' contract. However, a party's exclusion of a default term presumptively signals that the optimal terms do not include it.

UCITA's version of the knock out rule makes the opposite judgment about efficiency of UCC-supplemented terms. Its knock out rule applies only to contracts formed by the parties' conduct. Under § 210(a), the terms of these contracts are "determined by consideration" of a list of items, including terms and conditions agreed upon, course of dealing, trade usage. Default terms supplied by UCITA are not among the items listed. The implication of the omission is that they are not to be "considered" in determining the contract's terms. In other words, UCITA's default terms, unlike Proposed Article 2's default terms, do not become part of the contract. Official Comment 2 to § 210 makes clear its rejection of this aspect of the knock out rule: "Formalistic rules cannot account for the contextual nuances that exist in the rich environment of transactional practice... [Supplementation by default rules] is too rigid for information transactions where contracts terms often define the product and scope of the grant." The Comment apparently takes the position that computer information contracts that are created by conduct are so diverse that default terms create inefficient levels of performance for them.

## B. Under the CISG

The CISG's treatment of offer-varying acceptances differs from § 2-207. Article 19, the CISG's counterpart to § 2-207, adopts what can be described as a slightly modified mirror image rule. Article 19(1) announces a mirror image rule concerning acceptance: "A reply to an offer which purports to be an acceptance but contains additions, limitations or other modifications is a rejection of the offer and constitutes a counter-offer." To be an acceptance, a reply must contain only terms contained in the offer. A reply containing additional or different terms not in the offer cannot conclude a contract. Subsection (1) therefore states the mirror image rule.

Article 19(2) modifies the rule: "However, a reply to an offer which purports to be an acceptance but contains additional or different terms which do not materially alter the terms of the offer constitutes an acceptance, unless the offeror, without undue delay, objects orally to the discrepancy or dispatches a notice to that effect." Subsection (2) only applies to responses that contain non-material alterations of the terms of the offer. Responses containing material alterations therefore remain subject to Article 19(1). And under Article 19(1), such responses are rejections and counteroffers, not acceptances. No action need be taken by the offeror to prevent the response from creating a contract. If a response contains a non-material alteration of the terms of the offer, and the offeror objects to the alteration, the reply still does not constitute an acceptance. The response constitutes an acceptance only if the offeror makes no objection to non-material alterations contained in it. In this case subsection (2) modifies the mirror image rule and its corollary, the "last shot" doctrine: a contract is created by the offer-varying acceptance, and the terms of the resulting contract include the non-material alterations in the acceptance.

Article 19(2)'s modification of the mirror image rule at work in subsection (1) is slight. This is because almost any additional or different terms in a response will amount to a material alteration of the terms of the offer. According to Article 19(3), almost all matters that would be covered by a contract are "material" terms: "Additional or different terms relating, among other things, to the price, payment, quality and quantity of the goods, place and time of delivery, extent of one party's liability to the other or the settlement of disputes are considered to alter the terms of the offer materially." To see this, try to think of a term in a response which would not "relate" to one of the enumerated matters. Further, Article 19(3)'s enumeration is non-exhaustive, as indicated by the phrase "among other things." Given the breadth of the list of matters considered material, the phrase is properly interpreted broadly. Almost any additional or different term in a reply therefore will be a material alteration. To see this, take a matter that you think is not "related" to the matters mentioned in Article 19(3) and ask whether, given the phrase, it nonetheless is a material alteration. For example, suppose the reply prohibits the seller from using convict labor to produce the goods to be purchased. The seller's offer says nothing about how the goods are to be manufactured. Seemingly, the term does not relate to "quality," the only likely candidate in Article 19(3)'s list of materially altering terms. But, given the phrase "among other things," a restriction on the production of goods probably is a material term. And, again, if a term is material, Article 19(2) does not save the contract from the mirror image rule of Article 19(1). Almost all offer-varying replies therefore will not constitute acceptances but rejections and counteroffers.

Article 19 applies in two sorts of cases involving offer-varying acceptance: "no performance" and "performance" cases. A "no performance" case is one in which the contracting parties exchange writings without performance following. "Performance" cases are cases in which performance follows an exchange of writings containing non-identical terms. In "no performance" cases, no contract is formed under Article 19. In "performance" cases, a contract is formed on the terms of the last reply prior to performance. A simple "no performance" case is the following. Buyer dispatches a purchase order to Seller containing a clause imposing an implied warranty of merchantability on Seller. Seller responds with an order acknowledgment which accepts Buyer's order but disclaims all implied warranties of merchantability as to the goods. No further communication occurs between Buyer and Seller. Neither Seller nor Buyer performs. No contract is created under Article 19. Under Article 19(1), the term in Seller's reply excluding all implied warranties of merchantability is a "modification" of the terms of Buyer's offer. Seller's reply therefore constitutes a rejection and counteroffer. If Seller's "additional or different" term is a non-material alteration, Seller's acknowledgment would constitute an acceptance under 19(2) unless Buyer objected to the term. Since Buyer made no objection, Seller's reply constitutes an acceptance under Article 19(2) if the exclusion of warranties in Seller's acknowledgment is considered a non-material alteration. Article 19(3) treats terms relating to "quality" of the goods and "extent of one party's liability to the other" as material terms. Since an exclusion of a warranty clearly relates to both matters, Seller's term is a material alteration. Therefore, Seller's reply does not constitute an acceptance under Article 19(2). No contract is concluded under a "no performance" case. However, Seller's reply would operate to conclude a contract under § 2-207(1): the acknowledgment is seasonable and reasonably definite, and it is not made expressly conditional on Buyer's assent to Seller's exclusion of implied warranties of merchantability.

A simple "performance" case involves a slight variant on the previous case. Now suppose Seller performs by delivering the goods. The goods fail to conform to the ordinary purposes to which they are used by Buyer. Under Article 19(1), Seller's order acknowledgment is a rejection and counteroffer, not an acceptance. As before, Article 19(2) does not alter this consequence because the material alteration makes it inapplicable. Buyer's receipt and use of the goods, however, amounts to acceptance of Seller's counteroffer under Article 18(1): "A statement made or other conduct of the offeree indicating assent to an offer is an acceptance." Buyer's acceptance becomes effective under Article 18(2) when Seller receives notice of it — here, presumably when the goods were delivered and used. Under Article 23 the contract therefore is concluded at that time. The terms of the contract concluded are those of Seller's order acknowledgment. They do not include an implied warranty of merchantability. In other words, the last shot corollary to the mirror image rule would create a contract on Seller's terms.[17] The result under § 2-207 would be different. Here, as in the "no performance" case, under § 2-207(1) a contract would be created by Seller's acknowledgment. The terms of the contract would be established under § 2-207(2). A term in a responsive writing excluding the implied warranty called for in an offer probably is a materially altering, different term. Section 2-207(2) eliminates Seller's term from the resulting contract. The contract therefore includes as a term the implied warranty contained in Buyer's purchase order.[18] A "first shot" doctrine controls the terms of the contract.

Article 19's application is not always straightforward. For instance, whether a term in a responsive writing is "additional or different" from a term in the offer sometimes is not obvious. Suppose that it is the custom in the relevant trade that Seller can select the law governing the contract. Buyer sends Seller a purchase order containing no applicable law clause. Seller sends an order acknowledgment in response accepting Buyer's order. The acknowledgment contains a choice of law clause. Does Seller's reply constitute an acceptance? There are two ways to analyze the issue under Article 19; both yield the same result. One way is to construe the term in Seller's response as not being "additional or different" from the term in Buyer's order. Under Article 9(2), trade usage is made applicable to the formation of the contract under specified conditions. Trade usage therefore is applicable to determine the terms of Buyer's offer. Given governing trade usage, a term in Buyer's offer is that Seller can select the law applicable to the contract. Seller's acknowledgment does not therefore contain a term "additional or different" from the terms in Buyer's order. Accordingly, the acknowledgment constitutes an acceptance under Article 19(1). The alternative analysis construes Seller's acknowledgment as containing a non-materially altering "additional or different" term. Seller's acknowledgment alters a term of Buyer's offer. But given that Buyer's

---

[17] For expression of dissatisfaction with Article 19's adoption of the last shot doctrine, see John O. Honnold, Uniform Law for International Sales under the 1980 United Nations Convention 192 (3d ed. 1999).

[18] If the "knock out" doctrine is applied to § 2-207(2), an implied warranty of merchantability would be a term of the resulting contract. Here both Buyer and Seller's terms would be eliminated. The UCC-supplied term imposing an implied warranty of merchantability under § 2-314 would supplement the terms common to both Seller and Buyer's writings. The resulting contract therefore would include an implied warranty of merchantability.

offer incorporates trade usage allowing Seller to select governing law, the Seller's alteration complies with it. Seller's term therefore is not a material alteration under Article 19(3), and Seller's reply constitutes an acceptance under Article 19(2). Both analyses, in different ways, reach the same result: Seller's acknowledgment can conclude a contract even if it varies the express terms of Buyer's offer.

To date the few judicial applications of Article 19 receive mixed marks. *Filanto, S.p.A. v. Chilewich International Corp.*[19] is a "performance" case. The court gets Article 19's application right. *Filanto*'s facts are unexciting. On July 5, 1989, Chilewich (the buyer) sent Filanto (the seller) a letter to which was attached a contract Chilewich had concluded with a Russian buyer. The contract included an arbitration clause. Chilewich's July 7 letter incorporated by reference the terms of that contract. Filanto responded by letter on September 2, 1989, agreeing to the incorporation of only three of the terms in Chilewich's contract with its Russian buyer and asking for Chilewich's acceptance. On March 13, 1990, Chilewich dispatched a signed memorandum to Filanto reincorporating the terms of the Russian contract. On May 7, 1990, Chilewich opened a letter of credit in Filanto's favor, as required under the terms of its March 13 memorandum. On August 7, 1990, Filanto signed and returned Chilewich's March 13 memorandum, but deleted all but three of its terms.

Strictly speaking, *Filanto* did not rule on Article 19 or its application because its comments on the Article were dicta. At issue in the case was the existence of an agreement in writing to arbitrate disputes under a contract of sale. The court only had to decide whether such an agreement in writing to arbitrate existed. If one did, then the New York Convention on the Recognition and Enforcement of Foreign Arbitration Awards requires staying the proceeding and ordering arbitration in accordance with the agreement.[20] Based on a mixture of general contract principles, the Restatement (Second) of Contracts and the CISG as sources of law, the court found that a written arbitration agreement existed. Accordingly, the court ordered the parties to arbitrate. Therefore, the court's discussion of the rest of the agreement is dicta.

---

[19] 789 F. Supp. 1229 (S.D.N.Y. 1992).

[20] See Convention on the Recognition and Enforcement of Foreign Arbitral Awards, art. II(1), (2), 330 U.N.T.S. 38 (1959).

The question the court's dicta addresses is whether Filanto and Chilewich's exchange of communications created a contract and, if so, its terms. Chilewich's March 13 memorandum constituted an offer. (It might be a rejection and counteroffer, depending on the treatment of the pre-March exchange of communications.) Filanto's August 7 return of Chilewich's March 13 memorandum altered its terms by deleting a number of them. Filanto's response therefore constituted a rejection and counteroffer under Article 19(1). The deletions in the response eliminated the arbitration clause in Chilewich's March memorandum. An arbitration clause clearly is a material alteration under Article 19(3). Hence Article 19(2) is inapplicable to Filanto's response, and Article 19(1) continues to apply. Because under Article 19(1) Filanto's response is a rejection and counteroffer, the court concludes that no contract was formed by Filanto's August response. The fact that the response is described as an "acceptance" does not affect the conclusion. The *Filanto* court's application of Article 19 is correct.[21]

A German court's application of Article 19 in another "performance" case is mistaken. In a case decided by the Landgericht Baden-Baden,[22] a buyer apparently sent a purchase order to a seller of tiles. The seller responded with an order acknowledgment which required notice of nonconformities in the tile within 30 days of the buyer's receipt of the invoice as a condition of its liability. The seller repeated the requirement again in a subsequent written communication to the buyer. The buyer

---

[21] The court went on to find that Article 19 did not apply. Instead, it found Filanto to have accepted Chilewich's offer under Article 18(1). Filanto's August response was tardy, according to the court, and so did not operate as a rejection and counteroffer. Given a course of dealing between the parties, including Filanto's drawing on the letter of credit established in its favor by Chilewich, and its failure to make timely objections to the terms of Chilewich's March memorandum, Filanto accepted its terms. On the facts, the court might have been correct: Filanto's response might have been tardy and therefore ineffective to constitute a rejection and counteroffer under Article 19(1). But note the consequence if the *Filanto* court's factual finding is wrong. Filanto's response would have been a rejection and counteroffer under Article 19(1). Chilewich's performance would have constituted acceptance under Article 18(1). And according to the "last shot" doctrine adopted in Article 19(1), the contract's terms would have been those provided in Filanto's counteroffer. The terms of Filanto's offer therefore did not include an arbitration clause.

[22] Landgericht Baden-Baden (Germany), August 14, 1991, 1 UNILEX D. 1991-7 (M.J. Bonell ed.).

failed to notify the seller within the time required in the seller's order acknowledgment. When the seller sued for the contract price, the buyer tried to setoff the price by the damages to it resulting from the nonconformity. The court found that the seller's acknowledgment varied the terms of buyer's order and therefore was a rejection and counteroffer under Article 19(1). But it also found that Article 19(2) applied because the term in the seller's acknowledgment requiring notification was a non-material alteration of the terms in buyer's purchase order. Applying Article 19(2), the court concluded that seller's acknowledgment constituted an acceptance and the terms of the resulting contract included seller's term.

The court's application of Article 19 pretty clearly is wrong. A time limit for notification as a condition of liability limits a seller's liability for nonconformities in the tiles. Under Article 19(3), a term in a responsive writing relating to the "extent of one party's liability..." is a materially altering term. The term in the seller's reply therefore constitutes a material alteration of the terms of the buyer's offer. Hence Article 19(2) is inapplicable to the reply, and Article 19(1) continues to treat it as a reply and counteroffer. No contract was formed by the exchange of the buyer and seller's writings. The correct application of Article 19 would find that a contract instead was created by performance following dispatch of the seller's counteroffer. Delivery of the tile and its use by the buyer constituted an effective acceptance of the seller's counteroffer under Article 18(1). A contract therefore was concluded under Article 23. The contract's terms are those contained in the seller's offer, including its limitation of liability. The seller was not liable for the nonconformity in the tile. A proper application of Article 19 therefore reaches the same result as the court reached on a different basis.

An Austrian court's application of Article 19(3) to offer-varying terms in a reply probably is mistaken.[23] The case involved a Russian buyer's response to an Austrian seller's offer to sell a quantity of chemicals. The reply contained a range in the quantity that could be ordered that differed from the range specified in the seller's offer. Both also stipulated quantities "with respect to the ship chosen." However, the quantity range stipulated was within the range specified by the seller's offer, and allowed for less variation. Both the offer and the reply also agreed on the minimum quantity to be ordered by the buyer. On these

---

[23] See Oberster Gerichtshof (Austria), March 20, 1997, 1 UNILEX D.1997-6 (M.J. Bonell ed.).

facts the court found that Article 19(3) did not state a *per se* rule for the materiality of an alteration of a term in an offer. It instead read the subsection to consider the listed items as material unless "the circumstances of the case," including prior negotiations and trade usage, indicate otherwise.[24] Because the tighter permissible quantity variation in the buyer's reply was favorable to the seller if the seller could select the ship, the court concluded that the alteration of quantity in the reply was not material. The court remanded the case for a determination as to the party the contract allowed to select the ship.

The court, we think, reached the wrong conclusion because it confuses two different matters. It is one thing use trade usage, course of dealing, prior negotiations and the like to interpret the content of an offer or acceptance. Article 8(2) expressly requires this. It is another matter to use such evidence to gauge the materiality of a reply's alteration of terms of the offer. Article 19(3)'s language does not allow this use of trade usage and the like, probably for defensible reasons of contract administration. The subsection does not ask whether an alteration affects a party's costs of performance. Having used trade usage and the like to determine the quantity variations permitted by the seller's offer, the buyer's narrow variations are "different terms relating... [to the] quantity of goods." According to Article 19(3), the buyer's reply therefore materially alters the terms of the seller's offer.

## C.  § 2-207 and Article 19 Evaluated

We conclude with an evaluation. It is popular to criticize § 2-207 and Article 19's treatment of offer-varying acceptance. There is ongoing effort at the domestic level to revise Section 2-207.[25] At the international

---

[24] The court relied on Professor Peter Schlechtriem's interpretation of Article 19(3) in support; see 3 UNILEX 1997-6 at 627 (M.J. Bonell ed.). Shlechtriem claims that the subsection "does not rule out the possibility" that changes in the listed items may be considered immaterial alterations. See Commentary on the UN Convention on Contracts for the International Sale of Goods (CISG) 140 (2d ed., P. Schlechtriem ed. 1999). However, Article 19(3)'s language does not allow the possibility, and Schlechtriem offers no reason for finding that it does.

[25] See Proposed § 2-207; Richard Speidel, Article 2 Drafting Committee: Status of Article 2 Revision 6 (August 1, 1996); cf. 1 Ontario L. Reform Comm'n Report on Sale of Goods 83-84 (1979) (§ 2-207 unsatisfactory in present form); W. David Slawson, Binding Promises 147 (1996) (recommending repeal of § 2-207 without replacing it; courts to be allowed to decide terms based on reasonable expectations of the parties).

level moves are being made to blunt the effect of Article 19. The UNIDROIT Principles for International Commercial Contracts, for example, includes provisions dealing with the battle of the forms which differ from Article 19.[26] Clearly, § 2-207 is overly complex and indeterminate in important respects. But, statutory details aside, there is the broader question as to how offer-varying acceptance should be handled. We think that the answer turns on resolving three issues: a behavioral issue, a substantive issue, and an issue about comparative judicial competence. The behavioral issue concerns the way in which parties contract and the information they use to do so. Article 19 assumes that each contracting party reads the written communication it receives and does not take action until the form contains terms it finds acceptable. Section 2-207 assumes that the parties exchange written communications and act without reading them or insisting that the communications reflect the parties' agreement.[27] The substantive issue goes to the content of the terms incorporated in the writings exchanged by the parties. Article 19 assumes that the terms of a reply containing offer-varying terms do not systematically favor the party replying. For its part, § 2-207(1) assumes that the terms of the offer favor the offerer; and § 2-207(3) assumes that the non-identical terms in each party's writing favors the party dispatching the writing. The third issue is a matter of comparative judicial competence. Article 19 in effect assumes that the error costs of a judicial construction of contract terms are high. It therefore reads the terms from one of the parties' writings. Minimal judicial inquiry concerning the "materiality" of a term is required under Article 19(3). Section 2-207 requires resort to more judicial inquiry, both in determining when a contract is formed under § 2-207(1) as well as in finding terms to be "material" alterations under § 2-207(2).[28]

---

[26] See UNIDROIT Principles for International Commercial Contracts arts. 2.18, 2.20, 2.21 (1994).

[27] For a representative statement of the behavioral assumption, see Henry D. Gabriel, *The Battle of the Forms: A Comparison of the United Nations Convention on Contracts for the International Sale of Goods and the Uniform Commercial Code*, 49 Bus. L. 1053, 1063 (1994); for unstructured interview data suggesting that the assumption is false, see Daniel Keating, *Explaining the Battle of the Forms in Action*, 98 Mich. L. Rev. 2678, 2703-2704 (2000).

[28] For a recent proposal that a court adopt the terms in the form it finds "fairer," see Victor P. Goldberg, *The "Battle of the Forms": Fairness, Efficiency, and the Best-Shot Rule*, 76 Ore. L. Rev. 155 (1997). This is a "best shot" rule because it induces the parties to use terms in a form each thinks a court ex post

The behavioral issue relating to information read, in our view, is relatively unimportant. Whether contracting parties read or do not read the writings they receive is not decisive. The question is whether the parties who send them have incentives to take into account the interests of parties receiving the writings. Roughly, parties who send them have such incentives when there are "enough" parties who read writings received so that it pays to take receiving parties' interests into account.[29] If this happens, then whether parties read the writings they receive does not matter. Their interests often will be anticipated. Criticisms of § 2-207 or Article 19 that rely on a behavioral assumption about offerees in general therefore miss the point. The substantive issue, we think, is important. The terms of a writing may systematically favor one of the parties, whether or not a party reads the writings it receives. In our view, the possibility is remote. For the price of the party dispatching a writing to include a term systematically favoring itself is to lose the deal—again, assuming that "enough" parties read the writings they receive. Hence, if the receiving parties' interests are taken into account in advance, there is no reason to think that terms systematically favor one of the contracting parties.

The issue of judicial competence is equally important. Even if terms in a writing systematically favor a party, the question is whether courts are better able to find the term of the parties' bargain than is indicated by the parties' writings. The question is a comparative one. There is a risk that the writings might not reflect the terms of the parties' bargain. There is also the risk that a court might mistakenly impose the wrong terms on that bargain. The question is which risk is greater. In our view, a higher risk of judicial error is present when courts determine the "materiality" of an alteration or ignore the terms in the parties' writings and impose statutorily supplied gap-filling terms on the resulting contract. This also is the view of Article 19(1), which adopts the "last shot" corollary to the mirror image rule. As usual, our resolution of all three issues might be wrong. But any approach to offer-varying acceptances must identify and resolve them. Drafting details are only of secondary importance.

---

will find the fairer. Given the serious administrative problems a court faces in determining the fairness of a term in a transaction, the proposal arguably demands as much from a court as an inquiry into materiality. Arguably both inquiries ask too much of a court.

[29] See Douglas Baird & Robert Weisberg, *Rules, Standards, and the Battle of the Forms: A Reassessment of § 2-207*, 68 Va. L. Rev. 1233 (1982).

## D. Layered Contracts and Article 2

Sometimes the seller encloses terms with goods it delivers to the buyer. This practice is common with "shrinkwrap" and other ways of delivering licensed computer software, as well as with the sale of computers. In the latter case the additional terms are provided by the seller along with the goods, after the buyer has purchased and often paid for them. The buyer is given the opportunity to reject the terms by returning the goods. In such cases the question is whether these terms become part of the parties' contract when the buyer retains the goods. Two different answers are possible depending on when the sales contract is formed. One view is that the sales contract is formed at the time the acceptance of the offer to purchase occurs. The terms of the resulting contract are set at that time, unless the offer allows for terms to be added after performance has begun. Section 2-207 treats contract formation in this way. Another view is that the sales contract is formed at a point after performance has begun, usually after the buyer has inspected the goods, not when acceptance of the offer occurs. The contract terms include those provided at that later point. These are "layered" or "rolling" contracts. Section 2-204(1)'s allowance of contracts formed in "any manner sufficient to show agreement" is broad enough to include them. However, it is controversial when a contract is layered and when it is not.

*Hill v. Gateway 2000, Inc.*[30] is a leading case finding a layered contract. Its result turns on a particular interpretation of Article 2's formation rules. The buyers in *Hill* ordered and paid for a computer from Gateway by telephone. Terms enclosed in Gateway's subsequent shipment of the computer called for the arbitration of all disputes arising from the sales contract. They also provided that the failure to return the computer within a stipulated period constituted acceptance of the terms enclosed. In response to suit against it by the buyers, Gateway invoked the arbitration clause. The court concluded that the contract was layered and required arbitration. *Hill*'s conclusion relies on a questionable reading of § 2-207 and a questionable application of § 2-204. The court found § 2-207 to be irrelevant on the facts, according to it, because the subsection addresses only contracts concluded by an exchange of forms.

---

[30] 105 F.3d 1147 (7th Cir. 1997).

In *Hill* only Gateway used a form.[31]   This interpretation of § 2-207 is almost certainly wrong.  By its terms, § 2-207(1)'s applies to "*a* written confirmation," and Official Comment 1 makes clear that the subsection covers an oral agreement followed by a single confirmation.  The court's implicit application of § 2-204(1) also is unsupported.  *Hill* notes that an offer can propose terms inviting acceptance by later performance.[32]  Although an obviously true observation, *Hill*'s facts do not determine Gateway to be the offeror.  In fact, typically the buyer placing the purchase order is the offeror and the seller the offeree.[33]  If so, Gateway's shipment of the computer constitutes acceptance of the buyers' offer.  Their retention of the computer  therefore would not be "sufficient" to indicate under § 2-204 a contract containing an arbitration clause.

If § 2-207 is applied to *Hill*'s facts, the terms of the contract do not include an arbitration clause.  Under § 2-207(1), Gateway's enclosed terms are part of a written confirmation sent after the buyers and Gateway reached an oral agreement.  Because consistent with the terms of their agreement, the arbitration clause would an "additional" term.  Section 2-207(2) determines the terms of the resulting agreement.  Under it, when one of the parties is a non-merchant, additional terms become proposals for inclusion in the contract.  These terms do not automatically become part of the agreement.   Thus, because the buyers were consumers, Gateway's arbitration clause in its confirmation is not a term of the resulting contract.   Under varying facts, some courts have determined contract terms by § 2-207.   Others have found layered contracts under § 2-204.[34]  A proposed comment to Proposed § 2-207 states that the Proposed Revision does not take a position on the

---

[31] See also ProCD, Inc. v. Zeidenberg, 86 F.3d 1447, 1452 (7th Cir. 1996). In M.A. Mortenson Co., Inc. v. Timberline Software Corp., 998 P.2d 305, 312 (Wash. 2000), the court found § 2-207 irrelevant because it does not address contract formation, only "contract alteration." Section 2-207(1)'s language shows that this reading of the section also is wrong.

[32] Id. at 1149.

[33] Accord Klocek v. Gateway, Inc., 104 F.Supp.2d 1332, 1340 (D. Kan. 2000).

[34] Compare Klocek v. Gateway, Inc., 104 F.Supp.2d 1332, 1340 (D. Kan. 2000) (§ 2-207 applied) with Brower v. Gateway, 2000, Inc., 676 N.Y.S.2d 571 (N.Y. App. Div. 1998) (layered contract).

dispute.[35]  Article 2's formation rules can support both results.

Given the ambiguity about the proper application of § 2-204, it makes sense to resolve the issue of the offeror's identity by asking which interpretation would generate a more desirable result.   Judge Easterbrook's opinion in *Hill*, in fact, rather directly addressed this question without investigating all the technical niceties of Article 2's interpretation.  Clearly some contracts are concluded at the time the offer is accepted.  Others are concluded after acceptance of the offer and payment, when the full terms of the offer are disclosed to the buyer. These "pay now, terms later" agreements are layered contracts.  The question is when a particular transaction creates a layered or non-layered contract.   Some of the hostility to layered contracts is misplaced. Layered contracts are not concluded without the buyer manifesting asset. Only the point at which assent is manifested changes.  Assent occurs after acceptance of the offer and payment, when the offer's full terms are revealed to the buyer.  If the buyer does not like a term, it can reject the goods.   Thus, the resulting agreement is not imposed on a party. Rejection of terms requires the buyer to return the goods, and this may be costly and inconvenient.  But requiring the offeror to disclose full terms prior to the buyer's acceptance is also costly and inconvenient to the buyer.  It can result in delay, incomprehension and lost contracting opportunities.  So the charge of inconvenience is inconclusive.  Proper resolution of the issue requires comparison of the inconvenience and contracting costs associated with layered and non-layered contracts.

Layered contracts can reduce the cost of contract formation for both sellers and buyers.  They can achieve this by reducing the efforts that sellers must make at the time of contract to explain terms and that buyers must make to understand the seller's terms.  These savings would be offset by the costs associated with buyers' subsequent discovery of surprising and disadvantageous terms.  Thus, it is useful to ask whether buyers are likely to be surprised by the terms that they discover after acceptance.  In well-operating (though imperfect) markets, that is likely to be an infrequent event.   Sellers in such markets will suffer both economic and reputational harms by offering terms that are disadvantaged by a large number of buyers.  In the case of goods, such as computers, that are offered to both consumers and non-consumers, the latter group (which will make bulk purchases) is likely to read contracts carefully and consumers will be able to free ride on those efforts,

---

[35] See Rev. 2-207 Official Comment  4.

assuming that the seller offers similar terms to both groups. Thus, as long as sellers have incentives to offer efficient term, even consumers who never read the terms post-acceptance will receive protections that are inserted to attract non-consumer purchasers. Where a term is, in fact, highly exploitative, other contract doctrines, such as unconscionability, can apply to knock it out. The "no contract" argument is unnecessary to protect the purchaser in that situation. Thus, we conclude that, especially in a world of on-line and telephonic purchases, which attempt to take advantage of savings available from long-distance transactions, layered contracts ought not to be disfavored.

UCITA's formation rules expressly allow for layered contracts for computer information. Section 202(a) recognizes contracts formed "in any manner sufficient to show agreement." These can include agreements allowing for terms to be provided after performance has begun. Terms later provided are assented to by the party if it adopts them. Adoption occurs if a party fails to reject terms. Under § 208(2), a party adopts terms provided in a record after the beginning of performance if it had reason to know that terms would later be provided and lacked the opportunity to review them prior to beginning performance. Section 209 adds restrictions regulating the adoption of terms of a "mass market licence," which includes consumer transactions. Under § 209(b), the licensee who rejects the terms must be reimbursed for the cost of returning the computer information, if the licensee has previously paid for the license and did not have an opportunity to review its terms prior to payment. Section 208(2) follows *Hill* with respect to terms provided after a license has been made available and the licensing fee paid.[36] Section 209(b) adds to *Hill* the requirement that the rejecting licensee be reimbursed for the cost of returning the computer information.

## IV. Modification

Modification of an existing agreement comprises two steps: rescission of the original agreement and the creation of a new agreement with new terms. The steps can occur separately or at the same time. Modification is in play in a variety of instances in sales transactions governed by Article 2. A subsequent agreement might change the price, payment or delivery terms of an initial agreement. Alternatively, after the sale, the seller might make representations concerning the product it had

---

[36] See UCITA § 208 Official Comment 3.

not made before.   Or, in the course of a series of similar sales transactions, the terms of sale might be altered by one of the parties. The enforceability of the modification straightforwardly is in issue in the first of the examples. A post-agreement representation also can be an express warranty which modifies the warranties arising under the initial agreement.[37]   The parties' course of performance over a series of transactions can amount to a modification of the terms of sale for transactions within the series.   Each of these examples presents the difficult question of whether a modification of an existing contract is enforceable.

### A.  Under Article 2

Section 2-209 governs the enforceability of modifications under Article 2. The section is for the most part opaque. It is clear that the modified contract does not require fresh consideration. Section 2-209(1) says as much: "An agreement modifying a contract within this Article needs no consideration to be binding." (The subsection leaves untouched any non-UCC requirement under § 1-103 that the original contract be supported by consideration.) Official Comment 2 replaces a requirement of fresh consideration with the requirement that the modification be in good faith.[38] Strictly, good faith under the UCC is limited to good faith in the performance and enforcement of a contract.[39]   Good faith in modification goes to the formation of the modified contract, not its performance or enforcement—a different issue. This statutory limitation has not stopped Comment 2 to § 2-209 or case law from imposing a requirement of good faith on modifications.[40]

As a doctrinal matter, the requirement has two components. First, good faith requires that the modification be consistent with commercially reasonable standards.   Second, the modification must be motivated by a

---

[37] Cf. § 2-313 Official Comment 8.

[38] See § 2-209 Official Comment 2 ("However, modifications made thereunder must meet the test of good faith imposed by this Act").

[39] See § 1-203.

[40] See, e.g., Roth Steel Products v. Sharon Steel Corp., 705 F.2d 134 (6th Cir. 1983). Extra-UCC law, applicable to § 2-209 under § 1-103, also imposes a requirement that the modification not be the result of economic duress. See, e.g., Kelsey-Hayes Co. v. Caltaco Redlaw Castings Corp., 749 F. Supp. 794 (E.D. Mich. 1990); Essen Nutrition v. Electronic Liquid Fillers, (N.D. Ill. 1996).

legitimate reason for altering the original contract in light of supervening exigencies. The first component, based on Comment 3 to § 2-209, looks to an objective standard; the second to a subjective standard. *Roth Steel Products v. Sharon Steel Corp.*[41] illustrates the application of the doctrine. In *Roth Steel*, Roth and Sharon had contracted for the sale of steel by Sharon to Roth at a fixed price through 1973. Steel prices increased in early 1973 due to increased demand, and Sharon notified Roth that it would cease deliveries unless Roth agreed to pay a higher price for the steel to be delivered. Roth agreed to the price increase in part because it was unable to obtain substitute steel elsewhere within its production schedule. Even with the higher contract price agreed upon, Sharon continued to lose money on the deliveries to Roth. The court found the modification unenforceable because Sharon lacked good faith in eliciting it. In doing so the court applied the two-part test of good faith to the modification. Sharon satisfied the objective component of good faith: the increase in the price of steel had increased and Sharon's continued loss even on the modified contract were events which made a modification commercially reasonable, according to the court. Sharon did not satisfy the subjective component of good faith, according to the court: its notification to Roth did not justify the price increase. Not too much should be made of the distinction, here as elsewhere, between objective and subjective components. In determining subjective good faith, the *Roth Steel* court looked to objective elements too. Sharon provided a justification for the price increase ex post, in the course of litigation. It provided none before. Lacking verifiable evidence of a legitimate reason for the modification at the time it was made, the court concluded that Sharon was moved by bad faith.

A requirement of good faith, and its doctrinal interpretation, makes sense. It is reasonably effective at regulating party-induced alterations in contractually allocated risks. To see this, realize that contractual modification is a response by contracting parties to information acquired after the conclusion of an initial contract. The information acquired can be of two sorts: either that one of the parties has made contract-specific investments or that changed circumstances make performance obligations imposed under the initial contract unprofitable to one or both of the

---

[41] 705 F.2d 134 (6th Cir. 1983).

parties.[42] Modification can be a response to either sort of information. In the first case the party making contract-specific investments might lose more from nonperformance of the initial contract (net of recovering damages) than from agreeing to altering the terms of the initial agreement. Absent a market or remedial substitute for performance, the party will acquiesce to modify the contract. An altered agreement in this case reallocates the contractually agreed upon division of the gains from trade from one party to the other. Modification in this case is wasteful because it does not increase gains from trade. In the second case intervening events can alter the efficiency of performance risks allocated by the initial contract. Reallocation of these risks can increase gains from trade by assigning the risks to the now-cheaper risk bearer. Modification in this case is not wasteful. Modifications based on the first sort of information therefore should be unenforceable; those based on the second sort should be enforceable. A statutory or doctrinal proxy is needed to distinguish between the two cases.

The good faith requirement tracks the distinction between the two cases reasonably well. It certainly does better than a requirement of fresh consideration. A requirement of fresh consideration is both seriously under- and over-inclusive. It is underinclusive because it allows some modifications to survive even if they do not increase gains from trade. All that is needed is fresh consideration. The requirement also is overinclusive because it strikes down modifications which lack fresh consideration but increase the contractual surplus available to the parties. The good faith requirement does better. As applied, the requirement looks to objective evidence of changed circumstances making performance unprofitable as well as an absence of market substitutes or adequate remedies.[43]     It also looks to objective evidence of the contracting parties' motivation. Changed circumstances is pretty good evidence that a modification increases gains from trade. (And unaltered circumstances is pretty good evidence that the modification is a strategic ploy inducing wasteful transaction costs.) The modification is not likely

---

[42] See Richard A. Posner & Andrew M. Rosenfield, *Impossibility and Related Doctrines in Contract Law: An Economic Analysis*, 6 J. Legal Stud. 83 (1977); Varouj A. Aivazian, Michael J. Trebilcock & Michael Penny, *The Law of Contract Modifications: The Uncertain Quest for a Bench Mark of Enforceability*, 22 Osgoode Hall L. J. 173 (1984).

[43] See Alan Schwartz, *Relational Contracts in the Courts: An Analysis of Incomplete Contracts and Judicial Strategies*, 21 J. Legal Stud. 271, 308-11 (1992).

to simply redistribute an initially agreed upon division of contractual gains. Case law generally supports this use of the good faith requirement.[44]

But sometimes circumstances change at the same time a party seeks to reallocate the contractual surplus. When market substitutes or adequate remedies are not available, the objective evidence cannot distinguish between an opportunistic, redistributive modification and a surplus-increasing modification. The doctrinal requirement that consults a party's motivations in seeking modification handles such cases. Look at *Roth Steel* again in this connection. The court found that changed circumstances were present in the form of increased prices for steel. This objective evidence supported Sharon's claim that at the modified price it lost money on deliveries to Roth. At the same time Roth lacked access to substitute steel to meet its production schedule. Accordingly, Sharon was in a position to take advantage of Roth's lack of access to the market. The parties' 1973 agreement to increase price therefore might have been an opportunistic modification on Sharon's part. The *Roth Steel* court determined that it in fact was an opportunistic modification. It did so by finding that Sharon's insistence on increasing its price to Roth was not accompanied at the time by recital of such reasons. This also is apparently objective evidence for the court of Sharon's motive to reallocate some of Roth's profit from Sharon's performance to itself. Lacking objective evidence of a legitimate motive, the court concluded that Sharon acted in bad faith. Evidence of bad motive was used by the *Roth Steel* court to distinguish opportunistic from surplus-increasing modifications when changed circumstances are present at the same time as access to a market or legal substitute is unavailable.

Section 2-209's other statutory conditions are sometimes superfluous and unclear. Section 2-209(3) demands that the "requirements of the statute of frauds section of this Article (Section 2-201) must be satisfied if the contract as modified is within its provisions." A modified contract alters the terms of an initial contract and supersedes it. Section 2-201(1) requires that contracts for the sale of goods falling within it satisfy a set of writing requirements. So the modified contract must satisfy those requirements if the contract is within the scope of 2-201(1). Because § 2-209(3) says no more than this, the subsection is superfluous. The subsection also is unclear. When read in conjunction with 2-201(1),

---

[44] See, e.g., R.S. & V. Co. v. Atlas Van Lines, Inc., 917 F.2d 348 (7th Cir. 1990).

slightly creative interpretation can produce at least four possible readings of § 2-209(3).[45] First, § 2-209(3) might require that all modifications be evidenced by a legally sufficient memorandum under § 2-201(1). Second, it might require that modifications which bring the contract within § 2-201(1) for the first time satisfy § 2-201(1)'s requirements. Third, a legally sufficient memorandum might be needed when the modification removes the contract from the scope of § 2-201(1). Fourth, the subsection could demand that modifications satisfy § 2-201(1) when they alter one or more of the terms required in a legally sufficient memorandum.

The first possibility is barely plausible. Requiring a legally sufficient memorandum for all modified contracts imposes a requirement that is stronger than the writing requirement imposed under § 2-201. Section 2-209(3)'s reference to the modification falling within § 2-201's scope ("within its provisions") makes the enhanced requirement groundless. The other possibilities are more plausible, but the subsection does not favor any of them. A straightforward interpretation of § 2-209(3) has much to recommend it. Section 2-201(1) requires the existence of a legally sufficient memorandum for types of contracts that fall within its scope. If the modified contract falls within § 2-201(1)'s scope, it too must be evidenced by such a memorandum. Otherwise, not. The former is what § 2-209(3) says in slightly different words. The latter is a fair implication from § 2-209(3)'s cross-reference to § 2-201. Whether the initial contract need be evidenced by legally sufficient memorandum is irrelevant. The policy underlying the Statute of Frauds—reducing negative externalities induced by proof costs—does not justify extending a writing requirement to modified contract just because the initial contract either fell or did not fall within § 2-201(1)'s scope. True, this interpretation makes § 2-209(3) superfluous, but the alternative is to add requirements not imposed by either § 2-201(1) or the plain language of § 2-209(3).

Section 2-209 is unclear in other ways. One difficulty is in the connection between § 2-209(2) and (4). Section 2-209(2) explicitly enforces contractual clauses requiring that all modifications be in a signed writing: "A signed agreement which excludes modification or rescission except by a signed writing cannot be otherwise modified or rescinded...." Seemingly, the subsection strictly enforces such "no oral

---

[45] See James J. White & Robert S. Summers, Uniform Commercial Code 54 (5th ed. 2000) (outlining positions).

modification" (NOM) clauses. Section 2-209(4), however, allows later conduct of the parties to avoid the effect of a NOM clause: "Although an attempt at modification or rescission does not satisfy the requirements of subsection (2) or (3) it can operate as a waiver." Not all subsequent conduct works to avoid a NOM clause. If it did, § 2-209(4) would render all NOM clauses ineffective (and § 2-209(2) superfluous). The conduct, according to § 2-209(4), must be "an attempt at modification or rescission" that does not satisfy a NOM clause. Further, the subsection allows such conduct to operate as a waiver ("it can operate as a waiver"). Section 2-209(4) does not require that all attempts at modification be treated as waivers. The live question is when an attempted modification amounts to a waiver. Very roughly, two positions are possible. One is that a waiver here requires detrimental and reasonable reliance on an oral agreement altering a term subject to a NOM clause. Oral agreements without such reliance are not waivers under § 2-209(4). A second position is that a waiver does not require detrimental reliance. An oral agreement alone can be sufficient to be a waiver.

The two positions are neatly represented in the majority and dissenting opinions, respectively, in *Wisconsin Knife Works v. National Metal Crafters*.[46] In *Wisconsin Knife*, the buyer and seller agreed that the buyer was to purchase spade bits to be delivered on specified dates. The contract contained a NOM clause. After the seller failed to make delivery on several of the required dates, the buyer placed further orders and continued to accept spade bits originally ordered. No written modification was made changing the initial delivery dates. Subsequently, the buyer terminated the contract because the seller had failed to deliver on specified dates. The seller argued that the buyer's acceptance of tardily delivered spade bits amounted to a waiver of its right to receive them under the original delivery dates. The majority held that a waiver under § 2-209(4) requires detrimental reliance. The reliance requirement is needed, according to the majority, to make § 2-209(2) consistent with § 2-209(4). Section 2-209(2) does not allow enforcement of an oral modification when the initial contract contains a NOM clause. Section 2-209(4) enforces an oral modification when there is a waiver accompanied by detrimental reliance on the modification. (Section 2-209(5), for the majority, is in turn consistent with § 2-209(4) because it allows retraction of a waiver of an executory part of a contract when there has been no detrimental reliance.)

---

[46] 781 F.2d 1280 (7th Cir. 1986).

The dissent denies that a waiver under § 2-209(4) requires detrimental reliance. Section 2-209(4) does not mention the requirement, and reliance figures only in § 2-209(5), to bar retraction of a waiver of prospective performance. The inference from these two facts is that an oral modification can be a waiver under § 2-209(4) without reliance. Further, according to the dissent, the requirement is not needed to give both § 2-209(2) and § 2-209(4) effect. Because § 2-209(4) allows some later conduct, including an oral modification, to alter the terms of a contract containing a NOM clause, § 2-209(2) is not given full effect. But a waiver still is needed under § 2-209(4): not every sort of later conduct is enough to avoid a NOM clause. The dissent probably has the better reading of § 2-209(4). Case law also has mostly favored its interpretation.[47]

Statute aside, it is worth considering the fighting issue between the majority and the dissent. The issue concerns the conditions under which the legal effect of NOM clauses are to be limited. Everyone acknowledges the value of enforcing NOM clauses. Such clauses operate as a "private" statute of frauds of sorts, reducing both agency costs and proof costs associated with oral modifications. (The prospect of an employee binding its employer through an oral modification presents an agency cost; oral modifications raise the cost to the parties of proving that the terms of an initial contract have been altered.) The cost of NOM clauses is that they require a writing to modify the terms of an initial agreement, and a writing can introduce inflexibility into the agreement. Assuming that under some circumstances inflexibility comes at too high a price for the contracting parties, most parties would prefer to limit the effect of NOM clauses. The question is when. The dispute over the connection between § 2-209(2) and (4) addresses this question.

A NOM clause in a contract indicates a party preference for evidence of a modification provided by a writing. It is fair to conclude that the preference would be satisfied by events having the same evidentiary value as a writing indicating a modification. The dispute is over the sorts of events having the same evidentiary value as the writing. Possibilities include (1) oral relinquishment of a contractual right, (2) a course of performance by the parties recognizing the relinquishment of the right, or (3) detrimental reliance on the relinquishment of a contractual right. The majority in *Wisconsin Knife* seems to think that only detrimental

---

[47] See, e.g., Exxon Corp. v. Crosby-Mississippi Resources Ltd., 815 F. Supp. 977 (S.D. Miss. 1993).

reliance has the same evidentiary value of a modification as a written modification. The dissent thinks that the course of performance of the contract has evidentiary value equal to that of a written modification.[48] The disagreement is not over the party preference for limiting the effect of NOM clauses. Rather, it is over the sorts of evidence that serve as evidentiary substitutes for a written modification. The disagreement is reflected in the disparate interpretations of when an oral modification operates as a waiver under § 2-209(4).[49] Case law does not frame the matter in terms of evidentiary value, but the disparate interpretations of § 2-209(4) can be explained in this way.

### B. Under the CISG

The CISG's treatment of modification is significantly different from Article 2 treatment. Article 29(1)(1) allows a modification to be made by the "mere agreement" of the parties. A "mere agreement" means that no fresh consideration is required. Article 29(1) by itself therefore places no restrictions on the effectiveness of a modification of an existing agreement. Article 7 or domestic law, however, may do so depending on Article 7's interpretation. Article 7(1) provides that "[i]n the interpretation of this Convention, regard is to be had to...the observance of good faith in international trade." The different readings of the Article, rehearsed below, are important here. A natural way to read Article 7(1)'s reference to good faith is fairly literally: courts are instructed to interpret the CISG's provisions with an eye to good faith in international trade. There is no prescription that a duty of good faith is imposed on the parties' performance of the sales contract governed by the CISG. Another way to read Article 7(1) is to extend the prescription to courts to the parties' performance of the underlying contract. Article 7(1) in this way indirectly imposes a duty of good faith performance on the parties.[50] We argue below that Article 7, its inconclusive diplomatic

---

[48] 781 F.2d at 1292.

[49] See, e.g., Smyers v. Quartz Works Corp., 880 F. Supp. 1425 (D. Kan. 1995); Green Construction Co. v. First Indemnity of America Insurance Co., 735 F. Supp. 1254 (D.N.J. 1990). The Proposed Revision of § 2-209 requires reliance.

[50] See Robert A. Hillman, *Applying the United Nations Convention on Contracts for the International Sale of Goods: The Elusive Goal of Uniformity*, Review of the Convention on Contracts for the International Sale of Goods 21, 30 (Cornell International Law Journal ed. 1995); but cf. Robert A. Hillman,

history and fair inference drawn from both support the natural reading. Here we simply draw the obvious consequences of the two readings for Article 29. On the natural reading, modifications by "mere agreement" are not subject to a restriction of good faith. In this case, courts are enjoined to interpret Article 29(1) in good faith. The other reading would impose a requirement of good faith on modifications made under Article 29(1) by the "mere agreement" of the parties. As read, Article 29(1) would have the same restriction placed on it as is placed on § 2-209(1), its domestic law counterpart.

Domestic law may further restrict modifications of contracts governed by the CISG. In particular, a domestic law requirement that modifications be in writing may apply. Whether the requirement applies depends on two matters: whether the relevant Contracting State has made a reservation under Article 96 and whether conflicts rules select the law of that state. Take the matters in turn. Article 96 provides that a Contracting State whose domestic law requires modifications to be in writing can make a reservation under Article 12 excluding the portion of Article 29 "that allows a ...modification...to be in any form other than writing, ...where any party has his place of business in that State." Article 12 in turn says that the portion of Article 29 allowing a modification to be made in other than a writing does not apply when a party's place of business is in a Contracting State that has made an Article 96 reservation. Since Article 29 does not apply in the circumstances, there is an issue that is not now addressed by the CISG: the effectiveness of non-written modifications. Hence, given the principle of issue preclusion discussed in Chapter 2, the issue is determined by applicable domestic law. Conflicts of law rules will select that law. Whether non-written modifications are enforceable depends in this case on restrictions imposed by applicable domestic law.

The following is a simple illustration of the point. Suppose Seller's place of business is in Hungary and Buyer's place of business is in the United States. Some time after concluding a sales contract governed by the CISG, Seller and Buyer orally agree to reduce the contract price. Still later, Seller insists on the higher, initial contract price. Buyer claims that price was modified downward, and Seller resists. Is the reduced contract

*Article 29(2) of the United Nations Convention on Contracts for the International Sale of Goods: A New Effort at Clarifying the Legal Effect of "No Oral Modification" Clauses*, 21 Cornell Int'l. L. J. 449, 458 (1988) (reporting that diplomatic history does not support interpreting Article 7(1) to impose a good faith duty on contracting parties).

price enforceable? It depends on applicable domestic law. Hungary has made an Article 96 reservation requiring that all modifications be in writing,[51] and one of the contracting parties (Seller) has its place of business there.    Therefore, according to Article 12, Article 29(1)'s allowance that a modification is effective by the "mere agreement" of the parties does not apply. This means that there is an issue of the rights and obligations of Buyer and Seller which the CISG does not govern. The enforceability of an oral modification reducing the contract price. The CISG is silent on the matter. Hence, as applied, the principle of issue preclusion does not exclude domestic law to decide the issue. The forum's choice of law rules will select which domestic law applies—here, presumably the domestic law of either the United States or Hungary. If Hungary's domestic law applies, the oral modification is unenforceable. (For a signatory state to make an Article 96 reservation, Article 96 demands that its "legislation" require enforceable modifications to be in writing.) If the domestic law selected is Article 2 of the UCC, the oral modification may or may not be enforceable. It depends on the interpretation given to § 2-209(3) and (4), discussed above.

Further restrictions can be placed on modifications by the contracting parties themselves. Article 29(2) provides that a contract containing a NOM clause "may not otherwise [be] modified...by agreement." The provision itself contains an exception based on reliance: "a party may be precluded by his conduct from asserting such a provision [i.e., a NOM clause] to the extent that the other party has relied on that conduct." Both the restriction and its exception make sense. Contracting parties sometimes prefer to reduce agency and proof costs by insisting that modifications be in writing. A writing provides good verifiable evidence of an agreement to alter the terms of an initial agreement. Some parties also prefer to allow oral modifications to be enforceable even in the presence of a NOM clause if the evidence of modification is equal in evidentiary value to that of a written modification. Reliance on a party's conduct arguably has as much evidentiary value as a writing. In this way Article 29(2) and its reliance exception are justified by predominant party preference. They are the counterpart of the combination of § 2-209(2) and (4) when waiver under § 2-209(4) is interpreted to require reliance.

In general, Article 29(2)'s application is straightforward. "Conduct"

---

[51] So have seven other Contracting States: Argentina, Belarus, Chile, Estonia, Hungary, Lithuania, the Russian Federation, and the Ukraine.

by a party sensibly includes her statements, and the meaning of the parties' statements and other conduct is a matter of contract interpretation no different from deciphering the NOM clause in the first place. Reliance is a matter of fact, to be proven like any fact. NOM clauses present problems when they require that all modifications be in writing and expressly excludes application of Article 29 in its entirety. For example, consider the clause: "The parties agree that all modifications are to be in writing and that, in accordance with Article 6 of the CISG, Article 29 does not govern the enforceability of any modification of the parties' agreement." Suppose the parties orally agree to a modification, and they act upon it. The question is whether the oral modification is enforceable. Here Article 29's application can be controversial. Three positions are possible, and Article 29 and other CISG provisions do not conclusively favor any of them.

1. One position allows the parties to opt out of Article 29 entirely. The allowance is based on the permissibility under Article 6 of the parties derogating from "any" of the CISG's provisions not prohibited by reservations made by a contracting state. The NOM clause in question by its terms makes Article 29 inapplicable to the parties' contract. Therefore, Article 29(2)'s treatment of reliance on an oral modification in the face of a NOM clause is irrelevant. It does not determine whether the oral modification of the parties is enforceable. Instead, domestic law selected by the forum' choice of law rules would decide the matter.

2. A second position allows limited opting out of Article 29. It reads the reliance exception in Article 29(2) as a mandatory term from which parties cannot derogate under Article 6. At most their derogation makes Article 29(1) and the NOM part of Article 29(2) inapplicable. Therefore, at most, a NOM clause is effective according to the parties' initial agreement, *unless* reliance on an oral modification is involved. If there is reliance on an oral modification, Article 29(2) still applies to render the oral modification effective.

This position does not have much going for it. For one thing, it is inconsistent with Article 6. Article 6 in effect treats all of the CISG's provisions as default rules which can be varied by the parties (unless a signatory state has made a reservation). This includes Article 29 in its entirety. The second position simply treats the reliance exception in Article 29(2) as stating a mandatory rule--an unexplained exception to Article 6. Another difficulty is that the position in effect prohibits most opting out of Article 29(2). If a party orally agrees to a modification, the agreement constitutes "conduct" upon which the other party can rely. All reliance-inducing oral modifications therefore are ineffective under

Article 29(2). Only oral modifications not inducing reliance continue to be effective. Presumably those will be very few and far between. Hence, the second position prohibits almost all opting out of Article 29 by the parties.

3. The third position also restricts the parties' ability to completely opt out of Article 29. It does so, however, via either of two other provisions of the CISG. One provision is Article 7(1). Article 7(1) can be read as imposing a duty of good faith in interpreting the CISG's provisions. (As noted in earlier, we do not favor the reading, but it is a possible one.) Accordingly, Article 7(1) could require good faith in opting out of Article 29, as permitted by Article 6. This could mean that good faith is a condition of giving effect to a NOM clause.[52] Another basis is Article 8(2). Under Article 8(2), a party's statements are to be interpreted in the way a reasonable person in the listener's position would interpret them. On this objective standard, the oral modification, when made, would be interpreted by the other party as just that: an agreement to waive insistence on the NOM clause in the initial agreement as well as Article 29. The other party, interpreting the agreement in this way, could rely on the oral modification. In the circumstances, the party's statement might make Article 29(2) applicable to the modification and the oral modification effective.

It is worth putting aside the details of Article 29 and considering the issue of modification generally. Early evidence suggests that courts can miss a question of modification under the CISG presented by a set of facts. This arguably occurred in *Beijing Metals & Minerals Import/Export Corp. v. American Business Center, Inc.*[53] a case that considers the CISG in passing. *Beijing Metals* involved a contract for the sale of weight lifting equipment by a Chinese seller, MMB, to a Texan buyer, ABC. At first the contract called for payment to be made by a letter of credit. The contract later was changed to require payment by a 90 day time draft. After ABC refused to make payment for a number of shipments received because of nonconformities in equipment previously paid for, and MMB refused to make further shipments until it was paid, the parties apparently reached a compromise. A written agreement between the parties acknowledged ABC's debt to MMB and required ABC to pay MMB in scheduled installments. When MMB later refused

---

[52] Honnold, supra note 17, at 231-32.

[53] 993 F.2d 1178 (5th Cir. 1993).

to ship equipment to compensate for the nonconforming goods delivered and insisted on payment by a letter of credit, ABC notified MMB that it would not honor the payment schedule, and MMB sued ABC. ABC's defenses included the allegation that MMB orally agreed to ship equipment to replace the nonconforming equipment shipped and allow ABC to pay for new shipments by 90 time drafts. The district court granted summary judgment in MMB's favor.

Both the District Court and the Fifth Circuit saw the outcome of the case as turning on the parol evidence rule. Finding that deciding whether the CISG applied to the sales contract or the parties' written agreement was not necessary, both courts applied Texas' parol evidence rule. The courts further found that the ABC and MMBs' written agreement was completely integrated and barred evidence of the terms ABC alleged MMB orally agreed to. We believe that the facts in *Beijing Metals* are better analyzed as raising an issue of the modification of the contract. As an initial matter, discussed in Chapter 5, we believe that the CISG allows the admissibility of parol evidence. If so, both courts did not have the luxury of avoiding deciding whether the CISG applied to the sales contract. But there is a more basic trouble with the courts' decisions: Both courts assume that ABC and MMB's written agreement is simply a writing to which the parol evidence rule might apply. The written agreement obviously might be an integrated writing, but it is also a modification of an initial contract. The question therefore is whether the writing alone is the modification or whether it also includes the terms ABC alleged MMB orally agreed to at the time the parties executed the writing. Assuming that the CISG governed the sales contract—a safe assumption on the facts[54]—Article 29 applies to a modification of the sales contract. Since there is no evidence that the parties' initial contract contained a NOM clause, Article 29(2) is inapplicable. Therefore, Article 29(1) controls.[55] Under it, a modification can be effective by the "mere agreement" of the parties. "Mere agreement" implies that a

---

[54] Since ABC was a Texas corporation and MMB a Chinese corporation, the CISG almost certainly applied via Article 1(1)(a).

[55] Article 29 does not apply when a Contracting State in which one of the contracting parties is located has made an Article 96 reservation. China's accession to the CISG includes a declaration that it "does not consider itself to be bound...by Article 11 as well as the provisions in the Convention relating to the content of Article 11." Since China's declaration is not made in accordance with Article 96, it has not made a reservation under that Article. Therefore, Article 29 continues to apply in the sales contract at issue in *Beijing Metals*.

modification may be made orally as well as in writing. This means that on *Beijing Metals'* facts, the parties' modification might have included terms orally supplied.[56] It is therefore an issue of fact as to whether ABC and MMBs' agreement included the terms ABC alleged MMB orally agreed to: the shipment of replacement goods and the 90 day payment term. The issue therefore is not properly decided by summary judgment.

---

[56] See also Article 8(1) (statements of parties to be interpreted according to party's intent where other party knew or could not not have known of that intent), Article 8(2) (where Article 8(1) does not apply, a party's statements to be interpreted according to the understanding of a reasonable person in other party's position). Since both Articles 8(1) and (2)'s application is not restricted to the parties' initial agreement, they apply to modifications as well. Their application makes the terms of an agreement to modify a contract a question of fact.

# CHAPTER 4
## IMPLIED TERMS

## I. Trade Usage, Course of Dealing, Course of Performance

### A. Under the UCC

Section 1-205(3) provides that trade usage and course of dealing may be used to give meaning to the terms of an agreement. Section 2-208(1) has the same effect with respect to course of performance. Indeed, the very definition of "agreement" in § 1-201(3) indicates that a course of dealing, trade usage, or course of performance becomes part of the understanding between the parties. The distinctions among these interpretive tools relates primarily to the nature of the relationship between the parties to the contract. Trade usages constitute customs or methods of dealing that are regularly observed within a trade or industry.[1] A trade usage does not assume any prior relationship between the parties to the agreement in which the trade usage is being incorporated. It assumes only that they are transacting in the trade to which the custom is applicable. A course of dealing, on the other hand, assumes that the parties to this transaction have been involved with each other in prior transactions. The course of dealing constitutes a pattern of behavior, or sequence of previous conduct between those parties that sets a standard for their subsequent dealings with each other.[2] A course of performance involves repeat performance within the same contract and thus also constitutes a pattern of behavior between the same parties that determines their expectations about each other's conduct during the remainder of that contract.[3] We use the phrase "custom" to capture all three of these behavior-based means of implying terms in the contract.

One might reasonably wonder why the introduction of custom to determine the meaning of a contract would every be allowed. After all, the parties have presumably set forth their expectations within a written agreement, and we might believe that inducing parties to draft complete and precise agreements will minimize ambiguities. It may be that parties

---

[1] § 1-205(2).

[2] § 1-205(1).

[3] § 2-208(1).

would want to incorporate practices into their contract, but they could do so if they so desired. Why, then, would we impose that evidentiary standard on them in the absence of any showing that they intended custom to be part of the contract?

Two explanations are possible, each of which is consistent with an efficiency rationale of commercial law. Under that rationale, parties would want to invest as few resources in actually negotiating a contract as possible, since transaction costs reduce the net value of the contract. Parties can write contracts more cheaply if they do not have to spell out all the provisions to which they agree to be bound. Recall the old story about the comedians' convention in which one comedian stands up and yells out a number, e.g., "34!" The rest of the audience breaks out in laughter because they all know what Joke #34 is and do not need to hear it told in its entirety. Similarly, if parties to a transaction are aware that, within their trade, the term "chicken" means chickens suitable for frying but not those only suitable for stewing,[4] then there is no need to incur the costs of being more specific in contractual drafting. No one suffers an informational disadvantage if all are familiar with the shortcut phrasing. When parties enter into a trade, they presumably know the jargon of the trade.[5]

This explanation, then, is consistent with a default rule explanation for sales law. Presumably, most parties involved in a trade are aware of the relevant customs and would prefer to minimize transaction costs. Thus, they can be assumed to have intended the words they use in a

---

[4] See Frigaliment Importing Co. v. B.N.S. International Sales Corp., 190 F. Supp. 116 (S.D.N.Y. 1960).

[5] Of course, some parties will be novices or ignorant of that jargon. They may indeed suffer a disadvantage. We discuss this possibility below in our discussion of trade usage under the CISG. But the bottom line is that nothing prevents such parties, who presumably are aware of their own limited comprehension of trade practices, from either opting out of the parol evidence rule or trade usage, or of becoming informed. The issue is whether we should impose on novices the obligation to undertake that effort or to impose on experienced parties the obligation to ensure that their trading partners are similarly aware of those practices. For the reasons discussed below, we believe that § 1-205(3) is correct in assigning the obligation to the novice. Section 1-205(3) incorporates into an agreement a course of dealing or usage of trade in the vocation or trade in which the parties are engaged or "of which they are or should be aware."

contract to have the meaning attributed to those words within the relevant trade. When a question of interpretation arises, these parties presumably intended the question to be resolved by reference to the customary meaning of the phrase. Of course, like all default rule explanations, this explanation assumes that the custom reflects the rule that a majority of parties would prefer if left to their own devices. As we saw in our general discussion of default rules in Chapter 1, a rule that reflects majoritarian preferences minimizes transactions costs because only those individuals who want an idiosyncratic rule will have to bargain about the particular term at all. The rest can simply leave a contractual gap to be completed by the default rule. Similarly, those who accept a customary definition or term need not specify a contract with precision if custom is used as an interpretive tool when questions of meaning arise.

Implying customary terms is also likely to reflect efficient allocations of risk between contractual parties. Customs in commercial transactions, at least subject to exceptional circumstances that we discuss below, are likely to arise because parties determine that they have repeatedly assigned risks to one party or another in the course of their more fully dickered contracts or in their post-contractual conduct. For instance, assume that there is an industry in which sellers and buyers enter into fully dickered contracts, and that in virtually all cases sellers accept risk of loss of the goods until buyers obtain actual receipt. That allocation is likely to occur because the parties to any particular transaction recognize that sellers are in a superior position to avoid loss of the goods until they are delivered to buyer. At some point, this allocation would become "customary" so that parties would not have to bargain about risk of loss at all, unless an idiosyncratic buyer or seller desired to alter the customary rule in a particular transaction. But because this custom will have arisen out of an efficient bargain, the custom itself is likely to be efficient. The same explanation applies with equal force to the use of course of dealing or course of performance.

The second explanation for using these implied terms has less to do with the parties to the transaction and more to do with minimizing the use of judicial resources. As we have seen in trying to interpret provisions of the UCC, language, even statutory language, can be inherently imprecise. What is meant in one context may have a different meaning in another context. "Plain language" meanings of a term may be perfectly comprehensible, and therefore unambiguous, when used by laypeople, but may differ substantially from the more specialized meaning that the same term possesses within a trade or industry.[6] If there exists a custom that can be readily identified, then third-party interpreters of the contract such as judges and juries have a relatively costless mechanism for understanding what the parties meant by the use of a particular phrase. If we believe that commercial contracts should be read to reflect the intention of the parties, then we would want their interpretation of contractual language, rather than lay definitions of the same language, to prevail. Thus, third-party interpreters need information about the content of that language. Once they have the information, phrases that might have previously seemed ambiguous may be crystal clear, while other phrases, that might have seemed free of ambiguity, may have previously unknown meanings (to them).

These justifications for implied terms do not mean that their application is obvious. Two questions necessarily arise whenever one party seeks to use custom to explain a contract. First, what is the custom, and second, does the custom apply to the facts of the case before the court? The difficulties involved in these issues can be illustrated by the case of *Columbia Nitrogen Corp. v. Royster Co.*[7] In that case, Royster agreed to sell a minimum of 31,000 tons of phosphate each year for three years to Columbia. The contract stated a price per ton for the phosphate, subject to an escalation clause. The contract also contained an integration clause that stated that the contract expressed all the terms and conditions of the agreement. During the contract term, phosphate prices dropped "precipitously." Columbia ordered only about 10 percent of the phosphate called for under the contract and refused to take any more. Royster sold the unaccepted phosphate at the sub-contract price prevailing in the market and sued Columbia to recover the difference. Columbia unsuccessfully offered testimony at trial that, because of uncertain crop and weather conditions, express price and quantity terms in phosphate contracts were customarily treated as mere projections to be

---

[6] Thus, § 2-202 incorporates the view that the "test of admissibility of extrinsic evidence [such as custom] to explain the meaning of a written instrument is not whether it appears to the court to be plain and unambiguous on its face, but whether the offered evidence is relevant to prove a meaning to which the language of the instrument is reasonably susceptible." Pacific Gas and Elec. Co. v. G.W. Thomas Drayage & Rigging Co., 442 P.2d 641 (Cal. 1968). See C-Thru Container Corp. v. Midland Manufacturing Co., 533 N.W.2d 542 (Iowa 1995).

[7] 451 F.2d 3 (4th Cir. 1971).

adjusted according to market forces.

*Columbia Nitrogen* reflects the difficulty of defining the initial existence or scope of trade usage or course of dealing.[8] Assume that the buyer in *Columbia Nitrogen* was correct in contending that there existed a custom of allowing deviations from stated terms. One might imagine that such a custom makes a great deal of sense in times of stable market prices. A buyer might need a little more or a little less phosphate than originally projected. If the industry involves repeat players, that is, the same buyers and sellers in multiple transactions, then one would predict that a seller might, given stable market prices, make a little bit more than anticipated in one transaction and a little less in another. But over a large portfolio of contracts, these discrepancies would be likely to cancel each other out so that accommodating the needs of buyers is relatively costless. Thus, one might anticipate that such accommodation would evolve as an efficient custom. But the conditions that led to *Columbia Nitrogen* were not those we have just described. Rather, the court indicates that phosphate prices had declined "precipitously." If the market deviations were ahistorically steep, then the conditions that prevailed were not those that had generated the custom in the first place. In addition, one would not expect the custom to evolve under these conditions, because substantial variations in market prices could mean that sellers could lose a substantial amount on individual contracts that could not be recovered in subsequent contracts because those latter contracts would command prices that reflected the substantially lower market prices. In short, Royster may have been attempting to employ a custom under conditions (substantial deviations between contract prices and market prices) in which the custom simply did not exist.

It is not clear that the court should be criticized for failing to dig more deeply into the conditions under which the custom applied. A more refined judicial analysis of the relevant custom would require ad hoc judicial inquiry into the origin and applications of the custom. Parties to subsequent transactions would litigate not only the existence of the custom, but also its provenance and the conditions under which it had been applied in the past and the extent to which those conditions applied

---

[8] There is also the obvious problem, finessed in *Columbia Nitrogen*, of defining the "trade" in question. See Nanakuli Paving & Rock Co. v. Shell Oil Co., 664 F.2d 772 (9th Cir. 1981); Clayton P. Gillette, *Cooperation and Convention in Contractual Defaults*, 3 S. Cal. Interdiscip. L.J. 167, 183-84 (1993); Roger W. Kirst, *Usage of Trade and Course of Dealing: Subversion of the UCC Theory*, 1977 U. Ill. L. Forum 81.

in the case before the court.  Each of these inquiries increases the opportunity for judicial error.  The determination of industry custom is a classical example of the difficulties of judicial verification.  That is, even if commercial parties are aware of an industry custom, and can readily observe its violation, they may have difficulty proving the violation to a third party.  For instance, in *Columbia Nitrogen*, the parties may understand the conditions under which deviation from contract terms have been permitted historically, but those conditions may be so dependent on technicalities within the industry that proving them to a court is extremely costly.  It is simply not clear that this effort would be worth undertaking or whether error costs would be minimized by a relatively broad default rule that induced parties to be more precise in their contractual language.  Indeed, some commentators have gone so far as to suggest that readily verifiable customs rarely exist,[9] so that claims of custom are likely to constitute ex post rationalizations for a party's behavior.

In addition, careful consideration of the facts of *Columbia Nitrogen* suggests that the parties might not have intended to apply any custom about adjustment to their contract.  The court observes that the 31,000 ton figure was achieved after "extensive negotiations" during which the parties rejected each other's proposals for specific contractual terms concerning adjustments to prices and quantities before settling on their written agreement.  In the face of such arrangements, it would be reasonable to characterize a custom that would allow the buyer subsequently to take only 10 percent of the contractual amount as a "contradiction" of the dickered contract as well as an "explanation" of that term.  After all, one way to contradict a custom would presumably involve the creation of a specific, dickered term covering the same ground as the custom, and that appears to be exactly what the parties did in this case.[10]  It is difficult to think of what else could constitute a

---

[9] See, e.g., Lisa Bernstein, *The Questionable Empirical Basis of Article 2's Incorporation Strategy: A Preliminary Study*, 66 U. Chi. L. Rev. 710 (1999).  But see, Jody S. Kraus & Steven D. Walt, *In Defense of the Incorporation Strategy,* in The Jurisprudential Foundations of Corporate and Commercial Law 193 (Jody S. Kraus & Steven D. Walt, eds. 2000).

[10] For example, in Brunswick Box Co. v. Coutinho, Caro & Co., 617 F.2d 355 (4th Cir. 1980), the court found that evidence of substantial negotiations between the parties about who was to bear certain charges could be admitted to override statutory and trade usage understandings of the term "F.A.S. Port,"

contradiction of trade usage or course of dealing, except for an explicit statement that customs cannot be used to supplement or explain the writing. Since the UCC does not require such an explicit opt-out clause, but only the existence of contradiction, the court should have paid more attention to the possibility that the substantial negotiations between the parties, including implicit allocation of risk of price declines, was equivalent to a rejection of trade usage and course of dealing.[11]

As a second problem, note that the justifications for employing custom make sense where there is reason to believe that the custom or course of performance makes sense where there is a reason to believe that the practice has evolved out of dickered transactions between similarly situated parties. But that presumptively efficient evolutionary pattern is not the only source of recurring practices. A pattern of allowing adjustments to contractual quantities may also arise because one party has chiseled on the original understanding, but the deviation is too small for the other party justifiably to incur litigation costs to enforce the literal contract terms. That practice, of course, should not be the kind of behavior that constitutes a waiver binding on a seller who suffered such losses that it *was* worthwhile to initiate an action against a breaching buyer.

This was the rationale used by the court in *Southern Concrete Services, Inc. v. Mableton Contractors, Inc.*[12] In that case, a buyer of concrete who ordered significantly less concrete than was called for under the explicit terms of a contract sought, pursuant to § 2-202 and *Columbia Nitrogen*, to introduce evidence that the quantity stipulated in the contract was not mandatory on either of the parties. The court concluded that the failure of sellers in prior cases to enforce their rights strictly did not mean that there was a custom or course of performance to allow adjustment. Rather, an aggrieved party might prefer to renegotiate a contract, knowing that "he may resort to those enforceable contract rights if necessary." Thus, the mere fact that parties had previously treated contract terms as the subject of renegotiation did not imply that sellers in the industry had waived their contractual rights or that the

---

which was used in the contract.

[11] Even here, the court in *Columbia Nitrogen* would give effect to such a statement unless it made specific reference to the relevant trade usage excluded. Cf. § 2-202, Official Comment 2.

[12] 407 F. Supp. 581 (N.D. Ga. 1975).

parties did not initially contemplate full performance.

## B. Under the CISG

The incorporation of customs into contracts governed by the CISG is explicitly authorized by Article 9. Subsection (1) of that Article applies to the parties' agreement any usages that the parties have agreed to or established by practice between themselves. Thus, Article 9(1) parallels course of dealing or course of performance under the UCC. Subsection (2) parallels the UCC's concept of usage of trade and applies to the contract any usage "of which the parties knew or ought to have known and which in international trade is widely known to, and regularly observed by, parties to contracts of the type involved in the particular trade concerned." In addition, Article 8(3), which concerns the determination of a party's intent, requires consideration of any practices that the party has established with trading partners, the conduct of the parties, and any "usages," which presumably include the trade usages incorporated into the contract under Article 9.

The efficiency case for applying custom is the same under the CISG as it is under the UCC. That is, the use of custom serves as an efficient means of interpreting contractual language, if we believe that the parties to the contract were aware of the custom and intended to apply it to their contract. The result is likely if the custom arose out of a series of bargains between similarly situated parties who consistently allocated a particular risk in such a manner that it developed into a custom. In addition, use of custom serves as an efficient interpretive tool to the extent that courts can economize on the costs of resolving ambiguity in contractual language by invoking a customary definition.

In international sales, however, the efficiency case for custom may be more difficult to make than in domestic sales. Recall that custom can be assumed to constitute an efficient allocation of risk if the custom arose out of a series of arm's length bargains between similarly situated parties. In domestic sales, that assumption seems appropriate, at least in the case of commercial transactions. In international transactions, however, one can tell a more malign story about customs that undermines its use as a surrogate for efficient practices. Where customs involve trade in goods or raw materials that have historically been exported by less developed countries, it is conceivable that relevant trade usages were imposed rather than the result of bargains. Colonial practices, for instance, may well have intended to capture benefits for the colonial power rather than to achieve an optimal allocation of risks between the parties. Thus, retention of those customs cannot be assumed to embody an efficient norm. This concern led some countries to resist the incorporation of custom into the CISG. While a Chinese proposal that would have required trade usages to be "reasonable" in order to be incorporated into a contract was defeated,[13] some commentators have indicated that developing countries and socialist countries resist the possibility that usages that have been generated by developed countries should bind commercial parties in other countries.[14]

Nevertheless, there is some risk in asking courts to make a determination of the origin of a trade custom. There is little reason to believe that courts are armed to make the historical inquiry that would be necessary to discern the evolution of a custom, any more than courts can easily define the parameters of the trade usage. Indeed, the inquiry into evolution is very much of a piece with the concern about defining the scope of the custom. For instance, a party disfavored by a trade usage that evolved as an exploitative measure might argue that the "custom" should be ignored because it only applies under circumstances that no longer obtain. This is not to suggest that such an inquiry is either easy or desirable. It may be preferable to minimize judicial intervention into the area by simply applying custom broadly, as long as we do not believe that there remain a significant number of exploitative customs. After all, even traders from less developed countries have incentives to become more sophisticated and to bargain around preexisting customs that were initially created to take advantage of them. It is difficult to say, however, that any effort to invoke custom substantially increases the ability of the judiciary to intervene and police the fairness of the contract.

Article 9(2) incorporates trade usages of which the parties "knew or ought to have known." This language roughly parallels the application of trade usage under § 1-205(3) to parties who "are or should be aware of" the usage. In either case, the objective appears to be to deny to the novice who engages in the ability to plead ignorance of the customs that govern that trade. The reason for disallowing subjective ignorance is consistent with the reason for incorporating custom in the first place. The objective of reducing negotiation costs will be defeated to some degree if transacting parties must determine the state of knowledge of their trading partners in order to know how much they are required to

---

[13] Fritz Enderlein & Dietrich Maskow, International Sales Law 69 (1992).

[14] See Albert H. Kritzer, International Contract Manual 108 (1994). Note that the last phrase of Article 9(1) is elastic enough to avoid trade usage of developed countries from being imposed on developing countries.

disclose before trade usage becomes part of the binding contract.[15] Thus, we could either have a rule that says "trade usage always applies unless one party opts out" or one that says "trade usage never applies unless the parties opt in." Since novices will only be parties to the contract occasionally, it makes sense to assume in any given contract that both parties have the requisite experience and the knowledge that typically attends that experience. Of course, this does not preclude an unsophisticated party from announcing his or her ignorance and thus invoking the "unless otherwise agreed" clause of Article 9(2).

The capacity of courts to treat usage of trade with more breadth than it arguably deserves is evident in *ICC Arbitration Case No. 5713.*[16] *Case No. 5713* involved a contract concluded in 1979 which was silent as to the applicable law and the rights of the buyer to inspect the goods that were the subject of the contract. The buyer apparently gave the seller notice of nonconformity some time after delivery of the goods. The arbitral award notes that the CISG did not apply, since neither the country of the buyer nor of the seller was a party to the CISG. Nevertheless, the arbitration tribunal looked to the CISG as evidencing "the generally recognized usages regarding the matter of non-conformity of goods in international sales." Even though the CISG was at odds with the otherwise applicable law of the seller's place of business, the tribunal believed that it should apply trade usages to the contract, and hence the CISG's terms. There are at least three problems in making this determination.

First, the finding applies the CISG, which came into effect in 1988, to a contract concluded in 1979. Any trade usage found in the CISG may not have been present almost ten years prior to its codification. Second, Article 9(2)'s conditions for applying trade usage are ignored. In particular, there was no finding by the tribunal that the usage was known or should have been known to the parties or that is was a usage of "parties to contracts of the type involved in the particular trade concerned." Third, even if the CISG provisions did reflect trade usage, there remains the issue of what priority exists between incorporation of that usage into the law of the seller's residence. The tribunal said nothing about the issue, even though it identified applicable law as the law of the

---

[15] See Elizabeth Warren, *Trade Usage and Parties in the Trade: An Economic Rationale of an Inflexible Rule,* 42 U. Pitt. L. Rev. 515 (1981).

[16] 20 Yearbook Comm. Arb. 70 (1990).

seller's residence. In short, the tribunal failed to realize that, while the CISG may itself allow the incorporation of trade usages, this is an entirely different matter from concluding that the provisions of the CISG themselves are representative of pre-existing trade usage. Indeed, since most CISG provisions evolved from a multi-year process of substantial negotiation and compromise, it would be difficult to conclude that they simply codified custom.

## II. Open Terms

Recall that the sales contract does not specify the rights and obligations of the buyer and seller in every possible future state of the world. There will be some contingencies left unaddressed. The resulting contract is, to borrow jargon from transaction cost economics, incompletely state contingent. Some terms are left open by the parties. Uncertainty about the future, imprecision of language, sheer oversight, unwillingness to disclose information, and an aversion to raising issues that could prevent reaching agreement can lead to an incompletely contingent contract. Sometimes incompleteness is unavoidable because no amount of expenditure by the contracting parties can eliminate it (e.g., uncertainty, linguistic imprecision). More often contracts remain incomplete because reducing or eliminating incompleteness is not cost-justified for the contracting parties. Both Article 2 and the CISG supply some terms where the sales contract is silent on the matter. By doing so, they make more complete an otherwise incomplete contract. At least three questions can be asked about the terms supplied. First, which terms are supplied? (Derivatively, which terms are not supplied by Article 2 and the CISG?) Second, how do the supplied terms allocate relevant risks between the parties? Third, what is the standard by which to evaluate the terms supplied by Article and the CISG? Take the questions in turn.

To begin with, Article 2 and the CISG reduce the number of unprovided for contingencies by in effect broadening the notion of the parties' agreement. They do so by incorporating into the parties' agreement a set of implied terms. In addition to the express terms of the parties' deal, Article 2 defines "agreement" to include the parties' previous pattern of conduct and trade usage: "'Agreement' means the bargain of the parties in fact as found in their language...including course of dealing or usage of trade or course of performance as defined in this

Act..."[17] The CISG provides the same, in different language. Article 9(1) in so many words binds the parties to any agreed-upon usage and previous contractual pattern of conduct, and Article 9(2) makes trade usage "impliedly" applicable to the parties' agreement. Trade usage, course of performance and course of dealing supply norms that allocate rights and obligations over some matters where express terms of a contract do not. But, even supplemented with a set of implied terms, the parties' contract will be incomplete. There will be a set of terms that the contract leaves open.

Both Article 2 and the CISG provide a set of "gap filling" terms to complete the parties otherwise incomplete contract. The terms govern price, time and place of delivery, inspection rights, and time, place and form of payment. With important exceptions, Article 2 and the CISG's gap-filling terms are for the most part the same. As gap-filling terms, they state default rules and apply only when the parties do not otherwise provide the relevant term. Under § 2-305(1), price is the "reasonable price at the time of delivery." The place of delivery under § 2-308(a) is the seller's place of business. Time of shipment or delivery is a reasonable time under § 2-309(1). Under § 2-310(a) payment is due at the time and place at which the buyer is to receive the goods. (Hence, when § 2-308(a) applies to the contract, the buyer is required to pay the contract price at the seller's place of business when it is to receive the goods.) Section 2-310(b) gives the buyer the right to inspect the goods prior to making payment, unless the contract provides otherwise. Payment is to be in cash or non-postdated check, according to the ready implication of § 2-511(1).[18] The CISG puts the place of delivery at the seller's place of business under Article 31(c), when the sales contract does not involve carriage.[19] Under Article 33(c), the time of delivery is

---

[17] § 1-102(3); cf. §§ 1-205(2) (trade usage), 1-205(3) (course of dealing), 2-208(1) (course of performance).

[18] Cf. §§ 2-511(2), 2-511 Official Comments 2, 6.

[19] Whether the sales contract "involves" carriage presents a minor interpretive difficulty. Since almost all goods being sold require transportation-- the more so in international sales--seemingly almost all sales contracts "involve" carriage. Therefore, seemingly, under Article 31(a) the seller is required to deliver the goods to the first carrier for shipment to the buyer. But appearances are deceptive. "Carriage" presumably refers to transportation by a third party. Cf. United Nations Convention on Carriage of Goods by Sea; ICC Incoterms 1990 (definition of "carrier"). "Involves" also presumably means more than that

a reasonable time after the conclusion of the contract. Payment of price is at the seller's place of business under Article 57(1)(a) unless the goods or documents covering the goods are to be delivered elsewhere. The buyer has a right to inspect the goods prior to making payment under Article 58(3), unless the contract provides otherwise. Article 58(1) requires that the price be paid when the goods are made available to the buyer. Payment is to be in cash, according to a fair implication of Article 58(1). The CISG is silent on the currency in which payment is to be made, although a respectable argument can be made that the currency is the legal tender of the place where delivery is to be made.

## A. Open Price Terms Under the CISG

The CISG's treatment of open price terms is unclear and its diplomatic history too disparate in opinion to be helpful. Quite simply, the CISG may or may not supply a price term when the parties' agreement fails to provide one. Given the practical importance of the term, the matter is worth discussing. To focus discussion, call the demand that an agreement expressly or implicitly provide for the contract price "the definite price requirement." Article 14(1) appears to incorporate the requirement. It does so indirectly, by requiring that the terms of the offer be sufficiently definite. An offer is in turn sufficiently definite, according to Article 14(1), "if it indicates the goods and expressly or implicitly fixes...the price." This condition seems to state the definite price requirement. Since Articles 14-23 take a contract to be concluded by an offer and an acceptance, there cannot be an acceptance of an offer insufficiently definite in its terms. Therefore, if an offer does not satisfy the definite price requirement, a contract cannot be concluded under Article 23. As far as Article 14(1) goes, the CISG does not supply a price term.

But other Articles in the CISG deny the definite price requirement. Article 55 provides that a "validly concluded" contract which does not expressly or implicitly state a price is to have "impliedly made reference" to the price generally charged in the trade at the time of the conclusion of the contract. The Article presupposes that a contract can be "validly

---

the goods will be transported at some time or other. Otherwise, there would be no need for the qualification, "involve," in Article 31(a). Article 31(a) therefore must be restricted to contracts which call for carriage of the goods by a third party. It is of course a matter of fact as to when a contract contemplates such carriage.

concluded" without a price term.[20] In other words, Article 55 denies the definite price requirement. Otherwise, Article 55 would have no point because it would never apply. More generally, Article 55 assumes that a contract can be formed other than on the basis of Articles 14-23—other than via offer and acceptance. Article 14 appears to require that an offer fix the price, and Article 23 stipulates that contracts are concluded by the acceptance of an offer. Since Article 55 provides that a contract can be "validly concluded" without price being fixed, it follows that a contract can be formed without an offer and acceptance. Given Article 55, Articles 14-23 therefore cannot state the exclusive means by which contracts are formed under the CISG.

What is going on here? Articles 14 and 55 seem contradictory. Article 14 seems to state the definite price requirement. Article 55 presupposes that there is no definite price requirement under CISG. Both provisions are part of the same treaty. In our view, there are four positions that can be taken on the matter. We favor one of them, as we make clear below, but all are respectable positions, and all find some support in the inconclusive diplomatic history.

1. Articles 14 and 55 are in fact contradictory. Appearances are not deceiving. The contradiction is the consequence of a failed attempt to reach a compromise between countries whose domestic law adopts the definite price requirement and those whose law rejects the requirement.

---

[20] There are a couple of possible interpretations of what a "validly concluded" contract lacking a price term under Article 55 amounts to. One interpretation has "validity" referring to validity under applicable domestic law. This fits with Article 4(a)'s exclusion of matters of validity from the CISG. See Helen Elizabeth Hartnell, *Rousing the Sleeping Dog: Validity Exception to the Convention on Contracts for the International Sale of Goods*, 18 Yale J. Int'l L. 1, 68 (1993). Accordingly, if applicable domestic law does not adopt the definite price requirement (e.g., § 2-305), then a contract governed by the CISG could be concluded without a price term. If applicable domestic law insists on a provision of a price term (e.g., Article 1591 of the French Civil Code), offers lacking a price term could not conclude a contract under the CISG. A second interpretation reads "validity" as referring to validity under the CISG. This too fits with Article 4(a) because the Article's rider states that "except as otherwise provided in this Convention...," and Article 55 may be such an exception. Accordingly, if a contract is validly formed on a basis other than that provided in Article 14-23 of CISG, Article 55 fixes ("implies") price. Because both interpretations allow a contract to be formed without fixing price, the apparent inconsistency between Articles 14 and 55 noted just below in the text remains.

At the 1980 Vienna Diplomatic Conference, UNCITRAL's chairman noted the contradiction between the two Articles.[21] The contradiction persists in the final version of CISG.

2. Articles 14 and 55 are consistent because they do not apply at the same time. Article 55 applies to sales contracts only when the relevant signatory state has made an Article 92 reservation declaring that it will not be bound by Part II of the CISG (Article 14-23). If not bound by Part II, then Article 14 does not apply. The UNCITRAL Secretariat Commentary on the 1978 draft of the CISG reflected this understanding.[22] Some delegates to the Vienna Conference also understood the operation of Articles 14 and 55 in the same way.[23] The trouble with the position, of course, is that it says nothing about the Articles' operation when a signatory state *has not* made an Article 92 reservation. In that case the two Articles remain contradictory. Since very few states have made such a reservation, the contradiction is significant.

3. Articles 14 and 55 are consistent because they apply to two different ways of forming a contract. Article 14 applies to a contract formed by an offer and acceptance. Article 55 applies to contracts formed by a single document, multiple communications or exchanges which cannot be analyzed as offers and acceptances. This is Professor Honnold's position.[24] It is weak in two respects. First, Part II of the

---

[21] See 11th Meeting, First Committee Deliberations, Documentary History of the Uniform Law for International Sales para. 49 at 513 (J. O. Honnold ed. 1989) [hereinafter, "Documentary History"]; id., 24th Meeting, First Committee Deliberations, para. 38 at 585 (statement of Soviet representative). See also Peter Schlechtriem, Uniform Sales Law 50 (1986); Helen Elizabeth Hartnell, supra note 19, at 69 (1993) (Articles 14(1) and 55 inconsistent; Article 14(1) controlling); but cf. Enderlein & Maskow, supra note 12, at 208 ("total solution" found at the diplomatic conference).

[22] See Secretariat Commentary, Article 51 comm. 2, Diplomatic History, supra note 20, at 435.

[23] 24th Meeting, First Committee Deliberation para. 34, Diplomatic History, supra note 20, at 585; cf. E.A. Farnsworth, *Formation of Contract*, International Sales: The U.N. Convention on Contracts for the International Sale of Goods 3-9 (N. Galston & H. Smit eds. 1984).

[24] See John O. Honnold, Uniform Law for International Sales Under the 1980 United Nations Convention 152-53 (3d ed. 1999); cf. Gyula Eorsi, *Open-Price Contracts* Commentary on the International Sales Convention 407 (C.M.

CISG follows Anglo-American law in analyzing contract formation as one of offer and acceptance. To do so inevitably may invite some artificiality, but it does require adherence to the form of offer and acceptance. Even contracts that are formed through performance, and thus might fall within § 2-305 if the UCC applied, are properly construed under the rubric of offer and acceptance in the CISG, given the broad definition of "acceptance" in Article 18(1).

Second, Professor Honnold's position achieves consistency at the price of placing arbitrary restrictions on scope. What is he to do with a clear offer which lacks a price term? He is committed to finding that it is insufficiently definite and therefore an acceptance cannot conclude a contract. That is fine, but why impose a definite price requirement on Article 14 offers while not insisting on it when contracts are formed by the other means that his analysis presumes can exist? The different imposition of the requirement appears to us arbitrary.

4. Articles 14 and 55 are consistent because, appearances to the contrary, Article 14 does not state the definite price requirement in the first place. The second sentence of Article 14(1), properly read, states only a sufficient condition for the definiteness of an offer. In other words, it says that an offer is sufficiently definite if it fixes price: "A proposal is sufficiently definite if it indicates..." The second sentence does not say that an offer is sufficiently definite only if it fixes price. It does not state a necessary condition of definiteness. A literal reading of Article 14(1) therefore allows offers to be sufficiently definite while lacking a price term. Some representatives at the Vienna Conference had this understanding.[25] There is also an excellent reason to adopt a literal reading of Article 14(1)'s second sentence: doing so avoids what would otherwise be a contradiction in CISG. We favor this position.

The Hungarian Supreme Court recently decided a case, *Pratt & Whitney v. Malev Hungarian Airlines*,[26] which turns on the interpretation

---

Bianca & M.J. Bonell eds. 1987) (Article 14 deals with offers; Article 55 deals with contracts).

[25] See 8th Meeting, First Committee Deliberation, para. 68, Documentary History, supra note 20, at 496 (statement of representative from United Kingdom).

[26] Gf. I. 31 349/1992/9 (Hungary), reported in 13 J. Law & Comm. 31 (1995).

of Articles 14 and 55.  Unfortunately, it does not clearly announce in favor or against the definite price requirement.   Pratt & Whitney presented a written proposal to Malev Airlines offering to sell Malev any of several described types of its 4000 series aircraft engines.  Prices were attached to each engine type.  Later, it extended an offer to include another type of engine in the series.  No price was stipulated.  Malev subsequently accepted the offer by letter.  When Malev declared that it would not purchase the engines, Pratt & Whitney sued.   In finding no enforceable agreement, the Hungarian Supreme Court says things that both support and detract from reading the definite price requirement into Article 14(1).   On the one hand, the Court says that Article 14(1) incorporates the requirement: to be sufficiently definite, "price is an essential element of a bid [i.e., offer]."  Since the Court finds that Pratt & Whitney's offer lacked prices for some of the "engine systems" and "engines," Malev's putative acceptance could not conclude a contract. This seems clearly to support finding the definite price requirement in Article 14(1).  On the other hand, the Court also says that the price of unpriced "engine systems" could not be determined under Article 55 because they "have no market price."  (The Court does not bother to notice the possible contradiction between Articles 14 and 55.)  The Court's willingness even to consider market price under Article 55 suggests that it would allow market price to make definite an offer lacking a price term.  It suggests that the Court is considering Articles 14 and 55 together.  Doing so indicates that the Court does not read Article 14(1) to incorporate the definite price requirement.

But there may even be less than meets the eye here.  The *Malev* court could be saying something like the following: "Article 14(1) requires an offer to fix price.  Pratt & Whitney's offer for some engines and engine systems did not fix price.  Therefore, Malev's acceptance could not conclude a contract.  But suppose we are wrong about Article 14(1)'s interpretation and have to read Article 55 in conjunction with it.  We still would reach the same conclusion here.  This is because the price term of the offer cannot be fixed by market price in this case where there is no market price."  The Court's opinion is simply too disorganized to distill a consistent interpretation of Articles 14 and 55.

UCC- and CISG-supplied terms have a couple of consequences.  One is that otherwise unenforceable bargains can be enforceable.  This is because the presence of provided terms can make an otherwise indefinite agreement definite in terms.  For instance, at common law an agreement lacking essential terms is not enforceable.  Section 2-204(3) alters the rule by allowing enforcement of a sales contract which leaves terms open as long as the parties intend to contract and "there is a reasonably certain basis for giving an appropriate remedy." Article 2's provision of price, delivery, payment terms and the like can allow such a remedial basis. The question then is only whether the parties' omission of particular terms indicates that they did not intend to contract.[27] The absence of UCC-provided terms by itself show that there was no contractual intent.

Another consequence concerns the allocation of costs and risks provided by UCC- and the CISG-supplied terms. These terms indirectly allocate the costs of performing the contract between the parties. Take the seller's delivery obligations under § 2-310(a) and Article 31(c), respectively. The seller's obligation of delivery under both provisions requires delivery of the goods at her place of business. Once delivered there, in almost all cases the goods have to be transported to their final destination. Given § 2-310(a) and Article 31(c), the buyer bears costs (and risks) of transportation. The provisions therefore indirectly impose transportation costs on the buyer. The payment terms supplied by Article 2 and the CISG also allocate cost. Section 2-511(2) and Article 58(1) require that the contract price be paid in cash. The provisions thereby impose on the buyer the cost of financing the goods between the time of sale and resale to another buyer. The seller, by receiving cash, does not have to finance the sale to its buyer. Inspection rights allocate cost and risk too. The seller not only has to incur the obvious cost of making the goods available to the buyer for inspection. It also bears the risk of damage to the goods arising from the buyer's inspection, when proof of such a causal connection between inspection and resulting damage is not convincing to a trier of fact.

Price terms also indirectly allocate between the parties the risk of price fluctuations. To see this, notice the obvious risk that market price can alter between the time the contract is executed and the time delivery of the goods is required. A price term assigns this interim market risk to the buyer or seller. Where contract price is fixed by the parties, the buyer bears all interim risks of price fluctuations. For instance, suppose the parties' contract is silent on price, the market price at the time the contract is executed is $100, and the contract price at the time of delivery can either be $50 or $150. The buyer bears the risk of both upward and downward changes in market price between the time the contract is concluded and the date of delivery. Where the parties' contract is silent, the UCC and the CISG assign the risk of price fluctuations differently.

---

[27] See § 2-204 Official Comment.

Under § 2-305(1), the contract price is a reasonable price at the time of delivery, whereas Article 55 puts the contract price as the price generally charged at the conclusion of the contract. Therefore, § 2-305(1) places the risk of interim market increase on the buyer; the seller bears the risk of interim market decreases. Article 55 places the risk of both market increase and decrease on the buyer, as in a fixed price contract. Under § 2-305(1), the buyer bears the risk of the price increasing from $100 to $150 (buyer's costs increase by $50). The seller, however, bears the risk of the price dropping from $100 to $50 (seller's cost increases by $50). Under Article 55, the buyer bears both the risk of upward and downward market risk. This is because the contract price is fixed as of the date the contract is concluded. Of course, since UCC- and the CISG-supplied rules are default rules only, the parties can alter the cost and risk of contractual performance assigned by them. The point here is only that these supplied terms allocate costs and risks to the parties initially.

## B. Open Quantity Terms

Article 2 and the CISG's treatment of open quantity terms is slightly complex. As usual, the complications arise from unclarity in statutory standards compounded, in the case of Article 2, by sometimes careless case law. An agreement contains an open quantity term when it calls for quantity to be determined by the buyer's requirements for particular goods or by the seller's output of particular goods. The former provision in an agreement creates a requirements contract; the latter, an output contract. Requirements and output contracts contain open quantity terms in that the parties fail to specify a particular amount of goods to be bought or sold. (An agreement contains no quantity term when it does not state a particular quantity term and is not a requirements or output contract.) Open quantity terms are common features of contracts where future supply and demand conditions cannot reliably be gauged by the parties.

Surprisingly, the CISG does not explicitly address the enforceability of requirements or output contracts. However, a good argument can be made for their recognition under the CISG. The argument is based on Article 14(1). The first sentence of Article 14(1) requires that an offer be sufficiently definite in its terms. This obviously includes quantity terms. Article 14(1)'s second sentence says that an offer is sufficiently definite if it "indicates the goods" and provides for "determining the[ir] quantity." It may or may not state a definite quantity requirement: the demand that an offer is sufficiently definite only if it contains a quantity term. Given our previous argument that the second sentence of Article 14(1) states only a sufficient condition of a sufficiently definite offer, and therefore does not announce a definite price requirement, we reach the same conclusion here. Article 14(1) does not announce a definite quantity requirement. But we need not rely on that argument because the terms of second sentence of Article 14(1) allow for open quantity contracts. "Indicates the goods" does not by itself demand that an agreement implicitly or expressly state a specific quantity. A quantity term calling for requirements or outputs is enough to "indicate the goods." It "determines" quantity as the amount a buyer requires or a seller produces. Quantity in this case presumably would be determined by amounts supplied or demanded in good faith,[28] supplemented by course of dealing and trade usage where possible.[29] Hence, even if Article 14(1) announces a definite quantity requirement, requirements and output contracts satisfy it.

Article 2 explicitly recognizes requirements and output contracts. Both are subject to two standards provided by § 2-306(1): any requirements and output must be demanded or supplied in good faith, and cannot be unreasonably disproportionate to any stated estimates or "normal or comparable" prior requirements or output "tendered or demanded." The standards make definite an otherwise indefinite offer containing an open quantity term.[30] A straightforward reading of § 2-306(1) considers the two standards as conjunctive and unrestricted: demands for requirements or supply must both be made in good faith and within reasonably proportionate stated estimates or "normal or comparable" prior requirements or output. Both standards also must be satisfied by any requirements demanded or output supplied. But some of § 2-306(1)'s language, Official Comments and case law create three uncertainties. First, it is uncertain whether the reasonably proportionate standard applies to decreases in quantities demanded or supplied. Section 2-306(1) speaks of "prior output or requirements...tendered or demanded." Relying on a bit of lexicography, one might argue that the

---

[28] Good faith would be determined under either of two standards. Either the standard would be one articulated in Article 7(1) or under domestic law selected by conflicts principles of the forum.

[29] See Article 9(1), (2).

[30] Comment 2 to § 2-306 notices that the good faith standard has this consequence; see § 2-206 Official Comment 2 ("...a contract for output or requirements is not too indefinite since it is held to mean the actual good faith output or requirements of the particular party.").

buyer is not "tendering or demanding" disproportionate requirements when it orders less than prior requirements. In this case the buyer is not "tendering or demanding" anything more than it is asking for.[31] By § 2-306(1)'s terms, then, the unreasonably disproportionate standard seems to apply only to quantity increases. Most but not all of the sparse case law takes this view.[32]

Second, the Official Comments to § 2-306 make it uncertain whether the standards themselves are conjunctive. The Comments disagree with each other. Comment 2, in glossing the good faith standard, says that a "shutdown by a requirements buyer for lack of orders might be permissible when a shut-down merely to curtail losses would not." The distinction between a requirements buyer having no requirements because there is no demand for its products and having no requirements because it is losing money itself is artificial. In both cases the requirements buyer shuts down in order to minimize its losses. But, the distinction aside, Comment 2 allows a requirements buyer to satisfy the good faith standard without satisfying the unreasonably disproportionate standard. Comment 3 makes matters worse by seemingly contradicting Comment 2. In interpreting the unreasonably disproportionate standard, it says that any "agreed estimate is to be regarded as a center around which the parties intend the variation to occur." The statement suggests that requirements or output must be within an undefined range of any stated estimate—in other words, not "unreasonably disproportionate" to it. Comment 3, contrary to Comment 2, therefore suggests that the unreasonably disproportionate standard must be satisfied by all requirements or output demanded or supplied. Quantity decreases as well as increases, Comment 3 has it, are subject to the standard. A good deal of case law has simply ignored the unreasonably disproportionate standard and applied only the good faith standard.[33]

---

[31] Cf. Empire Gas Corp. v. American Bakeries Co., 840 F.2d 1333, 1337 (7th Cir. 1988) ("delivery" does not "naturally" apply to requirements buyer ordering less than stated estimate; point a bit of "verbal skirmishing).

[32] See, e.g., id.; R. Weaver & Assoc. v. Asphalt Constr. Inc., 587 1315 (D.C. Cir. 1978). Proposed § 2-306 would apply the unreasonably disproportionate standard to both quantity increases and decreases.

[33] See, e.g., Lakeland v. Union Oil, 352 F. Supp. 758 (M.D. Fla. 1973); Eastern Air Lines v. Gulf Oil Corp., 415 F. Supp. 429 (S.D. Fla. 1975); Laing

The third uncertainty centers on the content of the two standards. The standards are themselves slippery, and § 2-306 gives little hint as to their meaning. In principle, "good faith" and "not unreasonably disproportionate" describe distinct standards. Good faith focuses on the requirements buyer or output seller's conduct. Its requirement for merchants under § 2-103(1)(b) that they comply with commercially reasonable standards of fair dealing, for instance, looks at least to the behavior of the requirements buyer or output seller. The unreasonably disproportionate standard concerns the range of variation in quantity demanded or supplied. So the standards are different. But they are otherwise vague in their terms. Hence, in practice, the good faith and unreasonably disproportionate standards can be applied on the basis of the same factors. Some well-known case law does this.

*Orange & Rockland Utilities, Inc. v. Amerada Hess Corp.*[34] nicely illustrates the problem. Here the buyer, a public utility, and the seller entered into a requirements contract for the supply of fuel oil at a fixed price for use in the one of the buyer's generating plants. The contract contained estimated requirements over the period of the contract. Due to an apparent substitution effect of increased demand for gas, the market price of fuel oil rose and the buyer increased its requirements for oil. After the seller refused to satisfy all of the buyer's annual demands for oil, the buyer sued. The *Orange & Rockland* court read § 2-306 to require the buyer to satisfy both the good faith and not unreasonably disproportionate standards. It found the buyer to have violated the good faith standard in its demand for oil during 1970. The buyer's increased demand was in bad faith, according to the court, because it sold increased amounts of energy to other utilities and reduced its consumption of natural gas.[35] Apparently the buyer was strategically manipulating its demand under a favorable fixed price to sell energy. Turning to the buyer's increased demand for oil in 1971 and 1972, the court refused to draw an unfavorable inference from the buyer's failure to explain the

---

Loggin, Inc. v. International Paper Co., Lexis 6695 (Sup. Ct. N.Y. 1996).

[34] 397 N.Y.S.2d 814 (Sup. Ct. 1977).

[35] Id. at 820. The court conveniently ignored a provision in the contract, mentioned in its recitation of the facts, under which the buyer reserved the right to burn as much gas as it chose. Id. at 816. Had it considered the provision, the buyer's substitution away from gas to oil would have been harder to characterize as in bad faith.

source of the demand.[36]  Instead, it held as a matter of law that, because the seller could not have reasonably expected the magnitude of price rise in fuel oil, a demand for requirements twice that of a stated estimate was unreasonably disproportionate.  The buyer therefore violated the unreasonably disproportionate standard too.

Notice, however, that the *Orange & Rockland* court could have found on the same facts that the buyer's demand was in bad faith.  The buyer had acted strategically in manipulating its demand for oil during 1970.  It could not explain why its need for natural gas declined in 1971 and 1972 while the market price of fuel oil increased.  The ready inference is that the buyer continued to manipulate its demand for oil and therefore continued to act in bad faith.  The *Orange & Rockland* court might not disagree since it allows the reason for increased demand to be a factor in determining whether  the quantity demanded is unreasonably disproportionate to any stated estimate.[37]  If so, the same facts bearing on good faith also bear on the reasonable proportionateness of a quantity demanded.  Therefore, as applied, the two standards in fact may be one standard.

### C.  Evaluating Supplied Terms

This brings us to the standard by which UCC- and the CISG-supplied terms should be evaluated.  The majoritarian default standard argued for in Chapter 1, we suggest, should be applied to open terms.  Used as a normative standard, a majoritarian default rule recommends supplying terms which would be provided by most contracting parties if bargaining costs were zero.  Such terms save most parties the cost of contracting for terms already provided for by background rules.  Assuming that the costs of contracting into and out of any particular default rule are the same for all parties, contracting costs are lower when a default rule adopts terms most parties prefer than when the rule adopts terms preferred by atypical parties.  Total contracting costs in this way therefore are optimally minimized.  The question then is which terms most parties prefer.  Most parties arguably prefer to have contractual rights and obligations turn on verifiable variables: events which third parties have access to information

---

[36] Id. at 821.

[37] Id. at 821-22.

needed to determine whether they obtain or not.[38] In general, they prefer not to have their contractual rights and duties determined by information available only to the other contracting party. Otherwise, the party with the relevant information ex post can act strategically to alter the initial contractual assignment of risks between the parties in its favor. Other things being equal, parties do not expose themselves to a risk of being exploited. Because verifiable variables prevent this possibility, most parties would prefer to select such terms. UCC- and the CISG-supplied terms can be evaluated by predominant party preference to condition contractual terms on verifiable variables.

Evaluated in this way, the UCC and the CISG do pretty well. Delivery terms, for instance, are consistent with predominant party preference for verifiable variables. Both § 2-308(a) and Article 31(c) set the place of delivery as the seller's place of business. Also, both § 2-503, combined with § 2-301, and Article 31(c) set the seller's obligation of delivery as one of making the goods available. The location and manner of delivery are verifiable variables. True, sometimes it can be difficult to decide where the seller's place of business is located or whether seller has made the goods available to the buyer there. But this information, even when difficult to come by, is not available to only one of the contracting parties. Price terms are the same way. Section 2-305(1) supplies a "reasonable price" at the time of delivery, which can be the prevailing market price at that time. Article 55 provides the price "generally charged at the time of the conclusion of the contract," clearly the market price. Market price is a verifiable variable. It is determinable independently of the facts about the seller (e.g., seller's production costs) that are not observable by third parties. Even a "reasonable price," although less specific than market price, allows for determination of contract price without reference to facts known only to the seller.[39] Article 55 can be criticized here in one respect. By relying market price at the conclusion of the contract, it relies on an event (conclusion of the contract) which is less verifiable than other possible candidates (e.g., delivery). The time and place at which a contract is concluded often can be difficult to determine. Still, the information relevant to this

---

[38] See Alan Schwartz, *Relational Contracts in the Courts: An Analysis of Incomplete Agreements and Judicial Strategies*, 21 J. Legal Stud. 271 (1992).

[39] Cf. Robinson v. Stevens Industries, Inc., 290 S.E.2d 336 (Ct. App. Ga. 1982) (federal support price for peanuts on date of delivery a "reasonable price"); Ogelby Norton Co. v. Armco, Inc., 556 N.E.2d 515, 519 (Ohio 1970).

determination is not available to only one of the contracting parties. Price under Article 55 is simply being conditioned on an observable verifiable which can be hard to verify.

Some UCC- and CISG-supplied terms are vague. Section 2-309(1) and Article 33(c), for instance, put the time of delivery at a "reasonable" time. In the case of open quantity contracts, § 2-306(1) sets the enforceable quantity required or supplied at the amount reasonably proportionate to a stated estimated or normal requirements or output. More generally, a number of UCC and CISG terms call for conditioning a contractual duty on reasonableness.[40] Such terms specify events which a party is enjoined to bring about or avoid. They instead leave the conditioning of duties to an ex post determination by a third party trier of fact. But vagueness does not make a term unverifiable. This is because the circumstances under which a party is under a duty is not determined by information available only to the buyer or the seller. "Reasonable," for instance, does not mean "at cost to the party under a duty finds acceptable" or "within the discretion of the party under the duty." At most a vague term only makes the full details of contractual performance difficult for the contracting parties to determine ex ante. (The difficulty presumably is cost-justified for the parties ex ante because they omitted terms which would have made aspects of their duties more precise.) Hence UCC- and CISG-supplied vague terms are consistent with a majoritarian preference for terms which condition contractual performance on verifiable variables.

The majoritarian standard also can justify the *absence* of particular terms from the UCC and the CISG. Neither supplies a nonzero quantity term where the parties' agreement and trade usage are silent on quantity. In these circumstances, an agreement lacking a quantity term is unenforceable. The UCC and the CISG, by not enforcing the agreement, can be thought of as supplying a zero quantity term to the agreement. Why doesn't the UCC and the CISG supply a nonzero quantity term in these circumstances? Ayers and Gertner suggest that only a "penalty" default standard, not a majoritarian standard, can justify a zero quantity term: a standard which supplies terms that most contracting parties would not want.[41] A penalty default, by supplying a zero quantity term not

---

[40] See Articles 39(1), 48.

[41] See Ian Ayres & Robert Gertner, *Filling Gaps in Incomplete Contracts: An Economic Theory of Default Rules*, 99 Yale L. J. 87, 95-97 (1989); see also Ian Ayres, *Making a Difference: The Contractual Contributions of Easterbrook*

wanted by most parties, induces them to supply a nonzero quantity term. Ayers and Gertner's suggestion is premature because a majoritarian standard can also account for a zero quantity term. True, most contracting parties would want their contract enforced even when it lacks a quantity term. But most parties also would want their contract only enforced by a court supplying terms based on verifiable variables. The two preferences are perfectly consistent. In order to supply a nonzero price term, a court needs to rely on nonverifiable variables. It needs to look to demand conditions facing the buyer to determine the quantity of goods the buyer would order at the contract price. The buyer's demand in turn depends on facts about the value of alternative uses to which it could put the contract price for a particular quantity. Both matters require information to which only the buyer has access. In other words, the information needed to supply a nonzero quantity term is unverifiable. Therefore, given the parties' preference for verifiable information, most contracting parties in the circumstances would prefer a court not to supply a nonzero quantity. The UCC and the CISG mimic this majority preference by in effect setting the quantity term at zero. A majoritarian standard therefore can justify the absence of a nonzero quantity term from both sets of provisions. There is no need to justify it as an instance of a penalty default rule.

The majoritarian standard has another virtue: it can give content to UCC-supplied terms that otherwise appear vacuous. This is the case with the well-known difficulty concerning § 2-306(2)'s requirement of best efforts in an exclusive dealing contract. Where the contract obligates the seller to sell goods only to the buyer, § 2-306(2) charges the parties with obligations to make best efforts: the seller with making best efforts to supply the buyer and the buyer with making best efforts to resell and market the goods.[42] A requirements contract, for instance, in which the seller promises to sell only to the buyer creates an exclusive dealing contract. There are impeccable reasons why parties sometimes create one. The buyer's distribution costs for seller's goods may be lower than the seller's due to investments in distribution and advertising networks already incurred by the buyer. At the same time the buyer might fear that

---

*and Fischel*, 59 U. Chi. L. Rev. 1391, 1395-1400 (1992).

[42] Although § 2-306(2)'s terms limit an obligation of best efforts to sales contracts ("the seller to use best efforts...and by the buyer to use best efforts..."), Official Comment 4 to § 2-306 extends the obligation to exclusive agency agreements.

the benefits from distribution costs it incurred would be captured by other buyers of seller's products. It therefore might insist on being the seller's exclusive dealer. Finally, given uncertainty about future supply and demand conditions, the parties might prefer not to set quantities of goods to be supplied by the seller and bought by the buyer. An exclusive dealing contract with an implied or express best efforts clause can suit the parties.[43] The problem, of course, is to set the standard of what constitutes best efforts when the parties' contract is otherwise silent on the matter. Section 2-306(2) and its associated Comments are entirely unhelpful here.

The absence of a well-defined standard creates a practical difficulty concerning remedies. A best efforts standard is needed not only to determine whether the parties have performed their contractual obligations in an exclusive dealing contract. It is also needed to calculate damages in the event that a party has breached its contractual obligations. To see this, recognize that damages, D, in a contract with a fixed price, P, are given by the following simple measure: $D = P(Q^* - Q)$, where $Q^*$ is the quantity supplied or sold if the party in breach had made best efforts to do so, and Q is the quantity actually supplied or sold with the effort the party in breach expended. Since Q is the quantity actually supplied or sold, its size is easily determined. A best efforts standard is needed to determine the value of $Q^*$, the amount required to be supplied or sold.

*Bloor v. Falstaff Brewing Corp.*,[44] the most important case discussing a best efforts term, unwittingly demonstrates the difficulty of its application. Falstaff purchased Ballantine's beer labels, trademarks and distribution network, and promised to use best efforts to sell Ballantine beer in exchange for paying Ballantine four million dollars and a royalty

---

[43] It is fair to ask why the parties do not vertically integrate their operations, the buyer purchasing the seller's product line or the seller purchasing the buyer's distribution and advertising network. A straight sale might be infeasible because of asymmetrical information: the buyer has information about the value of its network or the seller has information about the value of its product that the other party lacks. Risk aversion is another possibility: The buyer might not want to take the chance by itself that the asset purchased can be profitably resold. An exclusive dealing contract shares this risk between seller and buyer. The presence of exclusive dealing contracts lacking best efforts standards supports both possibilities.

[44] 454 F. Supp. 258 (S.D.N.Y. 1978), *aff'd* 601 F.2d 609 (2d Cir. 1979).

of 50 cents per barrel of Ballantine beer it sold. In this way part of Ballantine's profit depended on the effort Falstaff exerted in selling the Ballantine brand. When Falstaff closed a depot that served small stores selling Ballantine beer, selected a distributor who owned competing brands, failed to accept offers to distribute Ballantine beer, favored its own brands over Ballantine, and relaxed sales goals of Ballantine for its salesmen, the court had to decide what efforts Falstaff was required to expend in selling the Ballantine brand. The Second Circuit held that Falstaff was not required to "spend itself into bankruptcy"[45] selling the Ballantine brand but that it was required to incur some loss on Ballantine's behalf[46] and to perform "as well as 'the average prudent comparable' brewer."[47] The holding seems to describe three different standards of best efforts. None specifies exactly what quantity of Ballantine beer the best efforts term required Falstaff to sell. In order to calculate damages, a best efforts standard has to provide that quantity.

At least four different standards are available: a market standard, a fiduciary standard, a joint maximization standard, and a verifiable effort standard. The market standard requires the best efforts supplier to provide the quantity up to the point at which its marginal costs equal its marginal revenues. A fiduciary standard requires the best efforts supply to supply quantity up to the point at which the other party's marginal revenue is zero. Joint maximization requires supplying the quantity that maximizes the sum of the net marginal revenues of the parties. A verifiable effort standard requires supplying only the quantity associated with incurring some observable marginal cost. To exemplify and make concrete these different standards, consider a manufacturer who grants the right to a distributor to exclusively distribute its products. Their contract is silent as to what effort the distributor is to exert on the manufacturer's behalf. Suppose that the following table represents the

---

[45] 601 F.2d at 614.

[46] Id.

[47] Id. at 613 n.7 (case citation omitted). A different parsing of the case might find different candidates; see, e.g., Mark P. Gergen, *The Use of Open Terms in Contracts*, 92 Colum. L. Rev. 997, 1066-67 (1992). The *Bloor* court is aware that the possible standards are not themselves transparent. After describing them, the court notes that "[t]he net of all this is that the New York law is far from clear and it is unfortunate that a federal court must have to apply it" (Bloor, 601 F.2d at 613 n.7).

marginal cost to the distributor ("Distrib.") associated with each level of effort it expends and the marginal revenues to the distributor and manufacturer ("Manuf.") yielded by that expenditure.

| Effort Level | Marginal Costs to Distrib. | Marginal Revenue to Distrib. | Marginal Revenue to Manuf. | Total Marginal Net Revenue |
|---|---|---|---|---|
| 1 | 7 | 10 | 12 | 15 |
| 2 | 10 | 12 | 14 | 16 |
| 3 | 10 | 10 | 17 | 17 |
| 4 | 12 | 10 | 20 | 18 |
| 5 | 14 | 0 | 21 | 7 |

The market standard requires the distributor to exert effort level 3. That is the level at which its net profits are maximized because its marginal costs (10) equal its marginal revenue (10). The *Bloor* court implicitly describes this standard by the performance required of the "average prudent comparable" brewer in that case. A market standard fails, we think, because it is unnecessary: it would discourage a rational distributor from exerting more or less effort than is required by the standard. In other words, even without being under an obligation to exercise best efforts, the distributor would expend the effort required by the market standard. The standard therefore would regulate only irrational or unwitting production decisions— presumably very few cases.

A fiduciary standard requires the distributor to exert effort level 5. This is because under it the distributor is required to expend effort, at whatever cost to it (14), that maximizes the manufacturer's marginal revenue. At effort level 5, the manufacturer's marginal revenue is 21, more than yielded by any other effort level. Revenues yielded to the distributor (0) are irrelevant. The *Bloor* court may be employing the fiduciary standard when it says that Falstaff is not required to spend itself into bankruptcy but that it is required to incur some ("trivial") loss to itself. Fiduciary standards fail because they do not plausibly reflect the parties' preferences. After all, the distributor does not plausibly assume the risk of having to incur costs that would render it insolvent. As for the constraint that the distributor risk incurring some loss to itself, it is indeterminate. How much loss is that?

The joint maximization standard urged by Professors Goetz and

Scott[48] demands that the distributor exert effort level 4. This is because at effort level 4 the total marginal revenue to both parties (30) is highest. Total net profit also is highest there too (18 = 30 - 12). Effort level 4 is the level of effort that would be expended if the manufacturer and distributor formed a single integrated firm selling the same product. Professors Goetz and Scott suggest that this is, therefore, the effort level that most contracting parties would bargain for the distributor to expend.

We are less certain of that conclusion. We base our doubts on two points. First, although this standard certainly reflects the result that would be achieved in an integrated firm that both produced and distributed the good, in cases like *Bloor*, the parties most emphatically did *not* vertically integrate. They may have wanted to retain organizational independence for a variety of reasons, some of which have no implications for the "best efforts" standard, but some of which do. For instance, Falstaff might have wanted to remain independent because it had a comparative advantage monitoring the credit of customers, or because Falstaff's performance might have been easily monitored by Ballantine (thus, no monitoring advantages would be realized by integration). Alternatively, Ballantine's owners might have been unwilling to sell the whole business to Falstaff because they had private information about the value of the firm that they could not credibly convey to Falstaff and for which Falstaff was unwilling to pay. None of these reasons for retaining organizational autonomy necessarily entails that the parties would not want to maintain the same level of effort that would be required if they had merged. Thus, the absence of integration does not require that the parties intended Falstaff's effort to diverge from what would maximize joint interests. It might mean only that the parties could not come up with a more satisfactory way of expressing that thought than "best efforts." But it is equally conceivable that at least one of the parties avoided integration for the very reason that it wanted to be able to avoid the joint maximizing obligation that integration entails. In this case, it would be perverse to impose on that party (or both of them) an obligation of joint maximization by using a standard taken from an organizational form (vertical integration) that the parties assiduously avoided. While the resulting "best efforts" clause in a contract between independent firms may be sufficient to preclude either party from acting

---

[48] See Charles J. Goetz & Robert E. Scott, *Principles of Relational Contracts*, 67 Va. L. Rev. 1089, 1119-26 (1981); cf. Robert E. Scott & Douglas Leslie, Contract Law and Theory 303 (2d ed. 1991), Mark P. Gergen, *The Use of Open Terms in Contracts*, 92 Colum. L. Rev. 997, 1064-72 (1992).

strategically, it may also reflect an implicit agreement that the parties are not required to treat each other with the same deference that is reserved for partners in a joint enterprise.

Second, we believe that in placing parameters on strategic behavior under a "best efforts" clause, most parties would prefer to assign contractual duties on the basis of variables verifiable to third parties. Effort levels and their associated costs to the distributor are unverifiable, and we have little faith that courts will be able to exact information that allows the development of something like the table above.[49] The manufacturer, for instance, lacks reliable access to the distributor's cost data and actual expenditures of effort. They are artifacts of the table, not frequently and reliably known by the non-best efforts party or triers of fact. Because the joint maximization standard requires verification of unobservable events, most contracting parties would not prefer to hinge the distributor's required efforts on them. The verifiable efforts standard is more modest, requiring only that the distributor incur some observable cost in association with yielding revenue to the manufacturer. The standard allows the distributor to exert significant effort level, and presumably levels 1 through 5 would all qualify. In other words, the distributor's best efforts obligation is violated only if the distributor incurs no or de minimis observable cost. Clearly, because the standard turns on verifiable events (observable costs incurred by the distributor), it satisfies a majoritarian preference for conditioning terms on events observable to a third party. By limiting judicial inquiry into the proper level of investment in producing revenues for the other party, the standard reduces judicial error, while allowing (indeed, encouraging) parties to state their intentions more explicitly where that is their intention. At the same time the standard is not useless. "Verifiable efforts" is more than a term expressing an aspiration about the quantity that the best efforts party is to supply. The best efforts party is required by the standard to do something: to make observable efforts on the other party's behalf in selling goods. A majoritarian default rule, we conclude, supports the verifiable efforts standard as defining best efforts. For what it is worth, ample case law is consistent with the verifiable efforts standard.[50]

---

[49] See Alan Schwartz, supra note 38.

[50] See, e.g., CKB & Associates Inc. v. Moore McCormick Petroleum, Inc., 809 S.W.2d 577, 581 (Tex. App. 1991); United Roasters v. Colgate-Palmolive, 649 F.2d 985, 990 (4th Cir. 1981). Although not put in such terms, these cases

all find that satisfying a best efforts obligations depends on verifiable costs incurred by the best efforts supplier. Case law does not fit the "verifiable efforts" standard perfectly. The "verifiable efforts" standard measures damages for a breach of best efforts as the price adjusted difference between the output that the exercise of verifiable efforts would produce and the output that existing efforts actually produced. Case law finding a lack of best efforts does not articulate the damages measure in this way. At most it is consistent with the measurement of damages compelled by a "verifiable efforts" standard.

## I. Introduction: Permissive Rules, Mandatory Rules, and Externalities

Sales law consists of a set of rules addressing the contingencies that can occur in connection with a sales contract. The contingencies range from unprovided terms in an agreement to the circumstances in which performance is excused under the contract, to the remedies available when the contract is breached. For the most part, Article 2's rules are permissive, not mandatory. That is, most are default rules which can be altered by the contracting parties. Section 2-308(a), for instance, provides that the place of delivery of the goods is the seller's place of business, "unless otherwise agreed."[1] Section 2-501(1) defines when goods are identified to the contract "[i]n the absence of an explicit agreement" to the contrary. Both sections allow parties to set a place of delivery and a manner of identifying the goods to the contract. Parties can agree that delivery occur at a place other than the seller's place of business and that the goods be identified to the contract in a manner not described in § 2-501(1). In fact, § 1-102(3) allows the parties to vary the effect of all of the UCC's provisions, subject to a few exceptions.[2] Not all of Article 2's rules, however, can be altered by the agreement of the parties. An important subset of its rules (sometimes supplemented by common law) are mandatory, not permissive. Article 2's Statute of Frauds, parol evidence rule and provisions on unconscionability are mandatory. Sometimes called formal requirements, they regulate the parties' agreement in different ways. This chapter describes and assesses Article 2's formal requirements.

It is worth beginning by asking whether any rules should be mandatory. There are two different bases for making a rule mandatory: considerations having to do with costs the parties' contract imposes on

---

[1] Cf. §§ 2-309(1) (time of shipment), 2-316(2) (implied warranties can be excluded).

[2] The exceptions concern the duties of good faith, reasonableness, diligence and care. But even here § 1-102(3) allows the parties' agreement to provide the standards for these duties. To the extent that parties can set standards of good faith, reasonableness, diligence and care, they can determine by agreement what the duties require.

those who are not parties to the contract, and considerations concerning the effect of the contract on the parties' own welfare. The first sort of consideration focuses on what economists call "negative externalities." The second focuses on the reduction in the parties' welfare produced by a contractual term. To see how these considerations might become relevant, recall our discussion in Chapter 1 of the justification for default rules in commercial law. We noted that a default rule, which is a form of permissive rule, is warranted where it can reduce contracting costs for most parties who enter into the kind of transaction that the rule governs. If parties to sales contracts, left to their own devices, would usually bargain for a rule that places the risk of loss of the goods on the seller until the buyer receives actual possession of the goods, then a legal rule that reflects that same result makes bargaining about risk of loss unnecessary in the majority of transactions. Parties who desire the result embodied in the default rule can be silent about risk of loss and still satisfy their desires, because any court will fill that contractual silence with the state-supplied risk of loss allocation. Of course, it is in the nature of a default rule that those parties in the minority—for instance, an idiosyncratic seller who wants to shift the risk of loss while the goods are still in its possession—can bargain for their preferred rule. But if the default rule reflects what a majority of parties would do, the savings in contract costs for the majority is greater than the increase in cost imposed on the atypical few, with the result that aggregate costs are reduced.[3] Permissive rules therefore do not prevent parties from maximizing their interests, unless the costs of bargaining away from the default rule become too great.

If default rules are so beneficial, why would we ever have mandatory rules that parties cannot escape? First, a permissive rule may impose costs on other commercial actors who enter into similar contracts so as to produce a net social cost. For instance, if X and Y can alter a permissive rule, a court might be called upon to decide whether they have in fact done so. The court's determination might increase contracting costs in a similar type of contract subsequently entered into by A and B, since they will want to eliminate any uncertainty about whether they have

---

[3] This assumes, of course, that the costs of altering a default rule are the same for all contracting parties. If the assumption does not hold, the contracting costs incurred by atypical parties can exceed the contracting costs of most parties under permissive rule reflecting their preferences.

retained the permissive rule to govern their contract.[4] The increased uncertainty and costs of resolving it might not be cost-justified.

Second, a permissive rule may impose costs on those who are not parties to the contract, and those costs may more than offset the benefits that the majoritarian default rule confers on contracting parties. A court's determination that a rule has been altered by contract requires the expenditures of tax revenues that may not be cost-justified and takes up judicial effort that might better be expended resolving other disputes. Third, the justification may be paternalistic. Allowing contracting parties X and Y to alter a rule might not be in their best interests, whatever their preferences and information.

Paternalistic justifications of mandatory rules are least persuasive when the contracting parties are commercially sophisticated. Article 2's mandatory rules are better justified, if at all, by negative externalities: the adverse effects that default rules impose on those who are not parties to the contract. This obviously does not mean that the presence of negative externalities is enough to justify making a rule mandatory. All contracting imposes some costs on third parties. If Smith agrees to sell her widget to Jones, Clay loses the opportunity to purchase Smith's widget. Clay's lost opportunity can be a cost to him. Smith and Jones' agreement nonetheless is enforceable because enforcing contracts yields net aggregate benefits. A mandatory rule is not justified just because a contract imposes costs on third parties that exceed the benefits realized by the contracting parties. A court or legislature must also be able to select a mandatory rule which improves on the contract by optimally reducing negative externalities.

## II. The Statute of Frauds

### A. Introduction

Even if a sales contract exists, the question arises as to whether it is enforceable. The Statute of Frauds states a formal requirement that has to be satisfied for certain contracts governed by Article 2 to be enforced. Article 2's Statute of Frauds provision is contained in § 2-201(1), and requires that certain sales contracts be evidenced by a legally sufficient writing. Section 2-201(1) provides that a contract for the sale of goods

---

[4] See Jeffrey N. Gordon, *The Mandatory Structure of Corporate Law*, 89 Colum. L. Rev. 1549, 1567 (1989); Charles J. Goetz & Robert E. Scott, *The Limits of Expanded Choice: An Analysis of the Interactions Between Express and Implied Contract Terms*, 73 Cal. L. Rev. 261 (1985).

with a price of at least $500 is enforceable against a party to the contract only if there exists a legally sufficient memorandum signed by that party.[5] The memorandum need not have been executed as part of the sales contract; it could be produced before or after the contract was concluded. And, of course, the memorandum can, but need not be, the sales contract itself. It need only exist at the time enforcement is sought against a party to the sales contract. If the sales contract falls within the scope of § 2-201(1), a legally sufficient memorandum is necessary. Otherwise, the contract is unenforceable, unless one of the exceptions in § 2-201(2) or (3) is satisfied. The Proposed Revision of § 2-201(1) would not substantially alter § 2-201(1).

A couple of points should be emphasized. One is that satisfaction of § 2-201(1) is a necessary but not sufficient condition for enforcement of a sales contract. In other words, if a sales contract falls within the scope of § 2-201(1), it is unenforceable unless evidenced by a legally sufficient memorandum or one of the exceptions in § 2-201(2) or (3) applies. But the existence of a legally sufficient memorandum does not mean that an enforceable sales contract will be found. Satisfaction of the Statute of Frauds is one thing. The existence of an enforceable agreement is another, distinct matter. On occasion courts mistakenly run together the two matters.[6] The practical implication is apparent. Satisfying Article 2's Statute of Frauds allows the case to go forward to the fact-finder. But the fact-finder still might find that there is no sales contract. The other point is a warning: Failure to satisfy the Statute of Frauds does not mean that a sales contract is unenforceable. It only means that the sales contract is unenforceable *as a contract*. Recovery remains available "off the contract," on an extra-contractual basis. For instance, even without a legally sufficient memorandum, a party can recover on a restitutionary basis the value of any benefits conveyed to the

---

[5] The UCC contains other Statute of Frauds provisions, which govern the sale of personal property other than goods (§ 1-206(1)), the lease of goods (§ 2A-201(1)), and the creation of security interests (§ 9-203(b)(3)(A)). Revised Article 1 eliminates § 1-206's Statute of Frauds requirement.

[6] For cases making the mistake, see Nelson v. Union Equity Co-operative Exchange, 548 S.W.2d 352, 354 (Tex. 1977) (Johnson, J., dissenting); Trilco Terminal v. Prebilt Corp., 400 A.2d 1237, 1238-39 (Super. Ct. 1979) (effect of § 2-201(2)'s "merchant's exception" is to bind merchant to contract he did not sign).

other party.[7]

### B. Justifying the Statute of Frauds

Evaluating and interpreting the Statute of Frauds requires us to have some idea of what the provision is trying to accomplish. This issue is more complicated than one might think, as there is considerable sentiment that the Statute of Frauds accomplishes little that is worthwhile. The Statute is not part of the sales law of most common and civil law countries, and the CISG's default rule, Article 11, eliminates it. Further, there has been considerable sentiment in favor of discarding the Statute of Frauds provision in Article 2 of the UCC. Drafts of Proposed Revisions of Article 2 varied between removing the Statute and weakening its requirements.[8] Revisions of other UCC Articles have eliminated the Statute.[9] On the other hand, UCITA contains a Statute of Frauds provision,[10] and the Proposed Revision of Article 2 would retain § 2-201's basic requirements. Given these different statutory responses, it is worth asking whether a Statute of Frauds can be justified.

We think it can. We are less moved, however, by the traditional justification, which is that the writing requirement prevents fraudulent allegations that a contract exists. For one thing, there is a virtual absence of good data about this essentially empirical issue.[11] One would like

---

[7] Compare in this respect the operation of the Statute of Frauds in the case of a security interest governed by Article 9. The counterpart of a sales contract not evidenced by a legally sufficient memorandum is a debt secured by collateral without an authenticated security agreement. Upon debtor's default, the absence of an authenticated security agreement makes the creditor's security interest unenforceable against the debtor. See § 9-203(b)(3)(A); § 9-203 Official Comment 3. The creditor still can recover from the debtor on the debt, however.

[8] Cf. PEB Study Group: Uniform Commercial Code--Article 2 50-53 (1990) (recommending elimination); Revised Article 2--Sales (November 1996) (eliminating 2-201); Revised Article 2--Sales 2-201 (May 17, 1997) (reinstating § 2-201 in weakened form); Revised Article 2--Sales 2-201 (June 7, 1997).

[9] See 8-113; Revised Article 1 (§ 1-206 eliminated).

[10] See UCITA § 201.

[11] The exceptions are a few informal and dated surveys of contracting practices; see, e.g., Comment, *The Statute of Frauds and the Business Community: A Re-Appraisal in Light of Prevailing Practices*, 66 Yale L. J. 1038

some comparative data on the rate of fraud, for example, in jurisdictions with and without Statutes of Fraud, with controls for other variables. Ideally, one might try to measure the price effect of formal requirements. The debate pro and con proceeds with assertions unsupported by any evidence.

We can imagine two other potential objectives for a writing requirement. The first is to give the parties an incentive to make sure they understand their agreement. This would be consistent with the paternalistic justification for a mandatory rule. As we have said, however, paternalistic justifications for imposing rules on sophisticated commercial actors are not very strong. Since commercial actors enter into transactions in order to achieve certainty and predictability in their business lives, they have their own incentives to reach an optimal level of precision without having an obligation to memorialize their understanding imposed on them by the state.

The second potential justification for a Statute of Frauds may be more persuasive. This justification asserts that the Statute avoids the costs that would be imposed on nonparties if agreements were not in writing. Writing requirements force contracting parties to internalize some of the costs of their contracting.[12] Even parties who agree that a contract has been made may disagree about contractual terms. When the disagreement must be resolved by litigation, the ensuing debate produces proof costs. Some of those costs are borne by the parties litigating the dispute. But the remainder of the proof costs are incurred by third parties in the form of tax revenues paid to judges and court officials, and in the form of delay to other parties who have disputes to be adjudicated. Since the contracting parties do not bear all proof costs, they contract (and litigate) without taking into account the full social costs of their behavior. A Statute of Frauds, by requiring a legally sufficient memorandum as a condition of enforceability, shifts some of the proof costs otherwise borne by third parties ex post to the contracting parties negotiating the dispute ex ante. It does so by placing on the parties the cost of producing written evidence prior to litigation as a condition of enforceability. By

---

(1957); Bradley Crawford, *Formalities of Formation (Statute of Frauds)*, cited in 1 Ontario Law Reform Commission, Report on Sale of Goods 108-9 (1979).

[12] See Alan Schwartz & Robert E. Scott, Commercial Transactions: Principles and Policies 32 (2d ed. 1981); Ian Ayres & Robert Gertner, *Filling Gaps in Incomplete Contracts: An Economic Theory of Default Rules*, 94 Yale L. J. 97 (1989).

internalizing some of the costs of contracting, the parties are more likely to weigh marginal costs and benefits to obtain an optimal amount of contracting (and litigation). At the same time, the parties reduce the costs of litigation, because the terms of a written agreement can be proven in court more readily than the terms of an oral agreement.

Of course, the Statute of Frauds does not force the contracting parties to fully internalize proof costs. The size of the proof costs internalized depends on the stringency of the writing requirement. Insisting that the contract itself be written, for instance, significantly reduces the cost of proving its terms ex post. On the other hand, § 2-201(1)'s requirements of a signature, quantity term and some indication of a contract are minimal. They have less evidentiary value than a requirement that the terms of a contract be written, and therefore externalities are produced in proving the existence and terms of a contract. But § 2-201(1)'s justification is that the size of externalities associated with proof costs is reduced: § 2-201(1) reduces proof costs ex post at little ex ante cost to the contracting parties. Considered in this light, the different Statute of Frauds provisions of the UCC require the contracting parties to internalize proof costs ex ante to different extents.[13]

Given the justification of internalization of proof cost, different sorts of empirical evidence become relevant. The rate of fraudulent allegations of a contract is unimportant because the Statute of Frauds is justified, if at all, by a reduction in externalized proof costs associated with establishing all contracts. Case law provides doubtful data about fraud rates, due to the bias in the sample of litigated disputes. The responsiveness of contracting parties to a writing requirement is an open initial question, but there is no a priori reason to believe that they behave differently here than they do toward any cost-increasing rule. The size of the marginal benefits brought by the Statute of Frauds in the form of a reduction in proof costs needs to be estimated. It is possible that § 2-201(1)'s minimal requirements for a legally sufficient memorandum yield so slight a reduction as to not be cost-justified. Our point is simply that debate on the mandatory nature of a Statute of Frauds should focus on these empirical questions.

## C. Article 2's Statute of Frauds

### 1. § 2-201's Statutory Requirements

Section 2-201(1)'s requirements are fairly minimal. Two are

---

[13] See supra note 5.

apparent from the section and a third is fairly implied.  First, the writing must be "sufficient to indicate that a contract for sale has been made."[14] Official Comment 1 to § 2-201 weakens the demand, only requiring that the writing "afford a basis for believing that the offered oral evidence rests on a real transaction."  A written purchase order, price schedule or statement about the availability of products, without more, are not enough to indicate a contract of sale has been made.  Writings may be interrelated so that, although not individually, taken together they evidence that a sales contract has been made, even if individual writings do not compel that conclusion.[15]  Electronic transmissions stored in an electronic medium and capable of being retrieved arguably are writings too.[16]  Second, the writing also must be signed by the party against whom enforcement is sought.  A "signature" includes any symbol adopted by a party with a present intention to authenticate.[17]  A letterhead, existing signature or even a statement on a videotape can count as a "signature." "Signature" is broad enough to include a personal identification code used to access e-mail, for instance.[18]

Third, § 2-201(1) arguably requires that the writing state a quantity of goods.  This is a fair implication of § 2-201(1)'s restriction that a contract is not enforceable beyond the quantity mentioned in the writing.

---

[14] A "writing" is any "intentional reduction to tangible form."  See § 1-201(46).  A videotape, tape recording, compact disc, and the like therefore all can count as "writings."

[15] See, e.g., Sea-Van Investments Associates v. Hamilton, 861 P.2d 485, 488 (Wash. 1993), Int'l Products & Technologies, Inc. v. Iomega Corp., 10 UCC Rep. Serv.2d 694 (E.D. Penn. 1989).

[16] See Sharon F. Dipaolo, *The Application of the Uniform Commercial Code Section 2-201 Statute of Frauds to Electronic Commerce*, 13 J. L. & Com. 143 (1993); Deborah L. Wilkerson, *Electronic Commerce Under the U.C.C. Section 2-201: Are Electronic Messages Enforceable?*, 41 U. Kan. L. Rev. 403 (1992); Mare E. Szafran, *A Neo-Institutional Paradigm for Contracts Formed in Cyberspace: Judgment Day for the Statute of Frauds*, 14 Cardozo Arts & Ent. L. J. 491 (1996).

[17] Cf. §§ 1-102(39), 1-201 Official Comment 39 ("sign"); Southwest Engineering Co. v. Martin Tractor Co., 473 P.2d 18 (Kan. 1970).

[18] See Douglas Robert Morrisson, *The Statute of Frauds Online: Can a Computer Sign a Contract for the Sale of Goods?*, 14 Geo. Mason U. L. Rev. 637 (1993); Wilkerson, supra note 16.

Official Comment 1 to § 2-201 supports the implication by its insistence that the writing specify a quantity. There is room for argument here, however. Section 2-201(1) does not say that the writing mention quantity. It only says that a contract is unenforceable for more than the quantity mentioned in a writing. So § 2-201(1) allows the inference that the writing need not contain a quantity term. It is just that if the writing mentions quantity, the contract is enforceable only up to the quantity mentioned. Although case law and commentary is mixed, most courts require that the writing contain a quantity term.[19] Indefinite quantity terms in writings reflecting requirements or output contracts will satisfy the requirement.[20]

The fight over whether § 2-201(1) requires a quantity term cannot be settled decisively. Because § 2-201(1) does not expressly state the requirement, opposing plausible inferences can be drawn from its language. Section 1-102(1)'s injunction to "liberally construe[]" UCC provisions to promote the its underlying policies, invoked by the court in *Bazak International Corp. v. Mast Industries, Inc.*,[21] is not enough to waive mention of quantity. It depends on the UCC's policy underlying the Statute of Frauds provision in § 2-201(1). The trouble is that the underlying policy is not enough to determine whether § 2-201(1) requires that a legally sufficient memorandum mention quantity.

Considered generally, a Statute of Frauds requires that there be some written evidence that a contract exists. The writing, in other words, serves an evidentiary purpose. How much evidentiary value a writing must have depends on the requirements set by a particular Statute of Frauds provision. Different Statute of Frauds provisions vary as to the minimum evidentiary value concerning a contract. Section 1-206, the Statute of Frauds provision governing the sale of personal property other

---

[19] See Caroline N. Bruckel, *The Weed and the Web: § 2-201's Corruption of the UCC Substantive Provisions--The Quantity Problem*, 1983 U. Ill. L. Rev. 811; James J. White & Robert S. Summers, Uniform Commercial Code 49 n.9 (4th ed. 1995) (raising doubt about requirement that quantity term be mentioned); cf. Monetti, S.P.A. v. Anchor Hocking Corp., 931 F.2d 1178 (7th Cir. 1991); Omega Engineering, Inc. v. Eastman Kodak Co., 908 F. Supp. 1084 (D. Conn. 1995) (requiring mention).

[20] See, e.g., Upsher-Smith Laboratories, Inc. v. Mylan Laboratories, Inc., 944 F. Supp. 1411 (D. Minn. 1996).

[21] 535 N.E.2d 633 (Ct. App. NY 1989).

than goods, requires mention of a price term, a "reasonable" identification of the subject matter of the sale, and a signature.[22] Failure to mention price limits enforcement of the contract to $5000. No quantity term is required. The Statute of Frauds provision governing leases of personal property, § 2A-201(1), requires that the leased goods and lease term be "described."[23] No quantity or price term is required. A Statute of Frauds provision that does not require mention of quantity means that a writing can have less evidentiary value concerning the terms of a contract. This is because the writing might indicate that a contract exists but contain nothing about the quantity term of the contract. If so, the trier of fact has to determine the quantity term, unaided by evidence provided by a writing. Hence the fight over § 2-201(1)'s treatment of quantity is really a debate over how much evidentiary value the section requires a writing to have. Because the optimal evidentiary value to be demanded depends on consideration of the array of marginal benefits and costs associated with writing requirements, recourse to the policy underlying § 2-201(1) does not help. The debate cannot be settled in the abstract.

The Proposed Revision of § 2-201(1) leaves existing requirements essentially unaltered. Its proposed changes are matters of detail. Proposed § 2-201(1) increases the minimum dollar amount necessary for contracts to fall within the Statute of Frauds from $500 to $5000.

---

[22] The buyer in Advent Systems Limited v. Unisys Corp., 925 F.2d 670 (3d Cir. 1991) probably missed an opportunity to take advantage of § 1-206. It argued that the sale of a computer software in connection with hardware was not a sale of a good governed by Article 2. The buyer also raised § 2-201(1) as a defense to the seller's enforcement of the contract. After the court found that the contract was governed by Article 2 and that § 2-201(1)'s requirements were satisfied, the jury awarded the seller $4,550,000 in damages. The buyer might better have raised the Statute of Frauds provision of § 1-206(1) as a bar to enforcement of the contract. The documents between the buyer and seller arguably did not mention price. Because § 1-206(1) limits enforcement to $5000 "in amount or value of remedy" when writings do not mention price, the seller's recoverable damages would be comparatively modest if § 1-206(1) applied.

[23] See § 2A-201(1); cf. 2A-201 Changes, § 9-203(b)(3)(A) (authenticated security agreement must contain a "description of the collateral").

Although the amounts differ in early-1950s constant dollars,[24] when Article 2 began to be adopted, it is not clear that the change would bring many more contracts under the Proposed Revision than were initially brought by § 2-201.

Proposed § 2-201(1) also expressly requires mention of a quantity term. Omitting or misstating a term does not render a writing "insufficient...other than a quantity term." The most significant change in detail concerns the form in which a memorandum may appear. A legally sufficient memorandum need not be a writing; the information can be stored in an electronic medium. Proposed § 2-201(1) adopts the now-predominant principle of medium neutrality: agreements and signatures will not be denied legal effect solely because they appear in electronic form. It does this by requiring an "authenticated record." Proposed § 2-103(1)(o) defines a "record" to include a writing as well as information "...that is stored in an electronic or other medium and is retrievable in perceivable form." "Authenticate" is defined by Proposed § 2-103(1)(a) to include a signature as well as an act "to attach to or logically associate with a record an electronic sound, symbol, or process, with the intent to sign the record." (Corresponding changes have been made in Revised Article 1 and Article 9, and are adopted in UCITA.) Thus, memoranda in email, computer disk, or tape recorded form easily can constitute authenticated records.

This change reaches a result already required by federal law. Under the Electronic Signatures in Global and National Commerce Act ("E-Sign"), transactions in interstate or foreign commerce involving signatures or contracts cannot be denied effect solely because they are in electronic form.[25] In other words, E-Sign generally demands that state and other law be medium-neutral. E-Sign's exceptions to this requirement do not apply to § 1-206, Article 2 and Article 2A.[26] Thus, E-Sign preempts § 2-201(1)'s non-media neutral writing requirement, for instance. However, E-Sign restricts its own preemptive effect by allowing state or other law to "modify, limit or supersede" the requirement of medium-neutrality. The restriction operates when that law basically itself

---

[24] For instance, according to the consumer price index, goods purchased in 2001 for $5000 would cost $750 in 1953 dollars. See Federal Reserve Bank of Minneapolis <http://woodrow.mpls.frb.fed.us/economy/calc/cpihome.html>.

[25] See 15 U.S.C. § 7001(a)(1), (2).

[26] See 15 U.S.C. § 7003(a)(3).

requires medium-neutrality and makes specific reference to E-Sign.[27] Proposed § 2-201(1)'s demand for an authenticated record satisfies medium-neutrality. And Proposed § 2-108(4) expressly "modifies, limits and supercedes" E-Sign, except with respect to consumers. Thus, E-Sign does not apply to Article 2 transactions; Proposed § 2-201(1)'s authenticated record requirement continues to control. But it controls only because it mimics E-Sign's demand for medium-neutrality

## 2. Exceptions to the Statute of Frauds

Section 2-201 contains exceptions to § 2-201(1)'s Statute of Frauds requirements. The exceptions work to allow enforcement of a contract which falls within the scope of § 2-201(1) and does not satisfy its requirements. Some difficult spots in the exceptions are worth noting. They turn on the evidentiary value demanded by § 2-201(1)'s Statute of Frauds requirement.

Section 2-201(3)(a), for instance, makes an exception for contracts for the manufacture of specially manufactured goods unsuitable for sale to others, where the seller has substantially begun manufacturing. Section 2-201(3)(b)'s exception allows enforcement for goods accepted and paid or accepted and received. Both sections take particular sorts of nonwritten evidence (manufacture, acceptance and payment) as indicating a contract. The nonwritten evidence is a substitute for the written evidence of a contract demanded by § 2-201(1). Two questions are raised by the opaque statutory language in the exceptions. First, how much evidentiary value must a writing have under § 2-201(1)? Second, how much evidentiary value must the exceptions to § 2-201(1) have?

Section 2-201(2) states what is sometimes called the "merchant's exception" to § 2-201(1). The subsection allows enforcement of a contract, even when § 2-201(1) is not satisfied, if (1) a written confirmation of a contract is received, (2) the confirmation is enforceable against the sender under § 2-201(1), (3) the recipient does not make written objection to the confirmation within 10 days of receiving it, and (4) both the sender and recipient are merchants. The merchant status of parties under § 2-201(2), discussed in Chapter 2, is not transparent. Condition (1), which calls for receipt of a written confirmation, requires distinguishing confirmations from offers or preliminary negotiations.[28]

---

[27] See 15 U.S.C. § 7002(a)(2)(A), (B).

[28] See Arcuri v. Weiss, 184 A.2d 24 (Pa. 1962); Alice v. Robert Manufacturing Co., Inc., 328 F. Supp. 1377 (N.D. Ga 1970).

Condition (2)'s requirement is open to dispute, reflected in the case law. Section § 2-201(2) calls for a written confirmation "sufficient against the sender... [which] satisfies the requirements of subsection (1)." The confirmation therefore must be a legally sufficient memorandum under § 2-201(1). So it must also be "sufficient to indicate that a contract for sale has been made." The question is what "sufficiency" amounts to. In everything but name, the question asks how much evidentiary value § 2-201(1) insists a writing have.

The majority and dissent in *Bazak International Corp. v. Mast Industries, Inc.*[29] divide over the matter. With the aid of Official Comment 1 to § 2-201, *Bazak*'s majority reads "sufficiency" in § 2-201(1) to require only that the writing provide "a basis for believing" that a contract exists. "A basis" for belief can mean that the writing provide merely some evidence for a contract. The buyer in *Bazak* sent the seller purchase order forms, described as "offers," with an annotation to the effect that it was presented by the buyer's agent. For the majority this was enough written evidence of an agreement.[30] If the working standard of evidentiary value is the majority's, we agree. A written offer annotated as presented, we suppose, increases the probability of there being a contract over its prior probability. The dissent reads "sufficiency" in § 2-201(1) to require a higher evidentiary standard. It requires that the writing makes it more probable than not that a contract exists.[31] The buyer's purchase orders, described as "offers," even with the annotations, do not make it more likely than not that the buyer and seller had reached agreement. For the dissent, the written evidence is not "sufficient" to indicate a contract. If the dissent's working standard of "sufficiency" governs, we agree. Our point is that the majority and dissent in *Bazak* disagree over the evidentiary value § 2-201(1) requires a writing to have.

Evidentiary value also determines the scope of condition (3), that the recipient of a confirmatory memorandum not have made written objection to its contents. The narrow statutory question goes to the sort of objection required. For example, suppose a buyer sends its seller a signed memorandum which says: "This is to confirm our agreement that

[29] 535 N.E.2d 633 (N.Y. 1989).

[30] Id. at 634; cf. id. at 639-40 (Alexander, J., dissenting); GPL Treatment, Ltd. v. Louisiana Pacific Corp., 914 P.2d 682 (Or. 1996).

[31] Id. at 641.

you sell me 10 widgets, delivery at your place of business." The seller's written response states: "I object to your memorandum; our agreement called for me to sell you 5 widgets." In a recognizable sense, the seller's response obviously is an objection to the contents of the buyer's confirmation. The question is whether it counts as an objection for purposes of § 2-201(2). Two standards are possible. One is "blanket objection," and requires that the response deny that an agreement exists. The second is "term objection," and requires denial that a term in the confirmation accurately reflects the agreement. The choice between standards turns on the evidentiary value required by § 2-201(1). Section 2-201(1), among other things, demands that the writing evidence an agreement. The writing need not state the material terms of the agreement, much less state them accurately. (A trier of fact may even find that no agreement exists.) Given this miminal requirement, a "blanket objection" seems appropriate. Objecting to the contents of a confirmation is the counterpart of a writing which insufficiently indicates an agreement. A "term objection" implicitly admits an agreement but merely denies that the confirmation accurately reflects its terms. The standard therefore requires more of the confirmation (accuracy) than is required of a writing satisfying § 2-201(1). In other words, it requires that the confirmation have a higher evidentiary value than a legally sufficient memorandum. This argues for a "blanket objection" being the proper standard under § 2-201(2). The little case law on the subject agrees.[32] On the standard of "blanket objection," the seller's response would not count as an objection to the contents of the buyer's written confirmation.

"Blanket objection" leaves some difficult possibilities. Suppose the seller's written response had read "I object to your memorandum; we didn't have an agreement on 10 widgets." The response does not deny the existence of an agreement but only a quantity term in that agreement. However, unlike the initial hypothetical, no quantity is conceded by the seller. Section 2-201(1) serves as a substitute for satisfaction of § 2-201(1)'s requirements. Accordingly, failure to object to the contents of a confirmation satisfying § 2-201(1) must provide as reliable evidence of a contract as the items in § 2-201(1) provide. Without more, objection to a quantity term without supplying a substitute quantity gives less reliable information about a contract than is provided by the items in § 2-201(1). But there may be more. There are a couple of competing

---

[32] See *Simmons Oil Corp. v. Bulk Sales Corp.*, 498 F. Supp. 457 (D.N.J. 1980).

inferences here. One inference is that objection to a quantity term with no substitute term is the counterpart of a writing without a quantity term. The two suggested quantity terms cancel each other out, as it were. If a quantity term is required in a legally sufficient memorandum, "blanket objection" would treat the case as an objection to the contents of the confirmation. Another inference is that an objection with no substitute quantity term renders the quantity term in the confirmation indefinite. If so, the objection would concede an agreement as to some number of widgets. Courts allowing parol evidence to prove an intended quantity[33] would consider the buyer's confirmation to be a legally sufficient memorandum notwithstanding the indefinite quantity term. The seller's objection in this case would not amount to an objection to the contents of the buyer's confirmation. Thus, the "blanket objection" standard does not itself decide between the inferences.

Section 2-201(3)(b)'s exception for in-court admissions also raises a problem of the evidentiary value of nonwritten evidence. The section allows enforcement of a contract without satisfaction of § 2-201(1) "if the party against whom enforcement is sought admits in his pleading, testimony or otherwise in court that a contract for sale was made." An initial difficulty is to know when the exception even applies. That is, does (3)(b) provide a right to compel an admission from a defendant in a judicial proceeding such as a deposition or trial, or does it simply state the consequence of the defendant making an admission? The question presents a dilemma of sorts. If (3)(b) gives a right to compel an admission, then plaintiff go forward in the hope of obtaining an admission from the defendant at some point in a trial before the case goes to the jury. In that case (3)(b) undermines the purpose the Statute of Frauds: to reduce proof costs associated with enforcing an agreement by making contracts unenforceable when accompanied by only oral testimony. Granting plaintiff a right to compel an admission reintroduces the proof costs the Statute of Frauds is designed to eliminate. Alternatively, if (3)(b) only states the consequence of an in-court admission, the exception is effectively useless. This is because the defendant simply can raise the Statute of Frauds as a defense and be entitled to judgment in its favor, on the pleadings or by summary judgment. Subsection (3)(b) would have a use only in the infrequent case of an inadvertent admission in pleading, pretrial discovery or the like. So

---

[33] See, e.g., Fishermen's Marketing Ass'n v. New England Fish Co., 548 P.2d 348 (Wash. 1976); Hankins v. American Pacific Sales Corp., 499 P.2d 214 (Wash. 1972).

the dilemma is that (3)(b) either undermines the Statute of Fraud's purpose or almost never applies. Subsection (3)(b) is silent on the matter, but Official Comment 7 and pre-UCC pleading practice support reading § 2-201(3)(b) to only state the consequences of an in-court admission.[34] An admission in court probably refers to the relatively infrequent occurrence of an admission in a collateral proceeding (e.g., a contract admitted in defending against a tort claim). Absent an admission, a sworn denial of a contract, accompanied by evidentiary materials and the affirmative defense of the Statute of Frauds, ends the case.[35]

The other difficulty concerns what constitutes an admission under § 2-201(3)(b). The evidentiary value of a statement again is in play. To see this, consider the following five statements made in the course of a judicial proceeding.

1. "I offered to buy the widget."[36]

2. "I deny that there was a contract, but I agreed to buy 10 widgets, delivery at my place of business."[37]

3. "I admit that there was a contract, but we didn't agree on how many widgets I was to buy."

4. "I admit that we came to an agreement."[38]

5. "I said 'I agree to buy 10 widgets,' but I meant 'I agree to buy 10 widgets if we come to agrement on credit terms.'"[39]

---

[34] See § 2-201 Official Comment 7 ("Under this section it is no longer possible to admit the contract in court and still treat the Statute as a defense"); cf. Uniform Sales Act § 4 (no equivalent to exception based on in-court admissions); Robert S. Stevens, *Ethics and the Statute of Frauds*, 37 Cornell L. Q. 355, 374 (1952) (majority position that admission in answer does not prevent raising Statute of Frauds as a defense).

[35] See DF Activities Corp. v. Brown, 851 F.2d 920 (7th Cir. 1988).

[36] See Dairyland Financial Corp. v. Federal Intermediate Credit Bank of St. Paul, 852 F.2d 242 (7th Cir. 1988).

[37] Cf. Cargill, Inc., Commodity Marketing Division v. Hale, 537 S.W.2d 667 (Mo. 1976).

[38] Cf. Radix Organization v. Mack Trucks, 602 F.2d 45 (2d Cir. 1979).

[39] Cf. Lewis v. Hughes, 346 A.2d 231 (Md. 1975).

If § 2-201(3)(b) serves as a substitute for § 2-201(1), it must provide information having at least the same evidentiary value as is provided by a writing containing the items required by § 2-201(1). This suggests an easy comparison: A statement is an admission for purposes of § 2-201(3)(b) if it provides as much information about a contract as would be provided by a signed legally sufficient memorandum. The statements above can be quickly assessed using this test.[40]

Statement 1 concedes only that there an offer was made, not that a contract was concluded. It therefore gives less information than is given by a writing sufficient to indicate that a contract was made, as required by § 2-201(1). Therefore, statement 1 does not contain an admission for purposes of § 2-201(3)(b). Statement 2 contains a denial along with a concession of enough facts to indicate that a contract was made. Put it this way: If the facts conceded were in a writing, the writing would be deemed sufficient to indicate the existence of a contract. So statement 2 contains an admission. Statements 3 and 4, because lacking mention of quantity, contains less information than is contained in a writing satisfying § 2-201(1). Neither amounts to an admission. Statement 5 makes a statement which reasonable listeners could interpret as indicating agreement to buy a quantity of widgets. The speaker's undisclosed condition (agreement on credit terms) does not affect the reasonable meaning of his utterance. The utterance, as reasonably interpreted, provides as much information about a contract as is provided by a legally sufficient memorandum. Therefore, statement 5 is an admission. The Proposed Revision of § 2-201(3) does not clarify what counts as an admission.[41]

### 3. Ethics and the Statute of Frauds

A final question focuses on professional ethics and the propriety of invoking the Statute of Frauds. Good morals and prudence suggest that lying to the opposing party or counsel about the existence of a contract is wrong. The rules of legal ethics do too. Rule 3.1 of the ABA Model

---

[40] See, e.g., Harper Plastics, Inc. v. Amoco Chemicals Corp., 29 UCC Rep. Serv. 985 (7th Cir. 1980); Litzenberg v. Litzenberg, 514 A.2d 476 (Md. 1986).

[41] An earlier draft of Proposed § 2-201's "admission" exception treated as an admission statements of "facts from which an agreement may be found." Revision of Uniform Commercial Code: Article 2–Sales (March 1, 1999) § 2-201(3)(c). UCITA's admission exception considers statements of "facts sufficient to indicate a contract" an admission. See UCITA § 201(c)(2).

Rules of Professional Conduct prohibits a lawyer from asserting a frivolous defense.[42] Rule 4.1 prohibits a lawyer from knowingly making a false statement of material fact to a third party.[43] Both rules make it improper for a lawyer to deny in pleadings or elsewhere that a contract exists when she knows that one exists. Since the denial goes to the contract and does not concern formal requirements for its enforcement, the prohibition on lying does not touch the lawyer's use of the Statute of Frauds.

There are three circumstances in which professional propriety and the Statute of Frauds are implicated. None presents a difficult question of professional responsibility. One circumstance is where the client denies that a sales contract exists and good judgment calls for invoking § 2-201(1). Raising § 2-201(1) as an affirmative defense here does not violate Rules 3.1 and 4.1. Rule 3.1 is not violated because the absence of a legally sufficient memorandum is a perfectly good defense to enforcement of a contract. Section 2-201(1) states a formal requirement of enforcement, and the defense is that the requirement isn't satisfied. The defense clearly is not frivolous. Rule 4.1 also is not breached because raising § 2-201(1) as a defense is not making a "false statement of material fact." This is because the Statute of Frauds again states only a formal requirement for enforcement. Invoking it as a defense to enforcement therefore at most amounts to a representation ("statement") that the contract at issue does not satisfy the Statute of Frauds. The defense therefore does not amount to a "false statement" (unless, of course, the contract satisfies the Statute).[44]

A second circumstance is where the client admits to her lawyer that a sales contract exists. Again, no problem of professional responsibility is presented. If the client is willing to admit in pleadings or pretrial discovery that an agreement exists, § 2-201(3)(b) treats the admission as

---

[42] ABA Model Rules of Professional Conduct Rule 3.1 (1983); cf. ABA Model Code of Professional Responsibility DR 7-102(A)(2) (1969).

[43] Model Rules Rule 4.1(a); cf. ABA Model Code of Professional Responsibility DR 7-102(A)(5).

[44] In this respect the Statute of Frauds is similar to a statute of limitation as a defense. Both raise a barrier to enforcement of an underlying claim. Neither defense works by denying the underlying claim itself. For a discussion of the professional propriety of raising the statute of limitations as a defense, see David Luban, Lawyers and Justice: An Ethical Study 9-10, 47-48 (1988).

an exception to § 2-201(1).[45]   Invoking § 2-201(1) as a defense to enforcement therefore would be useless and good judgment would not recommend it.  The third circumstance is the hardest.  Here the client admits to her lawyer that a sales contract exists but says that she will deny its existence in pretrial discovery and elsewhere.  Good judgment, however, suggests that raising § 2-201(1) would end the case.  Although the hardest of the circumstances, it does not present a difficult problem of professional responsibility.  The circumstance presents a question about the professional responsibility of a lawyer in the course of representation to disclose their client's lies.  It is answered fairly easily. Rule 3.3 of the ABA Model Rules of Professional Conduct requires that the lawyer who knows of a "fraudulent act by the client" to disclose it to the court when material.[46]  The client's denial of a contract is a lie, a material, "fraudulent act."  (The point at which the client's denial becomes a lie is another matter.)  Disclosure to the court therefore is required.  Alternatively, when the lawyer "reasonably believes" that the client's statement is a lie, she may refuse to offer it as evidence.[47]  Either way, the problem of professional responsiblity raised has nothing to do with the propriety of using the Statute of Frauds as a defense.  It concerns the lawyer's obligations or rights when she knows or reasonably believes that her client has lied about the existence of a contract.

### D.  The CISG and the Statute of Frauds

The CISG eliminates formal writing requirements for enforceability, including the Statute of Frauds.  At the same time it allows signatory nations to make a reservation which imposes formal writing requirements. Article 11 eliminates the requirements: "A contract of sale need not be concluded in or evidenced by writing and is not subject to any other requirement as to form."  The Article's scope is broad.  It not

---

[45] See § 2-201(3)(b).   .

[46] Model Rules, Rule 3.3(a)(2).  Model Rule 1.6(a) prohibits a lawyer from revealing confidential information related to representation of the client, but makes an exception for information covered by Rule 3.3.  See Model Rule Rule 1.6(a), (b).  The Model Rules require the lawyer to take remedial action to rectify fraud if he has offered material evidence resting on it; see Model Rules Rule 3.3(a)(4).  For a succinct discussion of a lawyer's obligations in the face of client perjury, see George Rutherglen, *Dilemmas and Disclosures: A Comment on Client Perjury*, 19 Amer. J. Crim. L. 267 (1992).

[47] See Model Rules Rule 3.3(c).

only makes a contract enforceable when not evidenced by a legally sufficient memorandum. Article 11 also removes requirements of some domestic law, such as the Chinese foreign contract law,[48] that a contract be concluded in writing. The CISG recognizes writing requirements imposed via trade usage. Article 9(2), for instance, provides that "[t]he parties are considered, unless otherwise agreed, to have impliedly made" trade usage applicable to their contract.[49] But, absent trade usage which demands documentation, a contract is enforceable without a writing. The CISG's elimination of written formalities is in line with the domestic law of most civil and common law countries.

Both the Oregon Court of Appeals and Oregon Supreme Court in *GPL Treatment v. Louisiana-Pacific Corp.*[50] miss the point. GPL Treatment consisted of three Canadian corporations with places of business in Canada and Louisiana-Pacific was a United States corporation whose place of business was in the United States. In defending against the plaintiffs' allegation that the defendant breached a contract with them concluded in May 1992, Louisiana-Pacific raised § 2-201(1) as a defense to enforcement. GPL Treatment countered with § 2-201(2)'s "merchant's exception." Both the Court of Appeals and Supreme Court saw this as a question of whether the document received by the defendant from the plaintiffs constituted a confirmation, and the majority and dissents in both courts divide over the answer. Once the CISG's applicability to the underlying sales contract is noticed, the case is easy. Article 100(2) of the CISG provides that it governs contracts concluded on or after the CISG enters into force in a signatory nation. The CISG entered into force in the United States on January 1, 1988 and in Canada on January 5, 1992. Since the contract in dispute in *GPL Treatment* was concluded in May, 1992, the CISG applies under Article 1(1)(a) because the GPL Treatment and Louisiana-Pacific have places of business in Canada and the United States, different Contracting States. Under Article 11 of the CISG, to be enforceable, a contract need not satisfy the Statute of Frauds. Hence the "merchant's exception" in § 2-

---

[48] See Rui Mu & Wang Guiguo, *Chinese Foreign Economic Law*, Foreign Trade Laws & Foreign Economic Contract Law 14-17 (R. Mu & W. Guiguo eds., 1992).

[49] Cf. Oberster Gerichtshof (Austria), February 6, 1996,1 UNILEX D.1996-3.1 (M. J. Bonell ed.) (Austrian seller's defense of unenforceability based on lack of writing rejected; trade usage did not require writing)..

[50] 894 P.2d 470 (Or. Ct. App. 1995), *aff'd* 914 P.2d 682 (Or. 1996).

201(2) also is not needed. Clearly the contract in dispute is enforceable under the CISG.[51]

Other provisions complicate but do not alter the CISG's treatment of formal writing requirements. One complication is Article 4(a), which says that the CISG is not concerned with "the validity of the contract..." Suppose domestic law provides that a contract is "invalid" when not evidenced by a writing, and defines "invalidity" to mean that the contract is unforceable. Is a contract not evidenced by a writing nonetheless enforceable? On the one hand, the CISG allows enforcement because Article 11 eliminates writing requirements. On the other hand, domestic law prevents enforcement because a writing requirement is considered by it to be a matter of validity. The problem, of course, is created by two different possible descriptions of the issue raised by a transaction: an issue of "validity," which the CISG leaves to domestic law, or an issue of formal writing requirements, which the CISG addresses.

The better view is that the contract is enforceable, even if domestic law describes formal writing requirements as presenting issues of "validity." The principle of issue-displacement, discussed in Chapter 2, justifies the result. According to the principle, if the CISG defines an issue and addresses it under the CISG by creating contractual entitlements, domestic law addressing the same issue is displaced, however domestic law describes the issue. If the CISG either does not define an issue and addresses it or leaves its resolution to domestic law, domestic law is not displaced. Applying the principle here, Article 11 of the CISG defines the identifies an issue--is a contract enforceable without a writing?--and addresses it by saying that a writing is not needed. A contract need not satisfy any "requirement as to form," according to Article 11, to be concluded. Domestic law therefore is displaced even if domestic law describes a writing requirement as a matter of "validity."[52]

---

[51] The trial court excluded the plaintiffs' invocation of the CISG because tardily raised. The dissent in the Court of Appeals noticed the CISG's potential applicability, but would have had the appellate court consider whether the trial court abused its discretion in refusing to consider the CISG. See GPL Treatment, 894 P.2d at 477 n.4 (Leeson, J., dissenting). We take no position on the application of Oregon abuse of discretion standard to the facts in the case.

[52] Honnold suggests that Article 11 "probably" does not displace domestic law on matters of validity where domestic law imposes special formal requirements on an entity, such as a government agency. See John O. Honnold, Uniform Law for International Sales Under the 1980 United Nations Convention

Another complication results from the ability of Contracting States to opt-out of Article 11. Article 12 allows a Contracting State to make a reservation to Article 11 under Article 96. Article 96 in turn provides that "[a] Contracting State whose legislation requires contracts of sale to be concluded in or evidenced by writing may make a declaration in accordance with Article 12 that any provision of Article 11... does not apply where any party has his place of business in that State." The effect of the reservation, according to Article 12, is that Article 11 "does not apply where any party has his place of business in a Contracting State...." The consequence of a Contracting State making a reservation is open to slight debate. Does the reservation have the effect of making the reserving State's domestic law writing requirements applicable to the contract? If so, the reserving State's domestic law on the matter supplements the CISG provisions. Or does the reservation simply eliminate Article 11 of the CISG, leaving it to the forum's conflict of laws principles to select the appropriate domestic law? If so, the reserving State's domestic law concerning writing requirements might not be selected.

The question is illustrated by the following example. Suppose a Mexican buyer and an Argentinian seller orally agree to a sale of widgets. The agreement is negotiated in Argentina; delivery of the widgets is to be made by the seller in Mexico City. Later, when the buyer repudiates the agreement and the seller sues, the buyer raises the lack of a writing as a defense. Is the defense good? Since Argentina and Mexico are Contracting States and the sale is otherwise governed by the CISG, the CISG applies to the contract under Article 1(1)(a). Argentina, however, has made a reservation to Article 11 in accordance with Article 96. The reservation states that "any provision of Art. 11... that allows a contract of sale... or any offer, acceptance or other indication of intention to be made in any form other than in writing does not apply where any party

---

on Contracts for the International of Goods 135-37 (3d. 1999). The principle of issue-displacement rejects the suggestion, and Honnold does not justify it. If a government agency's contract is governed by CISG and Article 11 applies, domestic law which insists on formal writing requirements is displaced. There is no room in the principle to qualify it according to the type of entity regulated by domestic law, and Honnold does not describe an alternative principle.

had his place of business in the Argentine Republic."[53]  Mexico has not made a reservation to Article 11 under Article 96.  If the effect of Argentina's Article 96 reservation is to have its domestic law governing writing requirements apply, the seller's suit will be unsuccessful.  The agreement is unenforceable because not concluded in writing.  If the effect of the Article 96 reservation is only to eliminate Article 11, then Article 11 "does not apply."  The forum's conflict of laws rules would then select the domestic law governing the issue of writing requirements. Since the agreement was negotiated in Argentina but to be performed in Mexico, conflicts principles probably could select either the domestic law of either Argentina or Mexico.  If Mexican law is selected, the agreement could be enforceable.  If the law of Argentina is selected, then, again, it is unenforceable.

Text and good sense favor giving Article 96 the more limited effect. The terms of both Article 96 and 12 say that Article 11 "does not apply" when a Contracting State has made an Article 96 reservation.  Neither Article goes further to say that the *reserving State's* domestic law concerning writing requirements applies when the reservation has been made.  The slight diplomatic history suggesting this understanding by some participants at the 1980 Vienna Conference not only concerns an earlier version of Article 96.[54]  Article 12 and 96s' language also does not support this understanding.  Further, there is a serious problem with applying the reserving State's law: sometimes the directive is indeterminate in outcome.  This is so where two States make Article 96 reservations and their domestic law differs as to formal written requirements.  Which States' domestic law governs the contract?  There is no difficulty under the interpretation of Article 96 which limits its effect to simply eliminating Article 11 from the CISG.  The forum's conflicts principles will select the law of one of the reserving States (or

---

[53] See 1 UNILEX B.2 (M.J. Bonell ed.) (Reservations and Declarations). Belarus, Chile, China, Estonia, Hungary, Lithuania, the Russian Federation, and the Ukraine also have made Article 96 reservations.

[54] See Seventh Meeting, Diplomatic Conference, A/CONF.97/C.1/SR.8, Documentary History of the Uniform Law of International Sales 492 (J. Honnold ed., 1989) [hereinafter "Diplomatic History"] (statement of Austrian representative concerning understanding of Article (X), Article 96's predecessor; statement of United Kingdom representative pointing out "difficulty" under Article (X) of Contracting State being bound by the reserving State's domestic law on formal requirements); Larry DiMatteo, *CISG and the Presumption of Enforceability*, 22 Yale J. Int'l L. 111 (1997).

possibly the law of a third country). No answer can be given under the interpretation which applies the domestic law of the reserving State. Most commentators and cases on the subject adopt the more limited, sensible interpretation of the effect of an Article 96 reservation.[55]

## III. The Parol Evidence Rule

### A. Article 2's Parol Evidence Rule: § 2-202 Outlined

The parol evidence rule states a formal requirement for the admissibility of evidence. It is a different restriction than is imposed by the Statute of Frauds. The Statute of Frauds asks the question: Can a party enforce a contract, given that it falls within § 2-201(1)? The parol evidence rule asks a separate question: Assuming that a party can enforce a contract, what evidence is admissible to prove its terms? The rule limits the evidence that can be used to prove a contract's terms, not whether the contract is enforceable in the first place. A convincing justification of the parol evidence rule, if there is one, is administrability. The rule allows contracting parties in advance to know how their contract will be interpreted by restricting the sort of evidence that can be used to interpret it should litigation occur. And increased confidence about the judicial administration of a contract, in turn, reduces the costs of taking contractual precautions ex ante against determinations of a contract's terms ex post.[56]

---

[55] See Joseph Lookofsky, Understanding the CISG in the USA 25 (1995); Peter Schlechtriem, Commentary on the UN Convention on the International Sale of Goods (CISG) 91-92 (2d ed. 1998); Jerzi Rajski, *Article 96*, Convention on International Sales Law 659 (C.M. Bianca & M.J. Bonell eds. 1987); Metropolitan Court of Budapest (Hungary), March 24, 1992, 1 UNILEX D.1992-8 (M.J. Bonell ed.) (court applies German domestic law to contract between Hungarian buyer and German seller; Hungary has made an Article 96 reservation); cf. Quilmes Combustibles v. Vigan S.A., Jazgado Nacional de Primera Instancia en lo Comercial No. 18 (Argentina), October 20, 1989, 1 UNILEX D.1989-5.1 (M. J. Bonell ed.) (dicta to the effect that forum selection clause naming Belgium not contrary to Argentina's public policy requiring international contracts to be made in writing). For a dissenting view, see Honnold, supra note 52, at 139-40.

[56] A few jurisprudentially minded writers say that the parol evidence rule is "philosophically indefensible" or rests on the questionable assumption that the meaning of the terms in an integration require no interpretation. See Sanford Levinson, *Law as Literature*, 60 Texas L. Rev. 373, 377 n.18 (1982) ("philosophically indefensible"); Stanley Fish, Doing What Comes Naturally 511 (1989); Stanley Fish, *The Law Wishes to Have a Formal Existence*, The Fate of

Article 2 deviates from the common law understanding of the parol evidence rule. The common law rule makes inadmissible evidence of prior or contemporaneous agreements to contradict a writing intended to be a final expression of the parties' agreement. Evidence of prior or contemporaneous agreements of terms consistent with the writing is admissible, however, unless the writing is also intended to be the complete expression of the parties' agreement. The evidence made inadmissible by the rule is not limited to oral (parol) evidence and can include prior written agreements. Application of the rule turns on the purpose for which the evidence is attempted to be introduced. If evidence is not being introduced to contradict or add to the terms of a writing, the parol evidence rule does not bar it. Evidence aimed at establishing fraud, lack of consideration, or mistake therefore is not affected by the rule. Also, evidence is admissible when directed at establishing that a writing is not a final or complete expression of the parties' agreement. In general evidence bearing on the interpretation of the terms of a writing is admissible too, even if the writing is considered the complete expression of the parties' agreement. And, of course, the rule does not bar evidence of subsequent agreements, such as modifications, and waivers of contractual rights.

Section 2-202, Article 2's parol evidence rule, is more complicated. The provision is in places difficult to understand, and considerable litigation focuses on its interpretation. Section 2-202's basic outlines are clear. Terms in an integrated writing ("a final expression of their agreement") "may not be contradicted by evidence of any prior agreement or of a contemporaneous oral agreement."[57] Since the bar on evidence operates only if the writing is integrated, any evidence, including prior or contemporaneous written agreements, can be used to show that the writing is not integrated. Evidence of inconsistent terms in such agreements therefore is admissible to show that the writing was not intended as an final expression of the parties' agreement. If the writing is integrated, however, evidence contradicting the terms of the integration

---

the Law 141, 147 (A. Sarat & T. Kearns eds. 1991) (meaning must be self-evident and not involve interpretation). The charge is mistaken. The rule only operates to restrict the evidence used to interpret an agreement. It makes no general assumptions about language, including an assumption that meaning can be determined without interpretation. In fact, § 1-205(3) has trade usage give meaning to the terms of the agreement. The terms of the integration therefore must be interpreted in light of it.

[57] § 2-202.

is inadmissible. If the writing is completely (totally) integrated, evidence of consistent terms based on prior or contemporaneous agreements is inadmissible too. Section § 2-202 puts it obliquely: the terms of the integration "may be explained or supplemented... (b) by evidence of consistent additional terms unless the court finds the writing to have been intended also as a complete and exclusive statement of the terms of the agreement."

Evidence about trade usage, course of performance and course of dealing is handled differently. Section 2-202 allows the terms of an integrated agreement to be "explained or supplemented... by course of dealing or usage of trade... or by course of performance." There is no restriction on their admissibility when the writing is completely integrated, as there is for "consistent additional terms" in § 2-202(b). Trade usage and the like therefore is treated under § 2-202(a) differently from "consistent additional terms" under § 2-202(b).[58] The easy inference from this is that trade usage and the like is admissible to "explain or supplement" the terms of even a completely integrated writing. It is excluded only when inconsistent with the terms of an integration or the terms of the integration excludes it. The standard for exclusion by the terms of the integration is high according to Official Comment 2 to § 2-202, requiring a "careful negation" of trade usage and the like.

## B. Excluding Trade Usage

### 1. Two Standards of Contradiction

An important difficulty comes in determining when trade usage and the like contradicts a term in the integration. Two different standards of

---

[58] The same conclusion can be reached by a short chain of UCC definitions. "Terms" is defined as "that portion of an agreement" relating to a particular matter. See § 1-201(42). "Agreement," in turn, is defined as the parties' bargain, as found by circumstances including trade usage, course of performance, and course of dealing. So "terms" includes trade usage and the like. Section 2-202(b) excludes evidence of "consistent additional terms" when a writing is completely integrated. Since § 2-202(a) does not contain a similar restriction in the case of trade usage and the like, the "terms" referred to in § 2-202(b) cannot include the "terms" mentioned in § 2-202(a)--trade usage and the like. Trade usage and the like therefore are admissible even when the agreement is completely integrated.

contradiction are possible.[59] Under the first standard, a contradiction is an inconsistency, so trade usage contradicts a term when it is inconsistent with the term.[60] This broad and obvious standard works well with the express terms in a contract (as opposed to implied terms such as trade usage) . For example, if a quantity term in an integration calls for 50 tons, and a prior agreement called for 40 tons, the quantity terms are inconsistent. Similarly, if a completely integrated option contract gives an option to purchase to be exercised at a given price, evidence conditioning its exercise on the seller receiving an offer from a third party is inconsistent with the option. Many courts have been unwilling to apply a broad standard of contradiction to implied terms such as trade usage. They instead adopt a second, narrow standard. According to it, inconsistency occurs only when trade usage "totally negates" a term in the integration.[61] The *Nanakuli Paving & Rock Co. v. Shell Oil Co.*[62] court, for instance, found trade usage guaranteeing price protection for a period consistent with the price term "posted price at time of delivery." A term calling for "500 tons" of steel was held by the *Michael Schiavone & Sons, Inc. v. Securalloy Co., Inc.*[63] court to be consistent with trade usage allowing for delivery of "up to 500 tons." In each case trade usage did not totally negate the term, but only qualified it, and therefore was

---

[59] Some courts use a "reasonable harmony" test to assess consistency. The test unhelpfully finds a contradiction when a term is not in "reasonable harmony" with a term in the integration. As applied, the "reasonable harmony" test sometimes mimics the narrow standard (e.g., Snyder v. Herbert Greenbaum & Assoc., Inc., 380 A.2d 618 (1977) or the broad standard (e.g., ARD, Inc. v. E-Systems, 663 F.2d 189 (D.C. Cir. 1980)).

[60] See, e.g., Seessel Holdings, Inc. v. Flearing Companies, Inc., 1996 WESTLAW 735277 (W.D. Tenn. 1996); Vogel v. W.A. Sandvi, Inc., 898 F. Supp. 254 (D. Ver. 1995); Island Creek Corel Co. v. Lake Shore, Inc., 636 F. Supp. 285 (W.D. Va. 1986); Trailways Finance & Acceptance Corp. v. Euro-Flo Tours, Inc., 572 F. Supp. 1227 (D.N.J. 1983); Alaskan Northern Development, Inc. v. Alyeska Pipeline Service Co., 666 P.2d 33 (Alaska 1983).

[61] See, e.g., Wayman v. Amoco Oil Co., 923 F. Supp. 1322 (D. Kan. 1996), Tigg Corp. v. Dow Corning Corp., 822 F.2d 358 (3d Cir. 1987); Nanakuli Paving & Rock Co. v. Shell Oil Co., 664 F.2d 772 (9th Cir. 1981); Michael Schiavone & Sons, Inc. v. Securalloy Co., Inc., 312 F. Supp. 801 (D. Conn. 1970).

[62] 664 F.2d 772 (9th Cir. 1981).

[63] 312 F. Supp. 801 (D. Conn. 1970).

consistent with it. Presumably only trade usage allowing indefinite price protection in *Nanakuli* and no tonnage to be delivered in *Michael Schiavone* would contradict a term in the respective integrations.

The narrow standard of contradiction has some support in the UCC. Section 2-202, again, says that the terms of an integration may not contradicted but can be "explained or supplemented" by trade usage and the like. Section 1-205(3), in turn, provides that trade usage and its ilk "give particular meaning to and supplement or qualify term of an agreement." And § 2-105(4) says that the express terms of an agreement and trade usage and the like must be construed "wherever reasonable" as consistent with each other.[64] Because trade usage gives meaning to express terms, it is often "reasonable" to construe the two as consistent. For example, a reasonable way to interpret a quantity term "500 tons" is to read it, in light of trade usage allowing for varying tonnage, as "500 tons or an amount up to 500 tons." In fact, since trade usage gives meaning to express terms, it is almost always possible to find a reading of a term which is "reasonably consistent" with trade usage. A consistent reading is unreasonable only when trade usage, for instance, allows delivery of no tonnage. In other words, inconsistency occurs only when trade usage totally negates an express term.

The different standards of contradiction are at work in *Columbia Nitrogen Corp. v. Royster Co.*[65] and *Southern Concrete Services, Inc. v. Mableton Contractors, Inc.*.[66] The *Columbia Nitrogen* court allowed evidence of trade usage concerning adjustments in orders of fertilizer components to supplement an express term calling for delivery of 31,000 tons of phosphate. As supplemented, the quantity term was found to be an estimate. In doing so, the *Columbia Nitrogen* court held that trade usage is displaced only by language in the contract specifically negating the particular usage in question.[67] By assuming that the relevant trade usage does not contradict the plain meaning of the quantity term "31,000 tons," the court implicitly adopts the narrow standard of contradiction. A broad standard of contradiction is adopted by the court in *Southern Concrete*. There the court found trade usage allowing for significantly

---

[64] Cf. § 1-205(4).

[65] 451 F.2d 3 (4th Cir. 1971).

[66] 407 F. Supp. 581 (N.D. Ga. 1975).

[67] 451 F.2d at 583.

varying quantities of concrete ordered to be inconsistent with a quantity term calling for delivery of "about 70,000 cubic yards" of concrete. It was enough for the court that trade usage contradicts the terms of a "clear and explicit" contract. For the *Southern Concrete* court, the plain meaning of terms is enough to exclude trade usage; an explicit exclusion is unnecessary.

The narrow standard of contradiction is the better standard, although we admit that the case is a close one.[68] To begin, observe that the ability of parties to opt-out of trade usage and the like is not at stake. Both the narrow and broad standards allow it. If the parties' integration provides, for instance, that "trade usage does not explain or supplement the terms of our agreement," evidence of trade usage is inadmissible because it would clearly contradict a term of the integration. The difference in standards concerns the cost of opting-out of trade usage. The narrow standard requires exclusion of trade usage, either generically or by *Columbia Nitrogen*'s enhanced requirement that specific trade usages be excluded by mention. The broad standard requires only the use of terms whose plain meaning is inconsistent with trade usage. Because the narrow standard requires mention of trade usage in addition to express terms while the narrow standard only requires express terms, the costs of opting-out of trade usage under it are higher than under the broad standard. For example, assume that under a contract calling for "blue widgets," trade usage allows delivery of either blue or red widgets. Assume also that the buyer wants only blue widgets. Can the seller comply with the contract by delivering red widgets? Under the broad standard of contradiction, red widgets do not conform to the contract description. Under the narrow standard, they conform to the contract.

The benefit of the narrow standard is that it forces idiosyncratic parties to send very clear signals that they are opting-out of trade usage. By requiring mention that trade usage is being excluded, the risk of judicial error in interpreting agreements is reduced. This reduction in error increases the value of more typical parties' contracts because the risk to them of having a court wrongly find that they have opted out of trade usage is reduced. Of course, the narrow standard comes at a cost. Idiosyncratic parties are (wrongly) saddled with contract terms they did not bargain for—in our example, the buyer's obligation to take delivery of red widgets when it specified "blue widgets." The broad standard of contradition sets costs in the opposite direction. By not requiring that

---

[68] For an opposing view, see Goetz & Scott, supra note 4, at 311-12, 314.

trade usage be expressly excluded, idiosyncratic parties need not send as clear a signal that they are opting-out of trade usage. They thereby are saved the costs of doing so. However, the risk of judicial error in interpreting more typical parties' contracts is increased. Those parties now have to indicate that they prefer to have trade usage continue to govern their contracts.

Trade usage presumably reflects the preferences of most contracting parties in a particular industry. If so, it forms the background against which most parties prefer to have their expressions interpreted. By interpreting express terms against this background, the narrow standard imposes on idiosyncratic parties the cost of excluding trade usage from their contracts. The majority of parties, whose preferences reflect trade usage, are saved the cost of providing that it is applicable to their contracts. Since the narrow standard reflects the preferences of most contracting parties, and assuming that the costs of contracting in and out of trade usage are the same, the narrow standard of contradiction reduces aggregate contracting costs. On balance, then, it is the better standard of contradiction.

## 2. The Process of Exclusion

A final question concerns what it takes to exclude trade usage and the like. Official Comment 2 to § 2-202 requires that trade usage must be "carefully negated" to be displaced. The court in *Columbia Nitrogen* reads this to demand that trade usage and the like be excluded by a specific reference to the particular usage being excluded.[69] A provision in a merger clause such as "trade usage shall not be used to explain or supplement this agreement" apparently is insufficient. The *Columbia Nitrogen* court requires that specific reference to the trade usage being excluded be made.

The above case for the narrow standard suggests that this stringent requirement is unjustified. By excluding trade usage, parties are signaling their idiosyncratic preferences. They are indicating a preference that a trier of fact not use typical norms of contracting to set the terms of their agreement. In doing so they incur a contracting cost, imposed on them by the narrow standard of contradiction. A more specific reference to particular trade usages imposes additional contracting costs on the parties with no offsetting benefits. For the generic exclusion of trade usage is enough to signal that the contracting

---

[69] See 451 F.2d at 10.

parties' preferences are not those of most contracting parties, so there's little risk that trade usage will not be applied to contracts between parties with typical preferences. As for benefits to the contracting parties in the form of increased accuracy in the determination of the terms of their contract, the exclusion of trade usage indicates that increased accuracy isn't cost-justified for them. In excluding trade usage, the parties think that the risk that a trier of fact will misconstrue the terms of their contract is worth it. Hence a better view of "careful negation" requires only that trade usage and its ilk be excluded by generic reference.

### C. Warranties and the Parol Evidence Rule

The interaction between the parol evidence rule and the law of warranties is worth noticing. The parol evidence rule only controls the evidence that can be used to prove the terms of a contract. It filters evidence, as it were. A warranty is an express or implied term of an agreement. As a term, a warranty assigns the risk of nonconformity in the goods to the seller. It concerns the underlying obligations of the parties, not the evidence used to prove them. Since warranties and the parol evidence rule involve different matters--evidence versus an obligation--strictly there is no conflict between the two. However, the parol evidence rule can operate to affect the content of a seller's warranties. This is because what evidence is admissible to prove a warranty obviously can determine whether a trier of fact finds that a warranty was made. When this occurs, there is a tension, as lawyers like to put it, between the policies underlying warranty law and the parol evidence rule. A justification of the parol evidence rule is needed.

To see the tension between warranty law and the parol evidence rule, consider the following three stylized hypotheticals:

(1) The buyer purchases a widget from her seller, a merchant. The written sales contract, signed by the buyer, recites in prominent type: "Seller makes no implied warranties of any sort, including but not limited to a warranty of merchantibility, concerning the widget. This agreement is a final and exclusive expression of Seller and Buyers' agreement."[70] If the widget does not work as well as ordinary widgets, and the buyer sues, the case is easy. The seller has effectively disclaimed an implied warranty of merchantibility as to the widget under § 2-316(2). Since the

---

[70] Cf. Apollo Group, Inc. v. Avnet, Inc., 26 UCC Rep. Serv.2d 1099 (9th Cir. 1995); Duquesne Light Co. v. Westinghouse Electric Corp., 66 F.3d 604 (3d Cir. 1995); Earman Oil Co., Inc. v. Burroughs Corp., 625 F.2d 1292 (5th Cir. 1980).

writing probably is completely integrated, evidence of the existence of an implied warranty of merchantability as to the widgets is inadmissible as well. So no tension exists here between warranty law and the parol evidence rule.

(2) The same facts as in the first hypothetical, except that the relevant portion of the written agreement simply reads: "This agreement is the final and exclusive expression of Seller and Buyers' agreement."[71] Now the seller has made an implied warranty of merchantibility under § 2-314, which has not been effectively disclaimed under § 2-316(2) or (3). Since the writing still could be found to be completely integrated, the parol evidence rule excludes evidence that the implied warranty exists. Section 2-314, however, allocates the risk to the seller that the widget is unfit for ordinary purposes to which it is put. There is a tension between warranty law and the parol evidence rule.

(3) During the course of negotiations with the buyer, the seller says "this widget will work for the ordinary purposes to which it is put." The sales contract contains the same clause as in the first hypothetical.[72] The seller's statement creates an express warranty under § 2-313(1) because it is an affirmation of fact or promise relating to the widget and forming the basis of the bargain. As an express warranty, it cannot be disclaimed under § 2-316(1), but the ineffectiveness of the disclaimer under § 2-316 is made "subject to the provisions of this Article on parol or extrinsic evidence (2-202)."[73] Without this qualification in § 2-316(1), the seller's express warranty continues to be effective. However, because the writing is completely integrated, the parol evidence rule bars evidence bearing on the express warranty. Again, there is a tension between warranty law and the parol evidence rule.

There are ways of reducing, without eliminating, the tension. A court could find that a merger clause is effective to create a complete integration only when it contains the canonical language of disclaimer required by § 2-316(2) or (3). Although the statutory basis for doing so

---

[71] Cf. Credit Alliance Corp. v. Cornelius & Rush Co., Inc., 508 F. Supp. 63 (N.D. Ala. 1980).

[72] Cf. Webster v. Sensormatic Electronic Corp., 389 S.E.2d 15 (Ga. 1989); Jaskey Finance & Leasing v. Display Data Corp., 564 F. Supp. 160 (E.D. Pa. 1985).

[73] § 2-316(1).

is weak,[74] it would make warranty law and the parol evidence rule consistent. In hypothetical (2), for instance, because the writing would be deemed at most partially integrated, evidence would be admissible to show that the implied warranty was not disclaimed. A court also could ignore § 2-316(1)'s qualification and find that an attempt to disclaim express warranties renders writings unintegrated.[75] If so, evidence that an express warranty had been made by the seller in hypothetical (3) always would be admissible. These findings, although possible, are ad hoc. Their only purpose is to recognize warranties at the expense of the parol evidence rule. Not every attempted disclaimer of an express warranty or disclaimers of implied warranties violating § 2-316(2) or (3) indicates that the parties did not intend writings to be the complete expression of their agreement. And not every such attempt renders an otherwise effective integration unenforceable. Sometimes the parol evidence rule conflicts with warranty law.

How the conflict is handled depends in part on whether the parol evidence rule is justified. An noted above, the parol evidence rule allows the parties to better administer their contracting by allowing them certainty in the sorts of evidence admissible to prove its terms. There are malign and benign reasons why parties might exclude evidence concerning a warranty or its disclaimer by executing a completely integrated writing. The malign reason is the result of asymmetric information: one party knows the details and legal consequences of the writing while the other party remains ignorant. By obtaining the ignorant party's (the buyer's) assent to the integration excluding warranties, the knowing party (the seller) gains an unpaid-for advantage. The seller shifts the risk of a nonconformity to the buyer without compensating her.

The benign reason is that "agency costs" (the losses suffered by principals when their agents misbehave) or vagueness in the legal standard for warranties or their disclaimer can justify reliance on a completely integrated writing. Sellers sometimes cannot easily control

---

[74] A finding of unconscionability, based on § 2-302, sometimes might be possible. See, e.g, Adams v. American Cyanamid Co., 498 N.W.2d 577 (D. Neb. 1992); Seibel v. Layne & Bowler, Inc., 641 P.2d 668 (Or. Ct. App. 1982). There is no guarantee that the finding always will be supportable by evidence.

[75] See, e.g., L. S. Heath & Son, Inc. v. AT & T Information Serv., Inc., 9 F.3d 561 (7th Cir. 1993); Beatco, Inc. v. Cessna Aircraft Co., 32 F.3d 1126 (7th Cir. 1994); Sierra Diesel Injection Service v. Burroughs, Inc., 890 F.2d 108, 113 (9th Cir. 1989).

the representations their employees make to buyers that create express warranties. In addition, the legal standards for warranties are themselves sometimes uncertain. For instance, the distinction between "affirmations of fact" which create express warranties and "commendations" which do not often is a fine one, as is what does and does not form the basis of the parties' bargain.[76] The parties can reduce some of the seller's agency costs and avoid the consequences of legal vagueness, at a price, by agreeing in advance on the sorts of evidence that will be admissible to prove their contract's terms. The seller purchases from the buyer the exclusion of evidence bearing on warranties not contained in the integration. The buyer in turn bears the risk of forgoing use of evidence concerning warranties in exchange for a price reduction or other more favorable terms of sale. We suspect, but obviously cannot prove, that the benign reason dominates with commercially sophisticated parties. Our claim is modest: Given that courts are not good at making ad hoc determinations as to which sort of reason operates, a good case can be made for giving effect to the parol evidence rule when it conflicts with warranty law.

## D. The CISG and the Parol Evidence Rule

### 1. Is the Parol Evidence Rule Displaced?

The CISG does not explicitly deal with the evidence that is admissible to prove the terms of a contract. Not surprisingly, its relevant provisions therefore can be read either as rejecting the parol evidence rule or allowing the rule's continued operation under applicable domestic law. Article 11 states that a contract "may be proved by any means, including witnesses."[77] Article 8(3) provides that "[i]n determining the intent of a party...due consideration is to be given to all relevant circumstances of the case including the negotations, any practices which

---

[76] See § 2-313(1)(a), (2).

[77] We recognize that, strictly, Articles 11 and 8(3) deal with different matters. Article 11 concerns the enforceability of a contract, not its terms, while Article 8(3) is expansive enough to include the terms of a contract. However, the diplomatic history of Articles 8 and 11 suggests that the CISG does not recognize the nice distinction. The history shows that the second sentence of Article 11 first appeared as a separate subsection in a precursor of Article 8. See, e.g., U.N. Doc. A/CN.9/128 para. 155, reprinted in Diplomatic History, supra note 54, at 287. Proposals to introduce a species of parol evidence rule also focused on Article 11, so the distinction between a contract and its terms apparently was not taken too seriously.

the parties have established between themselves, usages..."[78] And Article 7(2) requires that where the CISG does not "expressly settle" a matter governed by it, the matter is settled by the CISG's "underlying principles" or, if none are applicable, by applicable domestic law.[79] The three Articles allow the inference that a fact finder can use parol evidence to ascertain the terms of a contract governed by the CISG. If so, the CISG displaces the operation of the parol evidence rule under domestic law. But Articles 7(2), 8(3) and 11 also support the opposite inference. Article 7(2) allows the continued application of the parol evidence rule because none of the CISG's provisions "expressly settle" the question of admissible evidence going to the terms of a contract. Article 8(3) can be read as consistent with the parol evidence rule, by allowing parol evidence ("all relevant circumstances...") to be used to determine whether a writing is integrated. This includes testimony given by witnesses, also allowed by Article 11. If the parties intend a writing as the final expression of their agreement, the exclusion of evidence of prior or contemporaneous agreement is consistent with both Articles. The CISG therefore does not displace the parol evidence rule governed by domestic law.

As is often true of the CISG, pertinent diplomatic history is inconclusive. Supporting the continued operation of the parol evidence rule is the deletion of a predecessor to Article 8(3). A 1977 draft of Article 8(3) included the phrase, "...and any applicable legal rules for contracts of sale."[80] The draft was rejected, in part because the subsection was thought "unnecessary."[81] Although unexplained, one reason why the draft could be thought "unnecessary" was that the CISG's provisions did not upset applicable rules of domestic law, including the parol evidence rule. Later pieces of diplomatic history, however, support the CISG's rejection of the parol evidence rule. The Australian

---

[78] Article 8(3).

[79] See Article 7(2) ("Questions concerning matters governed by the Convention which are not expressly settled in it are to be settled in conformity with the general principles on which it is based or, in the absence of such principles, in conformity with the law applicable by virtue of rules of private international law.").

[80] See U.N. Doc. A/CN.9/128 para. 155, reprinted in Diplomatic History, supra note 54, at 287.

[81] Id. para. 166, reprinted in Diplomatic History, supra note 54, at 288.

representative commented at the Vienna Diplomatic Conference that a immediate predecessor to Article 8(3) required that the parol evidence rule be "amended" in the case of contracts governed by the CISG.[82] And a Canadian proposal to incorporate in Article 11 a version of the parol evidence rule was rejected by the Austrian representative because it denied to the judge "the free appreciation of evidence."[83] These actions suggest that the version of the CISG adopted at the Diplomatic Conference rejects the parol evidence rule. The trouble, of course, is that the diplomatic history is unclear because none of the CISG's provisions expressly address the question.

Here the principle of issue-displacement which we have used before by itself is not very helpful. Recall that the principle says that where the CISG defines and addresses an issue, domestic law governing the issue is displaced; otherwise, domestic law continues to govern it. The CISG does not expressly specify the evidence admissible to prove the terms of a contract. Article 8(3), for instance, only requires that "due consideration" be given to various sorts of evidence of contractual intent. It does not say whether "due consideration" allows or prohibits the introduction of prior or contemporaneous negotiations or agreements. So it is unclear whether the principle of issue-displacement in fact displaces the parol evidence rule or not. A case against and in favor of displacement can be made.

The case against displacement relies on Articles 8(3) and 7(2).[84] Article 8(3), again, requires that contractual intent be determined by giving "due consideration" to prior negotiations, course of dealing, trade usage and the like. Since Article 8(3) does not specify how such evidence is to be "considered," rules withholding some evidence from the fact finder are consistent with it. The parol evidence rule, for instance, implements Article 8(3) by allowing all of this evidence in determining whether a writing is integrated. It excludes prior or contemporaneous

---

[82] See U.N. Doc. A/CONF.97/C.1/SR.6 para. 51, reprinted in Diplomatic History, supra note 54, at 483.

[83] See id. paras. 82, 83, reprinted in Diplomatic History, supra note 54, at 491.

[84] See, e.g., David H. Moore, *The Parol Evidence Rule and the United Nations Convention on Contracts for the International Sale of Goods: Justifying Beijing Metals & Minerals Import/Export Corp. v. American Business Center, Inc.,* 1995 B. Y. U. L. Rev. 1347.

negotations or agreements when inconsistent with the terms of the integration and entirely when the integration is complete. The parol evidence rule also is consistent with Article 7(2). Article 7(2), again, requires that matters not expressly settled by the CISG be settled by its underlying "general principles" or, if none are applicable, by applicable domestic law. Since the CISG does not "expressly settle" precisely how evidence of contractual intent is to be considered, applicable domestic law governing the matter can do so. In this way the CISG does not displace the parol evidence rule.

The case for displacement understands the same Articles of the CISG differently. Article 8(3) requires that contractual intent be determined by giving "due consideration" to all relevant evidence, including prior or contemporaneous negotations or agreements. To withhold some evidence from a fact finder when the court determines the writing to be integrated, as the parol evidence does, does not give "due consideration" to the excluded evidence. By being excluded, the evidence gets no consideration. Article 8(3) therefore does not allow the continued operation of domestic law rules which restrict evidence of contractual intent. It displaces the parol evidence rule. Since Article 8(3) "expressly settles" the question of what evidence is admissible to determine a contract's terms--all evidence--Article 7(2) does not come into play. As we have indicated, we think the case for displacement is the stronger position, principally because it does not require reading Article 8(3) in a Pickwickian fashion to say that "no consideration" is "due consideration." For all that, we should note that the question is relatively unimportant to the CISG's implementation. This is because in most legal systems the judge is the fact-finder, and with a single fact finder the parol evidence rule is useless. Anglo-American legal systems retaining the rule are a distinct minority.

Most courts addressing the matter conclude that the CISG displaces the parol evidence rule.[85]  *MCC-Marble Ceramic Center, Inc. v.*

---

[85] See Filanto, S.P.A. v. Chilewich International Corp., 789 F. Supp. 1229, 1238 n.7 (S.D.N.Y. 1992); Claudia v. Olivieri Footwear Ltd., 1998 Lexis 4586 (S.D.N.Y. 1998); MCC-Marble Ceramic Center, Inc. v. Ceramica Nuovo D'Agostino S.P.A., 144 F.2d 1384 (11th Cir. 1998); Mitchell Aircraft Spares, Inc. v. European Aircraft Service AB, 23 F. Supp.2d 915 (N.D. Il. 1998); but cf. Beijing Metals Minerals Import/Export Corp. v. American Business Center, Inc., 993 F.2d 1178 (5th Cir. 1993).

*Ceramica Nuova D'Agostino*[86] is the leading case taking this position. The Italian seller and the American buyer in that case reached an oral agreement on particular terms. The buyer, who did not speak Italian, executed the agreement on one of the seller's standard forms. The form, printed in Italian, contained terms that were not part of the oral agreement. In the buyer's breach of contract action against the seller, the seller relied on terms in the form. The buyer argued that the terms were not part of the parties' agreement. In support the buyer sought to introduce an affidavit stating that the buyer had no subjective intent to be bound by the terms in the seller's form and that the seller was aware of its intent. The court held that the parol evidence rule did not apply to contracts governed by the CISG. It admitted the affidavit as evidence showing that the parties' did not intend to include the terms in the seller's form as part of their agreement. The court based the CISG's displacement of the parol evidence rule on articles 11 and 8(3).[87] Article 11 is irrelevant. It only allows a contract to be concluded and enforceable without a writing. The parol evidence rule restricts evidence to prove the terms of a contract, not the formation or enforceability of the contract itself. Thus, strictly article 11 has no effect on the parol evidence rule. Only article 8(3)'s directive to consider prior negotiations and the like in determining the parties' intent supports the court.

The *MCC-Marble* court did not need to decide whether the CISG displaces the parol evidence rule. It could have reached the same result it reached even if the rule applies. This is because the parol evidence rule only operates to bar evidence when the court has found a writing to be integrated. The rule does not bar evidence introduced for the purpose of showing that the writing was not a final expression of the parties' agreement. For this purpose, evidence is not being introduced to establish terms not present in the integration. Rather, the purpose is to show that the writing is not integrated. A court must receive extrinsic evidence when introduced for this purpose. The buyer in *MCC-Marble* was claiming that the seller's standard form did not reflect the parties' final agreement. According to the buyer, the operative agreement was oral. The affidavit of the buyer's president stating his intent not to be bound by the seller's form he signed was offered to support the claim. Because the affidavit goes to the integrated status of the seller's form, the

---

[86] 144 F.3d 1384 (11th Cir. 1998).

[87] See id. at 1389.

parol evidence rule does not bar its introduction.[88] The *MCC-Marble* court left to the jury the question whether the form was the final expression of the parties' agreement. It could have done the same even had it applied the parol evidence rule.[89]

## 2. Contracting for the Parol Evidence Rule

A remaining question concerns the ability of parties to opt-in to a parol evidence rule under the CISG. Assuming that the CISG displaces the rule, can parties contract around the CISG to manufacture their own parol evidence rule? One way to do so, of course, is to opt-out of the CISG entirely, as Article 6 allows. Once parties have done so, the forum's conflicts principles might select a law which contains a parol evidence rule. But suppose the parties do not want to opt-out of the CISG entirely. Can they manufacture their own parol evidence rule while having the CISG continue to govern their contract? We are not sure. Initially it seems as if the CISG poses no barrier to the parties doing so. Article 6 allows the parties to derogate from any of the CISG's provisions, except for a few provisions irrelevant for present purposes. Because Article 8(3) permits contractual intent to be determined by the full range of evidence, the parties might exclude Article 8(3)'s application to their contract. For instance, they might include a merger clause, perhaps mimicking Article 8(3)'s language (e.g., "This writing reflects the entire agreement of the parties, and in determining its terms no consideration is to be given to negotiations, any practices which the parties have established among themselves, or usages"). The clause

---

[88] The buyer's counsel apparently failed to make clear this argument. The court notes that the buyer "makes much" of the buyer's president's inability to understand Italian. See id. at 1387  n.9. Apparently the buyer argued on the basis of the affidavit that it was not bound by a writing it signed in a language its representative could not read. Although the *MCC-Marble* court rejected this argument as "astounding," the buyer's real argument is different. It is that a writing in a language the seller knows the buyer's representative is unable to read, preceded by an oral agreement (by translation), is not a final expression of the parties' agreement. In short, the buyer's position is that it not bound by the seller's form it signed because the form is not the contract. The buyer was introducing the affidavit to prove this fact. The parol evidence rule does not prevent introduction of extrinsic evidence for this purpose.

[89] Compare Mitchell Aircraft Spares, Inc. v. European Aircraft Service AB, 23 F. Supp.2d 915 (N.D. Il. 1998), in which the court acknowledged that the CISG displaces the parol evidence rule while finding that the rule, even if applicable, admits parol evidence when the contract is ambiguous.

seemingly would prevent prior or contemporaneous negotiations from being used to determine the terms of the parties' contract. But such a clause might present an issue of validity. If so, Article 4(a) leaves the issue to domestic law, and some domestic law might not give effect to the parties' merger clause. Domestic law, together with the CISG, could prevent parties from opting-in to the parol evidence rule.

## IV.  Unconscionability

### A.  Under the UCC

Another formal requirement is that the sales contract not be unconscionable under § 2-302. Unconscionability functions as a barrier to enforcement. Courts have traditionally refused to enforce agreements which are the product of duress, fraud or other irregularities. Sometimes a contract's terms appear to a court to be unreasonable or reflect objectionable features of the circumstances in which agreement was reached. Although not described as unconscionable, nonenforcement traditionally has been justified by artful interpretation of contract terms or findings of duress or fraud. Section 2-302 avoids these judicial dodges. It allows a court to find that the agreement is unconscionable even when fraud or duress is not involved. Under § 2-302, court can refuse to enforce part or all of the agreement, as well as limiting the effect of agreement. Considered abstractly, the values of both autonomy and party welfare support unconscionability as a ground for nonenforcement. If an agreement is the product of irregularities, for instance, it probably does not reflect the genuine consent of the contracting parties. The autonomy of a party is unlikely to be exercised in the circumstances. Irregularities also mean that the agreement is unlikely to maximize the welfare of the contracting parties. Two difficult questions are raised by § 2-302: (1) what is its working standard of unconscionability? and (2) given a working standard of unconscionability, are courts competent to apply it? The first question is conceptual; the second is largely normative.

### 1.  § 2-302's Standard of Unconscionability

Section 2-302 does not define a standard of unconscionability.[90] It instead simply gives a court the power to withhold enforcement when a contract or contract term is found to be unconscionable.  Official

---

[90] For statements of doubt about the possibility of defining unconscionability, see White & Summers, supra note 18, at 137; Melvin A. Eisenberg, *The Bargain Principle and its Limits*, 95 Harv. L. Rev. 741, 754 (1982).

Comment 1 to § 2-302 helps slightly by describing the underlying principle as one of the "prevention of oppression and unfair surprise...and not of disturbance of allocation of risks because of superior bargaining power." "Unfair surprise" suggests defects in the bargaining process focused on the limited information available to a party. It connotes a procedural defect in bargaining to a deal. "Oppression" suggests that the terms of the deal struck are unreasonable or one-sided or otherwise unfair. A defect in the substance of the bargain is suggested. According to Official Comment 1, procedural and substantive defects are independent of disparities in the bargaining positions of the parties. Strictly, Official Comment 1's implicit standard of procedural unconscionability is unworkable. All contract terms reflect the bargaining power of the parties, as measured by the comparative cost to the parties of altering them. Because terms allocate risks between the parties, the allocation also is the product of disparities in bargaining power. Hence refusing to enforce a contract or contract term disturbs risk allocations resulting from superior bargaining power. A finding of unconscionability therefore must do so too. Courts generally ignore this part of Official Comment 1 and allow gross disparities in bargaining power to test for procedural unconscionability.

The law of unconscionability is fairly easily stated. Justifying it and its applications in particular cases is more difficult. Unconscionability, according to most courts, contains both procedural and substantive elements. A contract or contract term is unconscionable only if it is both procedurally and substantively unconscionable.[91] Procedural unconscionability consists in some flaw in the formation of the contract. The commonly listed menu of flaws include the absence of "meaningful choice" in entering into the contract, the absence of meaningful negotiation of contract terms, and gross disparities in bargaining power between the parties.[92] Also included are incapacities of contracting parties, such as limited information about the nature of the contract or an

---

[91] See, e.g., Brower v. Gateway 2000, Inc., 676 N.Y.S.2d 569 (N.Y. App. Div. 1998); Adams v. American Cynamid Co., 498 N.W.2d 577 (Neb. App. 1992); cf. A & M Produce Co. v. FMC Corp., 186 Cal. Rep. 114 (Cal. App. 1982); Williams v. Walker-Thomas Furniture Co., 350 F.2d 445 (D.C. Cir. 1965); Arthur Leff, *Unconscionability and the Code--The Emperor's New Clause*, 115 U. Penn. L. Rev. 485 (1967).

[92] See, e.g., Kerr-McGee Corp. v. Northern Utilities, Inc., 673 F.2d 323 (10th Cir. 1982); Hahn v. Ford Motor Co., Inc., 434 N.E.2d 943 (Ind. 1982); Frank's Maintenance & Engineering, Inc. v. C.A. Roberts Co., 408 N.E.2d (Ill. 1980).

inability to accurately assess risks associated with its terms.[93] Substantive unconscionability occurs when the outcome of a bargain is so one-sided as to be unfair. A price term, cancellation option, limitation on remedies and exclusion of recoverable damages have been found to be substantively unconscionable. Several courts have invoked a mathematical metaphor, holding that the more substantively unconscionable a term, the less procedural unconscionability is necessary to refuse enforcement.[94] Although more often invoked in consumer contracts, the doctrine has been applied to contracts between commercially sophisticated parties.

Unconscionability doctrine is difficult to apply. This is so for at least three reasons. First, and obviously, the standards of procedural and substantive unconscionability are vague. For instance, the distinction between a gross inequality of bargaining power, which is a procedural flaw, and mere bargaining inequality, which is not, is hard to draw. The same is true of a term which unfairly favors one party, a substantive flaw, and one which does not do so. Second, application of the doctrine depends on information to which courts have limited access. For example, information about market structure or parties' cognitive capabilities is inaccessible by courts in all but the easiest cases. It is therefore unsurprising that the run of cases often have an air of arbitrariness about them. Third, the doctrine's application turns on the wrong sort of factors. Case law illustrates the second and third problems.

### 2. Unconscionability Applied

Unconscionability doctrine principally has been applied to three sorts of contract terms: price terms, termination clauses, and warranty disclaimers, remedy limitations and damage exclusions. Consider just price unconscionability and warranty disclaimers, remedy limitations and damage exclusions, respectively. Price unconscionability requires a finding of substantive unconscionabitly: that the contract price is excessively high. An indication of an excessive price is that it is higher than the price charged for comparable goods. In other words, price

---

[93] See Eisenberg, supra note 83, at 763-773 (summarizing and justifying the principle of transactional incapacity supported by case law).

[94] See Stanley A. Klopp, Inc. v. John Deere Co., 510 F. Supp. 807 (E.D. Pa. 1981); Tacoma Boatbuilding Co. v. Delta Fishing Co., Inc., 28 UCC Rep. Serv. 26 (W.D. Wash. 1980); Richard Craswell, *Property Rules and Liability Rules in Unconscionability and Related Doctrines*, 60 U. Chi. L. Rev. 1, 16 (1992).

dispersion in a product market is evidence of price unconscionability. So, for example, in *Jones v. Star Credit Corp.*,[95] a refrigerator sold to a welfare recipient in a   door-to-door sale for $900 was found to be unconscionable when its retail price was $300. And in *Ahern v. Knecht*[96] a $762 service bill was deemed unconscionable when the same service was performed by another outfit for $72. These might appear to be easy cases, and they might in fact be so. But, if the cases are easy, they are easy because courts assume that the products being sold in different markets are homogeneous. In *Jones*, the assumption is being made that the refrigerator sold in a door-to-door sale has no nonprice benefits not shared by the same refrigerator sold retail, such as product information provided by the salesman, convenient in-home shopping or a favorable return policy. When products are sold under different sorts of contracts, product homogeneity is difficult to determine. In these cases price dispersion is a bad proxy for price unconscionability.[97] Whether it is generally a bad proxy depends on whether courts are competent at determining product homogeneity in the full range of cases. We doubt they are.

Warranty disclaimers, remedy limitations and damage exclusions can present issues of both substantive and procedural unconscionability. There is an initial statutory question about the applicability of unconscionability doctrine to warranty disclaimers. In particular, the question is whether § 2-302 limits the operation of disclaimers otherwise effective under § 2-316(2) and (3). Section 2-316(2) and (3) provide that warranties of merchantability and fitness for a particular purpose may be disclaimed by the use of the appropriate language of disclaimer.[98] The section does not include a requirement that the disclaimer be conscionable. Section 2-719(3), which governs the effectiveness of damage exclusions, by its terms requires that the exclusion not be

---

[95] 298 N.Y.S.2d 264 (N.Y. 1969).

[96] 563 N.E.2d 787 (Il. App. Ct. 1990).

[97] Cf. California Grocers Ass'n v. Bank of America, 22 Cal. App.4th 205 (Cal. App. 1994); Beasley v. Wells Fargo Bank, 235 Cal. App.3d 1383 (Cal. App. 1990) (refusing to apply unconscionability doctrine to bank service fees; courts not competent to regulate price); Alan Schwartz, *Unconscionability and Imperfect Information: A Research Agenda*, 19 Can. Bus. L. J. 437, 439-440 (1991).

[98] See Chapter 8.

unconscionable. Courts have drawn opposing inferences from the combination of these sections. Some courts find that there is no requirement that a warranty disclaimer be conscionable.[99] They do so by noticing the mention of unconscionability in § 2-719(3) and its omission in § 2-316(2) and (3). The inference from the omission is that § 2-302 does not apply to otherwise effective warranty disclaimers. Most courts require that an otherwise effective warranty disclaimer be conscionable.[100] They justify the requirement by noticing that § 2-302, by its terms, applies to "any clause of the contract."[101] The inference is that § 2-302 therefore applies even to warranty disclaimers satisfying § 2-316(2) or (3). The mention of unconscionability in § 2-719(3) is treated as surplusage. These courts also could have noted Comment 1 to § 2-302, which gives as illustrations of unconscionable terms some warranty disclaimers.[102] The majority view probably has the better inference, although § 2-719(3)'s mention of unconscionability is mildly embarrassing. Unconscionability doctrine most likely applies to warranty disclaimers, remedy limitations and damage exclusions.

The frequent treatment of damage exclusion clauses shows the difficulty of judicial vetting a contract for substantive unconscionability. A clause often present in a sales contract excludes the seller's liability for incidental expenses and consequential damages resulting from a breach of warranty. The sales contract also often contains a remedy limitation clause, restricting buyer's remedies in the event of a breach of warranty to a refund of the purchase price or repair or replacement of the goods. Section 2-719(3) gives effect to the damage exclusion clauses unless they are unconscionable. In cases where the buyer's damages are predominantly consequential damages, a number of courts have found a damage exclusion clause to be substantively unconscionable. The finding is based on characterising the clause as "one-sided" because it leaves the

---

[99] See, e.g., Reibold v. Simon Aerials, Inc., 859 F. Supp. 193 (E.D. Va. 1994).

[100] See, e.g., U.S. Roofing, Inc. v. Credit Alliance Corp., 14 UCC Rep. Serv.2d 746 (Cal. App. 1991); Lecates v. Hertrich Pontiac Buick, 515 A.2d 163 (Del. Super. Ct. 1986); Hanson v. Funk Seeds International, 373 N.W.2d 30 (S.D. 1985); Martin v. Joseph Harris Co., 767 F.2d 296 (6th Cir. 1985), A & M Produce Co. v. FMC Corp., 135 Cal. App.3d 473 (1982).

[101] § 2-302(1).

[102] § 2-302 Official Comment 1.

buyer without any significant remedy for the seller's breach.[103]

The characterization is questionable for two reasons. First, the characterization confuses ex post with ex ante assessments of the contract. Ex post, of course, the buyer is left without a significant remedy against the seller. But the buyer is compensated ex ante to bear the relevant risk. A damage exclusion clause shifts the risk of specified damages (e.g., consequential damages) resulting from seller's breach to the buyer. Because the risk is a cost to the buyer, the clause reduces the value of the contract to it. Hence, other things beings equal, the buyer will offer a lower price for a contract containing the clause. The buyer receives a reduced contract price in exchange for bearing the risk of, say, consequential damages, and the seller receives less revenue in exchange for bearing less of the relevant risk. Both parties therefore "pay" for allocating the risk of consequential damages to the buyer. Described in this way, the damage exclusion clause is not appropriately characterized as "one-sided." The label ignores the price effects of damage exclusion clauses. Second, the accuracy of the characterization depends on facts about market structure which courts typically do not possess. For example, if the seller has market power, so that as a monopolist it prices a contract with a damage exclusion above marginal cost, the damage exclusion could be "one-sided" in favor of the seller. Alternatively, if the buyer is unable to assess the risks associated with the exclusion, the seller can take advantage of the buyer's ignorance to price the contract inefficiently in its favor. These possibilities require findings about a seller's production costs and the entry and exit costs of sellers, as well as about buyer's capacities to accurately assess risks. As with product homogeneity, courts are not well placed to assess such facts. Judicial findings of substantive unconscionability therefore often appear as unsupported or conclusory assertions.

Procedural unconscionability often is an issue when contracts contain warranty disclaimers, remedy limitations or damage exclusions. It also is difficult for courts to assess. This is because some of the tests courts use to detect irregularities in contract formation are bad ones. Recall that procedural unconscionability is present when there is gross disparities in bargaining power, a party lacks a meaningful choice, and it cannot negotiate over particular terms. Courts applying this test find procedural

---

[103] See, e.g., Adams v. American Cyanamid Co., 498 N.W.2d 577 (Neb. App. 1992); Construction Associates, Inc. v. Fargo Water Equipment Co., 446 N.W.2d 237 (N.D. 1989); Durham v. Ciba-Geigy Corp., 315 N.W.2d 696 (S.D. 1982).

unconscionability even between commercial parties when standard form contracts are used and are uniform in the industry. The test often gives the wrong result. To see this, consider *Martin v. Joseph Harris Co.*,[104] an often-cited case. The buyers in *Martin* purchased some cabbage seeds. The sales contract was a standard form contract containing a disclaimer of a warranty of merchantability and a remedy limitation clause. When the buyers' cabbage developed "black leg," the buyers argued that both terms of the contract were unenforceable. The District Court and Court of Appeals agreed. Both courts found the warranty disclaimer and remedy limitation to be procedurally and substantively unconscionable. Two facts indicated procedural unconscionability, according to the District Court: the buyers were unaware of the clauses, and they were unable to bargain for different terms. The Court of Appeals also found there to be procedural unconscionability, adding a third fact: that all sellers sold the cabbage seed under contracts containing the same warranty disclaimer and remedy limitation. Apparently, the buyers' lack of awareness made for "unfair surprise," and the use of a nonnegotiable standard form contract offered by all sellers in the industry made for an absence of "meaningful choice" on the buyers' part.

The basis of a finding of procedural unconscionability in *Martin* is weak. Use of a nonnegotiable standard form contract need not indicate a defect in the bargaining process. Nonnegotiable standard form contracts lower the per unit cost of contracting for mass produced goods, where most buyers have predictable preferences. Bargaining clause by clause does not allow the contracting parties to capture the economies of scale often realized by standard form contracts. Rather than nonnegotiability indicating a defect in the bargaining process, standardization can be a contractual device that both buyer and seller prefer. A reduction in contracting costs yielded by standardization, here as elsewhere, is a benefit that can be divided between the buyer and seller. The District Court in *Martin*, along with other courts,[105] therefore is wrong to infer a procedural flaw from the seller's use of a

---

[104] 767 F.2d 296 (6th Cir. 1985).

[105] See, e.g., Cate v. Dover Corp., 790 S.W.2d 559, 564 (Tex. 1990) (concurrence); Construction Associates, Inc. v. Fargo Water Equipment Co., 446 N.W.2d 237 (N.D. 1989).

nonnegotiable standard form.[106] A uniformity among sellers' standard forms also does not indicate a procedural flaw in the bargain. Convergence in contract terms among sellers is consistent with both a perfectly competitive market or a well-functioning cartel. A profit-maximizing contract can require all seed sellers to shift the risk of nonconformity in seeds to their buyers. If so, buyers cannot obtain without a warranty disclaimer from a seller because no seller can maxmize profits by offering one. A buyer of cabbage seeds therefore has no alternative to entering into a contract which contains a warranty disclaimer. Collusion among sellers need not be present. This means that unformity among the contracts offered by sellers is a bad test for a flaw in the bargaining process. The Court of Appeals in *Martin* therefore is wrong to infer procedural unconscionability from the absence of different terms offered by competing sellers of cabbage seeds.[107]

### 3. Unconscionability Evaluated

It is worth summarizing the case against judicial regulation of unconscionability. Findings of substantive and procedural unconscionability are difficult. They depend on courts ascertaining facts to which they have little reliable access. Courts are not good institutions for determining the market structure in which a product is sold or its homogeneity. They also cannot be relied upon to accurately evaluate across a range of cases the cognitive capacity of buyers and sellers. Findings of unconscionability also invoke the wrong sort of standards. Nonnegotiable standards forms and convergence of contract terms offered by sellers do not reliably test for unconscionability. Given the difficulties identified, courts are not competent to engage in the kind of

---

[106] Trebilcock suggests a more sophisticated test to the effect that a term in a standard form is unconscionable if it is inferior to the terms offered economically similar buyers in the same product market; see Michael J. Trebilcock, The Limits of Freedom of Contract 120 (1993). The test has the virtue of not wrongly inferring term unconscionability from the use of standard forms. But it has two defects. First, it is limited in application to markets in which products are sold under contracts using both standard and nonstandard forms. Where a product market does not have this characteristic, Trebilcock's test cannot be applied. Second, as argued, the determination of the product market and the comparable economic circumstances of buyers exceeds the competence of courts.

[107] See also Allen v. Michigan Bell Telephone, 171 N.W.2d 689 (Mich. Ct. App. 1971); A & M Produce Co. v. FMC Corp., 135 Cal. App.3d 473 (Cal. Ct. App. 1982); Henningsen v. Bloomfield Motors, 161 A.2d 69 (N.J. 1960).

inquiry unconscionability doctrine requires. Courts can enforce or not enforce an contract or contract term. They cannot reliably adjust the terms of the contract or even identify the price effects of a particular terms. Case law outcomes are consistent with this assessment: very few contracts or terms are invalidated on grounds of unconscionability. As the unconscionability doctrine stands, we therefore do not think that § 2-302 should be applied often. In saying this we are not suggesting that contracts should not be regulated for unconscionability. We only suggest that judicial regulation is inferior to feasible alternatives, such as legislative regulation. Experience with federal schemes regulating product warnings suggests that administrative oversight of unconscionability might be preferrable to episodic judicial oversight induced by litigation.[108] Legislative determinations of disclosure and disclaimer requirements, as well as data about relevant market structures, are more likely to accurately guage "oppression and unfair surprise." The question, as is usually the case, is "compared to what"? As we see it, legislatures are better social institutions than courts at regulating contracts for unconscionability.

The history of recent proposed revisions of § 2-302 is consistent with our evaluation. Early drafts of proposed changes to § 2-302 allowed for a finding of unconscionability when a contract or contractual term was "unconscionable at the time the contract was made or was induced by unconscionable conduct."[109] This would have allowed a finding of unconscionability based on the presence of "unconscionable conduct," even when the contract or its terms were both substantively and procedurally conscionable. More types of conduct potentially would have been effected by the proposal than under the current version of § 2-302. By its terms, the proposal required a court to determine that conduct is unconscionable apart from both the process by which the bargain is concluded and the bargain's terms. The proposal therefore placed even greater informational demands on courts than is placed on them under current unconscionability analysis. The Proposed Revision of Article 2 rejects the proposal and leaves the substance of § 2-302 unchanged. A plausible explanation for this outcome is that the Proposed Revision views courts as being comparatively bad assessors of

---

[108] Cf. Richard A. Epstein, Simple Rules for a Complex World 233-236 (1995).

[109] See Draft Revision of Uniform Commercial Code: Article 2–Sales (August 1997) § 2-105(a).

unconscionability, given on the informational constraints usually facing them.

## B. The CISG and the Domestic Law of Unconscionability

The CISG does not expressly address unconscionability as defense to enforcement of the sales contract. A question therefore arises: If a contract governed by the CISG is unconscionable under applicable domestic law, is it nonetheless enforceable under the CISG? Article 4 of the CISG restricts the CISG's scope to issues governing contract formation and "the rights and obligation of the seller and the buyer arising from" the sales contract. Article 4(a) excludes issues concerning the validity of the contract from the CISG's scope. So the question just raised in effect asks whether unconscionability is an issue excluded from the CISG by Article 4. If unconscionability either presents an issue unrelated to the rights and obligations of the parties arising from the contract or presents an issue of validity, applicable domestic law of unconscionability continues to govern. Otherwise, not. Along with others, we think that applicable domestic law of unconscionability almost certainly continues to govern contracts subject to the CISG.

Both Articles 4 and 4(a) can be read to exclude unconscionability from the CISG's scope. Consider Article 4 first. Article 4 mentions specific issues excluded from the CISG's scope, introducing the specific issues excluded in Article 4(a) and (b) using the phrase "[i]n particular." By the use of "in particular" in Article 4, the Article can be read to say that issues set out in Article 4(a) and (b) are not the only matters outside of the CISG. So matters of validity, for instance, are not the only issues the CISG does not govern. The CISG more generally does not govern any matter which does not involve the rights and obligations of the parties "arising from" the sales contract.[110] The power of a court under § 2-302 to refuse to enforce a contract is not a power that the sales contract creates. And a party's right to have a contract not enforced under § 2-302 in the proper circumstances is not a right created by the contract at all. Section 2-302 is a regulatory power the UCC gives to the court independent of the sales contract. Article 4 therefore by itself excludes unconscionability from the scope of the CISG. The consequence of exclusion, again, is that applicable domestic law of unconscionability continues to control.

The same conclusion can be reached under Article 4(a). Article 4(a),

---

[110] See Article 4.

which excludes issues of validity from the CISG's scope, can be read so that unconscionability is a matter of validity. Most commentators have interpeted it in this way.[111] We agree, but the interpretation is not absolutely overwhelming. "Validity" is undefined by Article 4 and the rest of the CISG.[112] Since the term is part of the CISG and nothing suggests domestic law definitions should be consulted, Article 4(a) excludes only issues that *the CISG* considers matters of "validity." So the question here is which issues are considered matters of validity when the CISG does not describe them as such. Fraud, illegality, incapacity and the like affect the enforceability of a contract, and therefore clearly are issues of validity. Other issues addresses by the CISG clearly are not--damage measures, for instance. Which side does the issue raised by unconscionability fall on.

The relevant diplomatic history is sparse but somewhat helpful. There was discussion among an early Working Group drafting a version of Article 4 to the effect that validity touches on "sensitive issue of domestic policy."[113] Fraud and legality are issues of this sort. Unconscionability also presents a "sensitive issue of domestic policy": the extent of judicial regulation of contracts. (Our argument that § 2-302 resolves the issue wrongly of course does not mean that § 2-302 does not reflect a "sensitive issue of domestic policy.") Therefore it presents an issue of validity excluded from the CISG which continues to be governed

---

[111] See Helen Hartnell, *Rousing the Sleeping Dog: The Validity Exception to the Convention*, 18 Yale J. Int'l L. 1 (1993); Lookofsky, supra note 49, at 105; Honnold, supra note 52, at 116; Jacob S. Ziegel, *Canada Proposes to Adopt the International Sales Convention*, 18 Can. Bus. L. J. 1, 13 (1991); but see Sara G. Zwart, *The New International Law of Sales: A Marriage Between Socialist, Third World, Common and Civil Law Principles*, 13 N.C. J. Int'l L. & Com. Reg. 112 n.32 (1988).

[112] A concern that addressing validity would delay completion and impair acceptance of the CISG apparently surrounded the failure to define the term. See UNCITRAL Yearbook I, U.N. Doc. A/CN.9/35/1970, para. 52(b), reprinted in Diplomatic History, supra note 54, at 34. It was thought that a definition of validity would be difficult to draft and obtain acceptance among signatories to the CISG. A definition would reduce the difficulties of applying Article 4 and diminish the risk of nonuniform application of the Article. This is a good example of UNCITRAL trading off "enactment" costs against "enforcement" costs. Whether the tradeoff optimally reduces the relevant total costs is another matter, which we leave unaddressed.

[113] Id.

by applicable domestic law. We could put the same point in terms of the principle of issue-displacement employed earlier.[114] Recall that the principle in brief says that if the CISG defines and addresses an issue, applicable domestic law addressing the same issue is displaced; otherwise, applicable domestic law continues to apply. The CISG does not define unconscionability or "validity," and expressly excludes issues of validity from the CISG's reach. Therefore, the principle of issue-displacement says that applicable domestic law of unconscionability is not displaced. It continues to govern a contract otherwise subject to the CISG.[115]

The continued application of the domestic law of unconscionability has two drawbacks. One is that the different countries' courts might interpret Article 4(a) differently, so that unconscionability sometimes is and sometimes is not considered a matter of validity. The second drawback is that the domestic law of unconscionability can differ, so that whether a sales contracts governed by the CISG is enforceable depends on the applicable domestic law.[116] For instance, some legal systems might consider a particular sort of warranty disclaimer or damage exclusion unconscionable, and others not. In other words, there is a risk of nonuniformity in the result of applying Article 4(a). The first

---

[114] See Chapters 2 & 3.

[115] An early application of Article 4(a) suggests that courts will treat unconscionability as raising an issue of validity. In *Inta S.A. v. MCS Officina Meccanica S.p.A.* (Argentina), Camara Nacional en lo Commercial, sala E, October 14, 1993, 1 UNILEX D.1993-24 (M. J. Bonell ed.), a buyer of machinery tried to avoid enforcement of a forum selection clause in a standard form contract governed by the CISG by arguing that the clause was invalid. The Argentinian court tested the validity of the clause by Argentinian domestic law. Argentinian law apparently considers valid a clause in an offer which is implicitly accepted by the buyer. Presupposed by the court is the view that even contracts effectively concluded under the CISG's formation rules still can be invalid under applicable domestic law. The Argentinian court's finding of validity could be understood as a finding that the forum selection clause at issue was conscionable in the circumstances.

[116] For descriptions of some of the comparative law of unconscionability, see A.H. Angelo & E.P. Ellinger, *Unconscionable Contracts: A Comparative Study of the Approaches in England, France, Germany, and the United States*, 14 Loyola L.A. Int'l & Comp. L. J. 455 (1992); Franco Taisch, *Unconscionability in a Civil Law System: An Overview of Swiss Law*, 14 Loyola L.A. Int'l & Comp. L. J. 529 (1992).

drawback is inevitable, given UNCITRAL's decision to leave validity undefined. Without a definition, the risk of inconsistent application of Article 4 cannot be avoided, even heeding Article 7's injunction to interpret the CISG's provisions so as to achieve uniformity. The second drawback is a simple consequence of the limited scope of the CISG. By leaving matters of validity to domestic law, conflict of laws principles selects the domestic law applicable to the contract. And different domestic law will treat the same contractual terms differently. This is a simple result of there being variety among legal systems. A uniform application of Article 4(a) therefore will yield different outcomes, depending on the applicable domestic law selected by the forum court. If there is a failure here, it is the CISG's limited scope, not the CISG's application within that scope. UNCITRAL got what it bargained for, purchasing consensus at the price of compromise.

## I. Introduction: Allocating Losses and Monitoring Performance

We are now at the stage of the transaction where we assume that the parties have entered into a binding contract and have agreed on its terms. The obligations of each party at this point are straightforward. As succinctly put in § 2-301, "[t]he obligation of the seller is to transfer and deliver and that of the buyer is to accept and pay in accordance with the contract." The CISG is of the same tenor. Article 30 imposes on the seller the obligation to "deliver the goods, hand over any documents relating to them and transfer the property in the goods, as required by the contract and this Convention." Article 53 imposes corresponding duties on the buyer to "pay the price for the goods and take delivery of them as required by the contract and this Convention."

These obligations are consistent with both fairness and efficiency objectives of commercial law. Fairness requires that a party to a voluntary transaction receive what it bargained for. A norm that allowed a party to chisel or renege on its obligations with impunity would violate virtually any plausible norm of fairness, whether it be treating individuals with respect, or making burdens commensurate with benefits received. Allowing parties to negate their promises would also undermine the practice of promising, and thus the capacity of individuals to rely on the word of others. Parties would be less willing to enter into any transaction that did not involve contemporaneous exchange. The lack of trust that parties would have in the forthcoming performance of other parties would make transactions more costly, as parties would insist on being compensated for the risk that they would not receive the bargained-for consideration. In short, mutually beneficial transactions would either be avoided or entered into only at a cost greater than would otherwise be the case. It is for this reason that the success of a system of commercial transactions is frequently assumed to depend on the existence of a background set of legal rules that clearly assign entitlements to parties and a legal system that enforces those assignments.

This same desire to encourage efficient transactions at minimal cost can also serve as a guideline for allocating losses that arise after the parties have entered into a contract. When contract performance is defective, some principle is necessary to decide how to allocate the loss that results. As we have noted, commercial transactions do not simply allocate goods between the parties, they also affect the distribution of goods throughout society. Presumably we would want to ensure that social resources dedicated to any particular transaction are minimized so that more resources can be dedicated to other transactions. We can think of minimizing the costs of the transaction as equivalent to avoiding waste. In order to achieve this objective we might allocate any loss to the party in the best position to avoid its occurrence, on the theory that we thereby provide that party with incentives to take precautions against behavior that produces waste. Typically, this means sellers should bear the risk of nonconformity and buyers should bear the risk of nonpayment. This principle is obviously consistent with the doctrinal obligations of buyers and sellers to perform in accordance with the contract.

But even if we provide incentives against defective performance, some breakdowns in transactions will continue to occur. Occasionally, with or without the seller's knowledge, defective goods will be delivered. When that occurs, it may be that the buyer who has received the goods is in a superior position to minimize the adverse consequence of the nonconformity. Even if the buyer cannot make use of the goods, or at least as productive use as if the goods had conformed to the contract, it may be that the goods will be useful in the hands of others. This implies two obligations that we might impose on buyers. First, we want the buyer to indicate as quickly as possible whether it is satisfied with the seller's performance. A seller who believes that a performance was satisfactory will move on to other transactions, and returning to the "completed" transaction will impose additional costs. In addition, if the buyer fails to notify the seller promptly of any defect, the goods may further deteriorate or the seller may lose opportunities to transfer the goods to someone who could use them or to obtain and deliver conforming goods.

Second, we may want the buyer to take action with respect to the defective goods, even though it is the seller who is in breach. If the seller is in a distant jurisdiction, or if the goods are susceptible to spoilage, or if the buyer is better situated to take advantage of the relevant resale market than the seller, then the buyer may be better able to avoid waste, regardless of who was at fault for the initial defective performance. This might seem to violate the fairness norm, however, insofar as it requires the buyer to take measures for which it has not bargained and requires the buyer to avoid losses that its conduct did not create.

To a substantial degree, both the UCC and the CISG reflect these concerns for minimizing the risk of defective performance and the losses that result when defective performance occurs. It is important to keep in mind, however, that the law is not the only safeguard against chiseling or reneging. As we discussed in Chapter 1, the need for a commercial party (especially one in a relational contract) to maintain a reputation as a fair dealer and a keeper of promises may provide a far more powerful inducement to full performance than legal sanctions. In "repeat play" situations, fear that the other party will terminate relations provides insurance of performance and forgiveness of small defects that are not obviously a result of bad faith conduct. Although law may play a secondary role, it is important to understand what legal obligations and rights parties have when less formal norms of cooperation fail to deter breach.

## II. Insecurity and Adequate Assurances of Performance

### A. Under the UCC

### 1. Introduction

Parties who enter commercial contracts may come to regret their decision. They may realize that performance will be more difficult or expensive than initially contemplated, that changes in market prices make the contract less profitable, or that they have alternative uses for the time and effort that must be expended in fulfilling the contract. Since each party to the contract is subject to regret, and each party knows that the other is subject to regret, there is likely to be some degree of mutual suspicion about ultimate performance of the contract. The result is that neither party will want to commit too much to its own performance without some assurance that the other party is similarly committed. These general suspicions can, of course, be exacerbated by specific events. A seller may learn that a buyer with whom it has contracted for specially manufactured goods has filed for bankruptcy, and thus be concerned about whether payment will be forthcoming; a subcontractor may hear rumors that a contractor has fallen behind in payments; a buyer may discover that a seller to whom progress payments are being made has been having difficulties getting materials required under the contract. In each of these cases, the insecure party will want to know its rights to withhold performance until the uncertainty about the other party's performance is resolved.

The common law was not very helpful in these situations. An insecure party had little choice other than to perform or withhold performance, and would be justified in the latter course only if the conduct of the other party amounted to a repudiation of the contract. Given ambiguity about what conduct constitutes a repudiation, stopping performance for insecurity was risky. A wrong guess that the other party's conduct constituted a repudiation meant that the insecure party who failed to perform became the wrongful breacher.

In the face of this uncertainty, parties had limited options. They could have drafted more explicit clauses about what would constitute a breach under their contract. But negotiating such a clause could be costly, especially in light of the infrequency of default, so that we would expect to see such clauses only when their expected value is high, either because there is an above average likelihood of default or the contract goods are very costly. Even in these situations, parties may be unwilling to signal to each other (or to admit to themselves) that default is a potential outcome of their transaction and thus might not focus on that possibility.

Parties who desire more certainty about performance might favor a state-supplied mechanism for reducing insecurity about the other party's prospective performance. Arguably, that is the function of § 2-609 of the UCC. That provision creates a process by which a party can determine whether or not an expected performance from the other party will be forthcoming. At least, that is the ideal. Whether it works is a more complicated issue.

As a technical matter, § 2-609's requirements are straightforward. A party who has "reasonable grounds for insecurity" with respect to the performance of the other party may, in writing, demand adequate assurance of due performance. Once the request is sent, the insecure party may suspend its own performance for which it has not yet received the agreed return, as long as that suspension is commercially reasonable. This statutory authority to withhold performance arguably reduces the common law's uncertainty about whether such an act constitutes a breach. Nevertheless, because withholding performance is permissible only when the vague standard of "commercially reasonableness" is satisfied, that uncertainty is not eliminated. A recipient of such a demand has a "reasonable time," not exceeding 30 days from the time of receipt, to provide assurance of due performance. Failure to provide assurances that are "adequate under the circumstances of the particular case" will constitute a breach.

Obviously, for any provision that contains as many vagaries as § 2-609, the devil is in the details. Courts will ultimately have to make fact-specific interpretations of the meaning of such phrases as "commercially reasonable," "reasonable grounds for insecurity," and "adequate assurances of due performance." Efforts to attach concrete meaning to the terms of § 2-609 have been frustrated by the tendency of courts to becloud even those terms that one might have thought were relatively unambiguous. For instance, notwithstanding the explicit requirement that a demand for adequate assurances be "in writing," some courts have considered this formality superfluous where the other party clearly understands that the insecure party will halt performance unless assurances are forthcoming.[1]

## 2. Demand for Adequate Assurances

Not every writing evidencing the insecure party's uncertainty will qualify as a demand for adequate assurances. A letter in which the buyer refused to accept shipments from the seller until quality problems had been redressed was not a request for assurance,[2] and a letter asking why a shipment was late also did not constitute a demand under § 2-609.[3] A writing that expressed concerns about the other party's acceptance of a draft and the settlement of outstanding claims and discussed possible amendments to the contract did not constitute a demand for adequate assurances where the parties had a long course of dealing in which the buyer had always paid.[4] On the other hand, a letter that explicitly spoke of past due payments qualified as a demand for assurances with respect to future payments,[5] and a letter confirming a telephone conversation that requested a reply was held to be a valid request for assurances.[6]

If it is difficult to distinguish among these cases, it may be because courts do not consider the alleged demand in isolation. Those cases in which the court finds that an ambiguous writing did not qualify as a

---

[1] See, e.g., Atwood-Kellogg, Inc. v. Nickeson Farms, 602 N.W.2d 749 (S.D. 1999) (collecting cases).

[2] See Quaker Alloy Casting Co. v. Gulfco Industries, Inc., 686 F. Supp. 1319 (N.D. Ill. 1988).

[3] See SPS Industries Inc. v. Atlantic Steel Co., 366 S.E.2d 410 (Ga. Ct. App. 1988).

[4] See Petroleo Brasilerio, S.A., Petrobras v. IBE Group, Inc., 1995 WESTLAW 326502 (S.D.N.Y.).

[5] See Land O'Lakes, Inc. v. Fredjo's Enterprises, Ltd., 1992 WESTLAW 153619 (N.D. Ill.).

[6] See Ward Transformer Co. v. Distrigas of Mass. Corp, 779 F. Supp. 823 (E.D.N.C. 1991).

demand for assurances tend also to be cases in which the court concludes that there were no reasonable grounds for insecurity. Conversely, cases in which a writing is construed as a demand tend to be cases in which the court finds grounds for insecurity.[7] It is conceivable that these conclusions reinforce each other in the court's mind, so that the courts might be more deferential to the adequacy of demands for assurances where they believe that a basis for insecurity existed. In any event, a party who desires to invoke § 2-609 is well advised to track the language of the provision closely and to assert explicitly that it is invoking rights under that section in order to signal its intent to the court.

### 3. Reasonable Grounds for Insecurity

Although any inquiry into the existence of a reasonable basis for insecurity is necessarily fact-specific, and will normally be a question for the finder of fact, the cases reveal some patterns. Market price changes that increase the cost of performance may lead a court to look askance at efforts to use a request for adequate assurances as a pretext for avoiding an unprofitable contract. In *BAII Banking Corp. v. UPG, Inc.*,[8] market prices declined significantly after the buyer agreed to purchase oil from the seller. The buyer would have saved $1.47 million if it could get out of the contract. The buyer thus allegedly began looking for a basis to deem itself insecure, in part by inhibiting the ship carrying the oil from docking, and then demanding adequate assurances in the hope that they would not be forthcoming. The court concluded that the buyer "used [§ 2-609] to avoid accepting the cargos from [the seller] at a time when these transactions had become unprofitable. . . ."[9] The court, then, was particularly attentive to the risk that parties who wish to escape a contract obligation may strategically employ § 2-609 to make an unfounded claim that their "expectation of receiving due performance" has been "impaired." The possibility of such abuse suggests that courts should be cautious in applying § 2-609.[10]

Market price fluctuations played a smaller role in *S & S, Inc. v.*

---

[7] See, e.g., Universal Builders Corp. v. United Methodist Convalescent Homes of Conn., 508 A.2d 819 (Conn. App. 1986).

[8] 985 F.2d 685 (2nd Cir. 1993).

[9] Id. at 704.

[10] 1 Report of the Law Revision Commission for 1955: Study of the Uniform Commercial Code, Article 2--Sales 537 (1955).

*Meyer*.[11]  The sellers of grain in that case did stand to profit if their contract with the buyer were terminated.  But the buyer had filed a petition in bankruptcy, written checks against insufficient funds, and assigned contracts to a third party after the buyer had lost its license to sell grain.  The court determined that these factors outweighed the possibility that sellers were acting strategically and held that reasonable grounds for insecurity existed.

It is unclear whether market price fluctuations, standing alone, are sufficient to provide reasonable grounds for insecurity Official Comment 3 to § 2-609 provides that "a ground for insecurity need not arise from or be directly related to the contract in question."  This Comment certainly allows external events to trigger insecurity.  An obvious case may be a seller who learns that its buyer has breached a contract with another seller, so that the former demands assurances of performance of its own contract.  But arguably that Comment is broad enough to cover circumstances unrelated to any action or omission of the parties, such as severe market price fluctuations since the time of contracting or statements by authorities that the contract at issue is unenforceable.[12]

### 4. Adequate Assurances of Performance

A promisor who has received a demand and does not want to terminate the contract is required by § 2-609 to respond with adequate assurances of performance within a reasonable time, not exceeding 30 days.  This standard, too, is defined by reference to "the circumstances of the particular" case.  Promisors who are uncertain about their own performance, but who are hoping that matters work out are likely to respond as ambiguously as possible within this standard.  For example, a response to a proper demand for assurances might state, "We have every expectation of fulfilling our contractual obligations."  Such general expressions of hope will do little to comfort the insecure party, but, more importantly, their status as adequate assurance is also uncertain.  The assertions in Official Comment 4 that what constitutes adequate assurances will depend on whether the assuring party has a good reputation or is known as a "corner-cutter," or that the assurances must be given in "good faith" and in accordance with "commercial standards" and must be "based upon reason and must not be arbitrary and

---

[11] 478 N.W.2d 857 (Iowa Ct. App. 1991).

[12] See Top of Iowa Cooperative v. Sime Farms, Inc., 608 N.W.2d 454 (Iowa 2000).

capricious" do little to predict results in specific cases.

Case law is not very helpful in this area, in part because the cases are few in number and in part because most cases that ultimately generate litigation and in which the court finds reasonable grounds for insecurity involve a party who provides no assurances at all. If the promisor has truly provided an irrefutable assurance, litigation is unlikely to ensue. Assume, for instance, that the promisee hears that the promisor has been late in paying bills and is on the verge of bankruptcy. The promisee thus dispatches a proper § 2-609 writing that demands assurances of performance. If the promisee responds with a current Dun & Bradstreet report that the promisor is creditworthy and notarized letters from recent creditors attesting to timely payment, it is unlikely that the promisee will withhold further performance or that the promisee will fail to perform. Thus, the cases tend to involve situations in which the very reasons that warrant the demand also render the pale efforts of the promisor inadequate. As a result, although the issue of "reasonable grounds for insecurity" is conceptually distinct from the issue of "adequate assurances," the courts often apply the same underlying facts to both inquiries.

In *Waldorf Steel Fabricators, Inc. v. Consolidated Systems, Inc.*,[13] for example, Consolidated entered two separate contracts with Waldorf. For various reasons, Consolidated became anxious about Waldorf's ability to make payments under both contracts. The court found that the first contract did not give rise to reasonable insecurity because Waldorf had offered to enter into a "joint check" agreement whereby Consolidated would be paid at the same time that Waldorf was paid. The court reasoned that since the drawer of the joint check was known to and trusted by Consolidated, it had no reasonable grounds for insecurity. Alternatively, the court could have concluded that although there were originally grounds for insecurity, the willingness of Waldorf to enter the joint check agreement constituted adequate assurances of performance. With respect to the second project, Consolidated had reasonable grounds for insecurity because Waldorf had ignored the explicit payment terms on two past projects. Waldorf's response to a demand for assurances was not only late (i.e., past the 30-day limitation), but was also inadequate insofar as it promised a similar joint check arrangement, but this time from a drawer with whom Consolidated had no prior experience and was of unknown creditworthiness. Again, the "reasonable grounds for

---

[13] 1996 WESTLAW 480902 (S.D.N.Y.).

insecurity" analysis is not entirely severable from the "adequate assurance" analysis. Both inquiries essentially look at the capacity of the promisor to perform.

One point about adequate assurances must be reiterated. A party who requests adequate assurances is essentially demanding that the other party provide something that is not required under the explicit terms of the contract. If reasonable, however, that demand does not constitute a repudiation of the contract. Thus, the party to whom the demand is made might claim that it is required to provide something for which it was not compensated. Nevertheless, because § 2-609 provides a default rule of which commercial parties should be aware, its implications are presumably considered in the initial bargain. Parties who must comply with its obligations presumably have been compensated in other contractual clauses for the additional tasks they must undertake.

## B. Suspending Performance Under the CISG

Article 71 of the CISG incorporates many of the principles of § 2-609 into international sales law. The standard for suspending performance, however, varies somewhat from the standard under the UCC. A party is entitled to suspend performance under Article 71 if "it becomes apparent that the other party will not perform a substantial part of his obligations," and if that expected nonperformance will result from a serious deficiency in "his ability to perform," or in "his creditworthiness," or in "[h]is conduct in preparing to perform or in performing the contract." For instance, failure of a buyer to provide an agreed bank guarantee of payment would justify the seller in suspending shipments. At least one court has held that the apparent nonperformance need not relate to a "fundamental breach of contract."[14] This appears to be the correct result. The drafters of the CISG used the phrase "fundamental breach of contract" with sufficient frequency that one would imagine that they would have used it in Article 71 if it was intended to be the standard for suspension of performance. In addition, since Article 72(1) makes "fundamental breach of contract" the standard for avoidance of the contract, and Article 71 is intended to deal with uncertainties and opportunistic acts before they evolve into acts that warrant avoidance, it would make little sense to allow suspension of performance only when

---

[14] See Landgericht Berlin, 52 S 247/94, Sept. 15, 1994 (Germany), 1 UNILEX D. 1994-22.1 (M.J. Bonell, ed.). Article 25 recites that a breach of contract is fundamental if it results in "such detriment to the other party as substantially to deprive him of what he is entitled to expect under the contract."

matters had reached the point where avoidance was appropriate.

One who suspends performance must notify the other party. If that other party provides "adequate assurance of his performance," the promisee must continue its own performance. A seller who has dispatched, but not delivered, goods prior to the time that the buyer's expected nonperformance becomes apparent may order the goods withheld from the buyer, even though the buyer holds a document of title for the goods. The seller, however, may not reclaim the goods from a third party, such as a good faith purchaser from the buyer.

Note that Article 71 varies in important ways from § 2-609. First, the CISG omits the writing requirement of § 2-609. It also provides no time period within which adequate assurances must be received before insecurity is automatically transformed into repudiation. Instead, a party who has suspended performance occupies the same position as any other party who claims a repudiation. That is, only if it is "clear that one of the parties will commit a fundamental breach of contract"[15] will the aggrieved party be entitled to avoid the contract prior to the date for performance. Perhaps the wider variance of transactions and lower reliability of communication in international transactions makes any bright line rule on these matters less useful than in domestic transactions. The party who has suspended performance but not received assurances will, of course, claim that the absence of assurances makes it "clear" that a fundamental breach will ensue. The result, however, is that Article 71 provides even less certainty about the rights of the parties than § 2-609, even though it creates a rough framework for permitting parties to resolve suspicions and rumors concerning contractual performance.

Perhaps most importantly, Article 71 limits suspension to situations in which insecurity is based on "a serious deficiency in" the other party's ability to perform or in its creditworthiness, or the conduct of the other party in preparing to perform or performing the contract. These limits appear to foreclose one party from suspending performance based either on market conditions generally or on breach by the other party of some other contract. As we have indicated above, each of these conditions might justify suspension under the UCC.

---

[15] Article 72(1).

## III. Anticipatory Repudiation

### A. Under the UCC

A party who fears nonperformance by the other party is not required to use the procedures created by § 2-609 and Article 71 to obtain assurances of performance. Those measures are permissive, not mandatory. There may exist situations in which the aggrieved party is so certain that the other party will fail to perform that it is appropriate to cancel the contract prior to the time of performance, so that damages can be minimized and alternative arrangements made. Of course, this remains a risky decision for the aggrieved party. If calling a repudiation entails ceasing one's own performance, and a court subsequently determines that no repudiation existed, the "aggrieved" party will turn out to be the breacher.

The UCC purports to clarify the issue of what constitutes a repudiation. Official Comment 1 to § 2-610 recites that an "overt communication of intention or an action which renders performance impossible or demonstrates a clear determination not to continue with performance" will qualify. But such overt acts are rarely the stuff of which repudiations are made. Commercial parties do not easily admit that they have entered an agreement they cannot perform. Even under difficult circumstances, they may believe that new financing will be found, or the weather will change, or their ship will arrive in time to save the contract. Thus, Official Comment 2 to the same section recognizes that repudiation can result from actions that reasonably indicate an end to one party's continuing obligation. Recent proposals to revise Article 2 include provisions based on § 250 of the Restatement (Second) of Contracts. Those provisions include as a repudiation the use of language that a reasonable party would interpret to mean that the speaker will not or cannot make a performance or voluntary affirmative conduct that would appear to a reasonable party to make a future performance impossible. Note that the focus here is on a repudiation of a performance rather than on the contract as a whole. Thus, a party who is unable to perform part of its obligations, but would like to reaffirm the contract may still commit a repudiation.

Obviously, the inquiry into whether a repudiation has occurred will be fact specific. (Where adequate assurances have been properly demanded and are not forthcoming, a repudiation automatically exists.[16]) Some patterns, however, emerge from the cases. As a general matter, attempts to condition performance on requirements not included in the contract will be considered a repudiation. Filing for bankruptcy, however, will not automatically constitute a repudiation, and expressions of difficulty in fulfilling contractual obligations will not amount to a refusal to perform that constitutes a repudiation.

Once a repudiation occurs, the aggrieved party has several options. It may simply wait for the repudiating party to change its mind and perform.[17] But inaction is permitted only for a "commercially reasonable time." Waiting beyond that period of time will preclude the aggrieved party from recovering damages that could have been avoided by earlier action. Alternatively, the aggrieved party may immediately resort to any remedy for breach, and may do so even if that party has notified the repudiating party that it would await performance. Finally, the aggrieved party may suspend its own performance or identify or salvage goods that have been identified to the contract.

---

[16] See § 2-609(4). There does appear to be a small glitch in the link between § 2-609 and § 2-610. The former permits an insecure party to demand assurances whenever reasonable grounds for insecurity to arise. That insecurity is not limited to a fear that the other party's performance will substantially deviate from contractual requirements. Any deviation appears to be sufficient. Should those grounds exist, the insecure party may suspend performance and declare a repudiation if assurances are not forthcoming within a reasonable time. Section 2-610, which states the consequences of a repudiation, however, recites that those consequences occur only if the repudiation will "substantially impair" the value of the contract. Among those consequences is the right of the aggrieved party to suspend his or her own performance. It would be somewhat odd to say that an aggrieved party with respect to a minor deviation that does not "substantially impair" the contract can suspend performance until the time that a repudiation exists, but cannot continue that suspension after a repudiation exists. Assume, for instance, that the seller of goods fears that the buyer will not pay more than 95 percent of the contract price. If this fear is reasonable, the seller would be authorized to suspend performance under § 2-609. But if the five percent shortfall is not "substantial," then once assurances were not forthcoming and a repudiation existed, a strict reading of § 2-610 would require seller to resume performance. We believe that this interpretation is perverse and that the language that gives seller greater leeway on performance pre-repudiation than post-repudiation was not intended.

[17] § 2-610(a).

The interaction of these principles is evident in the well-known case of *Oloffson v. Coomer*.[18] A seller of corn agreed in April to sell grain to a dealer for delivery in October and December. On June 3, the seller informed the buyer that he was not going to plant corn because the season had been too wet and advised the buyer to procure substitute corn elsewhere. The following September, the buyer inquired about delivery of the corn and was again told that it would not be delivered. After the scheduled delivery times passed, the buyer covered the contracts at prices significantly above the contract price and the June 3 market price. The buyer claimed that § 2-610 permitted him to await performance by the repudiating party for a commercially reasonable period of time. The court, however, concluded that, in light of the seller's unequivocal repudiation, that period expired when the first notification of nonperformance was given. Thus, the buyer was limited to damages for non-delivery based on the market value of grain on the date of repudiation. The court may have been influenced by the fact that the buyer was awaiting performance in a rising market. Therefore, the buyer was essentially gambling with the seller's money. If the market price continued to climb, the buyer's interpretation of a "commercially reasonable time" would have allowed it to recover the difference between the contract price and the cover price at the time of performance and thus be in as good a position as if performance had occurred. If, on the other hand, the market price declined below the contract price during that period, the buyer could have covered at the lower market price and avoided what would have been a bad deal. The buyer, on this interpretation of "commercially reasonable time," would have no incentive to minimize the seller's damages.

Notwithstanding this apparent opportunistic behavior by the seller, the court's reasoning seems problematic. At the very least, the explicit option of waiting a "commercial reasonable time" would appear to permit the buyer some period after the repudiation before being required to cover. That period may not be as long as the time of performance, but it might at least include a period of time for the buyer to determine whether the current market prices are likely to increase or decrease. After all, if market prices declined within a reasonable time after the repudiation and the buyer covered within that period, the breaching seller would have been better off. Of course, there is no reason to believe that the buyer would be a better predictor than the market of subsequent price fluctuations, and given that the gamble was with the seller's money, it

---

[18] 296 N.E.2d 871 (Ill. Ct. App. 1973).

might make sense to limit the buyer to a period of time reasonably necessary to make a cover contract and no longer.

Basing our sympathy for the seller on the buyer's opportunism, however, may prove too much. If the seller feared that increasing market prices would increase his damages for non-delivery, he could have entered the market as a buyer and covered his own contract. After all, the post-June inquiries made by the buyer indicated that no cover contract existed. If the seller failed to cover, perhaps he was also involved in a gamble, since he could have been waiting for prices to decline before covering his broken contract.

There may be cases in which either party could enter a cover contract, but we would prefer that one rather than the other make the effort. For instance, professional buyers may be able to reduce transactions costs related to cover more easily than professional sellers, because the buyers will be more aware of markets in which cover contracts can be obtained. In those situations, we may want to interpret a "commercially reasonable time" as a period sufficiently brief as to induce the buyer to act or forfeit damages that could otherwise be obtained. But *Oloffson* does not look like such a case. Even the court which demonstrated such sympathy for the seller in that case refers to the existence of a "well organized and easily accessible market for purchases of grain to be delivered in the future." If that market was as accessible to seller as to buyer, then the need to compel prompt action by the buyer is less clear.

### B. Under the CISG

The CISG provides no greater guidance on the occurrence or consequences of an anticipatory repudiation. Article 72 simply permits one party to declare a contract avoided if, "prior to the date for performance of the contract it is clear that" the other party will commit a fundamental breach. Obviously, "clarity" of the repudiation may be in the eyes of the beholder. A German court determined, for instance, that an Italian seller of shoes was entitled to avoid a contract with a German buyer where the buyer had not paid for shoes ordered under a previous contract and had not responded to requests for payment and assurances of performance under the later contract.[19] The "clarity" requirement, however, likely does mean that one party's request for modifications to

---

[19] Oberlandesgericht Düsseldorf, 17 U 146/93, Jan. 14, 1994 (Germany), 1 UNILEX D.1994-1 (M.J. Bonell, ed.).

the contract or expression of difficulty of performance without modifications is insufficient, in itself, to constitute a repudiation.

Article 72 requires that, if time permits, the declaration of avoidance be preceded by reasonable notice so that the allegedly repudiating party can provide adequate assurances of performance under Article 71. But the notice requirement does not apply if the declaration of avoidance is precipitated by the other party's own declaration of nonperformance.

## IV. Tender, Acceptance, Rejection, Cure

### A. Tender and Inspection

Let us now assume that there has been no repudiation at the time of performance. At this point, we assume that the parties have entered into a valid contract, that is, there are no formation problems; the seller is actually willing to deliver the goods; and the buyer is willing to accept and pay for them. The potential difficulties at this stage begin with the possible failure of the seller's performance to meet contractual requirements.

The technical requirements for performance are set forth in § 2-301. The seller is obligated to transfer and deliver the goods or documents contracted for and the buyer is obligated to pay for and accept goods that conform to the contract. Tender of delivery requires that the seller put and hold conforming goods at the buyer's disposition and give the buyer any notification reasonably necessary to enable it to take delivery. Issues of time, place, and manner of delivery are open to agreement between the parties, but tender must be at a reasonable hour and any tender of goods must be kept available for the period reasonably necessary for the buyer to take possession. The buyer, however, is responsible for furnishing facilities suitable for receipt of the goods.[20] "Receipt" for these purposes means taking physical possession of the goods.

The buyer is obligated to pay for the goods at the time and place where the buyer is "to receive" them.[21] Note that the effect of this provision is that in a shipment contract, which requires the seller to deliver goods to the carrier and in which the risk of loss passes to the buyer on delivery of the goods to the carrier, the buyer's payment obligation is not activated until the buyer actually obtains the goods. Of course, a buyer may agree to prepay, as when the buyer agrees to pay

---

[20] § 2-504(1).

[21] § 2-310(a).

against documents that arrive prior to the goods. Nevertheless, in the absence of a contrary agreement, the default rule of payment on receipt applies. The reason for this presumption is that most buyers will not want to pay until they are certain that they have received the goods for which they have paid. Presumably, sellers have control over the goods that are delivered and thus are in the best position to ensure that buyers receive what they have actually ordered. Hence, the UCC induces the seller to take advantage of its position to ensure quality by making the seller wait for payment until the buyer determines conformity.

Buyers determine conformity through the process of inspection. Where goods are tendered or delivered or identified to the contract for sale, the buyer has a right prior to making payment or accepting the goods to inspect them as long as inspection occurs at a reasonable time and place and in a reasonable manner. The buyer must also bear the expenses of inspection, although those expenses may be recovered from the seller if the goods are rightfully rejected.[22]

Inspection presents a substantial risk for the buyer because, as we will see, a buyer who fails to find defects that warrant rejection of the goods may be deemed to have accepted them and to have incurred the obligation to pay for them. It is essential, therefore, that a buyer understand what constitutes an opportunity to inspect.

Assume that a buyer has agreed to purchase an automobile from the dealer's lot. Prior to taking delivery of the automobile, the buyer takes a test drive, agrees to purchase the automobile, and makes a down payment of $500, but requires the seller to install a new stereo system. On returning the next day, when the new system has been installed, the buyer notices some defects in the paint that were observable the prior day, but that the buyer failed to notice. If the buyer attempts to reject the goods at that stage, claiming that it noticed the defects on "inspection," can the seller retort that the time for inspection already occurred, either when the $500 down payment was given or the test drive taken, so that the attempted rejection comes too late?

First, we should get rid of the red herring of the $500 down payment. Section 2-512(2) is quite explicit that payment is not acceptance, at least where the contract requires payment before inspection. Thus, as long as the down payment was required by the seller to process the order, it bears no evidence on the issue of inspection. The buyer might claim that there

---

[22] § 2-512.

was no inspection prior to delivery of the goods, because inspection cannot occur until the goods are tendered, and that does not occur until the seller puts conforming goods—an automobile with the new stereo system—at the buyer's disposal. That argument seems plausible in light of the wording of § 2-513, which grants the buyer a right of inspection when goods are "tendered or delivered." But that same clause also grants buyer a right of inspection when the goods are "identified to the contract for sale." That event presumably has occurred when the buyer picked out the car and the stereo system to be installed, even though the goods were not ready for tender or delivery.[23]

The problem with § 2-513(1) is that it does not tell us whether the right to inspect is triggered by the first or the last of the listed events. The use of "or" suggests that passage of any of them will be sufficient, so that the buyer's examination of the automobile even prior to its delivery will constitute the requisite inspection. This interpretation is also consistent with the rationale behind the inspection requirement. It is certainly true that the buyer should have a right of inspection prior to payment, since this entitlement induces sellers to perform in accordance with the contract. But we would presumably want sellers to know at an early point that the transaction they believed would be complete has in fact gone awry. Prompt notification to the seller has a series of desirable effects. First, it enables the seller to cure any defect at a time when the goods may still be useful to the buyer. Second, it enables the seller to salvage the goods by reselling them in their current condition to an alternative buyer prior to any further deterioration. Third, it allows seller to avoid deterioration by taking steps to preserve goods that might otherwise be perishable. These objectives combine to favor prompt notice by the buyer, and we are most likely to get that result if we make the buyer bear losses that result from tardy action.

Notwithstanding that rationale, assigning a proper time for the buyer to inspect can be difficult in some cases. The nature of the goods and the use to which the buyer will put them are the primary factors to which

---

[23] Under § 2-501, the goods were identified either at the time when the contract was made (if we treat the automobile and the stereo system as goods that were independently existing and identified when the contract was made) or no later than the time when the stereo system was installed by the seller (if we treat the sale as one for an automobile that included the particular stereo system, which, by virtue of installation, was designated by the seller as goods to which the contract refers). Either of these events would have preceded tender or delivery.

courts look in deciding whether a reasonable time for inspection has passed. Sellers may deliver goods to buyers prior to the time that buyers are able to determine whether they conform to the contract, because the goods must interact with other goods that are not yet available or the goods' conformity may be determinable only after lengthy tests. For instance, in *Figueroa v. Kit San Co.*,[24] the acceptability of the chemical compound bentonite could be determined only after a 200-day permeability test, and failure to reject within that period did not constitute an acceptance. The court reasoned that the goods were not perishable and the buyer had a contractual right to ensure that the goods met specifications satisfaction of which could only be determined by the lengthy testing period. Indeed, the court concluded that even use of some of the bentonite did not constitute acceptance of the whole, especially with respect to that part of the delivery that had been employed for testing.

## B. Inspection in Documentary Transactions

Not all transactions are face-to-face. Sellers and buyers may be geographically distant. Inspection in these cases creates additional burdens because the costs of transactional breakdown increase when goods must be recovered from or salvaged in foreign jurisdictions. Certainly the UCC permits buyers to delay inspection until receipt. Section 2-513(1) provides that inspection can occur after the arrival of the goods where the seller is authorized to send them to the buyer. But sellers may be reluctant to accept these terms. If the buyer rejects goods after delivery, the seller must bear the costs of reclaiming the goods or reselling them at a distant location that may be beyond the seller's normal market. If the seller believes that the buyer was not justified in rejecting the goods, the seller has to decide whether to pursue a lawsuit in a distant jurisdiction. Sellers would prefer to obtain payment prior to shipment so that buyers must initiate any long-distance lawsuit to recover what they have paid. Sellers anticipate that buyers will only bring such a lawsuit where warranted by sellers' nonperformance, thereby reducing the risk of buyer misbehavior.

Buyers, of course, face the flip side of these risks. They fear that prepayment will remove sellers' incentive to perform in accordance with the contract. Buyers are no more enamored of long-distance litigation than sellers, so they will not want to make payments that require them to bring lawsuits in foreign jurisdictions if the transaction breaks down.

---

[24] 845 P.2d 567 (Idaho Ct. App. 1992).

Unless we could resolve the tension between these conflicting concerns, long-distance transactions that were otherwise mutually beneficial would not occur. The UCC accommodates a variety of mechanisms for reducing these risks. The buyer could, for instance, appoint an agent in the seller's jurisdiction to inspect the goods prior to their shipment, or the parties could agree on a neutral third-party inspector who would confirm the quality of the goods prior to shipment. This mechanism provides the buyer the certainty that goods are conforming prior to making payment and allows the seller the certainty that the goods have been accepted, so that buyer's payment obligation has been triggered, prior to shipment. The problems that might arise here are those associated with any agency relationship. Agents and other third parties do not perfectly share the interests of their principals. Through shirking or negligence, an agent may accept goods that the buyer would personally reject.[25] Thus, buyers may prefer alternative arrangements unless they have a means of monitoring the agent or are confident that the agent's determination of quality will be substantially similar to their own. Third-party inspection, therefore, may be more appropriate where the determination of conformity can be readily made than where it is highly nuanced. Buyers, for instance, may be more willing to allow others to determine that the goods to be shipped are of a required color or size than that they are of a particular grade or quality.

An alternative means for resolving the tension between the interests of distant buyers and sellers is the documentary transaction. In this transaction, described further in Chapter 11, the seller ships the goods to the buyer prior to receiving any payment. Simultaneously, the seller sends to its agent in the buyer's jurisdiction certain documents that evidence the shipment. These documents will typically include a bill of lading or other document of title that describe the goods that have been shipped, an invoice, and a sight draft that the seller has drawn on the buyer. The bill of lading serves as the key to obtaining the goods from the carrier. It is, in effect, the key to the safe deposit box without which

---

[25] This may be the explanation for the difference between the condition of the goods as approved by a government inspector and as delivered in Bartlett & Co., Grain v. Merchants Co., 323 F.2d 501 (5th Cir. 1963), a pre-UCC case. The court found that the parties had agreed that, for purposes of acceptance, the condition of the goods would be governed by the weight and grades assigned by a federally licensed grain inspector. That inspector designated the goods as No. 2 yellow corn. When the goods arrived at their destination, however, the buyer had an additional inspection that designated the corn at a lower grade. The court found that the inspection at the time of shipment governed under the contract.

access to the box will not be allowed. The sight draft is essentially a check drawn by the seller on the buyer. These documents will typically arrive in the buyer's jurisdiction prior to the goods. On arrival, the seller's agent will notify the buyer, who can inspect the documents to ensure that the description of the goods matches contractual specifications. At that point, the buyer will be required to make payment to the seller against the sight draft in order to receive the documents of title. Thus, when the goods arrive, the buyer will have paid, but will also have access to the goods by virtue of the document of title and will have received assurances that conforming goods have been shipped.

Note the security that this transaction offers to the parties. The seller can ship the goods to a distant jurisdiction without surrendering control over them. As long as the seller, or the seller's agent, retains the document of title, it possesses the ability to direct delivery of the goods. Since the seller's agent will not surrender the document of title until the buyer has paid, the seller's risk of nonpayment is minimized. Sellers do not have to worry about opportunistic rejection by a buyer who has changed its mind about the deal, because the buyer will not have an opportunity to inspect the goods for nonconformities until payment has been made. Similarly, the buyer's risk that the seller has shipped nonconforming goods is reduced. The buyer must pay before obtaining physical possession of the goods and before having an opportunity to inspect them. But the buyer does have the right to inspect the documents that describe the goods. Only if that description conforms to the contract will the buyer make payment against the sight draft.

Use of the documentary transaction may displace the buyer's right to make a pre-payment inspection of the goods when they arrive and to reject them. As we noted above, payment does not constitute acceptance where it is required prior to inspection. Thus, in the rare case in which the goods arrive prior to the documents, the buyer may wish to inspect the goods prior to payment. The UCC takes the position, however, that the buyer's right to such an inspection has been bargained away by the buyer's agreement to the documentary transaction. Section 2-513(3)(b) makes clear that the buyer is not entitled to inspect prior to payment when the contract provides for payment against documents of title, unless the contract provides otherwise. Comment 5 to that section emphasizes that any delay in the transmission of the documents does not alter the risk allocation made by the parties concerning inspection.[26]

One potential anomaly does exist in this scenario, however. Assume that the buyer has ordered 100 cases of peaches. When the truck carrying the goods arrives, it bears an overwhelming stench of rotting fruit. Nevertheless, the documents, which arrive simultaneously with the goods, are in proper order. Must the buyer make payment against the documents? Section 2-512(1)(a) provides that where the contract requires payment before inspection, as in the documentary transaction, non-conformity of the goods does not excuse the buyer from making the payment unless "the non-conformity appears without inspection." One might claim that the apparent nonconformity in this case falls within that exception, so that the buyer is not required to pay. This interpretation, however, appears inconsistent with the risk allocation made by the parties. Recall also that if this was the normal case of a shipment contract, the risk of loss would have passed to the buyer so that if the cause of the fruit's rotting materialized after the goods were loaded on the carrier (e.g., the truck's air conditioning broke down), the buyer would bear the loss (or have an action against the carrier). Perhaps the buyer would claim that it does not have to pay until a determination of whether the nonconformity existed prior to or after the risk passed. But that argument should not help the buyer in a variation of this case. Assume, for instance, that the buyer learns that the goods have been destroyed en route when the carrier was involved in an accident. There is now no basis for the buyer's believing that the goods were nonconforming. Since the risk would have passed to it, the buyer should presumably pay the seller and make what claim is appropriate against the carrier. But the wording of § 2-512(1)(a) may be read to suggest that the buyer is now aware of a "non-conformity" even without inspection because the goods it ordered will not arrive.

The seller, on the other hand, may contend that the nonconformity to which § 2-512(1)(a) refers is nonconformity in the documents, not the goods. Thus, there would be no relevant nonconformity in this case and the buyer would be required to pay. While this reading seems more consistent with the rationale behind the documentary transaction, it is difficult to force into the wording of the UCC. When the drafters wanted to speak of nonconformity in the documents, as opposed to the goods,

---

[26] Buyers similarly have no right to inspect in transactions that are understood to require payment against documents or prepayment such as C.O.D. transactions and C.I.F. contracts. See §§ 2-310(a), 2-320(4), 2-513(1), 2-513(3), § 2-503, Official Comment 2.

they knew how to say so. They did exactly that in the same section; § 2-512(1)(b) speaks explicitly of "tender of the required documents." "The non-conformity" in § 2-512(1)(a), on the other hand, refers back to the "non-conformity" in § 2-512(1), and that non-conformity is quite explicitly "non-conformity of the goods."

While we conclude that the seller cannot claim that the reference to "non-conformity" in § 2-512(1)(a) is to non-conformity in the documents, we also believe that the buyer should not be able to avoid payment in the latter of these cases. Notwithstanding the violence that allowing nonpayment does to the documentary transaction and risk of loss allocation, we conclude that the buyer has a stronger argument in the former scenario. Official Comment 3 to § 2-512 states that the nonpayment exception is triggered by a non-conformity that "is evident in the mere process of taking delivery." This suggests that if the buyer is physically present and it is clear that the seller shipped goods that did not conform to the contract, there is no commercially valid reason for requiring a payment that will be returned in subsequent litigation. But as we indicate above, the first scenario does not inexorably lead to the conclusion that the non-conformity, albeit apparent, was the fault of the seller. The goods may have been conforming when shipped and became defective en route. This possibility, of course, will be reduced with nonperishable goods, and maybe those cases are more readily subsumed within the exception of § 2-512(1)(a). We note only that in at least some cases, the exception seems broader than is appropriate.

### C. Inspection under the CISG

At first glance, the terms of the CISG concerning inspection appear to be entirely consistent with the UCC. Article 38 seems even more precise in that it speaks of the need for inspection (or examination) "within as short a period as is practicable under the circumstances," and thus avoids the difficulty inherent in § 2-513 about which event triggers the obligation to inspect. Article 58 entitles a buyer, who is bound to pay for the goods when they are put at its disposal, to make an examination prior to payment unless the terms of the contract are inconsistent with that right. As with the UCC, examination can be delayed until the time of arrival if the goods are to be transported by seller to buyer. Article 39 also requires notification to the seller if the buyer discovers a nonconformity.

Nevertheless, the CISG terms contains some ambiguities and differences from the UCC provisions. Article 39(1) limits the buyer's right to rely on a nonconformity unless the buyer gave notice within a reasonable time after the buyer did find or *should have* found the defect during an examination—an objective test. Article 39(2) generally provides an absolute bar to the buyer's claims of nonconformity unless the seller receives notice within two years from the date on which the goods were delivered to the buyer. But Article 44 excuses the buyer from making the requisite notification under Article 39(1) if the buyer has a "reasonable excuse." It is difficult to fathom what would constitute a "reasonable excuse" under Article 44 other than reasonable failure to discover the nonconformity, which already excuses the notification requirement under Article 39(1). If the latter provision is not superfluous, it must refer to a situation in which it would have been unreasonable not to notice the nonconformity, but in which the buyer has a reasonable excuse for not giving notice.

Perhaps a scenario like the following reconciles the two provisions. Assume that the buyer orders 1000 bushels of red peppers and receives instead 1000 bushels of yellow peppers. The perishable nature of the goods indicates that any nonconformity must be noticed immediately if it is to be noticed within a reasonable time. The buyer does immediately notice the discrepancy, but due to communications failure (after all, in international sales, it is likely that we will frequently be dealing with unreliable communications), the buyer cannot inform the seller of nonconformity for 12 hours. As a result, no carrier can be found and the goods spoil awaiting reshipment. Arguably, the buyer satisfied both the requirements of Article 39 and Article 44, even though it was required to make an immediate notification and (reasonably) failed to do so.

This scenario also raises a question that became important in the drafting of Article 44. What does Article 39 mean by the phrase "ought to have discovered"? The phrase appears to incorporate an objective standard, but objective from whose perspective? Assume that intricate computer equipment is shipped from the United States, where the equipment is commonly used, to Moldova, where it is uncommon. The equipment fails to operate properly for reasons that the unsophisticated users believe is attributable to operator error or ignorance, but that is actually caused by defects in the equipment. If the defect would have been noticed much earlier in the sophisticated country of the seller, we may conclude that the subsequent notification by unsophisticated users comes too late. This may smack of unfairness in that the unsophisticated buyer could not have done better, or of inefficiency in that, as between the sophisticated seller and unsophisticated buyer the former could have most easily avoided any losses, assuming that the buyer acted as quickly as could be expected given its level of knowledge. That may mean that we should use a subjective standard and ask whether *this* buyer "ought to have discovered" the defect. Or it may mean that we use the objective standard in Article 39(1), but allow lack of sophistication to serve as an excuse under Article 44. Indeed, the drafting history of Article 44 suggests that it was included to permit consideration of the particular difficulties buyers that buyers from developing countries would face and thus to allow "excuse" for those buyers under circumstances that would not be applicable under Article 39. In short, Article 39(1) may be seen as applying an objective test that does not consider the personal circumstances of the particular buyer, while Article 44 does allow further consideration of individual circumstances.

Article 44 may exempt a buyer from the strictures of Article 39(1), but does not relieve the buyer who runs afoul of the two-year statute of repose in Article 39(2). Furthermore, the buyer excused under Article 44 preserves only two remedies: reduction of the price and recovery of damages other than loss of profit. Other remedies of requiring performance, avoiding the contract, and delaying passage of the risk of loss are denied buyers who do not meet the notice requirements of Article 39(1), even if they have an excuse under Article 44.

### D. Acceptance and Rejection

### 1. Introduction: Neutralizing Strategic Behavior

The inspecting buyer must make a decision: accept the goods or reject them. As we have indicated, failure to act at this time constitutes an acceptance; affirmative action is necessary to reject. A rule that requires action for rejection but not acceptance follows logically from the assumption that most tenders will be acceptable to buyers. Requiring buyers to signal acceptance would be wasteful, since sellers can almost always correctly assume that goods have been satisfactory if they have heard nothing to the contrary. But the need for affirmative action raises the question of what constitutes rejection and when it must occur. The interests of the parties place them in tension with one another on these issues. Sellers will want to limit the method and period of rejection so they can be certain that the transaction is complete at the earliest possible time. Buyers, on the other hand, will want to hedge their acceptance and extend the period for rejection in order to ensure that they are satisfied with the goods. In short, each party will want to prevent the other from acting strategically, that is, self-interestedly, while retaining flexibility for itself. Since uncertainty about the other party's performance will interfere with otherwise mutually beneficial transactions, one measure of the UCC's success is the extent to which it prevents either party from engaging in strategic behavior.

Compounding this tension is the possibility that a party who is actually satisfied with the goods, but who has come to regret the deal because the same goods are now available on better financial terms, may use an immaterial nonconformity to reject. Section 2-601 adopts the common law concept of "perfect tender," permitting rejection of the goods should the seller's performance fail to conform to contractual specifications "in any respect." The perfect tender rule means that the extent of nonconformity is not a condition of rejection. It rejects the "substantial performance" rule applicable in service and construction contracts. Thus, the seller is exposed to some risk of strategic rejection. As we will see, the UCC reduces that risk by granting sellers certain rights to take a second bite of the performance apple. But sellers will also rely on the absence of an explicit rejection by buyers, and hence the implicit indication of acceptance, to reduce the buyer's capacity to act strategically. Our analysis, therefore, begins with an investigation of the basis for rejection and the signals that buyer must send in order to reject properly.

## 2. Perfect Tender

As a doctrinal matter, the basis for rejection seems straightforward: failure of the tender of delivery or of the goods themselves to conform to the contract "in any respect" justifies rejection. But, after paying lip service to that standard, the UCC, sometimes aided by courts that seem to dislike the perfect tender rule, retreats substantially from its implications.

The perfect tender rule may initially appear to be inconsistent with the efficiency objectives of commercial law. After all, if the seller's performance does not affect the buyer's capacity to use the goods, then why would we want to permit the immaterial nonconformity to unravel the transaction and force the goods back on the seller? This seems especially odd, given that a rejection for insubstantial nonconformities would likely occur only because the buyer was dissatisfied with the deal it had made rather than with the goods. Thus one might believe that a substantial performance rule that prevents buyers from rejecting goods with immaterial nonconformities is superior to a perfect tender rule. Further thought suggests that the issue is more complicated. Requiring buyers to accept goods that deviate even immaterially from what they ordered imposes on those buyers the costs of nonconformity, even if they receive a reduction in price for the nonconformity. In addition, sellers who need only tender substantially conforming goods have incentives to chisel by making a delivery that is nonconforming, but only insubstantially, in the hopes that buyers either will not notice or will not complain. Of course, sellers may respond that buyers have the opposite incentive under a perfect tender rule. Thus, either a perfect tender or a substantial performance rule creates incentives to chisel on the deal, but each rule induces the undesirable behavior from a different party.

Some courts have been sympathetic to the claims of sellers and have essentially eviscerated the perfect tender rule. They have done so in large part by invoking the obligation of § 1-203 to perform contracts in "good faith." "Good faith" for these purposes has traditionally been interpreted as creating a subjective test, although the proposed revision to Article 2 would incorporate into the Article 2 definition of "good faith" a requirement to comply with reasonable commercial standards of fair dealing. (The current version of § 2-103(1)(b) defines "good faith" for merchants to include observance of reasonable commercial standards of fair dealing, but that may apply only where the phrase "good faith" is used in Article 2 rather than to create a general obligation of acting in accordance with that objective definition.)   While violation of the obligation currently requires an actor's dishonesty rather than a negligent failure to comply with commercial standards, courts retain significant leeway to decide what conduct amounts to dishonesty.

There is some support in the commentary for the proposition that a buyer's seizing on a trivial defect in order to reject under the perfect tender rule, where the buyer's true concern is a drop in market price for the goods, violates the obligation of good faith.[27] Some courts have also accepted this rationale. In *D.P. Technology Corp. v. Sherwood Tool, Inc.*[28] the court, applying Connecticut law, refused to dismiss seller's action for the price of a computer system notwithstanding buyer's allegation of a late, and hence noncomplying, tender.   The court concluded that a rejection of specially manufactured goods because of an insubstantial delay that caused buyer no damage might not constitute good faith. The court relied on Connecticut cases that interpreted § 2-601 as requiring "substantial nonconformity" in order to trigger the right to reject, though the court was unclear whether a rejection for immaterial defects is authorized by § 2-601 itself, or whether § 2-601 is subject to some overriding obligation of good faith.   But the position comes

---

[27] See, e.g., John O. Honnold, *Buyer's Right of Rejection*, 97 U. Pa. L. Rev. 457, 475 (1949).

[28] 751 F. Supp. 1038 (D. Conn. 1990).

dangerously close to creating an independent obligation of good faith, a position that the Permanent Editorial Board of the UCC rejects.[29]

Nevertheless, other courts, perhaps fearful of buyers' strategic behavior, have similarly embellished the perfect tender rule, either by invoking a good faith requirement or by construing § 2-601 in a manner that it was clearly intended to avoid, such as a rule of substantial performance. For instance, although the court in *National Fleet Supply, Inc. v. Fairchild*,[30] permitted a buyer to reject nonconforming goods, the court stated that "it is generally understood" that when tender is deficient "in some small respect," rejection is not available. And a Connecticut appellate court, relying on the admonition of Professors James J. White and Robert S. Summers that perfect tender has been properly diminished by courts, concluded that § 2-601 "requires a substantial nonconformity to the contract before the buyer can rightfully reject the goods."[31]

If the perfect tender rule were the only remedy available to a disappointed seller who was a victim of a rejection for trivial defects, we might agree that buyers have too many opportunities for misbehavior. But at least two additional restrictions limit the buyer's capacity to avoid the transaction. The first of these is doctrinal. Even a rightful rejection does not mean the end of the transaction. Under quite broad conditions, the UCC offers a seller whose tender of goods is rightfully rejected to "cure" the defect and to deliver conforming goods. We discuss the conditions of cure below. For the moment, note that if sellers have the right to remedy a defective tender, there is little reason for buyers to engage in strategic behavior, and even less reason for courts to enter the muddy waters of distinguishing substantial from insubstantial nonconformities. Indeed, as we will see, there is some risk that the right to cure confers too much discretion on *sellers* and induces them to chisel in their initial performance. Nevertheless, the combined rights of buyer rejection and seller cure may provide the best mechanism for neutralizing both sellers' motivation to underperform and buyers' motivation to reject for reasons unrelated to product quality.

---

[29] See Permanent Editorial Board Commentary No. 10: Section 1-203 (1994).

[30] 450 N.E.2d 1015, 1017 n.4 (Ind. Ct. App. 1983).

[31] Franklin Quilting Co. v. Orfaly, 470 A.2d 1228, 1229 n.3 (Conn. Ct. App. 1984). The White and Summers position can be found in James J. White & Robert S. Summers, Uniform Commercial Code § 8-3 (5th ed. 2000).

The second restraint on buyer misbehavior evolves from the power of reputation in commercial markets. Buyers who reject strategically may obtain a one-time benefit by purchasing goods at a market price that is lower than the original contract price. But they are unlikely to have cordial dealings with that same seller in the future. And if networks among sellers are sufficiently robust, as they often will be, a buyer who misbehaves with respect to one seller will have a sullied reputation with other sellers. The result is that buyers, at least those who anticipate future dealings in the same market, will often stick to a bargain that they regret rather than incur the long-term costs of reputational injury. Indeed, the fact that buyers who are repeat players in a particular market are unlikely to risk their reputation in that market suggests that allegations of bad faith rejection may simply misunderstand the buyer's need for a conforming tender that precipitated a rejection.

### 3. What Constitutes Acceptance?

Section 2-606(1) provides that acceptance occurs when the buyer:

(a) after a reasonable opportunity to inspect the goods signifies to the seller that the goods are conforming or that he will take or retain them in spite of their non-conformity; or

(b) fails to make an effective rejection . . . but such acceptance does not occur until the buyer has had a reasonable opportunity to inspect them; or

(c) does any act inconsistent with the seller's ownership; but if such act is wrongful as against the seller it is an acceptance only if ratified by him.

Under subsection (a), indications of acceptance will be binding, even if the buyer simultaneously notes defects in the goods. Indications of acceptance, moreover, require no overt statement such as "I accept" or signatures on documents that acknowledge delivery in good order. An act such as commingling seller's goods with buyer's other goods of the same type can signify acceptance.

But statements of satisfaction do not necessarily constitute acceptance. Even though a buyer may waive the pre-acceptance inspection right provided by § 2-513, courts may be wary of purported contractual waivers, especially where consumer contracts or form contracts are involved. Assume, for instance, that a purchaser signs a receipt for a new car that contains an acknowledgment of conformity. If the buyer has, in fact, not yet had an opportunity to inspect the goods and discovers defects on a test drive, we would not be surprised to find a court conclude that the acknowledgment was not binding on the grounds that acceptance could not have occurred until a reasonable time for inspection had passed.

Acceptance through failure to reject essentially incorporates our discussion of inspection. Since acceptance in this manner cannot occur until a reasonable opportunity for inspection has passed, the issue of whether acceptance has occurred requires investigation of the proper period for inspection. The negative implication of § 2-606(1)(b) is that failure to reject on passage of that period will constitute an acceptance. As we indicated in our discussion of inspection, that period will depend on the nature of the goods (are they perishable so that prompt inspection is necessary to avoid waste?) and the nature of the alleged defect (could it be remedied by seller, could it have been caused by the buyer?). But notice the effect of this analysis: Not only is there not a single proper time for an inspection of all goods, but with respect to the same good the proper time for inspecting against one set of defects may not be the same as the proper time for inspecting for other defects. If a buyer of new furniture fails to complain of scratches until a week after delivery, we might be unsympathetic since the intervening period makes it difficult to discern whether the seller or buyer was responsible for the defect. But if the same buyer had ordered a twelve-foot table and she discovered a week after delivery that it was only eleven feet long, we would be more willing to say that the period for inspection had not expired. It is unlikely that the table shrunk in the intervening period or that the buyer sawed off a foot's length.

### a. Burden of Proof Concerning Defects

This logic is consistent with one of the major consequences of acceptance. After acceptance, § 2-607(4) imposes on the buyer the burden of proof with respect to any defect in the goods. By negative implication, the seller bears the burden of proving conformity until acceptance. This allocation of proof makes sense, since the buyer's pre-acceptance inspection should reveal any defects. Hence, we would presume that any subsequent problems with the good were as likely caused by some act of the buyer as of the seller. Since the buyer will usually have the best evidence about treatment of the good after acceptance, and thus be best able to contravene the assumption that the previously undiscovered defect did exist at the time of acceptance, it makes sense to place the burden of proving that fact on the buyer.

This suggests that expiration of the proper time for inspection, and hence acceptance, will occur at the time when the buyer is the party best positioned to explain the origins of the alleged defect. That point occurs, for instance, at a different time with respect to scratches in furniture than to improper measurements. Similarly, it will occur sooner after perishable or fragile goods fall into the possession of the buyer than when the buyer takes possession of durable goods. Inspection, however, is not costless. Buyers may have to incur substantial expense in order to make the kind of inspection that would reveal all defects. A buyer of a horse in a distant market might not be expected to travel with a veterinarian to make an inspection of the horse's health, even though waiting for the horse to arrive at the buyer's residence creates substantial risk of interim injury.

Professors Alan Schwartz and Robert Scott have used these criteria to propose a standard for calculating the reasonable time for inspection in any given situation.[32] Their analysis improves on the simple admonition that courts should balance the relevant factors, such as nature of the goods and nature of the defect. The analysis reflects that the issue of time for inspection and rejection must be determined in light of our overall objective of minimizing the costs of transactional breakdown. There are two risks possible in deciding when a reasonable time for inspection has passed. One is the risk that the seller will erroneously have to bear the cost of a defect that actually arose after tender. The other is the risk that buyer's delay will increase damages suffered, and hence the costs of breach. Each of these risks has a value that should be discounted by its probability. A reasonable time for inspection can be considered to have passed when the sum of the values of those discounted risks exceeds the costs of inspection that the buyer would have to bear. The upshot of this analysis is that while, chronologically, we think of acceptance as preceding the assignment of the burden of proof under § 2-607(4), conceptually the reverse may be true. It may be that we first decide whether it makes sense to assign the burden of proof with respect to the defect at the time of delivery to the buyer or seller, and then conclude whether acceptance has occurred or not, depending on the party to whom it is appropriate to allocate that burden.

### b. Acts Inconsistent with Seller's Ownership

Acts that are inconsistent with the seller's ownership under subsection (c) of § 2-606 are essentially those that evince a failure to reject. Rejection is a means of contending that the goods tendered are not those ordered by the buyer. Hence the rejecting buyer is claiming that it

---

[32] See Alan Schwartz and Robert E. Scott, Commercial Transactions: Principles and Policies 272 (2d ed. 1991).

does not want the goods and asserts no ownership of them. Any act that implies that the buyer has the kind of control and dominion over the goods that we typically associate with ownership negates this claim and allows the seller to maintain that the goods do, in fact, belong to the buyer. These acts usually consist of use or alteration or installation of the goods in a way that makes them substantially less valuable for other users. For instance, a buyer of computer hardware and software who used the goods for approximately 19 months before rejection was deemed to have acted in a manner inconsistent with the seller's ownership.[33] Similarly, a purchaser of cabinets could not reject after cutting them to fit over pipes and installing them notwithstanding an apparent nonconformity.[34]

Mere taking possession of the goods, however, does not constitute an act inconsistent with the seller's ownership. Indeed, rightfully rejecting buyers are obligated to hold defective goods at the seller's disposition and to take reasonable care of the goods for a period of time sufficient to permit the seller to remove them. The tricky part is walking the fine line between this obligation and an exercise of dominion and control that constitutes a wrongful exercise of ownership. The classic case in this area is *Clark v. Zaid, Inc.*[35] Ms. Clark had ordered dining room furniture from Zaid, Inc. which arrived in damaged condition. Clark immediately called the seller and demanded that it take back the furniture and cancel the transaction. Instead, the seller offered to repair. A few months later, with the furniture still in Clark's home and lawsuits flying between the parties, employees of a linoleum company badly damaged one of the contested pieces of furniture. This posed a problem for Clark. If she pursued no remedy against the linoleum company, she might be characterized as failing to take reasonable care of the goods. But any act she took to repair or salvage the goods could be characterized as inconsistent with the seller's ownership and leave her open to a claim that she had accepted the goods and was therefore required to pay for them. Clark complained to the linoleum company. The company's insurer delivered a draft for the full purchase price of the damaged furniture, but

---

[33] See Softa Group, Inc. v. Scarsdale Development, 632 N.E.2d 13 (Ill. Ct. App. 1993).

[34] See United States for Use and Benefit of Whitaker's Inc. v. C.B.C. Enterprises, Inc. 820 F. Supp. 242 (E.D. Va. 1993).

[35] 282 A.2d 483 (Md. 1971).

(on advice of wise counsel for Clark) made the draft payable to Clark and Zaid Co. The court found that if Clark had made an effective and rightful rejection, then retaining the furniture did not constitute an exercise of ownership. The court noted that the buyer can take a series of measures with respect to rejected goods, and will not be deemed to have acted inconsistently with the seller's ownership as long as those actions are taken on behalf of the seller. Thus, the buyer is authorized to resell the goods for the account of the seller (less the costs of resale). The court also noted that a buyer who rejects has a security interest in goods in his possession or control for any payments made on their price and for any expenses reasonably incurred.[36] Since Clark had made a substantial down payment, she was also entitled to resell under this provision or to hold them as a possessory security interest.

There may be cases in which making some use of the goods is not inconsistent with the seller's ownership. Any interpretation of the buyer's actions under this provision requires some understanding of what the UCC is trying to accomplish. Rejection signals the seller that the buyer is not in a position to make effective use of the goods. That is not to suggest, however, that the goods are without value. There may be other buyers who would take the goods in their current condition or as repaired. As between buyers and sellers, the assumption is that the latter has superior knowledge about the market for the goods in their defective or repaired condition. Thus, one function of the acceptance/rejection paradigm is to induce sellers to take unwanted goods back and return them to commerce before they deteriorate further. In short, the objective is to avoid waste. Buyers, however, may occasionally be in a superior position to avoid waste. When that is the case, the conditions of acceptance should not be read to deter buyers from taking advantage of that position. In *CPC International, Inc. v. Techni-Chem, Inc.*,[37] a buyer continued to use a fructose processing system after complaining of defects. The seller maintained that the use precluded return of the goods. The court found, however, that continued use of the system pending the arrival of a replacement might minimize the buyer's losses (which would reduce social waste) and thus could constitute a proper exercise by the buyer. One might explain *Clark v. Zaid* along these lines. Clark would have been authorized to store the goods for the account of the seller pending the seller's retaking of them. If placing the goods in a

---

[36] § 2-711(3).

[37] 660 F. Supp. 1509 (N.D. Ill. 1987).

commercial warehouse had been more costly than maintaining them in Clark's apartment, then a court would want to encourage such waste-reducing activity and conclude that retention did not constitute an act inconsistent with the seller's ownership.

The issue becomes more difficult if the buyer makes actual use of the goods subsequent to rejection. In some cases, even that use should not be considered equivalent to acceptance. Assume, for instance, that a homeowner rejects kitchen floor tiles installed by the seller because of defects that are apparent in an inspection that first occurs after installation. We would be reluctant to require the homeowner to stay out of the kitchen until the tiles were removed, since allowing use would mitigate the seller's damages and minimize the social waste resulting from the defect.[38] Again, the nature of the goods and the buyer's use would appear relevant to the inquiry into whether acceptance had occurred. A purchaser of a mobile home who complains of defects apparent when the buyer first moves in should not be allowed to remain for a substantial period of time and make major alterations to the structure without being held to have accepted the goods. But if the buyer properly rejects and notifies the seller of the defects, makes no non-essential alterations to the structure, and minimizes use of the goods, then (assuming that the rental value of the mobile home is sufficiently low) we should prefer buyer's mitigating use of the goods to the more costly alternative of renting another home or moving into a hotel.

Similarly, inspection under some circumstances might require use of the goods in order to determine whether they conform to the contract. Under these conditions, use is part of the inspection process that precedes the acceptance/rejection decision and thus does not constitute the act of ownership that defines acceptance. In *Stratton Industries, Inc. v. Northwest Georgia Bank*,[39] the buyer purchased a novel system for dyeing carpeting. When the system did not function properly, the buyer dismantled it, modified it, and used it in combination with products of another manufacturer. The court found that the revolutionary nature of the equipment, combined with its failure to function properly and the failure of the seller to respond to an initial rejection warranted the efforts

---

[38] But see Robertson Mfg. Co. v. Jefferson Tile Co., 5 UCC Rep. Serv. 119 (N.Y. Sup. Ct. 1968) (subcontractor accepted tiles notwithstanding defects where tiles were installed notwithstanding discovery that they were improperly mounted).

[39] 382 S.E.2d 721 (Ga. Ct. App. 1989).

of buyer without transforming them into an act of acceptance.

### 4. Buyer's Obligations on Rejection

As our discussion of *Clark v. Zaid* indicates, the buyer who rightfully rejects has some obligations with respect to the goods. The obvious reason for placing obligations on a party who has committed no breach is to mitigate the buyer's damages and avoid social waste by preserving the goods or getting them into the hands of some party who can make use of them. It makes sense for the aggrieved buyer to bear these obligations only when it is in a superior position to minimize waste. Merchant sellers may have better information about alternative uses for the goods than buyers. Of course, sellers cannot take advantage of this information unless they are aware of defects. Thus, § 2-602(1) makes effective rejection dependent on seasonable notification to the seller. Once that prerequisite is satisfied, however, it makes little sense to require mitigation by a buyer who cannot easily salvage the goods. In addition, if the seller is not distant from the goods, then the seller may be in a superior position to recover and resell them.

Section 2-603, therefore, imposes no obligation on the buyer with respect to rightfully rejected goods when the seller has an agent or place of business at the market of rejection. If the seller has no presence in that market, however, a merchant buyer must follow reasonable instructions from the seller with respect to the goods. If no instructions are forthcoming, the merchant buyer must make reasonable efforts to sell them for the seller's account if they are perishable or threaten to decline in value speedily. The buyer is entitled to indemnity for expenses before following the seller's instructions and to reimbursement from the seller for reasonable expenses of selling or caring for the goods. As we have indicated, the exercise of these obligations in good faith does not constitute acceptance or conversion of the goods. Even a buyer who rightfully rejects goods but who is not obligated to resell them has the option of reselling if the seller gives no instructions within a reasonable time after rejection. Alternatively, the buyer in such circumstances may store the goods for the seller's account or reship them to the seller. In each case, § 2-604 provides the buyer the right to reimbursement for reasonable expenses.

Whether the buyer can exceed these explicit options will depend largely on the facts of the case. In particular, buyers may wish simply to destroy or discard nonconforming goods. Although destruction of goods initially seems inconsistent with the objective of avoiding waste, there may be situations where it is the most efficient solution. In *Home*

*Shopping Club, Inc. v. Ohio International, Ltd.*,[40] the court found that the buyer had timely rejected or revoked its acceptance of 12,000 Care Bear lamps delivered to it by the seller. The tendered lamps suffered both cosmetic and safety defects that made them unsuitable for their intended installation in childrens' bedrooms. The seller did not contest the unsuitability of the goods and was provided an opportunity to cure. Nevertheless, the seller gave no instructions with respect to the goods, even after being notified that the buyer would hold the goods as security for its purchase costs and that it was no longer interested in repairs. Seven months later, the buyer destroyed approximately 12,000 Care Bear Lamps. The court held that this action was not unreasonable. The buyer could not reasonably resell the goods, since it might thereby incur liability if the lamps were to fall into the hands of consumers through a secondary market. The cost of storage had reached $33,000 and the estimated cost of testing and repairing each lamp, if undertaken by buyer, would have approached the original cost of each unit.

Compare this situation with *United States for Use & Benefit of Whitaker's Inc. v. C.B.C. Enterprises, Inc.*[41] A buyer of cabinets rejected the tendered goods after discovering nonconformities. Some of the cabinets were installed based on assurances of cure by the seller, but no cure occurred. When the seller failed to retrieve and remove the nonconforming cabinets as the buyer requested, the buyer removed them and disposed of them. The court determined that installation of some of the nonconforming cabinets constituted acceptance of all the nonconforming units. But the court also noted that, even if the buyer had rightfully rejected the cabinets, it had no right to remove and discard them. While the court concluded that the options offered to the buyer under § 2-604 were not exclusive, destruction of rightfully rejected goods for the seller's benefit was inconsistent with the buyer's salvage obligation. The court's decision seems to be correct. The cabinets or their components may or may not have been salvageable for some other buyer. Whether that is the case was arguably best determined by the merchant seller. The buyer, moreover, had the option of simply reshipping the goods to the seller at the latter's expense. In light of this possibility, there seems little reason to give the buyer the discretion to determine the best use of the goods. Perhaps the failure of the seller to respond to the request to reclaim the goods, however, constituted an

---

[40] 27 UCC Rep. Serv. 2d 433 (Fla. Cir. Ct. 1994).

[41] 820 F. Supp. 242 (E.D. Va. 1993).

admission that it had neither the desire nor the capacity to make some alternative use of the goods. That reasoning seems implicit in *Home Shopping Club,* given the delay in the seller's response to the buyer's claim of nonconformity. In light of the objective of avoiding waste, however, there would seem to be few cases in which destruction of the goods is appropriate, and those cases would have to characterized by relatively clear signals that the seller is unwilling to take the goods back combined with low likelihood of significant resale value and high probability of significant costs involved in salvage or storage.

## E. Cure

### 1. Introduction

The seller's ability to cure an initial defective performance substantially retreats from the effect of the perfect tender rule. Cure may be conceived of as a remedy to one of the major risks created the perfect tender rule. A seller who cures can prevent the buyer from escaping a transaction out of regret about entering the deal rather than because of dissatisfaction with the seller's performance. Thus, a buyer who can purchase goods more cheaply than the contract price has less incentive to act strategically where cure is available. The court in *T.W. Oil Inc. v. Consolidated Edison Co.*[42] recognized this feature explicitly. The plaintiff had purchased a cargo of fuel oil whose sulfur content was represented to be no greater than 1 percent and that later was calculated at .52 percent. The plaintiff sold the oil to the defendant under a contract that, consistent with trade practice, described the sulfur content of the oil as .5 percent. Defendant was authorized to use oil with a sulfur content up to 1 percent. Testing after defendant received the oil determined that it bore sulfur content of .92 percent. Defendant rejected the oil and refused offers to accept it at an adjusted price. Instead, defendant insisted on paying no more than the latest prevailing price for the oil, which was 25 percent below the level that existed when the contract was made. Defendant also rejected plaintiff's offer to cure with a substitute shipment of conforming oil. In a subsequent action for breach of contract, the court found that the function of cure was to prevent undue surprise to a seller as a result of some technical nonconformity claimed by the buyer. In order to prevent chiseling by buyers who reject goods in response to price fluctuations that lead them to regret the original bargain, the court subjected the right to refuse cure to a good faith test. Cure was to be permitted as long as the seller "had reasonable grounds,

---

[42] 443 N.E.2d 932 (N.Y. 1982).

tested objectively, for its belief that the goods would be accepted." The court's attempt to merge good faith notions with an objective test of opportunistic rejection is frustrated somewhat by the subjective definition of good faith in § 1-201(19). But it is clear that the court in *T.W. Oil* was less interested in the purity of textual consistency than with the commercial objective of neutralizing strategic rejections.

But if cure is successful in reducing the risk of strategic rejection, it creates the offsetting risk of reducing incentives for the seller to provide conforming deliveries and may allow sellers to reduce their effort with relative impunity. Some buyers will not discover the nonconformity, or at least not discover it until it is too late. Once buyers do discover nonconformities, sellers may have to exert additional effort. But if the expected value of that effort, discounted by the probability that buyers discover the defect that triggers the cure, is projected to be less than the expected savings involved in chiseling (and less than the loss of reputation that results from providing nonconforming goods), then the possibility of cure may induce sellers to provide nonconforming tenders. Unless we think that courts can readily identify strategic rejections (and thus allow cure) and strategic tender (and thus deny it) in appropriate cases, it is unclear whether the opportunity to cure after rejection generates more or less opportunistic behavior than either a perfect tender rule without cure or a substantial performance rule.

## 2. Technical Requirements

The technical requirements of cure are, for the most part, straightforward. They depend on whether the time for delivery set by the contract has passed. A seller who makes a nonconforming tender prior to the scheduled time for performance may seasonably notify the buyer of his intention to cure. A notification of intent to cure, however, must be specific. A request that a customer make a list of all problems, without further communication, may not constitute an offer of cure. Sellers who do choose to cure a prior nonconforming delivery have complete discretion to make another attempt within the contractual period for performance. Buyers who resist cure will be in breach of the contract and will be precluded from rescinding the contract. Sellers, on the other hand, are not required to cure and buyers may not enforce an obligation to cure. The seller's latitude to cure is limited only by the ubiquitous "reasonableness" standard. A buyer who has allowed its seller several efforts to repair an engine that continued to leak oil could ultimately refuse additional attempts at cure,[43] and the buyer of an automobile that spent half of its life in the repair shop was not bound to permit the seller "to tinker with the article indefinitely."[44]

If the time for performance under the contract has expired, § 2-508(2) still provides the seller with an additional opportunity to perform within a "further reasonable time." At this point, however, the seller is subject to two constraints. First, the seller must have had "reasonable grounds to believe" that the initial tender would be acceptable. Second, the seller must substitute a "conforming tender."

The second requirement is somewhat of an oxymoron. A tender can be "conforming" only if it is in accordance with the obligations under the contract. A tender that is late, therefore, cannot be conforming at all. Thus, one must read § 2-508(2) as requiring a tender that is conforming in all respects, other than time of delivery.

The meaning of the first requirement is somewhat more complex. A seller might have reasonable grounds to believe that a nonconforming tender would be acceptable for either of two reasons. First, the seller might be unaware of the nonconformity. Second, the seller might be aware of the nonconformity, but believe it to be sufficiently trivial that the buyer would still accept the goods, with or without cure, and with or without a price adjustment. If the first scenario gave rise to a right to cure, then a seller who was unaware of even substantial nonconformities would have the opportunity to cure. This would seem inconsistent with the objectives of the UCC, insofar as it rewards seller's inattention to the quality of performance. Nevertheless, even an optimally attentive seller arguably could fail to notice some nonconformities, so it is not clear that ignorance alone should disqualify the seller. Of course, if the nonconformity was so substantial that only a careless seller could fail to notice it, one might conclude that the "reasonable grounds" condition was not satisfied.

Some commentators have suggested that the language of the UCC limits the right to cure to the second scenario. The seller's right to cure exists when the seller believed the tender would be acceptable "with or without money allowance." A seller who was unaware of the defect

---

[43] See Tucker v. Aqua Yacht Harbor Corp., 749 F. Supp. 142, 146 (N.D. Miss. 1990).

[44] Orange Motors of Coral Gables, Inc. v. Dade County Dairies, Inc., 258 So.2d 319, 321 (Fla. Dist. Ct. App. 1972).

would have no reason to contemplate whether the buyer would take the goods with an appropriate price reduction for defects in quality or quantity.[45] This interpretation suggests that cure would be available under subsection (2) only if the seller actually had knowledge of the defect and the defect was insubstantial. Official Comment 2 to § 2-508 seems to support this reading insofar as it suggests that the function of cure is to avoid the effects of a "surprise" rejection. Arguably, the seller only could have been "surprised" if it had been aware of the nonconformity, yet still reasonably believed that the buyer would accept the goods. (Of course, the seller who is unaware of a defect may be "surprised" that the buyer has found one.) The Comment, however, creates an additional confusion. It implies that the seller could have anticipated acceptance because, for instance, price adjustments for deviations from contractual quantity or quality are common in the trade. But if the seller's reason for believing the goods would be acceptable was that the tender was consistent with trade usage, then it is unclear that there was any nonconformity in the first place. Recall that trade usage and course of dealing always supplement the contract unless explicitly disclaimed. If acceptance of goods that deviate from contract specifications fall within a trade usage or course of dealing, then the tender would appear to be conforming. Hence, any rejection would be wrongful.

We believe that the focus on the seller's knowledge does little to advance the analysis of who should bear the risk of minor deviations from contractual specifications. One can interpret § 2-508(2) to allow cure where the seller would have reasonable grounds to believe that the goods would be acceptable with a money allowance *if* there was a nonconformity, even though the seller was unaware of the particular nonconformity at the time of tender. For instance, a retailer who sells goods believes that a particular sale of a good that has been sold to many customers without incident will be acceptable to the next customer who purchases one. But the retailer may also reasonably believe that any buyer who finds a minor defect would be willing to take it at a discount rather than terminate the transaction. Indeed, this may have been the effect of the Proposed Revision, which deleted the requirement that the seller have reasonable grounds to believe that the nonconforming tender

---

[45] This argument was originally made by Professor Nordstrom. See William Nordstrom, Handbook of the Law of Sales 321 (1970). For an argument that sellers who are ignorant of defects may also fall within § 2-508(2), see White & Summers, supra note 31, at § 8-5.

would be acceptable and permitted cure after the original time of performance if the seller had made an initial tender in good faith and the cure was "appropriate and timely under the circumstances."

### 3. Curing with a Conforming Tender

A seller who falls within § 2-508(2) may only cure by tendering a conforming delivery. In most cases, that will mean compliance with contractual specifications. Deviations from the contract will not satisfy the seller's obligation. For instance, where the seller agreed to provide the buyer with a mobile home that had dual roof air conditioning, and the proffered unit contained a single air conditioner, the seller's offer to install an additional air conditioner did not constitute a "conforming tender," since the alteration could result in a hole in the middle of the mobile home.[46]

But the issue of conformity may be more complex, and thus raise the same issues of seller and buyer opportunism that underlie the whole issue of whether cure is a desirable remedy. In *David Tunick, Inc. v. Kornfeld*,[47] the buyer of a signed Picasso print determined that he had purchased a forgery. The gallery that sold the print offered to substitute a different print of the same series. The buyer rejected the offer and filed suit alleging fraud and breach of warranty. The court found that the buyer had no obligation to accept cure because "two prints from a series produced by an artist each possess distinctive qualities that may impact their aesthetic and economic value." The court determined that the subjective value that a buyer might place on having a particular print within the series meant that even prints from the same plates and by the same artist were not fungible for purposes of cure. In addition, the court found that prints could look different because they had been handled differently over time. Finally, the court determined that the "aesthetic sensibilities" of the purchaser might have caused the purchaser to favor one print over another, so that the two would not be fungible; thus, imposing on the buyer an obligation to accept a print other than the one selected would impose on the buyer the costs of the seller's breach.

The court's position is a bit overstated, at least as applied to the facts on which the court concentrates. While prints produced by certain processes may have different value because of the wearing of the plates

---

[46] See Worldwide RV Sales & Service, Inc. v. Brooks, 534 N.E.2d 1132, 1133 (Ind. Ct. App. 1989).

[47] 838 F. Supp. 848 (S.D.N.Y. 1993).

over a long run, the court pointed to no evidence that the proffered substitute print in this case suffered from that defect. It might make a difference whether the prints were the 8th and 9th of a run of 10, or the 12th and 950th of a run of 1000. For this very reason, prints carry market values, and one would expect that lower numbered prints of large runs would have different values from higher numbered prints of the same run. Similarly, prints that reflect poor handling would presumably have lower market value than prints that were stored more carefully. But the court provided no information about whether the tendered substitute had the same market value as the print for which the buyer had contracted.

Indeed, there is a nice question, unaddressed by the court, as to who had the burden of proof with respect to the relative values of the prints.[48] Perhaps that means that the court was really relying on the idiosyncratic value that each print has to the buyer. The court found that prints were not interchangeable in that "the purchaser chose a given print because he viewed it as uniquely beautiful, interesting, or well suited to his collection or gallery. Nothing else will satisfy that collector but that which he bought." Perhaps. But if prints have little difference in market value, and cure is to be denied because of the subjective value that is not priced in the marketplace, then the buyer has substantial capacity for strategic rejection of essentially fungible substitutes. Assume, for instance, that the buyer in *Tunick* found no aesthetic difference between the two prints, but regretted the initial transaction on other grounds. For instance, suppose the buyer felt resentment and embarrassment at purchasing an alleged forgery and thus wanted out of the transaction even though there was no claim of forgery with respect to the proffered substitute. It is less clear that those subjective reactions of the buyer should be credited, or that requiring acceptance of cure would amount to the imposition of breach costs on the buyer. The subjective feelings of the buyer would be real enough, but if courts cannot use them to

---

[48] Since the case involved cure after revocation of acceptance, there is at least some claim that the buyer had the burden of proving that the tender was not conforming. Initially, one might imagine that the seller who proffers cure must demonstrate that the cure conforms to the contract. But § 2-607(4) places on the buyer the obligation to establish any breach with respect to goods accepted. Certainly that requires buyer to establish that the original print was forged. Does it require the buyer also to prove that any post-acceptance cure was not conforming? Arguably not, since that claim is not related to "the goods accepted." Yet once the seller offers a particular good in substitution and claims that it is conforming, the buyer may have the burden, under ordinary burden shifting rules, to demonstrate the contrary.

distinguish reliably between cases of buyer opportunism and cases of seller chiseling, then it is less clear that they should have legal significance. Certainly, if we assume that buyer simply wanted out of the transaction because, like the buyer in *Bartus*, it simply decided it had made a bad deal, allowing the unprovable subjective value of the print to serve as a basis for rejecting cure permits buyers to act in the very manner that the cure option is intended to preclude.

### 4. Cure in the Courts: Repair and Interpretation

As we indicated earlier, we might feel more comfortable about the availability of cure if we believed that courts were institutionally capable of distinguishing cases of strategic rejection by buyers from cases of strategic nonconforming tenders by sellers. The cases, however, suggest the difficulty of those inquiries. Take, for instance, a couple of well-known early cases in this area. In *Wilson v. Scampoli*,[49] the purchaser of a color television set complained about the quality of the picture, but refused to permit the seller to adjust or repair it. The court found that the seller had a statutory right to cure the initial tender, including removing the television chassis for a short period of time in order to determine the cause of the malfunction and to ascertain the degree of repair necessary. The buyer complained that she had not bargained for a repaired set, but for a new one. There are contexts in which such a claim is perfectly sensible. A good that has been repaired does not command the same market price as a good that is new and unrepaired. Thus, a buyer of such a good who is required to accept a defective performance that has been cured through repair will be paying a price for the good in excess of its market value and in excess of what was bargained for. The seller who cures through repair and does not provide an offsetting money allowance gets to impose the costs of breach on the buyer. This imposition suggests that cure would be inappropriate, given the objective of avoiding seller chiseling. The knowledge of the seller about the condition of the television at the time of tender is irrelevant to this determination.

But we should perhaps not leap so quickly to the result that the seller was imposing breach costs on the buyer. There are some goods that are sufficiently complex that reasonable buyers will anticipate that some adjustment is likely to be necessary subsequent to delivery. The need for "repair" of such goods is presumably factored into their price, and most buyers normally bargain about the price of such a good with the understanding that it could need adjustment. A buyer who discovers that

---

[49] 228 A.2d 848 (D.C. 1967).

such a good requires adjustment is not the victim of a breach and does not bear the costs of breach. Indeed, if no adjustments are necessary, the buyer may believe that it received a better than average good of that kind. Where adjustment is anticipated, we might conclude the need for adjustment does not constitute a nonconformity, so that any rejection by buyer would be wrongful. Alternatively, we might say that the tender was nonconforming, but that the seller reasonably anticipated that the good would still be acceptable, so that the seller has a right to cure any rejection. (Of course, an idiosyncratic buyer would have the right to bargain for a "no cure" clause; but the objective of the UCC, again, is to provide default rules that most parties in the situation would accept.)

The one caveat, recognized by the court in *Wilson,* is that the source of the rejection must fall within the normal range of adjustment. We all understand that when we purchase a new car, some adjustments will be necessary after it is broken in. Thus, a rejection for a broken window regulator after 1200 miles may be either "wrongful" or "curable." But that does not mean that the buyer should be prevented from making a rejection of the same automobile when the engine falls out within that same period of time. In *Wilson*, it is conceivable that adjustments to "new" color televisions in the ancient years of the 1960's were sufficiently commonplace that the seller's efforts to repair did not impose any costs that a reasonable buyer would not have thought were reflected in the price of the good.

Cure by repair may also minimize the costs of transactional breakdowns. Assume, for instance, that the original price of the television was $675, that the seller could have fully repaired the television for $25, that Wilson would place a value of $625 on the "repaired" television (on the theory that she might be concerned that it would be more likely to need additional repairs), and that the resale costs to the seller (costs related to picking up the television, restocking it, and reselling it) amount to $100. Under these circumstances, it would be less costly to allow repair of the television ($25 in repair costs and $50 in lost value) than to terminate the contract ($100 in resale costs). Of course, those costs would be visited on the innocent buyer rather than on the seller who delivered nonconforming goods, but perhaps that loss is worth incurring to avoid additional social waste. (It would be ideal to require the seller to reimburse the buyer for the lost value of $50, but that value is difficult to measure and would induce buyers to overstate the amount by which they devalued the nonconforming good.)

While courts do not speak in these terms, the analysis seems to be consistent with the results that courts reach. The more complex the good, the more the courts are willing to allow adjustment. The more serious the defect, the less willing courts seem to be to allow cure. Unfortunately, it is not always easy to determine whether the possibility of adjustment was anticipated by the parties, and hence whether it is the buyer or seller who is acting opportunistically. Consider in this light another classic cure case, *Bartus v. Riccardi*.[50] The purchaser of a hearing aid ordered a particular model. The manufacturer delivered a different model when it determined that the model that was ordered had been modified and improved. The purchaser complained that the hearing aid was noisy, gave him a headache, and was not the model he had ordered. He returned the hearing aid after using it for approximately two weeks and refused the seller's offer to obtain the model originally ordered. The court found that the seller had made a proper tender of a conforming good under § 2-508(2) which the buyer was required to accept.

Our initial reaction to the court's decision might be hostile. It is easy to conclude that the buyer had simply lost faith in the seller or manufacturer of the hearing aid. To require the purchaser to accept another product of the same manufacturer, especially with an item as personal and important as a hearing aid, might seem to impose significant breach costs on the buyer. Indeed, the fact that the buyer never returned to retrieve his $80 deposit may have reflected just how much he wanted to avoid dealing with the seller.

But there is an alternative explanation of *Bartus* that is less sympathetic to the purchaser. Maybe, having tried the hearing aid, he discovered he did not want one after all, but for reasons unrelated to its performance. Perhaps he found it displeasing aesthetically or discovered that he did not like wearing one. After all, the court stated that the purchaser had not bought a replacement in the interim. Maybe he left his deposit behind because he realized that he had breached the agreement and hoped to liquidate his damages. If this explanation for the buyer's reluctance to accept cure is more probable, then it is buyer opportunism, rather than seller chiseling, that explains the case, and the court was correct in permitting the seller another opportunity to provide a conforming tender. Indeed, this might be the quintessential case of a nonconforming tender that the seller had reason to believe would be acceptable to the buyer, since the seller apparently thought that he was tendering a good that was *better* than what was required under the contract.

---

[50] 284 N.Y.S.2d 222 (N.Y. City Court 1967).

In sum, once a breach has occurred the desire to minimize the costs of the breakdown suggests that the question of cure's desirability should be answered asking whether the buyer or seller is in the superior position to avoid waste. One way of reducing waste is to get the defective goods back into commerce. If the seller repairs, either the seller could resell them, or the seller could put the goods back into the buyer's hands and the buyer who felt dissatisfied could resell them. If we believe that sellers are generally better able to resell damaged goods (because sellers better know the market for them), then cure is a bad idea. But we reach that conclusion only by looking at that variable in isolation. If we also take into consideration that the likelihood of a "no cure" rule increases the likelihood of strategic rejection by buyers, it might be that we would prefer a cure rule because the risk of strategic rejection more than offsets the risk of seller "overreaching" by imposing breach costs on buyers.

### 5. Cure and Avoidance Under the CISG

The CISG provides seller with an opportunity to cure defective tenders, and, as with the UCC, makes the nature of the right contingent on whether the time for performance has passed. Article 37 grants the seller the right to cure any "deficiency" in the goods so long as the "date for delivery" has not passed. Article 34 explicitly extends this right to cure to deficiencies in documents up to the date of delivery, "if the exercise of this right does not cause the buyer unreasonable inconvenience or unreasonable expense."

The seller's right to cure extends beyond the date for delivery if cure occurs "without unreasonable delay and without causing the buyer unreasonable inconvenience or uncertainty of reimbursement by the seller of expenses advanced by the buyer."[51] One arbitral tribunal has intimated, without citing Article 48, that the seller's right to cure after delivery is contingent on the buyer's consent.[52] This interpretation is too strict. The prerequisites to cure state an objective test, so that even a nonconsenting buyer should be required to accept a cure if a court finds that no unreasonable inconvenience or uncertainty would result. Otherwise, the cure provision will not be able to accomplish its apparent objective of avoiding buyer opportunism.

A seller, however, may wish to avoid the uncertainty of proffering a

---

[51] Article 48(1).

[52] ICC Arbitration Case No. 7531, 2 UNILEX 1994-31 (M.J. Bonell, ed.).

cure that the buyer may find unacceptable. Thus, a seller may request a buyer to decide whether it will accept a substitute performance. If the buyer does not comply with that request within a reasonable time, the seller may perform within the time stated in the request.

The seller's right to cure is explicitly constrained by Article 49. That Article allows the buyer to declare the contract avoided under certain circumstances, and an avoided contract cannot be cured. Under Article 49, the buyer may avoid the contract if the seller's nonconforming performance amounts to a "fundamental breach of contract," or, in the case of non-delivery, if the seller does not deliver the goods within an additional time for delivery fixed by the buyer or declares that it will not deliver within that time. A "fundamental breach of contract," in turn, is defined in Article 25 as a breach that results in such detriment to the other party that it substantially deprives that party of what it was "entitled to expect under the contract." Presumably, if the seller is willing and able to cure promptly, the buyer will have difficulty meeting this standard.

The buyer, therefore, has a limited period of time in which to declare the contract avoided and thus to prevent seller from attempting to cure. If the seller has delivered goods, but the delivery is late, the buyer must declare the contract avoided within a reasonable time after it becomes aware that the delivery has been made. Presumably, the buyer could then avoid the contract if the late delivery precluded buyer from making use of the goods. But if the only nonconformity in the contract is late delivery that deprives the buyer of its contractual expectations, the seller will obviously have no opportunity to cure with a subsequent delivery.

Where the seller has made a timely delivery but the goods fail to conform in quantity or quality, the buyer must also act promptly to avoid the contract. The buyer cannot declare the contract avoided if it acts more than a reasonable time after it knew or ought to have known of the breach, after the expiration of any additional period that the buyer has fixed for the seller's performance, or after the expiration of any period of time that the seller has fixed for offering a cure or after the buyer has declared that it will not accept the cure. Thus, assume that Buyer orders morel mushrooms to be delivered on July 1 and on that date receives a delivery of mushrooms that are not morels. Buyer immediately notifies Seller who offers to ship conforming mushrooms. Buyer agrees to accept a subsequent conforming delivery, but only if they arrive by July 8. The buyer's fixing of an additional time for performance by the seller is explicitly authorized by Article 47(1), and is known as a *Nachfrist* notice. Buyer will now be required to accept the conforming shipment under

Articles 47 and 48. If delivery is, in fact, made on July 7, but Buyer does not realize until July 20 that the second delivery is also nonconforming, a court could find that Buyer cannot declare the contract avoided because it waited more than a reasonable time after it should have learned of the breach and after the expiration of the additional period fixed for performance under Article 47. This is not to say, however, that Buyer was ever required to provide Seller with the opportunity to send a second shipment. If Buyer had no use for the mushrooms that arrived after July 1, e.g., Buyer had to fill a downstream contract due shortly after that date, then the failure to comply on that date would have substantially deprived Buyer of what it was entitled to expect under the contract and the breach would have been "fundamental."

The issue of fundamental breach, however, may not be entirely severable from the issue of cure. Assume that Buyer could fill the downstream contract as long as a conforming delivery was received by July 8. Buyer bargained with seller for a July 1 delivery date in order to give itself some leeway in the event that seller failed to perform. If Buyer no longer needs the mushrooms, however, can it immediately avoid the contract under Article 49 for a fundamental breach? Arguably not. When Seller delivers nonconforming mushrooms on July 1, Buyer stands to lose what it was "entitled to expect," that is, mushrooms that could be resold by July 8, only if Seller cannot deliver a curative tender within the next week. Even if Buyer no longer needs those mushrooms, it should not be able to avoid the contract without permitting the cure. If Seller provides conforming mushrooms by July 8, then the breach will turn out not to be fundamental and Seller is entitled, under Article 48, to remedy the original nonconforming tender. The problem is that we cannot know whether the original breach was fundamental unless we know whether cure is forthcoming. If it is forthcoming, then the original breach would have been nonfundamental and Buyer has no right to avoid the contract. The result is that the link between fundamental breach and the right to cure imposes substantial uncertainty on Buyer. Of course, if that uncertainty is too great, Buyer may claim that Seller has no right to cure under Article 48(1), since that provision limits cure to situations in which Buyer does not suffer unreasonable inconvenience, of which uncertainty in performance would seem to be a prime example.

Thus, assume that on July 1, Seller is notified of the nonconformity and indicates that it will perform by July 8. Under Article 48(2), this notice of cure to Buyer implicitly serves as a request that Buyer make known whether it will accept performance. This provision might be read to give Buyer a unilateral right to reject an offer to cure. But that reading seems too narrow. First, it is inconsistent with the conditions for cure in Article 48(1) that give the seller autonomy over the cure decision, as long as the buyer does not suffer inconvenience or uncertainty. Second, as we have suggested above, it is inconsistent with the rationale of precluding buyer opportunism. If cure were limited to situations in which the buyer acceded, there would be no need for the provision, since buyers can always agree to accept a repair or replacement for a nonconforming delivery. Thus, Article 48 must be read as imposing on the buyer a duty to accept cure even where it would prefer not to. The only caveat is that the request by the seller under Article 48(2) provides the buyer with an opportunity to serve notice that no cure will be acceptable because it cannot be accomplished without imposing on the buyer unreasonable delay or inconvenience. But if there is no basis for that claim, then a seller who gives notice of cure will suffer a wrongful avoidance of the contract should the buyer refuse to accept a substitute tender.

## F. Revocation of Acceptance

### 1. Introduction

Even a thorough inspection may not reveal all defects in a good. Latent nonconformities may not be revealed until the good has been used in such a way that acceptance has occurred. When defects appear at a late date, two policies are implicated. On the one hand, we do not wish to impose breach costs on buyers who have complied with their obligations to inspect, but who nevertheless cannot detect defects. On the other hand, there is something to be said for finalizing transactions and allowing sellers to rely on the buyer's silence. The UCC recognizes a limited set of cases in which the second objective is trumped by the first and permits buyers in such cases to revoke their acceptance of the good.

As we would expect, the conditions for a proper revocation of acceptance are more stringent than for an initial rejection. Presumably the buyer has used the good in the interim, so it is less clear that, even if there are defects, seller occupies the best position to salvage the goods. Sellers of new goods are not necessarily purveyors of used goods. If our objective is to minimize breach costs and avoid waste, it may be that the buyer is in as good of a position as the seller to salvage the maximum value from the transaction. (Of course, the buyer would still have a remedy against the seller for breach of warranty for any difference in value between the goods as contracted for and as accepted.) This rationale suggests that, unlike the case of rejection, revocation should not be permitted when the good fails to conform to the contract "in any respect." Instead, consistent with this rationale, § 2-608 permits a buyer to revoke acceptance only if the nonconformity "substantially impairs" the value of the good to him.

In addition, the right of revocation undercuts buyers' incentives to make thorough inspection of goods on initial tender. If buyers can subsequently revoke acceptance with ease, there is less need to incur the cost of an early inspection. Of course, there are countervailing incentives that would induce buyers to make a proper inspection. For instance, a buyer who is required to pay on acceptance would prefer to discover defects and avoid payment rather than proceed against a seller who has been paid. But the right of revocation at least provides a basis for the buyer's reducing his inspection effort, with the result that defects that might have been easily discovered and cured will go undiscovered. In order to avoid this wasteful result, § 2-608(1) permits revocation of acceptance only if (1) the buyer discovered the nonconformity, but accepted the goods nonetheless on the reasonable assumption that the nonconformity would be cured and it has not been seasonably cured, or (2) without discovery of the nonconformity, if the acceptance was reasonably induced by the difficulty of discovery before acceptance or by the seller's assurances.

Typically, the buyer's reasonable assumption that a discovered nonconformity will be cured will be based on seller's assurances. For instance, in *Beal v. Griffin*,[53] a purchaser of a window-blind cleaning machine was entitled to revoke acceptance when the initial acceptance was made only after the purchaser noted nonconformities on delivery and was informed that they would be remedied if the buyer signed an acknowledgment of satisfactory delivery. A seller's statements that apparent defects will "work themselves out" or will require "only minor adjustment" will excuse the buyer's failure to make an earlier rejection or revocation. Most frequently, buyers will revoke acceptance after sellers have unsuccessfully attempted to repair defects brought to their attention by buyers.[54] The traditional response of sellers in these cases is that the buyer has held onto the goods for a period that exceeded the "reasonable time" within which § 2-608(2) permits buyers to discover the nonconformity. These claims typically ring hollow. A buyer who permits its seller to attempt to repair is attempting to minimize breach costs, even if that requires accepting goods that have been repaired rather

---

[53] 849 P.2d 118 (Idaho Ct. App. 1993).

[54] See, e.g., Cato Equipment Co. v. Matthews, 372 S.E.2d 872 (N.C. Ct. App. 1988).

than goods that are new. Alternatively, the buyer is agreeing that the good at issue is of the type that a reasonable buyer would expect might need adjustment. It would be perverse to invite the buyer to permit such repairs, but then deny the buyer the right to revoke should the repair effort prove fruitless. If that were the case, buyers might more readily reject goods or refuse offers to repair, notwithstanding that repairs could make them whole in a substantial majority of cases, because risk-averse buyers would fear the occasional responsibility for accepted goods that were irreparable.

The buyer's revocation also must occur prior to the time of any substantial change in condition of the goods that is not caused by their own defects. Assume, for instance, that a buyer of fabric does not discover a defect until the goods had been cut into pieces. The buyer would be barred from revoking acceptance, even if it had not been negligent in failing to discover the defect at an earlier time.[55] This limitation applies even where the changed conditions result from circumstances beyond the buyer's control (unless changes result from the defects themselves, as where a faulty engine in a machine causes a fire that destroys the good). Assume, for instance, that the fabric had been destroyed in a fire that was not caused by any defect in the fabric. The buyer would be unable to revoke by offering burned remains back to the seller. The rationale for the requirements appears to be consistent with our objective of minimizing breach costs. If the seller is in the best position to repair goods and get them back into commerce, the parties would want a default rule that induces the seller to take advantage of that position. Nevertheless, the seller's salvage advantage probably exists only with respect to goods that are of the type that the seller traditionally handles. Once the goods have been altered while in the hands of the buyer, the seller's advantage likely disappears. If the buyer's actions with respect to the goods increases the market for them, that change should not preclude revocation, since the seller's advantage in resale will not be adversely affected.[56] But if the alteration removes the goods from the seller's traditional market, it makes more sense to require the buyer to dispose of them and claim damages from the seller than to force the goods back into the seller's hands. Of course, this rationale would apply even if the goods were destroyed as a result of their defects. For

---

[55] See Trinkle v. Schumacher Co., 301 N.W.2d 255 (Wis. Ct. App. 1980).

[56] See J.F. Daley International, Ltd. v. Midwest Container & Industrial Supply Co., 849 S.W.2d 260 (Mo. Ct. App. 1993).

instance, the seller of the machine that burns up as a result of its own defective engine will not necessarily be better at salvaging the remains than the buyer. But § 2-608(2) permits revocation when the change in condition is caused by the defect in the goods. Thus, there appears to be at least some fairness rationale underlying the revocation provision, perhaps reflected in the principle that the change in condition rule seeks to "provide substantial justice to the seller in regard to the condition of goods restored to him and to prevent unjust enrichment to the buyer."[57]

There is one area in which the courts have been less stringent in requiring buyers to maintain the original condition of the goods. Where buyers have, in good faith, attempted to make defective goods operable, courts have been reluctant to accept sellers' argument that the alterations void the right of revocation. In *ARB, Inc. v. E-Systems, Inc.*,[58] for instance, a purchaser of a system for electronically monitoring televisions installed certain equipment notwithstanding discovered defects. It also allegedly damaged the equipment, albeit in an effort to make the system operate properly. The court concluded that neither the installation nor the "changes" occurring in the process of a good faith attempt to make the equipment work constituted "substantial changes in condition." The court may have believed that a contrary rule would deter buyers from good faith efforts to complete the contract satisfactorily.

Conceptually, revocation constitutes an assertion that the goods belong to the seller rather than to the buyer. Thus, post-revocation acts by the buyer that amount to an exercise of ownership of them are inconsistent with the purported revocation, and, just as in the case of rejection, would be wrongful against the seller.[59] Courts have concluded, therefore, that continued use of the goods after an attempted revocation nullifies the effort to throw the goods back at the seller.[60] The attempted revocation is ineffective and the buyer's acceptance remains operative.

---

[57] Stridiron v. I.C., Inc., 578 F. Supp. 997, 1002 (D.V.I. 1984).

[58] 663 F.2d 189 (D.C. Cir. 1980).

[59] See § 2-602(2)(a). Under § 2-608(3), a buyer who revokes acceptance has the same rights and duties with regard to the goods as if it had rejected them. Thus, the duty to abstain from acts of ownership under § 2-602 would apply equally to the buyer attempting to revoke.

[60] See, e.g., L.S. Heath & Son, Inc. v. AT&T Information Systems, Inc., 9 F.3d 561, 568 (7th Cir. 1993).

A buyer, presumably, would have the right to exercise dominion and control over the goods for security or salvage purposes, however, since § 2-608(3) provides revoking buyers with the same rights they have under §§ 2-603 and 2-604 as rejecting buyers. Nevertheless, courts have been rather forgiving of buyers, especially consumer buyers, who use goods post-revocation. If use is precipitated by the seller's continued assurances of repair, courts have correctly found that failure to repair does not preclude the revocation.[61]

But some courts have gone further and allowed juries to determine whether the buyer's post-revocation use of the goods has been "reasonable," taking into account a number of factors. These include the seller's instructions to the buyer after revocation of acceptance; the degree of economic and other hardship that the buyer would suffer if it discontinued using the defective goods; the reasonableness of the buyer's use after revocation as a method of mitigating damages; the degree of prejudice to the seller; and whether the seller acted in bad faith.[62] The reasonableness test is not overly helpful, and has been applied by some courts in a manner that seems inconsistent with the functions of revocation. For instance, courts have considered seller silence about how to redeliver goods as a justification for subsequent use by the buyer.[63] While seller's failure to give instructions may justify the buyer's storage or retention of possession of the goods in order to preserve their value, it does not necessarily warrant their further use, which is likely to depreciate their value.[64] Most cases that permit continued use involve purchasers who make limited use of the goods by buyers who would

---

[61] See, e.g., Wilk Paving, Inc. v. Southworth-Milton, Inc., 649 A.2d 778, 782 (Vt. 1994).

[62] See, e.g., Liarikos v. Mello, 639 N.E.2d 716, 719 (Mass. 1994).

[63] See Erling v. Homera, Inc., 298 N.W.2d 478 (N.D. 1980); Minsel v. El Rancho Mobile Home Ctr., Inc., 188 N.W.2d 9 (Mich. Ct. App. 1971).

[64] See, e.g., Bryant v. Prenger, 717 S.W.2d 242 (Mo. Ct. App. 1986). One commentator has called the failure to compensate for depreciation of the goods during the period between acceptance and revocation an "obvious oversight in the drafting of section 2-608." See George L. Priest, *Breach and Remedy for the Tender of Nonconforming Goods Under the Uniform Commercial Code: An Economic Approach*, 91 Harv. L. Rev. 960, 979 (1978). Our discussion concerns post-revocation use of the goods.

otherwise have incurred significant expense in procuring a substitute.[65]

Perhaps one mechanism for avoiding inappropriate post-revocation use of the good is to grant the seller a setoff for the market value of the post-revocation benefit received by the buyer. This strategy has been employed by a few courts,[66] and rejected by others.[67] The Proposed Revision of § 2-608(4)(b) indorses something similar, making the revoking buyer liable to the seller for the value of buyer's use. That remedy would appear to be an effective mechanism for avoiding the kind of waste that the requirement of prompt revocation is intended to address. Assume, for instance, that a buyer continues to use a mobile home after revoking acceptance. Presumably, we would want the buyer to take this action if, but only if, use of the home reduced losses that it would otherwise suffer. If, for instance, the buyer could obtain reasonable alternative accommodations in a hotel for $30 per night, we would prefer that the buyer remain in the home if its per diem value were less than that amount. While all might agree with that objective, it is less clear that granting the seller a right of setoff is necessary to bring about the correct result. It might be preferable to deny the buyer full recovery of the purchase price and to allow a setoff only if the seller demonstrates that the buyer had a less costly alternative to use of the good. This would give the buyer an incentive to use the good only when it is efficient to do so, without imposing on the buyer the more onerous burden of risking full loss of the right to revoke in the event of a wrong guess about the value of the good and its substitutes.

There is also a doctrinal difficulty with awarding the seller a setoff for continued use by the buyer. Assume that the buyer of an automobile that suffered defects justifying revocation simply stored the vehicle rather than using it. The buyer then rented another automobile for use during the period between revocation and return of the purchase price. The storage charges would appear to be incidental damages and the rental charges consequential damages incurred as a result of the seller's breach,

---

[65] See, e.g., Steers Security Inc. v. Sportscoach Corp. of America, 781 P.2d 1267 (Ore. Ct. App. 1989). But see Aluminum Line Products Company v. Rolls-Royce Motors, Inc., 649 N.E.2d 887 (Ohio Ct. App. 1994).

[66] See, e.g., Lawrence v. Modern Mobile Homes, Inc., 562 S.W.2d 729 (Mo. Ct. App. 1978).

[67] See, e.g., Stridiron v. I.C., Inc., 578 F.Supp. 997 (D.V.I. 1984).

both recoverable in addition to return of the purchase price.[68]  Thus, we may view the buyer's failure to rent another vehicle as a means of avoiding consequential damages that the seller would otherwise have to pay.  The seller in effect obtains a double savings if it not only avoids reimbursement of consequential damages but also receives an offset for the use of the defective vehicle.  Of course, this means that the buyer who continues to use the good and is not required to pay for it receives some windfall.  But that windfall may be explained in a variety of ways.  First, we may believe that the buyer who recovers only the purchase price suffers some undercompensation because there is no payment for the time and aggravation involved in the revocation process.  Second, the alternative of giving the seller an offset when the seller would have had to reimburse the buyer for the costs of storage and use of a substitute may similarly be characterized as a windfall gain to the seller.  Hence, invocation of "windfalls" does little to allocate the loss here.

### 2. "Substantial Impairment to Him"

The requirement that revocation be preceded by a substantial impairment raises additional issues about the proper scope of revocation.  Two elements of the requirement warrant discussion.  First, is the measurement of impairment subjective or objective?  Second, does the requirement inappropriately impose breach costs on the buyer?

The subjective/objective inquiry is raised by the language of § 2-608 that allows revocation by the buyer if the defect causes a substantial impairment "to him."  The argument that this language embodies a subjective standard is bolstered by Official Comment 2, which states that the test of impairment "is not what the seller had reason to know at the time of contracting; the question is whether the nonconformity is such as will in fact cause a substantial impairment of value to the buyer though the seller had no advance knowledge of the buyer's particular circumstances."  Perhaps not too much should be made of the difference between subjective and objective standards.  In practice a finder of fact very often will come to the same conclusion under either standard.  For instance, a buyer's allegation of great suffering from a nonconformity that the factfinder considers trivial may be met with disbelief.

Even where the buyer is credible, § 2-608 and Official Comment 2 should not be interpreted to permit revocation by a buyer who is so idiosyncratic as to be bothered by "defects" that would be acceptable to

---

[68] See § 2-715.

reasonable purchasers in the same conditions. Some indication of reasonable behavior must exist. Consider, for instance, the facts of *Colonial Dodge, Inc. v. Miller.*[69] The buyer revoked acceptance of a new car when he discovered that it had no spare tire and one could not be procured immediately. He made no further use of the automobile. The seller claimed that a spare tire was a trivial defect and that a proper construction of "substantial impairment" would not permit revocation where the difference between the value of proper performance and the value of the good as delivered was so small. The court, however, noted that the "to him" language required that impairment be measured by reference to the circumstances of the particular buyer. Since the buyer had to travel substantial distances at odd hours, absence of a spare tire could constitute a substantial impairment to him, even though it would have been a minor omission to other drivers who did not drive under the same circumstances: "The dangers attendant upon a stranded motorist," the court noted, "are common knowledge, and Mr. Miller's fears are not unreasonable." In short, the court concluded that although the particular circumstances of this buyer did not have to be known to the seller, revocation would be appropriate if the buyer's sense of impairment would have been shared by a reasonable person in those same circumstances. Thus, the court likely would have reached a different decision had the missing part consisted of a hub cap that had no operational effect on the automobile, but Mr. Miller claimed an idiosyncratic insistence on the aesthetic integrity of the automobile.

Interpreted in this manner, the "substantial impairment" requirement describes a mixed standard. It has a subjective element, insofar as the particular circumstances that leads the buyer to have subjective needs may be taken into account. But once those circumstances are known, the buyer is not entitled to have a wholly subjective reaction that creates a substantial impairment under conditions that would be considered trivial by others in the same position.[70] The buyer's rejection must be fairly typical, an objective standard. This appears to be a commonly reached conclusion.[71] For instance, a buyer who needed a sun lamp to treat a rare

---

[69] 362 N.W.2d 704, 707 (Mich. 1984).

[70] See also Jorgensen v. Pressnall, 545 P.2d 1382 (Ore. 1976).

[71] See, e.g., Hays Merchandise, Inc. v. Dewey, 474 P.2d 270, 272 (Wash. 1970) (court interprets existence of substantial impairment in light of "objective factual determination of the buyer's particular circumstances rather than some unarticulated desires").

skin condition could revoke acceptance of a bath/shower unit advertised as including a sun lamp when he discovered that it had no such capacity, even thought the unit otherwise operated perfectly.[72] A mixed standard is also an appropriate one. Permitting buyers to revoke for wholly subjective reasons would impose on sellers breach costs that could more readily be avoided by buyers, who presumably are aware of their idiosyncracies. Subjectivity also threatens the desire for verifiability. Buyers who could make wholly subjective claims could assert substantial impairment for idiosyncratic reasons that courts could not distinguish from opportunistic behavior. A more objective test allows courts to deny revocation under circumstances in which buyers suffer minor defects that can be remedied through damage actions rather than though the more costly mechanism of unraveling the entire transaction.

Much as the car seller in *Colonial Dodge* believed that the "substantial impairment" test imposed too great of a burden on sellers, others conclude that it imposes too great of a burden on buyers. Professors Alan Schwartz and Robert E. Scott have suggested that the test can prevent dissatisfied buyers and breaching sellers from reaching efficient bargains about the repair of defective goods.[73] Assume, for instance, that a defect lowers the market value of a good with a contract price of $2000 by $75, but that the seller could repair the good for $50. (One might wonder why, if full repair could be made for $50, the market price would decline by $75. The greater market price decline may reflect the greater costs that buyer has to incur in obtaining a repair from a third party than for the seller to repair the goods himself.) If the $75 defect did not qualify as substantial, then the buyer would be unable to revoke and would have to bring a warranty action for $75 or personally bear the costs of breach. If the buyer were able to revoke, on the other hand, the seller would repair for $50 and breach costs would decline from $75 to that level. Thus the substantial impairment requirement imposes breach costs on buyers (including the potential costs of bringing a warranty action), even though they would have revoked if permitted. The substantial impairment requirement, therefore, interferes with minimizing the costs of transactional breakdown. At the same time, as suggested above, the substantial impairment requirement reduces the ability of buyers to act strategically to undo completed transactions. But as Schwartz and Scott argue, while strategic revocations are possible, their likelihood is reduced

[72] See Scott v. Noland Co., 1995 LEXIS 505 (Tenn. Ct. App.).

[73] See Schwartz and Scott, supra note 32, at 309-311.

by the fact that § 2-607(3) imposes on accepting buyers the burden of proof that they do not bear for rejection. The relevant issue is whether the increase in strategic revocations that would remain if we eliminated the substantial impairment requirement more than offsets the social losses that the requirement creates by deterring efficient resolutions of buyer complaints.

If the drafters of the Proposed Revision of Article 2 were attentive to these arguments at all, they did not find them convincing. The most recent proposed revision of the revocation provision retained the substantial impairment requirement, and defined the application of the requirement in terms of the value of the good "to the buyer."

### 3. Post-Revocation Cure

Nothing in Article 2 explicitly allows cure after a revocation. Commentators and a majority of courts that have addressed the issue agree that a strict reading of the UCC provides sellers with a right to cure only after rejection.[74] In *Grappelberg v. Landrum*,[75] a seller of a defective television set offered to replace the set with an identical model. The court concluded that allowing cure after revocation places the seller in a better position to maximize profits at the expense of buyers by saving itself the cost of storing items and the expense and risk involved in reselling goods. The court seemed to believe that allowing cure at the revocation stage would undercompensate buyers whose faith in the particular brand and model of good was shattered by the defective performance. Other courts view cure as a remedy only for minor defects, and thus preclude sellers from demanding it where, as in a revocation situation, the defect is necessarily "substantial."[76]

Nevertheless, some courts and commentators have required revoking buyers to accept a proffered cure. The doctrinal basis for the requirement is § 2-608(3), which imposes on buyers who revoke the same duties with regard to the goods that they have after rejection. Arguably, that

---

[74] See, e.g., U.S. Roofing, Inc. v. Credit Alliance Corp., 279 Cal. Rptr. 533 (Cal. App. 1991); John A. Sebert, Jr., *Rejection, Revocation, and Cure Under Article 2 of the Uniform Commercial Code: Some Modest Proposals*, 84 N.W.U.L. Rev. 375, 392-93 (1990).

[75] 666 S.W.2d 88 (Tex. Ct. App. 1984).

[76] See, e.g., Johannsen v. Minnesota Valley Ford Tractor Co., 304 N.W.2d 654 (Minn. 1981).

provision includes the "duty" to accept a cure under § 2-508.[77] One can plausibly read the seller's right to cure as imposing on the buyer a correlative obligation to accept the cure, and thus within the realm of buyer duties incorporated into § 2-608(3). But the reading stretches, if not to the breaking point, the concept of the buyer's duties. The duty to allow the seller to exercise a right is of a different nature than the independent duties imposed on buyers by provisions such as §§ 2-603 and 2-604 with respect to salvage and storage of rejected goods. These are the types of duties that are clearly implicated by § 2-608(3). Thus, the question of whether there does or should exist a post-revocation right of cure cannot be resolved on the basis of statutory language alone. Some underlying policy must be used to resolve the issue. That policy should reflect the same objective that is addressed in the rejection/cure scenario. That is, given that the seller's right to cure will induce sellers to chisel in their initial performance, since they have a second opportunity to perform if "caught," do we believe that cure is still helpful because it will offset strategic behavior by revoking buyers? If we believe that buyers systematically revoke acceptance strategically when they regret having entered into the transaction rather than when they are dissatisfied with seller's performance, then we would prefer to allow sellers the opportunity to save transactions by curing defects, even at this late stage. On the other hand, if we believe that buyer revocations tend to reflect substantial defects in seller performance, then there seems less reason to provide sellers with additional opportunities for performance that likely impose breach costs on buyers.

As noted above, there are some reasons to believe that buyers are less likely to act strategically in making revocations than in making rejections. Perhaps most importantly, the revoking buyer, unlike the rejecting buyer, bears the burden of proving defects.[78] In addition, the standard for revocation is higher than that for rejection; the buyer must prove not just nonconformity, but substantial impairment. If the expected loss that the buyer will suffer from the defect is less than the expected cost of proving substantial impairment, the buyer will simply retain the defective good. While this statutory scheme may impose certain breach costs on the buyer (the costs of defects that do not amount to substantial impairments), it suggests that buyers who do not in fact suffer substantial impairments

---

[77] See, e.g., David Tunick, Inc. v. Kornfeld, 838 F. Supp. 848 (S.D.N.Y. 1993); White & Summers, supra note 31, at 333.

[78] § 2-607(4).

(those buyers who would simply be acting opportunistically to get out of a bad deal) are less likely to bring revocation actions. If the statutory scheme discourages opportunistic revocation claims, then the claims we are likely to see will be those in which buyers really do suffer substantial impairments. Consequently, there is little reason to believe that opportunistic revocation will be as frequent as opportunistic rejection, and there is less need to provide seller with a right to cure. Given the risk that cure can be used strategically by sellers to chisel at initial performance, it is by no means clear that post-revocation cure is a good idea.

The most recent Proposed Revision of Article 2 nevertheless explicitly granted sellers the right to cure after a rejection or a justifiable revocation of acceptance. Proposed § 2-508(1) places two significant limitations on post-revocation cure, however. First, it would not be available in consumer transactions. Second, the post-revocation right to cure would be limited to situations in which the defect had not been discovered when it was accepted. Thus, if a buyer noticed nonconformities on tender, but accepted the goods anyway because of the seller's assurances that cure was forthcoming, a seller who failed to cure would not have an additional opportunity after buyer revoked acceptance. The proposed comment to that provision stated that the post-revocation right to cure "expands" the seller's rights. This reference implies that the drafters of the Proposed Revision believed that the right to post-revocation cure does not exist under current Article 2. It is less clear that they suggested a change for the better.

## V. Excuse

### A. Introduction.

Parties enter into contracts with certain assumptions about the conditions that will exist while the contract is in force. A manufacturer of widgets may assume that its plant will not burn down. Purchasers of grain in a long-term supply contract may assume that the market price of grain during that period will stay within historical parameters. When conditions change so significantly that those assumptions are no longer true, one of the parties may stand to profit from the transaction much more than it initially anticipated, while the other stands to lose much more than it intended to risk. In these situations, the latter party is likely to claim that the contract was never intended to apply to the changed situation and to seek excuse from its performance.

The law of excuse, therefore, constitutes a mechanism by which to allocate the risk of changed circumstances. If we believe that parties essentially assume all risks that they do not explicitly allocate to the other party, then there is little room in which the risk of changed circumstances should apply. If, on the other hand, we believe that parties implicitly intend to adjust their performance when circumstances change, then judicial intervention may be necessary to enforce that expectation, as the party who stands to benefit from the change may wish to deny that the obligation to adjust exists.

### B. Under the UCC.

Prior to the UCC, these cases were decided under principles of "impossibility" or "frustration of purpose." The UCC integrates these principles into excuse or "commercial impracticability" under § 2-615. That provision states that "[e]xcept so far as a seller may have assumed a greater obligation ... (d)elay in delivery or non-delivery ... by a seller ... is not a breach of his duty under a contract for sale if performance as agreed has been made impracticable by the occurrence of a contingency the nonoccurrence of which was a basic assumption on which the contract was made . . . ." Before analyzing this test, note that, by its terms, it applies only to sellers. The negative implication is that buyers have no parallel claim to relief. If, for instance, market prices drop precipitously after a buyer has agreed to enter a long-term contract with a fixed price, the literal language of § 2-615 does not give the buyer any claim for relief. In addition, Official Comment 1 speaks explicitly of excuse for a seller, without any mention of buyers. Nevertheless, some courts have been more generous towards buyers and have held that the provision applies with equal force to them.[79] Thus, we apply our analysis to both buyers and sellers.

Courts have routinely denied the relief made available under § 2-615, regardless of who requests it.[80] Narrow construction of excuse strikes us as the correct result. We reach this conclusion primarily because we believe that the parties are better able to allocate risks of changed circumstances at the time of negotiation than courts are able to allocate them after a risk has materialized. A rule that regularly denies claims of excuse, therefore, induces parties to reach an optimal bargain. This is so

---

[79] See, e.g., Power Engineering & Manufacturing, Ltd. v. Krug International, 501 N.W.2d 490 (Iowa 1993); Syrovy v. Alpine Resources, Inc., 19 UCC Rep Serv. 995, 841 P.2d 1279 (Wash. Ct. App. 1992).

[80] See, e.g., Alamance Cty. Bd. Of Educ. v. Bobby Murray Chevrolet, Inc., 465 S.E.2d 306 (N.C. Ct. App. 1996).

because courts have difficulty verifying that the prerequisites for excuse have been satisfied, while parties can more easily consider the conditions under which the contract will not operate either explicitly in the contract or implicitly as a trade usage.

How do courts interpret the terms of § 2-615 to reach this result? Consider first the condition that excuse will not be permitted when a party has "assumed a greater obligation." Essentially, this allows a party to assume the risk that circumstances will change between contract formation and performance in a manner that causes that party to regret having entered into the contract. Risk assumption may be explicit, as where a seller negotiates to exclude a "force majeure" clause in return for a higher price for the goods. But parties may also implicitly assume risks. Official Comment 8 to § 2-615 suggests that a greater assumption may also be inferred from circumstances. Assume, for example, that the parties negotiate a five-year coal supply contract and tie the contract price to the consumer price index. Subsequently, the spot market price for coal increases at a significantly greater rate than the selected index. The seller may seek to be excused, contending that the parties assumed that changes in the market price for coal would parallel changes in the consumer price index. At the very least, the seller might contend, the assumption underlying the selection of the index was that coal prices would stay within their historical range or within their historical ratio to consumer prices. The buyer may respond, however, that the selection of a particular index, rather than some other available index, implicitly allocated the risk that the selected index would fail to perform as the seller anticipated.[81]

It is difficult to adjudicate such claims. Without knowing the reasons why a specific term was selected, it is unclear whether its presence in the contract constitutes an assumption of a particular risk. We might simply conclude that *any* consequence that follows from the inclusion of each clause was accepted by the party who would be adversely affected by operation of the clause. But unless we make that assumption, it will typically be unclear whether the parties actually bargained about that clause. Perhaps, for instance, the buyer was willing to pay a higher initial price if that particular index for subsequent price increases was selected. The investigation into assumption of the risk, therefore, requires courts

---

[81] See Northern Indiana Public Service Co. v. Carbon County Coal Co., 799 F.2d 265 (7th Cir. 1986).

to reconstruct the bargain reached by the parties.[82]  But attempting to unpack the relationship among different clauses to the contract is a task bound to be filled with erroneous guesses.

A similar judicial difficulty occurs if the court finds that a clause was not bargained for and therefore seeks to adjust the parties' relationship in light of changed conditions.  A court has little ability to make other contractual adjustments, such as delivery dates or quantities, that may have been traded against the price term implicitly or explicitly during negotiations.  Thus, when a court focuses on the term of the contract about which one party complains, therefore, it may poorly serve the party who benefitted from the inclusion of that clause. A better approach would be for courts to signal that they will not intervene to impose contractual adjustments unless parties have explicitly indicated their desire to have such an obligation.  That signal might take the form of a renegotiation clause or other contractual provision that indicates the parties' intent to allow adjustment when circumstances change dramatically.  This does not mean that most parties would prefer to take a winner-take-all approach when those circumstances alter the parties' initial expectations.  Rather, the preferred default rule may simply reflect the difficulty courts have in either discerning the parties' intent or imposing a sharing of losses where the parties have been silent.

If the risk has not been assumed, excuse is permitted only if the condition that causes regret makes performance "impracticable."  The Official Comments provide little guidance as to the what constitutes impracticability.  If a seller's plant is destroyed in a fire, it may purchase the goods elsewhere and resell them to buyer.  The question is whether it is required to do so.  We are told that "[i]ncreased cost *alone* does not excuse performance"[83] and a rise or a collapse in the market, "in itself," also does not make performance impracticable.[84]

The problem, of course, is that price increases and shortages never occur "alone" or "in itself;" they occur due to some other conditions, such as economic crisis, oil embargo, or war.  Some courts have concluded that excuse is permissible only when the background

---

[82] See, e.g., Stinnes Interoil, Inc. v. Apex Oil Co., 604 F. Supp. 978 (S.D.N.Y. 1985).

[83] § 2-615, Official Comment 4 (emphasis added).

[84] Id.

conditions that make performance more difficult are unforeseeable.[85] As we discuss below, however, the concept of foreseeability, however, may be too slippery to serve as a valid predictor of circumstances that would warrant excuse. Before we turn to a critique of foreseeability, however, we note that one way to consider the issue of impracticability is by reference to the reasonable assumption that the parties at least expected their agreement to produce net gains. Thus, the limiting case for claims of excuse based on increased seller's costs would exist where that increase exceeded the gain that the buyer would enjoy from performance.

Consider, in this light, *International Minerals & Chemical Corp. v. Llano, Inc.*[86] A buyer of natural gas claimed that it could not comply with new environmental regulations without shutting down gas-powered boilers and thus its need for gas fell below contractual expectations. The court concluded that the contract should be interpreted to allow buyer to accept below-contract quantities of gas if full performance had become impracticable. The court properly did not equate impracticability with impossibility, but instead contended that performance was impracticable if it could only be accomplished at "excessive or unreasonable cost." That phrase begs the question of what makes increased costs "excessive or unreasonable." But it also gives rise to a possible solution. If the other conditions of § 2-615 were satisfied, we would not expect the buyer to incur an additional cost of $10,000 in order to ensure buyer a profit of $100. But the reason is not simply the dramatic differences between buyer's loss and seller's gain. Rather, we are moved to this conclusion because it turns the contract into one that produces a net social loss, insofar as losses exceed gains. Of course, the logic of our position means that the buyer should also be excused if it suffers a loss of $10,000 and seller would gain $9999 from performance. Even if that is true as a logical position, parties and courts will be unable to quantify gains and losses with such precision, and the presumption against granting excuse (which we defend below) will lead courts to require significant discrepancy (hence the strong language of "excessive or unreasonable") between gains and losses before allowing excuse in order to ensure that the estimates of gains and losses reflects a net loss situation.

In *International Minerals & Chemical*, the court considered an additional cost of performance. The seller contended that the buyer could

---

[85] See Waldinger Corp. v. CRS Group Engineers, Inc., Clark Dietz Division, 775 F.2d 781 (7th Cir. 1985).

[86] 770 F.2d 879 (10th Cir. 1985).

have forestalled implementation of the governmental regulations and continued to accept and use gas under the contract. The court replied that any such action would have the effect of increasing pollution, which would be unacceptable as a matter of public policy. "Public policy," perhaps somewhat empty of itself, suggests that the court properly considered the additional pollution as a cost to be considered in determining whether the social benefits of completing the contract as drafted exceed the costs of performance. The combined social costs of pollution and increased costs to the buyer, the court seemed to conclude, exceeded the benefits of performance to the seller and thus permitted a finding of impracticability.

Of course, in many cases, the obligor's loss will offset the obligee's gain. Where market prices diverge from their anticipated range during the course of the contract, the consequences for sellers and buyers will produce a zero-sum effect: dramatic increases in prices mean that the seller will receive from the buyer an amount equal to what the buyer will have to pay in excess of its expectations. Thus, unless the buyer can demonstrate some additional losses, such as significant losses on downstream contracts or impending bankruptcy if performance is required (and if the other conditions of § 2-615 are satisfied), Official Comment 4 correctly suggests that increased cost alone does not warrant excuse.

Even a finding of impracticability does not necessarily excuse performance. The third element of § 2-615 requires that the impracticability result from a contingency the nonoccurrence of which was a basic assumption of the parties. This could mean either that the parties did not contemplate the contingency or that they considered it and affirmatively believed that it would not occur. In either event, the test boils down to an inquiry into foreseeability.[87] But it leaves open the issue of *what* must be foreseeable. Return to our example of the coal contract. Assume that the spike in coal prices was caused by an unprecedented drought that reduced the production of hydroelectric plants and increased demand for energy generated by coal-fired electric plants. As a result, coal that was selling (in current dollars) for $40 per ton at the time of contract and that in the past 50 years has sold at (in current dollars) for between $25 per ton and $60 per ton was now selling at $80 per ton. Even if the "consumer price index" clause does not impose a higher risk

---

[87] See Eastern Air Lines, Inc. v. Gulf Oil Corp., 415 F. Supp. 429 (S.D. Fla. 1975).

on the seller and even if the dramatic increase renders performance impracticable, whether that impracticability resulted from an unforeseen occurrence ("a contingency the nonoccurrence of which was a basic assumption" of the parties) remains open. The precise cause, the historic drought that reduced the energy generating capacity of rivers, may have been unforeseeable.

But why should we define the relevant "contingency" as that particular event? Instead, we might ask whether it was foreseeable that within the contract period *some* event would materialize that could cause coal prices to increase by a third over their historic high. On that interpretation of the relevant contingency, the precise cause of the increase would not matter. If the parties could anticipate that *something* might occur to increase prices, although the more precise cause is unknown and unprecedented, then the event that materialized was, in a very real sense, foreseeable. Indeed, if the reason for a foreseeability test is a concern that parties should not be liable for the consequences of events that they could not control, a broad reading of that contingency is appropriate. Commercial actors, as we have indicated above, can control through contract for consequences, even if they cannot control the materialization of the particular event that requires adjustment. Parties can deal with uncertainty by including renegotiation clauses, or by hedging one contract with a broad portfolio of other contracts. There is no need to identify a specific event in order to allocate the risk emanating from externally imposed shocks to contractual expectations.

Even if we define the precise event as the one that must be unforeseeable, that standard proves problematic. What does it mean to be unforseeable? It need not mean that no one would ever have thought of it, or that if bargainers with unlimited time and resources had thought up a list of events that might interfere with contractual expectations they never would have considered the event that materialized. To some, this difficulty is resolved by interpreting foreseeability in terms of an inquiry that asks which party was in a superior position to avoid the materialization of a risk or to insure against it.[88] This analysis is consistent with appeals to efficient allocations of risk. Nevertheless, it takes an ex post view of risk, insofar as it asks, once a remote risk materializes, which party could best have avoided it. Insofar as excuse is directed at the capacity of parties to allocate remote risks, we prefer an

---

[88] See Richard A. Posner & Andrew M. Rosenfield, *Impossibility and Related Doctrines in Contract Law: An Economic Analysis*, 6 J. Legal Studies 83 (1977).

ex ante approach cast in terms of the effort that we expect rational parties to devote to risk allocation. The results are typically consistent with efficient risk allocation, but the test requires more attention to the bargaining process. At some point in that process, the expected value of a contingency is so small that it is not worth bargaining about at all. Assume, for instance, that there is an event that will cause the seller a loss of $1 million, if it materializes at all. Assume further that the seller estimates that there is a no greater than 1:100,000 risk that is will materialize. A rational seller would not invest more than $10 in time to negotiate about that risk. But what are the implications for that calculus should the remote risk materialize? One might conclude that the risk has been unallocated because it was not worth considering. But failure to reallocate the risk from the party on whom it would fall may also imply that that party implicitly assumed the risk because the cost of reallocating it elsewhere was not worth incurring. This result not only has the benefit of avoiding difficult judicial efforts to adjust obligations, but also induces each party to make rational calculations of which risks are, in fact, worth including in the contract.

Indeed, judicial intervention may significantly reduce incentives of those best able to avoid risks to take advantage of their position. Assume, for instance, that the parties identify a commercial risk that would reduce the expected value of the contract to the seller by $50,000. Assume further that the seller could avoid the loss at a cost of $30,000, while the buyer could avoid it only at a cost of $55,000. We would certainly prefer that the loss be allocated to the seller, in order to induce him to take the cheaper cost avoidance measure. Assume further, however, that the probability of occurrence is sufficiently remote that the seller believes that a court would adjust the parties' obligations or excuse performance should the risk materialize, and that the seller believes that judicial intervention would take the form of loss splitting. Thus, the expected value of the contract to the seller would decline by ½ x $50,000, or $25,000. This loss is less than the investment the seller would have to make to avoid the loss ($30,000). Thus, the seller will allow a $50,000 loss to materialize, even though it could have efficiently avoided it. A flat rule that imposes the loss the seller induces it to take efficient loss avoidance measures.

To the extent that this approach reduces judicial intervention, it might be thought a harsh rule that threatens to impose significant losses on commercial parties who fail to negotiate for specific risk allocations. Two mediating possibilities, however, suggest that parties can control for significant changes in circumstances. First, clauses that require renegotiation when spot market prices deviate significantly from contract prices may be negotiated with less difficulty, insofar as they do not require identification or allocation of a particular risk. Instead, they simply impose an obligation to share risks when any event causes a clear divergence from contractual expectations. Second, the nature of long-term supply contracts that are most frequently the source of cases involving claims of excuse suggests that the buyer and seller will each have a portfolio of contracts at any given time. That is, our coal supplier will simultaneously have contracts with several buyers and the buyer will have contracts with several sellers. Each party can adjust for risks by entering into contracts that have different price, quantity, and delivery terms. In this way, parties can allocate risks among contracts rather than within a single contract.

Finally, it might be thought that a rule of no adjustment induces those who would benefit from changed circumstances to act strategically. Thus, even if a seller knows that the implicit deal was to adjust the contract price if the market price for the good fell precipitously, the seller might be reluctant to give the buyer that benefit should the risk materialize. If the seller knows that courts will be reluctant excuse the buyer, it might be thought that the seller would have nothing to lose from such opportunism. That fear, however, ignores the likelihood of extra-legal sanctions available to the aggrieved buyer. Reputation will be particularly important in long-term transactions, for the very reason that parties are susceptible to opportunism. To the extent that buyers and sellers transact in common networks and can inform others within the network of chiseling by a trading partner, they can credibly threaten to punish chiselers without the use of legal sanctions. These reputational sanctions may be far more effective than the possibility of judicial intervention and reformation in ensuring that commercial parties adhere to their original understandings.

### C. Under the CISG.

The CISG accommodates the UCC's analysis of excuse to a significant degree, though the CISG employs a different language. Article 79 of the CISG exempts either the seller or the buyer from liability for failure to perform contractual obligations if that party proves (1) that the failure was due to an impediment "beyond his control," (2) that "he could not reasonably be expected to have taken the impediment into account at the time of the conclusion of the contract," and (3) that once the impediment materialized, he could not reasonably have avoided or overcome it or its consequences. Although the Article avoids language of "impracticability" and phrases such as "the occurrence of a contingency the non-occurrence of which was a basic assumption," the principles behind those terms appear also to inform the CISG standard.

The requirement that materialization of the impediment must be beyond the control of the party seeking exemption suggests that some inquiry into reasonable precautions is necessary. One commentator concludes that the obligor "is always responsible for impediments when he could have prevented them but, despite his control over preparation, organization, and execution, failed to do so."[89] This suggests something close to a strict liability rule in which an obligor guarantees performance. As an interpretation of Article 79, the rule is too strict. At some cost, an obligor will often be able to avoid loss. Fire can be prevented by hiring round-the-clock guards armed with fire extinguishers; shipping disasters can be avoided by shipping the goods twice, in case something goes awry with the first shipment. But these possibilities make the possibility of an exemption superfluous. The language of "beyond his control" should be read in terms of what we would expect a reasonable obligor to do under the circumstances in which the contract is being performed. Thus, an impediment sufficient to trigger a right to exemption would exist only if the event materialized notwithstanding reasonable precautions against its occurrence by the obligor. Whether unreasonable precautions are equivalent to "impracticable" ones under the UCC, however, is a different matter. The most we can say is that efforts that would be impracticable because (as we discussed above) they eliminate the net value of the contract should certainly not be required under the CISG.

The second requirement is that the impediment must be one that the obligor could not reasonably be expected to have taken into account at the time the contract was concluded. This requirement reflects the same concerns we saw under the UCC analysis that permits excuse only when the contingency that arises is one the non-occurrence of which was a basic assumption of the contract. As in the case of the "beyond his control" standard, the requirement calls for some inquiry the reasonableness of the obligor's conduct. But the inquiry into reasonableness is directed at different issues. Assume, for instance, that an Italian seller ships goods to an Australian buyer through a zone in which hostilities are occurring. The goods are lost when the seller's ship is seized in the hostile zone. Here, the seller may claim that the hostile seizing of the cargo constituted the relevant impediment that exempts him from performance. There may have been little that the seller could have

---

[89] Peter Schlechtriem, Uniform Sales Law 101 (1986).

done to avoid the seizure. Hence, it was "beyond his control" and qualifies as an impediment. At the same time, if the seller could reasonably have foreseen that an attack could have occurred, then it should have taken that possibility into account at the time of contract and expressly allocated it to the buyer through a force majeure or other clause. Failure to do so in the face of foreseeability would deprive the seller of the exemption claim.

Here, we use the term "foreseeability" with all the scepticism to which we alluded above. At the very least, we mean by that term that a person who devoted a reasonable amount of time and resources into contemplating what might occur during performance of the contract would not have considered the risk that materialized. We reiterate, however, our previous concern for the slippery nature of unforeseeability. If we define the risk as "seizure of goods by hostile forces," for instance, the risk may have been "unforeseen." If we define the risk more broadly as "loss of goods at sea," however, we could more readily conclude that the seller did or should have contemplated what occurred. In any event, the claimed impediment could not have existed at the time of the conclusion of the contract. Hence, a Bulgarian buyer who did not open a documentary credit as required by its contract with an Austrian seller could not claim exemption due to a Bulgarian government order suspending the payment of foreign debts, since that suspension had been declared at the time of the conclusion of the contract and the buyer could thus have foreseen the difficulties that subsequently arose.[90]

Under the third requirement of Article 79, exemption is permitted only if the obligor could not have avoided or overcome the impediment or its consequences. Assume in our previous example that the seizure of the goods constituted an impediment and that the seller could not reasonably have anticipated the attack. Assume further that seller could still have performed the contract by purchasing and delivering a fungible substitute for the lost goods, although the seller would have had to pay a price for the goods in excess of the price he was to receive from the buyer. The buyer may now contend that seller is capable of performance, although at a loss, and thus should not be exempt. The seller must again respond with the concept of reasonableness. We believe that the phrase "reasonably be expected," which modifies the "taken the impediment into account" clause of Article 79(1), should be read to modify this obligation ("to have avoided or overcome" the impediment) as well. The question

---

[90] See ICC Court of Arbitration Paris, No. 7197/1992, UNILEX D. 1992-2.

then arises whether the seller acts reasonably when he fails to provide a conforming substitution that imposes a loss on him. The answer is not clear, but some guidance is available from a comparison with the Official Comment to § 2-615 that states that excuse under that section is not available due to "increased cost alone," but that is more forgiving towards "a severe shortage . . . which either causes a marked increase in cost or altogether prevents the seller from securing supplies." Here, as with the inquiry into impracticability, we believe the best way to interpret these clauses is to look at the effect of nonperformance on the joint interests of the parties. A small loss incurred by the seller may be justified if it would prevent a larger loss by the buyer.

Assume in the above example, for instance, that the seller knows (1) that substituted performance will cause him a loss of $100 on a $10,000 contract, and (2) that if he does not provide the substitute performance, the buyer will lose $5000 on a downstream contract for which the buyer needs the goods. We would be reluctant under those circumstances to find that the seller was exempted from the contract, since performance would increase the joint product of the seller and buyer. On the other hand, we would exempt the seller from performance and conclude that it could not reasonably avoid the consequences of the impediment if it could only avoid the buyer's loss with an expenditure of an additional $6000. This appeal to joint maximization principles, however, is subject to the need for verifiability. If courts cannot easily determine the costs to the parties of performance or nonperformance, they may be better off allowing losses to lie where they fall and deny exemption in an effort to induce parties to allocate risks more explicitly.

Article 79(2) restricts exemption by allowing an obligor to rely on some third party's non-performance only if both the obligor and that third party could have claimed exemption under Article 79(1). The diplomatic history suggests that this provision is intended to have narrower scope than might first seem apparent. It does not apply, for instance, to cases of suppliers of raw materials who might face difficulty in providing seller with goods that are necessary for the seller to complete a contractual obligation to buyer. Rather, the provision is intended to cover cases in which the obligor subcontracts with others to perform its own obligations under the contract. The distinction may be difficult to draw at times, since raw materials suppliers themselves can often be looked on as subcontractors. Indeed, in at least one case, the arbitral court refused to apply Article 79(2) to exempt a subcontractor who was to perform the very obligations of the seller (provision of contracted-for fertilizer, rather than raw materials for the fertilizer), holding that the seller was responsible for the nondelivery of subcontractors without any inquiry into the latter's ability to claim exemption.[91]

The intended application of Article 79(2) can be analyzed through the following example. Assume that a Canadian buyer agrees to purchase a machine from a Hungarian manufacturer. The manufacturer, in turn, contracts with a manufacturer of electrical equipment to produce the motor for the machine. (Note that the manufacturer and subcontractor need not be in different Contracting States for the CISG to apply, since the contest is between the Canadian buyer and the Hungarian seller.) The motor producer's plant explodes just before the contract performance date and the motor is lost. The Hungarian seller can claim exemption only by showing that (1) the explosion constitutes an impediment under Article 79(1) as applied to the motor manufacturer; and (2) the Hungarian seller is himself exempt because he cannot readily obtain a substitute for the motor, i.e., cannot avoid or overcome the consequences of the impediment. Thus, non-performance of the subcontractor alone does not exempt the seller.[92] Where the party who was to perform the seller's obligations simply goes out of business or declares bankruptcy, nonperformance is unlikely to qualify as an impediment that could not have been taken into account, and thus will not exempt the seller. Similarly, a buyer who contracts with a third party to make payment cannot claim exemption if the third party never transfers the payment to seller, as the third party's default cannot be attributed to an Article 79(1) impediment.[93]

Exemption applies only as long as the impediment to performance exists.[94] Temporary difficulties in performance may extend the time for delivery of goods or payment, but do not necessarily eliminate them. Exemption also requires notice to the other party within a reasonable time after the party seeking exemption knew or should have known of the

---

[91] See ICC Court of Arbitration—Paris, Number 8128/1995, 1 UNILEX 1995-34 (M.J. Bonell, ed.).

[92] See Tribunal of International Commercial Arbitration at the Russian Federation Chamber of Commerce, 155/1994 March 3, 1995, (Russian Federation) 1 UNILEX D.1995-10.0.1 (M.J. Bonell, ed.).

[93] See Amtsgerich Alsfeld, 31 C 534/94 December 5, 1995 (Germany), 1 UNILEX D.1995-15.2 (M.J. Bonell, ed.).

[94] See Article 79(3).

impediment.[95] Even in the case of a valid exemption, moreover, the effect is only to preclude a claim for damages.[96] Literally read, a party who successfully asserts an exemption may still be vulnerable to the other party's right to demand specific performance or to avoid the contract. This provision poses significant difficulties. There is something anomalous about saying that one who cannot perform because of an impediment can be required to perform specifically, although the party is not liable for damages for nonperformance. If substituted performance were available, then one would imagine that the conditions justifying exemption did not exist in the first place. Perhaps the drafters were thinking in terms of a reduced price under Article 50. That conclusion is sensible once one understands that reduced price is not considered an award of damages, which are precluded under the explicit terms of Article 79(5). Perhaps the provision is best interpreted as allowing the aggrieved party some non-damages recourse where the impediment does not totally preclude the obligor's performance. Under those circumstances, the provision may be interpreted as allowing the aggrieved party to salvage as much of the contractual performance as is not exempted by the impediment or (at the aggrieved party's option) to avoid the contract entirely if the nonperformance constitutes a fundamental breach.

A final debate that has emerged with respect to Article 79 involves efforts by sellers to use excuse to avoid damages for nonconforming deliveries, rather than for non-delivery. May a seller, for instance, who delivers goods that are not of the quality required by the contract claim an exemption from the obligation (under Article 35) to make a conforming tender as a result of a qualifying "impediment?" The language of Article 79, the seller might claim, provides exemption from "any of his obligations" in a case where the requisite impediment can be demonstrated. Certainly this would be a deviation from the understanding under the UCC that impracticability applies to non-delivery, not to defective delivery. Nevertheless, the language of Article 79 offers at least a theoretical argument for a different rule in international sales. Some commentators suggest that the legislative history of the provision disproves any intention to extend exemption to

---

[95] See Article 79(4).

[96] See Article 79(5).

defects.[97] In addition, Article 79 appears to apply when sellers are not at fault for their defalcations. It would be anomalous to apply that exemption to obligations, such as those created by Article 35, that impose liability regardless of fault. Finally, even if Article 79 does apply, it would be the exceedingly rare case in which a defect arose but the seller "could not reasonably be expected to have taken the impediment into account." Sellers in commercial transactions, as repeat players, are likely to be familiar with the kinds of defects that might arise in the goods that they sell, and thus to be able to adjust contractual terms to take the possibility of such defects into account.

In a case from the Federal Supreme Court in Germany,[98] the court took note of the debate about the applicability of Article 79 to defects, but concluded that events within that provision had to outside the seller's control. The court then broadly interpreted the scope of seller control over product quality. In that case, a seller of vine wax contended that it could use Article 79 to avoid liability for a defective tender of goods. The seller claimed that it had received the wax from the manufacturer and resold it without inspection or alteration. Thus, the seller claimed, the condition of the wax was not within its control. The court rejected the claim. It concluded that the buyer had contracted for a particular quality of wax, which the seller had agreed to provide, and was indifferent as to whether the seller or some other supplier manufactured the wax. Where the seller obtains goods from suppliers, it is required to ensure that those suppliers provide defect-free goods. The seller's "risk of acquisition" precluded it from subsequently claiming an exemption if the defect was beyond the control both of itself and of any supplier. In this case, the defect was apparently due to the manufacturer's use of inappropriate raw materials, a fact that the court considered within the manufacturer's control. Although the court did not provide any deeper analysis of the concept of control, the effect of its logic implies that sellers lose control only with respect to the type of unallocated external events that are seen as the basis for excuse under § 2-615.

---

[97] See, John O. Honnold, Uniform Law for International Sales 477-79 (3d ed. 1999); Joseph M. Lookofsky, *Fault and No-Fault in Danish, American and International Sales Law: The Reception of the 1980 United Nations Sales Convention*, 1983 Scandinavian Studies in Law 109, 135-37.

[98] Bundesgerichtshof, 24 March 1999 (Germany), 1 UNILEX D.1999-6 (M.J. Bonell, ed.).

CHAPTER 7
RISK OF LOSS

## I. Introduction: Loss Allocation in Transactional Settings

During the period between the formation of a contract and its successful completion, the goods that are the subject of the contract may be lost, damaged, or stolen. Commercial law principles allocate the risk of loss when one of these events materializes. There are four scenarios that create risk of loss problems. In the first, the loss occurs while the goods are in the seller's possession. In the second, the goods are in the possession of a third-party bailee when the loss occurs. The buyer is expected either to obtain the goods from the bailee or to resell the goods without ever receiving physical possession of them from the bailee. In the third scenario the loss materializes while the goods are in transit from the seller to the buyer. In the final scenario, the loss occurs after the goods have reached the buyer, but prior to the time when the buyer has accepted them.

Both the UCC and the CISG allocate the loss in each of these cases. They vary from the principles that existed under pre-UCC law, in which risk of loss was closely linked to title. A seller who parted with goods, but who had not yet passed title to the buyer, retained the risk that the goods would be damaged. A moment's thought reveals that this arrangement appears inconsistent with an efficiency rationale. If the objective of commercial law is to reduce the costs associated with transactions, including the risk that goods will be damaged, lost, or stolen, then that risk should be placed on the party who is in the best position to avoid the loss from materializing or to insure against risks that do materialize, that is, the party who can perform these functions at lowest cost. That party then will have an incentive to take advantage of its position by caring for or insuring the goods. Typically, the party who possesses or controls the goods can best avoid loss to them. Similarly, that party will be best able to insure goods, because insurers know that the party in control can minimize losses that the insurer will have to pay. On these assumptions, efficiency principles require that risk of loss follow possession and control rather than title.

Indeed, the parties themselves should prefer to allocate risk of loss in this manner. Assume, for instance, that Seller is willing to sell goods that have a price, consisting of cost of production plus profit, of $100. It would cost it $2 to insure the goods until they are accepted by Buyer.

Assume that the same insurance would cost Buyer $3, perhaps because the Seller is better able to care for the goods until completion of the transaction.  Presumably, Seller is indifferent between (1) selling the goods to Buyer for $100 and having Buyer accept the risk of loss, and (2) selling the goods to Buyer for $102 while personally bearing the risk of loss.  Buyer, on the other hand, would presumably prefer paying $102 and having Seller accept the risk of loss rather than paying $100 for the goods plus an additional $3 for insurance.  Thus, we would expect Buyer and Seller to agree that Seller should accept the risk of loss and sell the goods to Buyer for $102.  If sales law adopts majoritarian default rules, and if most sellers are better positioned to accept the risk of loss for goods in their possession, then we would expect legal doctrine to place risk of loss on sellers in cases like this in order to reflect the results that would occur if there had been an actual negotiation.

## II. Risk of Loss Under the UCC

The UCC appears to embrace this efficiency rationale.  Official Comment 3 to § 2-509, the  primary provision that allocates risk of loss, states that

> the underlying theory of [loss allocation] is that a merchant who is to make physical delivery at his own place continues meanwhile to control the goods and can be expected to insure his interest in them.  The buyer, on the other hand, has no control of the goods and it is extremely unlikely that he will carry insurance on goods not yet in his possession.

Courts have similarly adopted this rationale.  Thus, in an action to recover the purchase price paid for a motorcoach which was extensively damaged by fire while still on the seller's premises, the court concluded,

> the rationale of the risk of loss rules . . . is to place the risk of loss on the party most likely to insure the goods.  The rules recognize that a merchant who is to make physical delivery at his own place of business continues to exercise dominion and control over the goods and can be expected to insure his interest in them until delivery.[1]

Nevertheless, the UCC does not simply direct courts to apply this standard.  That is, the UCC does not tell courts to place the loss on the party best positioned to avoid it.  Rather, the UCC defines a variety of

---

[1] Galbraith v. American Motorhome Corp., 545 P.2d 561 (Wash. 1976).

situations in which the tendency will be for control and dominion to rest with either the seller or the buyer and allocates the risk of loss accordingly.

## A. Risk of Loss Where Seller Retains the Goods

According to § 2-509(3), risk of loss passes to the buyer on receipt of the goods if the seller is a merchant. If seller is not a merchant, risk passes to the buyer on tender of delivery. Recall that "receipt" requires taking physical possession of the goods.[2] The receipt requirement is entirely consistent with the efficiency rationale. A buyer who has not obtained the goods has little opportunity to care for them. But note that the rule applies only where the seller is a merchant. The "tender of delivery" condition in non-merchant seller cases can cause difficulty. Assume, for instance, that the consumer-seller of a used car agrees to sell the car to a buyer. One of the contract terms requires the buyer to leave the car with the seller until the following Tuesday evening so that the seller has an opportunity to remove personal effects. The seller also informs the buyer that he expects to be out of town, but will leave the key under the floor mat. After the seller complies with all his obligations, but before the buyer arrives to claim the car, it is damaged without the fault of either party when a tree limb falls on the car's hood. The seller, a non-merchant, may claim that he had tendered the goods by making them available to buyer.[3] Nevertheless, the seller controlled the location of the car and thus was in a superior position to avoid the loss. Of course, in this situation, the seller might claim that he canceled his insurance after completion of the sale, so that the "best position to insure" rationale may point to placing the risk of loss on the buyer, while the "best position to avoid the loss" may point to the seller.

We can imagine cases in which both rationales point to placing risk of loss on the seller, but § 2-509(3) provides otherwise. For instance, assume our buyer agrees to purchase a dining room table at an estate sale, and the table is damaged in the seller's home while buyer is obtaining a truck to cart the table away. The seller is best positioned both to avoid the loss and to insure, but has a colorable claim that it had tendered the table to the buyer, so risk of loss had passed.

---

[2] § 2-103(1)(c).

[3] According to § 2-503(1), the seller will have tendered delivery by holding conforming goods at the buyer's disposition and giving the buyer notification reasonably necessary for the buyer to take delivery.

Perhaps for these reasons, the Proposed Revision eliminated the distinction between merchant and non-merchant sellers for risk of loss purposes.[4] Unless the case falls within an exceptions, risk would always pass to a buyer on receipt of the goods.

## B. Risk of Loss Where Goods are Held by a Bailee

Goods may suffer injury while in the hands of a third-party, typically a bailee, such as a warehouseman, who is holding the goods at the time of the transaction. If the goods are to be delivered to the buyer without being moved from the bailee's premises, § 2-509(b) dictates that risk of loss passes on the first of three events. First, risk of loss passes if the buyer receives a negotiable document of title covering the goods. A person who holds a negotiable document of title has the ability to control the disposition of the goods. Thus, rights with respect to the goods and the document are essentially merged and possession of the negotiable document constitutes constructive possession of the goods. As a result, the buyer who has possession of the document has the same rights as if it actually received possession and risk of loss passes with that control.

Second, risk of loss passes when the bailee acknowledges that the buyer has a right of possession. For instance, in *Jason's Foods, Inc. v. Peter Eckrich & Sons, Inc.*,[5] a seller of ribs brought an action for the price after the ribs had been destroyed in a fire. The ribs were held in the warehouse of a bailee and the sale was to occur by a transfer from the seller's account to the buyer's account on the warehouse books. This transaction occurred on January 13, but the buyer did not receive a confirmation until January 24. The fire occurred on January 17. The seller contended that it surrendered all control over the ribs once the paper transfer was effected and that it could not insure what it no longer owned. Therefore, the seller argued, risk of loss had passed to the buyer. The buyer, on the other hand, contended that it could not be responsible for goods that it did not know it owned. The court did not address the issue of whether an "acknowledgment" for purposes of § 2-509(2)(b) consisted of mailing notice or receiving it, as that issue had not been raised by the parties. Nevertheless, the court did conclude that the relevant acknowledgment had to be made *to the buyer*. The court found the language of the provision to be at best suggestive of that result. The court further indicated that the policies underlying risk of loss were

---

[4] See Proposed Revision § 2-509(3).

[5]  774 F.2d 214 (7th Cir. 1985).

inconclusive. Once the seller ordered the transfer, it had no reason to insure the goods or care for them, and until the buyer learned of the transfer, it similarly had no reason to insure or protect. The fact that the buyer had a "well-founded expectation" that the transfer had been finalized prior to the loss was insufficient to shift the risk of loss. Ultimately, the court determined to follow textual analysis and Official Comments that revealed a desire to retain pre-Code law. Since risk of loss in transactions governed by § 2-509(2)(a) and (c) clearly passed only when buyer received evidence of the transfer, the court imposed a similar requirement on § 2-509(2)(b) transactions. Thus, the seller bore the risk at the time that the goods were destroyed.

A bailee, however, must truly be independent of the buyer if receipt by the bailee is not to be attributed to the buyer under agency law. For instance, in *In re Julien Co.*,[6] a representative of cotton sellers delivered cotton to a warehouseman pursuant to contracts under which the cotton was sold to the buyer. After the buyer's drafts in payment of the cotton were dishonored, the representative demanded return of the goods. The buyer subsequently declared bankruptcy. In those proceedings, the representative contended that the warehouseman served as bailee, from whom the representative could reclaim the cotton. The court, however, concluded that the warehouseman was an agent of the buyer. The warehouse was owned by an affiliate of the buyer and was managed primarily for the benefit of the buyer. Furthermore, the cotton was to be retained by the warehouse only so long as it took to re-ship the cotton to the buyer's own customers.

The third loss-allocating event in a bailee situation is receipt by the buyer of a non-negotiable document of title or other written direction for the bailee to deliver the goods. The receipt of such a document or direction constitutes tender of the goods under § 2-503(4)(b). Once tender has occurred, buyer has the type of control and dominion over the goods that the efficiency explanation dictates should also impose risk of loss.[7]

In some cases, the buyer may ask the seller to retain goods until the buyer can procure delivery. If the goods are lost or damaged during this period, a seller who would bear the risk of loss under § 2-509(3) might

---

[6] 44 F.3d 426 (6th Cir. 1995).

[7] See Commonwealth Propane Co. v. Petrosol International, Inc., 818 F.2d 522 (6th Cir. 1987).

claim that it had been transformed into a bailee or agent of the buyer. If the seller became a bailee, risk of loss would have passed on the seller's acknowledgment that the buyer could obtain the goods at any point. If the seller served as the buyer's agent, the risk would have passed because the buyer "received" the goods under agency principles. Courts, however, have justifiably been reluctant to accept such arguments. In *Conway v. Larsen Jewelers, Inc.*,[8] goods that a seller was holding for a buyer under a "layaway" purchase were stolen from seller's store. The seller claimed that it was serving as a bailee for the buyer. The court found that the seller was not holding the goods for the buyer's benefit, but for its own benefit, to secure the purchase price. Similarly, in *Caudle v. Sherrard Motor Co.*,[9] the court rejected the claim of a seller of a trailer home that it was a bailee for the buyer. The trailer was stolen from seller's premises while it was being prepared for delivery to the buyer. The seller maintained that it was acting as a bailee while the trailer remained on its premises and that by executing the contract, it had acknowledged the buyer's right to possession. The seller further contended that, because it did not agree to deliver the trailer to Caudle, the trailer was to be delivered to Caudle "without being moved." The court, however, concluded that the only parties who qualified as bailees under § 2-509(2) were persons in the business of storing goods for hire. Since the seller did not fall into that category, it could not take advantage of the "acknowledgment" term.

### C. Risk of Loss During Transit

The contract of sale between distant buyers and sellers will frequently require or authorize the seller to ship the goods by carrier. In these situations, risk of loss is typically tied to the payment terms under the contract with the carrier. Note that the term "carrier" in these provisions relates to an independent carrier. A seller who uses its own trucks to transport goods to the buyer will be deemed to retain possession and thus be governed by § 2-509(3) rather than the "carrier" provisions of the UCC.

Section 2-509 recognizes two basic forms of carrier contracts, a "shipment" contract and a "destination" contract. Where the parties use a shipment contract, the seller is not required to deliver the goods to "a particular destination." This is a rather unfortunate phrase, since the

---

[8] 429 N.Y.S.2d 378 (N.Y. Civ. Ct. 1980).

[9] 525 S.W.2d 238 (Tex. Civ. App. 1975).

seller is obviously required to deliver the goods somewhere. Where the parties enter into a shipment contract, § 2-509(1)(a) passes the risk of loss to the buyer when the goods are duly delivered to the carrier. Thus, under a shipment contract, the buyer will bear the risk of loss during transit. Due delivery will require the seller to comply with § 2-504 by entering into a reasonable contract for the transportation of the goods with a carrier and placing the goods in the possession of that carrier. What constitutes a reasonable contract will vary with the nature of the goods. For instance, a seller's failure to contract for refrigeration of perishable goods may be unreasonable.[10] In addition, an agreement between the seller and the carrier to an inadequate valuation of the goods will be unreasonable because it deprives the buyer of an opportunity to recover the full value of the goods from the seller.[11] In *Cook Specialty Co. v. Schrlock*,[12] however, the court found that the seller had entered into a reasonable contract for transportation, even though the carrier's insurance was below the value of its cargo. "Reasonableness," the court concluded, required only that the mode of transportation be satisfactory in light of the nature of the goods. It did not require the seller to investigate the amount or terms of the carrier's insurance.

Section 2-509(1)(b) provides that the risk of loss under a destination contract passes to the buyer when the goods are duly tendered to the buyer at the designated destination in a manner that enables the buyer to take delivery. Thus, under a destination contract, the seller bears the risk of loss during transit. "Tender," according to § 2-503, requires that conforming goods be placed at the buyer's disposition and that the buyer receive any notification reasonably necessary to enable it to take delivery.

There is a strong commercial presumption that contracts of carriage fall under the category of shipment contracts.[13] Thus, in cases of doubt, courts should construe contracts as placing the risk of loss on the buyer during transit. Indeed, some courts indicate that the presumption can only be rebutted by an explicit agreement that imposes on the seller an obligation to deliver at a particular destination; a mere agreement to ship

---

[10] See Larsen v. A.C. Carpenter, Inc., 620 F. Supp. 1084 (E.D.N.Y. 1985).

[11] See, e.g., § 2-503 Official Comment 3.

[12] 772 F. Supp. 1532 (E.D. Pa. 1991).

[13] In re Priority Finishing Corp., 246 B.R. 459 (Bankr. D. Mass. 2000). See § 2-503 Official Comment 5.

"to" a particular city will not suffice.[14] Parties can avoid ambiguity, however, by using a shipping term that is understood either as a matter of law or trade usage to mandate a shipment or destination contract. Under the current version of the UCC, several shipping terms are specifically defined to coincide with the risk of loss terms of § 2-509. As we will see, these terms may be inconsistent with their counterparts in international sales.

Under the UCC definitions, a contract that includes an F.O.B. ("free on board") shipping term allocates the costs of shipment, but does so in a way that meshes with the risk allocation of § 2-509. Where, for instance, the shipping term is "F.O.B. place of shipment" (such as the seller's business), the parties clearly intend a shipment contract rather than a destination contract, since no particular destination is mentioned in the shipment term. Under § 2-319(1)(a), such a term imposes on the seller both the expense and risk of placing the goods into the possession of the carrier. This obligation restates the position of § 2-509(1)(a) with respect to the passage of risk of loss in shipment contracts generally. Similarly, under § 2-319(1)(b) an "F.O.B. place of destination" contract places on the seller the expense and risk of transporting the goods to the named destination and making an appropriate tender. This obligation obviously comports with the seller's risk under § 2-509(1)(b).

Other shipment terms similarly elaborate the obligations of the parties. For instance, goods sold under a "C.I.F." (cost, insurance, and freight) term require the seller to bear the risk of loss only until the goods are put into the possession of the carrier at the port of shipment. Thus, the C.I.F. contract is a form of shipment contract. But the seller has additional obligations under this term. The seller must also load the goods and obtain a receipt from the carrier showing that the freight has been paid or provided for, obtain a policy of insurance for the goods, prepare an invoice, procure any other document necessary for shipment, and forward and tender with commercial promptness to the buyer any documents in the form necessary to protect its rights. At first glance, parts of this arrangement seem anomalous. If this is a shipment contract, with the buyer bearing the risk of loss, then why is the seller obtaining a policy of insurance? If the buyer bears the risk of loss during carriage, then one would imagine that it is the party who desires insurance. Careful attention reveals that the insurance obtained by the seller is for the benefit of the buyer. The seller is required to obtain a policy

---

[14] Windows, Inc. v. Jordan Panel Systems Corp., 177 F.3d 114 (2d Cir. 1999).

"providing for payment of loss to the order of the buyer or for the account of whom it may concern."[15] The underlying assumption is that the seller will be in the best position to obtain the required insurance, as evidenced by the language that the policy be "of a kind and on terms then current at the port of shipment in the usual amount. . . ."

Shipment terms, therefore, not only allocate the risk of loss; they also determine obligations of the parties, including the obligation to pay for particular services. Assume, for instance, that a New York seller of heavy equipment offers a Norfolk, Virginia buyer three separate terms of sale. The first is "F.O.B. New York" with a sales price of $1000. The second is "F.O.B. Norfolk" with a sales price of $1075. The third is "C.I.F. Norfolk" with a sales price $1100. Assume that Buyer could insure the goods during transit for $50 and that the carriage from New York to Norfolk would cost buyer $75. Under the first term, Buyer would pay $1000 for the goods, but would also have to pay for carriage ($75) and insure against loss during transit ($50) for a total of $1125. Under the second term, Seller bears the cost and risk of transporting the goods to Norfolk. Thus, Buyer does not have to purchase transportation or insurance and the stated price of $1075 is also Buyer's total cost. Under the C.I.F. term, the price includes insurance that the seller obtains on behalf of the buyer. The term also includes the cost of freight to the named destination, even though a shipment contract is intended. Thus, the $1100 sale price would also represent the total cost to Buyer.

Developments in international trade have created confusion in the meaning of some terms used in the UCC. The International Chamber of Commerce has compiled widely accepted international shipping terms in what has become known as "INCOTERMS." The most recent iteration, known as INCOTERMS 2000, created four categories that include 13 different shipment terms. As we noted above, these terms may vary from the meanings of the same terms in §§ 2-319 and 2-320.[16] For instance, an F.O.B. term, which is used only for waterway transport, the seller bears the risk of placing the goods past the ship's rail. Other terms are used to shift the risk of loss at the seller's place of business, so that an "FOB, seller's place of business" term, possible under the UCC, would be an anomaly under INCOTERMS.

---

[15] § 2-320.

[16] See ICC Incoterms (2000); John A. Spanogle, *Incoterms and the UCC Article 2--Conflicts and Confusions*, 31 Int. Law. 111 (1997).

The four categories of INCOTERMS are divided according to the responsibilities that they place on sellers of goods. Under the first category, (called "Group E") the seller need only make the goods available to the buyer at the seller's own place of business. This is referred to as an EXW, or Ex Works, term. Risk passes once the goods are placed at the buyer's disposal.

The second group (Group "F"), which includes such terms as "F.O.B." (Free on Board) and "F.A.S" (Free Alongside Ship), requires the seller to deliver the goods to a carrier designated by the buyer. Passage of risk, however, may vary depending on the specific term. For instance, risk would pass when the goods are delivered alongside a ship at a named port of shipment under a F.A.S. term, but would pass only when the goods pass the ship's rail under an F.O.B. term.

The third group (Group "C") requires the seller to contract for carriage without assuming the risk of loss after shipment. The final group of terms (Group "D") imposes on the seller all costs and risks related to bringing the goods to the country of destination. For instance, under a D.A.F. (Delivered at Frontier) term, the seller must contract and pay for the carriage of goods to the named point at the frontier, and must bear all risks until such delivery occurs. "Frontier" may be any point at which the goods have been cleared for export, but before the customs border of the adjoining country. It may be designated as the frontier of any country, including the boundary of the country of import or export, so that definition of the appropriate frontier is an essential element of the delivery term.

Recent proposed revisions of Article 2 recognize the discrepancy between existing UCC terms and INCOTERMS. In order to adjust domestic law to international commercial developments, the Proposed Revision eliminates any explicit definition of shipment and delivery terms. The proposed revisions have not, therefore, explicitly incorporate the INCOTERMS. Instead, trade usage and course of performance would be used to interpret trade terms. INCOTERMS would be used to interpret these terms if they reflect predominant usage. Until such a revision is adopted, however, current UCC definitions can be expected to prevail in domestic practice, an unfortunate example of the way in which legislation can lag behind trade practice.

### D. Opting Out of Risk of Loss Provisions

Section 2-509(4) confirms that the UCC risk of loss provisions are only default rules. In certain cases, idiosyncratic buyers may be better positioned to protect the goods that remain in the seller's possession, or may be willing to pay for some additional safeguards for the goods that a seller in possession would find unnecessary. Thus, parties are always entitled to alter the risk of loss rules set forth in § 2-509. Nevertheless, courts have been reluctant to conclude that parties have opted out of § 2-509. If the drafters have stated majoritarian default rules, then this reluctance is appropriate, since we would rarely expect to find parties that desire an alternative. Courts have required parties to use specific language to avoid the default risk allocation. In *Lynch Imports v. Frey*,[17] for instance, a purchase contract required the buyer to have insurance at the time he took possession of an automobile. The buyer took possession, but, pursuant to agreement, returned it to the dealer to have air conditioning installed. The automobile was damaged while in the dealer's possession. The court found that the seller retained the risk of loss during this period because the clause was not "conclusive on its face to pass the risk of loss of the buyer." A different result was reached in *Forest Nursery Co. v. I.W.S., Inc.*[18] There, the seller sought to recover the price of plants that had been damaged by heat in transit to buyer. The contract between the parties contained a conspicuous legend that shipment was at "No Risk to Supplier" and that all shipments were at the purchaser's risk.

Both decisions seem correct. Nothing in the contractual clause in the first case detracted from the traditional position of the seller as being a superior risk bearer or insurer while still in possession of the goods. Nothing about the buyer or the transaction suggested any idiosyncratic characteristic that would make it a better risk bearer until receipt of conforming goods. The fact that the buyer had taken the goods temporarily complicates the issue, but not even the seller contended that the risk had passed because buyer had received conforming goods. In the latter case, on the other hand, the seller was sending loud and clear signals about relative incapacity or unwillingness to accept the transit risk. Whether the seller was particularly risk averse or was an inferior risk bearer seems irrelevant, given the strength of that signal. In light of the prominence of the clause, the price term may well have reflected placement of the risk on the buyer, so that judicial reallocation would have imposed on the seller a risk for which it had not been compensated.

One way to vary from the default provisions of § 2-509, of course, is to utilize well understood shipping terms that assign the risk of loss. For

---

[17] 558 N.E.2d 484 (Ill. App. Ct. 1990).

[18] 534 N.Y.S.2d 86 (N.Y. Dist. Ct. 1988).

instance, § 2-319(1)(c) provides that an "F.O.B." term that calls for delivery at a particular vessel, car, or other vehicle will require the seller to load the goods on board at his expense and risk. In *Consolidated Bottling Co. v. Jaco Equipment Corp.*,[19] the seller sought to recover from the buyer the purchase price of can filling equipment that had been damaged before delivery to the buyer occurred. The equipment was sold under a "f.o.b. purchaser's truck" term. The equipment was damaged while awaiting delivery to the buyer but, according to the seller, after the equipment had been put at the buyer's disposal and thus tender had been made. The court concluded that the "f.o.b. purchaser's truck" term was a "contrary agreement" within the meaning of § 2-504 and prevailed over the default provision that would have shifted the risk of loss to the buyer on the seller's tender of the goods.

### E. Risk of Loss in the Event of Breach

Under the current version of Article 2, a breach by either party can alter the loss allocation provided in § 2-509. This risk shifting potentially diverges from our rationale for the risk allocation under that provision. Presumably, the drafters believed that the unfairness of requiring an aggrieved party to retain the risk of loss outweighed any efficiency gains that would materialize if the loss remained on the party best positioned to avoid the loss or insure against it. We are more doubtful that breach should be relevant to the risk of loss issue, given the underlying theory of efficient loss allocation. At least, that is true where the breach has no relationship to the damage or loss of the goods. A different result may be appropriate, for instance, if seller's breach consists of delivering a defective good that contains a fire hazard and the good is subsequently destroyed by a fire that the defect causes. That case might require allocating the loss to the seller even on efficiency grounds, as the seller may have been in the best position to avoid the loss through careful manufacture.

Section 2-510 shifts the risk of loss to a breaching party in three situations. In the first, a seller tenders or delivers goods that so fail to conform to the contract as to give a right of rejection. The buyer may then treat the risk of loss as resting on the seller until cure or acceptance. Since Article 2 adopts a perfect tender rule, this provision applies anytime there is a nonconformity in tender or delivery. Assume, for instance, that Buyer orders seven crates of grade A sawdust. The contract contains an "F.O.B. Seller's plant" term. On arrival and inspection,

---

[19] 442 F.2d 660 (2d Cir. 1971).

Buyer realizes that Seller has delivered seven crates of grade B sawdust. Buyer notifies Seller, who promises to send a truck to deliver conforming goods and pick up the nonconforming goods. Prior to the time that the truck arrives, the initial shipment is destroyed by a fire in Buyer's plant. But for the breach, Buyer would bear the risk of loss of the delivered goods. That assignment of risk makes sense under the efficiency rationale given that Buyer was in control and possession of the goods at the time the loss occurred. Nevertheless, under § 2-510(1), Buyer would be able to treat the risk as resting on Seller.

Assume in the same case that the goods were damaged en route to Buyer. Given the F.O.B. shipment term, both Buyer and Seller would have believed that Buyer bore the risk of loss during the period of shipment. Seller, therefore, would not have procured any insurance for the period of carriage or thereafter. Buyer, on the other hand, would have anticipated bearing any transit risk. If the goods were determined to have been nonconforming when delivered to the carrier (and assuming for the moment that the nonconformity did not cause the damage), Seller would bear the risk of the damage that occurred.[20] This result seems to confer a windfall benefit on Buyer, who would have expected to bear the transit risk and paid a commensurately low price, and a windfall loss on Seller, who believed that risk had already passed and charged accordingly. Of course, the windfall may be limited as, in most cases involving transit, allocation of the loss between buyer and seller is essentially a contest about which party will have a cause of action against the carrier, which will ultimately be liable for nondelivery of the goods.

The second situation in which breach affects risk of loss involves buyers who revoke acceptance after discovering a nonconformity. Section 2-510(2) allows the buyer to treat the risk of loss as having rested on the seller from the beginning, but only to the extent of any deficiency in the buyer's insurance coverage. Assume in the above case, for instance, that Buyer failed to recognize the nonconformity in the sawdust in a timely manner and is therefore deemed to have accepted the goods. Buyer subsequently notices the nonconformity, notifies Seller, and places the goods in an off-premises warehouse while awaiting replacement and pick-up by Seller. The goods are destroyed in the warehouse. Buyer subsequently discovers that it had no insurance for goods held off-premises. It may treat the risk of loss as resting on Seller. This result

---

[20] See Pantsmaker, Inc. v. Orbit Mfg. Co., 32 UCC Rep. Serv. 103 (N.Y. Sup. Ct. 1981) (seller retains risk of loss when he delivers nonconforming goods to carrier under "F.O.B. point of shipment" contract).

seems odd not only from an efficiency perspective, given the relative ability of Buyer to control and care for the goods, but also from a fairness perspective. After all, even if Seller breached by shipping nonconforming goods, Buyer perhaps deserves some reproach for failing to inspect with sufficient care to notice the nonconformity and reject at an earlier time.

The third situation involves breach by the buyer. If buyer breaches or repudiates prior to the time that risk of loss has passed to it, § 2-510(3) allows the seller to treat the risk of loss as resting on the buyer for a commercially reasonable time, but only to the extent of any deficiency in the seller's effective insurance coverage. Assume, for instance, that Buyer and Seller have an enforceable contract for the shipment of seven crates of grade A sawdust. After Seller has crated and addressed the sawdust to Buyer, thus identifying the goods to the contract, Buyer repudiates. Seller places the goods in an off-premises warehouse pending resale. The goods are subsequently destroyed in the warehouse, and Seller learns that it has no insurance coverage for such losses. Seller may treat the risk of loss as resting on Buyer, notwithstanding that it had full control and possession of the goods. The conclusion only follows, however, for a "commercially reasonable time." In *Multiplastics, Inc. v. Artch Industries*,[21] the seller agreed to manufacture and deliver specially made goods to its buyer. The buyer refused to send shipping instructions after manufacture was complete, notwithstanding the seller's requests. Nor did the buyer ever agree to receive the goods. The goods were ultimately destroyed by a fire at the seller's plant and its insurer did not cover the loss. The buyer contended that the "commercially reasonable time" should be limited to the period during which seller could have obtained the necessary insurance coverage, and that the fire occurred after that time had expired. The Supreme Court of Connecticut, however, concluded that the seller could treat the risk of loss as resting on the buyer. It reasoned that it was reasonable for the seller to believe that the buyer would soon comply with its contractual obligations, so there was no need for the seller to obtain insurance.

### III. Risk of Loss Under the CISG

Risk of loss is obviously a matter of some importance in international transactions, where goods are likely to travel over substantial distances and be involved in multiple forms of transportation (often referred to as "multimodal" transport). For instance, goods may be carried by truck

---

[21] 348 A.2d 618 (Conn. 1974).

from the seller's plant to a port, from which they are shipped to the buyer's jurisdiction. From that point, they may again travel by truck to the buyer's plant. The CISG sets forth a variety of default rules in Articles 66-70. It is important to recall, however, that Article 6 permits contracting out of these default rules. In the case of risk of loss, parties are likely to avail themselves of that possibility by contracting into the specific obligations and risk allocations offered by the INCOTERMS we have discussed above. Where parties use INCOTERMS, Article 9 will likely incorporate into contracts otherwise governed by the CISG the customary meanings given to those terms.

Widespread acceptance of INCOTERMS in international sales means that in most cases the CISG's risk of loss rules will be inapplicable. Where the parties do not take advantage of such customary shipment terms, however, the CISG's rules apply as they would to any contract.

There is one caveat to what we have just noted. INCOTERMS may define when risk of loss has passed, but they do not dictate the consequences of that event. Those consequences are determined by substantive legal provisions. In the case of contracts governed by the CISG, the applicable rule is set forth in Article 66. That Article defines when a seller of lost or damaged goods can continue to enforce the contract. It provides that loss or damage to the goods *after* risk of loss has passed does not discharge the buyer's payment obligation, unless the loss or damage is due to an act or omission of the seller. This provision thus gives the seller an action for the price of conforming goods if the goods suffer casualty after the risk of loss has passed to the buyer. Note, however, that a seller cannot bring such an action if the loss is due to the seller's breach. For instance, a seller who fails, under Article 35(2)(d), to package goods in a manner adequate to preserve and protect them would not be entitled to an Article 66 action if that failure causes the loss. Thus, a seller who packages cases of wine in a manner that allows the bottles to break during normal handling will not be able to obtain compensation from a buyer who suffers the loss, even though the breakage occurred after the risk of loss passed to the buyer. Indeed, since Article 66 denies an action for the price to a seller whose "act or omission" causes the loss, it is theoretically possible that the seller could be barred from bringing the action by committing an act that did not constitute a breach of contract. Professor Schlechtriem, for instance, posits a seller who has complied with its contractual obligations of loading goods under an F.O.B. contract, but whose servants damage the goods while removing their container from the ship.[22] In such a case, there may be no breach of contract, but their "act" arguably means that Article 66 allows the buyer to avoid the seller's action for the price.

Where the CISG does determine when risk of loss passes, the residual rule, which applies where no transportation is provided for in the contract, is found in Article 69. It states, consistent with § 2-509, that risk passes to the buyer when it "takes over the goods." If the buyer is to take the goods at a place other than the seller's place of business, the risk passes to the buyer when delivery is due and the buyer becomes aware that the goods have been placed at its disposal at the designated location.[23] Goods that have not been identified at the time of contracting, such as goods to be manufactured by the seller, cannot be placed at the disposal of the buyer, and thus risk of their loss cannot pass, until identification occurs. Assume, for instance, that a California wholesaler of wine maintains a significant inventory in a public warehouse and sells the goods in the warehouse by transferring warehouse receipts to buyers. An Egyptian importer of wines purchases receipts for twenty cases of wine. Prior to the time when the buyer can obtain the goods, the warehouse and its contents are destroyed. Risk may have passed if the delivery time was due and the buyer was aware of the availability of the goods. But that result can only occur if the goods were placed at the buyer's disposal, which in turn requires that the wholesaler identified the cases as the buyer's. If the warehouse held only fungible cases of wine for buyers generally, no such identification occurred, the goods cannot have been placed at the buyer's disposal, and risk will not have passed. Perhaps we can justify this distinction based on the likelihood that the buyer will have insurance for the goods. The buyer's insurance is less likely to cover its interest in an unidentified segment of a fungible set of goods. The seller, on the other hand, is more likely to have insurance on the entire set.

Under Article 69(2), a buyer who is to take over the goods from a place other than the seller's place of business bears the risk of loss once delivery is due and the buyer is aware that the goods have been placed at its disposal. Assume that the wine in the above example was marked for delivery to the buyer, the buyer was notified of the wine's availability, and the contract of sale permitted buyer to pick up the wine at the

----

[22]See Peter Schlechtriem, Commentary on the UN Convention on the International Sale of Goods 502 (2d ed. 1998).

[23]See Article 69(2).

warehouse by January 31. The goods are destroyed on January 10. Here, the buyer was aware of their availability and the goods have been identified. But the buyer had until the end of the month to take over the goods. Thus, delivery was not due and the seller retains the risk of loss.

Article 67 covers cases in which the contract of sale involves carriage of the goods. Two types of contracts are contemplated: contracts calling for delivery of the goods to a carrier "at a particular place" and contracts calling for delivery to a carrier but not at a particular place. With the first type of contract, the literal language of the Article states that risk passes to buyer when the goods are handed over to the carrier at the particular place. With the second type, it passes to buyer when the goods are handed to the first carrier. This literal language, however, contains some ambiguities that are best resolved by considering the underlying rationale for allocating risk of loss. We can explore these ambiguities by considering the following hypothetical. Assume that a Virginia winery contracts to sell wine to an Egyptian buyer where both parties have places of business in different Contracting States. The terms of the contract require the seller to "send by ship." The winery uses its own trucks to bring the wine to a port in New York, where the wine is to be loaded onto a ship for transport to Egypt. The wine is destroyed when the truck is involved in an accident in Pennsylvania. Who bears the risk of loss? The contract in this case does not call for delivery of the goods to the carrier at a particular place. If a specific ship were named, e.g., "send by U.S.S. Clinton, New York" the "particular place" condition would be satisfied and the risk of loss would pass to the buyer only when the goods were handed to the named carrier at New York. It is not necessarily the case that "particular" place for these purposes receive as restrictive of a reading as in the definition of a destination contract under § 2-509(1)(b). Destination contracts under the UCC typically require delivery at the buyer's place of business. In CISG contracts, the designation of a particular place indicates where the carrier that is transport the goods to the buyer will be located, not where the buyer is located. Thus, a general identification of a place will generally indicate where the seller is to hand the goods over to the carrier. Assume, for instance, that the contract reads, "goods shipped from Port of New York." While that place may not be sufficiently particular for purposes of § 2-509, it will be sufficiently particular to pass the risk under the second sentence of Article 67(1).

In the absence of a particular place designation, Article 67(1) provides that the risk passes to the buyer when the goods are handed over to the "first carrier for transmission to the buyer." If the seller had used an independent trucker to carry the goods from Virginia to New York, risk of loss would have passed when the truck was destroyed. But who is the "first carrier" where the seller uses its own trucks to transport goods? Given the rationale for assigning risk of loss, it makes little sense to include such a carrier within the definition of "first carrier." The seller retains control over the goods while they are transported by the seller's own trucks, and the seller is clearly better positioned both to protect the goods and to insure against their loss. Thus, we would conclude that the "first carrier" had not yet received the goods for transmission to the buyer and would impose the loss on seller.

Now assume that the parties agreed that the goods would be shipped on the "U.S.S. Clinton" from New York. Nothing is said, however, with respect to how the goods will get from Virginia to New York. The seller employs an independent trucker for this purpose. The goods are destroyed when the truck is involved in an accident in Pennsylvania. Was the seller "bound to hand the goods over to a carrier at a particular place"? If so, the second sentence of Article 67 states that risk passes when the goods are handed over at that place. The seller might claim that, notwithstanding the designation of a particular ship, it (the seller) was not obligated to "hand over" the goods to a carrier at that place. Instead, it might contend, its obligation was to "hand over" the goods to a carrier in Virginia. Such a reading would make the second sentence of Article 67 applicable only if the seller personally delivered the goods at the particular place. We think this reading is too restrictive. Given that the parties have agreed to the carriage *from* the particular place, the seller retains all control over how to get the goods *to* that place. We believe that risk of loss should travel with that responsibility and with the exercise of that control.

Article 67's language is a response to technological changes in the transportation of goods. Developments in multimodal transportation, particularly in containerization, allow delivery to a carrier at an inland location. The carrier then transports the goods to their destination by a combination of modes of transport such as rail, ship and truck. Given the predominance of multimodal transportation, contracts of carriage often call for delivery to the carrier's location without specifying the means of transport. Unlike shipment or destination contracts, which focus on a particular mode of transport or the buyer's location, Article 67(1) therefore focuses on the carrier's location.

The CISG also contains a provision concerning the passage of risk when goods are sold while they are in transit. For instance, a buyer of grain may resell the grain to another buyer after the seller has shipped them to the first buyer. Suppose the contract calls for the resale of five carloads of grain currently in transit to the seller. Assume that at the time of the sale, the grain has been destroyed, but neither the seller nor buyer had reason to know of the event. Under Article 68, risk passes to the buyer at the conclusion of the contract where goods are resold in transit. However, if "circumstances" indicate otherwise, risk passes retroactively to the buyer from the time the goods were first handed to a carrier who issued documents covering them. The relevant circumstances may include such matters as the purchase of transportation insurance by or on behalf of the buyer.[24] Article 68 also provides that the risk remains on the seller if, at the conclusion of the contract, the seller knew and failed to disclose information that the goods had been destroyed. In our hypothetical, the seller had no such knowledge. But the destruction had already occurred at the conclusion of the contract. As a result, the seller bears the risk of loss under Article 68.

The result is consistent with results that would be reached under the UCC, albeit through a different reasoning process. According to § 2-613 of the UCC, if goods identified to the contract are destroyed without fault of either party before the risk of loss passes to the buyer, the contract is "avoided." Avoidance of the contract would leave the goods, and hence the attendant risk of their loss, with the seller. The buyer would have no further obligations with respect to the goods and would not have to pay their price.

As is the case with the UCC, breach can alter these initial allocations. Breach by the buyer is addressed only in one situation. According to Article 69(1), a buyer who fails to take the goods in "due time" after they are placed at its disposal bears the risk of their loss. Assume that the buyer was obligated to pick up the goods from the seller's place of business on January 1. The goods are put at the buyer's disposal on the due date, but the buyer fails to take them over. Shortly thereafter, the goods are destroyed when the seller's place of business suffers a fire. The buyer bears the risk of loss and would be liable for the price of the goods under Article 66. The breaching buyer may also be liable for additional damages under Article 69(1). One might conclude that this provision inefficiently induces the aggrieved seller to ignore the care of goods once the buyer breaches. Some of this effect is moderated by the requirement in Article 85 that a seller in possession or control of goods take reasonable steps to preserve them where a buyer delays taking

---

[24] See Peter Schlechtriem, Uniform Sales Law 90 (1986).

delivery. This mitigation requirement recognizes the desire to impose losses on the party best positioned to avoid them. Article 85 provides the seller the concomitant right to reimbursement from the buyer for any reasonable expenses incurred in caring for the goods.

The situation is more complicated where a seller commits a fundamental breach.[25] Under Article 70, such a seller does not bear the risk of loss directly. Instead, the aggrieved buyer bears the risk if it would regardless of the breach; but the buyer retains the remedies available for breach of contract. Assume, for instance, that the contract requires a California winery to ship 50 cases of chardonnay wine, worth $10,000, to a buyer in Egypt. When the goods arrive, the buyer discovers that seller has shipped 50 cases of zinfandel wine, worth $8000, instead. The goods are destroyed while at buyer's business, but without buyer's fault. Under the UCC, recall, the risk of loss would now be deemed to have rested on the breaching seller because there had been no cure or acceptance. Article 70 of the CISG provides for a different analysis. Technically, the risk of loss has passed to the buyer, who has taken over the goods, and thus it is obligated to pay the price. Article 66 does not help because the damage was not caused by the seller's act or omission. But because the buyer retains its remedies after a fundamental breach, the buyer could avoid the contract entirely under Articles 49(1) and 51(2). A buyer who avoids the contract would have no payment obligation. Assume, however, that the buyer had not avoided the contract, but instead had demanded the seller replace the shipment with the appropriate wine and the zinfandel was destroyed while awaiting replacement by the seller. Now the buyer bears the risk of loss, but is entitled to damages. In the above example, for instance, the chardonnay for which the buyer had contracted had a market value in excess of the zinfandel. Under Article 74, the buyer would be entitled to recover the difference between the contract price of the goods ordered and the market price of the goods delivered, or $2000. The buyer, however, will bear the loss related to the underlying market value of the wine that was destroyed. Presumably, the buyer will recover that amount from insurance.

---

[25] Recall that a fundamental breach is one that "results in such detriment to the other party as substantially to deprive him of what he is entitled to expect under the contract." See Article 25.

## I. Introduction: Allocating the Risk of Quality

Sometimes goods do not perform as expected. When this occurs, warranty law provides a primary means for deciding whether the buyer or seller bears the costs of the product defect. Warranty is best viewed as a risk allocation device that, like other risk allocation schemes in the UCC, imposes losses on those best able to avoid them or to insure against their materialization. Thus, we attribute no blameworthiness to the seller of the defective good simply for selling a good that does not perform as expected. Concomitantly, warranty liability applies regardless of negligence or other fault. Warranty law allocates losses to merchant sellers not because they are wrongdoers, but because they have a comparative advantage as against their buyers at reducing or insuring against a risk of nonconformity in the goods sold. Comparative advantage, not culpability, is the basis for allocating the relevant risk. When a seller either expressly indicates that it has information about the probability of product defects or acts in a manner that permits a reasonable buyer to infer that the seller has such information, warranty law treats the seller as the party best able to take advantage of that information. Nevertheless, recovery for breach of warranty does require the buyer to demonstrate some causal relationship between the breach and the injury suffered.

The UCC provides for two kinds of warranty: warranties of quality and warranties of title. Warranties of quality, in turn, are divided into three types: express warranties, implied warranties of fitness for a particular purpose, and warranties of merchantability. The warranty of title is a guarantee that the seller had the rights to the good that it purported to have when the good was sold.

As a procedural matter, one can conceive of the issue of warranty as arising at either of two points in the transactions. First, it may arise once goods have been accepted. At that point, § 2-607(1) imposes on the buyer an obligation to pay for the goods, so that the warranty claim becomes a means by which the buyer can recoup some part of the price that is owed or that has been paid. Post-acceptance, the buyer must also bear the burden of proving any breach once accepted has occurred. Alternatively, a buyer may contend that the nonconformity in the good that gives rise to the right to rejection simultaneously constitutes a breach of warranty that gives rise to a claim for damages as well as to the right to reject.

## II. Warranties Under the UCC

### A. Express Warranties

#### 1. Who Can Make the Warranty?

Allocations of the risk of product defect may be made either by the parties or by law. Express warranty constitutes an allocation made by the seller. One who asserts or who commits an act that indicates that the goods offer a certain quality of performance or contain certain attributes assumes through express warranty the risk that the description or attribution of characteristics or quality is wrong.

Whether an express warranty arises in the first instance depends on the words or acts of a particular seller. Thus, unlike the implied warranties, an express warranty does not flow from any particular characteristic that the seller possesses apart from what the seller has explicitly given the buyer reason to believe. For this reason, any seller can make an express warranty. The warranty is not limited to commercial sellers or merchants, although such parties can, of course, make express warranties. A consumer seller of a used car who makes an affirmation of fact concerning whether the car has ever been in an accident, for instance, will have made an express warranty.

#### 2. How is the Warranty Created?

The basic express warranty can be found in § 2-313(1). It suggests that express warranties can be made by words, such as where a seller makes a statement of fact or promise "which relates to the goods;" by writings or symbols, such as where the seller provides a description of the goods; or by a sample or model. In each case, the words or conduct create a warranty only if they become a "basis of the bargain," about which we will say more momentarily. The substance of the warranty in each case is that the goods will conform to the affirmation, promise, description, sample or model. No words of warranty or guarantee need be used to create a warranty. A statement in sales brochures that a vessel was "a picture of sure-footed seaworthiness" and "a carefully well-equipped and very seaworthy vessel" could constitute a warranty that the vessel in question was not experimental in nature.[1] A statement in an appraisal form that jewels are of a particular quality may constitute a

---

[1] See Keith v. Buchanan, 220 Cal. Rptr. 392 (Cal. Ct. App. 1985).

warranty, notwithstanding that no prior discussion of quality occurred.[2] Under § 2-313(1)(c), a sample of a material may be treated as representative of what will be provided under the contract and hence serve as an express warranty.

Nevertheless, there is some language that falls outside of a warranty. A claim, that "this baby rides like the wind," or "this is the best treadmill on the market today" is likely to be dismissed as sales talk or puffing rather than language of warranty. Essentially vacuous statements such as "you meet the nicest people on a Honda," will not be considered to convey any qualitative information.[3] In between these extremes, there are close cases that are best resolved by considering the function of warranty law. We believe that an express warranty can best be explained as a solution to problems of asymmetric information between sellers and buyers. Sellers who offer descriptions or samples of goods implicitly signal that they have information about the quality of the goods on which buyers rely. Buyers who are concerned with the quality of the goods they propose to purchase and who might otherwise make further inquiries about those goods are induced by the seller's representations not to make further investigations. The seller who makes assertions about the qualities of the good, therefore, is essentially lulling the buyer into complacency about the good's characteristics. Thus, whether or not a statement constitutes an express warranty should depend on whether the statement is one that reveals the kinds of information that can reasonably be thought to have been within the knowledge of the seller. Sellers who deter buyers from making independent investigations concerning the goods provide a useful function, since it would be inefficient for buyers to duplicate information that the seller purports to have. Those efficiencies can only be realized, however, if the seller's information is accurate. Thus, to encourage sellers to convey correct information, and to encourage buyers to rely on that information, it is necessary to hold the seller responsible for the accuracy of the information they provide.

The application of this rationale for express warranty may be tested by the following hypothetical. Assume that a young attorney purchases a painting represented by the seller to be "one of the finest examples of Picasso's early work." Now take three possibilities. First, the work turns out to be universally considered by art experts to be an atypically poor

---

[2] See Daughtrey v. Ashe, 413 S.E.2d 336 (Va. 1992).

[3] See § 2-313(2); Federal Signal Corp. v. Safety Factors, Inc., 886 P.2d 172 (Wash. 1994).

piece of Picasso's early work, worth approximately 1/3 what our buyer paid. Second, the work turns out to be a Picasso, and a pretty good one, but was painted shortly before the artist's death. In short, it was not "early." Third, the painting turns out not to be a Picasso at all.

The first "defect," or error, is perhaps the most difficult to bring within the scope of express warranty. The seller, in suggesting that the work was "one of the finest examples" of Picasso's early work seems to have been expressing no more than a personal opinion. A statement that is inherently subjective may fall outside the scope of an "affirmation of fact." The buyer may understand that the seller believes that the painting is of the quality indicated. But if the underlying belief is simply a personal opinion, there is no basis for the buyer to conclude that the seller is representing that others would reach a similar conclusion. On the other hand, the seller may be indicating that the qualitative characteristic attributed to the work constitutes a consensus view of objective art experts. That claim sounds more like a verifiable, objective statement of fact that could be disproven by the buyer's own inquiry. The seller's assertion, however, deters the buyer from making such an inquiry. The buyer may reasonably interpret the statement as an expression of the seller's willingness to solve the informational asymmetry about the painting's quality at a lower cost than the buyer would have to incur by making an independent investigation. If that is the case, then our desire to reduce the costs of transactions should lead us to impose warranty liability on the seller should the implicit representation of quality turn out to be false. Imposing liability induces sellers to fill the buyer's informational gap only when doing so actually displaces the need for the buyer to obtain accurate and useful information. For the same reason, statements of opinion should not constitute warranties, since the seller's opinion, if it is only that, does not purport to respond authoritatively to the buyer's desire for additional information.

The second error, about the time when the painting was painted, sounds more like a factual indication than an opinion. Again, the verifiability of the statement helps to distinguish between fact and opinion. And, again, the statement by the seller discourages the buyer from making independent inquiry. The statement also reveals how levels of specificity can affect the existence or nonexistence of a warranty. The more general the statement, the more likely it is to fall within the category of "sales talk" rather than warranty. A statement that "this automobile will get 18 miles per gallon in city driving and 21 miles per gallon in highway driving" implies that the speaker has conducted the tests necessary to have knowledge of the good's performance with such specificity. That implication is simply absent in the remark that "this baby is a real gas miser."[4]

The third error, about the origins of the painting, initially looks like a factual statement. The seller, however, may contend that, given the painter's demise, we can never be *certain* of its author. Hence, any statement of provenance is inherently one of opinion.[5] We would reject that argument. It may be true that there is uncertainty about the origins of the painting, just as there is some uncertainty about whether any good will perform as expected. But by making an unqualified statement that the painting was done by Picasso, the seller has taken on the risk of error. After all, the seller could have stated that the painting was "attributed to Picasso," or "in the style of Picasso." Failure to qualify the statement indicates to the buyer that it need make no further inquiry to determine the genuineness of the painting, because the seller has done what is necessary to support the statement. Thus, we would conclude that this statement constitutes an express warranty, and that, if the statement was erroneous, the warranty has been breached.

The express warranty may also signal qualitative differences among otherwise fungible goods.[6] Buyers are unlikely to have the same information about goods as their sellers. Assume, for instance, that sellers of low-quality goods were not responsible for their quality claims. Such claims would be costless to make, so sellers would make unsupportable claims in order to compete with sellers of high-quality goods. Buyers would be unable to distinguish between sellers of high-quality goods and sellers of low-quality goods who were simply mimicking the behavior of the former sellers. As a result, buyers would pay more for low-quality goods than their characteristics justified. Alternatively, buyers would fail to purchase high-quality goods at the prices they should properly command, because buyers would not be able to determine that the goods were, in fact, of high quality. Now assume that sellers are responsible for their statements. As a result, warranties are costly for all sellers. All sellers will be required to charge prices that

---

[4] See, e.g., Web Press Services Corp. v. New London Motors, Inc., 525 A.2d 57 (Conn. 1987).

[5] See, e.g., Balog v. Cener Art Gallery—Hawaii, Inc., 745 F. Supp. 1556 (Haw. 1990).

[6] For discussion of signaling theories of warranty, see George Priest, *A Theory of the Consumer Product Warranty*, 90 Yale L.J. 1297 (1981).

reflect the costs of making the repairs or replacements necessary when the goods break down. This rate will, by definition, be higher for low-quality than for high-quality goods. As a result, sellers of low-quality goods will not be able to mimic the warranties of high-quality goods, since they will have to charge more in order the fund the higher rate of repair, replacement, or refund to which their goods will be subject. The result is that buyers will be able to compare the quality of goods by virtue of the signals implicit in the express warranties that are made with respect to the goods.

There are some circumstances in which it would be unreasonable for buyers to rely on sellers. This might be because the information is equally available to buyers, the statement is one on which no reasonable buyer would rely, or the content of the statement is essentially meaningless. Thus, when the UCC requires that the express statement or act be the "basis of the bargain" before a warranty is made, it is not suggesting that the statement or act be specifically bargained for. Rather, it suggests only that the term at issue be sufficiently within the knowledge of the seller, or reasonably believed to be within the knowledge of the seller, that the buyer can reasonably deduce that it has no need to make a further investigation. There is no need for the buyer to rely explicitly on the seller's statement in order to have an express warranty. It is in this sense that courts and commentators have distinguished the "basis of the bargain" language from the narrow requirement that the buyer have *relied* on the seller's representation. One court has gone so far as to maintain that any statement by one with "superior knowledge" about the goods is to be treated as a statement of fact, and hence an express warranty, unless the speaker qualifies the statement as mere opinion.[7]

This view of "basis of the bargain" is consistent with the recent case of *Rogath v. Siebenmann.*[8] Defendant had sold Rogath a painting, supposedly painted by a well-known artist. The seller warranted in the bill of sale that he was the sole owner of the painting, that it was authentic, and that he was not aware of any challenge to its authenticity. After Rogath resold the painting, however, the second buyer learned of challenges to its authenticity and the resale was canceled. The plaintiff then sued the defendant for breach of warranty. Defendant appealed a

---

[7] See Daugherty v. Ashe, 413 S.E.2d 336 (Va. 1992).

[8] 129 F.3d 261 (2d Cir. 1997).

grant of summary judgment for Rogath, contending that the representations made in the bill of sale did not qualify as warranties, as Rogath was fully aware when he bought the painting that questions of authenticity and provenance had already been raised. The court interpreted "basis of the bargain" to require "no more than reliance on the express warranty as being a part of the bargain between the parties."[9] The existence of an express warranty depended not on "whether the buyer believed in the truth of the warranted information . . . but whether [he] believed [he] was purchasing the [seller's] promise [as to its truth]."[10] If a seller personally disclosed facts that made representations in the contract untrue, the buyer "waived the breach." A buyer who learned of the misrepresentations from other sources, however, could still bring the warranty action, since the price of the goods included insurance that the representations were true.

This holding may initially seem inconsistent with the general objective of placing risk of defect on the party best positioned to avoid it. If the buyer already had information that the representation was false, arguably nothing is gained by requiring the seller to disclose. This claim, however, ignores the ways in which the desire to have legal tests that are easily verifiable and administrable may affect the substance of the law. If courts must adjudicate what the buyer knew and when it knew it, warranty litigation will become much more complex. If Rogath had heard a rumor that the painting might not be authentic, would that be enough? If he heard a series of rumors, some prior to his purchase of the painting and some subsequent, at what point would his suspicions have become "knowledge" sufficient to deprive him of the right to bring a warranty action? The uncertainty that ensues when legal tests depend on such difficult inquiries may justify having a precise, verifiable rule that makes the "basis of the bargain" test easier to administer. The "disclosure" rule adopted in *Rogath* may not always impose the risk on the party best positioned to avoid it, but it is relatively verifiable and arguably properly allocates the risk with sufficient frequency that its overall effect cannot be improved by ad hoc inquiries.

### a. Advertising and Warranty

If the seller can demonstrate that a buyer ignored or explicitly did not

---

[9] That view had previously been adopted in CBS Inc. v. Ziff-Davis Publishing Co., 553 N.E.2d 997 (N.Y. 1990).

[10] 129 F.3d at 264, quoting 553 N.E.2d at 1001.

rely on a statement, then the seller may be able to demonstrate that the statement was not part of the basis of the bargain.[11] This raises difficult issues particularly with respect to the issue of the extent to which advertisements give rise to warranties. Most courts now recognize that there are circumstances in which mass advertising can create warranties.[12] Nevertheless, difficulties of scope remain. In *Cipollone v. Liggett Group*,[13] involving cigarette warranties, the Court of Appeals limited the basis of the bargain to those representations of which the buyer had knowledge by virtue of hearing, reading, seeing or otherwise being aware of their contents. Once the buyer had such knowledge, however, the court created a presumption that the representation was part of the basis of the bargain, and that presumption could only be rebutted by "clear and affirmative proof" that the buyer knew the falsity of the representation. If the alleged warrantor could prove non-belief, the buyer could still recover under a warranty theory by showing explicit reliance notwithstanding non-belief.

The limitation on the consumer's ability to rely on advertising reveals a somewhat simplified view of consumer decision making. Consumers subjected to a bombardment of advertisements may not recall seeing explicit phrases or ads that ultimately influence their purchasing decisions. If the decision requires buyers to demonstrate that they saw and acted on specific claims made by the seller in a mass advertising campaign, the decision comes pretty close to embodying the reliance requirement that the Official Comments purport to abrogate. Indeed, the court appeared to use just this reasoning in rejecting an express warranty claim in *American Tobacco Co. v. Grinnell*.[14] In that case, the court rejected the claim that a cigarette manufacturer had made explicit warranties concerning the absence of health risks in its cigarettes. The court noted, in a strong statement at odds with most cases on the issue,

---

[11] See, e.g., Hauter v. Zogarts, 534 P.2d 377 (Cal. 1975).

[12] See Triple E, Inc. v. Hendrix and Dail, Inc. 543 S.E.2d 245 (S.C. App. 2001).

[13] 893 F.2d 541 (3d Cir. 1990), *aff'd in part, rev'd in part,* 505 U.S. 504 (1992).

[14] 951 S.W.2d 420 (Tex. 1997). In a similar case, plaintiff's specifically pleading of reliance on advertisements was sufficient to survive a motion to dismiss an express warranty claim. Wright v. Brooke Group Ltd., 43 UCC Rep. Serv. 2d 275 (N.D. Iowa 2000).

that the express warranty claim required proof of reliance. It then concluded that the company had negated reliance as a matter of law. As we have noted above, proof that the buyer did not rely on statements may be enough to remove the claimed statements from the "basis of the bargain." But what should be the standard for proving the absence of reliance? In *Grinnell*, the court found it sufficient that the plaintiff remembered seeing advertisements from cigarette manufacturers other than the defendant, that he began smoking because his friends smoked rather than because of claims in advertisements, and that when he did switch to cigarettes manufactured by defendant that had been the topic health claims in advertisements, he did so based on taste, rather than because of those advertisements. While the court properly rejected statements on which the plaintiff could not have relied because they were unavailable to the public at large or were made after he began smoking, the court may have been overly broad in its rejection of all advertising if the plaintiff had other reasons for beginning to smoke. The decision to purchase a good is often a complex one, comprising several factors that even the buyer will have difficulty disaggregating. To suggest that a decision to smoke was made for one reason rather than another is to ignore how multiple reasons, including claims made in advertising, can combine to cause a buyer to make a particular decision.

One might take a broad view of "basis of the bargain" and suggest that a seller who makes statements to the public at large through mass advertising should not be able to avoid warranty liability to purchasers who did not see or recall seeing promotional literature. After all, one might assert, the warrantor employed the advertisement to encourage purchase of the product and thus should not be heard to complain when a particular purchaser engages in the very transaction that the seller encouraged, even where the purchaser did not see the advertisement. One might go further and contend that, had this buyer not purchased the offending good, some other buyer who might have seen the advertisement could have. Thus, the seller is not disadvantaged by permitting this buyer from bringing the action. On this theory, the plaintiff who claims breach of warranty is akin to a private attorney general for all potential purchasers of the good.

This argument, however, may prove too much, at least with respect to those purchasers who demonstrably did not rely on the advertisement. Recall that recovery for breach of express warranty requires the plaintiff to demonstrate not only the warranty and its breach, but also a causal relationship between that breach and subsequent injury. Allowing a buyer who affirmatively did not see the advertisement to recover violates this requirement. In *Lowe v. Sproicidin International*,[15] the court found that even if a manufacturer's advertisements for a disinfectant misstated dangers from exposure, an injured hospital technical still could not recover for breach of express warranty, because the technician had never seen the offending advertisements. That logical leap might be less problematic if we did not think that causation played an important doctrinal role. But causation does limit the scope of liability in important ways and allows sellers to predict more reliably the extent of their exposure. In addition, the private attorney general argument allows too much latitude for buyers who do not rely on advertising. For instance, a seller may advertise in certain media in the expectation that a particular amount of goods will be sold through that media. Buyers outside that target audience are not perfect substitutes for buyers within the audience.

The Proposed Revision explicitly recognized that sellers could make express warranties through advertising, and distinguished between those buyers who were in a contractual relationship with the seller (termed an "immediate buyer"[16]) and those who were not (termed a "remote purchaser"[17]). With respect to the former, express warranties could be made through the affirmations, descriptions, and samples or models currently reflected in § 2-313. There is no reason to believe that the drafters of the Proposed Revision intended to scale back on court decisions that recognized warranties through advertising.

With respect to remote purchasers, the Proposed Revision would have added two new sections, § 2-313A and § 2-313B. The first would have made clear that remote purchasers could bring claims based on affirmations or descriptions of the goods contained in packaging or otherwise accompanying the goods in a sale of new goods in the normal chain or distribution. Although the drafters avoided the phrase "express warranty" since there was no contact between the seller and buyer, the effect of the provision would have been to impose the equivalent of warranty liability on remote sellers. Liability would apply as long as the seller reasonably expected the record to be furnished to the remote purchaser and the record was so furnished.

Proposed § 2-313B would have imposed liability for seller

---

[15] 47 F.3d 124 (4th Cir. 1995).

[16] Proposed § 2-313(a).

[17] Proposed §§ 2-313A, 2-313B.

affirmations or descriptions contained in "advertising or a similar communication to the public." The buyer would have been required to have "knowledge of and . . . the expectation that the goods will conform to" the affirmation or description. The knowledge requirement implied that the buyer actually read, heard, or saw the representation that forms the basis for the warranty claim. The "expectation" requirement essentially imposed a reliance test. The language of "basis of the bargain" would have been inappropriate, since there is no "bargain" between the advertiser and the remote purchaser. But the "knowledge" requirement created one potential anomaly. Notwithstanding the language of "basis of the bargain," there is no explicit "knowledge" requirement with respect to express warranties made to an immediate buyer. For instance, a warranty in a standard form contract that the buyer never read would presumably continue to serve as the basis of the bargain. Thus, one might infer that the advertising provision is more restrictive. Certainly, the combination of the "knowledge" and "expectation" requirements rejected the argument above that sellers who engage in mass marketing are essentially liable to any purchaser for any description or affirmation, even if the particular purchaser was, at time of purchase, unaware of the relevant language. Finally, the liability would have applied only if a reasonable person in the position of the remote purchaser would expect the goods to conform to the representation or perform as promised. This language essentially omits the kind of puffing or "sales talk" that arguably would not be considered language of warranty in the first place.

### b. Post-Bargain Warranties

This focus on relative access to information, rather than bargaining, also explains the initially odd assertion in the Official Comment 7 to § 2-313 that language used after the closing of the deal can constitute a warranty. One may question how a post-sale statement can constitute a "basis of the [completed] bargain," which appears to be the predicate for warranty liability. Nevertheless, Official Comment 7 to § 2-313 suggests that a post-sale statement *can* be considered a modification of the original bargain, which, under the UCC, requires no consideration to be effective. That leaves open the question whether, in a particular case, the statement *should* be considered a modification.

We believe that focus on a seller's assertions of superior knowledge, combined with the buyer's reliance on that knowledge, provides the basis for extending warranty protection to post-sale statements. Assume, for instance, that a buyer of a used car agrees to all terms with the seller, but subsequently asks whether the tires are in good condition. The seller assures the buyer that they are, but the automobile is shortly thereafter damaged due to the defective condition of one of the tires. The buyer, in seeking additional assurances after the close of the transaction, indicated reliance on any information imparted by the seller. The seller's unequivocal statements indicated the possession of sufficient knowledge to foreclose subsequent investigation by the buyer should be enough to constitute an express warranty.[18] We believe that this combination satisfies all the objectives underlying warranty liability, regardless of the time when the relevant statement was made.

Compare this situation with a variation on our Picasso example above. Assume that, subsequent to the sale of a nondescript painting, the seller informs the buyer, "You are very lucky; I happen to know that this is a Picasso." Even if that statement would have constituted a warranty if made pre-sale, and even if the statement is untrue, we would not impose warranty liability in this case unless the buyer could demonstrate that it had relied detrimentally on the statement. Perhaps the buyer subsequently announced that he was the owner of a Picasso and suffered embarrassment when proven incorrect. But without a showing that the buyer took some action taken as a of the seller's statement, we would not invoke post-sale warranty liability in this case.

### B. Implied Warranty of Fitness for a Particular Purpose

### 1. Who Can Make the Warranty?

The warranty of fitness for a particular purpose, created by § 2-315, is implied as a matter of law. The seller need make no statement or commit no act in order to trigger the warranty. It arises in circumstances that indicate that (1) the seller has special knowledge about what will satisfy the buyer's needs, and (2) the seller knows that the buyer is relying on the seller's skill or judgment to select suitable goods. Nothing in these criteria requires that the seller be a merchant with respect to the goods at issue. Again, the implicit rationale is that the seller has lulled the buyer into stopping any search for the optimal good. Once the seller has held itself out as capable of making a recommendation that will satisfy the buyer and has in fact made such a recommendation, the buyer is unlikely to make further investigation. The implied warranty induces sellers who are aware that they are being relied on only to make recommendations within their area of expertise and thus not falsely lull buyers into a sense of security.

---

[18] See, e.g., Downie v. Abex Corp., 741 F.2d 1235 (10th Cir. 1984).

## 2. How is the Warranty Created?

The warranty is created by the seller's selection or furnishing of goods suitable to the buyer's needs where the seller satisfies the criteria stated above. Assume, for instance, that a buyer asks the seller for a computer that is compatible with a particular program that requires substantial amounts of memory. The seller sells the buyer a computer that is incompatible with the proper operation of that program. The seller in these circumstances knew that the buyer had a particular purpose in mind and, by virtue of the question, that the buyer was relying on his judgment to select a proper computer.

This example also suggests a difficulty in determining what constitutes a "particular" purpose for a good. Official Comment 2 to § 2-315 contrasts a "particular purpose" with an "ordinary purpose" for which the goods are used. Warranties with respect to the ordinary purposes of a good are covered by the warranty of merchantability under § 2-314 rather than the warranty of fitness for a particular purpose. Comment 2 speaks of a "specific use" that is "peculiar" to the buyer's circumstances, as opposed to "uses which are customarily made" of the goods, which are the essence of merchantability. This might suggest that the "particular purpose" warranty is limited only to those cases in which a buyer has an idiosyncratic use for the good, such as where a buyer requests a chair that can be used as a stepladder. A buyer who communicates such an atypical use for a good and who receives a recommendation from the seller in return would, of course, be the beneficiary of a warranty of fitness for a particular purpose. An atypical use, however, need not be a purpose that transforms the good from its ordinary use into an entirely different use. A computer that does not have enough memory to run a specific software program, for instance, may be perfectly serviceable as a computer for a variety of purposes and thus constitute a merchantable computer. But if a computer user needs to be able to run that program and indicates her "particular" need to the seller, that buyer is indicating that it wants something more than a run-of-the-mill good that will satisfy the most general description of a "computer." The buyer's indication that it needs a computer that fits within a subset of the general description of the goods triggers the particular purpose warranty.

## C. Implied Warranty of Merchantability

### 1. Who Can Make the Warranty?

The warranty of merchantability is the most general of the UCC warranties of quality. It is made without any words being spoken by anyone or acts being committed other than the act of selling the good. It includes the serving of food or drink, whether they are to be consumed on the seller's premises or elsewhere. The warranty exists only if the seller is a merchant with respect to goods of that kind. This limitation suggests the basis for the warranty. In any contract for sale, a merchant who deals in goods of the kind involved is likely to be a repeat player with respect to the goods. The seller is likely to come into contact with the range of similar goods on a more frequent basis than the buyer. As a result, the seller is likely to have substantial information about the goods not readily available to the buyer. This information includes data relevant to the proper pricing of the good, taking into account such matters as its rate of breakdown, the kinds of damage that the goods are likely to suffer and inflict, and the cost of repair. A merchant of cars, for instance, will have a better idea of the reliability of its automobiles than any random customer. The warranty of merchantability addresses this information asymmetry and induces the seller to share information, implicitly or explicitly, with the buyer.

The warranty of merchantability effectively accomplishes this task by transforming the warrantor into a conduit for insuring the goods. Assume that the seller knows, based on frequent contact, that a good with a production cost plus reasonable profit of $99 has a breakdown rate of about one percent. Hence, the expected loss with respect to any unit is about $1.00. Armed with such information, a seller who is liable in warranty when the good breaks down can add approximately $1.00 to the price of each unit sold. When the buyer of the defective good appears, the seller will be able to provide compensation with the "insurance premium" collected from all buyers. Risk-neutral buyers should be willing to pay this amount, because it is a fair price for the insurance they are receiving and they, having less experience with the goods, will have comparatively unreliable information about breakdown rates and thus about the decision to insure against breakdown. At the same time, each buyer knows that if it is the unfortunate purchaser of the good that is defective, it will be able to shift the loss to the seller.

Warranty theory, therefore, shares many of the characteristics of strict liability. The merchant need not be negligent or reckless to create the warranty. Nor need the merchant have knowledge of the defect's existence or personal knowledge of the facts that trigger the warranty, such as breakdown rates for the goods. The mere fact that the seller, by virtue of being a merchant, occupies the position of one who is best positioned to have this information is sufficient. Recall that to be a merchant, it is not necessary for the seller actually to have the skills and practices associated with one who commonly sells the goods in question. The definition of merchant is satisfied if one simply "by his occupation hold himself out as having knowledge or skill peculiar to the practices or goods involved in the transaction."[19]  Similarly, the focus on "practices" in the definition of "merchant" indicates that it is not necessary that the seller have expertise in the particular good being supplied.   A manufacturer who uses certain practices or processes, for instance, may make widgets one day, gadgets the next day, and hoedads the third day. When one of the products fails to meet expectations the manufacturer may attempt to claim that it is not a merchant with respect to any of those goods, but only an occasional seller of each.  If the warranty claim involves the process by which the goods were made, however, the manufacturer is a merchant and, with respect to those processes, makes warranties of merchantability.

Doctrinally, warranty liability does not require the same proof of a defect that is often involved in many strict product liability cases. Product liability in cases of design defects and failure to warn cases have come to be dominated by cost-benefit analyses.  While those tests may be perfect appropriate, they vary from the test for merchantability, which looks more towards the acceptance of the product in the industry or the expectations of the buyer based on what passes without objection in the trade.  The analogy to products liability is closer when one is talking about those products that suffer manufacturing defects.  In these cases, the standard of liability for tort law is generally that the product is in a defective condition unreasonably dangerous to the user or consumer or her property even though the seller has exercised all possible care in the preparation and sale of the product.[20]  What makes the product defective and unreasonably dangerous is typically a characteristic that is unexpected given other products of that description that pass without objection in the trade or that are considered to be of fair average quality. Hence, the same evidence that demonstrates a product is unreasonably dangerous simultaneously demonstrates that the good is not merchantable.  For instance, the seller of a hammer that chips on its first use will not only run afoul of tort conceptions of products liability, but will also breach an warranty about the characteristics of the good.

---

[19] § 2-104(1).  See Proposed § 2-102(a)(23).

[20] See, e.g., Commonwealth v. Johnson Insulation, 682 N.E.2d 1323 (Mass. 1997); Restatement (Second) Torts, § 402A.

## 2. How is the Warranty Created?

The warranty of merchantability requires no special words or acts by the merchant seller. It inheres in the sale of goods by a merchant seller and may arise from course of dealing or usage of trade. Assume, for instance, that it is the practice of merchants who sell pedigreed dogs that they will provide papers testifying to the dog's pedigree. A merchant of pedigreed dogs impliedly warrants his ability to produce such papers simply by being a merchant within that trade.[21] The warranty exists, however, even if the buyer does not rely on any skill or judgment of the merchant seller. The insurance function of the warranty requires simply that the merchant be able to pass the costs of breakdown along to customers, and that objective implies only that the seller is in a better position than the seller to know breakdown rates and costs, not the specific needs of a particular customer.

One who is not a merchant of the defective goods, however, does not make the warranty. Thus, a consumer seller of a used car will not make an implied warranty of merchantability with respect to that car. This is not because of used nature of the goods; rather it is because the seller is not a merchant with respect to goods of that kind and therefore cannot be expected to have the knowledge that underlies the warranty. For instance, a restaurant may not be liable for breach of warranty when it serves a customer a glass of wine and the glass shatters in the customer's hand. The restaurant will claim that it is not a merchant with respect to the glass, but only to the wine. Nevertheless, the better view is that the restaurant had significant information about the defect rate of the glasses. Thus, the restaurant to be considered a person who "deals in" goods of that kind and is therefore a "merchant" under § 2-104(1) for purposes of serving drinks in glasses. If a non-merchant seller makes express claims about the quality of goods, however, § 2-314(2) may provide relevant information about the meaning of those general terms.[22]

The substance of the warranty differs from that in the warranty of fitness for a particular purpose. A merchantable good is fit for the ordinary purposes for which such a good is used. Thus, it passes without objection in the trade as being the good described, and is of fair average

---

[21] § 2-314 Official Comment 12.

[22] See § 2-314 Official Comment 4.

quality within that description.[23]  This may mean more than simply that the good contains all the ingredients or characteristics of the good in question.  It must also operate like the average and unobjectionable good within the contract description.  In *Delano Growers' Cooperative Winery v. Supreme Wine Co.*,[24] for instance, the buyer claimed that seller had furnished unmerchantable goods under a contract to deliver "finished wine."  The source of the defect was allegedly Fresno mold within the wine that seller supplied.  Seller contended that all wine within the contract description (California sweet wine) contained the offending mold.  Thus, seller argued, wine containing the mold passed without objection in the trade and was of fair average quality.  Nevertheless, the court concluded that even if mold was ubiquitous, its presence and its adverse effects could be controlled and was controlled by other producers of the same wine.  As a result, the warranty of merchantability was breached.

The warranty does not apply to idiosyncratic uses made by the purchaser (although if these uses were known to the seller and the buyer relied on the seller, a warranty of fitness for a particular purpose could apply).  Thus, the seller of an automobile made no warranty that a purchaser who locked herself in the trunk in an effort to commit suicide would be able to escape when she changed her mind and could not open the trunk, since the ordinary purpose of an automobile trunk is to transport and store goods, not to hold people who might seek to extricate themselves.[25]

Nor is the warranty breached by characteristics of a good but that are inherent in the good and therefore do not preclude its passing under the contract description.  Knives are sharp, fish chowder and enchiladas contain bones, raw clams contain bacteria that are usually harmless.  Each of these features can cause injury.  But their presence does not exclude the goods within which they are found from the category of "fair average quality."  To meet such cases, courts have devised a "reasonable expectations" test, under which the existence of characteristics that are "naturally" found in the goods of the contract description do not breach

---

[23] The Proposed Revision adopts the CISG language that the goods are fit for the ordinary purposes "for which goods of that description" are used.  See Proposed Revision § 2-404(b)(3).

[24] 473 N.E.2d 1006 (Mass. 1985).

[25] See Daniell v. Ford Motor Co., 581 F. Supp. 728 (D.N.M. 1984).

the warranty of merchantability.[26]

The content of the warranty becomes more complicated when the buyer's claim rests on information commonly available. If we perceive the warranty as a risk shifting device based on the seller's superior information, the exclusion of characteristics within common knowledge seems reasonable. At the same time, the issue of what constitutes common knowledge may be difficult to verify, especially if information about the characteristic at issue grew incrementally over a significant period of time. In that case, imposing warranty liability on sellers and manufacturers at least provides incentives for making cost-effective investments in obtaining and disseminating information about their products. These difficulties are demonstrated by the recent case of *American Tobacco Co. v. Grinnell*,[27] which we discussed above. Plaintiff had begun smoking cigarettes at age 19 in 1952. He died some 34 years later after contracting lung cancer. In a lawsuit against a cigarette manufacturer, the court rejected plaintiff's claim that the company had breached an implied warranty by marketing a product that was not safe for human consumption and that was addictive. The court rejected the first claim on the ground that no expectation arises with respect to cigarettes when they are purchased because their inherent health hazards are common knowledge. The court implicitly applied a standard of knowledge that existed during the latter years of the plaintiff's smoking. The addiction claim, however, was intended to demonstrate that once the plaintiff began smoking, he would have difficulty stopping, notwithstanding his knowledge of health risks. Thus, the court implied that the addiction claim had to be tested by reference to the state of common knowledge in 1952. The court concluded that the company had not conclusively established that the danger of nicotine addiction was common known at that time. That conclusion implicitly highlights the difficult issues inherent in any inquiry into common knowledge, as it is entirely unclear what has to be known and who has to know it. If what was known in 1952 was that cigarettes posed "health risks" of some kind, why would that include lung cancer, but not addiction? If there was

---

[26] Id. Earlier courts had adopted a "foreign-natural" test under which the food was deemed unfit for the ordinary purposes for which it is sold if an object found in the food did not occur naturally in that food. See Webster v. Blue Ship Tea Room, 198 N.E.2d 309 (Mass. 1964). The "reasonable expectations" test is more readily applicable to non-food goods.

[27] 951 S.W.2d 420 (Tex. 1997).

common knowledge of one risk, such as lung cancer, would people commonly infer that the same product could cause other respiratory ailments, such as bronchitis and emphysema? And if one assumed those diseases, would one also assume that there could be other non-respiratory health related risks such as breast cancer or stroke? These issues are raised by a dissenting judge in Grinnell, but give rise to little in the way of answers that suggests the desirability of so unverifiable of a test.

A buyer who is able to demonstrate that the goods it purchased from a merchant were not fit for their ordinary purposes faces one additional hurdle to recovery. There must be a causal relationship between the breach of the warranty and the injury suffered. Assume, for instance, that a farmer proves that it used the seller's herbicide, that the herbicide's formulation and application rate was inconsistent with the crops on which it was being used and on which the seller recommended that it be used, and that the farmer obtained a historically low crop yield. There are obviously other potential causes of low crop yield, including dry weather and the farmer's skill level. Thus, even if it can demonstrate that the herbicide was not as warranted, additional proof would be necessary to demonstrate the causal link between that breach and the low crop yield.[28] Even where there exists some causal relationship between breach and injury, courts will allow evidence of supervening cause to insulate sellers from liability. In *Porter v. Pfizer Hospital Products Group, Inc.*,[29] for instance, the court found that the injuries of a patient in a hip replacement operation were caused by the actions of the surgeon rather than by defects that existed in the artificial joint and that caused it to break during the operation. Similarly, the estate of a woman who died after ingesting cyanide-contaminated capsules could not recover from the manufacturer or the retailer, notwithstanding that the product was obviously unfit for its intended purpose. The intervention of a third party who tampered with the package, rather than any defect in the manufacturing process, caused the injury.[30]

The purchaser's own actions may also break the causal chain between defect and injury. In *Hubbs v. Joseph Enterprises*,[31] an elderly

---

[28] See In re L.B. Trucking, Inc., 163 B.R. 709 (Bankr. Del. 1994).

[29] 783 F. Supp. 1466 (D. Me. 1992).

[30] See Elsroth v. Johnson & Johnson, 700 F. Supp. 151 (S.D.N.Y. 1988).

[31] 604 N.Y.S.2d 292 (N.Y. Sup. Ct. 1993).

woman who suffered from arthritis and osteoporosis sustained injuries to her hand and wrist when she clapped her hands together in an attempt to activate a device designed to turn electrical appliances on or off by responding to sound. The plaintiff had failed to adjust the sensitivity control on the device, and seller had noted prominently that those who find clapping difficult (including senior citizens) should not use the device.

### D. Disclaiming Warranties

### 1. Should Warranties be Disclaimable?

Implied warranties, as we have noted, are predicated on an assumption that the seller who satisfies certain conditions is in a superior position to avoid the materialization of a loss, to insure against it, or to act as a conduit in passing along the costs of insurance or injury. Nevertheless, there may be cases in which the seller does not occupy a superior position to accomplish these objectives. Alternatively, there may be cases in which the buyer prefers to accept risks rather than to pay for shifting them to the seller. Assume that there exists a good, the price of which equals P without a warranty and P + $10 with a warranty, where the $10 is a fair price for the warranty. This price differential reveals that the seller believes that if it bears the costs of breakdown, it will incur an average cost of $10 per unit sold for repair or replacement. A buyer who anticipates expected breakdown costs of less than $10 would prefer to pay P for the good and abandon its warranty claim against the seller in the event that a defect materializes.

We can imagine three situations in which a buyer would fall in this category. First, a buyer might have an idiosyncratic use for the good that substantially reduces the risk that a defect will materialize or cause injury. For instance, if I purchase an expensive automobile only as an investment or as a work of art and never anticipate driving it in traffic, I may have no use for a warranty.

Second, I may use the good for its ordinary purpose, but may take above average care in my use of the good. The warranty will be based on the average level of care, and thus may be priced higher than my expected breakdown costs. Thus, assume that the expected value of breakdown in the hands of the average user is $12. An average user will want a warranty that costs only $10, because it can shift those breakdown costs to the seller. But if I take above average care of the good or can repair any defects myself at low cost, the value of breakdown to me may be only $8. I will not want to purchase for $10 a warranty that costs me more than the warranty is worth to me.

Third, I may simply have a preference for risk. It may be objectively worthwhile to me to purchase the warranty. That is, I may face an expected loss of $12 from a defect and could shift that risk to the seller by purchasing the warranty for $10. Nevertheless, I may view the purchase of a good without a warranty as the kind of risky situation that I find attractive, even though a rational, self-interested, risk-neutral individual would accept the warranty.

Finally, there may be situations in which neither the buyer nor the seller occupies a superior position to achieve the objectives of warranty. For instance, the buyer may understand that it is purchasing an experimental good or an untested prototype. Alternatively, the buyer may be cooperating with the seller in providing specifications or developing a product jointly. In these cases, it is more difficult to cast the seller as one with superior knowledge about breakdown rates and costs and the economies typically associated with placing warranty liability on the seller will not be realized.

For all these reasons, the UCC permits sellers who would otherwise make warranties to disclaim them. There exist, however, three respectable arguments that warranties should not be disclaimable. First, disclaimers may be written in language difficult to discover or decipher, so that parties who do not fall in the above categories and thus for whom a warranty would be a cost-effective purchase will be misled into accepting a disclaimer. Second, some buyers may prefer warranties to no warranties, but their preference may not be intense enough to be worth incurring the cost of negotiating around a disclaimer. Assume, for instance, that the warranty costs $10 and the buyer faces expected breakdown costs of $12, so that the buyer would prefer the warranty. The seller, however, sells the good with a disclaimer. The buyer, however, believes that negotiating for a warranty would cost $3. The rational, risk-neutral buyer will be unwilling to spend a total of $13 ($10 for the warranty, plus $3 in negotiation costs) to avoid an expected loss of $12, even though the same buyer would have preferred the warranty if it did not have to bargain for it, that is, if the warranty implied by law had not been disclaimed.

Third, some buyers may simply be unable to deal with the expected loss calculation and thus determine whether it is worth negotiating around the disclaimer. As we stated above, the primary rationale for implied warranties lies in the superior knowledge of the seller about breakdown rates and costs. If the buyer is unaware of the relevant data, it will be unable to determine whether to accept the disclaimer. Add to this the existence of cognitive phenomena that may interfere with calculations about the likelihood of breakdown. Theories of cognitive dissonance, for instance, predict that individuals will be unable simultaneously to believe that they are making a good purchase and that the product they have purchased may be defective. Thus, at least some buyers are likely to understate the risk of product failure and the need for a warranty.

These factors suggest that we are likely to confront occasional inefficiencies whether we permit or prohibit warranty disclaimers. Either individuals who do not desire or need warranties will be required to pay for them, or individuals who would (or should) prefer warranties will not be able to obtain them. The empirical issue, which we cannot address, is which result generates the greater inefficiency. But it may be that inefficiency alone does not answer the question. If we believe that the factors of ignorance and cognitive that would prevent buyers from bargaining for efficient warranties systematically affect consumers or the relatively poor, then there may be distributive reasons to prevent disclaimers, at least in cases that are most likely to involve those kinds of buyers. Perhaps for this reason, some states have adopted non-uniform amendments to the UCC that prohibits disclaimers in the case of consumer goods.[32]

Even where disclaimers are permissible (whether with respect to consumer or commercial transactions), the concern that sellers will attempt to obscure exclusionary language or that buyers will be ignorant of it led the drafters of the UCC to require sellers to meet certain criteria before disclaimers would be effective. It is to that issue that we next turn.

### 2. Disclaiming Warranties Under § 2-316

Section 2-316 creates the basic framework for disclaiming warranties. It provides plenty of room for judicial interpretation, and courts have not shied from the task. Subsection (1) concerns the practice of sellers simultaneously making statements that sound like express warranties and excluding or limiting those warranties. The problem typically arises when a seller allegedly makes express representations that are inconsistent with the form language of the contract. For instance, a seller who orally stated that a carpet was guaranteed for one year subsequently attempted to avoid warranty liability by pointing to a clause

---

[32] See, e.g., Md. Commercial Law Code Ann. § 2-316.1 (1997); 9A Vt. Stat. Ann. § 2-316 (1997).

in the sales agreement that disclaimed express and implied warranties. Section 2-316(1) provides that words of warranty and of the negation of warranty should be construed wherever reasonable as consistent with each other. Where consistency is unreasonable, however, the words of negation are inoperative. Sellers are presumably protected against false allegations of words of express warranty by the parol evidence rule.[33] This suggests that the buyer of the carpet could recover in warranty only if it could avoid the constraints of the parol evidence rule. This means that any contradictory language would be admissible only if the sales agreement was not intended as the final expression of the parties' agreement.[34] Otherwise, evidence of the express warranty would be admissible only if it was not contradictory to the sales agreement, but instead an explanation or supplement of it. Courts, which systematically disfavor warranty disclaimers, have found in this language an arsenal of weapons to invalidate sellers' efforts to give warranty with one hand while taking it away with the other. Some courts, as in the case of the defective carpet, have simply and boldly opined that the parol evidence rule has no effect where a prior oral express warranty is contradicted by a written disclaimer.[35] Other courts have admitted testimony of the oral warranty under the guise of determining whether the written contract containing the disclaimer was intended as the final expression of the parties' agreement.[36] Courts may also go to lengths to find that the writing was not intended as the final expression, such as by noting the absence of a merger clause in the contract, or by finding that the seller made post-contract statements that amount to warranties not covered by the contractual disclaimer.[37] Alternatively, courts may find that the expressions of the seller amount to fraud or otherwise invalidate the

---

[33] See § 2-316(1).

[34] See§ 2-202; Chapter 5.

[35] See Carpetland, U.S.A. v. Payne, 536 N.E.2d 306 (Ind. Ct. App. 1989).

[36] See, e.g., Husky Spray Service, Inc. v. Patzer, 471 N.W.2d 146 (S.D. 1991).

[37] See Muther-Ballenger v. Griffin Electronic Consultants, Inc., 387 S.E.2d 247 (N.C. Ct. App. 1990).

contract as a whole.[38] This is not to say that a seller could not effectively disclaim the statements of its agents who might too loosely express words or warranty. It is only to say that the task requires carefully worded contractual language, possibly including a merger clause that makes it clear that the disclaimer involves the parties' final expression, and that even the most careful drafter is vulnerable to the imagination of courts. Perhaps that is not an improper result. The problem typically arises where a seller's agent makes statements of warranty that the seller has not authorized and that the seller tries to negate through a written clause with the buyer. As between the seller and the buyer, however, the seller seems to be in a far better position to control its agents.

Consider next the efforts of sellers to disclaim implied warranties. The UCC places significant restrictions on the disclaimer of the implied warranty of merchantability, and the courts have read those restrictions narrowly, again demonstrating their disfavor of disclaimers. Section 2-316(2) requires that any exclusion or modification of the implied warranty of merchantability specifically mention the merchantability term. A clause that says "no guarantee" is unlikely to satisfy this criterion. In addition, any written disclaimer of the implied warranty of merchantability must be conspicuous, defined as "so written that a reasonable person against whom it is to operate ought to have noticed it."[39] A "conspicuous" term typically will be in a larger or different typeface or a different color than the surrounding text. Disclaimers of the implied warranty of fitness for a particular purpose must be both in writing and conspicuous, though the term "fitness" need not be mentioned.

These restrictions, however, are prefaced by a reference that makes them subject to § 2-316(3). That provision appears to take away much of the protection granted by § 2-316(2). The third subsection permits a seller to exclude all warranties, presumably including the warranty of merchantability, with language such as "as is," or "with all faults," or other language from which a reasonable buyer would infer that no warranties are intended. This caveat, however, is, in turn, subject to certain conditions. First, the language must "make plain that there is no implied warranty." Second, the effectiveness of these less rigorous forms of exclusion can be negated if "the circumstances indicate otherwise."

---

[38] See, e.g., George Robberecht Seafood, Inc. v. Maitland Bros. Co., 255 S.E.2d 682 (Va. 1979).

[39] § 1-201(10).

A court, for instance, might find that the presence of a consumer buyer indicates that the meaning of "with all faults" would not be understood as readily as the same phrase in a commercial context.

Finally, § 2-316(3) indicates that no warranty exists where the underlying assumption for the warranty--the superior knowledge of the seller--does not apply. For instance, a buyer who fully examines a sample or model, or refuses to do so when examination would have revealed defects, no warranty exists with respect to those defects that the buyer should or would have discovered. The assumption is that the inspecting buyer has as much information about the quality of the good as the seller, so there is no reason to shift risks from the buyer back to the seller when the buyer fails to observe them. Of course, this does not mean that a seller can impose on an unsuspecting buyer the duty to inspect and to bear risks of defects that the buyer did not detect. The inspection obligation is properly understood as triggered only where the buyer's investigation will place her level of knowledge on a par with that of the seller.

Similarly, § 2-316(3)(c) allows implied warranties to be excluded by course of dealing or course of performance or usage of trade. Again, we would expect exclusions to arise in these repeat circumstances only if the buyers in such situations are systematically as well informed about the rate and cost of product defects as the seller. As a result, situations in which sellers do not make warranties will tend to look like one of the cases we discussed above in which warranties will actually be inefficient, because buyers are superior risk bearers. In these cases, an idiosyncratic buyer who desires a warranty should have obligation of negotiating for one.

### E. Who Receives the Benefit of Warranties? Herein of Privity and Personal Injury

Those injured by a breach of a warranty need not be the purchasers of the warranted good or purchasers from the warrantor. Assume, for instance, that a passerby is injured when the purchaser of a gas-powered lawn mower, who bought the mower at a local hardware store, is using it and one of the blades throws a stone in the passerby's direction due to a defect that constitute's a breach of the manufacturer's warranty. Two questions arise: (1) was the passerby a beneficiary of the warranty entitled to bring an action for its breach? (2) is the manufacturer liable if it was not also the seller of the lawn mower? The first issue relates to "horizontal privity," that is, the range of those affected by the product who can properly be plaintiffs. The second issue concerns "vertical privity," that is, the susceptibility of a warrantor to suit where the warranty had no involvement in the ultimate sale of the good.

Taking vertical privity claims first, most courts have eliminated such requirements where personal injury is involved. Thus, if the bystander in our example were covered by the warranty (an issue of horizontal privity discussed below), he or she could bring the action against the manufacturer, even though the good was sold to the ultimate consumer through an intermediate seller. If the purchaser of the mower had been injured, he or she could certainly bring the action against the distant seller is almost all jurisdictions. Where economic loss alone is involved, courts have been more restrictive. Where the economic loss affects the value of the product itself, such as where a breach of warranty on a mobile home renders the home inhabitable, courts tend to permit actions against a distant seller. Where the economic loss is essentially consequential, such as where defective cattle feed does not injure the ingesting cattle, but induces abortions of pregnant cows, courts have been more divided, with several continuing to require privity before permitting recovery from distant sellers.

The decline of vertical privity makes significant sense in today's economy. It is clear that warrantors frequently anticipate that their warranty will be relied on by someone other than the warrantor's immediate purchaser. This is typically the case when a manufacturer warrants a product that it sells to a retailer for ultimate resale to a consumer. The Proposed Revision explicitly provides in Proposed § 2-408 that one who makes an express warranty has an obligation to the remote buyer where the representation or promise is in a record packaged with or accompanying the goods and the seller intends that record to be furnished to the remote buyer. A "record" for these purposes includes any information on a tangible medium or that is stored in an electronic or other medium retrievable in perceivable form. Thus, it would be irrelevant whether a warranty concerning a computer program is contained in an instructional booklet that accompanies a computer disk containing the program, is on the disk itself, or appears on a screen when the disk is activated. That representation or promise would be binding as against the remote buyer unless a reasonable person would not believe it or the representation or promise is merely a statement of value or opinion.

Issues of horizontal privity involve three questions. First, they address the issue of who can serve as a proper plaintiff in a warranty action. The current version of the UCC handles the issue of horizontal privity by permitting states to select among three alternatives of § 2-318 to define the beneficiaries of a warranty. Most states have adopted Alternative A, which restricts warranty coverage to "any natural person who is in the family or household of his buyer or who is a guest in his home if it is reasonable to expect that such person may use, consume or be affected by the goods and who is injured in person by breach of the warranty." Alternative B extends coverage to "any natural person who may reasonably be expected to use, consume or be affected by the goods and who is injured in person by breach of the warranty." Alternative C extends to "any person who may reasonably be expected to use, consume or be affected by the goods and who is injured by breach of the warranty." The beneficiary need not be a natural person under this alternative, nor need the injury be personal. In none of the cases is the seller permitted to exclude or limit the operation of the provision.

In our lawn mower example, the passerby would have the strongest claim to be an appropriate plaintiff under Alternatives B and C. The passerby is not expressly included within Alternative A, but is not necessarily excluded either. Official Comment 3 to § 2-318 provides that Alternative A is neutral beyond its stated scope "and is not intended to enlarge or restrict the developing case law on whether the seller's warranties, given to his buyer who resells, extend to other persons in the distributive chain." Some courts have seized on the Comment to extend the specific Alternative A categories, for instance by allowing recovery by employees of the purchaser.[40] But other courts have read the provision quite restrictively, denying recovery, for instance, to customers in defendant's place of business.[41] The application of Alternatives A and B to any natural person who may reasonably be expected to be "affected" by the goods might be seen as a tool by which courts could expand the coverage of the provisions. Nevertheless, courts have not systematically taken advantage of this opportunity. In *Umphlett Lumber Co. v. Trident Systems, Inc.*,[42] for example, the court held that guarantors of the debt of a closely-held corporation were not included within the scope of this provision.

Proposed § 2-409(a) extends express or implied warranties made to

---

[40] See, e.g., Salvador v. Atlantic Steel Boiler Co., 319 A.2d 903 (Pa.1974); Boddie v. Litton Unit Handling Systems, 455 N.E.2d 142 (Ill. 1983).

[41] See, e.g., Denton v. Sam Blount, Inc., 669 So.2d 951 (Ala. Ct. Civ. App. 1995).

[42] 878 F.Supp. 844 (D.S.C. 1995).

a person with whom the seller is in privity to "any member of the family or household or a guest of or a transferee from an immediate consumer buyer that may reasonably be expected to use or be affected by the goods and that is damaged by a breach of warranty." While the beneficiaries are limited to natural persons they do include at least some transferees, but the bystander seems excluded. Where an express warranty is made to a remote buyer, the seller's obligation under Proposed § 2-408 also extends to any member of the family or household or any guest of the buyer and to any transferee or subsequent transferee. These extensions are in addition to the obligations that a distant seller may incur through communications to the public such as advertising, discussed above.

The second issue under horizontal privity involves the type of injury for which non-privity plaintiffs can recover. Currently, Alternatives A and B to § 2-318 explicitly authorize actions for personal injury. At least that seems to be the most natural reading of "injured in person." Nevertheless, at least some courts have extended the phrase to include property damage.[43] And the South Carolina courts have gone so far as to hold that consequential economic damages in the form of lost profits qualifies as property damage within the provision.[44] Other courts have endorsed a more restrictive rule, holding, for instance, that non-privity purchasers cannot bring actions against warrantors for purely economic loss, even if privity purchasers could.[45] Nevertheless, there is reason to be wary of too great of an extension of warranty liability, and courts sometimes use these rationales to distinguish between the scope of recoveries available to privity and non-privity plaintiffs. The Minnesota Supreme Court, for instance, has held that under Alternative C, persons who purchase or use warranted goods may bring actions for any injury caused by a breach of the warranty, whether personal or economic. Proper plaintiffs under this theory would include non-privity users of the goods. Those who have not used or acquired the goods, however, may recover only for personal or property damage, not for pure economic loss

---

[43] See, e.g., Kassab v. Central Soya, 246 A.2d 848 (Pa. 1968).

[44] See Gasque v. Eagle Machine Co., Ltd., 270 S.C. 499, 243 S.E.2d 831, 832 (1978).

[45] See, e.g., Westchester County v. General Motors Corp., 555 F.Supp. 290, 294 (S.D.N.Y. 1983).

such as lost profits.[46]    The court feared the unlimited liability that warrantors would face under a broader rule. Unlimited liability of itself may seem unproblematic if we believe that warrantors have, in fact, misrepresented the character of the goods they sold and therefore caused injury.    But we think that there is some rationale for the court's conclusion in this case. The insurance function of warranty suggests that the warrantor has some capacity to predict losses and price the "insurance premium" into the cost of the good accordingly.    Courts may properly fear that as the scope of permissible plaintiffs and bases for recovery expands, warrantors will have increasing difficulty calculating the expected losses from use of their goods and will no longer have the informational advantage in pricing the legal consequences of defects that underlies contemporary conceptions of warranty liability.

As the lawn mower example suggests, the issues of warranty scope arise frequently where personal injury occurs.  In most of these cases, potential plaintiffs will have alternative causes of action for strict products liability in tort.  Unless procedural matters, such as a relatively short statute of limitations for tort, preclude such actions, plaintiffs may prefer to seek remedies.  The elements of a successful action under Restatement (Second) of Torts § 402A make it unnecessary for the plaintiff to demonstrate either privity or the making of a warranty. Instead, proof of that the good was sold in a defective condition that made it unreasonably dangerous, and a causal relationship to the plaintiff's injury (which would also have to be proven in a warranty action) will be sufficient.  Nevertheless, the elements of the cause of action may be sufficiently different that a plaintiff would prefer to bring a warranty action.  For instance, in *Denny v. Ford Motor Co.*,[47] the court held both that warranty and strict tort liability entail different proof and that the former is not subsumed within the latter.  The court concluded even a product of overall utility, which might insulate it from strict products liability, could still be unmerchantable if consumers have been misled into using it in a context where it was unsafe.  Hence a product with multiple uses could pass a strict liability test, but not be fit for "ordinary purposes" under warranty law.  Efforts to resolve the tension in the process of revising Article 2 by including special rules for personal injury claims resulting from breach of warranty were rejected.

---

[46] See Minnesota Mining and Manufacturing Company v. Nishika Ltd., 565 N.W.2d 16 (Minn. 1997).

[47] 662 N.E.2d 730 (N.Y. 1995).

## F. Federal Law and UCC Warranties of Quality

### 1. Introduction

Increasingly, federal law has addressed warranty issues previously within the exclusive domain of the UCC. Two areas of federal law are worth discussion. The first involves consumer products. Congress enacted the Magnuson-Moss Warranty Act in an effort to ensure that consumers received fuller disclosure of the scope of warranties and to reduce potential conflicts between written warranties and disclaimers. The second type of legislation has arisen out of contests concerning product liability. In certain cases, federal regulation of products has been construed to pre-empt state regulation through warranty law. In other cases, Congress has explicitly pre-empted warranty claims. We discuss these situations in turn.

### 2. The Magnuson-Moss Warranty Act

Congress enacted the Magnuson-Moss Warranty Act[48] in order to clarify warranties made by manufacturers or suppliers of consumer goods. Since the Act only applies when a written warranty has been made, however, the Act applies most frequently to manufacturers of goods who typically include such warranties in the sales material or on packaging that accompanies the goods. The Act does not compel anyone to make warranties at all. Indeed, the Act explicitly states that its provisions do not authorize the Federal Trade Commission ("FTC") to mandate warranties. It is simply a disclosure statute that requires manufacturers who do make warranties to do so in a particular manner that is considered less likely to deceive consumers and to restrict the ability of those who make some warranties to disclaim others. The Act authorizes the FTC to promulgate rules that regulate warranties in accordance with the Act,[49] and the FTC has taken full advantage of that authority.[50] Provisions of the Act may be enforced by the Attorney General, by the FTC,[51] or by a consumer damaged by the failure of the

[48] See 15 U.S.C. §§ 2301—2312.

[49] See 15 U.S.C. § 2302.

[50] See 16 C.F.R. Parts 700—703.

[51] See15 U.S.C. § 2310(c).

manufacturer or supplier of the good.[52]

A written warranty covered by the Act is not the same as an express warranty under § 2-313. It must be an affirmation of fact or promise about the characteristics of the good or an undertaking concerning the goods that is made "in writing."[53] Oral express warranties, samples, or models, all of which would be included in § 2-313 are not covered by the Act. The Act also excludes broad statements of opinion or policy, such as "satisfaction guaranteed."[54]

The Act applies only to consumer goods. These comprise tangible personal properly normally used for personal, family, or household purposes.[55] Note that the definition is an objective one that looks to normal rather than actual use. This restriction is necessary if manufacturers are to know in advance whether the goods they provide, and thus the warranty language that accompanies such goods, falls within the Act. The occasional purchaser of a helicopter for family vacations will not fall within the Act, even though her purchase is made in her capacity as a consumer, since the manufacturer will not have expected such a use and will not attempt to comply with the Act. On the other hand, the attorney who purchases a window unit air conditioner to install in her law office will be covered by the Act, notwithstanding that she is not making a consumer use of the good, since the manufacturer will have expected the product to be used "normally" by consumers.

The Act mandates that one who makes a written warranty clearly and conspicuously designate the warranty as either a "limited warranty" or a "full warranty."[56] In the latter case, the warranty may be limited in

---

[52] See 15 U.S.C. § 2310(d).

[53] 15 U.S.C. § 2301(6).

[54] 15 U.S.C. § 2303(b).

[55] See 15 U.S.C. § 2301(1).

[56] Certain exceptions apply, such as to goods that cost less than $10.00 and that are not designated as "full (statement of duration) warranties." See 15 U.S.C. § 2303(d). FTC regulations apply only to consumer products actually costing the consumer more than $15.00. Assume that a consumer purchases a package of 100 floppy disks for $100.00. Is this a purchase of more than the required amount and thus covered, or a purchase of 100 disks at $1 per disk, and thus outside the Act?

duration, but that duration must also be stated. A "full (statement of duration) warranty is one that meets the Federal minimum standards for warranty. A limited warranty does not meet those requirements. Whether a warrantor meets the minimum standards for warranty, therefore, is purely a matter of choice. There is nothing inappropriate or illegal about failure to meet those requirements, assuming that the disclosure requirements are satisfied and that the warranty clearly and conspicuously indicates that he is offering only a "limited warranty."

In order to meet the Federal minimum standards, and thus be entitled to use the language of a "full (statement of duration) warranty," the written warranty must contain certain provisions and avoid certain disclaimers. First, the warrantor must provide an effective and free remedy within a reasonable time in the event of defect, malfunction, or failure to conform to the written warranty. Second, the warrantor may not limit the duration of any implied warranty that arises under state law, such as the warranty of merchantability or the warranty of fitness. This applies even though the written warranty that triggers the Act has a limited duration. Third, the warrantor must not exclude or limit consequential damages for breach of any warranty (written or implied), unless the exclusion or limitation is conspicuous and on the face of the written warranty. Some states disallow such exclusions in the case of consumer goods. As a general rule, of course, federal law would prevail in the event of such a conflict. Section 111(b)(2) of the Act,[57] however, provides that the Act is not intended to supersede any state law concerning consequential damages for injury to the person or other injury. The UCC, in addition, makes the limitation of consequential damages for personal injury in the case of goods prima facie unconscionable.[58] As a consequence of this rationale, the FTC has promulgated regulations that require written warranties to contain the following statement if the warranty includes any exclusions or limitations on incidental or consequential damages:

> Some states do not allow the exclusion or limitation of incidental or consequential damages, so the above limitation or

---

[57] 15 U.S.C. § 2311(b)(2). Section 111(b)(1) provides more broadly that nothing in the Act invalidates or restricts any right or remedy of any consumer under state or federal law.

[58] § 2-719(3).

exclusion may not apply to you.[59]

Finally, warranties that satisfy the Federal minimum standards must permit the consumer to elect either a refund or free replacement for a product that continues to malfunction after a reasonable number of attempts by the warrantor to remedy the defect.

Warrantors of "full" warranties are not permitted to impose any duty other than notification on the customer as a condition of obtaining a remedy for a defect. The FTC may find, however that a particular condition is reasonable. Assume, for instance, that an automobile manufacturer were bold enough to offer a "full warranty" on its automobiles. If an automobile were to break down 500 miles from the nearest authorized dealer, it is not necessarily unreasonable to impose on the buyer the obligation of towing the automobile to the place where it can be repaired.

"Limited warranties," those that do not meet Federal minimum standards, allow warrantors greater discretion about the contents of the warranty. A warrantor who makes even this type of written warranty may not disclaim or modify an implied warranty.[60] Thus, assume that a seller of a refrigerator includes the following statement on the sales contract:

> LIMITED WARRANTY. Seller warrants against defects in materials, workmanship and installation. If defects are brought to the seller's attention within one year of the date hereof, seller will provide repair or replacement. Seller makes no other warranties, express or implied.

Assume further that the buyer had relied on the seller to recommend a refrigerator that would meet her particular requirements, and that the buyer subsequently discovered that the refrigerator did not satisfy those requirements. In response to buyer's complaint that the seller has breached a warranty of particular purpose, the seller points to the purported disclaimer. Who wins? Wholly apart from the issue of whether the language above satisfies § 2-316(2) (it probably does not), the fact that the seller has made a written warranty precludes him from making even an effective disclaimer of the implied warranty.

But the warrantor of a limited warranty may limit the duration of

---

[59] 16 C.F.R. § 701.3(a)(8).

[60] The same prohibition applies if the supplier of the good enters into a service contract with respect to the good within 90 days of the time of sale.

implied warranties to the period of the written warranty, if (1) that period is reasonable, (2) the limitation is conscionable, and (3) the limitation is stated in clear and unmistakable language and is prominently displayed on the face of the warranty.[61] Assume, for instance, that a seller of a refrigerator includes a "Limited Warranty" guaranteeing against defects for a period of 30 days and that simultaneously limits implied warranties to that same period. The seller has purported to limit the implied warranties to the duration of a written warranty, but it is not clear that the written warranty itself is of reasonable duration. Refrigerators are expected to last far longer than one month, and the effort to limit both express and implied warranties to that short of a period may be viewed as an effort to deceive the consumer into believing that it is receiving something of more value than the facts will support. As a result, the limitation would be ineffective for purposes of both federal and state law.[62]

The FTC requires, moreover, that even in the event of an effective limitation on the duration of implied warranties, the warrantor include the following statement:

Some states do not allow limitations on how long an implied warranty lasts, so the above limitation may not apply to you.[63]

In addition, all warranties must inform the consumer that "This warranty gives you specific legal rights, and you may also have other rights which vary from state to state."[64]

While the explicit requirements on remedial requirements that apply to "full" warranties do not apply explicitly to "limited" warranties, courts may have broader views of the obligations of warrantors. In *Gochey v. Bombarier, Inc.*,[65] for instance, the court found that the purchaser of a snowmobile that had been sold with a limited written warranty could revoke acceptance and recover the purchase price of the snowmobile after

---

[61] See 15 U.S.C. § 2308(b).

[62] See 15 U.S.C. § 2308(c).

[63] See 16 C.F.R. § 701.3(a)(7).

[64] See 16 C.F.R. § 701.3(a)(9).

[65] 572 A.2d 921 (Vt. 1990).

numerous repair efforts failed. The court concluded that the written warranty constituted an express warranty that created a sufficient relationship between the manufacturer and the purchaser to justify use of the revocation remedy, even if it was not explicitly authorized under the Act.[66]

The Act and the FTC rules that it authorizes impose additional regulations on warrantors that relate to such issues as making warranty terms available to consumer prior to the sale[67] and remedies for violations.[68] Our focus, however, has been on the substantive provisions of the Act that demonstrate its interplay with the UCC. As in the case of state law, the Act demonstrates an implicit recognition that manufacturers and sellers of products have superior information about the performance characteristics of the goods they sell. The emphasis of the Act is not on making those parties responsible for defects about which they should have information. Rather the emphasis of the Act is on the more subtle objective of ensuring that the claims they make about the information they purport to have are made clearly and in a manner consistent with the assumptions that would follow on the part of reasonable consumers.

### 3. Preemption by Federal Law

The Supreme Court initially considered the interplay of federal law and state warranty law in the context of cases involving federal regulation of cigarettes. In *Cipollone v. Liggett Group, Inc.*,[69] the court found that federal statutes regulating health warnings on each package of cigarettes pre-empted some, but not all, claims against cigarette manufacturers based on state tort and warranty law. A 1965 Federal Cigarette Labeling and Advertising Act mandated warnings on cigarette packages, but barred the requirement of such warnings in cigarette advertising. That Act explicitly pre-empted conflicting state law. The Court found that the 1965 law prohibited only state rule-making with respect to cautionary statements on cigarette packages or in cigarette advertising. It had no

---

[66] The court refused to extend the holding of *Gochey* to situations in which a breach of an implied warranty was claimed. See Vermont Plastics, Inc. v. Brine, Inc., 824 F. Supp. 444 (D. Vt. 1993), aff'd, 79 F.3d 272 (2d Cir. 1996).

[67] 16 C.F.R. § 702.3.

[68] 15 U.S.C. § 2310.

[69] 505 U.S. 504 (1992).

effect on other manufacturer obligations that might arise under state law. Thus, actions in tort, contract, or warranty survived the 1965 Act. A subsequent federal act, however, contained broader language. It strengthened the warning on packages and banned cigarette advertising in certain media. That act also prohibited any "requirement or prohibition . . . imposed by State law" with respect to advertising or promotion of cigarettes labeled in conformity with federal law. The Court found that the requirements covered by the phrase include those obligations that arise out of common law duties as well as from positive enactments of states. As a result, any such duty that constitutes a "requirement or prohibition based on smoking and health . . . imposed under state law with respect to . . . advertising or promotion" would be pre-empted. The Court then concluded that failure to warn claims were pre-empted insofar as they were based on an obligation to include more warnings than those required under state law. A claim of breach of express warranty, however, does not imposed by state law, the Court opined. Rather, the "requirements" imposed by the warranty arise from the words or conduct of the warrantor. This seems more than a little sophistic, insofar as the obligation to provide a product that complies with one's words or conduct is a requirement imposed by state law. Finally, the court concluded, federal law did not pre-empt claims based on intentional fraud and misrepresentation since those claims did not arise out of "advertising or promotion" of cigarettes. Since an implied warranty arise out of the nature of the goods and their fitness for their ordinary purpose, rather than out of any description involved in their promotion, § 2-314 claims would similarly seem to survive the pre-emption test of Cipollone.

The Court revisited the issue of pre-emption in *Medtronic, Inc. v. Lohr.*[70] Congress had enacted the Medical Device Amendments of 1976 ("MDA"), which explicitly pre-empted any "requirement" established by state law that applied to medical devices covered by the MDA, if that requirement was different from or added to requirements under the MDA and if the requirement related to the safety or effectiveness of the device. Although the number of plurality opinions in *Medtronic* make it difficult to discern any "holding," the case appears to stand for the proposition that the term "requirement" in the MDA does not constitute a blanket prohibition of all damage actions, at least where the device at issue had been marketed without FDA premarketing approval. Instead, preemption exists only where a particular state requirement threatens to interfere with

---

[70] 518 U.S. 470 (1996).

a "specific federal interest." Those state requirements must also relate "to the safety or effectiveness of the device or to any other matter included in a requirement applicable to the device." Thus, state requirements of "general applicability" are not preempted except where they have "the effect of establishing a substantive requirement for a specific device." Finally, a plurality of the Court determined that damage remedies survived where plaintiffs were seeking recovery for the seller's failure to comply with common law duties that parallel federal requirements.

### G. Warranty of Good Title

Purchasers of goods want to know that they are receiving valid title to the goods they buy. As we will see, a buyer of a good that has passed through the hands of a thief will not have good title, even though it has purchased from its immediate seller in good faith.[71] Thus, the original owner from whom the good was stolen will be able to recover the property from the buyer. The buyer, however, need not suffer the ultimate loss. Section 2-312 of the UCC provides that sellers of goods warrant that the title they convey is good and the transfer rightful. Thus, the buyer of a good that must be returned to the victim of a theft has an action against her seller for breach of the warranty of title. The same theory applies to a buyer who purchases a good that is subject to a security interest or other lien of which the buyer was ignorant at the time of contracting. If the lienholder is able to foreclose on the property, the buyer will be able to recover damages from her seller. The warranty is predicated on the same principle of asymmetric information that underlies warranties of quality. Sellers of goods are in a better position than buyers to know the origins of the goods they are selling. They can therefore both avoid the harms that result from title defects and predict the rate of those defects more easily than buyers. The warranty of title, like warranties of quality, induce those who occupy the superior position to avoid or insure against losses to take advantage of their position and minimize both the harms and the costs relating to insurance.

The warranty of title extends beyond those situations in which a successful claim of superior ownership is asserted. Even a buyer who must defend herself against non-frivolous claims of ownership, infringement, or other competing interest in the goods suffers the kind of disturbance of quiet possession that the warranty of title purports to

---

[71] See § 2-403.

protect.[72] The warranty is intended to protect against clouds on title, not simply hurricanes. Thus, in *Colton v. Decker*,[73] the buyer of a truck could recover for breach of warranty of title where the truck had been confiscated and dismantled by the state police after they discovered that vehicle the bore conflicting identification numbers and was possibly stolen. The state authorities subsequently determined that the buyer did have good title, but not until a nine-month investigation had ensued.

Merchant sellers make the additional warranty that the goods are delivered free of the rightful claim of nay third person by way of "infringement or the like." The claim of infringement need not be asserted against the buyer; it is sufficient that the buyer learns that the patent holder has brought an infringement action against the seller.[74] Thus, the buyer who discovers that the goods it has purchased infringe the rights of the patent holder may not only seek damages, but may also rescind the contract. But if the seller seeks to cure with non-infringing goods, is the buyer obligated to accept the cure? In *Yttro Corp. v. X-Ray Marketing Assn.*,[75] the seller agreed to supply buyer with filters. The buyer had earlier attempted to cancel the contract and had refused to take the contracted for number of filters, claiming that the filters did not perform as promised. While these claims were pending, the buyer discovered that the filters were alleged to infringe on a patent and sought to have the contract declared void from its inception. The seller did not contest the patent holder's claim, but entered into a licensing agreement that was retroactive to the time that the patent was issued. The seller conceded that the initial sale to buyer had breached the warranty of title, but insisted that it was entitled to cure that breach rather than have the contract invalidated or rescinded. The court agreed. Applying the rationales of § 2-508(2) and § 2-608, the court determined that the buyer suffered no substantial impairment with respect to filters it had accepted, and thus could not revoke their acceptance, and that cure was permissible as long as it was reasonable. Whether cure could occur in any particular case depended on whether the victim of the breach of warranty had

---

[72] See § 2-312, Official Comment 1.

[73] 540 N.W.2d 172 (S.D. 1995).

[74] See, e.g., American Container Corp. v. Hanley Trucking Corp., 268 A.2d 313 (N.J. Super. 1970).

[75] 559 A.2d 3 (N.J. Super. 1989).

suffered any loss, risk or inconvenience. Since the seller had subsequently obtained a license that validated its sales to buyer, and the buyer had not been threatened with any claim from the patent holder, the obstacles to cure do not appear to have arisen.

We think there is merit in this decision, even though it does not strictly follow the procedures of § 2-508. As we noted above, a breach of the title warranty can occur even in the absence of a successful claim of superior title or a finding of infringement. But in the Yttro case, the seller had effectively eliminated any risk of disturbance before the patent holder raised any claim against the buyer. The buyer's continued insistence of rescinding the contract had to be based either on the quality of the goods or on regret that it had entered into the contract in the first place. If the former, the claim of non-conformity should have been litigated directly. If the latter, the buyer was simply engaged in the very kind of strategic behavior that cure is intended to neutralize.

The warranty of title can be disclaimed, but typically that must occur by specific language. The warranty will be excluded, however, in situations such as sheriff's sales or estate sales in which the circumstances indicate that the seller has no superior knowledge about the true origins of the goods and is therefore making no warranty with respect to title.[76] The Proposed Revision, however, notes that an auctioneer who does not disclose that it is acting on behalf of a principal may make a warranty of title,[77] and the definition of "seller" for purposes of warranties includes an auctioneer or liquidator who fails to disclose its agency status.[78]

### III. Warranties Under the CISG

The CISG provisions governing product quality never employ the term "warranty." Nevertheless, their effect essentially mimics the UCC warranties, with the addition of provisions that reveal the long-distance nature of the covered transactions. Article 35(1) sets forth a general standard that essentially requires the seller to comply with the terms of the contract. The seller must, therefore, deliver goods of the quantity, quality and description required by the contract and that are contained or packaged in the manner required by the contract. The requirement that

---

[76] See § 2-312(2).

[77] See Proposed § 2-312, Note 5.

[78] See Proposed § 2-401(6).

the goods conform to descriptions is essentially a recognition that any such description constitutes an express warranty, breach of which means that the seller has not complied with his Article 35(1) obligations. The CISG is silent, however, about the sources of those descriptions, about whether only explicit statements made during negotiations count, or whether statements in advertisements or catalogues are included. Proving the existence of such a description may be a more important question under the CISG than under the UCC. Recall that the CISG contains no parol evidence rule. Thus, claims that a seller made particular oral statements concerning the quality of the goods will be admissible in contracts governed by the CISG under circumstances where the UCC, at least narrowly interpreted, would exclude the same statements.

The statements must, of course, be "descriptions" of the goods. While the CISG nowhere distinguishes statements that constitute descriptions from those that do not, it is arguable that puffing language and opinion would be no more a part of a CISG description than of a UCC description. Nevertheless, once we admit that possibility, the problem of distinguishing the statement of fact from the sales puff becomes more difficult, since international transactions are likely to entail cultural differences that complicate the inquiry. Assume, for instance, that an American seller of herbicide informs a Zambian buyer that, although the American product costs a little more, it "outperforms all competitors." After purchasing $50,000 worth of the herbicide, the buyer realizes that the product performs no differently than other products with the same chemical composition that cost significantly less. Has the seller breached a warranty? Under the UCC, the language sounds perilously close to mere sales talk and would not be the basis of a warranty. But what if Zambians are less disingenuous than Americans, so that the Zambian buyer was more likely to interpret the seller's words literally? Article 8, which deals with interpretation of parties' acts and words, may help in determining the scope of the warranty. That provision states that "statements made by . . . a party are to be interpreted according to his intent where the other party knew or could not have been unaware what that intent was." Here, the Zambian buyer certainly did not know and, given cultural differences, justifiably did not know, the intent of the seller. Article 8(3) tells us that we should consider "all relevant circumstances" in deciding what understanding a reasonable person would have, and the background understanding of a Zambian buyer would certainly count as one of those circumstances.[79] Thus, interpretation of the seller's statement will be governed by Article 8(2), which provides that, where the other party is reasonably ignorant of the speaker's intent, the speaker's statements are to be interpreted "according to the understanding that reasonable person of the same kind as the other party [that is, the addressee of the statement] would have had in the circumstances." Thus, if a reasonable Zambian buyer would interpret the statements as language of warranty, then a warranty exists. Thus, warranty law under the CISG not only places the risk of product quality on the seller who makes an express warranty. It also places on the seller who makes statements or engages in conduct during contract negotiations the risk of knowing under what circumstances its language or acts will reasonably be construed as warranty "descriptions" in the understanding of the buyer.

Article 35(2) then gives additional content to the concept of "conformity" required by Article 35(1), and that content essentially creates a basis for both express and implied warranties. Article 35(2)(a) borrows from the UCC's warranty of merchantability by limiting "conforming" goods to those that "are fit for the purposes for which goods of the same description would ordinarily be used." This limited definition of "conformity" may leave the buyer open to some degree of seller strategic behavior that is foreclosed by the more inclusive definition of "merchantability: under § 2-314. That provision requires that merchantable goods be of fair average quality within the contract description of the goods. Assume, for instance, that the seller and buyer enter a contract for the sale of three barges of "No. 2 yellow corn." Assume further, that it is acceptable within the trade for "No. 2 yellow corn" to contain no more than 2% other products, such as stones or cinders. An average barge of yellow corn may contain no more than 1% of such other products. Nevertheless, a barge with the higher percentage would be acceptable within the trade as meeting the contract description. Sellers may have incentives to ship the "dirtier" No. 2 yellow corn to distant buyers, since those buyers are less likely to complain or have opportunities to retaliate. The omission of the appeal to "fair, average quality" gives the buyer who suffers such behavior less recourse than might be available under the UCC.

---

[79] Of course, if trade usages or practices indicated that puffing was a common phenomenon in the international herbicide trade, then the buyer might have more difficulty proving ignorance of the seller's intent. See Article 8(3).

What if the concept of fitness for ordinary use is different in the seller's country than in the buyer's? In a case from the Austrian Supreme Court, a German seller agreed to sell four machines to an Austrian buyer, which intended to resell them.[80] The machines did not contain labeling necessary for resale under Austrian law. That labeling, however, was not necessary under German law. The court concluded that the standards of the seller's country apply in order to determine whether goods are fit for ordinary use under Article 35(2). The seller, the court opined, could not be charged with knowledge of special rules governing goods in the buyer's country, unless the buyer specifically bargained for them. In that case, noncompliance with the buyer's requirements would constitute a violation of Article 35(1).

Article 35(2)(b) embodies warranties of fitness for a particular purpose. It requires "conforming" goods to be fit for any particular purpose "expressly or impliedly known to the seller at the time of the conclusion of the contract." The warranty is excluded, however, where circumstances show that the buyer did not rely or could not reasonably rely on the seller's skill and judgment. The combination of the existence of a particular purpose, reliance by the buyer, and a seller with superior knowledge suggest that the warranty of particular purpose serves the same risk allocation function under the CISG as it does under the UCC. Article 35(2)(c) requires "conforming" goods to possess the qualities of goods that the seller has held out as a sample or model.

Finally, Article 35(2)(d) requires that conforming goods be contained or packaged in the manner usual for such goods or adequate to preserve and protect the goods. Shipping perishables without proper refrigeration or fragile goods without appropriate padding would constitute a breach of this implied warranty, even if nothing were said in the contract about packaging methods.

Nothing in the CISG explicitly addresses the issue of disclaiming these warranties. Nevertheless, it is clear that they are waivable. Article 35(2) makes the implies warranty subject to contrary agreement by the parties. Of course, Article 6, which respects the contract of the parties by allowing abrogation of any of the CISG provisions, would apply to permit disclaimers. Finally, Article 35(3) recognizes that disclaimer is possible simply by examining the circumstances in which a contract was made. It provides that the seller is not liable under Article 35(2) for any

---

[80] Oberster Gerichtshof, Austria, April 13, 2000 (http://cisgw3.law.pace.edu/cases/000413a3.html).

lack of conformity of which the buyer knew or could not have been unaware at the time of the conclusion of the contract.

Nevertheless, there is at least one issue of disclaimers that remains unresolved. Assume that the disclaimer is written in inconspicuously small type and does not mention "merchantability" and does not contain any of the language that would constitute a disclaimer under § 2-316(3) of the UCC. One might claim that the CISG contains no requirements similar to those in § 2-316, so that more general disclaimers than are recognized under the UCC might be acceptable. The problem is that the inquiry into the effect of the disclaimer can easily be cast as one concerning the validity of the disclaimer, and Article 4 explicitly removes issues of "validity" from the scope of the CISG. One might readily infer that these issues are therefore resolved under domestic law, and if United States law applies to the contract, the purported disclaimer would be ineffective, or invalid.[81] Thus, it is important to understand the scope of what is meant by "validity" in Article 4. If issues such as disclaimers are removed from the CISG, so they are covered by domestic law, then we will lose much of the uniformity that the CISG purports to achieve. At the same time, reading "validity" too broadly does not make much sense. For instance, any time we interpret a contract term under Article 8, we might limit the enforceability of the literal term in ways that might be construed as affecting its "validity." But no one would suggest that interpretations of contract terms are not governed by the CISG.

One way around the issue might be to assert that the effectiveness of a disclaimer simply involves interpretation of the contract terms concerning quality. Validity rules are omitted, according to Article 4, "except as otherwise expressly provided" in the CISG. One might contend, therefore, that since contract terms concerning quality are "expressly provided" in Article 35, the validity of a disclaimer can be addressed as a question of interpretation of that Article and the enforceability of a clause in the contract. Before concluding that this argument is too much of a stretch, recall that Article 35(2) applies unless "the parties have agreed otherwise." The reference to agreement otherwise contemplates the possibility of a disclaimer, so that one may even conclude that disclaimers, and hence issues of their validity, are "expressly provided" for by Article 4.

---

[81] For an argument to this effect, see Laura E. Longobardi, *Disclaimers of Implied Warranties: The 1980 United Nations Convention on Contracts for the International Sale of Goods*, 53 Fordham L. Rev. 863 (1985); see Chapters 2 & 5.

# CHAPTER 9
## REMEDIES

## I. Introduction: Allocating the Loss of Transactional Breakdown

Some sales contracts are performed defectively. Others are not performed at all. Defective performance or nonperformance may be due to regret or even simple inadvertence. When both parties regret entering into the contract, enforcing it would not maximize value. Resources are better allocated elsewhere. We would therefore expect the parties to agree to cancel or modify the contract without judicial intervention. When only one of the parties suffers regret and fails to perform, or performs defectively, the other party suffers a loss of the value of the bargain. Here we cannot be confident that nonconforming performance results in a superior allocation of resources. Viewed abstractly, the UCC's remedies for breach of contract allocate the loss from nonperformance. Whether its remedies are justified depends on whether they efficiently allocate the loss from breach.

In order to decide, a standard for evaluating the efficiency of remedies is needed. As in previous chapters, we ask whether the majority of contracting parties who bargained about remedies would agree to the terms reflected in the UCC. UCC remedies that satisfy this standard are efficient: they optimally minimize contracting costs for the majority of parties, while allowing atypical parties to opt out of the UCC and contract for their preferred remedy. As with most standards, its initial statement may be easier than its application to a particular case. Still, the majoritarian standard describes a criterion for evaluating remedies available under the UCC.

The majoritarian standard does not by itself select any particular measurement of damages. For instance, § 1-106 adopts an expectation measure of remedies. It says that the UCC remedies are to be applied to put the victim of the breach in the same position as performance.[1] An expectation measurement is a particular principle—a particular default term. The measurement may or may not be selected by the majority of parties if they were to bargain costlessly. Whether it would be selected depends on a number of factors, including whether courts typically have access to data that allow them to make reliable estimates of a party's expectation, whether the parties are consumers, and the incentive effects

---

[1] See § 1-106.

of different damage measures. Our point here is not to argue for the possibility of other measurements of damages. It is simply to observe that a majoritarian default standard does not determine the goal of compensation to be achieved by remedies. The majoritarian standard is one thing; the measurement of remedies selected by the standard is another.

The following table provides an overview of the UCC's scheme of remedies.[2]

| Seller's Remedies | Buyer's Remedies |
|---|---|
| 1. Contract Price - Resale Price (§ 2-706) | 1. Cover Price - Contract Price (§ 2-712) |
| 2. Contract Price - Market Price (§ 2-708(1)) | 2. Market Price - Contract Price (§ 2-713) |
| 3. Lost Profits (§ 2-708(2)) | 3. Value Differential (§ 2-714), Reduction in Price (§ 2-717) |
| 4. Incidental Expenses (§ 2-710) | 4. Incidental and Consequential Damages (§ 2-715) |
| 5. Action for the Price (§ 2-709) | 5. Specific Performance or Replevin (§ 2-716) |
| 6. Withhold Delivery (§ 2-702) | 6. Inapplicable |
| 7. Stop Delivery (§ 2-705(1)) | 7. Inapplicable |
| 8. Reclaim Goods (§§ 2-507, 2-702) | 8. Claim Goods on Payment (§ 2-502(1)) |
| 9. Cancellation (§ 2-703) | 9. Cancellation (§ 2-711) |

The table reveals that the UCC draws two different distinctions between

---

[2] Section 2-703 is titled "Seller's remedies in general," and § 2-711's partial title is "Buyer's remedies in general." Section 1-109 in turn expressly provides that section captions are part of the UCC. Nevertheless, one should not infer that the §§ 2-703 and 2-711 are exhaustive. Even a brief look at the provisions will show that they omit some of the remedies listed above and appearing in the associated sections of Article 2. Revised §§ 2-703 and 2-711 contain a complete list of remedies.

types of remedies. One distinction marks the familiar divide between substitutional and specific relief. Remedies describe different measures of money damages. Remedies 5-9 provide nonmonetary relief, ranging from specific relief to cancellation of the contract. The other distinction is between the type of remedies available when the breaching party retains the goods and remedies available when the nonbreaching party retains them. For instance, § 2-711(1) and (2) list remedies available to the buyer only when the seller breaches by failing "to make delivery or repudiates or the buyer rightfully rejects or justifiably revokes acceptance." When the seller delivers and the buyer retains nonconforming goods, § 2-714's "value differential" measures the buyer's damages. The buyer also can recover, where appropriate, incidental expenses and consequential damages under § 2-715.

All of the UCC's remedies are intended to protect the same interest: the expectation interest of the victim of the breach. Section 1-106 says as much. In theory, the UCC's remedies describe equivalent measures of that interest. Some simple examples of the seller's remedies illustrate the point. Begin by remembering that the expectation interest is the net value a party receives from performance of the contract. A seller's expectation interest therefore is its profit from performance: the difference between the contract price (K) and the seller's cost of performance (C). Suppose Buyer breaches by refusing Seller's tender of delivery of a conforming good. Suppose too that the market price (M) and the resale price (R) of the good has dropped below the contract price by the same amount, so that $M = R$. Seller's remedies under §§ 2-709(1), 2-708(1) and 2-706(1) give Seller its profit. Assuming that Seller has an action for the price against Buyer under § 2-709(1), its damages (D) therefore are equal to K, the contract price. Seller in turn has incurred C in producing the good. An action for the price therefore gives Seller $K - C$, its profit from performance. Alternatively, suppose that Seller measures its damages by the contract-market difference under § 2-708(1). Then $D = K - M$. Rearranging terms, $K = D + M$. Since the sum of the contract-market difference and the market price give Seller the contract price, and since its cost of performance is again C, § 2-708(1) gives Seller $K - C$, its profit from performance. Finally, suppose that Seller measures its damages by the contract-resale difference under § 2-706(1). Then $D = K - R$, and, rearranging terms again, $K = D + R$. The sum of the contract-resale difference and the resale price yields Seller the contract price. Seller's cost of performance being C, § 2-706(1) gives Seller its profit from performance: $K - C$. Thus, all three damages formulas yield the same measurement of Seller's expectation interest. Similar examples would show the same in the case of a buyer's damages.

## II. Money Damages

Although the UCC remedies all protect the expectation interest, the aggrieved party can have good reasons for preferring one remedy over others. The different formulations of the various remedies can result in different recoveries. The aggrieved party also might not satisfy the requirements attached to a particular remedy. Further, different remedies have different costs associated with their use, including proof costs. Where a plaintiff is not fully compensated for incurring these costs, its choice of remedy turns on minimizing relevant costs. Another reason for a preference among remedies concerns risks of undercompensation: The injured party has to convince a trier of fact of the extent of loss from breach, and it might be unable to present enough evidence to have a particular remedy accurately applied. If so, in applying the remedy, the trier of fact might underestimate the loss from breach, and these risks of undercompensation can vary among remedies.

### A. Under the UCC

### 1. Substitute Performance: Resale and Cover Under § 2-706(1) and § 2-712(1)

Under the UCC, the nonbreaching party can measure its damages by either the cost of obtaining substitute performance or the market price of substitute performance. If the buyer breaches and the seller resells the goods subject to the contract, the seller's damages under § 2-706(1) are measured by the difference between the contract price and the resale price. Alternatively, the seller can retain the goods and measure its damages under § 2-708(1), as the difference between the contract price and the market price. If the seller breaches, the buyer has corresponding remedies available to it. It can purchase substitute goods and measure damages under § 2-712(1), as the difference between the cover price and the contract price. Alternatively, it can abstain from making a substitute purchase and measure damages by § 2-713(1), as the difference between the market price and the contract price. Which damages formula an injured party prefers turns principally on the comparative size of proof costs and uncompensated resale or cover costs. Roughly, resale and cover measures require the victim of the breach to make uncompensated expenditures. Market price measures require the injured party to incur proof costs but no resale or cover costs. However, the proof costs associated with market price measures can exceed those associated with resale and cover measures.

Resale and cover measures allow the injured party to fix its damages by entering into a substitute transaction. These measures enable the party to avoid having a trier of fact determine market price—a determination that is sometimes costly to prove. Section 2-706(1) permits the seller to resell the goods in a reasonable manner and in good faith. Resale can be by either private or public sale, giving the buyer notice of the intended manner of disposing of the good.[3] Section 2-712(1) allows the buyer to cover by making a substitute purchase without reasonable delay and in good faith.[4] Failure to comply with §§ 2-706 or 2-712's requirements prevents the injured party from measuring damages under these sections. The party in that case is forced to measure its damages by market measures under §§ 2-708(1) or 2-713.[5]

In their broad outlines, §§ 2-706 and 2-708's procedural requirements are easily justified. Notice to the buyer of an intent to resell by private sale under § 2-706(2) or by public sale under § 2-706(3)(b), for instance, gives the buyer information it can use to assure that the resale price is not artificially inflated. The buyer, for example, can bid at the sale or, more likely, find others to do so. Creating an auction with more bids makes the resale price more competitive. Accordingly, the requirement of notice is a form of mitigation which serves to minimize damages assessed against the breaching buyer. Section 2-706(2)'s requirement of identification and § 2-712(1)'s requirement of a substitute purchase serve the same function. If the seller has to identify the goods to the breached contract, it cannot simply make a series of sales and select the sale fetching the highest price as the resale price under § 2-706(1). The seller has to connect the good sold to the good covered by the breached contract. Identification prevents the seller from increasing the buyer's damage bill by speculating at its expense. Similarly, § 2-712(1)'s requirement that cover be a substitute purchase forces the buyer to connect a purchase in some way with the breached contract. It limits the buyer's ability to make a series of purchases and select the highest purchase price as the cover price. A "substitute" purchase therefore prevents the buyer from increasing the seller's damage bill by speculating at its expense.

---

[3] See § 2-706(2)-(4).

[4] See § 2-712(1).

[5] See, e.g., § 2-706 Official Comment 2; § 2-712(3).

Fixing damages by resale or cover can be costly to the aggrieved party, however. For example, a seller incurs costs in satisfying § 2-706(1)'s requirement that the resale be "reasonable" as well as its procedural requirements. These costs are recoverable from the breaching buyer as incidental expenses[6] only if the seller can prove them to a trier of fact. Further, the indefiniteness of the requirements creates costly uncertainty for the seller. At the same time, by fixing its damages the seller avoids incurring the costs of proving market price. The same points apply to the buyer's cover formula under § 2-712(2). Thus, an aggrieved party using a resale or cover measure implicitly trades off uncompensated resale costs against the costs of proving market price.

*Sprague v. Sumitomo Forestry Co., Ltd.*[7] is a good illustration of the tradeoff. There the buyer breached by cancelling a contract to purchase logs and the seller filed suit. The seller subsequently resold the logs at less than the contract price without notifying the buyer. The court held that a buyer's knowledge of a lawsuit does not amount to notice of the seller's intention to resell under § 2-706(1). Thus, the seller could not measure its damages by § 2-706(1)'s resale formula. Accordingly, the seller could only measure its damages by § 2-708(1)'s market price measure.[8] Notice to the buyer is an expense the seller incurs in satisfying § 2-706(1). By requiring that the seller give notice to the breaching buyer of its intention to resell even when the buyer knows that the seller could resell, *Sprague*'s holding increases the seller's cost of fixing its damages. Section 2-706(1)'s measure of damages becomes correspondingly less attractive than § 2-708(1)'s market measure.

Section 2-712(1) allows the buyer to fix its damages by covering. Covering involves the buyer obtaining a substitute good in another transaction. One question is whether the buyer can cover either by manufacturing substitute goods itself or by substituting goods it has on hand for goods under the breached contract. In other words, can the buyer fix its damages by engaging in "self-cover"? Since § 2-712(1)

---

[6] See § 2-710.

[7] 709 P.2d 1200 (Wash. 1985).

[8] The *Sprague* court went on to find that the resale price in the circumstances was sufficient evidence of market price, so that the damage measures under §§ 2-706(1) and 2-708(1) gave the same amount of damages.

requires the cover transaction proceed by a "purchase" or "contract," and both transactions must involve another party,[9] the section seems to prohibit self-cover. Nevertheless, most of the few courts addressing the question have allowed the practice by invoking directive of § 1-102(2) that UCC provisions be interpreted in a liberal manner.[10]

There are two reasons for questioning the allowance of self-cover. First, stretching § 2-712(1)'s application to include self-cover often is unnecessary. This is because § 2-713(1)'s market measure usually can be used to obtain the same recovery of damages. Self-cover occurs when the buyer can manufacture or dip into its inventory to obtain a substitute good at a lower price than is demanded by other sellers.[11] Although above the contract price, the price of self-cover in such instances is lower than the cover price. But if it pays the buyer to have engaged in self-cover, the price of the good substituted is likely to equal the market price. In that case, § 2-713(1)'s market price formula gives the same measure of damages as § 2-712(1). Thus, there is no need to invoke § 2-712(1)'s cover formula in the first place. Second, self-cover is unlikely systematically to give a different measure of damages from the cover or market price formulas. Although the price of self-cover may ultimately prove to be above both market price and cover prices, from the ex ante perspective, there is no reason to believe that the self-cover price will be above rather than below those prices. In that case the value of self-cover to the buyer equals the value of market price and cover damages. Section 2-712(1)'s demand that cover involve a transaction with another party can be read to recognize this fact. Again, there is no need to stretch § 2-712(1)'s language to allow self-cover.

---

[9] See, e.g., § 1-201(32) ("purchase" is "taking by sale...or any other voluntary transaction creating an interest in property"); Chronister Oil Co. v. Unocal Refining and Marketing, 34 F.3d 462 (7th Cir. 1994). For a case allowing the buyer to "cover" by entering into a substitute purchase with the breaching seller, see Kelsey-Hayes Co. v. Galtaco Redlaw Castings Corp., 749 F. Supp. 794 (E.D. Mich. 1990).

[10] See, e.g., Cives Corp. v. Callier Steel Pipe & Tube, Inc., 482 A.2d 852 (Me. 1984).

[11] See, e.g., Dura-Wood Treating Co. v. Century Forest Industries, Inc., 675 F.2d 745 (5th Cir. 1982).

This brings us to § 2-712(2)'s cover formula. The formula itself is straightforward: the covering buyer's damages are equal to the difference between the (higher) cover price and the contract price, plus consequential damages and less expenses saved by the seller's breach. A difficult question concerns the offsetting of the buyer's profits against the buyer's cover damages. The question arises in the following situation. Suppose Seller and Buyer contract for Seller to sell goods to Buyer for $100. Seller breaches by tendering late delivery and Buyer refuses to pay. In the meantime the cover price of the goods increases to $150 and Buyer covers at that price. After receiving delivery of the goods, Buyer sells them to Buyer 2 for $125. Buyer seeks to recover $50 from Seller under § 2-712(2)'s cover formula. Seller in turn argues that Buyer's $50 cover damages should be offset by the $25 profit that Buyer realized on the sale of the goods to Buyer 2. Buyer, of course, resists, arguing that § 2-712(2) does not allow cover damages to be reduced by profits realized on the breached contract. Since § 2-712(2) is silent on the matter, the question is whether Buyer's cover damages should be reduced by its profits on the sale to Buyer 2.

The situation just described is deviant. Usually a buyer receiving a nonconforming tender will either reject the goods, revoke its acceptance, or accept them. If it rejects the goods or revokes its acceptance, the buyer can cover by purchasing substitute goods and the seller ends up with the nonconforming tendered goods. In that case cover damages are available to the buyer under § 2-712(2). If the buyer accepts the nonconforming tender, it cannot obtain cover damages. Instead, it ends up with the goods and its damages are measured by the "value differential" under § 2-714(2). In the unusual situation described, the buyer both accepts the goods and covers. The question here is whether the profit from the sale of accepted goods is to be offset against cover damages.

In *Fertico Belgium S.A. v. Phosphate Chemicals Export Ass'n., Inc.,*[12] on essentially the same facts as in the example given above, the majority and dissent disagreed. The majority did not offset the buyer's cover damages because it found that, absent the seller's breach, the buyer would have made two sales and two profits. Giving the buyer cover damages without reducing them by the profit on the second sale therefore puts the buyer in the position the seller's full performance would have put it. The dissent would have required an offset on the finding that the

---

[12] 510 N.E.2d 334 (N.Y. 1987).

buyer would not have made the second sale had the seller not breached. At bottom the dispute is over how many sales the buyer would have made had the seller fully performed.[13]

We think that the dispute, although genuine, is incorrectly formulated by both sides. The majority thinks that the buyer would have made a second sale because the supply of available goods is unlimited; the dissent thinks that a second sale would not have been made because supply is limited. For us, as for others,[14] the question is not whether the buyer could obtain enough goods to make two sales. It instead is whether the buyer *profitably* could have made both sales had seller fully performed. Requiring a profitable sale in turn requires determining the buyer's costs--more precisely, its marginal costs of each sale. So, for instance, in the example above, the cost to Buyer is the contract price charged by Seller—$100. We need to know the marginal cost of a good Buyer would have delivered to Buyer 2 had Seller performed. Given the increase in cover price in the example, the cost may be more than $100. If Buyer could have profitably made a second sale from the sale to Buyer 2 even if Seller had fully performed, there is no offset against its cover damages. If not, there is an offset to the extent of the profit on the second sale.

## 2. Market Price Damages

The injured party can measure its damages by the market price of substitute goods. It need not obtain substitute performance by reselling or covering. Sections 2-708(1) and § 2-713(1) state the seller and buyer's market price formulas, respectively. Both sections use the same damages measure: the difference between the market price of substitute goods and the contract price. Some of the details of the formulas differ, however. Under § 2-708(1), the aggrieved seller's market price is measured at the time and place of tender. Under § 2-713(1), the aggrieved buyer's market price is measured at the time the buyer learned of the breach. The buyer's relevant market is the place of tender or, when rejection or revocation of acceptance occurs after nonconforming goods arrive, at the place of arrival. Revised § 2-713(1)(a) determines market price as of the time for tender.

---

[13] For the counterpart problem in the case of the seller, with more details, see Chapter 8.

[14] See Charles J. Goetz & Robert E. Scott, *Measuring Sellers Damages: The Lost-Profits Puzzle*, 31 Stan. L. Rev. 323 (1979).

### a. Proof Costs

To use the market price measure, the injured party must establish market price. This is not always easy. The price of substitute goods, such as cover or resale prices, is not dispositive. The relevant markets in which these substitutes are available might not be the same markets as are required under § 2-708(1) or § 2-713(1). Think of the price at which a widget could be bought or sold in Los Angeles when the market price of a nonconforming widget delivered to the buyer is the New York price. Proof of widget prices in Charlottesville does not establish the price of widgets in New York. Further, the time at which resale or cover could occur does not establish the reqiured time under § 2-708(1) or § 2-713(1). While § 2-708(1) requires establishing market price at the time of tender and § 2-713(1) at the time the buyer learned of the breach, the resale or cover transactions occur later. Thus, the prevailing prices for resale or cover can deviate from the earlier market price. This is particularly true where the relevant market prices are volatile. The injured party's proof costs in establishing market price, which are uncompensated, therefore can be high. To be sure, the UCC anticipates this problem and provides for substitutes. Section 2-723(2) allows market price to be measured before or after the time of tender under § 2-708(1) or the time the buyer learned of the breach under § 2-713(1), when evidence of prevailing market price at these dates is hard to come by. It even allows another measure of market price to substitute when countenanced by trade usage. So, for example, if trade usage allows New York widget prices to be measured by Charlottesville widget prices in the circumstances, § 2-723(2) allows Los Angeles market prices to serve to measure damages under the market price formulas of § 2-708(1) and § 2-713(1). Thus, § 2-723(2) reduces the proof costs associated with use of the UCC's market price damage measures. However, it still does not eliminate them.

Proof costs also can be high because of uncertainty in law. Uncertainty occurs in at least two circumstances. One circumstance is where the sales contract authorizes shipment by carriage. Suppose the contract calls for shipment by carriage to the buyer in New York but is otherwise silent. The contract price is $100, the market price in Charlottesville, the seller's place of business, also is $100 and the market price in New York is $110. Suppose the seller breaches by cancelling the contract before the buyer has paid. Are the buyer's damages as measured under § 2-713(1) 0 or $10? It depends on which market price is used in § 2-713(1), and that in turn depends on where tender of delivery was to occur.[15] Since the contract calls for carriage but is otherwise silent, the UCC presumes that a shipment contract is authorized.[16] The seller therefore is authorized to deliver the goods to a carrier in Charlottesville for shipment to the buyer in New York. Thus, delivery of the goods is to occur in Charlottesville. Section 2-504(b), however, also requires a seller who enters into a shipment contract to "deliver or tender delivery" of any documents necessary for the buyer to obtain the goods from the carrier. Tendering delivery of documents presumably means making them available to the buyer in Charlottesville. Delivering the documents presumably means getting them into the buyer's hands in New York.[17] Since § 2-504(b) allows either delivery or tender of delivery of documents, and since tender can occur at Charlottesville while delivery can occur at New York, the place at which to measure market price under § 2-713(1) is indeterminate. We think but cannot be sure that the market price at Charlottesville is the proper market price because § 2-504(b) allows tender of documents, and tender would have occurred in Charlottesville.

The second circumstance that gives rise to legal uncertainty about market price involves buyer's damages in the case of anticipatory repudiation by the seller. Section 2-713(1) provides that the buyer in such a situation must measure market damages as of the time when "the buyer learned of the breach." That phrase may be defined as including at least the following: the time the buyer learns of the repudiation, the time within which the buyer could obtain substitute performance, or the time when the seller was to perform under the contract.[18] If we are seeking equal treatment for buyers and sellers, the last option should apply, since § 2-708(1) says quite clearly that in the case of repudiation by the buyer, the relevant market price for fixing seller's damages is the price "at the time and place for tender." The first option seems inconsistent with both seller's remedies and with § 2-723(1). That

---

[15] See § 2-713(2).

[16] See § 2-503 Official Comment 5; Chapter 6.

[17] Cf. § 2-503(5) (where contract calls for delivery of documents, seller must tender them through customary bank channels).

[18] See, e.g., Oloffson v. Coomer, 296 N.E.2d 871 (Il. Ct. App. 1973) (time for cover); James J. White & Robert S. Summers, Uniform Commercial Code 237 (5th ed. 2000) (time for performance); Baker v. Ratzlaff, 564 P.2d 153 (Kan. Ct. App. 1977) (time learned of repudiation).

provision fixes market price under § 2-708(1) and § 2-713(1) as of the time the aggrieved party learned of the repudiation in the case when recovery is sought before performance is due. The negative implication is that some other time is to be used in the more typical case where recovery is sought subsequent to the time of performance. If the time that buyer learned of the repudiation was to be used in the more common case, § 2-723(1) would be superfluous.

Fixing damages as of the time of performance allows the party aggrieved by a repudiation to speculate with the repudiator's money. Assume, for instance, that seller has repudiated. The aggrieved party may await the time of performance and simply cover in the market if prices decline between the time of repudiation and the time of performance. If market prices for the goods increase above the contract price during this period, the buyer can simply fix damages as of time of performance and recover the difference under § 2-713(1). Thus, a reading that restricts the aggrieved party's time to decide whether to obtain substituted performance might be desirable to constrain opportunism. On the other hand, maybe we should not feel too sorry for the repudiating party. After all, if that party fears that the market price differential between the time of repudiation and the time of performance threatens to become too large, it may enter the market itself and obtain substitute performance by finding another buyer or seller to satisfy the contract in a manner that minimizes its damages.[19]

Most case law and commentary sets market price as of the date substitute performance could be effected. This interpretation puts market price as of the last date cover or resale could have occurred. Our point, however, has less to do with determining whether any particular time creates the best incentives than with the fact that the different possibilities create costly uncertainty in the application of market price measures to cases of anticipatory repudiation. Revised 2-713(1)(b) reduces this uncertainty somewhat by measuring market price as of a commercially reasonable period after repudiation (but not later than the time for tender). Presumably this is the period in which the buyer could obtain substitute performance. Uncertainty remains in identifying the point at which substitute performance becomes available, taking into account the buyer's right to await for a reasonable period performance by

---

[19] On the incentives created by different damage measures, see Thomas H. Jackson, *Anticipatory Repudiation and the Temporal Element of Contract Law: An Economic Inquiry into Contract Damages in Cases of Prospective Nonperformance*, 31 Stan. L. Rev. 69 (1978)

the repudiating seller.

### b. Election of Remedies

A final question about market price measures concerns their availability once plaintiff has engaged in a course of conduct that might be considered an election of some alternative remedy. As noted, the UCC allows the injured party to choose between market price damages measures and cover or resale damages measures. The party is not forced to pursue one or another remedy. But suppose the injured party obtains substitute performance — by the buyer covering under § 2-712(1) or seller reselling under § 2-706(1). Can the injured party still elect to measure its damages by a market price formula? The question would be completely unimportant if the two sorts of damages measures always gave the same recovery. But they do not. Section 2-712(2), for example, measures the buyer's damages as the difference between the (higher) cover price and the contract price. Section 2-713(1) measures damages as the difference between the (higher) market price at the time it learned of the breach and the contract price. Since reasonable cover can occur after the buyer learns of the breach, and since the price of substitute goods could have changed in the interim, the cover price under § 2-713(1) could be different from the market price under § 2-712(1). Thus, the cover measure might be more or less generous than the market price measure.

Election of remedies would also be merely academic if it is impossible to tell whether the injured party obtained substitute performance. As a practical matter, in most cases it is hard to tell. For example, the injured seller can always say that the good it is reselling is not the good subject to the breached sales contract. For its part, the injured buyer can say with a straight face that it would have made the purchase it made even without the seller's breach, and therefore that it was not a substitute for the breached contract. However, in some cases a resale or cover transaction can be identified.[20] In these cases at least, whether the UCC allows an election of remedies remains an important question.

Surprisingly, the UCC's answer is inconclusive. Some UCC provisions appear to allow election while others appear to prohibit it. Sections 2-703 and § 2-711 list the seller and buyer's remedies, and

---

[20] See, e.g., Tesoro Petroleum Corp. v. Holborn Oil Co., Ltd., 547 N.Y.S.2d 1012 (N.Y. 1993).

neither section prevents use of a market price measure when cover or resale has been effected. Official Comment 1 to § 2-703 adds that whether pursuit of one remedy bars another depends on "the facts of the individual case."[21] These provisions seem to allow election of remedies. But Official Comment 5 to § 2-713 says that the market price measure applies only when the buyer has not covered.[22] This denies election of remedies to the buyer. (No comparable comment applies to the seller.) On the reasonable assumption that election should either be available to both the buyer and seller or neither, the UCC simply does not say whether the injured party can elect between remedies. The little available drafting history on point is equally inconclusive.[23]

We think that election should be permitted, although the answer is slightly complicated and reasonable disagreement is possible. One popular argument against election clearly is mistaken. The argument is that election sometimes can overcompensate the injured party. An illustration of the supposed possibility goes as follows. Assume that the contract price of a good is $100. The buyer has not prepaid the contract price. At the time tender of delivery is called for under the contract, when the market price has dropped to $70, the buyer repudiates the contract. Later the seller resells the good for $80 in conformity with the requirements of § 2-706. If the seller can elect to recover under § 2-708(1)'s contract-market price difference, its damages are $30 ($100 - $70 = $30). Since the seller resold the good for $80 as well, his total recovery is $110: $30 from the breaching buyer under § 2-708(1) plus $80 from the party to whom he resold the good. Had the buyer fully performed, the seller would only have received the $100 contract price. The argument concludes that election of § 2708(1) overcompensates the seller here.

This popular argument against election is weak because it wrongly focuses only on the actual outcome. The actual outcome in this case is that the resale price ($80) is higher than the market price at the time of tender ($70). The argument ignores the possibility that the expected value of the market price and resale measures are equal. In other words,

---

[21] § 2-703 Official Comment 1.

[22] § 2-713 Official Comment 5.

[23] See Ellen Peters, *Remedies for Breach of Contracts Relating to the Sale of Goods Under the Uniform Commercial Code: A Roadmap for Article Two*, 73 Yale L. J. 199, 260-61 (1963).

it looks only at recoveries ex post and not at the ex ante value of a recovery under a particular damages measure. To see why this is mistaken, remember that at the time the buyer breached, before the seller resold, the future resale price could have been either above or below the market price. In fact, since the seller cannot systematically outguess the market, the resale price is as likely to be above the market price as below it.[24] If so, the expected value of the contract-resale measure is equal to the expected value of a contract-market price measure. Assume, as before, that the contract price is $100, the resale price is $80 and the market price at the time of tender is $70. Suppose that the only other possible price that the good could have been resold for is $60. And suppose that at the time of the buyer's breach it is just as likely that the price of the good will be resold for $80 as it is that the good will be resold for $60. Then the expected values of the contract-market price and the contract-cover measures can be calculated. Since the market price of the good is known at the time of the buyer's breach, the probability of the market price being $70 is certain — its probability is 1.0. The expected value of the seller's damages under the contract-market price measure therefore is $30:

$$\$30 = \$100 - (1.0 \times 70)$$

Since at the time of the breach the resale price of the good may be either $80 or $60 with equal likelihood, the probability of each outcome is .5. Thus, the expected value of the seller's damages under the contract-resale measure also is $30:

$$\$30 = [.5 \times (100 - 80)] + [.5 \times (100 - 60)]$$

The expected value of damages under the two measures therefore is equal.

It would be convenient if this "ex ante" argument settled the case for the election of remedies. Unfortunately, the case is more complicated. Recall the assumption recited above to the effect that the injured party cannot outguess the market price, so that the future resale or cover price is as likely to be above as below it. That assumption supposes that the decision to resell or cover is made at the same time that the relevant market price is determined, either at the time of tender or the time the buyer learned of the breach. At that time the injured party has no special information about future resale or cover prices. Thus, it is safe to assume

---

[24] See Robert E. Scott, *The Case for Market Damages: Revisiting the Lost Profits Puzzle*, 57 U. Chi. L. Rev. 1155, 1190 (1990).

that future resale or cover prices are as likely to be above as below the relevant market price. But resale under § 2-706 and cover under § 2-712(1) can upset the assumption. Reasonable resale or cover takes time — more or less, depending on the circumstances. So the injured party does not have to decide to obtain substitute performance at the instant the other party breaches. While waiting, it can acquire information about future resale or cover prices. That information may allow the party to outguess the market price at the time of tender or when it learned of the breach. Since the injured party can have special information about resale prices, the expected values of market price and resale measures need not always be equal.

To see this, consider a variant on the last example. The contract price, market price and resale prices remain the same. But now the seller acquires information about the future resale prices in the interim between the buyer's breach and the resale. Suppose, for example, given the information, the seller believes that it is much more likely that the resale price will be $60 than it will be $80. To be precise, suppose the seller believes that the probability of resale fetching $60 is .8 and the probability of it fetching $80 is .2. Since the seller already knows that the market price was $70 at the time of tender, the probability of that price is 1.0. Thus, the expected value of damages under the contract-market price measure remains $30:

$$\$30 = \$100 - (1.0 \times 70)$$

But the expected value of damages under the contract-resale measure is $36:

$$\$36 = [.2 \times (100 - 80)] + [.8 \times (100 - 60)]$$

The expected value of damages under § 2-706 therefore is higher than it is under § 2-708(1).

The case favoring election of remedies, we think, must go back to first principles. One central principle is that damage measures are to give the injured party the economic value of full performance: its profit. So it needs to be asked what full performance amounts to. As Robert Scott remarks, the notion of full performance has no inherent meaning.[25]

---

[25] See Scott, supra note 25, at 1170 (1990). Years ago Judge Ellen Peters described market price measures of damages under the UCC as "statutory liquidated damages." See Peters, supra note 24, at 259 (1963). The description considers contractual performance as including contractually provided remedies. Put anachronistically, "statutory liquidated damages" is a way of saying that

Performance of a sales contract does not involve just delivery of goods, acceptance, and payment. Contractual performance also involves the payment of a sum in damages in the event goods are not exchanged for the contract price. The question is the amount of that sum agreed upon. A damages formula measures the sum. Thus, properly considered, the contract-resale and contract-market price measures are explicit or implicit terms of the parties' contract.

Those who oppose election of remedies label recovery of the contract-market difference "overcompensation" when the resale price is above the market price. The label begs the question because it simply assumes that full performance does not call for the payment of market damages in the circumstances. That assumption also is unsound. Parties can agree to allocate the risk of fluctuations in market price and resale price. Under the agreement, when a party breaches, the injured party can recover in damages the contract-market price difference, whatever it is. Market price damage measures therefore would give the injured party its economic value of full performance. They would not "overcompensate" the injured party. Contracting parties, of course, could explicitly agree to allocate the risk of fluctuations in market price. The harder issue is whether a market price measure is a default damages term. We believe that most parties would allocate the risk of market price fluctuations to the breaching party. Thus, we also believe that election of remedies only protects the economic value of performance and does not overcompensate the injured party. Even if we are mistaken, the case for or against election turns on arguments about the selection of a default damages term. Conclusory labels such as "overcompensation" and "full performance" do nothing to advance the argument.

### 3. Lost Profits: § 2-708(2)

Economic profits are the net gains a party receives from performing the contract. As noted above, all damages measures give the injured party its economic profits. For example, under § 2-708(1) the aggrieved seller who resells at a market price below the contract price and recovers damages still obtains its profit. But sometimes § 2-708(1) and § 2-706(1) will not give the seller its profit. One instance is when the buyer breaches before the seller completes production of the good, and the seller reasonably decides not to continue.[26] Since the completed good

---

market price measures are default damages terms.

[26] Cf. § 2-704(1).

will not be offered, contract-market price and contract-resale price formulas cannot be used to give the seller its profit. Another, more common instance in the case law occurs when, had the buyer performed, the seller would have sold goods to a second buyer too. In this case, the seller would have been able to make two sales and two profits. The seller, by selling only to the second buyer after the first buyer's breach, makes only one sale and one profit. He therefore has lost a profit. Section § 2-708(1)'s market price and § 2-706(1)'s resale formula will not compensate this seller for the lost profit resulting from the first buyer's breach. In both instances, § 2-708(2) allows the seller to recover lost profits under because § 2-708(1)'s damage measure is "inadequate" to put him in the position in which the buyer's performance would have put him.

### a. Measuring Lost Profits

Two issues are raised by § 2-708(2). First, how are the seller's lost profits measured under § 2-708(2)? Second, when should a seller be entitled to recover lost profits under the subsection? The first issue is the easier of the two to resolve. The seller's economic profit from the sale simply is the difference between the contract price and the variable costs of performing the contract. Variable costs are all costs which the seller incurs in performance and would not incur otherwise. Costs which would be incurred even if the contract had never existed are fixed costs, not variable costs. For example, labor costs, rent and interest payments on debt are fixed costs for the seller when he incurs them whether or not he has contracted with the buyer. Because performance of the contract almost certainly involves fixed costs, they are considered "overhead" and part of the seller's profit. The seller can allocate them among its contracts and reduce or increase its "accounting" profits accordingly. The allocation does not affect the seller's economic profits from performance. Hence, strictly, fixed costs are part of the seller's economic gain from performance, measured as the difference between contract price and variable costs.[27]

Read literally, § 2-708(2) does not measure the seller's lost profits. As is well-recognized, the formula described by the subsection sometimes

---

[27] A simple arithmetic formula establishes the conclusion. Let K = contract price, VC = variable costs, FC = fixed costs, and P = profit. The contract price is the sum of variable and fixed costs and the seller's profit: VC + FC + P = K. Rearranging terms, FC + P = K - VC. Given this equality, profits could be defined to include fixed costs.

gives the seller no damages.[28] This can be easily shown. Section 2-708(2) measures the seller's recovery as "the profit (including reasonable overhead). . . together with any incidental damages. . ., due allowance for costs reasonably incurred and due credit for payments or proceeds of resale."[29] Since profit is equal to the contract price less variable costs, and ignoring incidental damages, § 2-708(2)'s damages formula is as follows:

(Contract Price - Variable Costs) + Costs Reasonably Incurred - Proceeds of Resale

Now suppose that the contract price is $50, the seller's total costs of performance are $40, and the resale price of the good remains equal to the contract price ($50). The buyer breaches by repudiating the contract after the seller has completed production of the good, and the seller resells the good for $50. Section 2-708(2) calculates the seller's lost profits as zero:

$$(\$50 - \$40) + \$40 - \$50 = 0$$

This is because the seller's variable costs are $40, as are its costs reasonably incurred in producing the good, and the proceeds of resale are $50. In general, a seller recovers nothing under § 2-708(2)'s formula when the seller completes performance and the contract and resale prices remain equal. Courts recognize the infelicity of § 2-708(2)'s formula and do not use it in cases of the sort just described. Instead, they read § 2-708(2) to award lost profits, the difference between the contract price and variable costs, ignoring "Costs Reasonably Incurred" and "Proceeds of Resale" in the formula above.[30] Revised § 2-708(2) eliminates § 2-

---

[28] See, e.g., White & Summers, supra note 18, at § 7-13; John A. Sebert, Jr., *Remedies Under Article Two of the Uniform Commercial Code: An Agenda for Review*, 130 U. Pa. L. Rev. 360, 393-94 (1981).

[29] § 2-708(2).

[30] See, e.g., R.E. Davis Chemical Corp. v. Diasonics, Inc., 826 F.2d 678 (7th Cir. 1987); Neri v. Retail Marine Corp., 285 N.E.2d 311 (N.Y. 1972). Section 2-708(2)'s formula applies to component sellers and intermediate sellers ("jobbers"). A component seller is one who reasonably decides not to complete production of the good after the buyer's breach. An intermediate seller decides not to buy the good from another seller for delivery to the buyer after the buyer breaches. Since both sorts of sellers decide not to complete performance, costs reasonably incurred will not equal variable costs, and the proceeds of resale will not equal the contract price.

708(2)'s formula and simply allows the seller to recover "profits (including reasonable overhead)."

### b. Recovering Lost Profits Under § 2-708(2)

The second issue is harder: When should a seller be entitled to recover lost profits under § 2-708(2)? If the seller made a sale after the buyer breached and would have made the sale regardless of the buyer's breach, the second sale is not a replacement for the first sale. The seller in this case has "lost volume" as a result of the breach. If the buyer had not have breached, the seller would have made two sales and two profits. Thus, offsetting the profit that the seller would have made on the breached contract by the proceeds of the second sale does not provide the seller with the economic gain from the breached contract. Proceeds of resale by a "lost volume" seller therefore should not be offset against the seller's profit on the breached contract under § 2-708(2). The question, of course, is when a seller is a "lost volume" seller. The question is exactly the same question asked where the buyer is the nonbreaching party and disposes of goods after rejecting them.

A number of courts find that a seller has lost volume as long as he has the capacity to make an additional sale.[31] In *Neri v. Retail Marine Corp.*,[32] the buyer repudiated a contract for the purchase of a boat after the seller had ordered it from the manufacturer. The seller resold the boat to a second buyer for the contract price and sued the breaching buyer to recover its profit on the breached contract. The court awarded the seller its profit because it found that the seller had available an unlimited supply of relevantly similar boats. Another boat therefore could have been provided to the second buyer. The implicit rationale is that if the injured party has an unlimited supply of goods available to it, then it always could make an additional sale.

The thought, although reflected in some case law, is mistaken. It is not enough to show that a seller has the capacity to acquire additional units of a good. It is not even enough to show that, having this capacity, the seller could have made an additional sale but for the buyer's breach. The seller must also show that an additional sale would have been

---

[31] See Islamic Republic of Iran v. Boeing Co., 771 F.2d 1279 (9th Cir. 1985).

[32] 285 N.E.2d 311 (N.Y. 1972).

profitable for the seller.[33] This is because the variable costs associated with producing units typically does not remain constant over the entire range of output produced by the seller. Thus, the profitability of producing an additional unit (and therefore an additional sale) must be determined. To see this, consider the following illustration.

| Units | Marginal Cost | Marginal Revenue | Profit |
|-------|---------------|------------------|--------|
| 1 | $10 | $20 | $10 |
| 2 | $10 | $20 | $10 |
| 3 | $15 | $20 | $5 |
| 4 | $30 | $20 | -$10 |

The seller's marginal costs are the sum of its variable costs, and its marginal revenues are the contract price received from the sale of a unit of a good. The seller has the capacity to produce four units here, either by manufacturing them himself or buying them from another seller. In other words, he has an available supply of four units. But the seller will produce and contract for the sale of only the first three units of the good. The seller will not produce or contract to sell unit 4 because its marginal costs of doing so exceed its marginal revenues from the sale, $20, the contract price of unit 4. Thus, even though the seller has the supply available to make four sales, he can only profitably sell three units. Thus, if the buyer of unit 3 breaches and the seller sells the unit to another buyer, the sale replaces the breached contract and is not an additional sale. The seller, therefore, does not "lose volume" as a result of the buyer's breach.

*R.E. Davis Chemical Corp. v. Diasonics, Inc.*[34] correctly analyses when a seller is a "lost volume" seller. According to *R.E. Davis*, the seller's capacity to make a second sale is not sufficient to make it lose volume. Two other requirements also must be satisified. First, the seller must prove that he profitably could have made the second sale. The court here seemed to require a showing that the marginal costs of making an additional sale did not exceed marginal revenues. Second, the seller must

---

[33] Goetz & Scott, supra note 14, at 346-47 (1979); Morris Shanker, *The Case for a Literal Reading of UCC Section 2-708(2) (One Profit for the Reseller)*, 24 Case W. L. Rev. 697 (1973).

[34] 826 F.2d 678 (7th Cir. 1987); see also Miguela A. Diaz, Rodriguez v. Learjet, Inc., 946 P.2d 1010 (Kan. Ct. App. 1997).

establish that it probably would have made the second sale had the buyer not breached. The epilogue to *R.E. Davis* is not so encouraging. On remand, the District Court found that the seller met its burden as to profitability by the presentation of favorable average cost data, and the Court of Appeals for the Seventh Circuit upheld the finding.[35] Average cost data do not show the marginal cost of producing a particular unit of a good. As the term suggests, the data only show the average costs of producing a range of output, which are lower than marginal costs over part of the range. They therefore are irrelevant to establishing the seller's variable costs in making a second sale. The *R.E. Davis* court should have demanded that the seller produce the right sort of data: data about its marginal costs.

Whether the seller loses volume depends on the structure of the market in which he is selling. In a competitive market, the seller by definition cannot influence the price of the product. He can sell as many units as he wants at the prevailing price. Our illustration above describes a competitive product market, in which the seller's marginal revenue equals the contract price and remains the same whether the seller sells 1 or 4 units. In this market the seller will supply units up to the point where marginal costs equal marginal revenues. Breach is irrelevant to its decision as to the number of units to supply through sales contracts. Thus, when the buyer breaches and the seller resells, the seller replaces the breached sale at the same price and does not lose one.[36] In a competitive market, there are therefore no "lost volume" sellers. If the market is imperfectly competitive, so that seller has some market power, the analysis is more complicated. Here the seller by definition can effect the price of output by its supply of units. The seller will supply units up to the point at which marginal costs equal marginal revenue. If the buyer breaches, the seller has a choice. It can resell the good at a lower price or not resell at all. Reselling means that the seller's volume remains unchanged; its profit on the sale merely is reduced. Its damages therefore are equal to the contract-market or resale-market difference, with an

---

[35] See R.E. Davis Chemical Corp. v. Diasonics, Inc., 924 F.2d 709, 712 (7th Cir. 1991).

[36] Of course, given the buyer's breach, the market demand for units has diminished by one unit. There is one fewer unit sold in the relevant market than otherwise would be sold. The market demand curve facing the industry has shifted downward by one unit. But the lost sale is not a loss *to* the seller; it replaces the lost sale by reselling to another buyer.

offset for the reduced profit realized on the replacement sale. If the seller decides not to resell, it loses volume and can recover lost profits on the breached contract. The seller's decision either to resell or not depends roughly on the effect on all of the seller's contracts of reducing the contract price of the resold good.[37]

So a court needs to know the structure of the market in which the seller is selling. Courts generally lack the requisite information about market structure, marginal costs, marginal revenues and prices also are unobservable variables for them. Accordingly, courts need to assume facts that obtain more often than not. Thus, the use of presumptions about market structure seems appropriate. Since most products are sold in competitive markets, we would have courts presume that the relevant product market is competitive. The seller therefore does not lose volume as a result of the buyer's breach and is not entitled to lost profits. Being only a presumption, it is open to the seller to show that the relevant market is uncompetitive. In addition, the seller needs to show whether he lost volume by not reselling or resold at a reduced price. The case law on lost profits does not set presumptions by market structure. However, by requiring the seller to prove its damages with reasonable certainty, case law in effect requires the seller to prove facts about market structure. Assigning the burden of proof in this unexceptional way therefore is consistent with setting the presumptions in the way we suggest.

### 4. The Accepting Buyer's "Value Differential"

If the buyer has accepted nonconforming goods and not effectively revoked acceptance of them, it cannot cancel the contract or obtain substitute performance through use of either the market or cover measures to recover damages. The accepting buyer instead must retain the goods and recover damages. If the buyer has not prepaid the contract price, under § 2-717 it can reduce the contract price by the amount of damages resulting from the nonconformity. If the buyer has prepaid the contract price, § 2-714 measures the damages it can recover from the seller. Section 2-714 contains two different measures, cast in unhelpfully vague language. Section 2-714(1) allows the buyer to recover "damages for any nonconformity of tender for loss resulting in the ordinary course of events from the seller's breach as determined in any manner which is reasonable." Section 2-714(2) measures the buyer's "value differential":

---

[37] See Robert Cooter & Melvin Aron Eisenberg, *Damages for Breach of Contract*, 73 Cal. L. Rev. 1432, 1451-55 (1985).

> The measure of damages for breach of warranty is the difference at the time and place of acceptance between the value of the goods accepted and the value they would have had if they had been as warranted, unless special circumstances show proximate damages of a different amount.

Section 2-714(1) is the more general measure because it applies to "any nonconformity of tender." It applies, for example, to defective or tardy tender of delivery. Section 2-714(2) is a damages measure only for breaches of warranty. Although Official Comment 3 to § 2-714 describes subsection (2)'s measure as the "standard" measure for breach of warranty, § 2-714(1) is broad enough to measure damages resulting from a warranty breach. In fact, § 2-714(2) itself allows recourse to subsection (1) when "special circumstances" show a different amount of damages resulting from a breach of warranty.

### a. § 2-714(2)'s Measure of "Value"

Section 2-714(2)'s meaning is not transparent. It provides that the accepting buyer recovers the difference between "the value of the goods" at the time of acceptance and "the value" they would have had at that time if they had been as warranted. The relevant notion of value is undefined for purposes of this section. Section 2-714(2)'s references to "value" omit mention of "market value," invoked in other remedial provisions such as § 2-708(1) and § 2-713(1). As a matter of statutory interpretation, then, the most that can be concluded is that "value" in § 2-714(2) need not mean market value. Thus, the case for a particular notion of value cannot rest on statutory interpretation alone. Courts generally have opted for four different notions of § 2-714(2)'s "value differential": market price, subjective value, repair cost and replacement cost.[38] Using each of these notions, § 2-714(2)'s measures sometimes may undercompensate the accepting buyer for the seller's warranty breach.

The case against using the "value differential" based on subjective value is particularly strong. Subjective value is difficult to verify, and therefore evidence bearing on it can be used strategically by both the buyer and seller. There is no reason to believe that its use brings systematic gains in the accuracy of gauging damages. More important, subjective value can differ among buyers depending on their idiosyncracies. Because buyers and not their sellers have information

---

[38] See, e.g., Shroeder v. Barth, Inc., 969 F.2d 421 (7th Cir. 1992).

about their own subjective values, there is asymmetric information. A seller will price the good on the assumption that its buyer places subjective value on the good equal to the average value placed on it by buyers. "Low value" buyers subsidize "high value" buyers, producing a higher average price than if the buyers could be identified and handled differently. Measuring damages by objective measures such as market price induces buyers to disclose information about their subjective values to their sellers when value is above market price. The seller then can respond by adjusting price or disclaimers to reflect the information. Measuring § 2-714(2)'s "value differential" by subjective value gives buyers no incentive to disclose. In other words, the objection to subjective value is that it does not serve the information-forcing function needed in this case. Readers will recognize the similarity of this argument for objective measures of value to the justification for the rule of *Hadley v. Baxendale* restricting the recovery of consequential damages.

### b. The Relation Between § 2-714(1) and (2)

An initial curiosity is an unexplained asymmetry between § 2-714 and other remedial provisions in the UCC. Section 2-714 and other UCC remedies allocate the risk of fluctuations in market price differently. To see this, first recall that a fixed price contract allocates increases in market price ("upside risk") to the seller and decreases in market price ("downside risk") to the buyer. In other words, if market price increases, the seller incurs the opportunity cost of selling at the higher price; if it decreases, the buyer bears an opportunity cost of buying at the lower price. Section 2-714 retains this allocation of market price risk. Other UCC provisions, however, do not. The following example illustrates the point. Suppose the contract price of a conforming good is $100 and that the seller breaches a warranty covering the goods. Given the breach, the goods are worth $70. At the same time the market price of conforming goods at the time of delivery has dropped to $90. Under § 2-711(1), the buyer can cancel the contract. The buyer can cancel by rejecting the goods or effectively revoking acceptance of them. Cancellation shifts the downside market risk of $10 ($100 - $90) to the seller. Now suppose the buyer accepts the goods and cannot effectively revoke its acceptance. Section 2-714(2) gives damages of $20, the difference between the value the goods would have had at the time of delivery if they had been as warranted ($90) and the actual value of the goods given the breach of warranty ($70). Assuming that the buyer has prepaid the contract price, it therefore recovers $20 from the seller, and pays a total of $80 ($100 - $20) for a good having a value of $70. The disparity is justified because the buyer retains the downside market risk. Thus, rejection or effective revocation allows a buyer to reallocate the market risk to the seller which a fixed price contract initially allocated to itself. Acceptance keeps the risk on the buyer. The curiosity is that the UCC allows market risk to be shifted on the basis of acceptance and rejection. There seems to be no correlation between these acts and an efficient reallocation of market price risks.

In most cases, § 2-714(1) and (2) yield the same measurement of damages. This is because the diminution in value resulting from a breach of warranty measured by § 2-714(2) is the loss ordinarily resulting from the breach of warranty under § 2-714(1). If the market price of a conforming widget is $100 while a nonconforming widget has a price of $60, the buyer can recover $40, the "value differential" under § 2-714(2). The $40 diminution in value also is the loss ordinarily resulting from the nonconformity in the widget. Thus, usually it is unimportant whether a court awards damages to the accepting buyer under either subsection. In *Holm v. Hansen*,[39] the buyer ran together its own herd with a brucellosis-ridden herd it had bought. The court found that damage to the buyer's own herd was a "special circumstance" taking the buyer's damages out of § 2-714(2)'s "value differential" and measuring its damages by § 2-714(1). Under § 2-714(1), the loss of the buyer's own herd was considered a loss resulting in the ordinary course from the seller's breach of warranty. The *Holm* court could have awarded the same damages under § 2-714(2), without considering that "special circumstances" obtained. This is because § 2-714(3) allows recovery of consequential damages, where appropriate, under § 2-715(2). Accordingly, loss of the buyer's own herd from the brucellosis-ridden purchases could be considered consequential damages resulting from the seller's breach of warranty. If so, the loss of the purchased herd could be measured by § 2-714(2)'s "value differential." Loss of the buyer's own herd also could be recovered under § 2-715(2). The buyer's total recoverable damages therefore would be the same as the damages recovered under § 2-714(1).

Sometimes, however, the two measures can give different recoveries. This occurs in either of two circumstances. In one circumstance a loss is not reasonably foreseeable by the seller at the time the contract is entered into but nonetheless ordinarily results from a breach of warranty. An example would be a situation in which it is generally recognized only after the contract is concluded that a loss to other property is a direct

---

[39] 248 N.W.2d 503 (Iowa 1976).

result of the breach. In such a case the loss would be recoverable under § 2-714(1) because ordinarily resulting from breach. There is no recovery under § 2-714(2) because the nonconformity results in losses to property other than the goods. Nor is the loss recoverable under § 2-714(3) because not a type of consequential damage. Thus, § 2-714(1) would yield more damages than § 2-714(2). A second circumstance occurs when the sales contract contains a damages exclusion clause excluding recovery of consequential damages. By allocating the risk of such damages to the buyer, the clause prevents recovery of them under § 2-714(3). Thus, recovery of consequential damages cannot supplement recovery under § 2-714(2)'s "value differential." Considered as a type of direct damages, however, it is possible that they are recoverable under § 2-714(1).

*Hill v. BASF Wyandotte Corp.*[40] illustrates the possibility. The sales contract in *Hill* contained a damage exclusion clause excluding consequential damages. The seller's breach of warranty apparently resulted in the buyer losing profits, and the buyer sought to recover them under § 2-714(1). Finding uncertainty in applying the "value differential" to the facts, the court deemed there to be "special circumstances" making it appropriate to use § 2-714(1) to measure the buyer's damages. Applying § 2-714(1), the buyer's lost profits were recoverable as direct damages, nothwithstanding the exclusion clause. *Hill*'s outcome is indefensible. It upsets the contracting parties' allocation of risks of consequential damages, and it does so inconsistently. Either the damages exclusion clause is effective or not. If the clause is effective, then the buyer bears the risk of consequential damages. It should continue to bear the risk whether it recovers damages under § 2-714(1) or (2). The subsection under which recovery is sought should not matter. Recovery also should not turn on whether the loss is labeled as "direct damages" or as "consequential damages." Under *Hill*'s outcome, lost profits can be recovered under § 2-714(1) but not § 2-714(3) (and therefore not in conjunction with § 2-714(2)). Consistency aside, the outcome also upsets the parties' ex ante assignment of risks. If the damages exclusion clause is ineffective, then the seller bears the risk of consequential damages. In that case, the buyer should be able to recover its lost profits under both § 2-714(1) and (2). Thus, damage exclusion clauses should be treated the same under both subsections and honored when effective. *Hill*'s only virtue is to create a litigation tactic in which the buyer's lawyer can improve the client's prospects by artful

---

[40] 311 S.E.2d 734 (S.C. 1984).

labeling to avoid the effect of contractual provisions.

### c. Measuring Damages for Breach of Warranty of Title

The difference between § 2-714(1) and § 2-714(2)'s damages measures is apparent in setting damages for a breach of warranty of title. Under § 2-714(2), absent "special circumstances," damages equal the difference at the time and place of acceptance between the value of the good with good title and the value of the good given its impaired title. The value of the good at the time and place of acceptance typically is either the contract price or the market price. Call this measure an "acceptance measure." Under § 2-714(1), or § 2-714(2) if "special circumstances" obtain, damages are determined by the value of the good at the time the buyer is dispossessed of the good. Call this a "dispossession measure." The UCC's language does not favor either measure of damages, and the case law is mixed (although tending to favor a dispossession measure[41]). We think that a dispossession measure is the better measure of damages under both § 2-714(1) and (2).

To see this, recognize that damages measures can overcompensate or undercompensate the buyer. There are three different factors that might result in imperfect compensation. First, a buyer uses the purchased asset between the time of purchase and the time of dispossession. A good approximation of the value of that use is cost of depreciation. An acceptance measure overcompensates the buyer by not deducting depreciation costs. Because a dispossession measure gauges the value of the asset at the time of disposession, it takes depreciation occurring before dispossession into account. The buyer therefore is not overcompensated on this score. Case law adopting a dispossession measure recognizes this as a reason for preferring the measure.[42] Second, the buyer values the asset at more than its market price. Otherwise, it would not have retained the asset before dispossession occurred. Damages measures that look to market price therefore can undercompensate the buyer. Since this is true whether an acceptance or dispossession measure is used, the disparity between value and market price does not favor either measure. Third, the market price of the asset

---

[41] Compare Metalcraft, Inc. v. Pratt, 500 A.2d 329 (Md. Ct. Spec. App. 1985) with Canterra Petroleum, Inc. v. Western Drill & Mining Supply, 418 N.W.2d 267 (N.D. 1987).

[42] See, e.g., Itoh v. Kimi Sales, Ltd., 345 N.Y.S.2d 416 (City Civ. Ct. N.Y. 1973).

can fluctuate between the time of purchase and dispossession. A fixed price contract allocates the risk of a price increase to the seller and a price decrease to the buyer. Because an acceptance measure looks only at the market price at the time of acceptance, it operates to allocate the upside risk to the buyer and the downside risk to the seller. This reverses the risk allocations of a fixed price contract. A dispossession measure preserves the risk allocation, placing upside risk on the seller and the downside risk on the buyer. Again, case law opting for a dispossession measure recognizes the point. Since all three sources of imperfect compensation are present with an acceptance measure while at most only one source is present with a dispossession measure, we favor a dispossession measure.

It is worth emphasizing the third source of imperfect compensation through an example. Suppose the contract price is $100, the same as the market price at the time of acceptance of the goods. Suppose too that the market price increases to $130 at the time the good is retrieved from the buyer. An acceptance measure under § 2-714 would give the buyer only $100 ($100 - 0). The buyer does not get the benefit of appreciation in the asset's value of $30. A dispossession measure gives it $130 ($130 - 0), which includes the $30 upside risk. The seller therefore bears the cost of the $30 price increase. Now suppose the market price declines to $50 at the time the good is retrieved. An acceptance measure still gives the buyer $100. The seller therefore bears the $50 decline in the asset's value. A dispossession measure gives the buyer $50 in the circumstances, placing the downside risk of $50 on the buyer, not the seller. Thus, the dispossession measure, unlike the acceptance measure, allocates the cost of a price increase on the seller and a price decrease on the buyer. A contract with a fixed price of $100 allocates the cost of a price increase of $30 to the seller and a price decrease of $50 to the buyer. An acceptance measure allocates the cost of a $30 price increase to the buyer and a $50 price decrease to the seller.

An illustration of § 2-714's application and the use of a dispossession measure of damages might be useful. Suppose that Owner has a car with a current market value of $2000. Thief steals the car and sells it to Buyer 1, who pays Thief $2000 without notice that the car is stolen. Buyer 1 uses the car, thereby reducing the car's value from $2000 to $1500. Later, Buyer 1 sells the car to Buyer 2, who pays Buyer 1 $1500 and also has no notice that the car was stolen. Buyer 2's use of the car diminishes its market value by $500, to $1000. Still later, Owner discovers the location of the car and recovers it from Buyer 2. At the time the car has a market value of $1000. Besides recovering the car, Owner can recover damages from Buyer 2 in tort, based on conversion. Owner's damages in conversion are equal to the lost value of the car when it was in the hands of Buyer 2. Buyer 2 converted the car when it purchased it from Buyer 1 for $1500. Since Owner recovers the car with a market value of $1000, Owner can recover $500 from Buyer 2. In addition, Owner can recover the remaining $500 in damages from Buyer 1, also based on conversion. The Owner's total recovery of $2000 makes him whole. He obtains the car with a market value of $1000, $500 in damages from Buyer 2, and $500 in damages from Buyer 1.

Buyer 2 in turn can recover $1500 in damages from Buyer 1. Assuming that the implied warranty of title was not effectively disclaimed, Buyer 1 breached the agreement with Buyer 2. Under § 2-714(1) or if "special circumstances" obtain under § 2-714(2), a dispossession measure gives Buyer 2 $1000: the difference between the market value of the car at the time Owner recovered it had the warranty of title not been breached ($1000) and the car's value given that the warranty was breached (0). (Buyer 2 bears the $500 in depreciation costs of using the car before it was returned to Owner.) Buyer 2 also can recover from Buyer 1 the additional $500 Owner recovered from it either as a type of direct damages under § 2-714(1) or as consequential damages under § 2-714(3). Buyer 2's total recovery from Buyer 1 therefore is $1500. The result makes sense because Buyer 1, who dealt with Thief, is in a better position than Buyer 2 to take precautions against acquiring or selling stolen goods.[43] Thus, the dispossession rule operates efficiently to place the risk of theft on the party in the best position to prevent its materialization. Of course, Buyer 1 in turn can recover $1500 from Thief based on a breach of an implied warranty of title. But if, as is likely, Thief cannot be located or is judgment proof, Buyer 1 ultimately bears the loss.

Revised Article 2 indirectly adopts a dispossession measure of without saying so. Revised § 2-714(1) leaves the section substantially unchanged. It therefore continues to be neutral between acceptance and dispossession measures. However, under Revised § 2-608(4)(b), a justifiably revoking buyer must compensate the seller for its value of its use of the goods prior to revocation. Justified revocation occurs in most cases involving a breach of warranty of good title: the challenge to buyer's title usually comes after it has accepted the goods. Since

---

[43] We discuss the justifications for the Article 2 rules concerning theft in Chapter 10.

depreciation costs reflect the value of the buyer's use of the good, Revised § 2-608(4)(b) forces Revised § 2-714(1)'s measure to reduce the buyer's damages accordingly. The reduction is consistent only with a dispossession measure of damages, not an acceptance measure.

## B. Under the CISG

In its main outlines, the CISG's scheme of remedies parallels that of the UCC. There are, however, some differences, both as to when particular remedies are available and the remedy itself. The CISG, like the UCC, makes two distinctions among remedies. One distinction is between substitutional and specific relief. For example, the CISG recognizes the difference between money damages and specific relief. The second distinction is between remedies available when the breaching party retains the goods and remedies available when the nonbreaching party retains them. Here the CISG and the UCC differ. The UCC makes particular remedies available to the nonbreaching party according to whether the buyer has accepted the goods or ineffectively revoked its acceptance. Thus, in place of the UCC concepts of rejection, revocation and acceptance of the goods to select among remedies, the CISG employs uses the notion of "avoidance" of the contract. "Avoidance" means putting the contract to an end based on the other party's breach. Its closest counterpart under the UCC is cancellation of the contract.[44] Under the CISG, the remedies available to the nonbreaching party therefore do not turn on whether the buyer has accepted or rejected the goods. Rather, they depend on the avoidance or nonavoidance of the contract.

A contract can be avoided in either of two circumstances. First,

---

[44] See § 2-106(4) ("cancellation" puts contract to an end for breach of other party; right to remedy retained). The UCC occasionally refers to "avoidance" of the contract, as in § 2-613, where a party's performance is excused. The excused party is given the privilege of nonperformance without liability for breach. Cancellation gives the nonbreaching party the privilege of putting the contract to an end and preserves the liability of the breaching party.

Strictly, the CISG considers avoidance itself to be remedy. Articles 45 and 61, the index of the buyer and sellers' remedies, respectively, refer indirectly to avoidance (e.g., Article 45(1)(a) and Article 61(1)(a)). The headings of the remedial sections of the CISG also begin "Section II: Remedies..." and "Section III: Remedies..." Thus, the CISG divides remedies between those available when the remedy of avoidance has been exercised and those available when the remedy has not been exercised.

under Articles 49(1)(a) and 64(1)(a), a "fundamental breach" by one party allows the other party to terminate the contract. Article 25 of the CISG somewhat unhelpfully characterizes a "fundamental breach" as a breach that "results in such detriment to the other party as substantially to deprive him of what he is entitled to expect under the contract..." Second, a party also can avoid the contract if the breaching party fails to deliver conforming goods within the reasonable additional time set by the injured party.[45] This is the so-called *Nachfrist* (loosely translated: "deadline") period. Article 26 requires that notice of avoidance be given to the breaching party in both cases.

The effects of a requirement of a fundamental breach contrasts with the effects of the UCC's "perfect tender" rule. Where markets are distant and substitute performance is costly, a "perfect tender" rule allows the nonbreaching party to bargain strategically with the breaching party. In this way bargaining costs are increased. For example, assume the market price of a conforming widget is $20 and Seller tenders a nonconforming widget with a resale price of $10. Assume further that the seller faces no additional cost in substituting a conforming widget for the nonconforming one. If Seller tenders a conforming widget for $20, it can resell the nonconforming widget for $10 for a net loss of $10. Alternatively, Buyer can keep the nonconforming widget and Seller can pay damages. Seller will pay Buyer no more than $10 in damages. This is because Seller's net loss is $10 if it delivers a substitute widget and resells the nonconforming widget. Thus, where there are no costs in retrieving and replacing the defective widget, Buyer cannot bargain for damages greater than Buyer's actual loss.

Costly substitute performance allows for strategic bargaining by Buyer. Suppose that the cost of retrieving the nonconforming widget and substituting a conforming one is $7. Then Seller's net loss if it tenders a substitute widget is $17: $20 for the conforming widget less $10 received by reselling the nonconforming widget plus $7 in retrieval and substitution costs. Buyer's damages if it keeps the widgets are again $10, the difference between the price of a conforming widget and the nonconforming widget it received. There is therefore a $7 "surplus" realized if Buyer agrees to keep the widget. Since a "perfect tender" rule allows Buyer to reject the widget, Seller has to bargain to have Buyer keep it. He will pay no more than $17 to have Buyer do so, and Buyer will accept no less than $10. Bargaining costs are incurred in the

---

[45] See Articles 49(1)(b), 64(1)(b); cf. Articles 47(1), 63(1).

negotiations to divide the $7 surplus. A requirement of fundamental breach, like a "substantial performance" rule, eliminates these bargaining costs. This is because Buyer cannot avoid the contract if the nonconformity in the widget does not rise to a fundamental breach. Seller therefore does not have to negotiate with Buyer to keep the widget. Negotiating to divide the surplus is a wasteful transaction cost. Because international sales often involve sales where markets can be remote and therefore substitute performance is costly, bargaining costs are a concern. A requirement of fundamental breach eliminates them.

The requirement of a *Nachfrist* period, although trickier, also can be justified. Articles 49(1)(a) and 64(1)(a) allow the nonbreaching party to set an additional reasonable period in which the breaching party is to perform. The nonbreaching party can avoid the contract if performance does not occur within that period. Thus, even a nonfundamental breach allows avoidance if the breach continues past the *Nachfrist* period. Accordingly, because the nonbreaching party can insist on conforming performance, the requirement of a *Nachfrist* period might appear to function as a "perfect tender" rule. Appearances are deceiving, however. The *Nachfrist* period serves as a rough proxy for a fundamental breach. For the failure to perform within an additional reasonable period diminiishes the value of the contract to the nonbreaching party. Estimates are rough, but often the diminution in value at the end of the *Nachfrist* period can deprive the nonbreaching party of a significant portion of the value of performance to it. If so, nonperformance within the period is highly correlated with a fundamental breach under Article 25. Of course, there are obvious counterexamples. A minutely scratched widget probably does not seriously diminish the value of the contract to a buyer, even when the seller refuses to tender an unscratched widget within a period set by the buyer. But this only shows that the *Nachfrist* period is a rough proxy for a fundamental breach. The worth of the proxy has to be tested against the likely range of international sales contracts falling under the CISG. It is not crazy to find that over this range failure to perform within the *Nachfrist* period often indicates that a fundamental breach has occurred.

### 1. Substitute Performance: Article 75

If the aggrieved party cannot or chooses not to avoid the contract as a result of a breach, Article 74 permits it to accept the breaching party's performance and recover damages. A party who does avoid the contract may either obtain substitute performance and recover damages under Article 75 or not obtain substitute peformance and recover damages under Article 76. Substitute performance under Article 75 involves either the seller reselling the goods or the buyer obtaining replacement goods. Article 75 measures the nonbreaching seller's damages as the difference between the contract price and the resale price, and the nonbreaching buyer's damages as the difference between the cover price and the contract price. The damages measure is the counterpart of the measures described in § 2-706 and § 2-712 of the UCC, respectively.

## 2. Market Price Damages: Article 76

A nonbreaching party who has avoided the contract need not measure its damages by the formula in Article 75. It has the option of measuring damages by Article 76's market price formula. Under Article 76(1), damages are equal to the difference between the contract price and "current price." The "current price" undoubtedly is the market price. Although the measure is the counterpart of § 2-708(1) and § 2-713(1)'s market measures, there are two differences. First, the nonbreaching party can use Article 76's market measure only if it has not obtained substitute performance. The UCC may or may not allow use of a market measure in the same circumstances. Article 76 applies only if the party "has not made a purchase or resale under article 75." Thus, the CISG expressly bars the nonbreaching party from electing its remedies. Unlike the UCC, the CISG's choice here is clear.

Second, the market price selected differs from the price selected under the UCC. Article 76(1) sets market price as of the time of avoidance when avoidance occurs before the nonbreaching party takes delivery. When avoidance occurs after delivery, Article 76 sets market price as of the time of delivery. Section 2-708(1) sets market price as of the time of tender of delivery, and § 2-713(1) puts it as of the time the buyer learned of the breach. In volatile markets, the different times at which market price is set can result in different recoveries. There is some reason to favor the UCC's approach. While market price under both the CISG and the UCC is a verifiable variable, arguably the cost of verifying market price under the CISG is higher than under the UCC. If avoidance occurs before the goods are delivered, Article 76(1) sets market price at the time of avoidance. To be effective, avoidance requires notice to the breaching party.[46] The date at which notice is received as well as its content therefore is in play, and sometimes can be subject to dispute. When tender was to occur under the contract or when the buyer learned of the breach can be disputed too, but here evidence about such matters is relatively easy to supply. The comparative availability of evidence

---

[46] See Article 26.

means that the costs of proving market price can be lower under the UCC than under the CISG. Thus, although not a conclusive consideration, the lower costs of verifying market price favor the UCC's market measures.

### 3. Reduction of the Price

#### a. Article 50's Formula

Article 50 provides a form of substitutional relief that has no UCC counterpart. It takes the form of a money allowance by way of a reduction in the amount owed to the seller. Technically speaking, Article 50 is not regarded by the CISG as a form of damages. Damage measures are given in Articles 74 through 77, and these measurements differ from the measurement given by Article 50. Article 50 therefore cannot be considered as allowing an offset or counterclaim to the contract price due, where the offset or counterclaim is for damages. Accordingly, Article 50 is not a counterpart of the buyer's self-help remedy provided by § 2-717, which allows buyer to offset the contract price by the amount of damages resulting from nonconformity in the good tendered by seller.

Article 50's measurement of recovery, however, is familiar to civil law systems.[47] The measurement allows reduction of the contract price in the proportion that the value of the nonconforming good had on the date of delivery to the value that the good would have had on the same date had it conformed to the contract. Article 50's measure can be stated in a simple formula. If we designate X as the reduced price of the nonconforming good, K as the contract price, VNC as the value of the nonconforming good on delivery, and VC the value that a conforming good would have had on the same date, Article 50's measure is:

$$X/K = VNC/VC$$

Rearranging terms:

$$X = VNC/VC \times K$$

X is the reduced price that the buyer must pay, not the amount by which the price due may be reduced. An example will help. Assume that the buyer contracts to pay $50 and receives a nonconforming good valued at

---

[47] See, e.g., E.E. Bengston & A.J. Miller, *The Remedy of Price Reduction*, 27 Am. J. Comp. L. 275 (1979); Harry M. Flechtner, *More US Decisions on the UN Sales Convention: Scope, Parol Evidence, "Validity" and Reduction of Price Under Article 50*, 14 J. L. & Comm. 153 (1995); A.M. Honore, *The History of the Aedilitan Actions from Roman to Roman-Dutch Law*, in Studies in the Roman Law of Sale 132, 150-58 (D. Daube ed. 1959).

$45. At the time of delivery, however, the market price of a conforming good is $55. The reduced price that the buyer must pay equals the value of the nonconforming good divided by the value of a conforming good and multiplied by the contract price, or $45/$55 x 50. Thus, the price owed by the buyer under Article 50 is $40.90. The contract price has been reduced by $9.10. Section 2-717 of the UCC would allow the buyer to reduce the contract price due by $10, using the "value differential" of § 2-714(2).

Because the CISG does not consider Article 50 a form of damages, restrictions placed on recoverable damages do not apply to recovery under Article 50. Accordingly, awards under Article 50 are not subject to a mitigation requirement or a foreseeability limitation. For the same reason, recovery under Article 50 can be combined with the recovery of damages under Articles 74 through 77. The remedies, in short, are cumulative. This means that consequential damages, for instance, are recoverable along with a price reduction.

### b. Article 50's Use

When would an aggrieved buyer prefer to use Article 50 rather than a damage remedy? As the formula suggests, the desirability of Article 50 depends largely on what happens to the market price of the good between the time of the contract and the time of delivery. Three scenarios are possible: (i) the market price remains stable; (ii) the market price increases; and (iii) the market price decreases. In case (i), Article 50 and Articles 74-77 give the same measure of recovery. If K = $50, VC = $50 and VNC = $45, damages are equal to $5 under Article 74 ($50 - $45 = $5). Article 50 requires the buyer to pay $45 [$45/$50 x $50] and thus also reduces the contract price by $5. In case (ii), where market price has increased, a damage remedy gives a more generous recovery than does Article 50. Assume K = $50, VC = $55 and VNC = $50. Damages would again be $5 [$55 - $50 = $5]. But Article 50 reduces the contract price by $4.55 [$50/$55 x $50 = $45.45]. Thus, the aggrieved buyer would prefer to recover damages.

In case (iii), where market price falls, the buyer's remedy is greater under Article 50 than with a damage measure. Assume, for instance, that K = $50, VC = $45, VNC = $40. In this case, of course, the buyer would prefer to get out of the contract because market price is below contract price. The buyer would prefer to avoid the contract and purchase the goods elsewhere at the new market price. By avoiding the contract, the buyer could shift the risk of market decline back to the seller. But what if the buyer needs the goods immediately and must take these nonconforming goods? Or what if the nonconformity is insufficient to constitute a fundamental breach so the buyer has no right to avoid the contract? The buyer must now pay the contract price of $50 for goods worth $40, but is entitled to damages of $5, the amount of the loss suffered as a consequence of the breach. Hence, the buyer ultimately pays only $45 for the nonconforming goods. But Article 50 allows the buyer to pay only $44.44 [$40/$45 x $50] for the goods, giving the buyer a price reduction of $5.56. Note that Article 50 does not measure the buyer's expectation interest in either case (ii) or (iii).

### c. Why Allow Price Reduction?

The final question is a normative one. Is Article 50 defensible? As we have noted, it has long been available in civil law systems. But we have difficulty understanding its justification. When market price remains unchanged, damage measures and Article 50 give the same recovery. Article 50's measure therefore can be justified in the same way that damage measures are — say, by protecting buyer's expectation interest. When market price changes, however, the two measures do not give the same recovery, and other justifications for Article 50's measure are required. None of the candidate justifications is persuasive. Consider some.

One justification appeals to the distribution of risk of fluctuations of market price. In a fixed price contract, expectation measures of damages allocate the upside and downside risks of market price to buyer. Article 50, it might be said, simply distributes some of the upside and downside risks to the seller. There is nothing compelling in ex post allocating all of that risk to one party or the other, the justification concludes. This "distribution of risk" justification fails. It is accurate in describing Article 50's distribution of risk where market price rises or declines. For instance, in the ongoing examples, where market price rises seller obtains $.55 of the $5 increase in market price. Where market price falls, seller bears $.60 of the $5 decrease in price. But the justification fails to explain two features of Article 50. First, and less seriously, the particular distribution of market increase or decrease is not explained. Why is there an unequal distribution of gain and loss, for instance? Again, in the ongoing examples, the seller obtains 11 percent of the market increase ($.55 divided by $5 gain) and bears 12 percent of the market decrease ($.60 divided by a $5 loss). There is no salience to the distribution of market risk allocated by Article 50.

The second problem is more serious. It is that upside and downside market risk is *not* distributed to the seller. For Article 50 does not operate alone. Buyer also has the option of electing to recover damages. And it will do so when damages provide a more generous measure of recovery than is provided by Article 50. This will occur in case (ii), as noted, where market price increases. Here Article 45(2) allows the buyer to choose to recover damages. Damages in case (ii) allow the buyer to obtain the entire $5 increase in market price ($5 = $55 - $50). Seller gets none of it. Hence, when other available remedies are taken into account, Article 50 does not distribute any of the upside risk to seller. The "distribution of risk" justification therefore fails.

A variant on the "distribution of risk" justification does not help. Sometimes it is said that Article 50's measure of price reduction is a restitutionary measure, noncontractual in nature.[48] The measure is aimed at eliminating the amount by which the seller has been unjustly enriched by delivering nonconforming goods. If so, this restitutionary aim is not satisfied by Article 50's measure. For in a market decline, buyer receives more than the seller "gained" by its breach. In the ongoing example, the seller has gained $5 by breaching: the difference between the current market price of $45 for conforming goods and $40 for nonconforming goods. Article 50, however, allows the buyer to reduce the $50 contract price by $5.56 — $.56 more than the seller was enriched by its breach. The measure therefore is a very blunt tool for redistributing seller's gain from its breach to buyer.

A second justification appeals to systematic undercompensation. Assume that buyers are systematically undercompensated by damage remedies. Attorneys fees, proof costs and the prospect of legal error operate so that buyer's expectation interest is imperfectly secured. Article 50's measure allows a supercompensatory award where market prices decline. The buyer here obtains more than its expectation interest. The supercompensatory award is claimed to compensate for the risk of undercompensation buyer faces. The justification is weak because its supporting claim seems ad hoc. For one thing, Article 50's supercompensatory recovery is available only when the remedy is sought. When other remedies are sought (e.g., damages), the risk of undercompensation remains. It also seems miraculous that the proportional recovery given by Article 50 mirrors the extent of undercompensation buyer faces. Why is undercompensation even roughly correllated with the strict proportion of the contract price

---

[48] See, e.g., G. H. Treitel, Remedies for Breach of Contract: A Comparative Account 108 (1988).

required by Article 50? Even as a rough approximation, the asserted correlation seems ad hoc. It has no independent plausibility.

The third candidate justification appeals to the ex ante value of an Article 50 measure. Assume that the parties will both buy and sell with equal frequency. Also assume that the probability of breaching by delivering nonconforming goods is the same for every seller. Since the parties cannot systematically outguess the market, ex ante market price increases will be as likely as market declines. Accordingly, a damage measure is as likely to yield a higher recovery than Article 50's measure when market price increases as it is to yield a lower recovery than Article 50's measure when market price decreases. Hence, the justification concludes, the parties will assign the same expected value (ex ante) to recovery under Article 50 as to recovery of damages. The trouble with the justification is with its assumption about the parties' ex ante assessment of expected value. True, parties cannot outguess the market. But they do not have to under the CISG, because the buyer's remedial decision is not made ex ante. It can elect between damages measures and recovery under Article 50, as allowed by Article 46. Hence the buyer can wait and obtain information about market prices ex post. And given information about actual market prices, it will elect damages when market price rises and price reduction under Article 50 when market price falls. So the buyer will never in fact recover less than the amount measured by damages, and it sometimes can recover more. The expected value of recovery under Article 50 therefore is always higher than recovery under damages measures alone. A justification based on the same expected value of the two measures of recovery fails. Because we lack a good justification of Article 50's price reduction, we find it puzzling.

### III. Specific Relief

#### A. Under the UCC

#### 1. Seller's Action for the Price

#### a. § 2-709's Technical Requirements

The seller's action for the price is the counterpart of the buyer's right to specific performance. A sales contract calls for the seller to tender the goods and the buyer to pay the contract price. Specific performance allows the buyer to force the seller to deliver the goods. Similarly, an action for the price forces the breaching buyer to pay the seller the contract price. Reflecting a remedial preference for substititional over specific relief, the UCC restricts the availability of both an action for the price and specific performance. Section 2-703(e) allows the seller to recover the contract price "in the proper case" under § 2-709. Section 2-709(1) in turn allows its recovery in three cases.[49] The first is when the breaching buyer has accepted the goods. The second is when the conforming goods are damaged or destroyed while the buyer bears the risk of loss. The third case is when the seller is unable to resell the goods at a reasonable price. Case law has interpreted § 2-709(1) as describing the only cases in which a price action is available to the seller.

Acceptance of the goods and an inability to resell are the important occasions for granting a price action. Acceptance can occur directly under § 2-606(1)(a), as when the buyer signifies its willingness to take the goods.[50] But it can occur indirectly as well. The failure to make an ineffective rejection constitutes an acceptance under § 2-606(1)(c). An effective rejection requires that the buyer give notice to the seller that it rejects the goods.[51] Thus, failing to notify the seller of the rejection amounts to an acceptance. Further, revocation of acceptance includes the requirement that the good tendered be substantially nonconforming. An attempted revocation therefore is ineffective if the nonconformity is less than substantial. Thus, an acceptance continues to operate when the revocation is ineffective. Accordingly, acceptance of the goods as well as an ineffective rejection or revocation gives the seller a price action under § 2-709(1)(a). Under § 2-709(1)(b), a price action is available when the seller is unable to resell the goods. Sometimes, of course, both acceptance and an inability to resell can be present, and both § 2-709(1)(a) and (1)(b) satisfied. This occurred in *Plateq Corp. of Worth Haven v. Machlett Laboratories, Inc.*[52] There the breaching buyer failed to particularize the reasons for its rejection. The trial court found that the failure meant that the seller did not receive notice of the rejection and the rejection therefore was ineffective. By failing to effectively reject, the buyer accepted the goods. And since the buyer also failed to show that the nonconformity in the goods was substantial, it also failed to effectively revoke its acceptance. The trial court also found that, being specially manufactured goods, the seller was unable to resell them for a

---

[49] See § 2-709(1)(a)-(b).

[50] See § 2-606(1)(a).

[51] See § 2-602(1).

[52] 456 A.2d 786 (Conn. 1983).

reasonable price. Given these findings, the trial court and the Connecticut Supreme Court reached the same conclusion on different statutory bases. The trial court allowed a price action under § 2-709(1)(b) based on the seller's inability to resell. The Supreme Court agreed with the court's conclusion but based its decision on § 2-709(1)(a) and the buyer's acceptance of the goods.

A statutory question presented by § 2-709(1) is whether it displaces a duty of mitigation on the seller's part. For example, suppose the breaching buyer has accepted the goods and the seller sues to recover the contract price. The buyer demonstrates that the seller could resell the goods at a higher price than it would receive if it were to resell them. Can the seller still recover the price from the buyer or is it required to resort to the UCC's damage remedies? Almost certainly the seller can recover the price.[53] This is because § 2-709(1) almost certainly excludes a duty of mitigation. To be sure, § 1-103 continues to make pre-UCC law applicable, including a duty of mitigation, unless a particular UCC provision displaces it. But § 2-709(1) displaces the duty. For one thing, if § 2-709(1) did not supplant a duty of mitigation, § 2-709(1)(a)'s acceptance clause would be superfluous.[54] This is because acceptance would give a price action only if mitigation by the seller were infeasible, which means that resale by him at a reasonable price was not possible. But § 2-709(1)(b) gives a price action in precisely these circumstances. Thus, § 2-709(1)(a) would have no point. On the reasonable assumption that § 2-709(1)(a) is not a waste of words, § 2-709(1) supplants a duty of mitigation. Official Comment 2 to § 2-709 supports the conclusion. It provides that a price action is limited to cases where resale by the seller is infeasible "except where the buyer has accepted the goods..." The Comment makes no mention of the futher requirement of mitigation in the case of acceptance by the buyer.

### b. § 2-709's Justification

The UCC has a good reason for not imposing a duty of mitigation on an action for the price. Its justification depends on the reason for giving a seller a price action in the first place. An action for the price, we think, minimizes the seller's damage bill when the seller's resale costs are

---

[53] See F & P Builders v. Lowe's of Texas, Inc., 786 S.W.2d 502 (Tex. Ct. App. 1990).

[54] See Jody Kraus, *Decoupling Sales Law From the Acceptance-Rejection Fulcrum*, 104 Yale L. J. 129, 173 (1994).

greater than the buyer's resale costs.  The buyer breaches either because it no longer finds the contract as profitable to perform as the next best alternative or because of sheer mistake.  Otherwise, it would retain the goods without breaching and adapt them an alternative use.  Given the breach, the goods have to be resold either by the seller or the buyer. Allowing the seller to recover the price from the buyer forces the buyer to dispose of the goods: the seller gets the contract price and the buyer gets the goods. Denying the seller a price action forces the seller to resell the goods and recover damages from the buyer, including its resale costs. Allowing or denying a price action therefore determines whether the buyer or the seller resells the goods.[55]  Since resale costs figure in damages, the seller's damage bill is minimized when the goods are resold by the party facing the lowest resale costs.  Thus, when the seller's resale costs are lower than the buyer's, the seller and buyer would bargain not to give the seller a price action.  Conversely, when the seller's resale costs are higher than the buyer's, a price action would be agreed to by the parties.

Section 2-709(1) provides reliable proxies for when resale costs favor the buyer.  Acceptance of the goods usually occurs after the buyer is in possession or control of the goods.  At that point the seller is usually at a distance from them.  The buyer at the time also might have used the goods, which necessitates reselling them in a secondary market.  The seller's need to retrieve the goods as well as its lack of advantage in selling in a secondary market arguably signal that the resale costs favor the buyer.  Section 2-709(1)(a)'s acceptance clause therefore is a good indicator of the situation.  Similarly, when the goods have been damaged or destroyed and the buyer refuses to accept them, they must be resold (if still existing) in a secondary market.  The seller has no advantage at reselling in this market, and § 2-709(1)(a)'s "damage or destroyed" clause indicates the situation.  When resale by the seller at a reasonable price is not feasible, the seller also has no cost advantage at resale.  The buyer and seller's resale costs at most are equal.  Section 2-709(1)(b)'s clause signals that the seller's advantage in resale costs is absent.  Thus,

---

[55] A price action also can effect the risk of undercompensation a seller faces. Because a price action forces the breaching buyer to resell, the seller does not have to prove its resale costs in order to recover them from the buyer as incidental damages.  Thus, the seller does not risk having a trier of fact underestimate these costs.  Denying a price action requires the seller to resell and recover its resale costs by proving them to a trier of fact.  Here the seller bears a risk of undercompensation.

§ 2-709(1)'s statutory conditions for a price action minimize the costs of breach to the buyer.

Section 2-709(1)'s proxies, although reliable, are imperfect. Sometimes they fail to track the cost-minimizing comparative estimate of resale costs between the seller and the buyer. *Unlaub Co., Inc. v. Sexton*[56] presents circumstances in which § 2-709(1)(a)'s acceptance clause fails as a proxy. An Oklahoma seller agreed to sell an Arkansas buyer coal screens to be picked up by the buyer in Michigan. The buyer failed to effectively reject the screens, and the seller sued for the price. Finding that the buyer had accepted the screens, the court allowed the seller to recover the price under § 2-709(1)(a). There was no evidence that the buyer's costs in taking delivery in Michigan were lower than the seller's or that it had better access to the appropriate resale market in coal screens. Offhand we doubt that either situation obtained. Accordingly, *Unlaub* is a case in which acceptance occurs while resale costs favor the seller, not the breaching buyer. *Unlaub*'s facts, of course, does not show that acceptance is a bad proxy for comparative estimates of resale costs. While imperfect, acceptance might be a better proxy than other sorts of easily administerable proxies.

A tempting alternative is to not use proxies at all. Instead, one might directly estimate the size of comparative resale costs facing the particular seller and buyer. A duty of mitigation in effect rejects acceptance as a proxy and considers comparative resale costs directly. It does so by not allowing a price action upon acceptance when the seller has an advantage at reselling. Inquiring directly into the comparative size of resale costs on a case by case basis, however, itself is costly. Gains in accuracy must be traded off against the administrative costs of enhanced accuracy as well as the rate of erroneous determinations. Because proxies can reduce administrative costs and increase accuracy over the run of cases, they sometimes are better to use than direct tests of underlying variables such as resale costs. Borrowing Professor Richard Epstein's phrase, in law 95 percent is perfection.[57] Seen in this way, § 2-709(1)(a)'s displacement of a duty of mitigation might well be defensible.

## 2. Specific Performance

The buyer's right to specific performance assures it of the value of

---

[56] 568 F.2d 72 (8th Cir. 1977).

[57] Richard A. Epstein, Simple Rules for a Complex World iv (1995).

the seller's performance. The UCC restricts the circumstances in which the buyer can force the seller to deliver the goods. Section 2-716(1) allows but does not require a court to order specific performance in two situations: either when the goods are "unique" or in "other proper circumstances." These statutory conditions are not self-defining, and the Official Comments to § 2-716 do not help much. Official Comment 1 announces that the section is intended to liberalize the judicial attitude to specific performance, presumably by enlarging the occasions when the relief is made available. Official Comment 2 states that the uniqueness of goods is to be tested by the "total situation" of the sales contract. And Official Comment 3 says that the buyer's inability to cover is evidence of "other proper circumstances." Given § 2-716(1)'s statutory conditions of uniqueness or "other proper circumstances," specific performance is not routinely available to the buyer. At the same time, these conditions assure that the remedy is available. Section 2-716's official comments add almost nothing to the statutory language.

Pertinent case law is for the most part consistent, although there is some divergence. If a good is truly unique it has no substitutes, and the buyer cannot obtain substitute performance from another source. The stock examples of a Picasso painting or a numbered print in a series are familiar illustrations. Courts uniformly grant buyers' requests for specific performance in the circumstance, under the "uniqueness" condition of § 2-716(1). If goods are fungible, so that replacement from another source is feasible, specific performance will not be granted. Specific relief almost is never sought by the buyer where goods are fungible.[58] The case law divides when goods fall between being truly unique and perfectly fungible. When similar goods or conditions of sale are available, "uniqueness" of goods is at issue. Likewise, when the same goods can be obtained from another source with difficulty, "other proper circumstances" is the issue. Most courts find that the availability of only similar goods or sales conditions makes the good contracted for "unique." They also find there to be "other proper circumstances" when replacement by the buyer is difficult because costly.[59] In fact, these courts sometimes are not careful in distinguishing between "uniqueness" and "other proper circumstances," often ordering specific performance

---

[58] See Douglas Laycock, The Death of the Irreparable Injury Rule 101 (1991).

[59] See Steven Walt, *For Specific Performance Under the United Nations Sales Convention*, 26 Texas Int'l L. J. 211, 227-28 (1991).

on both statutory bases.[60] A minority of courts find that the buyer's difficulty in obtaining replacement goods does not amount to "uniqueness" or "other proper circumstances."

*Kaiser Trading Co. v. Associated Metals & Minerals Corp.*[61] is a representative example of the approach of most courts. The buyer in *Kaiser* ordered 3500 tons of cryolite from a seller. At the time of the seller's breach only a few hundred tons of cryolite were available on the open market. The remainder of marketable cryolite was otherwise committed under long-term contracts to other buyers. Kaiser, the buyer, could have covered partially by purchasing the uncommitted portion of cryolite from other sellers. Further, it could have covered completely by contracting with other buyers who already had long-tern contracts for cryolite. Presumably covering in this manner would have been costly but feasible. The court quoted approvingly Official Comment 2 to § 2-716 to the effect that an inability to cover was evidence of "other proper circumstances." However, cover was difficult, not impossible. Difficulty in covering was enough for the court to find that these were "other proper circumstances" in which specific performance could be ordered under § 2-716(1). Thus, the *Kaiser* court found that costly cover can warrant a grant of specific performance.

The minority approach is represented by *Duval & Co. v. Malcolm.*[62] The sellers in *Duval* agreed to sell their entire cotton crop to a buyer. A shortage of cotton increased the price and the sellers refused to deliver. The court rejected the buyer's attempt to force the sellers to deliver their cotton crop. It did so while acknowledging that the buyers would have to pay a higher price in covering on the open market. Having to pay a higher cover price is not enough for the court. According to the court, higher cover prices did not make the cotton "unique" or create "other proper circumstances" warranting specific performance. The additional cost to the buyer only increased its recoverable damages. Thus, the *Duval* court dismissed the increase in cover cost that the *Kaiser* court found sufficient to order the seller to perform. Courts adopting the majority approach have found increased cover cost to justify specific

---

[60] See, e.g., Copylease Corp. of America v. Memorex Corp., 408 F. Supp. 758 (S.D.N.Y. 1976); King Aircraft Sales, Inc. v. Lane, 846 P.2d 550, 556 (Wash. Ct. App. 1993).

[61] 321 F. Supp. 923 (N.D. Cal. 1970).

[62] 214 S.E.2d 356 (Ga. 1975).

relief on almost the identical facts as in *Duval*.[63]

The division among courts reflects a disagreement as to whether specific performance should be regularly available to the buyer. It is therefore worth asking about the justification of specific performance. As with an action for the price, a buyer should be entitled to force its seller to perform if doing so minimizes the costs of the seller's breach. Here matters get complicated. The buyer's damage bill is minimized when the obligation to cover is assigned to the party having the lowest cover costs. If the seller breaches, either the buyer can cover by obtaining substitute goods or the seller can deliver or itself arrange for cover on the buyer's behalf. Denying the right to specific performance requires the buyer to cover; specific performance forces the seller to deliver or arrange for cover. Where goods are unique, there are no substitutes, and the buyer's cover costs therefore are infinite. And in general the seller's activities typically give it a cost advantage at delivery or arranging for substitute goods. Thus, whether goods are unique or not, the seller's cover costs usually are lower than the buyer's costs. A comparison of only resale costs therefore favors specific performance.

The case for specific performance is complicated by two other variables: bargaining costs and undercompensation.[64] A complete assessment must consider the effect of these variables on the total cost of the seller's breach. Requiring the buyer to cover and recover damages avoids costs associated with the seller obtaining the buyer's agreement allowing him to allocate the goods elsewhere. The seller simply breaches and a trier of facts sets the buyer's damages; no agreement need be reached with the buyer. Because specific performance gives the buyer a right to insist on delivery of the goods, the seller has to bargain with the buyer to avoid delivering the goods. The seller can purchase the right only from the buyer, and the buyer can agree only with the seller not to insist on the seller's delivery. Thus, specific performance creates a bilateral monopoly, and a bilateral monopoly generates bargaining costs. Specific performance therefore produces bargaining costs and a damages

---

[63] See Mitchell-Huntley Cotton Co., Inc. v. Waldrep, 377 F. Supp. 1215 (N.D. Ala. 1974).

[64] Economic analyses of specific performance have considered both variables, reaching different conclusions. See Anthony T. Kronman, *Specific Performance*, 45 U. Chi. L. Rev. 351 (1978); Richard A. Posner, Economic Analysis of Law 145-46 (5th ed. 1998); Alan Schwartz, *The Case for Specific Performance*, 89 Yale L. J. 271 (1979).

remedy produces none. At the same time, a damages remedy creates a risk of undercompensation and specific performance creates none. (If damages threaten to overcompensate the buyer, the seller simply will perform.) Damages remedies require assessment of the price of reasonable cover and the cost of arranging for it. Both assessments present a risk that the trier of fact will fix damages at less than the amount of the buyer's costs resulting from the seller's breach. Forcing the seller to perform relieves a trier of fact of having to set damages for nondelivery. Specific performance therefore eliminates the risk of setting damages too low. Thus, bargaining costs favor damages remedies while the risk of undercompensation favors specific performance.

The case for or against specific performance turns on estimates of the relative size of bargaining costs and risk of undercompensation. These estimates are speculative and reasonable people can disagree over their magnitude. The disagreement is reflected among legal systems. The common law and § 2-716 implicitly presume that bargaining costs associated with specific performance exceed the risk of undercompensation generated by damages. Accordingly, both restrict the availability of specific performance. Most other legal systems presume that the risk of undercompensation associated with damages exceed bargaining costs generated by specific performance. They make specific performance regularly available, with some slight variations.[65] As a practical matter, the difference in legal rule does not usually make a difference in use of the remedy. This is because obtaining an order of specific performance, even when possible, takes time, and delay often results in damages which are difficult to prove or otherwise nonrecoverable. Thus, specific performance often increases the risk of undercompensation over a damages remedy. Most buyers therefore will prefer to cover and recover damages even in legal systems in which specific performance is available for the asking. The little anecdotal data

---

[65] See, e.g., Barry Nicholas, French Law of Contract 211-13 (1982); Denis Tallon, *Remedies: The French Report*, Contract Law Today 269 (D. Harris & D. Tallon eds. 1988) (France); Treitel, supra note 49, at 51 (1988) (Germany); Deborah E. Townsend, *The Foreign Economic Law of the People's Republic of China: A New Approach to Remedies*, 24 Stan. J. Int'l L. 479, 485 (1988) (China). For a description of differences among remedial regimes, see Walt, supra note 59, at 230-31.

available confirms as much.[66]

Still, this does not mean that the availability of specific performance makes no difference. It might. At least two testable implications could determine whether the unrestricted availability of specific performance matters. One implication concerns the frequency with which specific performance is requested. If buyers' prefer damages over specific performance, the availability of specific performance makes no difference. Thus, we would expect the rate at which it is requested to be the same in all legal systems.[67] Any difference among rates is consistent with remedial choice making a difference. Another implication concerns the pricing of sales contracts. If specific performance increases bargaining costs more than damages remedies increase the risk of undercompensation, the difference should be reflected in the contract price for the same sort of goods. Thus, holding other contract terms constant, the contract price in legal systems which make specific performance regularly available should be higher than the contract price in legal systems where it is an extraordinary remedy. Both implications, although difficult to test, show that the choice of remedy might make a difference.

Revised § 2-716(1) enforces provisions calling for specific performance in contracts between merchants. The court "may" enforce their choice of remedy. Goods need not be unique or cover costs high. (Revised § 2-716(1) does not allow specific enforcement of an obligation to pay money; to recover the price, the separate requirements for a price action must be satisfied.) By allowing merchant parties to contract for specific relief, the Revision in effect treats money damages as a default term. That is, damages remedies are available unless merchant parties agree otherwise. Where a contract calls for specific relief, the potential post-breach bargaining costs of "buying" the right not to deliver are avoided. The costs of negotiating for the right instead are incurred ex ante, as part of the negotiating for the sale contract. At the same time, a

---

[66] See N. Horn, H. Kotz & H. Leser, German Private and Commercial Law: An Introduction 109 (1982); G.H. Treitel, Remedies for Breach of Contract: A Comparative Account 53 (1988); John O. Honnold, Uniform Law for International Sales Under the 1980 United Nations Convention for the International Sale of Goods 286 (3d ed..1999).

[67] See Alan Schwartz, *The Myth that Promisees Prefer Supracompensatory Remedies: An Analysis of Contracting for Damage Measures*, 100 Yale L. J. 369, 389 (1990).

provision calling for specific relief signals that money damages present a significant risk of undercompensation. Such a term indicates that the parties are pricing the risk of undercompensation and finding that any increase in post-breach bargaining costs is justified. Thus, Revised § 2-716(1) specifically enforces these contracts when ex post bargaining costs are zero and the risk of undercompensation accompanying damages remedies likely to be high.

Damages remedies might be an inefficient default term, depending on the comparative size of bargaining costs and undercompensation risk. However, by allowing merchant parties to contract for specific relief, Revised § 2-716(1) allows them to select an efficient remedy for their contract. At most merchant parties incur a transaction cost in doing so. In this respect the Revised § 2-716(1) improves on present § 2-716(1).

### B. Under the CISG

### 1. The Routine Availability of Specific Relief

The CISG's provision for specific relief is somewhat tricky. In general, the CISG gives injured contracting parties a broad right to contractual performance. The seller can require the buyer to pay the contract price, and the buyer can require the seller to perform according to the contract. Neither need obtain damages or any other form of substitutional relief. The CISG's provision of specific relief is broad in three respects. First, the injured seller or buyer can elect between requiring performance and recovering damages. Article 46(1) provides that "[t]he buyer may require performance by the seller...unless the buyer has resorted to a remedy which is inconsistent with this requirement." Article 62, Article 46(1)'s counterpart, provides the same for the seller. Under Article 46 and 62, a court lacks the discretion to refuse the buyer or seller's request for specific relief. Second, the scope of the right to specific relief is broad. The breaching party can be forced to perform "his obligations," which includes all of the obligations under the contract. Thus, the breaching party can be required to abide by the terms of the contract, not just the obligation to deliver the goods or pay the contract price. Third, the restrictions on the availability of specific relief under Articles 46 and 62 are very limited. In fact, there is only one restriction: the injured party cannot have invoked a remedy "inconsistent" with obtaining specific relief. Such inconsistent remedies include avoiding the contract, reducing the contract price under Article 50, and securing substitute performance and recovering damages under Article 76. There is therefore no requirement that the injured party mitigate its damages by obtaining substitute performance. Other provisions in the CISG support this conclusion. Article 77 requires mitigation, but by its terms it applies only to "damages." That is, if the nonbreaching party fails to undertake measures to reduce its loss from breach, Article 77 allows the breaching party to "claim a reduction in the damages...." Because specific relief under Article 46(1) and 62 are not "damages," Article 77's requirement of mitigation therefore does not apply. Further support for Article 77's irrelevance to specific relief is found in Articles 45 and 61. Both Articles expressly distinguish between "damages" and "rights" provided by Article 46 and 62. Extending a mitigation requirement to specific relief is inconsistent with the CISG's careful distinction between substitutional relief ("damages") and other nonsubstitutional relief ("rights"). Relevant diplomatic history also supports the inapplicability of mitigation to the availability of specific relief.[68] Thus, as long as the injured party has not resorted to an inconsistent remedy, specific relief is freely available under the CISG.

### 2. Article 28's Restriction on Specific Relief

A complication comes in a limitation on specific relief imposed by Article 28. Article 28 provides as follows:

> If, in accordance with the provisions of this Convention, one party is entitled to require performance of any obligation by the other party, a court is not bound to enter a judgment for specific performance unless the court would do so under its own law in respect of similar contracts of sale not governed by this Convention.[69]

In other words, the forum court is not required to order specific relief, otherwise available under the CISG, unless it *would* order specific relief of a similar contract governed by its own law. The limitation is a result of a compromise between civil law countries, which routinely make the relief available, and common law countries, which consider the remedy extraordinary. Thus, Article 28 requires a court to engage in a two-step inquiry. First, it must determine whether specific relief sought is

---

[68] See supra note 59, at 215-16.

[69] The English version of Article 28 refers expressly only to "specific performance;" it does not provide the same for a seller's action for the price. It might therefore be thought that the Article therefore states a limitation only on the buyer's right to obtain performance from the seller. However, there is no principled reason why Article 28 should be limited to only one sort of specific relief.

available to a party under the CISG. Second, the court must determine whether it would order specific relief for similar sales contracts otherwise governed by its own law. The second inquiry is a counterfactual one-- what would the court do if it were providing a remedy under its own law?--and its terms are imprecise. This is what makes Article 28's limitation difficult to determine.

Two obviously key phrases in Article 28 are vague and require clarification: "its own law" and "similar contracts of sale not governed by this Convention." As to "its own law," the phrase probably refers to the substantive domestic law of the forum. For example, suppose the forum is a state court in New York and the sales contract governed by the CISG is between a United States seller and a German buyer. Suppose too that German domestic law would grant specific relief but that New York state law would not. The seller seeks the price from the buyer. New York state's "own law" includes its conflict of law rules, and these rules might lead to the application of the domestic law of Germany. If so, Article 28 would require the state court to order specific relief. If New York's "own law" referred only to its substantive domestic law, Article 28 would not require the court to allow the seller to recover the price from the buyer under Article 2 of the UCC. A defensible reading of "its own law" in Article 28 interprets the phrase to refer to the substantive domestic law of the forum court. In the example, the New York court therefore would have to determine whether the seller would have an action for the price under § 2-709(1) in a "similar contract" governed by Article 2 of the UCC.

"Similar contracts of sale not governed by this Convention" is more difficult to interpret. The phrase refers to contracts governed by substantive domestic law that share some of the same relevant features as a contract governed by the CISG. Put simply, the comparison is between a domestic sales contract having features relevantly similar to those of international sales contracts governed by the CISG. Of course, all sorts of different sales contracts are governed by domestic law and the CISG. There is no indelible set of features either sort of contract need possess, so some generalizations are needed. In general, we believe that international sales occur between geographically removed parties buying and selling goods in geographically distant markets. Otherwise, each party would transact with a domestic partner, and the sales contract would be governed by domestic law, not the CISG. Again, this is a rough generalization, but we think it holds. If so, determining the relevant markets in which to cover or resell is difficult, resale and cover themselves are costly, and the determination of damages risks error resulting in undercompensation. Thus, "similar" domestic sales contracts are contracts where proving the relevant resale or cover markets is hard, resale or cover costs high, and the risk of undercompensation serious. Article 28 therefore requires the forum court to order specific relief when it would do so under domestic law with domestic contracts having these features.

Where applicable domestic law is Article 2 of the UCC, specific relief very often will be available under the CISG. This is because the domestic sales contracts which are similar to international sales contracts often will call for specific relief under the UCC. Consider first the seller's right to recover the contract price under Article 62. Under § 2-709(1)(b), an action for the price is available when resale by the seller at a reasonable price is infeasible. When goods are sold domestically in thin markets, prices are dispersed and resale at a "reasonable" price is uncertain. Resale by the seller might fetch a significantly enhanced or depressed price. If so, a price action is available under § 2-709(1)(b). Contracts for goods sold in thin domestic markets are "similar" to some typical international sales contracts, where sellers and buyers sporadically enter the relevant market. Thus, because a forum court in the United States would allow recovery of the contract price in the relevant domestic sales contract governed by Article 2, it would be required to do so under Article 28 in contracts governed by the CISG.[70] Article 28 therefore would not limit the seller's right to the price under Article 62. The same argument applies to the buyer's right to specific performance under Article 46 of the CISG. According to § 2-716(1), specific performance may be ordered in the "proper circumstances." Where buyers and sellers are at a distance, markets can be thin, so that

---

[70] Early experience with a price action under Article 62 of the CISG is inconclusive. In particular, the few cases decided so far make it hard to tell how much attention, if any, tribunals are paying to Article 28's apparent limitation. The cases appear to allow recovery under Article 62 without considering Article 28 at all. See, e.g., Morales y/o Son Export, S.A. de C.V. v. Nez Marketing, Compromex, Comision para la Proteccion del Comercio Exterior de Mexico (Mexico), 2 UNILEX E.1993-13 (M.J. Bonell ed.); Tribunal of Int'l Commercial Arbitration, Russian Federation Chamber of Commerce 243/93, 1 UNILEX D.1994-8.1 (M.J. Bonell ed.); ICC Court of Arbitration-Paris, 7197/1992, 1 UNILEX D. 1992-2 (M.J. Bonell ed.). This may be for one of two reasons: either the domestic law of the forum makes a price action freely available, so that Article 28 requires a court to allow recovery of the contract price, or the tribunals are simply ignoring Article 28 and giving effect to Article 62. The case results are consistent with both possibilities.

obtaining substitute goods is difficult. The high cover costs in *Kaiser* or *Mitchell-Huntley Cotton Co. v. Waldrep, Inc.*[71] that satisfied the "other proper circumstances" clause of § 2-716(1) therefore also are present in typical international sales contracts. Because the majority of courts in the United States would order specific performance under § 2-716(1) when cover is costly, these courts are required to do the same under Article 28 with contracts governed by the CISG. Hence Article 28 also does not limit the buyer's right to specific performance under Article 46(1).

## IV. Contractually Stipulated Remedies

### A. Liquidated Damages

The remedies provided by the UCC are default terms. They set the compensation available to the injured party unless the contracting parties set other terms of compensation. The UCC permits the parties to supply their own damages at the time of contracting, thereby displacing UCC-supplied remedies. A risk of judicial error in computing damages, avoidance or reduction in litigation costs, signaling one's reliability as a contracting partner, recovery of elements of damages not otherwise recoverable, and possibly attitudes toward the consequences of breach are among the reasons parties might provide their own damages. They can do so by including a liquidated damages clause in the contract. The ability to set remedies contractually is consistent with the UCC because most of its provisions only set default rules which can be varied by agreement.[72] However, unlike other terms in a contract, the UCC regulates liquidated damages clauses through judicial scrutiny of them. Section 2-718(1) provides that damages may be liquidated by agreement "but only at an amount which is reasonable in the light of the anticipated or actual harm caused by the breach, the difficulties of proof of loss, and the inconvenience or nonfeasibility of otherwise obtaining an adequate remedy. A term fixing unreasonably large liquidated damages is void as a remedy." Courts therefore must vet a damages clause, describing it as "liquidated" if it is enforceable and as a "penalty" if unenforceable. The descriptions are conclusions reached by applying the standards set by § 2-718(1).

---

[71] 377 F. Supp. 1215 (N.D. Ala. 1974); cf. Magellan International Corp. v. Salzgitter Handel GmbH, 76 F. Supp.2d 919, 926 (N.D. Il. 1999)..

[72] See § 1-102(3) ("The effect of provisions of this Act may be varied by agreement...except that the obligations of good faith, diligence, reasonablenss and care may not be disclaimed by agreement....").

The common law test for enforceability generally is strict: a liquidated damages clause is enforceable only if stipulated damages bear a reasonable relation to the actual damages resulting from breach. Section 2-718(1)'s principal test is disjunctive and therefore more forgiving. Basically, a damages clause is enforceable if the stipulated damages either bear a reasonable relation to the anticipated or actual damages.[73] The first clause states an ex ante test: stipulated damages must be reasonable in light of the contracting parties available information at the time of contracting. The second clause states an ex post test: stipulated damages must be reasonable in light of the damages that actually resulted from breach. Stipulated damages which exceed (or fall short) anticipated or actual damages are unreasonable. A liquidated damages clause is enforceable if either the ex ante or the ex post test is satisfied. Since § 2-718(1) incorporates two different tests,   four different outcomes are possible: stipulated damages which are both ex ante and ex post reasonable, both ex ante and ex post unreasonable, ex ante unreasonable but ex post reasonable, and ex ante reasonable and ex post unreasonable. The first two possibilities are unimportant and can be ignored.   As to the second possibility, ex ante and ex post unreasonableness is strong evidence of the presence of procedural and substantive unconscionability. There is no need for courts to determine whether the damages clause works a penalty. The first possibility can be ignored for the same reason.   This is because ex ante and ex post reasonableness is strong evidence that the stipulated damages are procedurally and substantively conscionable. Thus, again, § 2-718(1) is superfluous. The section therefore only is needed when ex ante and ex post reasonableness come apart, as they do in the third and fourth possibilities.

We believe that liquidated damages clauses should not be judicially regulated by § 2-718(1). Courts, in our view, should not inquire into whether they operate as liquidated damages or penalties. The reason concerns the limitations of judicial competence in doing so, familiar from previous Chapters. To see this, consider first the determination of ex ante reasonableness. Contracting parties allocate all sorts of risks among themselves through the use of terms setting delivery, price, warranty and

---

[73] See Stock Shop, Inc. v. Bozell & Jacobs, Inc., 481 N.Y.S.2d 269 (Sup. Ct. 1984). Revised § 2-718(1) preserves this test for contracts between merchants. In contracts between a merchant and consumer, it adds the requirement that proof of loss be difficult and an adequate remedy be otherwise inconenient or infeasible.

damage exclusions. Courts do not vet these terms to see whether they are reasonable in light of the information available to the parties at the time of contracting.[74] The reasonable assumption here is that the parties are better able to make use of the information than a court to allocate the relevant risks. Since stipulated damages clauses allocate another risk (the risk that stipulated damages might be above or below actual damages in the event of breach), the same assumption operates. There simply is no good reason for supposing that courts have an advantage at allocating risks ex ante over the contracting parties. Thus, courts seldom will be able to improve on the contracting parties' stipulation of damages through an inquiry into the ex ante reasonableness of the stipulation.

Something similar is also true with the inquiry into ex post reasonableness. Ex post reasonableness requires that a court have all the information about the injured parties' damages and can assess it without error. Both the information and absence of error are needed to determine the actual damages resulting from breach. However, some elements of damages depend on unverifiable variables. Information about nonpecuniary losses, production costs, market demand and consequential damages sometimes is difficult to produce in order to convince the court. A court unconvinced by the evidence produced by the injured party might find actual damages to be less than they in fact are. The injured party therefore incurs a risk of undercompensation, even when a court takes into account § 2-718(1)'s requirement that difficulties of proof be considered. The ex post test creates a risk that the parties sought to avoid by opting-out of judicial determinations of damages. Perhaps for this reason, Article 2A of the UCC eliminates the ex post test of reasonableness for liquidated damages clauses in personal property leases.[75]

Case law shows that courts sometimes themselves doubt the judicial competence to apply the ex post test. One way to understand the treatment of "take or pay" clauses by a number of courts is as a refusal to consider unverifiable variables bearing on actual damages.[76] A "take or pay" clause requires the buyer to accept the entire quantity contracted for at the contract price or pay for a stipulated minimum quantity at the

---

[74] See Alan Schwartz, supra note 66, at 384.

[75] See 2A § 2-504(1); see also 2A § 2-504.

[76] See, e.g., Willisten Basin Interstate Pipeline Co. v. F.E.R.C., 931 F.2d 948 (D.C. Cir. 1991).

unit price. The clause is useful to the seller in part because it avoids the need to prove damages using market measures after the buyer's breach. The question faced by courts is whether "take or pay" clauses are liquidated damages clauses or part of the buyer's obligations of performance under the contract. If the former, § 2-718(1) regulates their enforceability; if the latter, it does not. By fashioning the clause as part of the buyer's performance obligations, judicial estimates of the seller's often-unverifiable variable costs and profit on the entire contract are avoided. The court does not have to exceed its judicial competence in determining whether the "take or pay" clause is unenforceable as a penalty. This might explain why courts often characterize the clause as a part of the buyer's performance obligation, not a party-provided remedy for nonperformance.

Section 2-718(1)'s ex ante and ex post tests in practice produce mischief. *Lee Oldsmobile, Inc. v. Kaiden*[77] applied an ex ante test to strike down a liquidated damages clause allowing an automobile dealer to retain a breaching buyer's $5000 deposit. The court found that the dealer's actual damages of $5080.07 were capable of accurate estimation at the time of contracting, and thus deemed the damages clause a penalty. The finding is mistaken. The dealer introduced evidence about the costs of reselling the car purchased by the buyer, such as sales commissions and interest on the car. These costs could vary with the time it took to sell the car, and the dealer might not have been able to estimate that time in advance. In the circumstances an accurate estimation of damages ex ante might be difficult. A provision giving the dealer the right to retain the buyer's $5000 deposit substitutes for actual losses which are difficult to prove. The *Lee Oldsmobile* court found no difficulty in an ex ante estimation because it implicitly considers the dealer's actual costs, an ex post inquiry. *Kvassay v. Murray*[78] is a case in which the ex post test goes wrong. There the court remanded the case to the trial court to determine the validity of the seller's liquidated damages clause. The court required that the profits the seller actually lost as a result of the buyer's breach be established. In doing so it noted that the seller had failed to prove its lost profits or its production costs. The seller's failure to provide the proof is understandable. Not having produced the product sold before, the seller might well not have enough evidence of production costs to convince a trier of fact. If so, a liquidated damages clause could serve as

---

[77] 363 A.2d 270 (Md. Ct. Spec. App. 1976).

[78] 808 P.2d 896 (Kan. Ct. App. 1991).

a substitute for actual damages which are themselves costly to prove. The *Kvassay* court's insistence on satisfaction of the ex post test defeats the utility of a liquidated damages clause.

Our argument against judicial regulation of liquidated damages clauses is incomplete. It also must consider the effects these clauses have on the contracting parties' behavior. The probability of breach obviously can be affected by the contracting parties. If damages are set by the parties above actual damages, a party can gain from the other party's breach. (If damages are set below actual damages, the party gains from its own breach.) At a minimum, a party benefitting from the other party's breach has no incentive to take precautions against its occurrence. Thus, liquidated damages clauses can generate wasteful opportunistic behavior in which parties try to induce breach in order to benefit.[79]

Although such opportunistic behavior is possible, we do not think it is a serious prospect. For one thing, there are relatively few occasions in which one contracting party's breach can be induced by the other party's behavior. Each party's performance usually depends only on variables within its control. Where performance requires the other's cooperation, failure to give it itself amounts to a breach. Two other considerations suggest that opportunistic behavior here is not a serious prospect. First, since such behavior when possible can be expected, the contracting parties contract with the contingency in mind. The contract therefore reflects the possibility, either in price or through use of extracontractual devices to control the contingency. Second, opportunistic behavior is costly to detect ex post, and the limited competence of courts to assess ex post reasonableness applies to determinations that opportunism is present. If courts are sometimes comparatively bad at guaging the reasonableness of actual damages, there is no reason to believe that they are good at detecting opportunism over the course of the contract. Our assessment that the case against judicial regulation is further supported by a datum about comparative law. The German Commercial Code enforces all liquidated damages clauses between merchants.[80] And although civil law systems generally allow some judicial scrutiny of such

---

[79] See Timothy J. Muris, *Opportunistic Behavior and the Law of Contracts*, 65 Minn. L. Rev. 521 (1981).

[80] German Commercial Code § 348 (M. Peltzer, J. Doyle & M. Allen eds., 3d rev. ed. 1995) ("A contractual penalty promised by a merchant in the course of his business cannot be reduced under the provisions of § 343 of the Civil Code.").

clauses, the level of scrutiny is less than under § 2-718.[81] Both treatments are consistent with finding minimal the prospect of opportunistic behavior in response to liquidated damages clauses.

## B. Remedy Limitations and Damage Exclusions

Since the UCC provides a set of remedies and recoverable damages as default terms, both can be altered by the parties' agreement. A remedy limitation is a term in the agreement which restricts access to UCC-supplied remedies or substitutes another remedy for them. If the limitation also excludes resort to other remedies, it is an exclusive remedy limitation. Section 2-719(1) allows the parties to provide for remedy limitations of both sorts. The most common sort of remedy limitation is one which gives the seller the exclusive right to repair or replace nonconforming goods. By restricting the buyer's remedies to repair or replacement, the buyer cannot cancel the contract or recover damages for the nonconformity. A damage exclusion is a term which limits or excludes liability for particular types of loss resulting from breach. Section 2-719(3), for example, allows consequential damages to be limited or excluded. Damage exclusions very often exclude the recovery of both consequential and incidental damages. Because remedy limitations restrict relief available to the nonbreaching party while damage exclusions restrict the sort of loss for which a breaching party is liable, they are distinct contract terms.

### 1. Allocating Risks of Nonconformity

Both remedy limitations and damage exclusions can be useful devices for allocating risk. Remedy limitations operate to liquidate damages, fixing the breaching party's liability. By fixing liability, the risk of error in judicial determination of damages is avoided. For example, an exclusive remedy of repair or replacement sets a limit on the seller's liability. If the seller repairs or replaces the good, a court is prevented from awarding damages to the buyer from the seller's breach. Since judicial determination of damages is avoided, the risk (and cost) of an incorrect assessment of damages also is avoided. Damage exclusions allocate the risk of certain sorts of damages between the seller and buyer. By excluding liability of the breaching party for particular sorts of damages, the excluded risk is allocated to the nonbreaching party. For

---

[81] For a description of the differences between common and civil law systems' regulation of liquidated damages clauses, see Ugo Mattei, *The Comparative Law and Economics of Penalty Clauses in Contracts*, 43 Am. J. Comp. L. 427 (1995).

instance, a damage exclusion clause making the seller not liable for consequential damages resulting from its breach places the risk of consequential damages on the buyer. This sometimes makes good sense where the buyer has a comparative advantage at reducing or eliminating the risk or impact of consequential damages. A damage exclusion clause allows the parties to shift the risk of consequential damages to reduce the expected cost of breach.

Sales contracts frequently contain warranty disclaimers, remedy limitations and damage exclusions together. The following is a prototypic example:

> SELLER DISCLAIMS ALL IMPLIED WARRANTIES OF MERCHANTABILITY AND FITNESS FOR A PARTICULAR PURPOSE AND MAKES NO WARRANTIES WHICH EXTEND BEYOND THOSE EXPRESSLY STATED HEREIN.
>
> Seller's liability arising out of warranties, representations or defects from any cause shall be limited exclusively to repairing or replacing the good.
>
> In no event will Seller be liable for consequential damages, including but not limited to loss of profits or other commercial loss, or incidental damages.

The warranty disclaimer in the first sentence allocates the risk of nonconformity in the goods between Seller and Buyer. Seller bears the risk of the goods not conforming to the express statements made. It does so by making an express warranty. Seller's disclaimer of implied warranties shifts the risk of all other nonconformities in the goods to Buyer. Buyer therefore bears the risk of nonconformities described by implied warranty, such as the failure of the goods to be fit for the ordinary purposes to which they are put. The second sentence is an exclusive remedy limitation, and fixes the extent of the seller's liability in the event of its breach. The damage exclusion in the third sentence places the risk of consequential damages resulting from Seller's breach on Buyer. These terms presumably allocate the risks of nonconformity, liability and damages between Seller and Buyer, presumably to optimally minimize costs associated with the contract.

The UCC's regulation of remedy limitations and damage exclusions is vague. Its vagueness has generated issues concerning the validity of remedy limitations and the relation between damage exclusions and invalid remedy limitations. Section 2-719(2) deems a remedy limitation invalid when it "fails of its essential purpose." If it does not satisfy this test, § 2-719(2) allows the injured party to make use of appropriate UCC remedies. The question, of course, is when a remedy limitation "fails of its essential purpose." Section 2-719(2) is completely silent on the matter, and Official Comment 1 is unhelpful. The Comment states that "it is of the very essence of a sales contract that at least minimum adequate remedies be available." The Comment's suggestion apparently is that a remedy limitation must provide basic (but unspecified) protection in the event of breach. If so, the Comment is meaningless. There is no "essence" of a contract requiring a minimum of remedial relief. Remedies are part of the total cost of administering the contract, and the contract price reflects the remedies agreed upon. Fewer effective remedies increases the loss to the nonbreaching party and therefore lowers the value of the contract to it. The nonbreaching party will pay a lower contract price. Conversely, more effective remedies increases the value of the contract to it and increases the contract price it will pay. Because the contract price is adjusted by available remedies, there are no minimum remedies. The notion has no more sense than the "just price." Revised § 2-719(2) nonetheless retains it.

Rather than asking about the essence of the contract, § 2-719(2) asks what remedies the contracting parties bargained for, taking into account the goods involved and the contracting price. The subsection requires determining the content of the bargain. In the buyer's case, for instance, it could promise to limit its remedies to repair or replacement of the goods in exchange for one of the following promises:

(P1) The seller will attempt to repair or replace nonconforming goods if it is feasible to do so.

(P2) The seller will make timely attempts to repair or replace nonconforming goods.

(P3) The seller will successfully repair or replace nonconforming goods in a timely manner.

Whether the remedy limitation fails of its essential purpose depends on which of the promises P1-P3 the buyer bargained for. It is not always clear which of these promises the buyer obtained from the seller in exchange for agreeing to limit remedies otherwise available to her. Although courts sometimes invoke a laundry list of factors ranging from the nature of the goods to the surrounding circumstances,[82] in practice

---

[82] See Myrtle Beach Pipeline Corp. v. Emerson Electric Co., 843 F. Supp. 1027 (D. S.C. 1993).

they decide the validity of a remedy limitation clause by determining the nature of the bargain. Where goods are experimental, novel or of uncertain capability, so that repair or replacement might not succeed, the remedy limitation is exchanged for merely the seller's attempt at effecting timely repair or replacement. Successful repair or replacement is not required, and the failure does not amount to a failure of essential purpose. Where the good's capabilities are predictable, timely and successful repair or replacement is required. The essential purpose of a remedy limitation fails when repair or replacement of a car or home construction kit sold to a consumer, a photoplotting system or logging equipment is unsuccessful or tardy.[83] These outcomes can be explained by consulting the promise the buyer received in exchange for agreeing to limit its remedies.

### 2. The Relation Between Damage Exclusions and Remedy Limitations

The other issue presented by § 2-719 is the relation between damage exclusions and the invalid remedy limitations. Suppose that a remedy limitation fails of its essential purpose and is therefore invalid. Section 2-719(2) allows the injured party to resort to remedies provided by the UCC. The issue is whether the invalidity of the remedy limitation renders the damage exclusion also invalid. By its terms, § 2-719(3) invalidates the exclusion if it is unconscionable. If unconscionable, the damage exclusion, as with any term, is invalid whether or not the remedy limitation also is invalid. The fighting issue, unaddressed by § 2-719, is whether the exclusion, even if conscionable, is invalidated by the invalidity of the remedy limitation. Three different positions that can be taken on the matter. One position is that the damage exclusion is dependent on the remedy limitation, so that if the limitation is invalid the exclusion is too. Early case law for the most part took this view.[84] A second position is that the damage exclusion and remedy limitation are independent of each other. The exclusion is invalid only if unconscionable. Most recent case law has adopted this position.[85] The third position is that the parties' bargain determines whether the

[83] See Bishop Logging Co. v. John Deere Industrial Equipment Co., 455 S.E.2d 183 (S.C. Ct. App. 1995).

[84] See Murray v. Holiday Rambler, Inc., 265 N.W.2d 513 (Wisc. 1978).

[85] See, e.g., Rheem Manufacturing Co. v. Phelps Heating & Air Conditioning, Inc., 726 N.E.2d 941 (Ind. 2001).

invalidity of the remedy limitation invalidates the damage exclusion. The parties' agreement, not per se rules, determines whether the exclusion is dependent or independent of the remedy limitation.

We think that the third position, although only sporadically reflected in case law,[86] has a lot going for it. As with deciding when a remedy limitation fails of its essential purpose, the contracting parties' exchange of promises needs to be determined. Otherwise, there is no nonarbitrary way of setting the relation between the remedy limitation and damage exclusion. A court has to construct the bargain to determine the promises exchanged by the parties. For example, assume that the sales contract contains an exclusive remedy limitation clause and a damage exclusion clause excluding the seller's liability for consequential damages from its breach. Assume also that the buyer's remedies are restricted to successful and timely repair or replacement of nonconforming goods by the seller. The seller here is promising to repair or replace nonconforming goods. In exchange for the seller's promise the buyer could have made either of the following two promises:

(P1) I will bear the risk of consequential damages arising from tender of nonconforming goods *only if* you succeed in repairing or replacing them.

(P2) I will bear the risk of consequential damages arising from tender of nonconforming goods *whether or not* you succeed in repairing or replacing them.

There is no reason to believe that buyers always make promise P1 rather than P2, or vice versa. Buyers having a comparative advantage at reducing the risk or impact of consequential damages might well make promises of the sort in P2. If the buyer makes the first promise, P1, the buyer is agreeing to the limitation clause and damage exclusion on condition that the seller succeeds in fixing the nonconformity in a timely manner. Thus, the seller's failure to do so invalidates the damage exclusion clause. If the second promise is made, P2, the buyer is not exchanging the damage exclusion for the remedy limitation. It is agreeing to bear the risk of consequential damages even if the seller fails to fix the goods. The damage exclusion is independent of the remedy

---

[86] See Cooley v. Big Horn Harverstore Systems, Inc., 813 P.2d 736 (Colo. 1991).

limitation.[87] Thus, the seller's failure to fix the goods does not invalidate it.

The other two possible approaches are weak. The first approach simply assumes that the damage exclusion always depends on the remedy limitation. It does so by assuming that the buyer always would condition its promise to restrict its recoverable damages on the seller's repair or replacement of nonconforming goods. In *Koehring Co. v. A.P.I., Inc.*[88] the court simply asserts that "the buyer, when it entered into the contract, did not anticipate that the sole remedy available to it would be rendered a nullity, thus causing additional damages." The *Adams v. J.I. Case Co.*[89] court makes the same assertion when it says that the buyer "could not have made [its] bargain and purchase with knowledge that [the seller] may be...wilfully dilatory or careless in making good [its] warranty in the event of its breach." Both assumptions are unsupported by evidence about the particular buyers in question. The second approach, although also weak, has something going for it: statutory language. Section 2-719(3) expressly invalidates exclusions of consequential damages if they are unconscionable. It does not hinge the invalidity of the exclusion on the invalidity of the limitation. The subsection seemingly therefore tests the invalidity of an exclusion clause independently of the invalidity of a remedy limitation. However, because both remedy limitations and damage exclusions are terms provided by the parties, the relation between them also should be tested by the parties' bargain. Thus, even if the exclusion is conscionable, the parties might intend that the invalidity of a remedy limitation also invalidate the damage exclusion. Since the second approach treats the validity of the exclusion as turning only on its unconscionability, not the parties' bargain, it is defective.

## C. The CISG: Liquidated Damages, Remedy Limitations, and Damage Exclusions

The CISG does not directly provide for liquidated damages, remedy limitations or damage exclusions. It instead does so indirectly, by allowing the parties to avoid application of its remedial provisions. Articles 74 through 77 describe damage measures that apply to measure

---

[87] See, e.g., Canal Electric Co. v. Westinghouse Electric Co., 973 F.2d 988, 997 (1st Cir. 1992).

[88] 369 F. Supp. 882 (E.D. Mich. 1974).

[89] 261 N.E.2d 1 (Ill. Ct. App. 1970).

the loss resulting from breach. These Articles are default rules only, however. This is because contracting parties can opt-out of them under Article 6, fixing damages for themselves in advance by use of a liquidated damages clause. Article 6 allows the parties to derogate from most of the CISG's provisions, including its damage measures. Providing for liquidated damages works to exclude the CISG's damages measures, substituting damages set by the parties. Remedy limitations have the same effect. Similarly, Article 74 allows the recovery of consequential damages.[90] Article 6 allows the parties to provide for a damages exclusion, which excludes recovery of these damages under Article 74.

The regulation of liquidated damages, remedy limitations and damage exclusions is not addressed by the CISG. It is left instead to applicable domestic law. The CISG simply allows parties to opt-out of its terms and allocate the risks of liability and damages for themselves. However, it says nothing about the validity of the terms set by the parties. Because regulation of liquidated damages, remedy limitation and damage exclusions is unaddressed, the principle of issue-displacement we have invoked elsewhere leaves the matter to applicable domestic law. The CISG considers such regulation a matter of "validity," left to domestic law under Article 4(a). Enforcement of liquidated damages clauses is an example.[91] Whether stipulated damages are enforced as liquidated damages or not enforced as a penalty depends on whether and how applicable domestic law recognizes the doctrine of penalties. In general, legal systems take one of three approaches to stipulated damages.[92] Some systems enforce stipulated damages whether or not they are supercompensatory. Others enforce supercompensatory stipulated damages as long as the compensation is not "manifestly excessive." A third sort of legal system enforces them only if they are compensatory. The forum's conflict of laws rules, by selecting applicable law,

---

[90] See Article 74 ("Such damages may not exceed the loss which the party in breach foresaw or ought to have foreseen at the time of the conclusion of the contract...").

[91] See Commentary on the Draft Convention on Contracts for the International Sale of Goods, Prepared by the Secretariat, Doc. a/CONF.97/5 (1979), Documentary History of the Uniform Law for International Sales 428 (J. O. Honnold ed. 1989) (Article 42, para. 10).

[92] See Ugo Mattei, *Comparative Law and Economics: Penalty Clauses*, 43 Am. J. Comp. L. 427 (1995); Rudolph B. Schlesinger et al., Comparative Law: Cases, Text, Materials 671-79 (5th ed. 1988).

determines which doctrine of penalties regulates the sales contract. For example, suppose a seller and buyer, both merchants, have entered into a sales contract governed by the CISG. The contract was negotiated in the United States and France, and called for delivery of goods in Germany. Suppose too that the contract contained stipulated a fixed sum in damages due in the event of breach. If the forum selects the domestic law of Germany, the stipulated damages would enforceable whether or not it worked a penalty. If French law is applied, they are enforceable only if the damages are not considered "excessive."[93] And if United States domestic law is selected, the stipulated damages are enforceable only if not considered a penalty. Under the CISG enforcement of liquidated damages therefore turns on applicable domestic law.

Early experience with the CISG confirms the conclusion. *ICC Court of Arbitration--Paris, 7197/1992*[94] involved a sales contract governed by the CISG which contained a liquidated damages and arbitration clause. The liquidated damages clause limited damages to X percent of the contract price if either party breached. The contract called for delivery of the goods at the Austria-Hungary border. Upon the buyer's breach, and without the liquidated damages clause, the seller would be entitled to recover the contract price under Article 62. If the liquidated damages clause were enforceable, Article 62 would be displaced and damages would be limited to X% of the contract price. Thus, the question was whether the contract's liquidated damages clause was enforceable. Noting that the CISG does not address liquidated damages clauses,[95] the arbitral tribunal applied Austrian law to answer the question. Austrian law apparently refuses to enforce stipulated damages when they are undercompensatory ex post. The seller therefore was entitled to recover full damages, including the contract price. There is no reason to believe that the analysis under the CISG would be any different if remedy limitations or damage exclusions were in play.

---

[93] See The French Civil Code article 1152 (J.H. Crabb trans. 1995) ("...[T]he judge, even on his own motion, may moderate or increase the penalty which had been agreed upon, if it is manifestly excessive or pitiful. Any contrary stipulation will be considered not written.").

[94] 1 UNILEX D.1992-2 (M.J. Bonell ed.).

[95] Accord Diepeveen-Drison B.V. v. Nieuenhoven Vichandel GmbH, Gerechtoshof Arnhem (Germany), 1 UNILEX D.1995-22 (M.J. Bonell ed.).

# CHAPTER 10
## RIGHTS TO GOODS: BONA FIDE PURCHASE AND RECLAMATION

### I. Good Faith Purchase Rules

One of the risks that attends a sale is the possibility that the seller does not have good title to the goods. The prototypical contest in which that risk creates a legal issue occurs when the original owner of the goods finds them in the hands of a purchaser and demands their return. The principles that determine whether the original owner or the purchaser is entitled to the goods are derived more from property concepts than from the contracts concepts that we have been discussing to this point. Those principles have been incorporated into the UCC in a way that makes the question of recovery depend on the rights of the buyer's transferor and the buyer's good faith. The CISG does not address the issue of rights to goods. Article 4 states explicitly that the CISG is not concerned with the effect that the contract may have "on the property in the goods sold."

The UCC employs the basic principle that a purchaser acquires all title that its transferor had power to transfer.[1] This is a codification of the common law doctrine of *nemo dat quod non habet*, or, one cannot give what one does not have. In the prototypical contest, the original owner has been dispossessed of goods by someone against whom the owner had a right of recovery. This right may exist because the party who obtained the goods from the owner was either a thief or someone who received the goods for a limited purpose, such as in the case of a bailee or a borrower of the goods. That party, in violation of the original owner's title, sells the goods to a third party. The *nemo dat* principle provides that the purchaser gets no better rights than the seller had. The original owner can reclaim the goods from the purchaser, just it he or she could have from the dispossessor. Similarly, we may have no difficulty allowing the original owner to recover where the goods are found in the hands of a donee or someone who has not yet parted with value. In that case, there seems little reason to favor the party in possession who gave up nothing for them as against the original owner of the goods, who was dispossessed of them without receiving any consideration.

But the issue becomes more complicated where the purchaser is a good faith purchaser (one without knowledge that the seller lacks good

---

[1] § 2-403(1).

title) who has given value for the good.[2] In that case, we are dealing with two innocents, the original owner and the purchaser, one of whom must suffer a loss. We might select any of a number of principles to resolve this contest. Under corrective justice principles, we might contend that the state should protect individuals' rights and interests in property against unconsented to interference. This principle might initially suggest that the original owner should be able to reclaim the goods. But such a principle assumes the conclusion by assuming that an original owner has "rights" in property even after the owner has been dispossessed of the good and it has been transferred to a good faith purchaser. One might with equal force claim that corrective justice principles protect the "right" of the good faith purchaser for value not to have its property subjected to an unconsented interference by requiring return of the goods to the seller. A notion of corrective justice that requires redress only against one who has acted wrongfully does not permit the original owner to reclaim the goods from one who, like a good faith purchaser, did not dispossess the original owner of the goods through some wrongful act.

Alternatively, we might adopt a principle that the loss from dispossession should be allocated to the party who was in the best position to prevent the original dispossession or who is in a superior position to insure against the loss that materializes when that dispossession occurs. Such a principle would induce that party to take relatively inexpensive measures to prevent losses, thus minimizing the costs of loss avoidance. The problem is that it can be difficult to identify the party best situated to avoid losses. Original owners could prevent some losses by taking better care of goods in their possession and checking the reputation of parties to whom they give their goods for safekeeping. Original owners may also be relatively better able to insure their goods against loss or theft, thus minimizing costs associated with those losses that do occur. On the other hand, allowing original owners to reclaim goods would induce good faith purchasers to purchase only from reputable sellers and thus to reduce the marketability of goods taken by wrongful dispossession.

Whether consciously or not, the UCC principles concerning rights to

---

[2] The expression "good faith purchaser for value" may seem redundant. But the UCC's broad definition of "purchase" to include any voluntary transaction, including a gift, § 1-201(32), requires that the "for value" clause be added if we are to restrict ourselves to "purchasers" who have parted with consideration. See § 1-202(44).

goods track a loss-minimization principle. This seems to be the best explanation for the Code's distinction among different sellers for purposes of granting or denying the original owner the right to recover goods. As we noted above, the provision that governs the contest between original owner and good faith purchaser, § 2-403, begins with the proposition that a purchaser acquires all title that its transferor had power to transfer. Thus, in the case of a thief, who has no title or void title to the stolen goods, the transferee similarly receives no title. In short, a person with void title cannot pass better title to a subsequent purchaser. As a consequence, the original owner can always recover goods from someone who traces title to the goods through a thief. Since the thief had void title, its transferee had void title, and all subsequent transferees will also have void title, since they will also receive "all title which his transferor had." The inference that one might draw from this rule is that, if the drafters of the UCC were attempting to create a loss-minimizing rule, they must have believed that it is generally easier for good faith purchasers to detect that their sellers are thieves than it is for original owners to prevent the theft from occurring in the first place. This is not an inappropriate conclusion. Even owners who take reasonable precautions are subject to theft, and stolen goods may tend to be sold outside of established markets in ways that raise suspicion about their origins. Thus, careful buyers may be able to determine with relatively little effort that the goods they are purchasing have passed through a thief. Nevertheless, many goods are not sold in such markets: used goods are frequently sold through markets in ways that make checking the origins of the goods difficult. Thus, a contrary rule would not necessarily be more costly than the theft rule adopted in the UCC.

The UCC, however, does permit exceptions to the *nemo dat* principle where it appears that the original owner was in a relatively good position to avoid the loss. These exceptions occur where the party who received the goods from the original owner did not have void title, as in the theft situation, but instead had voidable title. Voidable title suggests that the original owner consented to the original transfer of the good, but did so on a condition that, once defeated, allows the original owner to recover the goods. Even though the original owner can retrieve the goods from its transferee, however, the UCC provides that a person with voidable title may transfer *good* title to some third parties.[3] Where the original owner delivered the goods under a "transaction of purchase," which essentially means any voluntary delivery and thus excludes only a theft,

---

[3] § 2-403(1).

the "purchaser" (that is, the initial transferee) can pass good title to a subsequent purchaser as long as that subsequent purchaser (1) acts in good faith, and (2) gives value. In violation of the *nemo dat* principle, this rule allows someone with only voidable title to pass something better ("good" title) to a subsequent purchaser.

Under the current version of the UCC, the "good faith" necessary for a nonmerchant to be a "good faith purchaser" requires nothing more than "honesty in fact."[4] The test is considered to be subjective, and thus is often referred to as the test of the "pure heart and the empty head."[5] As a practical matter, however, objective standards will creep into the inquiry, as a jury will ultimately have to ask whether *anyone* could have believed the facts as the purported good faith purchaser presents them. The Proposed Revision explicitly alters the test to one that includes both "honesty in fact" and "the observance of reasonable commercial standards of fair dealing."[6] This more objective definition allows courts to deny "good faith" status a buyer either knew or should have known of the origin of the goods.[7]

The UCC's examples of the passage of good title through one with voidable title suggest that the reason for the rule lies in the relative ability of the original owner to avoid the loss. For instance, a person with voidable title includes an imposter who deceived the original owner as to his or her identity.[8] Presumably, a seller has an opportunity to determine the true identity of the person with whom it is dealing. If seller agrees to sell the goods on credit because the purchaser purports to be "William Gates," a wealthy owner of a major software company, seller has greater ability to ensure that it is dealing with that person than the subsequent buyer of the good from the imposter or one of the imposter's confederates has of confirming the good's origins. Similarly, the original owner who

---

[4] See § 1-201(19); Thorn v. Adams, 865 P.2d 417 (Or. Ct. App. 1993).

[5] See Karibian v. Paletta, 332 N.W.2d 484 (Mich. Ct. App. 1983).

[6] Proposed § 2-102(a)(19). The Proposed Revision adopts the good faith standard that Article 2 currently applies to nonmerchants. See § 2-103(1)(b).

[7] Some courts have applied an objective test even under the current version of the UCC. See, e.g., Monsanto Co. v. Walter E. Heller & Co., Inc., 449 N.E.2d 993 (Ill. App. Ct. 1983).

[8] § 2-403(1)(a).

sells a good in return for a check, rather than cash, can hold onto goods until the check clears. As a result, the original owner who releases the goods before that time cannot recover the goods when the check bounces, if the purchaser has resold the goods to a good faith purchaser for value.[9]

A similar rationale of "least cost avoider" explains the UCC's rules concerning the sale of goods that have been "entrusted." An entrusting consists of the original owner's delivery of goods to a third party and acquiescence in their retention by that party, notwithstanding that conditions are placed on that acquiescence.[10] For instance, an owner of a watch who delivers the goods to a watch repair shop in order to have the watch cleaned has "entrusted" the watch to that shop, even though delivery and acquiescence in possession were made for a limited purpose. According to the UCC, if an entrustment is made to a merchant who deals in goods of the kind that have been delivered, the merchant has the power to transfer all the rights of the entruster to a "buyer in the ordinary course of business."[11] That phrase includes any person who, in good faith and without notice that the sale to him is in violation of the ownership rights of a third party, buys in ordinary course from a person in the business of selling goods of that kind.[12] Thus, if the watch shop not only repairs watches, but also sells used watches, and an unscrupulous employee of the watch repair shop sells the watch to a buyer in the ordinary course, the original owner has no right to reclaim it from the purchaser. The original owner would, of course, have a conversion action against the watch repair shop. The owner would also be able to recover the watch from the buyer if it was clear that the watch was used and the shop only sold new watches. In that case, an entrustment would have occurred, but it would not have been made to a merchant who deals in goods of the kind that were sold to the buyer in the ordinary course.

---

[9] § 2-403(1)(b). The original owner stands in no better position if he claims that the original sale was intended as a "cash sale" or that he delivered the goods as a result of fraud, misrepresentation or some larcenous scheme perpetrated by his immediate purchaser. § 2-403(1)(c), (d).

[10] § 2-403(3).

[11] § 2-403(2). This reverses the common law rule, which held that the mere entrustment of goods to a merchant would not prevent the owner from recovering goods from a bona fide purchaser for value.

[12] See § 1-201(9). The definition explicitly excludes purchasers from pawnbrokers from the category of a buyer in the ordinary course.

Results in entrustment cases may be justified under a theory that the entruster has clothed the merchant with apparent authority, and thus is estopped from denying the merchant's right to sell the goods. But why would we want to apply such a theory, especially in light of a contrary allocation of loss in the event of a theft? Again, the underlying assumption seems to be that buyers will have a difficult time tracing the origins of the goods they purchase in these situations, at least relative to the ability of owners to ensure that they entrust their goods only to merchants of good reputation.[13] It is not clear that one could prove that claim empirically, but it seems to be a reasonable judgment that justifies a cost-minimizing rule.

Note that the merchant to whom goods have been entrusted only transfers the rights of the entruster. Thus, assume that a thief steals Smith's watch and brings it to Brown's watch store for repair. Brown sells the watch to Jones, a buyer in the ordinary course. If Smith finds the watch in the possession of Jones, he can reclaim it. Brown only transferred the rights of the entruster. In this case, the entruster was a thief who had void title. Thus, Brown could only transfer void title and Jones only received void title. As a consequence, Smith retains good title to the watch and can reclaim it from Jones.

The requirement that good faith purchasers and buyers in the ordinary course part with value in order to obtain rights under § 2-403 shows that loss minimization is not the only principle at work here. A donee from a thief or from a defalcating merchant to whom goods have been entrusted is in no better position than a good faith purchaser to question the origins of the goods they receive. Nevertheless, they must surrender the goods to the original owner. This implies that fairness concerns and the desire to avoid windfall gains and losses may trump the loss minimization principle. More troublesome is the case of the bona fide purchaser for value whose "value" consists of an executory promise to pay for the goods received from the person with voidable title. This person has given consideration for the goods sufficient to qualify as "value" under the UCC and thus to be a bona fide purchaser.[14] Thus, he or she is entitled to retain the goods as against the original owner. Nevertheless, insofar as the purchaser has not yet parted with money and

---

[13] See Heinrich v. Titus-Will Sales, Inc., 868 P.2d 169 (Wash. Ct. App. 1994).

[14] § 1-201(44).

surely has a valid defense against paying the party with voidable title the amount of the debt, he or she stands in the same position as the donee with respect to being able to avoid loss to the original owner.

## II. Seller's Right to Recover and Reclaim Goods

As a general matter, title to goods passes to the buyer at the time and place at which the seller completes his performance with respect to the physical delivery of the goods.[15] The fact that buyer has title to the goods, however, does not prevent the seller from recovering the goods should buyer fail to perform its obligation to pay for them.[16] As § 2-401(1) states, the rights of sellers and purchasers apply regardless of who has title. Although payment is generally not required until the seller has tendered delivery,[17] § 2-507(2) makes the buyer's right to retain or dispose of them "as against the seller" conditional on making payment when due. A seller may reclaim goods from a buyer who fails the make that payment. The quoted phrase, however, imposes a limitation on the seller's reclamation rights. As we have seen, a buyer of goods typically will have voidable title to them and will be able to pass good title to a good faith purchaser for value.[18] Thus, while § 2-507(2) governs the relationship between the unpaid seller and the buyer, § 2-403 governs the relationship between the unpaid seller and subsequent transferees from the buyer. Should that provision give priority to the transferee, as in the case of the good faith purchaser for value from a buyer with voidable title, nothing in § 2-507(2) gives greater rights to the seller.

There may be occasions, however, in which the seller can recover the goods or stop their delivery to the buyer even when the buyer's obligation to pay has not yet been triggered. Assume that on April 1, Smith agrees to sell walnuts to Jones. The terms of the sale require Smith to deliver the walnuts by July 1 and for Jones to make payment within 30 days after delivery. On June 15, as Smith is preparing to ship the walnuts, he obtains reliable evidence that Jones is insolvent. Insolvency for UCC purposes is not simply the common definition by which liabilities exceed assets, but includes any failure to pay debts in the ordinary course of

---

[15] § 2-401(2).

[16] The buyer's obligation to pay is stated in § 2-301.

[17] § 2-507(1).

[18] § 2-403(1).

business.[19] any formal proceedings intended to rehabilitate or liquidate
its estate.  At this point, § 2-702(1) enables Smith to refuse delivery,
except for cash, including payment of any outstanding indebtedness
between the parties.  Without the benefit of this provision, transforming
a credit transaction into a cash transaction would constitute a breach on
the seller's part.  Thus, the seller must be certain that the buyer is, in fact,
insolvent.

Assume that Smith obtains the information concerning insolvency on
July 1, after delivery of the walnuts, but prior to payment.  Smith's only
recourse other than hoping for payment is to reclaim the goods from
Jones.  Section 2-507(2) will not help here, because Jones' payment is not
yet due.[20]  Section 2-702(2), however, adds an additional, if limited,
weapon to Smith's arsenal: if Jones received the walnuts on credit while
insolvent, Smith may reclaim them on demand if he acts within ten days
after Jones has received the goods.  This ten-day limitation has no
parallel in the § 2-507(2) case where a payment has been duly demanded
but not made.

Section 2-702(2) has one additional caveat.  If Jones misrepresented
his financial status to Smith, in writing and within three months before
delivery, the ten-day limitation does not apply.  Thus, if Jones had
forwarded to Smith a fraudulent credit report or had even drafted a letter
making assurances of solvency at a time when those statements were
untrue, Smith will have a longer time in which to reclaim the walnuts
from Jones.  Note once again, however, that Smith's reclamation right
runs only against Jones.  If Jones has resold the walnuts to Brown by the
time Smith learns of the receipt while insolvent, Smith's rights against
Brown are determined by § 2-403 and Brown will be able to retain the
walnuts if she is a good faith purchaser for value.

Smith's rights to reclaim delivered goods from an insolvent buyer
might seem to entail the right to prevent the goods from reaching that
buyer in the first place.  Section 2-705 explicitly grants that right to
sellers who learn of their buyer's insolvency after they have authorized
delivery to the buyer, but prior to delivery.  A seller may stop delivery of
goods in the possession of a carrier or other bailee, such as a
warehouseman, when the seller discovers the buyer to be insolvent.

---

[19] § 1-201(23).

[20] Recall that § 2-507(2) provides that, where payment is due on delivery, the
buyer's right as against the seller is conditional on its making the payment.

Similarly, the seller may stop delivery of large shipments such as a truckload, carload, or planeload if the buyer repudiates or fails to make a payment due before delivery, or if the seller has a right to withhold or reclaim the goods. The right to stop delivery ceases when the buyer receives the goods, when a non-carrier bailee acknowledges to the buyer that the bailee holds the goods for the buyer, when a carrier provides such acknowledgment to the buyer by reshipment or as warehouseman, or when negotiable documents of title covering the goods have been negotiated to the buyer.[21]

The seller can only exercise a right of stoppage if it notifies the bailee in time to enable the bailee to prevent delivery. Thus, a seller who does not provide sufficient notice will not have any action against the bailee for making a delivery that the seller desired to stop. The bailee who receives sufficient notice, however, is obligated to hold and deliver the goods in accordance with the seller's instructions.[22] If the bailee has issued a negotiable document of title, such as a negotiable bill of lading, when picking up the goods, the bailee need not obey a notification to stop delivery until the negotiable document has been surrendered.[23] If the bailee has issued a non-negotiable document of title, the right of stoppage lies with the consignor.[24] Usually the consignor and the seller will be the same party, but where they are not, the seller who wishes to ensure that the insolvent buyer does not receive the goods will have to convince the consignor of the shipment to issue instructions to stop delivery.

While the UCC provisions concerning the seller's right to recover goods purport to cover any situation in which the buyer is insolvent, the federal Bankruptcy Code trumps state law, such as the UCC, where the buyer has actually filed for bankruptcy protection. Under the Bankruptcy Code, sellers retain some rights to recover goods, but on a more limited basis than is available through §§ 2-507, 2-702, and 2-705. Typically, the trustee in bankruptcy exercises authority over all property of the bankrupt's estate. If title to the goods has passed, as will ordinarily be the case where the buyer has obtained delivery or where the seller's obligations to deliver end with shipment of the goods, the trustee has

---

[21] § 2-705(2).

[22] § 2-705(3)(b).

[23] § 2-705(3)(c).

[24] § 2-705(3)(d).

those rights even with respect to goods for which the seller has not received payment. Section 546(c) of the Bankruptcy Code,[25] however, permits unpaid sellers to exercise common law or statutory (such as UCC) rights of reclamation where (1) the buyer has purchased the goods in the ordinary course of business; (2) the buyer received the goods while insolvent, as defined by the Bankruptcy Code; (3) the seller demands reclamation of the goods in writing; and (4) reclamation is demanded before ten days after receipt of the goods by the debtor, or if such ten-day period expires after the commencement of the filing of bankruptcy, before 20 days after receipt of the goods by the debtor.[26] Even where the seller satisfies these conditions, the court may deny reclamation by granting the seller's claim priority in the bankruptcy proceedings or securing the claim by a lien. Note that the writing requirement of § 546(c) has no parallel under § 2-507 or § 2-702. Nor does § 546(c) allow any extension of the ten-day period, as does § 2-702, where the buyer misrepresented solvency in writing. Indeed, it is not even clear that the ten-day periods of § 2-702 and § 546(c) pertain to the same period. The UCC provision requires a demand for reclamation to be made "within ten days after the receipt," while the Bankruptcy Code requires the written demand "before ten days after receipt." A literal reading of the latter would appear to give the seller one less day to act than the corresponding UCC provision.

### III. Goods-Oriented Remedies Under the CISG

The CISG does not address title concepts, and thus contains no provision that corresponds to § 2-403. Article 4(b) explicitly provides that the CISG is not concerned with the effect that the contract has on the property in the goods sold. Nevertheless, the remedies for fundamental breach by the buyer do include provisions that permit an aggrieved seller the right to reclaim goods that have been delivered. The more difficult issue is to determine the circumstances in which that right applies.

Nothing in the CISG provides an explicit distinction equivalent to that between § 2-507 and § 2-702 for buyers who have failed to make a payment when due and buyers who have received goods on credit while insolvent. Instead, the CISG grants to sellers who have performed their contracts in whole or in part a right of restitution from the other party "of

---

[25] 11 U.S.C. § 546(c).

[26] See In re Adventist Living Centers, Inc., 52 F.3d 159 (7th Cir. 1995).

whatever the first party has supplied" under the contract.[27]   Most
commentators have interpreted this provision to permit a seller to recover
goods that have been delivered to the nonpaying buyer. The Secretariat
Commentary supports this concept, as it refers to a restitutionary "return"
of what the aggrieved party provided rather than simply a right to
damages:

> Paragraph (2) authorizes either party to the contract who has
> performed in whole or in part to claim the return of whatever he
> has supplied or paid under the contract. Subject to [Article
> 82(2)], the party who makes demand for restitution must also
> make restitution of that which he has received from the other
> party. "If both parties are required to make restitution, they
> must do so concurrently," unless the parties agree otherwise.[28]

But the seller's right to return of the goods appears with those
provisions that detail the effects of avoidance of the contract.  Article
81(1) explicitly involves the consequences of avoidance, and it makes
sense to read Article 81(2) as a further itemization of those consequences.
That appears to be the intent of the Secretariat Commentary, which
introduces the discussion of Article 81(2) by stating that:

> It will often be the case that at the time the contract is
> avoided, one or both of the parties will have performed all or
> part of his obligations. Sometimes the parties can agree on a
> formula for adjusting the price to the deliveries already made.
> However, it may also occur that one or both parties desires the
> return of that which he has already supplied or paid under the
> contract.[29]

Thus, it appears that the seller has a right to recover the goods only when
the seller has the right to avoid the contract.  Recall that the right to avoid

---

[27] Art. 81(2).

[28] Commentary on the Draft Convention on Contracts for the International
Sale of Goods, Prepared by the Secretariat, Document A/CONF. 97/5 (1979),
reprinted in Diplomatic History of the Uniform Law for International Sales 447
(Article 66, para. 8) (J.O. Honnold ed. 1989) (commentary on then-Article 66,
draft counterpart to Article 81).

[29] Id.

is contingent on the existence of a fundamental breach,[30] which consists of a breach that "results in such detriment to the other party as substantially to deprive him of what he is entitled to expect under the contract."[31] This language surely entails the situation considered by § 2-507(2) of the UCC. A buyer who receives the goods but fails to make payment when due not only violates the primary duty owed by the buyer under the CISG,[32] but also deprives the seller of the primary benefit for which it entered the contract in the first instance.

A more difficult situation exists where the facts are closer to the scenario contemplated by § 2-702 and § 2-705. Assume that a French seller ships wine to an American importer on terms that allow the importer to make payment 30 days after receipt. Immediately after the importer receives the wine, the seller obtains reliable information that the importer is insolvent and was insolvent at the time of delivery. Can the seller procure the return of the wine? Since payment was not yet due, the buyer might contend that it has not committed any breach, much less a fundamental breach. This argument seems to be compelling, but for the clause in Article 25 that defines a breach in terms of a detriment to the seller that deprives him "of what he is entitled to expect" under the contract. The language of expectation implies that prospective breaches by one party may be sufficient to trigger a right of avoidance by the other party. If that is the case, then the current likelihood that an insolvent buyer will be unable subsequently to satisfy its obligation to pay for the goods should be sufficient to permit a seller to call a fundamental breach even before the time for payment has occurred. That would trigger the seller's right to avoid under Article 64 and the consequent right under Article 81 to obtain return of the goods.

None of these principles affects the rights of third parties. Should the buyer transfer the goods prior to the time that the seller exercises his right of restitution, nothing in the CISG permits the seller to pursue the goods into the hands of that purchaser. The Secretariat Commentary to Article 81 makes this clear by stating: "the right of either party to require

---

[30] Art. 64(1)(a). The seller may also declare the contract avoided if it has given the buyer an additional period of time to perform its obligations and buyer fails to perform within that time. .

[31] Art. 25.

[32] Art. 53 requires a buyer to "pay the price for the goods and take delivery of them as required by the contract and this Convention."

restitution as recognized by article 66 [draft counterpart of CISG article 81] may be thwarted by other rules which fall outside the scope of the international sale of goods."[33] These rules include the bona fide purchase rules that are derived from domestic law.

Finally, the right of the seller to reclaim goods may be affected by the ultimate bankruptcy of the buyer. Bankruptcy rules are also within the scope of "other rules" that may thwart the Article 81 right of restitution. The Secretariat Commentary recognized this possibility explicitly and thus seemed to suggest that domestic bankruptcy law could trump the CISG.[34]

---

[33] Commentary on the Draft Convention on Contracts for the International Sale of Goods, Prepared by the Secretariat, supra note 28, at 447 (Article 66, para. 10).

[34] Id.

## I. Introduction: Allocating Performance Risks

Performance of the sales contract presents the possibility that the seller might not deliver conforming goods and the buyer might not pay. The buyer might not pay, either because of dishonesty, insolvency or dissatisfaction with the goods delivered. The seller therefore does not want to relinquish control of the goods until the buyer pays the contract price. At the same time, the seller might not deliver the goods, either because of dishonesty or insolvency, or it might make a nonconforming tender. The buyer therefore does not want to pay for the goods until it has control over them. In summary, the parties face at least four sorts of risks: (1) a *nonperformance risk*: the likelihood that payment will not be forthcoming or that the goods will not be delivered; (2) *litigation risk*: the likelihood that the performing party will have to bring suit in a foreign jurisdiction when the other party fails to perform; (3) *interest rate risk*: the likelihood that interest or exchange rates will fluctuate between the time of shipment and delivery of the goods; and (4) *sovereignty risk*: the likelihood that political restrictions prevent payment or delivery of the goods. If these risks are substantial, parties might not transact at all. While these risks inhere in all sales contracts, they are particularly problematic where the parties are geographically distant from each other.

The UCC's default rules reduce all four sorts of risks associated with performance in face-to-face transactions. For instance, § 2-310(a) requires the buyer to pay at the time and place at which it is to receive the goods, and § 2-507(1) in turn requires the seller to tender the goods as a condition of the buyer's obligation to pay. Together, the two sections assure that the payment is not made before the goods are received and the goods are not received before payment is made. Thus, litigation need not proceed with the buyer without possession of the goods or the seller without the contract price.

When the transaction involves geographically distant parties, however, contracting parties may prefer to allocate performance risks differently from the UCC's default rules. For instance, a seller may be more willing to ship goods without advance payment if it has an instrument embodying the buyer's obligation to pay wholly apart from the seller's delivery of conforming goods. The buyer for its part may be more willing to make a binding commitment to pay if it has assurances that conforming goods are in transit. In short, the parties may agree to opt-out of the UCC's default rule requiring payment against receipt of the goods. A documentary sale accomplishes this objective. It is created by including in the sales contract a term calling for payment against an exchange of documents which reliably indicate that conforming goods have been shipped, rather than against inspection of the goods themselves.

Whether a documentary sale has been effected by the parties is a matter of contract interpretation. Section 2-513(3)(b) uncontroversially states that the buyer is not entitled to inspect the goods prior to payment when the contract provides for "payment against documents of title." Thus, an express term to that effect obviously creates a documentary sale. A shipment term "C.I.F." or "C. & F." also has the same effect.[1] An industry practice of paying against documents can create a documentary sale, even without express terms doing so. Beyond these indications, the question is one of contractual intent.

The simplest example of a documentary sale calls for a documentary draft. Here the seller is to be paid upon presentation of (1) a draft drawn on the buyer, and (2) accompanying documents of title, such as a bill of lading. The seller ships goods required by the contract by carrier. To do so it delivers the goods to the carrier and receives a negotiable bill of lading that describes the goods being shipped. As a negotiable document of title, the bill of lading also serves as the authorization for delivery of the goods. The carrier can only deliver them to the holder of the negotiable bill. The seller endorses the bill of lading and typically sends it through banking channels, along with a draft drawn on the buyer. The bank presents the draft together with the bill of lading to the buyer. But the buyer cannot retrieve the bill, which is necessary to take delivery of the goods from the carrier, without at the same time paying or accepting the draft. Prior to paying the draft, the buyer examines the bill and determines that the goods described in the bill conform to the goods ordered. Once the buyer has paid or accepted the draft, the bank surrenders the bill to the buyer. The buyer in turn surrenders the bill to the carrier, who then delivers the goods.

Notice how in this brief example performance and payment risks are reduced. The bank, acting as the seller's agent, does not surrender the bill of lading, which controls delivery of the goods, until the buyer has

---

[1] See §§ 2-513(3), 2-320(4), 2-320 Official Comment 12.

either paid it or accepted the draft. At the same time, the buyer does not pay the bank until it obtains control over the goods, represented by the bill that is endorsed to buyer. Thus, both the seller's and the buyer's nonperformance risks are reduced. (Of course, the goods might be nonconforming, but the description of them in the bill of lading reduces the risk of this sort of nonperformance. An inspection certificate, often required as one of the documents, reduces the risk even further.) Litigation risks are reduced for both parties: if the buyer fails to pay, the seller still controls the bill and therefore the goods, and does not have to recover them from the buyer; if the seller fails to deliver, the buyer still has the contract price and does not have to recover it from the seller. In both cases remedies need not be obtained in a foreign forum. Interest or exchange rate risks are reduced because the seller's bank does not surrender control of the bill until it is paid or the draft accepted, and the buyer does not surrender the price or accept the draft until it obtains control of the bill. As for sovereignty risk, the impact of political restrictions on payment or delivery is minimized because the exchange of payment and the documentary draft can occur in any jurisdiction.

## II. Payment Terms: Letters of Credit and Payment Risks

### A. Introduction

A documentary sale does not eliminate all payment risks, however. The buyer still may refuse or be unable to pay the contract price. For example, if the sale occurs through a documentary draft, the buyer simply may refuse to honor the draft. And if the buyer becomes obligated on the draft by accepting it,[2] it may later refuse or be unable to pay. In either event, although the seller has remedies against the buyer, pursuing them can impose uncompensated costs. Thus, the seller requires a payment mechanism that relies on the credit-worthiness of a third party to reduce the risk of nonpayment. The payment mechanism can be a guarantee or a letter of credit. If a guarantee is issued, the seller can seek payment from the guarantor if the buyer does not pay the contract price. Obtaining a guarantor that is more credit-worthy than the buyer enhances the value of the buyer's promise to pay. The trouble with a guarantee is that the guarantor is only secondarily liable to the seller: the guarantor must pay the seller only if the buyer fails to pay and the seller is entitled to payment. This means that any defenses that the buyer has to making payment are available to the guarantor. Since a trial can be required to

---

[2] See § 3-313(a); cf. § 3-409(a).

establish the existence of these defenses, during trial the seller is without the contract price.

A letter of credit does not have this drawback. Put simply, a letter of credit is a written undertaking by one person to pay a named person on that person's satisfaction of conditions, if any, stipulated in the writing. In its most basic form, the instrument involves three parties: the issuer (the party making the written undertaking), the customer or applicant (the party requesting the issuer to make the written undertaking), and the beneficiary (the party receiving payment).[3] The letter of credit is issued by the issuer to the beneficiary at the request of the customer or applicant. It provides that the issuer will pay the beneficiary upon the beneficiary's satisfaction of conditions, if any, stated in the credit. The legal relationship between the beneficiary and the applicant can vary, as can their identity. They may be a seller and buyer involved in a sales contract, contractor and owner in a construction contract, debtor and creditor, or donor and donee, respectively. The credit may even call for the issuer to deliver to the beneficiary value other than payment, such as stock certificates.[4] It also may undertake to make payment to parties other than the beneficiary, such as transferees of documents who present conforming documents. But the elementary form of the letter of credit is invariant: a written undertaking by the issuer to the beneficiary, made at the request of the applicant, to make payment to the beneficiary upon satisfaction of conditions, if any, stated in the writing.

Letters of credit may involve additional parties. The issuer can engage a party, called an adviser, to notify the beneficiary of the existence and terms of the credit.[5] Another party, called a confirmer, also may be engaged by the issuer to pay the beneficiary upon the presentation of conforming documents.[6] The same party may undertake both to advise and confirm the issuer's letter of credit. Advisers and confirmers, usually banks, often are used in international letters of credit transactions. This is because the applicant and beneficiary frequently are

---

[3] See § 5-102(a)(10); cf. §§ 5-102(a)(2), (3); cf. UCP art. 2 (1993 No. 500).

[4] See § 5-102(a)(8) ("'honor' means performance of the issuer's undertaking in the letter of credit to pay or deliver an item of value").

[5] See §§ 5-102(a)(1), 5-107(c); UCP article 5(c)(i).

[6] See §§ 5-102(a)(4), 5-107(a); UCP article 5(b).

unfamiliar with each other. Accordingly, the beneficiary might want reliable assurances about the terms of the credit as well as a known source of creditworthy payment. An adviser familiar to the beneficiary provides assurances of the genuineness of the credit and its terms. A local confirmer, trusted by the beneficiary, is a convenient source at which to present documents and obtain payment. Another advantage is that having a local confirmer avoids any restrictions in a foreign jurisdiction that might impede payment under the credit. Since a sales contract calling for payment by letter of credit does not require engagement of an adviser or confirmer, international sales contracts often expressly include terms calling for them.

The predominant use of letters of credit in sales contracts is as a payment mechanism. Under a commercial or documentary letter of credit called for by the sales contract, the seller is the beneficiary and the buyer the applicant.[7] A term of the sales contract requires the buyer to engage an issuer, usually a bank, to pay the seller the contract price upon the seller's presentation to the issuer of specified documents having a particular content. The documents specified can be any sort.[8] Documents called for by the typical commercial letter include a draft drawn on the buyer, a commercial invoice, a bill of lading or other document of title, and certificates of quality. Payment of the contract price is made by the issuer to the seller under the letter of credit upon the seller delivering to it documents complying with the terms of the credit. Note that in this typical transaction, three separate contracts are involved: (1) the sales contract between the seller/beneficiary and the

---

[7] Another increasingly frequent type of letter of credit is a standby (or "guarantee") letter. Here the issuer agrees to pay the beneficiary upon the beneficiary's satisfaction of conditions, if any, indicating breach by the applicant. When used in a sales transaction, the identity of the beneficiary and applicant of a standby letter are the reverse of a commercial letter. Now the beneficiary is the buyer and the applicant is the seller. The standby letter might provide, for example, that the issuer will pay the buyer a sum upon the buyer's statement or presentation of documents attesting to the seller's breach of the sales contract. When used in this way, the standby letter serves as security for the seller's performance. The standby letter does not function as a payment device, as it does when a commercial credit is used.

[8] See § 5-102(a)(6) ("'Document' means a draft, or other demand...or other record, statement, or representation of fact, law, right, or opinion..."); cf. UCP art. 2.

buyer/applicant; (2) the contract for payment against documents between the issuer/bank and beneficiary/seller; and (3) the contract of reimbursement between the issuer/bank and the applicant/buyer. It is standard to refer to (1) as the underlying sales contract, (2) as the letter of credit contract, and (3) as the reimbursement contract. The following triangular arrangement summarizes these points:

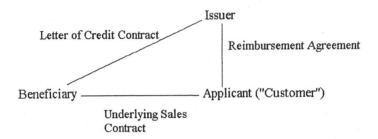

The letter of credit contract is not only distinct from the underlying and reimbursement contracts. It also has a different legal basis from them. A letter of credit contract, unlike other sorts of contracts, is not formed by an offer and acceptance between the issuer and beneficiary. It is enforceable without consideration too.[9] (Obviously, the reimbursement contract between the issuer and applicant almost always will be supported by consideration.) The contract is enforceable when transmitted by the issuer to the beneficiary.[10] Unless the credit states otherwise, it cannot be revoked by the issuer.[11] The contract cannot be assimilated to other sorts of contracts. It is not a type of guarantee because the issuer's liability to the beneficiary is primary while the guarantor's liability to the obligee is secondary. The issuer must pay the beneficiary if a documentary presentation complies, even if the underlying contract has been breached. Nor is the credit contract a type of third party beneficiary contract, since the issuer cannot invoke defenses available to the applicant to refuse payment to the beneficiary. Some courts and commentators conclude that a letter of credit therefore

---

[9] See § 5-105.

[10] See § 5-106(a); cf. UCP art. 5(d).

[11] See § 5-106(a); UCP art. 6(c).

is not a contract at all but a statutory obligation.[12] An equally good inference is that a letter of credit is a unique sort of contract, even if not assimilable to other sorts of contracts. Since enforceability of the issuer's undertaking by the beneficiary is the only central issue, the debate over the legal nature of the issuer's undertaking probably is unimportant.

It is apparent how a commercial letter of credit reduces the seller's risk of nonpayment. Since the letter of credit contract is separate from the underlying sales contract, the issuer's obligations to the seller are independent of the seller's obligations to the buyer. The credit requires the issuer to pay the seller the contract price upon his satisfaction of stipulated documentary conditions. This is true even if the seller breaches the terms of the underlying sales contract. Unlike a guarantee, the issuer's liability to the beneficiary is primary. It is not conditioned on the nonperformance of the underlying contract, and in general defenses to payment available to the buyer/applicant cannot be used by the issuer to refuse payment. The underlying sales contract also requires the buyer to pay the seller the contract price. Thus, the seller can look to two separate sources for payment: the issuer or the buyer. Put it this way: the seller goes unpaid only if *both* the issuer and buyer prove unwilling or unable to pay the contract price. As long as the risks of nonpayment by the issuer and buyer are uncorrelated, the probability of nonpayment therefore is the product of the probabilities of nonpayment from the issuer and the buyer. This product must be smaller than the probability of nonpayment from either the issuer or the buyer.[13] Since the

---

[12] See American Coleman Co. v. Intrawest Bank of Southglen, N.A., 887 F.2d 1382 (10th Cir. 1989); James J. White & Robert S. Summers, 3 Uniform Commercial Code 113 (4th ed. 1995); James G. Barnes & James E. Byrne, *Letters of Credit: 1996 Cases*, 52 Bus. Law. 1547, 1548 (1997); but cf. Comdata Network, Inc. v. First Interstate Bank, 497 N.W.2d 807 (Iowa 1993) (letter of credit a statutory obligation in the nature of a contract), John F. Dolan, The Law of Letters of Credit 2-4 (rev. ed. 1999) (letter of credit unique; law of contracts supplements it); § 5-101 Official Comment ("A letter of credit is an idiosyncratic form of undertaking..."). If credits are only statutory obligations, what does one make of letters of credit enforceable at common law, prior to the adoption of a governing statute?

[13] The point can be restated slightly more formally. Let $p$ and $q$ be the probability of nonpayment by the issuer and buyer, respectively. The seller will go unpaid only if both the issuer and buyer refuse payment. If these events are

issuer is usually a bank which is much more creditworthy than the buyer, the risk of nonpayment is significantly reduced by use of a letter of credit. The frequent use of letters of credit in international sales transactions, as well as their growth in domestic sales, is consistent with their risk reducing properties.

Most of the law governing letters of credit is domestic. Treaties play a relatively unimportant role in the area. The United Nations Convention on Independent Guarantees and Standby Letter of Credit, although in effect, has not been ratified by the United States. (Only five countries have ratified it to date.) Much of the domestic law governing letters of credit is found in Article 5 of the UCC, which has recently undergone revision. As of this writing, 46 states and the District of Columbia have adopted revised Article 5. But even Article 5 recognizes that the international nature of letter of credit transactions leaves substantial room for other law to govern the rights and obligations of the parties. By its own terms, Article 5 can be subject to rules of custom and practice to which the letter of credit is expressly made subject.[14] Section 5-103(b) also allows Article 5's provisions to be supplemented by statutory or common law rules.

The most important source of letter of credit custom is the Uniform Customs and Practices for Documentary Credits ("UCP"), compiled by the International Chamber of Commerce and currently published in what has become known as the UCP 500. (The International Chamber of Commerce's International Standby Practices (ISP98), a summary of standby letter of credit practices, is too recent to have much influence.) While the UCP has not been adopted as statutory law in any country, it is frequently incorporated by reference by commercial parties as the source for guiding principles of law in international letter of credit transactions. Almost all letters of credit issued in New York, for instance, are made subject to the UCP. Where parties explicitly incorporate the UCP into their letter of credit contract, those principles, rather than the UCC, will govern the transaction. Courts also sometimes rely on the UCP as a source of law even when the credit does not

---

uncorrelated, the probability of the conjunctive event (nonpayment by both issuer and buyer) is $q \times p$. For nonunitary probabilities, this probability must be smaller than the probability of either $q$ or $p$ alone. The probability of nonpayment from either the issuer or the buyer is $q + p$. Thus, $(q + p) > (q \times p)$.

[14] See §§ 5-103, 5-103 Official Comment 2, 5-116(c).

incorporate it. In our discussion of letters of credit we will make reference to the UCP where it deviates from or clarifies provisions of the UCC.

## B. Formal Requirements

A promise to pay a named person can be made orally or in writing, may or may not be supported by consideration, and can be made contingent on various sorts of conditions. Not all such promises, of course, constitute letters of credit. To be a letter of credit, a promise of payment must be in embodied in some tangible medium and indorsed by the promisor. Section 5-104 states this minimal condition as the requirement that a credit "be issued in any form that is a record and is authenticated..."[15] Section 5-102(a)(14) in turn defines a "record" as information inscribed in a tangible medium or retrievable in visual form from a medium.[16] The definition is broad, allowing letters of credit to be issued and stored electronically. A signed writing of course is the most common form that an authenticated record takes. Thus, an oral promise cannot constitute a letter of credit.

The next question concerns the content of a promise embodied in an authenticated medium. A typical letter of credit includes various information: the names of the issuer and beneficiary, the date the credit is established and will expire, a list of the documents the beneficiary must present and the office at which they must be presented, the amount of the credit, and the terms of payment. Very often the law governing the credit is stipulated as well, particularly with credits issued internationally. What information must be contained in an authenticated medium for the instrument to be a letter of credit? Apparently more than just an indefinite promise but less than a fully specified undertaking.[17] Section 5-102(a)(10) defines a letter of credit as a "definite undertaking that satisfies the requirements of Section 5-104..."[18] The adjective "definite" imposes the significant constraint. In *Transparent Products*

---

[15] § 5-104.

[16] See § 5-104(14).

[17] Cf. § 5-104 Official Comment 1 (neither § 5-104 nor § 5-102(a)(10) require that all terms of credit appear in the document).

[18] 5-102(a)(10).

*Corp. v. Paysaver Credit Union,*[19] Paysaver issued to Transparent Products a signed document stating that a letter of credit was established in Transparent's favor "up to the aggregate amount of fifty-thousand dollars ($50,000)."[20] Nothing was put in the document about the conditions under which Paysaver would pay Transparent or the identity of the applicant. In the circumstances the *Transparent* court found the undertaking to pay too indefinite to enforce as a letter of credit. The fact that the document was described as a letter of credit therefore was deemed unimportant.

In fact, the label a document carries is irrelevant to its character as a letter of credit. This is because § 5-102(a)(10) defines a letter of credit only in terms of the "definite undertaking" given, not how the undertaking is described. To see the point, consider the mirror image of the facts in *Transparent Products*. Suppose the signed document issued by Paysaver had read as follows: "We hereby establish our guarantee on behalf of, and at the request of, the applicant [i.e., Thomas Walls]...up to the aggregate amount of fifty-thousand dollars ($50,000), to be paid to you [i.e., Transparent Products] upon your written demand for that amount." The document requested by the applicant, although labeled a "guarantee," states a definite undertaking to pay a named beneficiary under a stipulated documentary condition. Thus, § 5-102(a)(10) would deem it a letter of credit. The character of Paysaver's definite undertaking would be unaffected by the label given it by the parties, whether a letter of credit or guarantee.[21] Indeed, European banks quite often describe some types of letters of credit as "independent guarantees."

The insistence on documentary definiteness is easy to justify. The utility of a letter of credit depends on parties being able to determine cheaply their rights and obligations from the face of the document. They must be able to gauge from the document at slight cost what the issuer has undertaken to do and the conditions under which the issuer will

---

[19] 864 F.2d 60 (7th Cir. 1988).

[20] Id. at 61.

[21] Cf. § 5-102, Official Comment 2; Wichita Eagle & Beacon Publishing Co. v. Pacific National Bank, 493 F.2d 1285 (9th Cir. 1974); Republic National Bank of Dallas v. Northwest National Bank of Fort Worth, 578 S.W.2d 109, 116 (Tex. 1979).

perform its undertaking. A document that only states that it is establishing "a letter of credit...up to...fifty-thousand dollars...," without more, requires costly inquiry by parties to determine what sort of payment device is being issued. In this way the net value of a credit as a low-cost payment mechanism is reduced. A formal requirement that the terms of the instrument state a definite undertaking saves parties the cost of inquiry and therefore increases the value of letters of credit. Form follows function. Of course, sometimes there can be a line-drawing problem here. There are degrees of definiteness in an undertaking, and some omitted terms do not affect an instrument's status as a letter of credit.[22] But difficult borderline cases do not undermine the justification of a definiteness requirement. Note that the justification is different from the justification of the Statute of Frauds. The Statute is justified by its function in reducing the costs of proving a contract ex post to a trier of fact.[23] Here the definiteness requirement is justified by its function in reducing the parties' costs of determining the nature of a payment mechanism ex ante.

## C. Issuer's Duty to Pay: The Strict Compliance Standard

The issuer has a duty to pay the beneficiary only if the documents presented comply with the terms of the letter of credit. This duty consists of two components. One is to exercise a degree of care in examining the documents presented. The other component is the standard by which documents presented comply with the terms of the credit. Strictly, revised Article 5 of the UCC does not impose a duty of care on the issuer. Section 5-109(2) of the predecessor to the revised version of Article 5 created the duty. Under then-§ 5-109(2), the issuer was obligated to examine documents "with care" to determine their compliance with the letter of credit's terms. The revised version of Article 5 eliminates the duty. Its elimination is probably ineffective for two reasons. First, provisions in other Articles of the UCC in effect impose a mandatory duty of care on the issuer. Arguably good faith requires the issuer to exhibit a degree of care in performing the letter of credit contract.

---

[22] For example, § 5-106(c) provides an expiration date of one year from the date of issuance if no expiration date is set in the credit. If no date of issuance is stated, § 5-106(c) sets it as of the date the letter is in fact issued. Omission of expiration or issuance dates in an undertaking therefore does not render it indefinite.

[23] See supra Chapter 5.

Section 1-203 provides that every contract governed by the UCC imposes an obligation of good faith in its performance.[24] And § 1-102(3) deems the obligation of good faith a term that cannot be varied by agreement.[25] Thus, in effect the duty of care eliminated by Article 5 is preserved by Article 1 of the UCC's obligation of good faith. Second, many letter of credit contracts subject the issuer to a duty of care. This is because most international and many domestic letters of credit incorporate the UCP, and Article 13(a) of the UCP imposes on issuing banks a duty of "reasonable care" in documentary examinations.[26] In such cases, the UCP supplements Article 5. Hence, as a matter of express terms or trade usage, a duty of care often exists even when Article 5 of the UCC continues to govern the letter of credit.[27]

The standard of documentary compliance under both Article 5 and the UCP is one of strict compliance. Section 5-109(2) of the predecessor to revised Article 5 simply insisted on compliance, leaving the standard of compliance to case law.[28] Most case law insisted on strict compliance. And the UCP continues to leave undefined the measure of compliance which documentary presentations must satisfy.[29] Section 5-108(a) of the

---

[24] See § 1-203.

[25] See § 1-203(3). The section allows atypical parties to define for themselves standards of good faith. Similarly, § 5-103(c) allows most of Article 5's provisions to be varied by agreement. Issuing banks sometimes try to avoid the consequence of a duty of care by limiting or excusing liability for defective documentary examination. Section 5-103(c) gives effect to such provisions as long as they are not part of a unbargained-for disclaimer or limitation; see § 5-103(c) ("A term in an agreement or undertaking generally excusing liability or generally limiting remedies for failure to perform obligations is not sufficient to vary obligations prescribed by this article").

[26] See UCP art. 13(a).

[27] See § 5-116(c). For a summary of the relevant revision to Article 5, see James J. White, *The Influence of International Practice on the Revision of Article 5 of the UCC*, 16 Nw. J. Int'l L. & Bus. 189, 199-202 (1995).

[28] See § 5-109(2) (1994) ("An issuer must examine documents...to ascertain that on their face they appear to comply...").

[29] See UCP art. 13(a) ("Banks must examine all documents stipulated in the Credit...to ascertain whether or not they appear...to be in compliance with the

revised version of Article 5, following predominant case law, expressly sets the standard at strict compliance: "...[A]n issuer shall honor a presentation that, as determined by the standard practice referred to in subsection (e), appears on its face strictly to comply with the terms and conditions of the letter of credit."[30] The standard referred to in § 5-108(e) is the letter of credit practice, usually the predominant practice of banks in handling letters of credit. The issuer's obligation to honor turns only on whether the documents presented and their content are strictly in accord with what is called for by the credit. Section 5-108(e) leaves to the court the determination of compliance with standard practice.[31]

Under the standard of strict compliance, the importance of a documentary discrepancy is irrelevant. As a Law Lord in a leading English letter of credit case put it, "[t]here is no room for documents which are almost the same, or which will do just as well."[32] The consistency of representations in the documents with the underlying sales transaction is irrelevant too.[33] If the documents presented correspond to the credit's terms, the issuer must honor. Otherwise, not. An issuer who honors a documentary presentation that does not strictly comply risks not being reimbursed by the applicant under the reimbursement contract. As with most of the UCC's rules, the standard of strict compliance is a default term. Section 5-103(c) allows the applicant and the issuer to alter

---

terms...of the Credit.").

[30] § 5-108(a).

[31] Adoption of the subsection has been controversial. Nonuniform amendments to § 5-108(e) omit its provision allocating to the court the determination of compliance. See, e.g., N.Y. U.C.C. § 5-108(e) (2001). The result is that the determination is left to the trier of fact. A court's authority to decide compliance issues on the basis of summary judgment presumably is unaffected.

[32] Equitable Trust Co. of New York v. Dawson Partners, Ltd., 27 Lloyd's List L.R. 49, 52 (1927) (Summer L.). An American court puts the same point more colloquially: "Compliance with the terms of a letter of credit is not like pitching horseshoes. No points are awarded for being close." Fidelity National Bank of South Miami v. Dade County, 371 So.2d 545, 546 (Fl. Dist. Ct. App. 1979).

[33] For the single qualification to this, see infra III.B.

the standard, relaxing it in light of the preferences of the parties.[34]

Strict compliance, however, does not mean absolutely literal compliance with the letter of credit's terms. It does not require letter-for-letter, word-for-word correspondence between documents presented and those called for in the credit.[35] Rather, under § 5-108(a) documents strictly comply when the issuer, using standard practices of issuers, determines that they on their face correspond to the credit's terms. The compliance of documents is tested only by the issuer's knowledge of letter of credit practices and terminology. An issuer's knowledge of other trade practices or facts to which the documents relate is irrelevant. For instance, § 5-108(f)(3) states that the issuer is not responsible for knowledge of any other trade usage. Thus, strict compliance requires the issuer to compare the documents presented to it with the terms of the credit and, on the basis of this comparison and knowledge of letter of credit practice alone, decide whether there is a discrepancy between the documents and the credit. Since letter of credit practices treat some documentary discrepancies as trivial, strict compliance does not demand a perfect correspondence between the documents and the letter's terms.[36] Put another way, a documentary presentation strictly complies if a reasonable issuer, examining only the documents and the credit, and charged with knowledge of the practices of issuers, would decide that a documentary discrepancy is insubstantial. The determination is one of

---

[34] Even without § 5-103(c), § 1-102(3) would allow the issuer and applicant to adopt a standard of documentary compliance other than one of strict compliance. For anecdotal evidence of an applicant who apparently does not even insist that its issuer inspect documentary presentations, see James J. White, supra note 27, at 201.

[35] See, e.g., New Braunfels National Bank v. Odiorne, 780 S.W.2d 313 (Tex. App. 1989); Documentary Credits: UCP 500 & 400 Compared 39 (C. del Busto ed. 1993). See also Boris Kozolchyk, *Strict Compliance and the Reasonable Document Checker*, 56 Brooklyn L. Rev. 45 (1990).

[36] Apparently issuers find it infeasible to insist on literal compliance. An informal survey of issuers indicates that about ninety percent of documentary presentations contain discrepencies; see James Byrne, 3 Letter of Credit Update 7 (July 1987). Other observers put the rate at no less than fifty percent; see, e.g., Robert M. Rosenblith, *Seeking a Waiver of Documentary Discrepancies From the Account Party: Unexplored Legal Problems*, 56 Brooklyn L. Rev. 81, 85 (1990).

fact, made by the court.[37]

The strict compliance standard, although somewhat vague, often is easily applied. Case law presents documentary discrepancies ranging from significant noncorrespondence to abbreviations to typographical errors. In some sense, of course, every discrepancy makes for a lack of correspondence between documents and the credit's terms. According to the strict compliance standard, however, the question is whether the discrepancy is considered substantial based on the letter of credit practices of issuers. Bills of lading describing the goods covered as "bags machine-shelled groundnuts" and referring to "O.T.C. C.R.S. Aarhus" do not correspond to the terms of a letter of credit calling for bills covering "about 1400 tons Coromandel groundnuts."[38] It is irrelevant that it was common knowledge in the nut trade that "C.R.S." was an abbreviation for "Coromandel." The reason for such a rule seems clear: If credits are to be efficiently employed to reduce the costs of long-distance transactions, issuers must be able to tell with relative ease the terms under which they are to pay drafts presented against the credit. To accomplish this objective, issuers cannot be required to be familiar with all the trade terms of the seller and buyer. Instead, issuers, according to the standard of strict compliance, are charged only with knowledge of banking usage. If issuers were charged with the requirement to learn or investigate the equivalency of "C.R.S." and "Coromandel" terms, they would presumably charge more for their undertaking (to compensate for the costs of investigation and the risk of erroneous decisions) than if they can make simple comparisons between the documents required under the credit and the documents presented. The desire to minimize investigation costs allows issuers to pay when bills of lading describing paper as having a range of tensile strength conform to a credit requiring bills reciting tensile strengths within that range, even if the issuer knows that the paper in fact lacks the strength represented.[39]

Isolated discrepancies in otherwise conforming documents press application of the strict compliance standard. Documents requesting payment under "Letter No. 86-122-S" conform when the credit specified

---

[37] See § 5-108(e); supra note 31.

[38] See J.H. Rayner & Co. v. Hambros Bank, Ltd., [1943] K.B. 36 (C.A.).

[39] See Maurice O'Meara Co. v. National Park Bank of New York, 146 N.E. 636 (N.Y. 1925).

"Letter of Credit No. 86-122-5." The "S" in the documents was considered to differ insubstantially from the "5" required by the credit.[40] The use of lower case letters when the credit is cast in upper case letters also is insubstantial. On the other hand, a misspelling of the beneficiary's name as "Sofan" when the credit lists the beneficiary as "Soran" renders the documentary presentation not strictly complying.[41] An intermediate case between a mere typographical error and a serious discrepancy might be the following: The documents presented refer to the beneficiary as "Swalt" while the credit refers to the beneficiary as "S. Walt." In determining strict compliance, the somewhat unhelpful question here is whether the practice of issuers considers the two proper names to refer to the same person.[42]

The strict compliance standard is tested when the documentary discrepancy involves omitted terms. *First State Bank v. Diamond Plastics Corp.*[43] illustrates the problem in an interesting way. The commercial letter of credit there stipulated that the documents to be presented were to be negotiated through the issuer, First State Bank. Negotiable bills of lading were required to be forwarded by the bank negotiating the documents. The beneficiary, the seller, presented nonnegotiable bills of lading to First State Bank, and the bank refused to pay. One of the issues on appeal was whether the documentary presentation strictly complied with the terms of the letter of credit. The answer might appear very easy: because nonnegotiable bills were presented while the credit called for negotiable bills, the documents did not strictly comply, and First State Bank was not obligated to pay the

---

[40] See New Braunfels National Bank v. Odiorne, 780 S.W.2d 313 (Tex. App. 1989); cf. Tosco Corp. v. FDIC, 723 F.2d 1242 (6th Cir. 1983) ("No." and "Number" considered insubstantial discrepancy).

[41] See Beyene v. Irving Trust Co., 596 F. Supp. 438 (S.D.N.Y. 1984).

[42] For doubts that banking practices exist covering all types of documentary discrepancies, see John F. Dolan, *The UN Convention on International Independent Undertakings: Do States with Mature Letter-Of-Credit Regimes Need It?*, 13 Banking & Fin. L. Rev. 1, 13 (1997).

[43] 891 P.2d 1262 (Okla. 1995).

beneficiary.[44] The trouble is that the documents were not negotiated to First State Bank by another bank. They were presented directly to First State Bank, the issuer, by the beneficiary. The letter of credit expressly required negotiable bills of lading when the documents were negotiated to the issuer. It was silent as to whether negotiable bills also were required when the beneficiary did not negotiate the documents but itself presented the documents to First State Bank. A term in the credit was omitted, as it were. Thus, the live issue was whether in the circumstances the presentation strictly complied with the credit.

The documentary presentation almost certainly did not strictly comply. To understand why, recognize that some letters of credit allow for negotiation of documentary drafts to the issuer. Such letters of credit, called negotiation letters of credit, are undertakings by the issuer to pay third parties who purchase complying documentary drafts or demands for payment made by the beneficiary. The letter of credit in *First State Bank* was a negotiation letter of credit.[45] First State Bank undertook to pay any bank who presented to it a draft accompanied by negotiable bills of lading which conformed to the terms of the credit. Thus, the real

---

[44] The majority takes this position; see id. at 1269 ("The letter explicitly requires 'a negotiable Bill of Lading of each set and consular invoice' to be forwarded to the Bank."). The dissent finds no requirement that a negotiable bill be presented by the beneficiary; see id. at 1276 ("The terms of the letter of credit do not require Diamond Plastics [i.e., the beneficiary] to submit a negotiable billl of lading.").

[45] The language in the credit creating a negotiation letter of credit was somewhat unusual. Usually a negotiation credit is created by language to the effect that "We hereby engage with the drawer, indorsers or bona fide holders of drafts drawn under and in compliance with the terms of this credit that the same will be duly honored on due presentation..." See, e.g., UCP art. 5(b)(iv). Cf. § 5-102 Official Comment 7; E.P. Ellinger, Documentary Letters of Credit 17 (1970). The language just recited creates what is called a "freely negotiation" credit: any person who has negotiated a conforming documentary draft is entitled to draw on the credit. The credit in *First State Bank*, using different language, had the same legal consequence. For the issuer's obligations to the negotiating bank, see UCP art. 14.

Negotiation credits are not negotiable instruments. A letter of credit does not take the form of negotiability. It is not payable to order or bearer, and is not an unconditional promise to pay. See § 3-104(c). A credit need not even promise to pay; it can promise to give value other than payment. See § 5-102(a)(10).

question in the case is whether the credit is reasonably read as insisting on the same documentary conditions when the beneficiary makes a documentary presentation to the issuer. The answer is that almost certainly it is to be read in that way. There are two reasons. First, negotiable bills of lading protect the issuing bank by providing it with security against nonpayment by the applicant. Once the issuer pays the beneficiary or a third party and obtains the negotiable bills, it controls access to the goods covered by the bill. The bill therefore serves as collateral securing the applicant's obligation to reimburse it. Nonnegotiable bills do not. The issuer's demand for security is the same whoever presents the documents. Hence, if an issuer insisted that negotiable bills be negotiated to it by a third party, it would do the same when the beneficiary makes the documentary presentation. Second, and more important, a negotiating bank delivers to the issuer the same documents that the beneficiary has delivered to it. This is the condition of it being paid by the issuer.[46] Thus, since the credit required the negotiating bank to present negotiable bills, it also required the beneficiary to present them. Presenting nonnegotiable bills of lading therefore does not strictly comply with the terms of the credit.

As we intimated above, the strict compliance standard can be justified on the basis of efficiency. Issuers already have significant incentives to use cost-effective mechanisms of inspection, since failure to do so would cause them to lose business to more efficient issuers or to other forms of payment. Thus, if the practice of issuers has evolved to create a strict compliance standard, there is reason to believe that the standard serves the interests of all parties relative to any alternative. Further, any alternative standard, such as "substantial compliance," would require substantial judicial intervention to determine whether the issuer should have paid against the documents presented. Even if practices in the issuer's industry are not net beneficial, courts are poorly positioned to improve on them.[47] Further, issuers are unfamiliar with the

---

[46] See, e.g., §§ 5-107(a), 5-102(a)(11).

[47] For an argument that evolved commercial norms need not be efficient and might be improved upon by premeditated legal design, see Jody S. Kraus, *Legal Design and the Evolution of Commercial Norms*, 26 J. Legal Stud. 377 (1997). Even if the practice of documentary inspection can be improved upon by legal design, the claim in the text is that judicial design is unlikely to be a vehicle for improvement. The substantial compliance standard adopted by a minority of courts illustrates the point. According to the standard, a documentary

industry practices bearing on the underlying sales contract. As statute and case law sometimes puts the point, issuers deal in documents, not goods.[48] Applicants, however, are familiar with the underlying sales contract and industry practices associated with it because they are parties to the contracts. An applicant therefore is better positioned to bear the risk that industry practice will affect the terms under which the demand for payment is made. Documentary compliance therefore is determined only by the documents presented, read in light of the issuer's industry practice.

### D.  Issuer's Duty to Pay:  Waiver, Estoppel and Preclusion

An issuer may be liable to a beneficiary even when a documentary presentation fails to comply strictly with the credit's terms. This can occur in two sorts of circumstances. One is by preclusion. Under § 5-108(b), the issuer has a reasonable time not exceeding seven business days after receipt of documents to honor or notify the presenter of its reasons for dishonor. According to § 5-108(c), if timely notice is not given, the issuer is precluded from claiming that the documents are noncomplying; if timely notice of reasons for dishonor is not given, it is precluded from relying on reasons for dishonor not mentioned.[49] Preclusion is based only on the issuer's failure to give timely notice of documentary discrepancies. It is not based on the presenter's detrimental reliance on the lack of timely notice or reasons for dishonor. In fact, the presenter's reliance is irrelevant to the limitation on dishonor. (The UCP

---

presentation complies with the credit's terms in all "significant respects." See, e.g., Flagship Cruises Ltd. v. new England Merchants National Bank, 569 F.2d 699 (1st Cir. 1978); Banco Espanol de Credito v. State Street Bank and Trust Co., 385 F.2d 230 (1st Cir. 1967). To apply the standard, a court ex post has to determine how important a term in the credit is to the underlying contract. Issuers in turn have to guess about a court's ex post determinations of importance. Because both courts and issuers are poorly positioned to make the determination, standards of compliance which look to the underlying sales contract are unlikely to optimally reduce the cost of using letters of credit as payment devices.

[48] See, e.g., UCP art. 4.

[49] See § 5-108(c). Section 5-108(d) limits the effect of preclusion by making it inapplicable when the basis of dishonor is fraud, forgery or the expiration of the credit.

contains the same rule about preclusion.[50]) Thus, in both Article 5 and the UCP, preclusion is not estoppel.

The doctrine of waiver provides the second circumstance in which an issuer is liable even when a documentary presentation fails to strictly comply. Waiver occurs when the issuer knowingly and intentionally relinquishes the right to insist on strict compliance.[51] The relinquishment of the right must be communicated to the presenter. Waiver is construed narrowly and found only when supported by significant evidence, so that an issuer does not waive its right to strict compliance in future presentations by waiving strict compliance in previous presentations.[52] Although not expressly contained in Article 5, waiver supplements the Article, presumably as an equitable principle incorporated under § 1-103.

Courts often are sloppy about distinguishing among preclusion, estoppel and waiver. Sometimes they use the terms interchangeably or simply attach the wrong label to notion they invoke. Some courts invent new synonyms, describing preclusion as "strict estoppel," for example.[53]

---

[50] See UCP art. 14(d), (e); cf. Integrated Measurement Systems, Inc. v. International Commercial Bank of China, 757 F. Supp. 938 (N.D. Ill. 1991); Toyota Tsusho Corp. v. Comerica Bank, 929 F. Supp. 1065 (E.D. Mich. 1996) (finding that article 16 of the 1983 revision of the UCP endorses preclusion without reliance).

[51] See, e.g., Todi Exports v. Amrav Sportwear Inc., 1997 Lexis 1425 (S.D.N.Y.); Voest-Alpine International Corp. v. Chase Manhattan Bank, N.A., 707 F.2d 680, 685 (2d Cir. 1983). By waiving strict compliance, the issuer risks not being reimbursed by the applicant. This is because § 5-108(i)(1) entitles the issuer to reimbursement when the issuer has "honored a presentation as permitted or required by this article." Since waiver operates by the issuer paying when the presentation does not comply with the credit's terms, the issuer is not entitled to reimbursement under the credit. The issuer can recover, if at all, only apart from the reimbursement agreement, on ordinary contract or restitutionary principles. This is why in practice issuers almost always obtain the applicant's permission to pay against nonconforming presentations.

[52] See § 5-108 Official Comment 7; cf. Alaska Textile v. Chase Manhattan Bank, N.A., 982 F.2d 813, 820 (2d Cir. 1992); Banco General Runinahui, S.A. v. Citibank International, 97 F.3d 480, 485 n.11 (11th Cir. 1996).

[53] See Alaska Textile v. Chase Manhattan Bank, 982 F.2d 813 (2d Cir. 1992) (describing preclusion as strict estoppel"); Kerr-McGee Chemical Corp. v. FDIC, 872 F.2d 971 (11th Cir. 1989). Dolan, who uses the term, is clear about the

To understand the distinction among these doctrines, consider the following three hypotheticals:

Hypothetical 1: The beneficiary presents discrepant documents to the issuer. Both parties are aware of the discrepancies. The issuer immediately informs the beneficiary of the discrepancies but states that nonetheless it will honor the presentation.

Hypothetical 2: The beneficiary presents discrepant documents to the issuer. The issuer refuses to pay but fails to specify the discrepancies and the beneficiary is unaware of them. If the discrepancies had been specified by the issuer, the beneficiary could have cured them and made a complying documentary presentation before the credit expired.

Hypothetical 3: The same as Hypothetical 2 except the beneficiary could not have cured the discrepancies even if the issuer had specified them when it refused to honor the beneficiary's presentation.

Waiver alone is present in Hypothetical 1. The issuer obviously knows that it has the right to insist on strict compliance. Its statement that it will honor the presentation notwithstanding the documentary discrepancies is an intentional relinquishment of that right. Preclusion and estoppel are not present. Because the issuer gave timely notice of the discrepancies, preclusion does not operate. Estoppel also is inapplicable because the beneficiary already was aware of the discrepancies and therefore could not rely on the issuer's notice of them. Preclusion and estoppel both are present in Hypothetical 2. By failing to give the beneficiary notice of discrepancies, § 5-108(c) precludes the issuer from relying on them to dishonor the beneficiary's presentation. Estoppel also is present because the beneficiary could have timely cured the discrepancies had they been brought to its attention. Thus, the beneficiary detrimentally relied on the issuer's failure to state the ground for dishonor. Waiver is inapplicable in Hypothetical 2 since, unlike in Hypothetical 1, there is no evidence that the issuer intended to relinquish its right to insist on strict compliance. In Hypothetical 3 only preclusion operates. As in Hypothetical 2, the issuer's failure to give notice of discrepancies precludes it from relying on them as grounds for dishonor. In Hypothetical 3, however, estoppel is not present. This is because there is no detrimental reliance by the beneficiary. Even had it been given timely notice of the discrepancies, it could not have cured them and made

distinction; see John F. Dolan, *Strict Compliance with Letters of Credit: Stricking a Fair Balance*, 102 Banking L. J. 18 (1985).

a conforming presentation. Thus, even if the beneficiary relied on the issuer's failure to give timely notice, its reliance is not detrimental. Waiver does not operate in Hypothetical 3 for the same reason it does not operate in Hypothetical 2.

The revised version of Article 5 eliminates estoppel as a limit on the issuer's right to dishonor. Section 5-108(c) expressly endorses preclusion as a limitation. It prevents the issuer from relying on unstated discrepancies to refuse honor if the issuer fails to give timely notice of dishonor or fails to state the basis for dishonor. The section does not contain a further requirement of detrimental reliance or even reliance by the presenter. It is enough that the issuer failed to give timely and particularized notice of the reasons for dishonor. Thus, § 5-108(c) displaces the limitation of estoppel previously imported into Article 5 via equitable principles under § 1-103. The revised version of Article 5 therefore is consistent with the rule of preclusion that always has operated under the UCP. It also makes things simpler. Previous case law implicating estoppel diverged in the statement of what constituted estoppel and when it applied. For instance, courts disagreed as to whether detrimental reliance was required or whether mere reliance was enough. Some courts also differed as to whether estoppel even applied when a letter of credit was subject to the UCP. Article 5's elimination of estoppel makes such divergence in case law unimportant. But since waiver and preclusion continue to operate under Article 5 via § 1-103, the distinction among waiver, estoppel and preclusion still matters.

A small question is whether waiver survives under the revised version of Article 5 when a credit incorporates the UCP. The UCP does not contain an article allowing waiver.[54] At least one court has inferred

---

[54] Although the UCP does not address the issuer's waiver when directed at the beneficiary, it addresses waiver when directed at the applicant. Article 14(c) allows the issuer "in its sole judgment" to request the applicant to waive documentary discrepancies. Article 14(c)'s purpose is avoid a waiver between the applicant and beneficiary binding the issuer. In this way the independence of the letter of credit contract and the reimbursement agreement is preserved. For a case in which a trial court wrongly saddles the issuer with a waiver directed at the beneficiary when it had obtained a waiver from the applicant, see Bombay Industries, Inc. v. Bank of New York, 27 UCC Rep. Serv.2d 987 (N.Y. Sup. Ct. 1995) *rev'd* Bombay Industries, Inc. v. Bank of New York, 31 UCC Rep. Serv.2d 1091 (N.Y. App. Div. 1996).

from this that the UCP does not support an equitable doctrine of waiver.[55] We find the inference less clear. Letters of credit incorporating the UCP can remain subject to Article 5 as well. Section 5-116(c) simply provides that in the case of a conflict between Article 5's nonmandatory rules and the UCP's provisions, the UCP's provisions apply. But the UCP's provisions do not address all aspects of the letter of credit contract. For instance, the UCP is silent on whether the issuer can resist payment in the face of the beneficiary's fraud. It also is silent on the operative standard of documentary compliance. A similar inference from the UCP's silence on these matters would mean that no fraud exception or standard of compliance is applicable to credits governed by the UCP. The inference obviously is unacceptable. Thus, the failure of the UCP to address waiver also does not mean that waiver is inapplicable to credits governed by the UCP. There is therefore no conflict between Article 5, which continues to make waiver available under § 1-103, and the UCP. Waiver, we believe, continues to be applicable to credits governed by both Article 5 and the UCP.

It is worth asking why there should be any limitation at all on the issuer's right to insist on strict compliance. Why should preclusion or waiver ever require an issuer to honor when there are discrepancies in the documentary presentation? There really are two questions here: one asking for a justification of any limitation on the issuer's right to require strict compliance, and a second asking about the justification of the particular limitations recognized by Article 5. As to the first question, the short answer is that limitations prevent strategic behavior by the issuer. Issuers usually have a strong incentive to honor complying presentations based on their desire to maintain reputation as a reliable payment source. However, sometimes loyalty to its applicant or short-term self-interest may induce an issuer to delay honor of presentations or renege on a prior commitment to honor a nonconforming presentation. For example, where the applicant regrets entering into the underlying sales contract or the issuer's prospect of reimbursement is jeopardized, the issuer may not want to honor. Delaying the decision to honor or notifying the documentary presenter of only some of the grounds for dishonor are good tactics for doing so. This is because the credit can expire while the issuer delays or the presenter fails to correct the documentary discrepancies not mentioned by the issuer. The issuer's

---

[55] See Banco General Ruminahui, S.A. v. Citibank International, 97 F.3d 480, 485 (11th Cir. 1996).

strategic behavior here obviously reduces the value of the letter of credit to the beneficiary, making it a less desirable payment device. By restricting the issuer's discretion, limitations on its right to insist on strict compliance control the prospect of strategic behavior. In this way limitations increase the value of the credit.

The second question asks about the justification of the limitations recognized by Article 5, and is harder to answer. Even if some constraints on the issuer are justified, it does not follow that Article 5's limitations are good ones. Their worth depends in part on the cost of applying the limitations when the issuer resists paying in the face of a noncomplying presentation. Here the assessment is mixed. Establishing waiver requires an open-ended inquiry in which the issuer's consent not to stand on its right to strict compliance is central. Exactly when the issuer's consent was obtained, and precisely which documentary conditions the issuer consented to not insist upon can be hard issues to resolve. Relevant facts and proof can be difficult to obtain. Whether waiver occurred can be uncertain ex post and even ex ante.[56] This is a problem because the issuer risks not being reimbursed by the applicant. Since the issuer is entitled to reimbursement from the applicant only if the documentary presentation conforms to the credit's terms, and waiver excuses noncomplying presentations, an incorrect finding of waiver means that the issuer bears the cost of noncompliance. Courts implicitly recognize the problem and cabin the doctrine by construing it narrowly and insisting on substantial evidence to support a finding of waiver. Without more, the doctrine of waiver is a costly way of controlling the issuer's strategic behavior.

Preclusion for the most part is a better restriction. This is because, unlike waiver, it provides some objective constraints on the issuer which are relatively cheap to administer. Section 5-108(d) (and article 14(e) of the UCP) prevents an issuer from grounding dishonor on a documentary discrepancy if the presenter has not been notified within a "reasonable

---

[56] Bank of Seoul v. Norwest Bank Minnesota, N.A., 27 UCC Rep. Serv.2d 982 (N.Y. App. Div. 1995) illustrates the point. There the issuer notified the beneficiary that it was requesting the applicant's permission to ignore documentary discrepancies in the beneficiary's presentation. Subsequently, the applicant gave its permission. The court found that in the circumstances a triable issue of fact existed as to whether the issuer waived its right to strict compliance. A factual issue exists only because the doctrine of waiver cannot exclude the possibility that the facts adduced can support waiver.

time" but not more than seven business days after receipt of the documents. In addition, § 5-108(d) (and article 14(e)) prevents the issuer from relying on discrepancies that have not been described to the presenter in the notice. Described abstractly, the section combines a rule ("seven days") and a standard ("reasonable time"). The rule is based on objective and easily determinable facts: a clock and calendar can determine when seven business days have passed. It sets the outer limit within which the issuer can delay its decision to honor. The standard, "reasonable time," does not rely on objective facts establishing undue delay and creates some uncertainty in application.[57] Notice, however, that even here preclusion does not depend on ascertaining some potentially inaccessible facts. Preclusion does not turn on the presenter's knowledge of discrepancies. Nor does it depend on reliance by the presenter on delay or notice given it by the issuer. Detriment to the presenter caused by delay or incomplete notice also is irrelevant to preclusion. These elements can be difficult to prove. Official Comment 3 to § 5-108 counts it a virtue that preclusion, unlike estoppel, avoids these sources of litigation.[58] Preclusion avoids these sources of litigation because it relies for the most part on objective and easily ascertainable facts: delay past seven business days or a failure to mention particular documentary discrepancies. Thus, preclusion functions as a relatively cheap way of controlling strategic behavior by the issuer.

## III. The Issuer's Right Not to Pay: The Independence Principle and the Fraud Exception

### A. The Independence Principle

With one exception, the issuer must pay if the documentary presentation strictly complies with the terms of the credit. The issuer's obligation derives from a legal rule commonly called the independence

---

[57] The uncertainty appears to have been reduced by letter of credit practice in some cases. The U.S. Council on International Banking, Inc. is on record to the effect that the "reasonable time" requirement is satisfied if the issuer gives notice of dishonor within three days of receipt of the documents. See 1997 Annual Survey of Letter of Credit Law & Practice 678 (James E. Byrne et al. eds. 1997). Apparently trade practice among issuers has transformed an otherwise indefinite standard into a rule by creating a "three day" safe harbor.

[58] See § 5-108 Official Comment 3 ("The virtue of the preclusion obligation adopted in this section is that it forecloses litigation about reliance and detriment.").

(or autonomy) principle. This principle holds that each of the three contracts involved in the standard letter of credit transaction--the sales contract between the applicant and the beneficiary, the reimbursement contract between the applicant and the issuer, and the letter of credit contract between the issuer and the beneficiary--is an independent contract, performance under which does not require performance under any of the other contracts. Hence, the independence principle provides that the issuer must pay regardless of whether the documents or performance conform to the underlying contract, as long as they comply with the requirements of the letter of credit contract.

Section 5-103(d) states a version of the principle: "Rights and obligations of the issuer to a beneficiary or a nominated person under a letter of credit are independent of the existence, performance or nonperformance of a contract...out of which the letter of credit arises or which underlies it..."[59] If the documentary presentation strictly complies, the issuer must pay even if the underlying sales contract has been breached or the documents falsely state that its performance is conforming. This is why courts and commentators (and the UCP[60]) frequently say that the issuer deals in documents, not in the goods or other performance to which the documents might relate.

A letter of credit's enhanced value as a payment device depends on the independence principle. Since the principle makes performance of all contracts other than the credit contract irrelevant to the issuer's duties to the beneficiary, the beneficiary is assured of prompt payment. It need only present complying documents, and need not be concerned that allegations bearing on other contracts will interfere with payment. To recognize the point clearly, compare the value of a guarantee with that of a letter of credit. Both are valuable when used as payment devices because both add a creditworthy person from whom payment can be obtained. However, a guarantor can employ defenses to payment available to the principal obligor on the underlying contract. There are therefore any number of circumstances under which the obligee will not be paid by the guarantor. Given the independence principle, the underlying contract and its performance is irrelevant to the issuer's duty

---

[59] See § 5-103(d); cf. UCP art. 3(a) ("Credits, by their nature, are separate transactions from the sale or other contract(s) on which they may be based and banks are in no way concerned with or bound by such contract(s)...").

[60] Cf. UCP art. 4.

to the beneficiary. The issuer therefore cannot use them to resist payment. Thus, there are fewer circumstances under which the beneficiary will not be paid by the issuer. Without the independence principle, the credit would not have an advantage over a guarantee as a payment device.

## B. The Fraud Exception

Fraud is the single exception to the independence principle. It is arguably recognized in common law and explicitly recognized under the revised version of Article 5. Section 5-109(a) contains the exception for fraud. Although its structure might appear complicated and some of its important terms imprecise, § 5-109(a)'s operation is clear. Basically, when fraud has been committed, the provision allows the issuer to refuse payment to some presenters while requiring payment to other presenters. In addition, § 5-109(b) allows a court to enjoin the issuer from paying some presenters when fraud has been committed while prohibiting injunctive relief against other presenters.[61] Section 5-109(a)(1) describes the class of presenters whom the issuer must pay even if fraud is involved ("the issuer shall honor..."). The fraud exception does not operate against this protected class. Under § 5-109(b), an issuer also cannot be enjoined from paying members of this protected class. Section 5-109(a)(2) describes another class of presenters whom the issuer can refuse to pay when fraud is involved ("the issuer...may honor"). Although the issuer is permitted to pay presenters in these class, it is not obligated to do so. Under § 5-109(b), the issuer nonetheless can be enjoined from paying members of this unprotected class of presenters.

### 1. Two Types of Fraud

Section 5-109(a) applies when "a required document is forged or materially fraudulent, or honor of the presentation would facilitate a

---

[61] There is a lack of uniformity in the adoption of unrevised Article 5 here. California and Nevada's adoptions of the model version of the predecessor to revised Article 5 deleted a portion of then-§ 5-114(2)(b). The deleted portion authorized courts to enjoin an issuer under some circumstances from honoring a credit when fraud had been committed. The inference drawn from the deletion is that California and Nevada state law prohibits courts from enjoining the issuer from honoring the credit. Both states have adopted revised Article 5 without altering § 5-109. See Cal. Civ. Code § 5109(b) (1998); Nev. Rev. Stat. Ann. § 104.5109 (2001).

material fraud by the beneficiary on the issuer or applicant..."[62] Two sorts of fraud are being described here, and only one of them states an exception to the independence principle. One sort of fraud involves fraud in the letter of credit transaction. Fraud of this sort occurs when "a required document is forged or materially fraudulent." For example, if the credit calls for presentation of an "on board" bill of lading, and the presenter simply writes "on board" across the bill presented, the written addition is a forgery. If the carrier has indorsed the bill as "on board" while the goods remain at the quay, and the presenter knows of the situation, the bill is a materially fraudulent document. When a letter of credit calls for presentation of particular documents, and the documents presented are forged or "materially fraudulent," the credit's terms are not satisfied. In both cases, the documents do not comply with the credit's terms. This is because its terms call for presentation of genuine documents without knowledge that they did not conform to the credit. The issuer therefore need not pay under the credit. Of course, where the fraud is in the letter of credit transaction itself, allowing the issuer to avoid payment under the letter of credit contract does not violate the independence principle.

A second sort of fraud provides the exception to independence. This involves fraud in the performance of the underlying contract, but the fraud excuses payment under the letter of credit contract. As § 5-109(a) describes it, the fraud occurs when "honor of the presentation would facilitate a material fraud by the beneficiary on the issuer or applicant." Since § 5-109(a)'s language preceding this phrase already has described fraud in the letter of credit transaction ("a required document is forged or materially fraudulent"), the "material fraud by the beneficiary" described must refer to fraud in the underlying transaction. Otherwise, the additional language would be superfluous. Prior to the revision of Article 5, then-§ 5-114(2) described the consequences of a document which "is forged or fraudulent or there is fraud in the transaction."[63] Courts and commentators debated whether "fraud in the transaction" referred to the documentary transaction or the underlying transaction. Section 5-109(a) pretty clearly settles the matter by distinguishing between the two sorts of transactions in which "material fraud" is involved and recognizing that fraud can involve the underlying transaction too. Official Comment 1 to

---

[62] § 5-109(a).

[63] § 5-114(2) (1993).

§ 5-109 confirms the conclusion.[64]

Obviously the two sorts of fraud often occur together. Suppose a letter of credit conditions payment on the seller-beneficiary presenting a bill of lading indicating shipment of widgets. If the underlying contract calls for the shipment of widgets to the buyer-applicant and the seller knowingly ships nothing, the failure to ship might count as fraud in the sales contract. If the seller obtains a bill of lading describing widgets delivered to the carrier and presents it to the issuer, the document is materially fraudulent. Thus, there also is fraud in the letter of credit transaction. But the two sorts of fraud can occur separately. If conforming widgets are shipped, there is no fraud in the performance of the sales contract. However, the seller might forge the bill of lading or alter the shipment date on it in order to expedite payment from the issuer or replace an original bill which was lost. Presentation of a forged or altered bill would be count as a presentation of a forged or fraudulent document--fraud in the letter of credit transaction.

Examples of the two sorts of fraud and their consequences might be useful. *Sztejn v. J. Henry Schroder Banking Corp.*[65] is the classic case illustrating fraud in the documentary transaction. There the buyer agreed to purchase bristles from a seller. A commercial letter of credit was opened in the seller's favor calling for presentation of bills of lading and invoices describing the goods being shipped as "bristles." A correspondent bank, the seller's agent, presented the documents to the issuer representing that crates of bristles had been shipped. In fact, according to the buyer's complaint, the seller had shipped rubbish and other worthless material. The buyer sought to enjoin the issuer's payment to the correspondent bank. In granting the injunction, the court assumed that the buyer-applicant's allegations were true. It therefore assumed that bills of lading indicating that bristles had been shipped when none had amounted to fraudulent documents. The buyer-applicant's allegation was based on documentary fraud: the beneficiary-

---

[64] See § 5-109 Official Comment 1 ("This recodification makes clear that fraud must be found either in the documents or must have been committed by the beneficiary on the issuer or applicant... The use of the word ["materially"] requires that the fraudulent aspect of a document be material to a purchaser of that document or that the fraudulent act be significant to the participants in the underlying transaction").

[65] 31 N.Y.S.2d 631 (N.Y. Sup. Ct. 1941).

seller's presentation (strictly, its agent's presentation) to the issuer of a document that made representations the seller knew to be false. Thus, although there was fraud alleged in the performance of the underlying sales contract, the *Sztejn* court prevented the issuer from paying, finding fraud in the documentary transaction. Section 5-109(a) continues prior-§ 5-114(2)'s likely codification of the result in *Sztejn*, allowing an issuer to refuse payment when the beneficiary commits documentary fraud.

*Itek Corp. v. First National Bank*[66] illustrates a finding of fraud in the underlying transaction. As part of a sales contract containing a force majeure clause, the seller was required to obtain a standby letter of credit.[67] The credit secured the beneficiary's obligations under a contract of guarantee to make payment to the buyer in the event the seller breached. The credit's terms called for the beneficiary simply to certify that it had been required to pay. After the guarantor had paid the buyer, it certified this fact to the issuer. The buyer-applicant obtained an injunction preventing the issuer from honoring the beneficiary's draw based on fraud in the performance of the underlying sales contract. In finding fraud, the *Itek* court interpreted the contract's force majeure clause and determined that the seller-applicant had properly canceled the contract.[68] The court also assumed that the credit incorporated the terms of the sales contract, so that the credit could be called on only if the contract remained in effect.[69] Since the sales contract was properly canceled, the buyer's demand on the guarantor had no basis and was fraudulent. Given the court's assumption, the guarantor's call on the letter of credit therefore had no basis and was fraudulent too. Thus, the *Itek* court enjoined the issuer's payment based on facts about the underlying sales transaction.

### 2. What is Fraud?

The fraud exception stated in § 5-109(a) uses but does not define the notion of fraud invoked. Apparently the committee drafting revised

---

[66] 730 F.2d 19 (1st Cir. 1984).

[67] See note 7, supra, for a short description of a standby letter of credit.

[68] 730 F.2d at 25-26.

[69] See id. at 25.

Article 5 could not agree on a definition.[70] Section 5-109(a) refers to "materially fraudulent" documents and a "material fraud" by the beneficiary on the issuer or applicant while omitting standards for determining when fraud occurs. The absence of a statutory standard can cause problems. To easily see the problems, consider the following two hypotheticals.

Hypothetical 1:    Buyer and Seller agree that Seller will sell new widgets to Buyer. The letter of credit calls for documents evidencing shipment of new widgets. The beneficiary, knowing that the widgets it has sent are slightly used, presents documents stating that new widgets have been shipped.

Hypothetical 2: The facts are the same as in Hypothetical 1, except that nothing is shipped.

In both hypotheticals, the beneficiary knowingly has breached the underlying sales contract. (A breach of an express warranty occurs in Hypothetical 1; a breach of a duty to deliver occurs in Hypothetical 2.) However, in Hypothetical 1 nonconforming goods have been shipped while in Hypothetical 2 nothing has been shipped. Letter of credit law considers the beneficiary to have committed fraud only in Hypothetical 2. Hypothetical 1 involves a breach of warranty, not fraud. Since a breach occurs in both hypotheticals, while fraud occurs only in one of them, a standard is needed to distinguish fraud from mere breach of contract.

Letter of credit law has difficulty in formulating a standard. If a knowing breach by the beneficiary is enough for fraud, then fraud exists in both hypotheticals. The problem in this case is that the letter of credit's allocation of payment risks is upset. After all, the credit's purpose is allocate to the applicant-buyer the risk that the beneficiary-seller will tender nonconforming goods and retain the contract price during the pendency of litigation. Allowing the issuer to refuse payment in the face of any knowing breach by the beneficiary defeats that purpose. If more than a knowing breach is needed for fraud, then Hypotheticals 1

---

[70] See 72nd Annual Meeting, The American Law Institute Proceedings 336 (1995) (statement of Professor White). An early version of revised Article 5 contained a definition of "fraud," construing it as intentional (common law) fraud. See Draft--Revised Article 5: Letters of Credit § 5-103(1)(g)(1), (2) (April 12, 1991). The definition was dropped in the March 31, 1993 draft of revised Article 5.

and 2 can be distinguished. The problem in this case is that distinguishing them requires distinguishing among the sorts of breach.

Courts recognized the conceptual difficulty of doing so early. In *Sztejn* the court distinguished between a "mere breach of warranty" and something it called "active fraud."[71] It said that "active fraud" in the credit transaction justified enjoining the issuer when the breach involved intentionally sending worthless rubbish. Sending goods of a lesser quality than the sales contract demanded did not constitute fraud. Nothing in the court's opinion suggests that intentionally sending goods of an inferior quality makes for fraud. The opinion also does not suggest that fraud exists if the documents represent that conforming goods are shipped. Thus, in distinguishing between mere breach of warranty and fraud, the court implicitly is distinguishing among degrees of breach. There apparently is an important difference between knowingly sending inferior bristles called for by the sales contract and knowingly sending worthless rubbish. Although both are breaches, the former is a "mere" breach of warranty and the latter is "fraud." The *Sztejn* court therefore would consider Hypothetical 1 above to involve a simple breach of warranty and Hypothetical 2 to involve fraud. The difficulty recognized but not resolved by *Sztejn*, of course, is when the difference in the extent of breach makes a difference.

Most courts follow *Sztejn* and find fraud only when a breach involves intentional and serious misconduct by the beneficiary. The case law and commentary sometimes phrases the standard of fraud differently, but the different phrasing is unimportant. This is because case results are consistent with a finding of intentional and very bad behavior by the beneficiary. Thus, according to every announced standard, fraud has been committed in such cases. For example, three different doctrinal formulations of the standard for fraud can be identified in case law and commentary: "intentional fraud," "egregious fraud," and a flexible standard that looks to the purpose of the letter of credit transaction. Intentional fraud, also known as common law fraud, requires satisfaction of the elements of common law fraud: (1) a misrepresentation of material fact, (2) made with the intent to deceive, (3) upon which the plaintiff reasonably relied, and (4) the reliance resulting in damages to

---

[71] See 31 N.Y.S.2d at 634.

the plaintiff.[72] Egregious fraud occurs when the intended breach gives the beneficiary no "colorable" right to expect honor by the issuer.[73] Some courts even insist that letter of credit fraud is not the same as intentional (common law) fraud.[74] The flexible standard finds fraud when breach so reduces the value of the contract to the victim that the purpose of the letter of credit is undermined.[75]

Fraud in the case law almost always involves intentional and serious misbehavior by the beneficiary. Intentional and serious misbehavior is easily fraudulent under all three standards when it takes the form of not performing at all. Where the sales contract calls for shipment of bristles or boxing gloves, and none are shipped, intentional fraud is unproblematically inferred. Egregious fraud can be inferred here too. So also can fraud under the flexible standard since shipping worthless material leaves the buyer without the value of the seller's performance to it. For the same reason, where there has been no default but a certification of default is submitted, intentional fraud, egregious fraud, and a flexible standard of fraud are satisfied. Thus, it is hard to discern the working standard of fraud in the cases. The most that can be done is to identify the conduct that courts deem fraud under letter of credit law: intentional and serious misconduct.

---

[72] See Dolan, supra note 12, at 7-78; Edward L. Symons, Jr., *Letters of Credit: Fraud, Good Faith and the Basis for Injunctive Relief*, 54 Tul. L. Rev. 388, 445 (1980); E.P. Ellinger, Documentary Letters of Credit 193 (1970); West Virginia Housing Development Fund v. Sroka, 415 F. Supp. 1107 (W.D. Pa. 1977).

[73] See Intraworld Industries v. Girard Trust Bank, 336 A.2d 316 (Pa. 1975); Henry Harfield, *Enjoining Letter of Credit Transactions*, 95 Banking L. J. 596, 602 (1978); The Task Force on the Study of U.C.C. Article 5, *U.C.C. Article 5 (Letters of Credit)*, 45 Bus. Law. 1521, 1615 (1990).

[74] See Emery-Waterhouse Co. v. Rhode Island Hospital Trust National Bank, 757 F.2d 399, 405 (1st Cir. 1985); Note, *"Fraud in the Transaction": Enjoining Letters of Credit During the Iranian Revolution*, 93 Harv. L. Rev. 992, 1009 (1980).

[75] See Roman Ceramics Corp. v. Peoples National Bank, 714 F.2d 1207, 1212, 1215 (3d Cir. 1983); GATX Leasing Corp. v. DBM Drilling Corp., 657 S.W.2d 178 (Tex. Ct. App. 1983).

Revised Article 5 is open to criticism here. Since § 5-109(a) leaves "fraud" undefined, the statute does not identify a standard of fraud. The addition of the adjective "material" and the adverb "materially" in the provision does not help. In order to know when fraud is material, one has to know when the beneficiary's behavior is fraudulent in the first place. Official Comment 1 to § 5-109 endorses different characterizations of fraud found in case law, to the effect that material fraud exists when the beneficiary has "no colorable right" to expect honor or that the draw has "absolutely no basis in fact."[76] However, these are somewhat vague and possibly nonequivalent characterizations. Breach of the sales contract by a beneficiary might range from simple nondelivery, to delivery of worthless goods, to the delivery of significantly nonconforming goods. A standard of fraud is needed to decide which sorts of breaches amount to serious misconduct making for fraud. Without one, issuers and beneficiaries can be uncertain in any particular case about whether fraud has occurred. Issuers therefore can be unsure about whether they are obligated to honor a documentary presentation, and beneficiaries the right to demand honor.

### 3. The Protected Class of Presenters: § 5-109(a)(1)

Even if there is fraud in the credit or underlying transaction, the issuer is obligated to honor presentation of documents by transferees identified in § 5-109(a)(1). Fraud does not excuse the issuer from paying members of this protected class of presenters. Section 5-109(a)(1) also defines the conditions under which fraud does not affect the issuer's obligations to members of the protected class. There are four sorts of transferees protected under the provision: (i) a nominated person, (ii) a confirmer, (iii) a holder in due course of a draft, and (iv) an assignee of a deferred payment obligation. Each is protected when it purchases for value conforming documents or drafts (or both) in ignorance of the relevant fraud. In other words, the transferees protected by § 5-109(a)(1) all are types of good faith purchasers for value. For purposes of the discussion below, assume that in all cases the beneficiary knowingly has committed fraud in the credit or underlying transaction.

One type of protected transferee is a "nominated person who has given value in good faith and without notice of forgery or material

---

[76] Cf. E.P. Ellinger, *Fraud in Documentary Credit Transactions*, 1981 J. Bus. L. 258, 262 (fraud when beneficiary draws "without any shred of honest belief in his rights").

fraud."[77]   A "nominated person" is a person authorized by the issuer under the letter of credit to give value and be reimbursed.[78]   For example, suppose the letter of credit provided in pertinent part that Issuer "agrees with bona fide holders or negotiating banks that all drafts drawn under and in compliance with the terms of this credit shall be paid." Beneficiary presents complying documents and a draft to Bank, and Bank pays Beneficiary.  Bank in turn presents the documents and the draft to Issuer.  At the time Bank paid Beneficiary, it did not know of the assumed fraud. Under § 5-109(a)(1)(i), Issuer must pay Bank. The letter of credit here is a negotiation credit.[79]  This means that the issuer's engagement to honor runs to parties other than the beneficiary.  In this case Issuer has undertaken to pay all negotiating banks and bona fide holders of drafts drawn under the credit.  Bank is a negotiating bank because the credit authorized it to pay Beneficiary in exchange for conforming documents and a draft.[80]  Thus, Bank is a nominated person. Since at the time Bank paid Beneficiary it was ignorant of the fraud, it paid in good faith and without notice.[81]  Section 5-109(a)(1) therefore requires Issuer to pay Bank when Bank presents the documents and an accompanying draft.   Beneficiary's fraud does not affect Issuer's obligation to pay.

Notice a couple of points about the example. First, the definition of "nominated person" excludes the beneficiary.   This is because a nominated person under § 5-102(a)(11) is a person whom the issuer agrees to reimburse if it gives value under the credit. The issuer does not agree to *reimburse* the beneficiary.  Rather, it agrees to pay the beneficiary if the beneficiary makes a conforming presentation to it. Thus, in the example, quite apart from Beneficiary's knowledge of its own fraud, Beneficiary is not among the transferees described by § 5-109(a)(1)(i).

---

[77] § 5-109(a)(1)(ii).

[78] See § 5-102(a)(11).

[79] See §§ 5-102 Official Comment 7; 5-107 Official Comment 4.

[80] Cf. UCP art. 10(b)(ii) (negotiation is giving value for drafts and documents by the bank authorized to negotiate them).

[81] See §§ 1-201(19), 1-201(25).

Second, Issuer's obligation to Bank in the example exists only because the credit is a negotiation credit. Otherwise, Issuer would have no obligation to pay Bank. For instance, suppose the credit simply had provided that "Issuer will pay Beneficiary upon the Beneficiary's drawing of a draft under and in compliance with the terms of this credit." Under this contract, known as a straight credit, Issuer's undertaking to pay on presentation runs to Beneficiary alone. Bank now is not a "nominated person" because the credit does not authorize Bank to give value to Beneficiary. Therefore, Issuer has no obligation at all to reimburse Bank. *A fortiori* it has no obligation to do so under § 5-109(a)(1)(i) given Beneficiary's fraud.

A second type of protected transferee is "a confirmer who has honored its confirmation in good faith."[82] A confirmer is a nominated person whom the issuer has requested to honor a presentation under the letter of credit.[83] The confirmer, usually a bank, becomes liable to the beneficiary by adding its own undertaking to the issuer's undertaking in the credit. It honors the confirmation by performing the terms of the credit, such as paying the beneficiary upon the beneficiary's conforming presentation. Section 5-109(a)(1)(ii) requires the issuer in turn to honor the confirmer's presentation to it, even if fraud has occurred, if the confirmer honored in good faith. So, for example, if Bank is a confirmer, Bank's payment to Beneficiary in the above example constitutes honor. When Bank paid Beneficiary, it did not know that Beneficiary had committed fraud. Thus, § 5-109(a)(1)(ii) requires Issuer to pay Bank upon Bank's presentation of documents and the draft required under the credit. Since a confirmer is a nominated person and honor involves giving value, there is an overlap between § 5-109(a)(1)(i) and § 5-109(a)(1)(ii). Therefore, § 5-109(a)(1)(i) would protect Bank as well. The overlap should not be surprising because (i) describes a general type of good faith purchaser for value while (ii) describes a subset of good faith purchasers for value.

The third type of protected transferee is "a holder in due course of a draft drawn under the letter of credit which was taken after acceptance by the issuer or nominated person."[84] In plain English, the protected

---

[82] § 5-109(a)(1)(ii).

[83] See § 5-102(a)(4).

[84] § 5-109(a)(1)(iii).

transferee described here is one who has given value for a draft called for by the credit and the draft has been taken by it after the issuer has become liable on the draft. A little statutory parsing confirms the point. Section 5-109(a)(1)(iii) protects the transferee only if it is a holder in due course. To be a holder in due course, the transferee must be in possession of a negotiable instrument.[85] Thus, the draft taken by it must be in negotiable form. In addition, three conditions stipulated in Article 3 of the UCC must be satisfied. First, the transferee must have given value, such as paying for it. Second, it must have done so in good faith.[86] Third, it must have done so without knowledge of a defense of the drawee (here, the issuer) to payment--for instance, the beneficiary's fraud. Section 5-109(a)(1)(iii) also requires that the issuer have accepted the draft before the transferee became a holder in due course. Acceptance makes the drawee liable on the draft.[87] It occurs when the drawee either signs the draft or makes a signed agreement on the draft to pay the draft.[88] Thus, the issuer is obligated under § 5-109(a)(1)(iii) to pay one who qualifies as a holder in due course of a draft after the issuer has become liable on the draft. The beneficiary's fraud does not affect the issuer's obligation to the holder.

Some examples illustrate § 5-109(a)(1)(iii)'s operation. Suppose in the above example involving Bank, Beneficiary, and Issuer the draft drawn by Beneficiary is negotiable and Beneficiary properly indorses it over to Bank. Section 5-109(a)(1)(iii) does not protect Bank. Bank is a holder in due course of the draft because it paid Beneficiary and took possession of the draft without knowledge of Beneficiary's fraud.[89] Since

---

[85] See § 1-201(20).

[86] Cf. § 3-103(a)(4).

[87] See § 3-408.

[88] See § 3-409(a).

[89] When an issuer discovers fraud, the common practice is to notify local banks of the fraud. Because only local banks typically will discount a beneficiary's drafts, notification prevents them from taking a draft in ignorance of the fraud and obtaining the status of holders in due course. It can happen that a draft is negotiated to a transferee and later the transferee gives value for it. If the transferee gives value before it discovers the fraud, it still is a holder in due course under § 3-302.

Issuer issued a negotiation credit, it is liable under the credit to anyone presenting conforming documents and a draft. However, Issuer did not accept the draft by signing it. Thus, although Issuer is liable to Bank under the credit, it is not liable to Bank on the draft. Because § 5-109(a)(1)(iii)'s protection applies only if the issuer is liable on both the draft and the credit, the provision does not protect Bank. This does not mean that Bank is unprotected here. Bank is a holder in due course of Beneficiary's draft. Accordingly, Bank still is a nominated person who has negotiated the draft and documents, authorized under Issuer's negotiation credit. Since Bank negotiated them in ignorance of Beneficiary's fraud, § 5-109(a)(1)(i) therefore requires Issuer to pay Bank.

Suppose in the ongoing example the letter of credit had been a straight, i.e., nonnegotiable, credit. Also suppose that Issuer signed the draft after Beneficiary presented it and accompanying documents. Issuer then returned the signed draft to Beneficiary. The facts otherwise remain the same. Section 5-109(a)(1)(iii) does not protect Bank here. A straight credit obligates the issuer to honor presentations made only by the named beneficiary. Although Issuer's signature amounts to an acceptance and therefore makes it liable on the draft, Issuer is not liable to Bank under the credit. Issuer's undertaking on the credit is only to Beneficiary, not Bank. It is only obligated *under the credit* to honor drafts presented by Beneficiary. Thus, although Bank took the draft after Issuer's acceptance, § 5-109(a)(1)(iii) does obligate Issuer to honor a conforming presentation made by Bank. To be sure, as a party to the draft, Issuer remains liable to Bank. It is just that Bank can recover from Issuer only on the draft, not on the credit. Under some circumstances, this might be an advantage. The most significant advantage is the recovery of consequential damages for dishonor, which § 5-111(a) makes unavailable under Article 5. Suppose, finally, Beneficiary drew a draft on Issuer and presented documents to it. Section 5-109(a)(1)(iii) does not protect Beneficiary. This is because he is not a holder in due course for three reasons. First, the draft was not negotiated to him. Rather, Beneficiary has issued the negotiable draft ordering Issuer to pay. Second, Beneficiary clearly exhibits bad faith because he committed the fraud. Third, he has notice of a defense to payment--his own fraud.

A fourth type of protected transferee is "an assignee of the issuer's or nominated person's deferred obligation that was taken for value and without notice of forgery or material fraud after the obligation was incurred by the issuer or nominated person."[90] The protection given here responds to a comparatively recent innovation in documentary credits and replicates the protection given under § 5-109(a)(1)(iii). A deferred payment obligation is a term of a deferred payment credit. Under such a credit the issuer undertakes to pay the beneficiary at a determinable date after conforming documents have been presented, often a fixed period after the shipment of the goods or the date on which the documents are presented.[91] The issuer does not accept the draft upon the beneficiary's presentation of conforming documents. In fact, deferred payment credits almost always do not require presentation of a draft. Rather, the issuer agrees to pay at a future date, sometimes providing the beneficiary with a document memorializing the promise to do so. Since the issuer has not accepted the draft, it is not liable on it. The beneficiary therefore cannot market the draft. Instead, the issuer's deferred payment obligation is marketable after it is incurred, and the beneficiary can assign it.[92] The assignee purchases from the beneficiary the issuer's undertaking under the credit to pay at a determinable date. Section 5-109(a)(1)(iv) mimics § 5-109(a)(1)(iii): the issuer or nominated person is obligated to honor its deferred payment obligation upon maturity if it was assigned to a person who took the assignment without knowledge of the fraud and after the issuer or nominated person became obligated. The issuer or nominated person becomes obligated under the deferred credit when it accepts the documents. If the assignee of the deferred obligation subsequently takes the assignment in ignorance of the fraud, the issuer or nominated party must pay the assignee of the credit when the deferred obligation matures. Fraud does not affect the issuer or nominated

---

[90] § 5-109(a)(1)(iv).

[91] See Gerald T. McLaughlin, *Should Deferred Payment Letters of Credit Be Specially Treated in the Revision of Article 5*, 56 Brook. L. Rev. 149 (1990); E.P. Ellinger, *Discount of Letter of Credit*, 1984 J. Bus. L. 379; Rolf Eberth & E.P. Ellinger, *Deferred Payment Credits: A Comparative Analysis of Their Special Problems*, 14 J. Mar. L. & Comm. 387 (1983); cf. UCP art. 10(a). A deferred payment obligation is functionally identical to a time draft: both allow the buyer to obtain the goods or their value on credit. Deferred credits are common in Europe and South East Asia and uncommon in the United States.

[92] Apparently there is no organized market in assignments on deferred credits, as there is for the discounting of accepted drafts. The point in the text is only that assignments have value, not that they are transferred in thick markets, where prices converge.

person's duty to pay.

## C.  Justification

Letter of credit law would be simpler if it did not protect some transferees from the fraud exception to the independence principle. Things would be yet simpler if the law did not recognize the fraud exception at all. It is not self-evident why there should be a fraud exception to the independence principle. Even if a fraud exception is justified, it does not follow that anyone should be protected from its operation. Thus, both § 5-109(a)(1)'s protection and the fraud exception itself require some explanation. We believe that the case for § 5-109(a)(1)'s protections is inconclusive. The case for the fraud exception, we think, is stronger although not overwhelming.

### 1.  Justifying § 5-109(a)(1)'s Protection

Described abstractly, § 5-109(a)(1) protects good faith purchasers of drafts or documents (or both) against dishonor by the issuer. The issuer is obligated to honor conforming presentations by them nothwithstanding fraud in the credit or underlying transaction. Upon honor, the issuer is statutorily entitled to be reimbursed by the applicant. Where the beneficiary or other person committing the fraud is judgment proof or has disappeared, the applicant in turn will not be able to recover from her. Thus, the applicant, not the protected purchaser or the issuer, ultimately bears the cost of fraud. Accordingly, § 5-109(a)(1) allocates the risk of fraud to the applicant. Is the allocation justified? Although we think there are considerations favoring the allocation, they do not decisively justify allocating fraud risk to the applicant.

A risk of fraud is an expected cost associated with the letter of credit contract. As with any cost, fraud risk should be optimally minimized. Doing so requires allocating fraud risk to the party who has a comparative advantage at reducing or eliminating it. Fraud in the credit or underlying transaction can be reduced or eliminated by taking precautions to deter or detect it. The precautions can be taken at the beginning of the credit or underlying transaction as well as later, after fraud has been committed. The first sort of precautions are ex ante precautions, and the second sort are ex post precautions. For example, provisions in a sales contract such as requiring an inspection certificate can make fraud more difficult to go undetected. Inquiring after the seller's reputation makes it less likely that the seller will be untrustworthy. Both measures are instances of ex ante precautions. Ex post precautions include inspecting the goods shipped, litigating the fraud claim or heavily discounting the price paid for a draft or document. As between the applicant or the purchaser of drafts or documents, fraud risk is properly allocated to the party facing the lowest total precaution costs. Although estimates of the comparative size of precaution costs necessarily are speculative, some guesses can be made.

By allocating the risk of fraud in the underlying sales contract to the applicant, § 5-109(a)(1) implicitly assumes that total precaution costs are lower for the applicant than for the purchaser of drafts or documents. We are not sure that the assumption is sound. The applicant clearly can take some ex ante precaution costs, since it deals with the beneficiary. It therefore can undertake a variety of measures to monitor the beneficiary or protect against fraud, ranging from contractual terms to verification of reputation. Transferees of drafts or documents only come on the scene later, after the credit or underlying transaction has been consummated. They deal in items generated by the underlying sales transaction, not the sale itself. Thus, the costs to transferees of detecting or deterring fraud ex ante are higher than are faced by the applicant.

Ex post precaution costs, however, do not always favor the applicant over the transferee. The law of negotiable instruments allows a holder in due course to take a draft free of defenses otherwise available to the drawer. The rule is justified because the holder in due course can be distant in the chain of negotiation leading from the drawer to her. The holder has information about the instruments it takes, not about facts creating a defense to payment of the instrument. The distance between the drawer and the holder, and the limited information available to the holder, therefore put the holder in an inferior position to detect or deter fraud that creates the drawer's defense to payment. Transferees of drafts or documents under a letter of credit may or may not be in the same position as holders in due course. Sometimes the chain of transfer between the beneficiary and the transferee is close. It can involve only a single transfer of a draft or documents. Where the link between transferee and beneficiary is direct, the transferee is in a good position to know facts about the beneficiary and discover others about the transaction giving rise to fraud. The transferee even might be in a better position than the applicant to do so. This is because the applicant might be geographically removed, perhaps never having dealt with the beneficiary before. In such cases the ex post precaution costs facing the transferee are lower than those facing the applicant.

For instance, letter of credits commonly authorize a bank to take up conforming documentary drafts and pay against them. The issuer agrees to repay the bank if it does so.   Article 5 deems the bank a nominated person who is functioning as a negotiating bank.[93]   Negotiating banks, typically local institutions, usually purchase documentary drafts only from beneficiaries known to them.  As such they know or can investigate the reputation of the beneficiary, and also can vet the documents presented.[94]  Although the available information bearing on fraud can be slight, negotiating banks might have better information, or can obtain it at less cost, than is available to the applicant.  The improved information about fraud can improve the transferee's position in litigation against the beneficiary.  This is true even if the applicant was in a better position to control against the beneficiary's fraud at the time the credit and underlying contracts were concluded.   If so, ex post precaution costs favor the transferee while ex ante precaution costs favor the applicant. Section 5-109(a)(1) implicitly assumes that the applicant's total precaution costs are generally lower than the transferee's total precaution costs.  We are not confident that the assumption is sound.  At the same time, we cannot say that the assumption is unsound.  Although the applicant's ex ante precaution costs are lower than the transferee's, the comparative size of ex post precaution costs is hard to gauge.  This is because reliable generalizations about the pattern of typical transfers of documentary drafts are hard to make.  To be sure, negotiation of a documentary draft by the beneficiary to a local bank is common.  But documentary drafts can be negotiated through multiple parties, so that the link between the ultimate transferee and the beneficiary becomes remote. Section 5-109(a)(1) recognizes the possibility that protected transferees can be remote by describing the transferee as "a holder" or "an assignee," for instance.  Where a documentary draft is negotiated many times, the informational advantage the transferee has over the applicant concerning the beneficiary's fraud disappears.   Advantages in litigation also disappear because the ultimate transferee and beneficiary may be geographically removed from each other.  For instance, banker's acceptances are traded in highly fluid and well-functioning markets. The purchasers of such acceptances can be far removed from the beneficiary, the drawer of the accepted draft.  Because they take drafts after

---

[93] See § 5-102(a)(11); cf. UCP art. 10(b).

[94] See Clayton P. Gillette, Alan Schwartz & Robert E. Scott, Payment Systems and Credit Instruments 603-04 (1996); Clayton P. Gillette, *Holders in Due Course in Documentary Letter of Credit Transactions*, 1 Ann. Rev. Bank. L. 21 (1982), E.P. Ellinger, supra note 76, at 264.

acceptance, the purchasers can qualify as holders in due course protected under § 5-109(a)(1)(iii).

In fact, some credits are not payable against drafts at all.  A credit can undertake to pay upon presentation of documents without a draft by the beneficiary or a transferee.[95]  Here the presenter's demand for payment does not even take the form of a draft.  These are "demand" credits and can involve an extended chain of transfers of documents. Where the demand credit authorizes payment to the presenter of conforming documents, the person who pays for the documents is a nominated person.   Because the nominated person need only be concerned about the conformity of the documents to the credit, it might be inclined to take up documents from a transferee far removed from the beneficiary.  The typical pattern of discounting drafts to local banks therefore may not hold when only documents need be transferred. Extended chains of transfer of documents put the nominated person in a poor position to know much about the beneficiary or fraud in the transaction.  In such cases, the applicant arguably is in a superior position to control against the risk of fraud.  Thus, our assessment is conditional: If documentary drafts or demands are negotiated to the ultimate transferee by the beneficiary, the transferee probably has a comparative advantage at controlling against fraud, and § 5-109(a)(1) therefore wrongly allocates fraud risk to the applicant.  If the ultimate transferee takes documentary drafts or demands from transferors other than the beneficiary or its agents, the applicant has the relevant advantage, and § 5-109(a)(1) correctly allocates fraud risk.

### 2.  Justifying the Fraud Exception

The fraud exception to the independence principle is justified, although the justification is not as straightforward as it might seem. Fraud by the beneficiary is an event that occurs after the letter of credit and underlying contracts have been concluded.  Thus, it is a future contingency that the applicant and beneficiary have to allocate between them.  To this extent fraud is similar to other supervening events that affect the value of the contract, such as destruction of the subject matter of the contract or an increase in input costs.  However, fraud is different from most other supervening events because they present exogeneous risks.  It is an endogenous rather than exogenous risk.  Increases in input costs, for instance, are not within the performing party's control.  At most

---

[95] Cf. § 5-102(a)(12) ("presentation"); § 5-102(a)(6) ("document").

their impact on the contract's value to the party can be controlled. Fraud obviously is entirely within the beneficiary's control: the beneficiary simply need refrain from committing fraud. Even if the applicant can employ contractual devices to detect or deter the beneficiary's fraud, the beneficiary obviously has a cost advantage at controlling its own behavior. Therefore, if bargaining were costless, the beneficiary and applicant parties would allocate the risk of fraud to the beneficiary. The allocation optimally minimizes a cost associated with the use of a letter of credit. Commentators sometimes put the point in a conclusory way by saying that the applicant does not agree to bear the risk of the beneficiary's fraud.[96]

Allocating fraud risk by comparative advantage also justifies a detail of Article 5's fraud exception: the circumstance in which § 5-109(a) permits the issuer to pay the beneficiary. Section 5-109(a)(2) allows the issuer to pay the beneficiary even when there is fraud. It simply does not require the issuer to pay. The issuer does not breach either the letter of credit or reimbursement contracts by paying or refusing to pay the beneficiary. However, § 5-109(a)(2) adds a constraint: the issuer is permitted pay when there is fraud as long as it does so "in good faith."[97]
The constraint of good faith is consistent with the justification by comparative advantage. Good faith imports a subjective standard of "honesty in fact."[98] If the issuer is ignorant of the fraud, it is in an inferior position to the applicant to avoid the impact of the fraud. When the issuer knows of the beneficiary's fraud, it is in a better position than the applicant to avoid the loss resulting from the beneficiary's conduct. Given the issuer's knowledge, positions are switched: the issuer's cost of avoiding the fraud now is less than the cost faced by the applicant. Thus, fraud risk in the circumstances properly is assigned to the issuer (and beneficiary). Section 5-109(a)(2)'s good faith requirement maintains the allocation of fraud risk to the beneficiary. For the issuer pays in bad faith when it pays the beneficiary knowing of the fraud.[99]

---

[96] See, e.g., Steve H. Nickles, John H. Matheson & Edward S. Adams, Modern Commercial Paper 520 (1994).

[97] § 5-109(a)(2).

[98] See § 1-201(19).

[99] Cf. § 5-109 Official Comment 2 ("...[the beneficiary] will have a claim against the issuer only in the rare case in which it can show that the issuer did not

Section 5-109(a)(2) therefore gives the issuer an incentive not to pay, leaving the fraud risk on the beneficiary. In a rough way, then, § 5-109(a)(2)'s good faith requirement tracks the circumstances in which the issuer is in a superior position to the applicant to avoid the impact of fraud.

The fraud exception is a default rule under Article 5. Section 5-103(c) allows the parties to vary the effect of all of Article 5's provisions, except enumerated provisions. Since the enumerated provisions do not include § 5-109,[100] which states the fraud exception, the applicant and issuer by contract could opt out of the fraud exception. The letter of credit contract also could do the same. The effect of doing so would be to require the issuer to honor a presentation by the beneficiary even when the beneficiary committed fraud in the credit or underlying transaction. Although possible, parties are unlikely to contract around the fraud exception. This is because fraud does not increase the surplus created by the credit or underlying transaction. It merely redistributes value from the applicant to the beneficiary. Since taking measures to prevent acts which only redistribute value is costly, most parties would prefer to prohibit fraud in the first place. Requiring the issuer to pay the beneficiary in the face of the beneficiary's fraud eliminates the value to the applicant of the letter of credit. Without a letter of credit, a contracting party can suspend its performance (e.g., by not paying the contract price) if the other party commits fraud. The party therefore avoids the cost of its performance and can recover damages from the breaching party. A letter of credit which excludes the fraud exception does not allow the applicant to do the same. The issuer here must pay the defrauding beneficiary and is entitled to reimbursement from the applicant. Functionally this is equivalent to

---

honor in good faith"). See James G. Barnes, *Defining Good Faith Letter of Credit Practices*, 28 Loy. L.A. L. Rev. 101 (1994). In practice applicants who discover the beneficiary's fraud often provide evidence of fraud to the issuer before the issuer decides to honor a documentary presentation. The tactic in part is intended to establish a foundation for bad faith in the event the issuer decides to honor.

[100] Section 5-103(c) treats § 1-102(3) as a mandatory term, and the latter provision prevents the parties from varying the obligation of good faith. As § 1-203 makes clear, however, good faith applies to the performance of the contract, not its terms. Therefore, paying under a reimbursement or letter of credit contract which derogated from the fraud exception would not be bad faith. The payment would be in conformity with the terms of the contract.

the applicant incurring the cost of its performance when the beneficiary commits fraud. Since the applicant has to recover its performance costs plus any damages from the beneficiary, it is worse off than if the credit had not been issued. The value of the credit to the applicant is lost.

One might wonder why the beneficiary could not offer to reduce the price of the underlying contract to reflect the probability that it might draw on the credit after committing fraud. After all, it might appear that for some reduction in price the applicant would agree to have a credit issued which required payment even if the beneficiary commits fraud. The trouble is that the process for setting the price of the underlying contract unravels. Whatever price is set reflects the probability of fraud by the beneficiary. Once the price is set, the beneficiary can "adjust" by increasing the probability of its own fraud. Knowing this, the applicant will demand a still greater reduction in price to reflect the anticipated further increase in the probability of fraud. In the limit the applicant will assume that the beneficiary's fraud is a certainty. Thus, it will price the underlying contract at the cost of its having to perform when the beneficiary has breached by committing fraud. This price is lower than the price of a contract which does not call for a letter of credit that contracts around the fraud exception.

A final question concerns the standard of fraud at work in the fraud exception. As a default rule, the fraud standard can be considered a term of an agreement between the applicant and beneficiary. It is the standard that most parties would agree governs the issuer's decision to honor a documentary presentation. Section 5-109(a)(2) allows the issuer, a third party, to decide whether to pay the beneficiary when the beneficiary commits fraud. The issuer is permitted but not obligated to pay in the circumstances. Even if the parties to a letter of credit would allocate to the beneficiary the fraud risk, nothing follows about the standard which they would prefer issuers to use to determine when fraud exists. Thus, the applicant and beneficiary's preferences for a fraud exception do not dictate a particular standard of fraud. The parties' preferences for a standard of fraud to be used by issuers have to be determined separately.

Here, where a third party has to determine fraud, the parties have to take into account the possibility of strategic behavior. This is because strategic behavior can upset the risk allocation set by the credit. For example, an applicant who regrets entering into the underlying contract might not want the issuer to honor the credit. If it can convince the issuer to find fraud in the credit or underlying transaction, the issuer will refuse to honor the beneficiary's presentation. This is a "false positive," as it were. A "false negative" occurs when the beneficiary after committing fraud convinces the issuer nonetheless to honor its presentation. Both sorts of cases interfere with the credit's allocation of payment risks. Absent fraud, the credit allocates to the applicant the risk that it has to litigate while the beneficiary is in possession of the contract price. Fraud allows the issuer to refuse payment and therefore place the nonpayment risk on the beneficiary. "False positives" shift back to the beneficiary the risk that the beneficiary is without the contract price during the pendency of litigation. "False negatives" shift back to the applicant the risk that the applicant is without the contract price during the same period. Thus, a standard of fraud applied by the issuer has to take into account the possibility of "false negatives" and "false positives" generated by the applicant or beneficiary's strategic behavior.

The preferences of the applicant and beneficiary justify a constraint on the standard of fraud. Contracting parties in general prefer to condition performance on verifiable events.[101] Events are verifiable when a third party can acquire information enabling it to determine whether the event obtains or not. In the case of a letter of credit, the issuer is the third party and the event to be determined is fraud by the beneficiary. For the letter of credit to effect payment without waiting for detailed inquiry into the credit or underlying contract, the issuer must detect fraud based on facts that clearly and reliably indicate it. These facts must be good proxies for fraud and also be accessible to the issuer, whatever the details of the credit or underlying contract. Obvious and reliable facts minimize the risk that evidence of fraud is manufactured by an applicant or hidden by the beneficiary. Thus, whatever standard of fraud is used, the applicant and beneficiary prefer that the issuer decide fraud by using verifiable facts.

The constraint of verifiable facts about fraud is consistent with much of the case law. "Egregious fraud," a presentation having "no colorable right," and other frequently used phrases all describe behavior that obviously and reliably indicates fraud to the issuer. Two observations about the case law support the point. First, there are relatively few cases in which an issuer refuses to pay based on fraud in the credit or underlying transaction. The textbook cases cited by courts and reproduced in casebooks present unusual fact patterns in which fraud is obvious. Courts regularly turn away complaining applicants, finding that there is insufficient evidence of fraud to enjoin payment by the issuer or

---

[101] See supra Chapter 3.

conclude that honor was in bad faith. The dearth of case law in which fraud is found suggests that the evidence of fraud must be clear and ample.[102] Second, in the few cases in which fraud is found, it is reliably indicated by the conduct described. Evidence that the beneficiary shipped nothing or shipped worthless goods or certified a default when none had occurred indicates fraud. The issuer does not have to know anything about the details of underlying contract to conclude that fraud is involved. It does not have to know how much the breach affected the value of the contract to the applicant because the breach is total. Thus, although case law and commentary invokes unhelpful phrases such as "egregious conduct," or "no colorable right to expect honor" to describe a standard of fraud, the conduct described easily indicates fraud to the issuer, not mere breach of contract. Party preference therefore can justify the requirement that fraud be verifiable by the issuer without resort to details of the credit or underlying contract.

---

[102] The revision to Article 5 also is consistent with the point. Section 5-109(a) requires a showing of "material" fraud before an issuer can refuse payment to a beneficiary under § 5-109(a)(2). The adjective "material" increases the evidentiary burden that needs to be met to establish fraud sufficient to allow the issuer to refuse payment.

# TABLE OF CASES

[References are to pages]

# INDEX

**References are to Pages**

463

**PERFORMANCE**—Cont'd

Acceptance and rejection—Cont'd
  Burden of proof as to defects, 217, 218
  Buyer's obligations on rejection, 222–224
  Cure, below
  Defects, burden of proof as to, 217, 218
  Introduction, 212, 213
  Neutralizing strategic behavior, 212, 213
  Perfect tender, 213–216
  Rejection, buyer's obligations, 222–224
  Revocation of acceptance, below
Adequate assurances of performance. insecurity and adequate assurances of performance, below
Anticipatory Repudiation, this index
Assurances. insecurity and adequate assurances of performance, below
Avoidance, cure and avoidance under CISG, 233–236
Burden of proof as to defects, 217, 218
Contracts for International Sales of Goods (CISG)
  Avoidance, cure and, 233–236
  Cure and avoidance, 233–236
  Excuse, 255–263
  Insecurity and adequate assurances of performance, suspension of performance, 197–199
  Inspection, 210–212
  Suspension of performance, 197–199
Cure
  Generally, 224
  CISG, cure and avoidance under, 233–236
  Conforming tender, curing with, 228–236
  Courts, cure in courts and repair and interpretation, 230–233
  Interpretation, cure in courts and repair and interpretation, 230–233
  Introduction, 224
  Post-revocation cure, 245–247
  Repair, cure in courts and repair and interpretation, 230–233
  Technical requirements, 225–228
Defects, burden of proof as to, 217, 218
Demand for adequate assurances, UCC, 193
Documentary transactions, inspection, 206–210
Excuse
  CISG, 255–263
  UCC, 248–255
Insecurity and adequate assurances of performance

**PERFORMANCE**—Cont'd

Insecurity and adequate assurances of performance—Cont'd
  CISG, 194
  Demand for adequate assurances, UCC, 193
  Reasonable grounds for insecurity, UCC, 194
  UCC
    Adequate assurances of performance, 194
    Demand for adequate assurances, 193
    Introduction, 191–193
    Reasonable grounds for insecurity, 194
Inspection
  CISG, 210–212
  Documentary transactions, 206–210
  Tender and inspection, 203–206
Losses, allocation of, 190
Monitoring performance, generally, 190
Post-revocation cure, revocation of acceptance and, 245–247
Reasonable grounds for insecurity, UCC, 194
Rejection. acceptance and rejection, above
Revocation of acceptance
  Generally, 236–242
  Introduction, 236–242
  Post-revocation cure, 245–247
  Substantial impairment, 242–245
Substantial impairment, revocation of acceptance, 242–245
Suspension of performance, CISG, 197–199
Tender
  Curing with conforming tender, 228–236
  Inspection, tender and, 203–206
  Perfect tender, 213–216

**PERSONAL INJURIES**
Warranties, personal injury and privity, 307–312

**PREEMPTION**
Warranties, pre-emption by federal law and warranties of quality, 317–319

**PRICE**
Implied terms, open price terms under CISG, 117–123

**PRIVITY**
Warranties, personal injury and privity, 307–312

**QUALITY**
Warranties, this index